Frommer's

W9-AVC-800

New York
State
from New York City to Niagara Falls

1st Edition

by Neil E. Schlecht, Rich Beattie,
Brian Silverman & Karen Quarles

Here's what the critics say about Frommer's:

"Amazingly easy to use. Very portable, very complete."
—*Booklist*

"Detailed, accurate, and easy-to-read information for all price ranges."
—*Glamour Magazine*

"Hotel information is close to encyclopedic."
—*Des Moines Sunday Register*

"Frommer's Guides have a way of giving you a real feel for a place."
—*Knight Ridder Newspapers*

WILEY

Wiley Publishing, Inc.

Published by:

Wiley Publishing, Inc.

111 River St.
Hoboken, NJ 07030-5744

Copyright © 2004 Wiley Publishing, Inc., Hoboken, New Jersey. All rights reserved. No part of this publication may be reproduced, stored in a retrieval system or transmitted in any form or by any means, electronic, mechanical, photocopying, recording, scanning or otherwise, except as permitted under Sections 107 or 108 of the 1976 United States Copyright Act, without either the prior written permission of the Publisher, or authorization through payment of the appropriate per-copy fee to the Copyright Clearance Center, 222 Rosewood Drive, Danvers, MA 01923, 978/750-8400, fax 978/646-8600. Requests to the Publisher for permission should be addressed to the Legal Department, Wiley Publishing, Inc., 10475 Crosspoint Blvd., Indianapolis, IN 46256, 317/572-3447, fax 317/572-4447, E-Mail: permcoordinator@wiley.com.

Wiley and the Wiley Publishing logo are trademarks or registered trademarks of John Wiley & Sons, Inc. and/or its affiliates. Frommer's is a trademark or registered trademark of Arthur Frommer. Used under license. All other trademarks are the property of their respective owners. Wiley Publishing, Inc. is not associated with any product or vendor mentioned in this book.

ISBN 0-7645-3929-9

Editor: Lorraine Festa
Production Editor: Donna Wright
Cartographers: Roberta Stockwell, Nicholas Trotter
Photo Editor: Richard Fox
Production by Wiley Indianapolis Composition Services

Front cover photo: Niagara Falls' *Maid of the Mist*
Back cover photo: Thoroughbred racing at the Saratoga Race Course

For information on our other products and services or to obtain technical support, please contact our Customer Care Department within the U.S. at 800/762-2974, outside the U.S. at 317/572-3993 or fax 317/572-4002.

Wiley also publishes its books in a variety of electronic formats. Some content that appears in print may not be available in electronic formats.

Manufactured in the United States of America

5 4 3 2 1

Contents

List of Maps

An Invitation to the Reader

In researching this book, we discovered many wonderful places—hotels, restaurants, shops, and more. We're sure you'll find others. Please tell us about them, so we can share the information with your fellow travelers in upcoming editions. If you were disappointed with a recommendation, we'd love to know that, too. Please write to:

Frommer's New York State, 1st Edition
Wiley Publishing, Inc. • 111 River St. • Hoboken, NJ 07030-5744

An Additional Note

Please be advised that travel information is subject to change at any time—and this is especially true of prices. We therefore suggest that you write or call ahead for confirmation when making your travel plans. The authors, editors, and publisher cannot be held responsible for the experiences of readers while traveling. Your safety is important to us, however, so we encourage you to stay alert and be aware of your surroundings. Keep a close eye on cameras, purses, and wallets, all favorite targets of thieves and pickpockets.

About the Authors

Neil E. Schlecht is a writer and photographer who travels frequently along the Hudson between an old farmhouse in northwestern Connecticut and New York City. He is the author of a dozen travel guides—including *Spain For Dummies* and Frommer's guides to Texas, Cuba, and Peru—as well as art catalogue essays and articles on art and culture.

Rich Beattie is a freelance writer who lives in New York City. Formerly the Managing Editor of *Travel Holiday Magazine* and Executive Editor of the adventure-travel site GORP.com, he now writes for *Travel & Leisure,* the *New York Times, Four Seasons Hotel Magazine, Boating Magazine,* and *Modern Bride,* among others.

Brian Silverman, author of *Frommer's New York City, Frommer's New York City From $90 A Day,* and *Portable New York City,* has written about travel, food, sports, and music for publications such as *Saveur, Caribbean Travel & Life, Islands, American Way,* the *New Yorker,* and the *New York Times.* He is the author of several books including *Going, Going, Gone: The History, Lore, and Mystique of the Home Run* (HarperCollins), and co-editor of *The Twentieth Century Treasury of Sports* (Viking Books). Brian lives in New York, New York, with his wife and son.

A native of Buffalo, New York, **Karen Quarles** now enjoys the temperate climate of New York City, where she works as a freelance writer and editor. Karen has also contributed to *Frommer's Los Angeles.*

Other Great Guides for Your Trip:

Wonderful Weekends from New York City
Frommer's New York City
Frommer's Memorable Walks in New York City

Frommer's Star Ratings, Icons & Abbreviations

Every hotel, restaurant, and attraction listing in this guide has been ranked for quality, value, service, amenities, and special features using a **star-rating system.** In country, state, and regional guides, we also rate towns and regions to help you narrow down your choices and budget your time accordingly. Hotels and restaurants are rated on a scale of zero (recommended) to three stars (exceptional). Attractions, shopping, nightlife, towns, and regions are rated according to the following scale: zero stars (recommended), one star (highly recommended), two stars (very highly recommended), and three stars (must-see).

In addition to the star-rating system, we also use **seven feature icons** that point you to the great deals, in-the-know advice, and unique experiences that separate travelers from tourists. Throughout the book, look for:

Finds	Special finds—those places only insiders know about
Fun Fact	Fun facts—details that make travelers more informed and their trips more fun
Kids	Best bets for kids, and advice for the whole family
Moments	Special moments—those experiences that memories are made of
Overrated	Places or experiences not worth your time or money
Tips	Insider tips—great ways to save time and money
Value	Great values—where to get the best deals

The following **abbreviations** are used for credit cards:

AE	American Express	DISC	Discover	V	Visa
DC	Diners Club	MC	MasterCard		

Frommers.com

Now that you have the guidebook to a great trip, visit our website at **www.frommers.com** for travel information on more than 3,000 destinations. With features updated regularly, we give you instant access to the most current trip-planning information available. At Frommers.com, you'll also find the best prices on airfares, accommodations, and car rentals—and you can even book travel online through our travel booking partners. At Frommers.com, you'll also find the following:

- Online updates to our most popular guidebooks
- Vacation sweepstakes and contest giveaways
- Newsletter highlighting the hottest travel trends
- Online travel message boards with featured travel discussions

The Best of New York State

Visitors to New York State who venture both downstate and upstate have an array of options unequaled elsewhere in the country. Besides the urban allure, culture, and shopping of Manhattan, much of New York State is still, in many ways, waiting to be discovered on a grand scale. The state is blanketed with outstanding beauty and diversity of scenery from one end to the other. Although New Yorkers have long vacationed in the Catskill and Adirondack mountains, for too long too few have seen too little of the state between its two tourist bookends, New York City and Niagara Falls. The historic Hudson Valley, a majestic river lined with elegant estates, is finally positioning itself as a destination, not just a day trip from the city. The great wilderness of the Adirondack and Catskill mountains is magnificent for outdoors and sporting vacations, but those spots are also home to the easygoing charms of small towns. The pristine glacial-lake beauty and outstanding wineries of the Finger Lakes make it one of the state's most deserving destinations. And Long Island is home to splendid sandy Atlantic Ocean beaches and the gulf of New York economic extremes, ranging from blue-collar immigrant enclaves to elite summer homes in the Hamptons.

Planning a trip to a state as large and diverse as New York involves a lot of decision-making, so in this chapter we've tried to give some direction. Below we've chosen what we feel is the very best the state has to offer—the places and experiences you won't want to miss. Although sites and activities listed here are written up in more detail elsewhere in this book, this chapter should give you an overview of New York State's highlights and get you started planning your trip.

—*Neil E. Schlecht*

1 The Best Places to Stay

- **Le Parker Meridien** (New York City; ✆ **800/543-4300**): New York's best all-around hotel, Le Parker Meridien has the perfect blending of style, service, and amenities. It's the best choice if you want a little of everything; luxury, high tech, family-friendly, comfort, and a great central location. See p. 96.
- **Hotel Metro** (New York City; ✆ **800/356-3870**): A Midtown gem that gives you a surprisingly good deal, including a marble bathroom; it's New York City's best moderately priced hotel. See p. 98.
- **Seatuck Cove House** (Eastport; ✆ **631/325-3300**). On the edge of the Hamptons, this enormous Victorian home sits right out on the water with gorgeous views. And because the inn has only five rooms, you'll feel like you own the place. The rooms are painted white and decorated with an appropriately beachy feel. Four of the five are also large enough to comfortably accommodate a separate sitting area. Take a walk along

New York State

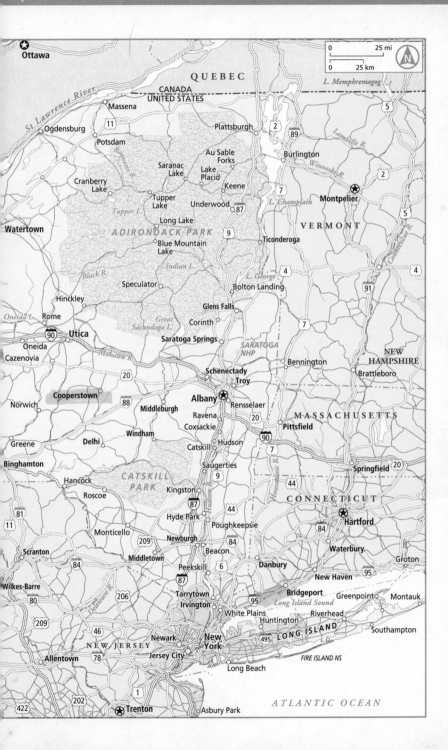

the waterfront or a dip in the pool, then grab one of the best B&B breakfasts on Long Island. See p. 181.

- **Mohonk Mountain House** (Lake Mohonk; ✆ **800/772-6646**): A legendary Victorian castle perched on a ridge overlooking the Catskill Region's Shawangunk Mountains, the Mohonk Mountain House is more than a hotel—it's a destination unto itself. Still in the hands of the original family, the whimsical lodge lives up to its exalted reputation, earned over the past 130 years. In the midst of the 6,400-acre Mohonk Forest Preserve, its setting is beyond compare and its outdoor activities include something for everyone. Rooms are decorated in Edwardian, Victorian, or Arts and Crafts style, and the massive place is loaded with fireplaces and pretty nooks. See p. 235.

- **Emerson Inn & Spa** (Mount Tremper; ✆ **845/688-7900**): The Catskills's only small luxury hotel, the Emerson—a grandly restored 1874 Victorian mansion—is all about pampering and escape. With a gorgeous spa, sumptuous restaurant, and exotic-themed rooms, it's a posh retreat few would expect to find in the midst of the region's outdoor offerings and more modest inns and large resorts. See p. 235.

- **The Morgan State House** (Albany; ✆ **888/427-6063**): One doesn't ordinarily expect elegance and luxury from the gritty state capital, which has few decent hotels, but this small inn goes against conventional wisdom. A lovely 1888 town house on "Mansion Row," it features spacious rooms that are as luxuriously appointed as any five-star hotel. But it's much more intimate and has more flair, with beautiful

19th-century period details and antiques and extraordinary linens and bedding. Sipping coffee in the serene interior garden courtyard, you'll never know how many trench-coated bureaucrats and lobbyists hover just down the street. See p. 285.

- **The Otesaga** (Cooperstown; ✆**800/348-6222**): The grand dame of central New York, dating from 1909, sits grandly on the shores of Lake Otsego. While renovations have brought bathrooms and air-conditioning into the 21st century, the hotel is firmly rooted in the past, maintaining its historic feel with high ceilings, heavy wooden doors, and formal furniture. Still, with a plethora of patios and balconies, along with a renowned golf course and plenty of watersports, this seasonal hotel is focused on the equally gorgeous outdoors that surrounds it. See p. 294.

- **Hillcrest Manor** (Corning; ✆ **607/936-4548**). A new and splendidly refined B&B in a gateway town to the Finger Lakes, this gorgeous 1890 Greek Revival mansion is minutes from downtown and the world-renowned Corning Museum of Glass in a peaceful residential neighborhood. The opulent inn owned by two art collectors who are new to Corning features eminently tasteful parlors and very spacious bedrooms. Few inns can match this level of sophistication and luxury, and fewer still for the relatively affordable prices you'll find here. See p. 319.

- **Hobbit Hollow Farm B&B** (Skaneateles; ✆ **315/685-2791**): Overlooking graceful Skaneateles Lake, this sumptuous and intimate small inn gives you a chance to make believe that you're a privileged country gentleman or woman, relaxing on your horse farm. The century-old Colonial

Revival, ensconced on 400 acres with panoramic lake views, is as luxurious and attentive to detail as they come. Rooms are charmingly elegant; for those on a budget, the smaller rooms are a decent value and you can still imagine yourself the prince of Skaneateles. See p. 349.

- **Mirbeau Inn & Spa** (Skaneateles; ℂ 877/MIRBEAU): A modern portrait of a French country château retreat, the Mirbeau is elegant and refined but with a chic contemporary sensibility. Rooms are richly appointed, the full-service spa stylish, and the restaurant extraordinary (in fact, dining here is one of the highlights of visiting this part of the Finger Lakes). In quaint Skaneateles, where the competition is extreme, this new hotel has jumped to the head of the class. See p. 350.

- **Lake Placid Lodge** (Lake Placid; ℂ 877/523-2700): Awash in rustic luxury, the Lodge is the quintessential Adirondacks experience. Sitting on the shores of secluded Lake Placid, this exclusive getaway features meticulous and personalized service, along with rooms filled with one-of-a-kind pieces of furniture, many built by local artists from birch or cedar (and for sale!). With lots of quiet nooks and a gorgeous stone patio, you can grab your own piece of the 'dacks and feel like you have the place to yourself. See p. 369.

- **The Sagamore** (Lake George; ℂ 800/358-3585): One of the last grand Adirondack lodges still standing, this 1883-era hotel sits on its own island in Lake George and comes with a stellar restaurant, a great spa, a terrific golf course, a wonderful waterfront, and loads of amenities. While a conference area keeps it open in the winter, this is mostly a summertime resort where you'll have your pick of room styles, restaurants (there are six), and activities—and you can always just grab an Adirondack chair and sit out on the patio overlooking the lake. See p. 362.

- **Mansion on Delaware** (Buffalo; ℂ 716/886-3300): This renovated mansion on Millionaire's Row blends in so well with the gorgeous private homes around it you'd never even guess it was a hotel. Inside, you'll find ultramodern (but comfy) furniture, luxurious (and huge) bathrooms, and ultrapersonalized service. Rooms have been styled around the existing mansion, creating unique spaces and the city's most unique property. See p. 392.

2 The Best Restaurants

- **Eleven Madison Park** (New York City; ℂ 212/889-0905): Higher praise has consistently gone to chef/restaurateur Danny Meyer's other restaurants, Gramercy Park Tavern and Union Square Café; as a result, Eleven Madison Park often gets unfairly neglected, which is a shame. It is a magnificent restaurant on every level. The Art Deco room is spectacular, the service almost otherworldly it is that good, and the food is truly memorable. See p. 107.

- **Peter Luger** (Great Neck; ℂ 516/487-8800). Hands down, one of the best steakhouses in the country. And people flock here for one thing and one thing only—porterhouse. In fact, if you try to order anything else (or even ask for a menu), you'll likely get a quizzical stare from your waiter. The dry-aged meat comes brushed with a tasty glaze and is tender enough to make vegetarians reconsider. See p. 162.

- **Culinary Institute of America (CIA)** (Hyde Park; © 845/471-6608): The most elite training ground in the country for chefs has not one but four on-campus restaurants run by students—but they're a far cry from what college students typically eat. Choose among the sophisticated Escoffier Restaurant (French), Ristorante Caterina de Medici (Italian), American Bounty Restaurant (regional American), and St. Andrew's Café (casual). You'll be impressed and unsurprised that so many of America's finest restaurants have CIA chefs at the helm. Plan ahead, though, because reservations are about as tough to come by as admission to the school. See p. 213.

- **Depuy Canal House** (High Falls; © 845/687-7700): A fabulously creative restaurant in a lovely, rambling 200-year-old stone tavern in the Catskills, Depuy Canal House is the longtime standard bearer in this part of upstate New York: It draws foodies from New York City and around the state for elegant and surprising selections served in a perfectly elegant but rustic setting. If you've brought an empty stomach and full wallet, check out the four- or seven-course prix fixe dinners; otherwise drop into the more casual downstairs bistro in the wine cellar. See p. 236.

- **Chez Sophie Bistro** (Malta Ridge; © 518/583-3436): Saratoga Springs is stocked with a number of excellent restaurants, but certainly the most unique is this charming French bistro housed in a 1950s stainless steel diner, about 5 miles from downtown. The original Sophie became something of a

local culinary legend, and her son is now the chef, continuing his mom's simple but refined approach and bringing French sophistication to upstate New York. The creative menu uses the best local ingredients and organic produce, meats and fish. One of the best bargains around is the "pink plate special" a three-course meal for just $25. See p. 274.

- **Alex & Ika** (Cherry Valley; © 607/264-9315): You'd never guess that this tiny, unassuming building in tiny Cherry Valley, about 15 miles north of Cooperstown, turns out some of the most amazing flavor combinations in the state. Open only on the weekends, this laid-back cuisine magic show is run by a couple that serves a tapas-style menu prepared with so many flavor combinations you'll be talking about the food long after you leave. With a menu that changes weekly, it's hard to believe they can hit a home run with every dish, but somehow they do. See p. 295.

- **The Carriage House at Rose Inn** (Lansing; © 607/533-7905): The restaurant connected to the elegant Rose Inn, near Ithaca and Cayuga Lake is worthy of mention on its own. In a fantastic 1842 carriage house, to the backbeat of live jazz on weekends, a romantic dinner here is one of the best bets in the Finger Lakes Region. The menu is creative, with surprises like grilled ostrich. See p. 312.

- **Jacques Cartier** (Riveredge Hotel, Alexandria Bay; © 800/ENJOY-US): This seasonal French-American restaurant, on the St. Lawrence River in the 1000 Islands, combines a stunning view of Boldt Castle with even more stunning cuisine. Dishes come infused with so many flavors you'll spend half the meal just trying to discern them all. Go at sunset to watch the sky turn red as it sets over the Canadian plain. See p. 383.

- **Richard's Freestyle Cuisine** (Lake Placid; © **518/523-5900**): This Adirondack newcomer, set right on Mirror Lake in the middle of town, has spurned the birch bark tradition of the area to focus on a more contemporary feel. With a clean, simple decor and a simple menu with names like The Soup and The Lasagna, Richard's takes a basic American menu to new heights with his surprisingly complex taste combinations. See p. 372.

3 The Best Places for Antiques Hounds

- **Jamesport:** You may miss tiny Jamesport, on Long Island's North Fork, if you blink, but keep your eyes open long enough and you'll see a Main Street lined with antique shops. There's the usual assortment of furniture and books, and a selection of nautical items to remind you of the area's history as a fishing community. See chapter 6.
- **Locust Valley:** Most antiques hunters head to Port Jefferson, farther east on Long Island's north shore. And that's exactly why you should hit this tiny town that's not even on many maps—their goods are less picked over and the antiques are of an excellent quality. See chapter 6.
- **Hudson:** This formerly rundown town along the Upper Hudson has exploded with high-end and eclectic antiques shops, making it *the* antiquing destination of the Hudson River Valley. Almost all the dealers are confined to the long stretch of Warren Street, making it ideal for window-shopping. See chapter 7.
- **Bloomfield Antique Country Mile:** Just west of Canandaigua, this mile-long cluster of antiques dealers along Routes 5 and 20 in Bloomfield is one of the best concentrations for antiquing in the Finger Lakes, with several multi-dealer shops lined up back-to-back. See chapter 11.
- **East Aurora:** This town outside Buffalo hosts a wealth of craftspeople, not technically sellers of antiques, who make furniture in the 100-year-old style of famed builder Elbert Hubbard. His movement of Roycrofters created some of the sturdiest and most beautiful pieces of wooden furniture anywhere, and while it's possible to find originals, you'll more likely find work from the expert builders who follow Hubbard's style. See chapter 13.

4 The Best Hikes

- **Mashomack Preserve, Shelter Island:** With more than 2,000 pristine acres in the southeastern part of the island, this preserve, run by the Nature Conservancy, is about as remote as you can get on Long Island. There are 11 miles of easy hiking trails that run through the oak woodlands, marshes, ponds, and creeks. Keep an eye out for osprey, ibis, foxes, harbor seals, and terrapins. See chapter 6.
- **Hudson River Valley:** Though the Hudson Valley is more hilly than mountainous, tucked in the southern highlands are several excellent spots for day hikes. Hudson Highlands State Park near Cold Spring contains a number of great day trails, as do Bear Mountain and

Harriman state parks, including on a section of the Appalachian Trail. Many are surprisingly challenging. See chapter 7.

- **Catskill Region:** Some of the most scenic hiking in New York State is through the dense forests and along the stony ridges lacing the Catskills, where there are nearly three dozen peaks above 3,500 feet. The 6,000-acre Mohonk Preserve, part of the Shawangunk Mountains, has 60 miles of trails. Nearby Minnewaska State Park Preserve offers another 12,000 acres perfect for hiking and mountain biking, with 30 miles of footpaths and carriage-ways. See chapter 8.

- **Southern Adirondacks:** How adventuresome are you feeling? Head to Lake George for a crazy steep climb up Black Mountain, an 8½-mile round-trip with a 1,100-foot vertical rise, for some amazing views of the lake and mountains. If you want a great view without so much work, Bald Mountain, east of Old Forge, is also steep but much shorter (2-mile round-trip). For a hike back in the woods, check out Cascade Lake, just north of Eagle Bay. It's an easy 5-mile walk to the lake that takes you past a gorgeous waterfall. See chapter 12.

- **Northern Adirondacks:** New York State's highest peak is Mt. Marcy, at 5, 344 feet. It's not the easiest climb, but for anyone with aspirations to nab the state's highest spot, it's a must. Just watch out for crowds: most people hike to the peak from the north, but take the Range Trail and you'll find fewer people and better views along the way. For an easier hike, check out High Falls Gorge, which offers a great and easy stroll along the Au Sable River and past waterfalls. See chapter 12.

- **Letchworth State Park:** This western New York park is home to a stunning 400-foot-deep gorge with all sorts of hiking trails taking you past views of the deep chasm that's cut by the Genesee River. There trails go either deep into the forest or along the rim of the canyon; the Gorge Trail hits the most scenic spots. It's a 7-mile trail one-way, and moderately difficult, but of course you can turn around at any time. Take the kids along the Pond Trail, an easy ¾-mile walk that lead you to a small pond stocked with fish. See chapter 13.

5 The Best Family Vacation Spots

- **Shelter Island:** Hardly the raging party scene that exists in the nearby Hamptons, Shelter Island makes for a quiet family retreat on the eastern end of Long Island. Hike, boat, or just relax. And since it's an island, there are very few ways to escape, meaning that—for better or worse—on this family vacation you'll always be together. See chapter 6.

- **Mount Tremper & Phoenicia:** This spot in the southeastern Catskills—two small towns bunched together off the main road—serves up a surprising roster of activities for families. In Mt. Tremper, at Catskill Corner, the Kaatskill Kaleidoscope Theatre is the world's largest kaleidoscope, occupying an old barn silo. Shows are similar to those kids have seen in a planetarium, but even cooler. In Phoenicia, just a couple of miles up the road, families can rent inner tubes and float down Esopus Creek, which slices the valley between towering mountains. The Catskill Mountain Railroad runs along Esopus Creek from Mount

Pleasant depot to Phoenicia's 1910 station; you can even float down in a tube and catch the train back. See chapter 8.

- **Healing Waters Farms/Delaware & Ulster Railride:** A fantastic farm in Walton, in the northeastern Catskills, Healing Waters overflows with cool things for kids. Its petting zoo, Little Boy Blue Animal Land, has an amazing array of gregarious animals, including camels, llamas, emus, and baby goats, and the farm holds all kinds of special events as well as hayrides. In Arkville, the Delaware & Ulster Railride transports visitors through the Catskill Mountains in a historic train that departs from the old depot. Kids will especially love the special "Great Train Robbery" train, where costumed actors playfully hijack and "rob" the train. See chapter 8.

- **Saratoga Springs:** This genteel resort town welcomes families with its plenitude of parks, the Saratoga Children's Museum, and Saratoga Springs Spa State Park, a huge and lovely urban park with miles of hiking trails, swimming pools, and a skating rink. But surely the most entertaining feature for kids is the Saratoga Springs Race Course and the opportunity to attend a thoroughbred horse race. Kids can take a walking tour of the stables, a tram ride, and starting gate demonstration, and learn how horses and jockeys prepare for races, even dressing up like a jockey. See chapter 9.

- **Skaneateles:** This charming village at the north shore of the Finger Lake of the same name has tons of shops, restaurants, and inns that parents will love, but also plenty of activities for the entire family. In summer, children are sure to love the nostalgic long pier that extends over the water, as well as swimming and boating in one of the state's most beautiful lakes. But best of all are the winter holidays, when Skaneateles comes alive with a Dickens Christmas celebration, with costumed Dickens characters taking over the streets, singing Christmas carols. There are free carriage rides around town, free roasted chestnuts, and hot chocolate. A good excursion from Skaneateles is the easy drive into Syracuse to visit the Museum of Science & Technology (MOST), whose excellent interactive exhibits and IMAX theater are huge hits with kids. See chapter 11.

- **Lake George:** This southern Adirondacks town is hardly a calm getaway in the summer, but it boasts distractions galore for kids, including amusement parks, haunted houses, family restaurants, and all the lake swimming you can handle. See chapter 12.

- **Niagara Falls:** It isn't just for honeymooners anymore—it's also jammed with families. The famous cascading water appeals to people of all ages; you can see it from high above, behind, or way down below on the ever-popular *Maid of the Mist.* But over on the Canadian side in the Clifton Hill area is where your kids will really want to go—there you'll find haunted houses, rides, and fun museums. See chapter 13.

6 The Best Places for Watersports

- **North Fork:** The protected waters of Long Island Sound (to the north of the fork) and Peconic Bay (to the south) make for the perfect place to head out with a boat. Whether it's a canoe, kayak, jet ski, or powerboat, you'll cruise around on relatively calm waters while keeping an eye out for herons, osprey, hawks, fish, and turtles. See chapter 6.

- **Hudson River:** One of the best ways to see the Hudson River, America's first highway and one of the great rivers in the nation, is from the middle of it: on a boat. You can board a sightseeing cruise at Rondout Landing in Kingston on the *Rip Van Winkle,* in Newburgh on The *Pride of the Hudson,* or take a sunset cruise aboard *Doxie,* a 31-foot sloop, or traditional-style yacht. See chapter 7.

- **Delaware River:** The western Catskills are one of North America's top fishing destinations, drawing serious anglers from around the world. Fly-fishing is legendary along the Delaware River and nearby Beaverkill and Willowemoc trout streams. The junction pool at Hancock, where the east and west branches join to form the main stem of the Delaware River, has long been celebrated for its preponderance of massive brown and rainbow trout. Pepacton Reservoir, also in the western Catskills, is perfect for open-water brown trout fishing. See chapter 8.

- **Finger Lakes & Erie Canal:** The gorgeous Finger Lakes are incredibly scenic spots for boating, water-skiing, and sailing. Seneca Lake has a picture-perfect port, where you can hire a yacht or sailboat, including a vintage 1930 schooner yacht. At Keuka Lake, held by many locals to be the prettiest of the Finger Lakes, there are boat cruises aboard the *Keuka Maid.* At several Finger Lakes, you can also rent kayaks and canoes if you're looking for an even more intimate experience on the water. Skaneateles Lake has one of the longest cruise boat

traditions in the region, and the lake is perfect for relaxed sightseeing and dinner cruises; for something even more novel, you can hop a U.S. Mail boat as it delivers mail to old-fashioned camps on the lake. Almost as unique is a cruise along the historic Erie Canal, which once ran unimpeded from the Great Lakes to the Hudson; boaters can pull up along the canal in Seneca Falls and dock for lunch, or even sleep along the canal in a houseboat. See chapter 11.

- **Alexandria Bay, 1000 Islands:** The miles-wide St. Lawrence River, dotted with somewhere between 1,000 to 1,800 islands, comes tailor-made for watersports. Tool around in powerboat, canoe, or kayak and check out the castles and mansions that some of America's wealthiest families have built. Just watch out for tankers and other big ships—this is one of America's busiest shipping lanes! See chapter 12.

- **Lake George:** Peppered with islands small and large, 32-mile-long Lake George offers endless exploration, whether you're in canoe, kayak, powerboat, or paddlewheel tour boat. Get out and experience the thrill of water-skiing, or just kick back and paddle quietly along the shores. Rent boats in the town of Lake George or in Bolton Landing. See chapter 12.

- **Mirror Lake, Lake Placid:** This lake, surrounded by the gorgeous peaks of the 'dacks, comes to life in the summer, with all kinds of boats plying the waters. The only drawback is that while it's super-convenient (Lake Placid sits right above it), it can get a little too crowded. See chapter 12.

7 The Best One-of-a-Kind Experiences

- **Walking the Brooklyn Bridge:** One of the great New York activities of all time. The skyline view heading toward Manhattan from Brooklyn is unparalleled. The walk takes 20 to 40 minutes, depending on your pace and every minute on this 19th-century architectural marvel is exhilarating. See chapter 5.

- **Reliving America's Glory Days:** Vintage "Baseball," a nostalgic sport played by old-school traditionalists partial to the 19th-century rules and uniforms of America's classic sport, is played in several parts of New York. In Roxbury, in the northwest Catskill Region, locals take it especially seriously. The best time to see a game is on Labor Day, when the Roxbury Nine hosts a home game and the town celebrates "Turn-of-the-Century Day." Locals turn out in period costume, and the opposing team arrives by vintage train. See chapter 8.

- **Attending a Baseball Hall of Fame Induction Ceremony:** Every July, a new generation of players are transformed from mortal to legendary as they take their place alongside Ruth, Gehrig, and the other greats in Cooperstown's Hall of Fame. See chapter 10.

- **Gorging on Grape Pie in Naples, Finger Lakes Region:** There's a reason grape pie hasn't earned a spot alongside apple, cherry, and peach in the pie pantheon: it's just too laborious to peel the grapes. But every year on the last weekend in September, the attractive little village of Naples near Keuka Lake becomes the grape pie capital of the world; nearly everyone seems to be selling, buying, and eating them. Grape fanatics and pie pilgrims come from all over to attend the Naples Grape Festival and stuff themselves silly with grape pie. See chapter 11.

- **Soaring the Friendly Skies:** The Finger Lakes are gorgeous from any angle, but a bird's-eye perspective—in a vintage warplane or a silent glider plane—is just about one of the most unique experiences to be had in New York State. At the National Warplane Museum, near Elmira, you can take to the sky in a PT-17 or even a B-17 bomber. And at the nearby National Soaring Museum, visitors can climb aboard sailplanes for peaceful, quiet rides that soar above the valleys around Corning. See chapter 11.

- **Ice Skating on the Olympic Rink, Lake Placid:** Slip on your silver skates and take to the same rink where Eric Heiden won his gold medals in the 1980 Olympics. It's a public rink, so there's no pressure to race, just glide at your leisure while taking in the majesty of the surrounding Adirondacks. See chapter 12.

- **Eating Chicken Wings in the Place They Were Invented:** It was a snowy night back in the '60s when the owners of Buffalo's Anchor Bar dumped some chicken parts into a deep fryer and served them with blue cheese and celery. The rest, as they say, is history. You can still sample the original recipe in the divey bar where they became an American staple. See p. 396.

- **Watching Fireworks over Niagara Falls:** On the Canadian side of the Falls, every Friday and Sunday from May to September, there's a concert from 8 to 10pm, followed by an amazing show as the sky lights up with fireworks and colored lights shine on the cascading water. Not going during the summer? No worries; you can see the falls lit up every night of the year. Walk along the railing of the Canadian side for the best view. See chapter 13.

8 The Best Historic Places

- **Sagamore Hill, Oyster Bay:** Theodore Roosevelt's Summer White House still stands out on his beloved stretch of earth overlooking Long Island Sound. The decor of this 23-room Victorian estate reflects the president's travels with the Rough Riders; it's jammed with animal skins, heads, and exotic treasures from East Africa to the Amazon. See chapter 6.
- **Hudson Valley's Great Estates:** American history was made up and down the Hudson River, and not just at Revolutionary War battle sites. The grand estates of important literary figures, railroad magnates, and finance barons—including Washington Irving's Sleepy Hollow, the Lyndhurst Estate, the Rockefeller Family's Kykuit Estate, and the Vanderbilt Mansion—are lasting portraits of a young country's great expansion and riches at the height of the Industrial Age. History lessons that go to the core of the country's development are sensitively presented at the Philipsburg Manor, an 18th-century farm that serves as a living history museum about slavery in the north, while the FDR Presidential Library and Home and Eleanor Roosevelt's Val-Kill Cottage in Hyde Park document another crucial period in the country's more recent history. See chapter 7.
- **Huguenot Street Stone Houses, New Paltz:** Founded in 1678, New Paltz is built around one of the oldest streets of surviving stone houses in North America. Along Huguenot Street are a half-dozen original colonial-era stone houses built by French religious refugees, the Protestant Huguenots. The earliest was built in 1692, and all have been restored with period furnishing and heirlooms and operate as house museums (but guided tours of the houses are conducted in summer months only). See chapter 8.
- **Seneca Falls:** The small town of Seneca Falls is where the women's and civil rights movements got their start in the mid–19th century. The first Women's Rights Convention was held here in 1848, and today the Women's Rights National Historical Park, a National Park, is a museum erected next to the chapel where brave activists like Elizabeth Cady Stanton, Lucretia Mott, and Frederick Douglass formalized the women's rights and abolitionist movements that would ultimately redefine the concept of individual liberty. Other important historic sites in the area, such as the Elizabeth Cady Stanton House, are part of a "Women's Rights Trail." See chapter 11.
- **Camp Santanoni, Newcomb:** Back when wealthy industrialists were exploring the concept of leisure travel, they discovered the Adirondacks. Of course, "roughing it" to the Vanderbilts wasn't exactly sleeping in a lean-to. This camp, 4 miles south of Raquette Lake, is a 27-building "Great Camp" filled with rustic luxury—there's even a bowling alley. Today you can check out what this camp in the woods was all about. See chapter 12.

- **Downtown Buffalo:** It's hard to believe that 100 years ago this area was home to more millionaires per capita than anywhere else in the U.S. Fortunately, those wealthy industrialists left behind a wonderful architectural legacy, and buildings designed by the likes of E. B. Green and H. H. Richardson still grace the city's skyline. From City Hall to the amazing Ellicott Square building, it's worth walking around downtown and checking out the sites. See chapter 13.

9 The Best Places to Commune with Nature

- **Fire Island, Long Island:** This slender island protecting the mainland is replete with trees, wilderness, and one entire side of gorgeous golden-sand beach. Best of all, cars aren't allowed, meaning bikes and little red wagons are the only things that can run you over. And because the island is 32 miles long but just a half-mile wide, you're never more than a short walk from the ocean's waves and beach. For a truly remote wilderness experience, head to the eastern end, where it'll likely just be you and the deer drinking in the gorgeous environment. See chapter 6.

- **Mashomack Preserve:** With more than 2,000 pristine acres in the southeastern part of Shelter Island, this preserve, run by the Nature Conservancy, is about as remote as you can get on Long Island. There are 11 miles of easy hiking trails that run through the oak woodlands, marshes, ponds, and creeks. Keep an eye out for osprey, ibis, foxes, harbor seals, and terrapins. See chapter 6.

- **Kaaterskill Falls:** The Catskill Mountains are all about the great outdoors, providing tons of invitations to hike, bike, ski, boat, and fish. But one of those unique spots where everyone is sure to feel just a little closer to nature is Kaaterskill Falls, the highest waterfall in New York State. It's not nearly as powerful and massive as Niagara Falls, though it is indeed higher. An easy but beautiful walk, wending along a flowing creek, takes you to the bottom of the falls. The truly adventurous can scale the sides of the cliff and climb up to the shelf that runs right behind the falls. Another great vantage point is from the top of the falls, where a short path delivers you right to the edge of the sheer drop. See chapter 8.

- **Montezuma National Wildlife Refuge, Finger Lakes Region:** Smack in the middle of the Atlantic Migratory Flyway, at the north end of Cayuga Lake, this 7,000-acres wetlands nature park, established in 1938, is superb for birding and a spectacular nature experience for families. The marshes draw thousands of Canada geese, blue herons, egrets, wood ducks, and other water birds on their sojourns from nesting areas in Canada, reaching temporary populations as great as two million birds during the fall and spring migrations. You can drive, cycle, or walk along a road that takes you up close and personal with birds and other creatures. Even "off season" it's a great spot, and if you're lucky, you may glimpse a bald eagle's nest. See chapter 11.

- **Watkins Glen State Park:** There are too many great nature spots in the Finger Lakes to even begin to discuss or hope to visit on a single trip, starting with the sinewy lakes themselves, but this 776-acre park is surely at the top of any list. Its centerpiece is an amazing slate gorge carved out of the earth at the end of the last Ice Age, gradually shaped by the waters of Glen Creek. Along the beautiful walking trails are 19 waterfalls. See chapter 11.

• **St. Regis Canoe Wilderness:** It's not easy these days to find a single body of water expressly reserved for nonmotorized boats, and it's even harder to find several bodies of water for the canoer/kayaker. But this remote area, tucked deep in the heart of the Adirondacks, is just that. Take your boat out on these waters and it'll likely just be you and the birds as you cruise quietly through this amazing backcountry. See chapter 12.

• **Navy Island, Niagara Falls area, Canada:** It's hard to believe that there's a place to get away from the crowds of Niagara Falls, but those in the know head to this undeveloped, quiet island at the northern tip of Grand Island. You'll see tons of deer and bird life, along with oak, hickory, and wild raspberries. It's a great spot for fishing, too. Just watch out for the poison ivy. See chapter 13.

10 The Best Leaf-Peeping

• **Hudson River Valley:** Fall is one of the best times to visit the Hudson Valley. Temperatures are perfect, the great estates, many of them set among large old trees, gardens, and with gorgeous views of the Hudson, are splendid for aesthetic visits. The light is always great on the Hudson, but it's really special during the fall. See chapter 7.

• **Catskill Region:** Pick a county and go on a hike. Or kayak down the Delaware River. This extremely rural region is ideal for fall leaf-peeping. It's full of dairy farms and farmer's markets, emboldened by mountains and laced with lakes. The dense Catskill Forest Preserve is a kaleidoscope of color in autumn. See chapter 8.

• **Finger Lakes Region:** Autumn in the Finger Lakes region is impossibly scenic, with the golden hues of vineyards that grace the banks of deep-blue slivers of lakes, set off against autumnal colors. It's a perfect time to visit the excellent wineries, take a boat cruise, or bike around the lakes. See chapter 11.

• **Warrensburg to Indian Lake:** This drive north nets you some amazing scenery and even more amazing fall colors. From I-87, take Route 73 through Keene Valley and Keene and you'll head straight into the Adirondack High Peaks area, one of the most scenic in the state, even without fall colors. You'll see mountains ablaze with oranges and reds; once you hit Lake Placid go north on Route 86 and you'll be driving along the west branch of the Au Sable River, also bright with color. See chapter 12.

• **Letchworth State Park:** Long and slender, the park's central feature is a 400-foot-deep cavern; the water from the Genesee River feeds tons of deciduous trees that absolutely light up with color during the fall. Go on a hike deep in the woods or see it all from above in a balloon. See chapter 13.

11 The Best Four-Season Towns

• **Saratoga Springs:** Although summer's the star in Saratoga, this small city is also an excellent year-round destination. In warm months, the one-time "Queen of the Spas" sees thoroughbred racing at the famed Race Course, where the season lasts from the end of July to Labor Day, open-air concerts in the park, the New York City Ballet and Philadelphia Orchestra in residence, as well as boating and fishing on Saratoga Lake. However, Saratoga is eminently enjoyable in spring, fall, and even winter. This "city in the country" has great restaurants and inns, a handful of small, family-friendly museums, and Saratoga Spa State Park, where visitors can take long walks among the spring blossoms or fall foliage or enjoy cross-country skiing and ice skating in the middle of winter. See chapter 9.

- **Ithaca:** This college town is a great place to visit no matter the season, with a varied menu of sports and culture available year-round. The great hikes along Cayuga Lake and to nearby gorges are perfect ways to enjoy spring, summer, and fall. Cornell University's attractions, including the Herbert F. Johnson Museum of Art and Cornell Plantations' botanical garden, wildflower garden and arboretum, can easily be enjoyed at any time of year. Ithaca is one of the most cosmopolitan small towns in New York State, with a great roster of restaurants and theaters. The nearby wineries of the Cayuga Wine Trail make great visits in any season (though they're perhaps best in fall during harvest), although the highest free-falling waterfall in the eastern U.S, at Taughannock Falls State Park, are best viewed in spring and fall but not in summer, there is often very little water. In winter, there's nearby downhill and tons of cross-country skiing. See chapter 11.

- **Lake Placid:** In the summer, go boating on Mirror Lake, hike the many trails just outside town, or canoe along your own quiet stretch of lake. In winter, things really swing; the home of two Olympic Games, Placid offers the opportunity to ski Whiteface Mountain, ice skate, try the bobsled run, or go dog-sledding on Mirror Lake. See chapter 12.

12 The Most Adorable Towns

- **Greenport:** This is the cutest town on Long Island's North Fork. Filled with colonial buildings, inns, homes and shops, the town sits right on the protected waters of Peconic Bay. There's a strong sense of the town's history as a fishing village, with the smell of salt in the air, but there are also nice galleries and restaurants that line Main Street. See chapter 6.

- **Cold Spring:** Perhaps the most visitor-friendly small town on the Hudson, warm and inviting Cold Spring has something for everyone. The historic waterfront, equipped with a Victorian band shell and park benches, has unequaled views of the Hudson River; Main Street is packed with antiques shops, cafes, and restaurants; and the nearby mountains are perfect for surprisingly rigorous hikes. Cold Spring's within easy reach of lots of historic estates along the river, and the town's excellent handful of restaurants and inns could easily entice you to a much longer stay than you might have planned. See chapter 7.

- **Saugerties:** Like an antiquing cousin to more developed Hudson across the river, laid-back Saugerties is no longer tiny and undiscovered, but it remains adorable. The lovely but not yet overly commercialized main drag, Partition Street, has several restaurants, art galleries, and a burgeoning roster of antiques dealers. Just beyond downtown is a charming mile-long walking trail out to the river and the picturesque 1838 Saugerties Lighthouse, where you can even stay the night. See chapter 8.

- **Cooperstown:** This chain store–free town is best known for being home to the Baseball Hall of Fame. But sitting on the shores of Lake Otsego, it's also one of the state's cutest small towns. Tiny buildings and shops line the small Main Street, which you can walk the length of in just a few minutes. You'll find cute inns, good restaurants, and plenty of base-ball-card shops; then walk down to the water and have a picnic lunch overlooking the quiet, undeveloped lake. See chapter 10.
- **Skaneateles:** They don't come any cuter (or harder to pronounce) than this graceful town, which is more reminiscent of New England than upstate New York. The

historic downtown, an attractive mix of 19th-century Greek Revival and Victorian homes and appetizing boutiques and antique shops lining East Genesee Street, sits right on the north shore of Skaneateles Lake. The beautiful and crystal-clear lake is one of the prettiest and cleanest in the state, and charming inns and restaurants back right up to it. In summer, bands play on the lakefront at a postcard-perfect gazebo and winter brings costumed actors who create a Dickensian holiday. See chapter 11.

- **Saranac Lake:** Less hectic than its neighbor, Lake Placid, this town boasts a charm all its own. With tiny clapboard shops mixed in with cute brick structures, there are a couple of gems of restaurants here, along with a pretty inn and clean streets. See chapter 12.

13 The Best Oddball Attractions

- **Big Duck, Long Island:** You knew Long Island was famous for its duck, but this statue on Route 24 at the Flanders/Hampton Bays border will likely surprise you—it's 20 feet tall. Even better, you can stop there and pick up tourist information. See p. 179.
- **Reviving the Borscht Belt:** The Catskill Region has come a long way since it was the so-called borscht belt vacation land where New York City families retreated to day camps in the mountains. But there are still some of those old-school, all-in-one resorts, many of them ethnic enclaves of group entertainment and back-to-back activities like bowling, shuffle board, and pale imitations of yesteryear game shows. They're nostalgic for some, high camp or cheese for others. Among the

many resorts hanging on to old ways of summer fun in the mountains, one stands out: the Scott family resort at Oquaga Lake, where generations of one family have been entertaining visitors, incredibly, since 1869. The resort is best known for the singing Scott family's nightly cabaret revues in which everyone from the costumed grandkids to the grandparents plays a rousing part. See p. 251 and chapter 8.

- **700 Mormons Interpreting the Bible in Full Technicolor:** The Mormon Church, also known as the Church of Jesus Christ of Latter-Day Saints, got its miraculous start in the Finger Lakes Region before heading west. Every year in July, hundreds of thousands of the faithful and curious make pilgrimages to witness the Hill Cumorah

Pageant, a giant spectacle that constitutes the largest outdoor theatrical production in the U.S.: the show sports a costumed cast of 700, a nine-level stage, and music by the Mormon Tabernacle Choir. It has to be seen to be believed, but even nonbelievers enjoy the over-the-top show. See p. 334.

- **The Winery Impersonating Hooters:** Wine tasting is all about protocol and pompous, highbrow terms like bouquet, nose, and body, right? Not at Hazlitt 1852 Vineyards, in the Finger Lakes, where occasionally a visit to the vineyard is more akin to something you'd stumble upon at the college frat house. To start, the winery's bestseller is the mass-market "Red Cat" a low-rent party wine that has earned a reputation as an everyman's aphrodisiac. The winery revels in party atmosphere, rock 'n' roll music, and irreverence toward traditional wine-tasting etiquette. Sometimes, wine tasting is accompanied by cheerful folks joining in chants laced with sexual innuendo; more than a few women have been know to doff their tops to demonstrate their preference for Hazlitt wines. See p. 316.

- **Kazoo Museum, Eden:** Who would go through the trouble of collecting wooden kazoos, gold kazoos, and liquor bottle-shaped kazoos (celebrating the end of Prohibition)? People driven indoors by the brutal western New York winters. This museum has the oddest collection of this peculiar little instrument and until recently was even making more. See chapter 13.

- **Town of Mediums, Lily Dale:** This haven for those in touch with otherworldly spirits has been celebrating its odd collection of residents for 125 years. You can stop by for a private reading any time of year, or come in the summer for daily events, along with meditation and healing services. See chapter 13.

2

Planning Your Trip to New York State

by Karen Quarles

In the pages that follow, we've compiled everything you need to know to handle the practical details of planning your trip in advance—from tips on accommodations to finding great deals on the Internet, plus a calendar of events and more.

1 The Regions in Brief

NEW YORK CITY Residents in the surrounding areas of New York, New Jersey, and Connecticut refer to it simply as "the City," as if there were no other. The city comprises about 300 square miles divided into five boroughs—the Bronx, Brooklyn, Manhattan, Queens, and Staten Island. Best known for world-class museums, Broadway theater, Madison Avenue shopping, four-star cuisine, and glamorous nightlife, it's also a great place for more low-key adventures, like grabbing a hot dog at Yankee Stadium or spending a sunny afternoon in Central Park. For more about New York City, see chapter 5.

LONG ISLAND & THE HAMPTONS At 188 miles, long is an accurate description of the island situated to the east of Manhattan, dividing the waters of the Long Island Sound from the Atlantic Ocean. As you may have guessed, the sea is the dominant theme here—charming ports, sandy beaches, and fresh seafood abound. Surprisingly, it's also an agricultural area that supports numerous farms and award-winning vineyards. The North Shore, or "Gold Coast," is strewn with mansions formerly belonging to Astors and Vanderbilts, now transformed into

museums open to the public. See chapter 6.

THE HUDSON RIVER VALLEY The stunning landscape along the 100-mile stretch of the Hudson River from Albany to New York City has been immortalized on canvas by the painters of the Hudson River School and on paper in classics such as *The Legend of Sleepy Hollow* and *Rip Van Winkle.* The Appalachian Trail cuts through the valley, offering hikers an up-close view of river and the wilderness. Antiquing is a favorite pastime here, as is touring historic homes. See chapter 7.

THE CATSKILL MOUNTAIN REGION The Catskill Park and Forest Preserve lies in the heart of the Catskill Mountains, about 100 miles to the northwest of New York City. Nature lovers can explore 300 miles of trails up and down mountain peaks and among unspoiled forests, lakes, and rivers. See chapter 8.

THE CAPITAL REGION: SARATOGA SPRINGS & ALBANY Albany and the city's impressive architecture reflect its status as the state's capitol since 1797. Saratoga Springs, about 20 miles north of Albany, is named for the natural mineral waters that have drawn visitors to the town's spas and baths since the 1800s. It's also home to the Saratoga Race Course, the oldest thoroughbred racetrack in the U.S. See chapter 9.

CENTRAL NEW YORK Just west of the Finger Lakes, this largely rural area is legendary among sports fans for the National Baseball Hall of Fame and Museum in Cooperstown. See chapter 10.

THE FINGER LAKES REGION Bounded by Lake Ontario to the north and the Pennsylvania border to the south, the aptly named Finger Lakes region contains 11 long, slender lakes plus rivers, streams, waterfalls, and smaller bodies of water. The lakes offer lots of water-related fun, from swimming to kayaking to fishing; parks such as Finger Lakes National Forest and Letchworth State Park keep

landlubbers happy. Finger Lakes wine is another big attraction here; more than 70 wineries are located around Canandaigua, Keuka, Seneca, and Cayuga Lakes. See chapter 11.

THE NORTH COUNTRY Adirondack Park accounts for the majority of land in New York State north of I-90. At 6.1 million acres, the park is almost the size of the neighboring state of Vermont. See chapter 12.

WESTERN NEW YORK On its journey from Lake Ontario to Lake Erie, the Niagara River pours between 50,000 and 100,000 cubic feet of water per second over spectacular Niagara Falls. Buffalo—the second-largest city in New York State and a good bet for restaurants and nightlife—is just a 30-minute drive from the falls. See chapter 13.

2 Visitor Information

Call or write the **New York State Division of Tourism,** P.O. Box 2603, Albany, NY 12220-0603 (© **800/CALL-NYS** or 518/474-4116; www.iloveny.com/main.asp), for a stack of free brochures, including the informative "I Love New York Travel Guide," the "Official NYC Guide," and pamphlets about seasonal events. They even throw in a free state map that's just as useful as any you'd pay $5 for at the gas station. While on the road, you can pick up brochures at one of the state's **information centers.** Call the toll-free number above or check the "I Love New York Travel Guide" for the locations along on your route.

If you're planning a tour of the great outdoors, contact the **New York State Office of Parks, Recreation and Historic Preservation,** Albany, NY 12238 (© **518/474-0456,** or 518/486-1899 for the hearing or speech impaired; www.nysparks.state.ny.us), to request a free brochure, order admission passes, or find out about camping, hiking, and a host of other activities within the state's parks and historic sites. To reserve a campsite or other accommodations, book online or call © **800/456-2267.**

For **fall foliage reports,** see **www.empire.state.ny.us/tourism/foliage**.

3 Money

New York City is consistently ranked among the top 15 most expensive cities in the world, and the most expensive in the U.S. Thankfully, costs elsewhere in the state are closer to the national average, and even in New

York City there are deals to be found. For tips on booking your trip for less see "Planning Your Trip Online" and "Tips on Accommodations," later in this chapter.

ATMS

The easiest and best way to get cash away from home is from an ATM even in a small town, there's likely to be at least one. The **Cirrus** (✆ **800/424-7787**; www.mastercard.com) and **PLUS** (✆ **800/843-7587**; www.visa.com) networks span the globe. In New York, you'll also come across ATMs that participate in the **NYCE** (www.nyce.net) and **Star** (www.star.com) networks. Look at the back of your bank card to see which network you're on, then call or check online for ATM locations at your destination. Be sure you know your personal identification number (PIN) before you leave home and find out your daily withdrawal limit before you depart. Also keep in mind that many banks impose a fee every time a card is used at a different bank's ATM. On top of this, the bank from which you withdraw cash may charge its own fee. The State of New York Banking Department has compiled a comparison of bank fees by region at **www.banking.state.ny.us/bf.htm**. You can also use this chart to see if your own bank operates in the area you plan to visit.

TRAVELER'S CHECKS

Traveler's checks are something of an anachronism from the days before the ATM made cash accessible at any time. Traveler's checks used to be the only sound alternative to traveling with dangerously large amounts of cash. They were as reliable as currency, but, unlike cash, could be replaced if lost or stolen. These days, traveler's checks are less necessary because most cities have 24-hour ATMs that allow you to withdraw small amounts of cash as needed. However, keep in mind that you will likely be charged an ATM withdrawal fee if the bank is not your own, so if you're withdrawing money every day, you might be better off with traveler's checks—provided that you don't mind showing

identification every time you want to cash one.

You can get traveler's checks at almost any bank. **American Express** offers denominations of $20, $50, $100, $500, and (for cardholders only) $1,000. You'll pay a service charge ranging from 1% to 4%. You can also get American Express traveler's checks over the phone by calling ✆ **800/221-7282**; Amex gold and platinum cardholders who use this number are exempt from the 1% fee. AAA members can obtain checks without a fee at most AAA offices.

Visa offers traveler's checks at Citibank locations nationwide, as well as at several other banks. The service charge ranges between 1.5% and 2%; checks come in denominations of $20, $50, $100, $500, and $1,000. Call ✆ **800/732-1322** for information. **MasterCard** also offers traveler's checks; call ✆ **800/223-9920** for a location near you.

If you choose to carry traveler's checks, be sure to keep a record of their serial numbers separate from your checks in the event that they are stolen or lost. You'll get a refund faster if you know the numbers.

CREDIT CARDS

Credit cards are a safe way to carry money, they provide a convenient record of all your expenses, and they generally offer good exchange rates. You can also withdraw cash advances from your credit cards at banks or ATMs, provided you know your PIN. If you've forgotten yours, or didn't even know you had one, call the number on the back of your credit card and ask the bank to send it to you. It usually takes 5 to 7 business days, though some banks will provide the number over the phone if you tell them your mother's maiden name or some other personal information. New York businesses honor most major credit cards, although Diners Club and Discover cards are somewhat less commonly accepted than MasterCard, Visa, and American Express.

For tips and telephone numbers to call if your wallet is stolen or lost, go to "Lost & Found" in the Fast Facts section of this chapter.

4 When to Go

Since New York State is a four-season destination, the best time to visit depends on what you want to do.

Summer is peak season, accounting for about 40% of New York State tourism. From June to August, the weather is pleasant and mostly sunny, though it tends to be humid. Temperatures usually remain below 85°F (29°C), except in the vicinity of New York City and Long Island, which is about 10°F (6°C) warmer than the rest of the state year-round. Summer weather is ideal for travel; the problem is that everyone else thinks so, too. Parklands and campgrounds are filled with vacationers, even more so on weekends. Cities throng with sightseers, making for long lines, sold-out events, and high prices.

Fall, from September through November, is another popular time to visit. Upstate, the air turns to crisp jacket-weather in September, but farther south summertime lingers until early October. New York's beautiful fall foliage is a huge draw, especially in mid-October—the best time to catch trees sporting brilliant reds and golds. Expect country inns, B&Bs, and state and national parks to be particularly busy over Columbus Day weekend.

Contrary to popular belief, winter temperatures aren't miserable—they normally range from about 15°F (–9°C) to as high as 40°F (4°C) in New York City. The snow, on the other hand, is brutal. Infamous "lake-effect" snowstorms can dump feet at a time on Buffalo and surrounding towns, prompting thruway and airport closings. Most of upstate New York is blanketed in snow from December to March. Although statistically winter is the slowest time for tourism in New York, it's high season for the state's ski destinations, and parks are still active with winter sports lovers. New York City, which welcomes a steady flow of visitors all year long, is extrajammed during the holidays thanks to Christmas festivities at Rockefeller Center, holiday shopping, and New Year's Eve in Times Square.

The spring thaw begins in March, but it's not unusual for snow to fall in April, or even May. There are spring showers, but the average amount of precipitation is no heavier than in summer or fall. Rainfall remains fairly constant from May to November at approximately 3 to 4 inches per month. If you enjoy the quietly melting snow and fresh spring breezes, this

Average Monthly Temperatures (°F & °C)

		Jan	Feb	Mar	Apr	May	June	July	Aug	Sep	Oct	Nov	Dec
Albany	°F	22	25	35	47	58	66	71	69	61	49	39	28
	°C	–6	–4	2	8	14	19	22	21	16	9	4	–2
Buffalo	°F	25	26	34	45	57	66	71	69	62	51	40	30
	°C	–4	–3	1	7	14	19	22	21	17	11	4	–1
New York	°F	33	35	42	52	62	72	77	76	69	58	48	38
	°C	1	2	6	11	17	22	25	24	21	14	9	3
Syracuse	°F	23	25	34	45	57	66	71	69	61	50	40	29
	°C	–5	–4	1	7	14	19	22	21	16	10	4	–2

season may be your golden opportunity to indulge in outdoor activities before the summer rush.

NEW YORK STATE CALENDAR OF EVENTS

January

Winter Festival of Lights, Niagara Falls, Ontario. A visual extravaganza of lighting displays featuring Disney's motion light displays in Queen Victoria Park. Call © **800/563-2557** or 905/374-1616 or visit www.niagarafallstourism.com/wfol/wfolmain.html. Early to mid-January.

Chinese New Year, New York City. Every year Chinatown rings in its own New Year (based on a lunar calendar) with 2 weeks of celebrations, including parades with dragon and lion dancers, plus vivid costumes of all kinds. Call the New York City Visitor's hot line at © **212/484-1222** or the Asian American Business Development Center at © **212/966-0100.** February 1, 2004; January 22, 2005.

World Cup Freestyle, Lake Placid. The world's best aerial skiers take off and fly, tucking and spinning their way to a championship. You'll see mogul action too, as the athletes' skis zig and zag among the mounds of snow. Call © **518/523-1655** or visit www.orda.org. Mid-January.

February

Olmsted Winterfest, Buffalo. Delaware Park becomes a magnet for fun seekers, with sledding, skating, snowmobiling, softball, ice sculpting, a chili cook-off, and races taking place all over the park. There's a Friday Fish Fry, naturally, and fireworks. Call © **716/884-9660** or visit www.buffaloolmsted parks.org. Four days in mid-February.

Empire State Winter Games, Lake Placid. The games for New York State's premier amateur athletes. Call © **518/523-1655** or visit www.orda.org. Mid-February.

March

St. Patrick's Day Parade. More than 150,000 marchers join in the world's largest civilian parade, as Fifth Avenue from 44th to 86th streets rings with the sounds of bands and bagpipes. The parade usually starts at 11am, but go extra early if you want a good spot. Call © **212/484-1222.** March 17.

April

Easter Parade, New York City. No marching bands, no baton twirlers, no protesters. It's more about flamboyant exhibitionism, with hats and costumes that get more outrageous every year—and anybody can join right in for free. It's along Fifth Avenue from 48th to 57th streets on Easter Sunday, from about 10am to 3 or 4pm. Call © **212/484-1222.** April 11, 2004; March 27, 2005.

May

Lilac Festival, Rochester. More than 1,000 lilac trees in Highland Park, with dozens of varieties of fragrant lilacs in full bloom, are the excuse for a big civic party; there are music and eats, but the highlight is easily the lilacs. Call © **585/256-4960.** Early May.

Bike New York: The Great Five Borough Bike Tour, New York City. The largest mass-participation cycling event in the United States attracts about 30,000 cyclists from all over the world. Call © **212/932-BIKE** (2453) or visit www.bikenewyork.org to register. First or second Sunday in May.

Tulip Festival, Albany. For more than 50 years, Albany has celebrated its Dutch heritage with this colorful festival, where in addition to thousands of beautiful tulips in Washington Park, there are plenty of foods, entertainment, and crafts—not to mention the annual crowning of the tulip queen! Call © **518/434-2032.** Second week of May.

Falls Fireworks & Concert Series, Niagara Falls, Ontario. Every Friday and Sunday you can enjoy free concerts by the falls at 8pm, followed by a fireworks show at 10pm, which bathes the falls in color. Call © **877/642-7275** or visit www.niagaraparks.com. Mid-May through mid-September.

Fleet Week, New York City. About 10,000 navy and Coast Guard personnel are "at liberty" in New York for the annual Fleet Week. Usually from 1 to 4pm daily, you can watch the ships and aircraft carriers as they dock at the piers on the west side of Manhattan, tour them with on-duty personnel, and watch some dramatic exhibitions by the U.S. Marines. Call © **212/245-0072,** or visit www.fleetweek.com. Late May.

June

Annual Hall of Fame Game, Cooperstown. The day begins with a lecture by Hall of Famers and moves into a game between pro teams. There's a home-run contest, and, of course, lots of hot-dog eating. Call © **888/HALL-OF-FAME** or visit www.baseballhalloffame.org. Early June.

Belmont Stakes, Elmont (Long Island). The third jewel in the Triple Crown is held at the **Belmont Park Race Track.** If a Triple Crown winner is to be named, it will happen here. For information, call © **516/488-6000,** or visit www.nyracing.com/belmont. Early June.

Caramoor International Music Festival, Katonah (Hudson River Valley). This idiosyncratic house-museum and performing arts center hosts one of the state's best music festivals, with a full slate of summer outdoor chamber and symphonic music concerts. Call © **914/232-1252.** Through August.

Hudson Valley Shakespeare Festival, Garrison (Hudson River Valley). On the gorgeous grounds of Boscobel Restoration, one of the prettiest spots along the Hudson, the performance of summer theater of Shakespeare seems suitably grand, and perfect for a summer's eve picnic. Call © **845/265-7858.** Through August.

Shakespeare in the Park, New York City. The Delacorte Theater in **Central Park** is the setting for first-rate free performances under the stars—including at least one Shakespeare production. Call © **212/539-8750** or point your browser to www.publictheater.org. Through August.

Shakespeare in Delaware Park, Buffalo. Free Shakespeare under the stars has been a Buffalo tradition for almost 30 years. Call © **716/856-4533** or visit www.shakespeareindelawarepark.org. Mid-June to mid-August.

Chautauqua season opens, Chautauqua Institution. This arts camp in western New York is one of the most prestigious in the nation. Its extensive grounds, right on the shores of Chautauqua Lake, play host to all manner of arts classes, lectures, and performances. Call © **800/836-ARTS** or go to www.chautauqua-inst.org. Mid-June to mid-August.

Museum Mile Festival, New York City. Fifth Avenue from 82nd to 104th streets is closed to cars from 6 to 9pm as 20,000-plus strollers enjoy live music, street entertainers, and free admission to nine Museum Mile institutions, including the Metropolitan Museum of Art and the Guggenheim. Call ✆ **212/606-2296.** Usually the second Tuesday in June.

Lesbian and Gay Pride Week and March, New York City. A week of cheerful happenings, from simple parties to major political fund-raisers, precedes a zany parade commemorating the Stonewall Riot of June 27, 1969, which for many marks the beginning of the gay liberation movement. Call ✆ **212/807-7433** or check www.nycpride. org. Mid- to late June.

U.S. Open Golf Championship, Southampton. In 2004, this major tournament comes to Shinnecock Hills in Southampton. Come see if Tiger can put another major tournament under his belt. Call ✆ **908/234-2300.** June 17 to 20, 2004.

Lake Placid Horse Shows, Lake Placid. Watch horses take to the air in this prestigious horse show set against the gorgeous Adirondacks. Call ✆ **518/523-9625** or visit www.lakeplacidhorseshow.com. Late June.

July

Glimmerglass Opera, Cooperstown. Central New York's famous opera gears up for another impressive season. Call ✆ **607/547-2255** or go to www.glimmerglass.org. Early July through end of August.

Hill Cumorah Pageant, Palmyra (Finger Lakes Region). Near the site where the Mormon religion was founded, the Church of Jesus Christ of Latter-Day Saints puts on an amazing theatrical spectacle, in the tradition of Middle Ages pageants, with 700 actors. Call ✆ **315/597-2757** or 315/597-5851. First 2 weeks of July.

Independence Day Harbor Festival and Fourth of July Fireworks Spectacular, New York City. Start the day amid the patriotic crowds at the Great July Fourth Festival in Lower Manhattan, and then catch Macy's great fireworks extravaganza (one of the country's most fantastic) over the East River (the best vantage point is from the FDR Dr., which closes to traffic several hours before sunset). Call ✆ **212/484-1222,** or Macy's Visitor Center at 212/494-2922. July 4th.

Hurley Stone House Tour, Hurley (Catskill region). Unlike New Paltz, where the ancient stone structures are open in season to visitors, Hurley's collection of two dozen stone houses, most privately owned, only open once a year for visits. Call ✆ **845/331-4121.** Mid-July.

Finger Lakes Wine Festival, Watkins Glen International Racetrack. The Finger Lakes is one of the country's great (but still up-and-coming) wine regions, and everybody gets together—locals, visitors, and some five dozen or so wineries—for tastings, crafts, food, and good spirits. It's anything but stuffy, though, as the annual toga party (or "Launch of the Lakes") attests. Call ✆ **607/535-2486,** ext. 230. Usually the third weekend in July.

Windham Chamber Music Festival, Windham (Catskill region). Opera stars from the Metropolitan in New York City descend upon the Catskills Mountains for some high culture at a higher altitude. Call ✆ **518/734-3868.** Through August.

Belleayre Music Festival, Highmount (Catskill region). The ski mountain of Belleayre races in summer with a wide-ranging mix of high-brow and popular music and entertainment, from classical and opera to folk and puppetry. Call ✆ **800/942-6904.** Through August.

Annual Wine Country Classic Boat Show, Hammondsport (Finger Lakes region). At the southern end of Keuka Lake, this antique and classic boat show features more than

100 boats, with judging, water parades, and demonstrations. On Sunday is the race regatta. Call ✆ **585/394-3044.** Third weekend in July.

Saratoga Summer Culture, Saratoga Springs. In July, the New York City Ballet makes its off-season home at the National Museum of Dance & Hall of Fame, and during the month of August, the Philadelphia Orchestra is in residence at the Saratoga Performing Arts Center (SPAC). Who would think that high culture could compete stride-for-stride with the horses over at the track for the big event of the summer? Call ✆ **518/584-2225** or 518/584-9330. July and August.

Baseball Hall of Fame Induction Weekend, Cooperstown. Come see which legendary swingers will make it in this year. Call ✆ **888/HALL-OF-FAME** or visit www.baseball halloffame.org. Late July.

Thoroughbred Horse Racing, Saratoga Springs (Capital region). At the famed Race Course, the oldest in the country, the race season lasts six weeks and turns the town upside down. Call ✆ **518/584-6200.** End of July through early September.

August

Antique Boat Show & Auction, Clayton. It's the oldest continuous boat show in the world—you can even bid on a boat at the auction. Cruise the commercial marketplace and flea market, sit in on an educational forum, listen to music, and sample food. Lots of kids' programs, too. Call ✆ **315/686-4104.** Early August.

Maverick Concert Series, Woodstock. America's oldest summer chamber music series, continuous since 1916, is this agreeable version of "Music in the Woods." Call

✆ **845/679-8217.** August through beginning of September.

Harlem Week, New York City. The world's largest black and Hispanic cultural festival actually spans almost the whole month to include the Black Film Festival, the Harlem Jazz and Music Festival, and the Taste of Harlem Food Festival. Call ✆ **212/484-1222.** Throughout August.

NASCAR Winston Cup at the Glen, Watkins Glen. Among legions of race fans, this huge event is unparalleled in the Northeast, and it draws NASCAR fans from across the state and the region, filling up just about every bed in the Finger Lakes. Call ✆ **607/535-2481.** Second week in August.

Republican National Convention, New York City. For the first time the elephants, as opposed to the donkeys, who last convened in New York in 1992, will be coming to New York to hold their national convention. Call ✆ **212/484-1200.** Last week of August 2004.

Toy Fest, East Aurora. The home of Fisher-Price toys comes to life with a toy parade along Main Street, an antique toy show, rides, and other activities. Call ✆ **716/687-5151** or visit www.toytownusa.com. Late August.

National Buffalo Wing Festival, Buffalo. This festival features many restaurants and sauces from Buffalo and around the country. Best wing and sauce competitions, wing-eating contests, and more. Call ✆ **716/565-4141.** Late August.

New York State Fair, Syracuse (Finger Lakes region). New York State's massive 12-day agricultural and entertainment fair, with all kinds of big-name music acts and food you'll be glad only comes 'round once a year. Call ✆ **800/475-FAIR.** Late August to early September.

U.S. Open Tennis Championships, New York City. The final Grand Slam event of the tennis season is held at the Arthur Ashe Stadium at the USTA National Tennis Center, the largest public tennis center in the world, at **Flushing Meadows Park** in Queens. Tickets go on sale in May or early June, and the event sells out immediately. Call © **888/OPEN-TIX** or 718/760-6200 well in advance; visit www.usopen.org or www.usta.com for additional information. Two weeks around Labor Day.

September

Turn-of-the-Century Day, Roxbury (Catskill Region). Reliving the glory days of baseball and hoop skirts, the town of Roxbury sheds about 100 years and celebrates with a vintage "base ball" game, horse-drawn wagon rides, and period foods and costumes on the former estate of Helen Gould Shepard in this Labor Day tradition. Call © **607/326-3722.** Labor Day.

West Indian–American Day Parade, New York City. This annual Brooklyn event is New York's largest and best street celebration. Come for the extravagant costumes, pulsating rhythms (soca, calypso, reggae), bright colors, folklore, food (jerk chicken, Caribbean soul food), and two million hip-shaking revelers. Call © **212/484-1222** or 718/625-1515. Labor Day.

Adirondack Balloon Festival, Glens Falls, Queensbury, and Lake George. Watch a rainbow of colors soar into the sky as 60-plus hot-air balloons lift off. Tons of activities surround this annual event. Call © **800/365-1050** or visit www.adirondackballoonfest.org. Mid-September.

Naples Grape Festival, Naples (Finger Lakes region). To celebrate the harvest of the grape in this grape-growing and wine-producing region, grape pie lives for a weekend in the tiny town of Naples. Connoisseurs rejoice, scarfing down as much pie as possible, and there's a "World's Greatest Grape Pie" contest and live entertainment. Call © **585/374-2240.** End of September.

October

Legend of Sleepy Hollow Weekend, Tarrytown (Hudson River Valley). At Washington Irving's Sunnyside home, as well as up the road at Philipsburg Manor, the specter of the Headless Horseman returns for one last ride. So as not to scare all concerned, there are also walks in the woods, storytelling, and puppet shows. Call © **914/631-8200.** Last week in October.

Halloween at Howe Caverns. Come check out the underground scare-a-thon with pumpkin-decorating contests, scary stories, and special kids' buffet. Call © **518/296-8900** or visit www.howecaverns.com. October 31.

Greenwich Village Halloween Parade, New York City. This is Halloween at its most outrageous. You may have heard Lou Reed singing about it on his classic album *New York*—he wasn't exaggerating. Drag queens and assorted other flamboyant types parade through the Village in wildly creative costumes. Call the *Village Voice* parade hot line at © **212/475-3333,** ext. 4044, or go to www.halloween-nyc.com for the exact route so you can watch—or participate, if you have the threads and the imagination. October 31.

November

New York City Marathon, New York City. Some 30,000 hopefuls from around the world participate in the largest U.S. marathon, and more than a million fans will cheer them on as they follow a route that touches on all five New York boroughs and finishes at Central Park. Call ✆ **212/423-2249** or 212/860-4455, or visit www.nyrrc.org, where you can find applications to run. First Sunday in November.

Lights in the Park, Buffalo. Delaware Park is transformed into a colorful wonderland throughout the holidays, with animated lighting displays and a collection of holiday scenes. Call ✆ **716/856-4533.** Begins mid-November.

Macy's Thanksgiving Day Parade, New York City. The procession of huge hot-air balloons from Central Park West and 77th Street and down Broadway to Herald Square at 34th Street continues to be a national tradition. The night before, you can usually see the big blow-up on Central Park West at 79th Street; call in advance to see if it will be open to the public again this year. Call ✆ **212/484-1222,** or Macy's Visitor Center at 212/494-2922. Thanksgiving Day.

Lighting of the Rockefeller Center Christmas Tree, New York City. The annual lighting ceremony is accompanied by an ice-skating show, singing, entertainment, and a huge crowd. The tree stays lit around the clock until after the new year. Call ✆ **212/332-6868** or visit www.rockefellercenter.com for this year's date. Late November or early December.

Christmas Traditions, New York City. Look for these holiday favorites: Radio City Music Hall's **Christmas Spectacular** (✆ 212/247-4777; www.radiocity.com); the New York City Ballet's staging of *The Nutcracker* (✆ 212/870-5570; www.nycballet.com); *A Christmas Carol* at The Theater at Madison Square Garden, 2003 final year (✆ **212/465-6741;** www.the garden.com); and the National

Chorale's singalong performances of Handel's *Messiah* at Avery Fisher Hall (✆ **212/875-5030;** www.lincolncenter.org). Call for schedules. Late November through December.

Dickens Christmas, Skaneateles (Finger Lakes region). Sweet nostalgia takes over this quaint Finger Lakes town as costumed characters—Father Christmas, Mother Goose, and Scrooge—roam the streets. Locals go door-to-door caroling, and there are carriage rides and free roasted chestnuts. Call ✆ **315/685-2268.** Last weekend in November to just before Christmas.

December

Great Estates Candelight Christmas Tours, Hudson River Valley. Some of the grandest mansions lining the Hudson River—Boscobel, Sunnyside, Van Cortlandt Manor, Lyndhurst, Olana, and others—get all decked out for the holidays, with special candlelight house tours, caroling, bonfires, and hot cider. It's one of the best times to experience the pageantry and customs of another era. Throughout December.

Holiday Trimmings, New York City. Stroll down festive Fifth Avenue, and you'll see doormen dressed as wooden soldiers at **FAO Schwarz,** a 27-foot sparkling snowflake floating over the intersection outside **Tiffany & Co.,** the **Cartier** building ribboned and bowed in red, wreaths warming the necks of the **New York Public Library**'s lions, and fanciful figurines in the windows of **Saks Fifth Avenue** and **Lord & Taylor.** Madison Avenue between 55th and 60th streets is also a good bet; **Sony Plaza** usually displays something fabulous as does **Barneys New York.** Throughout December.

Lighting of the Hanukkah Menorah, New York City. Everything is done on a grand scale in New York, so it's no surprise that the world's largest menorah (32 ft. high) is at Manhattan's **Grand Army Plaza,** Fifth Avenue and 59th Street. Hanukkah celebrations begin at sunset, with the lighting of the first of the giant electric candles. First day of Hanukkah.

New Year's Eve, New York City. The biggest party of them all happens in **Times Square,** where hundreds of thousands of raucous revelers count down in unison the year's final seconds until the new lighted ball drops at midnight at 1 Times Square. Hate to be a party pooper, but this one, in the cold surrounded by thousands of very drunk revelers, is a masochist's delight. Call © **212/768-1560** or 212/484-1222, or visit www.times squarebid.org. December 31.

5 Travel Insurance

Check your existing insurance policies and credit-card coverage before you buy travel insurance. You may already be covered for lost luggage, canceled tickets, or medical expenses. The cost of travel insurance varies widely, depending on the cost and length of your trip, your age, health, and the type of trip you're taking.

TRIP-CANCELLATION INSUR-ANCE Trip-cancellation insurance helps you get your money back if you have to back out of a trip, if you have to go home early, or if your travel supplier goes bankrupt. Allowed reasons for cancellation can range from sickness to natural disasters to the State Department declaring your destination unsafe for travel. (Insurers usually won't cover vague fears, though, as many travelers discovered who tried to cancel their trips in Oct 2001 because they were wary of flying.) In this unstable world, trip-cancellation insurance is a good buy if you're getting tickets well in advance—who knows what the state of the world, or of your airline, will be in nine months? Insurance policy details vary, so read the fine print—and especially make sure that your airline or cruise line is on the list of carriers covered in case of bankruptcy. For information, contact one of the following insurers: **Access America** (© 866/ 807-3982; www.accessamerica.com); **Travel Guard International** (© 800/ 826-4919; www.travelguard.com);

Travel Insured International (© 800/ 243-3174; www.travelinsured.com); and **Travelex Insurance Services** (© 888/457-4602; www.travelex insurance.com).

MEDICAL INSURANCE Most health insurance policies cover you if you get sick away from home—but check, particularly if you're insured by an HMO.

LOST-LUGGAGE INSURANCE On domestic flights, checked baggage is covered up to $2,500 per ticketed passenger. On international flights (including U.S. portions of international trips), baggage is limited to approximately $9.05 per pound, up to approximately $635 per checked bag. If you plan to check items more valuable than the standard liability, see if your valuables are covered by your homeowner's policy, get baggage insurance as part of your comprehensive travel-insurance package or buy Travel Guard's "BagTrak" product. Don't buy insurance at the airport, as it's usually overpriced. Be sure to take any valuables or irreplaceable items with you in your carry-on luggage, as many valuables (including books, money, and electronics) aren't covered by airline policies.

If your luggage is lost, immediately file a lost-luggage claim at the airport, detailing the luggage contents. For most airlines, you must report delayed, damaged, or lost baggage within 4 hours of arrival. The airlines are required to deliver luggage, once found, directly to your house or destination free of charge.

6 Health & Safety

STAYING HEALTHY

For the latest information about health issues affecting travelers, visit the **Centers for Disease Control and Prevention**'s travel page at www.cdc.gov/travel or call the **Travelers' Health Hotline** at © **877/FYI-TRIP.** The **New York State Department of Health** website (www.health.state.ny.us) is geared toward residents rather than visitors, but provides more specifics about issues concerning New York. If there's no link on the home page to the topic you're looking for, click on "Info for Consumers."

GENERAL AVAILABILITY OF HEALTH CARE

There's no shortage of doctors, hospitals, and pharmacies in New York. But it's true that cities have more facilities than rural areas. The New York State Department of Health provides a list of hospitals by county at www.health.state.ny.us/nysdoh/hospital/main.htm.

Pharmacy chains like **Rite Aid** (www.riteaid.com), **CVS** (www.cvs.com), and **Walgreens** (www.walgreens.com) are pretty easy to find should you need to fill or refill a prescription. Bring your doctor's telephone number with you so that the pharmacist can confirm the prescription with your doctor's office. It's also helpful to have the number of your home pharmacy on hand in case your doctor can't be reached.

COMMON AILMENTS

BUGS & BITES   Mosquitoes are a familiar annoyance, particularly in late summer and early fall when New York's mosquito population peaks. They were upgraded from pest to public health issue, however, when the first U.S. case of the mosquito-borne **West Nile virus** was reported in New York City in 1999. The virus can lead to a flulike bout of West Nile fever, or more serious diseases such as West Nile encephalitis or meningitis. Even if you get a few bites, though, the risk of illness is low. Not all mosquitoes carry the virus, and most people who are infected never even become sick, although people over 50 are more susceptible. Symptoms include fever, headache, stiff neck, body ache, muscle weakness or tremors, and disorientation. If you think you've been infected, see a doctor right away or go to the emergency room.

The best defense is an effective bug repellent worn whenever you're in a mosquito-friendly environment—this includes warm and wet urban areas as well as forests and fields. They can bite right through lightweight fabrics, so it's smart to give clothes a spritz, too. If possible, stay inside when mosquitoes are busiest: dawn, dusk, and early evening.

Ticks are common in the northeast. They stay close to the ground and prefer damp, shady grass and stone walls. **Lyme disease** is carried by deer ticks, which are 2 millimeters or less in size (smaller than dog ticks or cattle ticks). If you've been bitten by a tick, there's no reason to assume you've contracted the disease. Not all ticks are carriers, and removing the offender within the first 36 hours usually prevents transmission of the harmful bacteria. Seek medical aid if symptoms develop, such as the trademark "bull's-eye" bruise or red rash that grows outward from the area of the bite, or other signs like joint pain, fever, fatigue, or facial paralysis. If left unchecked, Lyme disease can lead to serious complications affecting the heart or nervous system.

Vigilance is the key to avoiding ticks, since they have a creepy habit of climbing up the body and settling in unexposed areas like the thighs, groin, trunk, armpits, and behind the ears (although they can attach anywhere). Wear light-colored clothes so they're easy to see before they latch on. Tuck shirts in at the waist, close up pant-leg access by tucking them into socks, and use bug repellent on clothes and skin. At the end of the day, check your entire body for ticks. If you have access to a dryer, set it on high and throw clothes in to kill any you may have missed.

Black flies are a nuisance in the Adirondacks, especially from late May to early June. Their bite can be itchy and painful, but they don't usually carry illness in this part of the country. As with mosquitoes, bug spray applied to skin and clothes will make you a less attractive target.

OTHER WILDLIFE CONCERNS
New York's national and state parks are great places to glimpse wild creatures. This can be exciting, but remember that wild animals are unpredictable, and it's wise not to get too close.

Raccoons, foxes, skunks, and bats are the most likely to spread **rabies.** The virus can be transmitted through the bite or scratch of an infected animal, or contact with the animal's saliva or nervous tissue through an unhealed cut. This means it's unsafe to poke around dead carcasses as well. If contact occurs, wash the wound thoroughly with soap and water and report to a doctor or hospital for treatment. Let a park ranger or other official know so the animal can be captured and tested for the disease.

Black bears are indigenous to the Adirondack, Catskill, and Allegany mountains. Although they're naturally inclined to avoid humans, they'll often raid campsites in search of food. Tuck food away and clean up campsites

after meals to keep them from sniffing around. And never approach a baby bear. The mother bear is usually not far away and may perceive you as a threat to the cub. A useful source for black bear safety tips is the Citizens for Responsible Wildlife Management website at **www.responsiblewildlife management.org/bear_safety.htm**.

Deer are frequently sighted in upstate New York—often crossing the road in front of your car. Hitting a deer can be an awful experience. Besides feeling as if you've just killed Bambi, you could also sustain major damage to your vehicle or yourself in the accident. Warning signs are posted at well-known deer crossings, but keep your eyes peeled in any wilderness area, especially during breeding season (Oct–Dec).

EXTREME WEATHER EXPO-SURE It's not typically cold enough in New York for **frostbite** to take hold during normal activities like sightseeing. But if you plan to spend all day on the slopes or take long winter hikes, dress appropriately and warm up indoors periodically. This is especially important for kids—they lose heat faster than adults and may not notice the cold if they're having fun. In summer, high temperatures and humidity combined with too much exercise can provoke **heat illness.** Stop and rest in the shade when you feel too hot, tired, or dehydrated, and always carry water with you.

WHAT TO DO IF YOU GET SICK AWAY FROM HOME
In most cases, your existing health plan will provide the coverage you need. But double-check; you may want to buy **travel medical insurance** instead. (See the section on insurance, above.) Bring your insurance ID card with you when you travel.

If you suffer from a chronic illness, consult your doctor before your departure. For conditions like epilepsy, diabetes, or heart problems, wear a **Medic Alert Identification Tag** (© **800/825-3785;** www.medicalert. org), which will immediately alert doctors to your condition and give them access to your records through Medic Alert's 24-hour hot line.

Pack **prescription medications** in your carry-on luggage, and carry prescription medications in their original containers, with pharmacy labels—otherwise they won't make it through airport security. Also bring along copies of your prescriptions in case you lose your pills or run out. Don't forget an extra pair of contact lenses or prescription glasses.

If you get sick, consider asking your hotel concierge to recommend a local doctor—even his or her own. You can also try the emergency room at a local hospital; many have walk-in clinics for emergency cases that are not life-threatening. You may not get immediate attention, but you won't pay the high price of an emergency-room visit.

STAYING SAFE

The crime rate in New York State has been steadily dropping for the last decade. New York City, once famous for muggings, is now considered one of the safest large cities in the country. That said, it's never a good idea to take your safety for granted.

First and foremost, know where you're going. If you look lost or distracted, you may seem like an easy mark. Ask for directions at the front desk before leaving your hotel, and try not to be obvious about checking maps on the street. Be wary of strangers who offer to act as guides. They may expect you to tip them, or they may try to lead you to a secluded place where they can rob you. Try not to use the subway to get around late at night; opt for the bus or a taxi instead.

Keep on the lookout for thieves and pickpockets. Common tactics include bumping into you, accompanying you through a revolving door, or spilling something on your clothes to distract you. When withdrawing money from an ATM at a bank after hours, note who enters the foyer with you or who is already inside. If it doesn't seem safe, find another ATM.

At the hotel, keep the door locked and use the bolt when you're inside the room. Before you answer the door, make sure you know who it is. If it's an unexpected visit from room service or maintenance, don't be embarrassed to call the front desk to make sure it's legitimate. Remember that the staff has passkeys, and your room is frequently opened when you're not there. Use the in-room safe for cash, traveler's checks, and valuables like your jewelry or your laptop. If there's no safe in your room, inquire about using the hotel safe.

Since the September 11, 2001, terrorist attacks, counteracting terrorism has become a major concern. The police urge everyone to report unattended bags or suspicious-looking packages through the **Statewide Public Security Tips Hotline** at **866/SAFE-NYS,** or 888/NYC-SAFE in New York City.

7 Specialized Travel Resources

TRAVELERS WITH DISABILITIES

Most disabilities shouldn't stop anyone from traveling. There are more options and resources out there than ever before.

Several travel agencies offer services for travelers with disabilities who are eager to explore the natural and cultural wonders of New York State. **People and Places** (© **716/937-1813** or 716/496-8826; www.people-and-places.org) offers escorted tours for developmentally disabled vacationers to the Adirondacks, Catskills, 1000 Islands, Finger Lakes, and other destinations in New York State. **Next Stop New York** (✆ 800/434-7554 or 718/264-2300; www.nextstopnew york.com) designs theater, food-tasting, and sightseeing tours of Manhattan for groups or individuals. **Alternative Leisure Co. & Trips Unlimited** (✆ 781/275-0023; www.alctrips.com) offers group excursions in New York and New England as well as a "Traveling Companion" program, which provides staff members to accompany individuals on customized trips. **Flying Wheels Travel** (✆ 507/451-5005; www.flyingwheels travel.com) arranges private tours in minivans with lifts. **Accessible Journeys** (✆ 800/846-4537 or 610/521-0339; www.disabilitytravel.com) caters specifically to slow walkers and wheelchair travelers and their families and friends.

The **U.S. National Park Service (NPS)** offers a **Golden Access Passport** that gives free lifetime entrance to all properties administered by the National Park Service—national parks, monuments, historic sites, recreation areas, and national wildlife refuges—for persons who are blind or permanently disabled, regardless of age. You may pick up a Golden Access Passport at any NPS entrance fee area by showing proof of medically determined disability and eligibility for receiving benefits under federal law. Besides free entry, the Golden Access Passport also offers a 50% discount on federal-use fees charged for such facilities as camping, swimming, parking, boat launching, and tours. For more information, call ✆ 888/467-2757 or go to www.nps.gov/fees_passes.htm. Keep in mind that this pass does not grant access to state-operated parks and facilities. For more about New York's state parks, see "Visitor Information," earlier in this chapter, and "Online Traveler's Toolbox," later in this chapter.

Organizations that offer assistance to disabled travelers include the **Moss Rehab Hospital** (www.mossresource net.org), which provides a library of accessible-travel resources online; the **Society for Accessible Travel and Hospitality** (✆ 212/447-7284; www.sath.org; annual membership fees: $45 adults, $30 seniors and students), which offers a wealth of travel resources for all types of disabilities and informed recommendations on destinations, access guides, travel agents, tour operators, vehicle rentals, and companion services; and the **American Foundation for the Blind** (✆ 800/232-5463; www.afb.org), which provides information on traveling with Seeing Eye dogs.

For more information specifically targeted to travelers with disabilities, the community website **iCan** (www.icanonline.net/channels/travel/index.cfm) has destination guides and several regular columns on accessible travel. Also check out the quarterly magazine *Emerging Horizons* ($15 per year, $20 outside the U.S.; www.emerging horizons.com); **Twin Peaks Press** (✆ 360/694-2462; http://disability bookshop.virtualave.net/blist84.htm), offering travel-related books for travelers with special needs; and *Open World Magazine,* published by the Society for Accessible Travel and Hospitality (see above; subscription: $18 per year, $35 outside the U.S.).

GAY & LESBIAN TRAVELERS

New York City is home to a gay, lesbian, bisexual, and transgender community of more than a million strong by some estimates. The highlight of the events calendar is the annual Pride Week (p. 24), but visitors year-round have plenty to explore in the gay-owned restaurants, bars, boutiques, bookstores, and art galleries of Manhattan's Greenwich Village and Chelsea neighborhoods. The central bulletin board for meetings, cultural events, and resources in New York City is **The Lesbian, Gay, Bisexual, and Transgender Community Center** (© 212/620-7310; www.gaycenter.org). Click on "NYC Resources" and "Accommodations" on their home page for a list of gay-friendly places to stay.

However, there's more to gay and lesbian life in the Empire State than cruising Chelsea and the Village. Travelers will find thriving networks in upstate, central, and western New York. **Outcome Buffalo** (www.outcomebuffalo.com), **GayBuffalo Online** (www.gaybuffalo.org), **Gay Rochester Online** (gayrochester.com), and **Capital District Gay and Lesbian Community Council, Inc.** (© 518/462-6138; www.cdglcc.org), are great sources of information about nightlife, social groups, news, and links to other gay and lesbian organizations.

The International Gay & Lesbian Travel Association (IGLTA; © 800/448-8550 or 954/776-2626; www.iglta.org) is the trade association for the gay and lesbian travel industry, and offers an online directory of gay and lesbian-friendly travel businesses; go to their website and click on "Members."

The following travel guides are available at most travel bookstores and gay and lesbian bookstores, or you can order them from **Giovanni's Room** bookstore, 1145 Pine St., Philadelphia, PA 19107 (© 215/923-2960; www.giovannisroom.com); *Out and About* (© 800/929-2268 or 415/644-8044; www.outandabout.com), which offers guidebooks and a newsletter 10 times a year packed with solid information on the global gay and lesbian scene; *Spartacus International Gay Guide* and *Odysseus,* both good, annual guidebooks focused on gay men; the *Damron* guides, with separate, annual books for gay men and lesbians; and *Gay Travel A to Z: The World of Gay &*

Lesbian Travel Options at Your Fingertips, by Marianne Ferrari (Ferrari Publications. Box 35575, Phoenix, AZ 85069), a very good gay and lesbian guidebook series.

SENIOR TRAVEL

Mention the fact that you're a senior citizen when you make your travel reservations. Although all of the major U.S. airlines except America West have canceled their senior discount and coupon book programs, many hotels still offer discounts for seniors. In most cities, people over the age of 60 qualify for reduced admission to theaters, museums, and other attractions, as well as discounted fares on public transportation.

Members of **AARP** (formerly known as the American Association of Retired Persons), 601 E St. NW, Washington, DC 20049 (© **800/424-3410** or 202/434-2277; www.aarp.org), get discounts on hotels, airfares, and car rentals. AARP offers members a wide range of benefits, including *Modern Maturity* magazine and a monthly newsletter. Anyone over 50 can join.

The **U.S. National Park Service** offers a **Golden Age Passport** that gives seniors 62 years or older lifetime entrance to all properties administered by the National Park Service (NPS)—national parks, monuments, historic sites, recreation areas, and national wildlife refuges—for a one-time processing fee of $10, which must be purchased in person at any NPS facility that charges an entrance fee. Besides free entry, a Golden Age Passport also offers a 50% discount on federal-use fees charged for such facilities as camping, swimming, parking, boat launching, and tours. For more information, call © **888/467-2757** or go to www.nps.gov/fees_passes.htm. Keep in mind that this pass does not grant access to state-operated parks and facilities. For more about New

York's state parks, see "Visitor Information," earlier in this chapter, and "Online Traveler's Toolbox," later in this chapter.

Many reliable agencies and organizations target the 50-plus market. **Senior Women's Travel** (© 212/838-4740; www.poshnosh.com) provides tours and customized itineraries for women 50 and older traveling alone or with a grandchild. **Elderhostel** (© 877/426-8056; www.elderhostel.org) arranges study programs for those aged 55 and over (and a spouse or companion of any age). Most courses last 5 to 7 days in the U.S., and many include airfare, accommodations in university dormitories or modest inns, meals, and tuition. The program schedule changes from year to year. Call or check the website to find out what's taking place in New York.

Recommended publications offering travel resources and discounts for seniors include: the quarterly magazine *Travel 50 & Beyond* (www.travel50andbeyond.com); *Travel Unlimited: Uncommon Adventures for the Mature Traveler* (Avalon); *101 Tips for Mature Travelers,* available from Grand Circle Travel (© 800/221-2610; www.gct.com); *The 50+ Traveler's Guidebook* (St. Martin's Press); and *Unbelievably Good Deals and Great Adventures That You Absolutely Can't Get Unless You're Over 50* (McGraw Hill).

FAMILY TRAVEL

New York's varied cultural landscape offers plenty of opportunities for family fun. You can pack up the station wagon for a Brady Bunch–style camping trip through the wilderness, visit the National Baseball Hall of Fame and Museum in quaint Cooperstown, New York, or take in a Broadway show amid the bright lights of Manhattan's now family-friendly Times Square.

A good source for family vacation suggestions is the **I Love NY** website (www.iloveny.com/asp)—click on "Travel Ideas." New York City's official tourism website, **NYC & Company** (www.nyvisit.com), details restaurants, museums, and tours designed to fascinate kids, plus a list of activities and neighborhoods that even the most blasé teen may actually enjoy.

Family-oriented vacation advice is available on other Internet sites like the **Family Travel Network** (www.familytravelnetwork.com) and **Family Travel Files** (www.thefamilytravelfiles.com), which offers an online magazine and a directory of off-the-beaten-path tours and tour operators for families.

For more money-saving and sanity-preserving ideas about traveling with your family in New York, grab a copy of *Frommer's New York City with Kids, Frommer's Family Vacations in the National Parks,* or *The Unofficial Guide to New England & New York with Kids* (Wiley Publishing, Inc.). *How to Take Great Trips with Your Kids* (The Harvard Common Press) is also full of good general advice that can apply to travel anywhere.

8 Planning Your Trip Online

SURFING FOR AIRFARES

The "big three" online travel agencies, **Expedia.com, Travelocity.com,** and **Orbitz.com** sell most of the air tickets bought on the Internet. (Canadian travelers should try expedia.ca and Travelocity.ca; U.K. residents can go for expedia.co.uk and opodo.co.uk.)

Each has different business deals with the airlines and may offer different fares on the same flights, so it's wise to shop around. Expedia and Travelocity will also send you **e-mail notification** when a cheap fare becomes available to your favorite destination. Of the smaller travel agency websites,

SideStep (www.sidestep.com) has gotten the best reviews from Frommer's authors. It's a browser add-on that purports to "search 140 sites at once," but in reality only beats competitors' fares as often as other sites do.

Also remember to check **airline websites,** especially those for low-fare carriers such as Southwest, JetBlue, AirTran, WestJet, or Ryanair, whose fares are often misreported or simply missing from travel agency websites. Even with major airlines, you can often shave a few bucks from a fare by booking directly through the airline and avoiding a travel agency's transaction fee. But you'll get these discounts only by **booking online:** Most airlines now offer online-only fares that even their phone agents know nothing about. For the websites of airlines that fly to and from your destination, go to "Getting There," later in this chapter.

Great **last-minute deals** are available through free weekly e-mail services provided directly by the airlines. Most of these are announced on Tuesday or Wednesday and must be purchased online. Most are only valid for travel that weekend, but some (such as Southwest's) can be booked weeks or months in advance. Sign up for weekly e-mail alerts at airline websites or check megasites that compile comprehensive lists of last-minute specials, such as **Smarter Living** (smarterliving.com). For last-minute trips, **site59.com** in the U.S. and **lastminute.com** in Europe often have better deals than the big-name sites.

If you're willing to give up some control over your flight details, use an **opaque fare service** like **Priceline** (www.priceline.com; www.priceline.co.uk for Europeans) or **Hotwire** (www.hotwire.com). Both offer rock-bottom prices in exchange for travel on a "mystery airline" at a mysterious time of day, often with a mysterious change of planes en route. The mystery airlines are all major, well-known carriers—and the possibility of being sent from Philadelphia to Chicago via Tampa is remote; the airlines' routing computers have gotten a lot better than they used to be. But your chances of getting a 6am or 11pm flight are pretty high. Hotwire tells you flight prices before you buy; Priceline usually has better deals than Hotwire, but you have to play their "name our price" game. If you're new at this, the helpful folks at **BiddingForTravel** (www.biddingfortravel.com) do a good job of demystifying Priceline's prices. Priceline and Hotwire are great for flights within North America and between the U.S. and Europe. But for flights to other parts of the world, consolidators will almost always beat their fares.

For much more about airfares and savvy air-travel tips and advice, pick up a copy of *Frommer's Fly Safe, Fly Smart* (Wiley Publishing, Inc.).

SURFING FOR HOTELS

Shopping online for hotels is much easier in the U.S. than it is in the rest of the world. However, many smaller hotels and B&Bs don't show up on websites at all. And even though there are plenty of options for reserving New York City hotels online, the selection narrows considerably when it comes to other parts of the state.

In general, **Expedia** may be the best choice of the "big three" sites, thanks to its long list of special deals. **Travelocity** runs a close second. Hotel specialist sites **hotels.com** and **hoteldiscounts.com** are also reliable. An excellent free program, **TravelAxe** (www.travelaxe.net), can help you search multiple hotel sites at once, even ones you may never have heard of.

Priceline and Hotwire are even better for hotels than for airfares; with both, you're allowed to pick the neighborhood and quality level of your hotel before offering up your money. *Note:* Hotwire overrates its hotels by one star—what Hotwire calls a four-star is a three-star anywhere else.

Frommers.com: The Complete Travel Resource

For an excellent travel-planning resource, we highly recommend Frommers.com (www.frommers.com). We're a little biased, of course, but we guarantee that you'll find the travel tips, reviews, monthly vacation giveaways, and online-booking capabilities thoroughly indispensable. Among the special features are our popular **Message Boards,** where Frommer's readers post queries and share advice (sometimes even our authors show up to answer questions); **Frommers.com Newsletter,** for the latest travel bargains and insider travel secrets; and **Frommer's Destinations Section,** where you'll get expert travel tips, hotel and dining recommendations, and advice on the sights to see for more than 3,000 destinations around the globe. When your research is done, the **Online Reservations System** (www.frommers.com/book_a_trip) takes you to Frommer's preferred online partners for booking your vacation at affordable prices.

SURFING FOR RENTAL CARS

For booking rental cars online, the best deals are usually found at rental-car company websites, although all the major online travel agencies also offer rental-car reservations services.

Priceline and Hotwire work well for rental cars, too; the only "mystery" is which major rental company you get, and for most travelers the difference between Hertz, Avis, and Budget is negligible.

9 The 21st-Century Traveler

INTERNET ACCESS AWAY FROM HOME

Travelers have any number of ways to check their e-mail and access the Internet on the road. Of course, using your own laptop—or even a PDA (personal desk assistant) or electronic organizer with a modem—gives you the most flexibility. But even if you don't have a computer, you can still access your e-mail and even your office computer from cybercafes.

WITHOUT YOUR OWN COMPUTER

It's hard nowadays to find a city that *doesn't* have a few cybercafes. Although there's no definitive directory for cybercafes—these are independent businesses, after all—three places to start looking are at **www.cyber captive.com, www.netcafeguide.com**, and **www.cybercafe.com**.

Aside from formal cybercafes, most **public libraries** offer Internet access free or for a small charge. Avoid **hotel business centers,** which often charge exorbitant rates.

Most major airports now have **Internet kiosks** scattered throughout their gates. These kiosks, which you'll also see in shopping malls, hotel lobbies, and tourist information offices around the world, give you basic web access for a per-minute fee that's usually higher than cybercafe prices. The kiosks' clunkiness and high price means they should be avoided whenever possible.

To retrieve your e-mail, ask your **Internet service provider (ISP)** if it has a web-based interface tied to your existing e-mail account. If your ISP doesn't have such an interface, you can use the free **mail2web** service (www.mail2web.com) to view and reply to your home e-mail. For more flexibility, you may want to open a free, web-based e-mail account with **Yahoo! Mail** (mail.yahoo.com). (Microsoft's Hotmail is another popular option, but Hotmail has severe spam problems.) Your home ISP may be able to forward your e-mail to the web-based account automatically.

If you need to access files on your office computer, look into a service called **GoToMyPC** (www.gotomypc. com). The service provides a web-based interface for you to access and manipulate a distant PC from anywhere—even a cybercafe—provided your "target" PC is on and has an always-on connection to the Internet (such as with Road Runner cable). The service offers top-quality security, but if you're worried about hackers, use your own laptop rather than a cybercafe to access the GoToMyPC system.

WITH YOUR OWN COMPUTER

Major Internet service providers have **local access numbers** around the world, allowing you to go online by simply placing a local call. Check your ISP's website or call its toll-free number and ask how you can use your current account away from home, and how much it will cost.

If you're traveling outside the reach of your ISP, the **iPass** network has dial-up numbers in most of the world's countries. You'll have to sign up with an iPass provider, which will then tell you how to set up your computer for your destination(s). For a list of iPass providers, go to www.ipass. com, click on "Reseller locator"; under "select a country," pick "United States"; under "Who is this service for?" pick "individual," and you'll get a list of iPass providers that take U.S. customers. One solid provider is **i2roam** (www.i2roam.com; ✆ **866/ 811-6209** or 920/235-0475).

Wherever you go, bring a **connection kit** of the right power and phone adapters, a spare phone cord, and a spare Ethernet network cable.

Most business-class hotels throughout the world offer dataports for laptop modems, and a few thousand hotels in the U.S. and Europe now offer high-speed Internet access using an Ethernet network cable. You'll have to bring your own cables either way, so **call your hotel in advance** to find out what the options are.

Many business-class hotels in the U.S. also offer a form of computer-free web browsing through the room TV set. We've successfully checked Yahoo! Mail and Hotmail on these systems.

If you have an 802.11b/**Wi-fi** card for your computer, several commercial companies have made wireless service available in airports, hotel lobbies and coffee shops, primarily in the U.S. **T-Mobile Hotspot** (www.t-mobile. com/hotspot) serves up wireless connections at more than 1,000 Starbucks coffee shops nationwide. **Boingo** (www.boingo.com) and **Wayport** (www.wayport.com) have set up networks in airports and high-class hotel lobbies. IPass providers (see above) also give you access to a few hundred wireless hotel lobby setups. Best of all, you don't need to be staying at the Four Seasons to use the hotel's network; just set yourself up on a nice couch in the lobby. Unfortunately, the companies' pricing policies are byzantine, with a variety of monthly, per-connection, and per-minute plans.

Community-minded individuals have also set up **free wireless networks** in major cities around the U.S., Europe, and Australia. These networks are spotty, but you get what you (don't) pay for. Each network has a home page explaining how to set up your computer for their particular system; start your explorations at www. personaltelco.net/index.cgi/Wireless Communities.

Online Traveler's Toolbox

Veteran travelers usually carry some essential items to make their trips easier. Following is a selection of online tools to bookmark and use.

- **Visa ATM Locator** (www.visa.com), for locations of PLUS ATMs worldwide, or **MasterCard ATM Locator** (www.mastercard.com), for locations of Cirrus ATMs worldwide.
- **Intellicast** (www.intellicast.com) and **Weather.com** (www.weather.com). Gives weather forecasts for all 50 states and for cities around the world.
- **Mapquest** (www.mapquest.com). This best of the mapping sites lets you choose a specific address or destination, and in seconds, it will return a map and detailed directions.
- **Travel Warnings** (http://travel.state.gov/travel_warnings.html; www.fco.gov.uk/travel; www.voyage.gc.ca; www.dfat.gov.au/consular/advice). These sites report on places where health concerns or unrest might threaten American, British, Canadian, and Australian travelers. Generally, U.S. warnings are the most paranoid; Australian warnings are the most relaxed.

NEW YORK STATE

- **I Love NY** (www.iloveny.com/main.asp). Maintained by the New York State Division of Tourism, this is the best site for general information about visiting New York. With the click of a mouse, you can search a vast database of state attractions, events, suggested itineraries, transportation options, and accommodations. View weather forecasts, check fall foliage reports or skiing conditions (in season), and download regional and city road maps.
- **New York State Office of Parks, Recreation, and Historic Preservation** (www.nysparks.state.ny.us). The official website for the state's parks and historic areas. Find out about events and activities, check admission fees, and make camping reservations.
- **Campground Owners of New York** (www.gocampingamerica.com/newyork/cony.html). A directory of independent private campgrounds and RV parks. Each profile includes a summary of the campground's facilities, including number of campsites, ability to accommodate RV's, and availability of phone and TV hookups.
- **ReserveAmerica** (www.reserveamerica.com). Thanks to partnerships with organizations like Campground Owners of New York, the NYS Department of Environmental Conservation, and the NYS Office of Parks, Recreation and Historic Preservation, ReserveAmerica allows campers to browse information about nearly 140 New York campgrounds, then reserve their campsites online.
- **Go Camping America!** (wwww.gocampingamerica.com/stateassoc/newyork). Sponsored by the National Association of RV Parks & Campgrounds, this site provides a directory of more than 250 privately owned campgrounds in New York. Each profile includes a summary of

the campground's facilities, including number of campsites, ability to accommodate RVs, and availability of phone and TV hookups.

- **New York State Department of Agriculture and Markets** (www.agmkt.state.ny.us). Ignore the latest information on organic pesticides and click on "Farm and Markets Search." This will lead you to the "Farm Fresh Guide," a database of farms, orchards, fields and the like that welcome visitors for activities such as apple-picking, hayrides, or just browsing bushels of freshly harvested fruits and vegetables. Perfect for day trips and lots of fun for kids.
- **New York State Department of Environmental Conservation** (www.dec.state.ny.us/website/dfwmr/huntfish.html). Scout public and private locations for fishing and hunting. Make sure to secure the proper license and review the regulations for the area you plan to visit.
- **Ski Areas of New York, Inc.** (www.skiareasofny.org). Skiers, snowboarders, and other winter sports fans can compare the stats of mountains and trails at more than 30 resorts.
- **NYS Wine and Grape Foundation** (www.nywine.com). A comprehensive list of New York wineries, categorized by region. Unfortunately, small font size makes the text on the site hard to read. Otherwise, it's a good place to start planning a wine-tasting tour of New York.

NEW YORK CITY

- **NYC & Company** (www.nycvisit.com). A clear and practical orientation to the city. Includes explanation of bus and subway lines, neighborhood descriptions, and suggested itineraries. Check out their advice for families, seniors, gay and lesbian travelers, travelers with disabilities, and couples looking to tie the knot during their stay.
- **Citysearch** (www.newyork.citysearch.com). Get the lowdown on New York City hangouts and happenings from opinionated New Yorkers themselves. The site provides editorial reviews of local venues and allows patrons to post their own sentiments about which spots are hot and which aren't worth the trip. Listings for other towns and cities across the state can be accessed through Citysearch's main menu; however, most of these consist only of addresses and phone numbers, making them not much more help than the phone book.
- **Village Voice** (www.villagevoice.com). The website of downtown Manhattan's alternative weekly paper. Click on "NightGuide" to search their database of events. Also the best source for a list of art films as well as mainstream Hollywood movies playing in the city.
- **Zagat Survey** (www.zagat.com). This handy guide to hundreds of New York City restaurants can now be viewed online. There is a subscription fee to read restaurant reviews ($1.50 per day; $2.50 per month; $15 per year), but nonsubscribers can still use the site to search for restaurants by neighborhood and type of cuisine.

USING A CELLPHONE
ACROSS THE U.S.

Just because your cellphone works at home doesn't mean it'll work elsewhere in the country (thanks to our nation's fragmented cellphone system). It's a good bet that your phone will work in major cities. But take a look at your wireless company's coverage map on its website before heading out—T-Mobile, Sprint, and Nextel are particularly weak in rural areas. If you need to stay in touch at a destination where you know your phone won't work, **rent** a phone that does from **InTouch USA** (© **800/872-7626**; www.intouch global.com) or a rental car location, but beware that you'll pay $1 a minute or more for airtime.

If you're venturing deep into state or national parks, you may want to consider renting a **satellite phone ("satphone"),** which is different from a cellphone in that it connects to a satellite rather than a ground-based tower. A satphone is more costly than a cellphone but works where there's no cellular signal and no towers. Unfortunately, you'll pay at least $2 per minute to use the phone, and it only works where you can see the horizon (i.e., usually not indoors). In North America, you can rent Iridium satellite phones from **RoadPost** (www.road post.com; © **888/290-1606** or 905/272-5665). InTouch USA (see above) offers a wider range of satphones but at higher rates. As of this writing, satphones were amazingly expensive to buy, so don't even think about it.

If you're not from the U.S., you'll be appalled at the poor reach of our **GSM (Global System for Mobiles) wireless network,** which is used by much of the rest of the world. Your phone will probably work in most major U.S. cities; it definitely won't work in many rural areas. (To see where GSM phones work in the U.S., check out www.tmobile.com/ coverage/national_popup.asp). And you may or may not be able to send SMS (text messaging) home—something Americans tend not to do anyway, for various cultural and technological reasons. (International budget travelers like to send text messages home because it's much cheaper than making international calls.) Assume nothing—call your wireless provider and get the full scoop. In a worst-case scenario, you can always rent a phone; InTouch USA delivers to hotels.

10 Getting There

BY PLANE

With flights from across the country and around the world converging in New York City, many visitors to New York State may find it convenient to arrive in New York City first and move on from there.

The Port Authority of New York and New Jersey operates three major airports in the New York City area: **John F. Kennedy International Airport (JFK), LaGuardia Airport (LGA),** and **Newark Liberty International Airport (EWK).** Together they're served by most major domestic airlines, including **AirTran Airways** (© 800/247-8726; www.airtran.com), **America West Airlines** (© 800/327-7810; www.americawest.com), **American Airlines** (© 800/433-7300; www. aa.com), **ATA** (© 800/435-9282; www.ata.com), **Continental** (© 800/ 525-0280; www.continental.com), **Delta** (© 800/221-1212; www.delta. com), **JetBlue Airways** (© 800/538-2583; www.jetblue.com), **Midwest Express** (© 800/452-2022; www. midwestexpress.com), **Northwest** (© 800/225-2525; www.nwa.com), **Spirit Airlines** (© 800/772-7117; www.spiritair.com), **United** (© 800/ 864-8331; www.ual.com), and **US**

Airways (© 800/28-4322; www.us
air.com).

However, arriving in New York
City isn't the only option. For those
traveling elsewhere in the state, several
of the airlines listed above offer direct
or connecting flights to Albany, Buffalo, Rochester, Syracuse, and 11 other
cities. US Airways covers more New
York destinations than any other carrier. AirTran Airways, American Airlines, Continental, Delta, JetBlue
Airways, Northwest, and United also
offer service, as does **Air Canada**
(© **888/247-2262;** www.aircanada.
ca) and **Southwest** (© **800/435-
9792;** www.southwest.com). For
more information about intrastate
flights, see "Getting Around," below.

GETTING THROUGH THE AIRPORT

With the federalization of airport security, security procedures at U.S. airports
are more stable and consistent than
ever. Generally, you'll be fine if you
arrive at the airport **1 hour** before a
domestic flight and **2 hours** before an
international flight; if you show up late,
tell an airline employee and she'll probably whisk you to the front of the line.

Bring a **current, government-
issued photo ID** such as a driver's
license or passport, and if you've got
an E-ticket, print out the **official confirmation page;** you'll need to show
your confirmation at the security
checkpoint, and your ID at the ticket
counter or the gate. (Children under
18 do not need photo IDs for domestic flights, but the adults checking in
with them need them.)

Security lines are getting shorter
than they were during 2001 and 2002,
but some doozies remain. If you have
trouble standing for long periods of
time, tell an airline employee; the airline will provide a wheelchair. Speed
up security by **not wearing metal
objects** such as big belt buckles or
clanky earrings. If you've got metallic
body parts, a note from your doctor

can prevent a long chat with the security screeners. Keep in mind that only
ticketed passengers are allowed past
security, except for folks escorting disabled passengers or children.

Federalization has stabilized **what
you can carry on** and **what you can't.**
The general rule is that sharp things
are out, nail clippers are okay, and
food and beverages must be passed
through the X-ray machine—but that
security screeners can't make you
drink from your coffee cup. Bring
food in your carry-on rather than
checking it, as explosive-detection
machines used on checked luggage
have been known to mistake food
(especially chocolate, for some reason)
for bombs. Travelers in the U.S. are
allowed one carry-on bag, plus a "personal item" such as a purse, briefcase,
or laptop bag. Carry-on hoarders can
stuff all sorts of things into a laptop
bag; as long as it has a laptop in it, it's
still considered a personal item. The
Transportation Security Administration (TSA) has issued a list of
restricted items; check its website
(www.tsa.gov/public/index.jsp) for
details.

In 2003, the TSA will be phasing
out **gate check-in** at all U.S. airports.
Passengers with E-tickets and without
checked bags can still beat the ticket-
counter lines by using **electronic
kiosks** or even **online check-in.** Ask
your airline which alternatives are available, and if you're using a kiosk, bring
the credit card you used to book the
ticket. If you're checking bags, you will
still be able to use most airlines' kiosks;
again call your airline for up-to-date
information. **Curbside check-in** is also
a good way to avoid lines, although a
few airlines still ban curbside check-in
entirely; call before you go.

At press time, the TSA is also recommending that you **not lock your
checked luggage** so screeners can
search it by hand if necessary. The
agency says to use plastic "zip ties"

instead, which can be bought at hardware stores and can be easily cut off.

FLYING FOR LESS: TIPS FOR GETTING THE BEST AIRFARE

Passengers sharing the same airplane cabin rarely pay the same fare. Travelers who need to purchase tickets at the last minute, change their itinerary at a moment's notice, or fly one-way often get stuck paying the premium rate. Here are some ways to keep your airfare costs down.

- Passengers who can book their tickets **long in advance,** who can **stay over Saturday night,** or who **fly midweek** or **at less-trafficked hours** will pay a fraction of the full fare. If your schedule is flexible, say so, and ask if you can secure a cheaper fare by changing your flight plans.

- You can also save on airfares by keeping an eye out in local newspapers for **promotional specials** or **fare wars,** when airlines lower prices on their most popular routes. You rarely see fare wars offered for peak travel times, but if you can travel in the off-months, you may snag a bargain.

- Search **the Internet** for cheap fares (see "Planning Your Trip Online," earlier in this chapter).

- Try to book a ticket **in its country of origin.** For instance, if you're planning a one-way flight from Johannesburg to Bombay, a South Africa–based travel agent will probably have the lowest fares. For multileg trips, book in the country of the first leg; for example, book New York-London-Amsterdam-Rome-New York in the U.S.

- **Consolidators,** also known as bucket shops, are great sources for international tickets, although they usually can't beat the Internet on fares within North America. Start by looking in Sunday newspaper travel sections; U.S. travelers should focus on the *New York Times, Los Angeles Times,* and *Miami Herald.* **Beware:** Bucket shop tickets are usually nonrefundable or rigged with stiff cancellation penalties, often as high as 50% to 75% of the ticket price, and some put you on charter airlines with questionable safety records. Several reliable consolidators are worldwide and available on the Net. **STA Travel** is now the world's leader in student travel, thanks to their purchase of Council Travel. It also offers good fares for travelers of all ages. **Flights.com** (© 800/TRAV-800; www.flights.com) started in Europe and has excellent fares worldwide. It also has "local' websites in 12 countries. **FlyCheap** (© 800/FLY-CHEAP; www.1800 flycheap.com) is owned by package-holiday megalith MyTravel. **Air Tickets Direct** (© 800/778-3447; www.airticketsdirect.com) is based in Montreal and leverages the currently weak Canadian dollar for low fares.

- Join **frequent-flier clubs.** Accrue enough miles, and you'll be rewarded with free flights and elite status. It's free, and you'll get the best choice of seats, faster response to phone inquiries, and prompter service if your luggage is stolen, your flight is canceled or delayed, or if you want to change your seat. You don't need to fly to build frequent-flier miles—**frequent-flier credit cards** can provide thousands of miles for doing your everyday shopping.

- For many more tips about air travel, including a rundown of the major frequent-flier credit cards, pick up a copy of *Frommer's Fly Safe, Fly Smart* (Wiley Publishing, Inc.).

Travel in the Age of Bankruptcy

At press time, two major U.S. airlines were struggling in bankruptcy court and most of the rest weren't doing very well, either. To protect yourself, **buy your tickets with a credit card,** as the Fair Credit Billing Act guarantees that you can get your money back from the credit card company if a travel supplier goes under (and if you request the refund within 60 days of the bankruptcy). **Travel insurance** can also help, but make sure it covers against "carrier default" for your specific travel provider. And be aware that if a U.S. airline goes bust midtrip, a 2001 federal law requires other carriers to take you to your destination (albeit on a space-available basis) for a fee of no more than $25, provided you rebook within 60 days of the cancellation.

BY CAR

Drivers approaching from the west or east can take **I-90,** a toll road that crosses the country from Seattle to Boston and runs straight through New York, connecting Buffalo, Rochester, Syracuse, Utica, Schenectady, and Albany. **Route 17 (I-86** in western New York) roughly follows the state's southern border through Jamestown, Olean, Corning, Elmira, and Binghamton, then heads southwest into the Catskills and Orange County.

I-95 connects major cities along the East Coast from Florida to Maine, including New York City. **I-87** runs north to south, from New York City to Newburgh, Kingston, Albany, Saratoga Springs, and Plattsburgh; it then crosses into Canada where the road extends to Montreal.

Travelers from the south can also use **I-81,** which enters the state near Binghamton and continues north to Cortland, Syracuse, and Watertown. **I-88** links Binghamton and Schenectady. **I-390** provides a route between I-90 and NY Route 17 in the Finger Lakes region.

There is a toll on the **New York State Thruway,** which is I-90 from western New York to Albany and I-87 from Albany to New York City. The New York State Thruway Authority hot line dispenses recorded updates on road conditions; dial ℂ **800/THRUWAY,** or check the website for construction schedules at www.thruway.state.ny.us.

The **American Automobile Association** (ℂ **800/836-2582;** www.aaa.com) will help members find the best routes to their destinations and provide free customized maps. AAA also offers emergency roadside assistance; members can call ℂ **800/AAA-HELP.**

Another great way to plan your route is on the Internet site **Mapquest** (www.mapquest.com). Simply type in your start and end points, and Mapquest will give full step-by-step directions to your destination. A free state map is also available from the **New York State Division of Tourism.** See "Visitor Information," earlier in this chapter.

All the major rental-car companies operate in New York State, including **Alamo** (ℂ 800/462-5266; www.goalamo.com), **Avis** (ℂ 800/230-4898; www.avis.com), **Budget** (ℂ 800/527-0700; www.budget.com), **Dollar** (ℂ 800/800-4000; www.dollar.com), **Enterprise** (ℂ 800/736-8222; www.enterprise.com), **Hertz** (ℂ 800/654-3131; www.hertz.com), **National** (ℂ 800/227-7368; www.nationalcar.com), and **Thrifty** (ℂ 800/847-4389; www.thrifty.com). It's worth noting that the only companies located at Kennedy, La Guardia, and Newark airports are Avis, Budget, Dollar, Hertz, and National. Enterprise is also available at La Guardia and Newark, but not at Kennedy.

When renting a car, there is always some kind of deal to be found—check company websites or ask reservations agents about specials before you rent. If you're a member of AAA, AARP, or another organization, find out if you qualify for a discount. For tips on booking a rental car on the Internet, see "Planning Your Trip Online," earlier in this chapter.

BY TRAIN

Rail travel can be less cramped than airline flights and affords some amazing views of the American landscape. **Amtrak** (© **800/USA-RAIL;** www.amtrak.com) connects New York with many American cities from coast to coast, and a handful of Canadian cities, too. However, a cross-country trip can last for days (Los Angeles to New York City is about 70 hr.) and require one or more connections. Unfortunately, despite the extended travel time, there isn't much savings here; train reservations cost almost as much as air travel, and sometimes more.

Three main Amtrak routes cross New York State, connecting major metropolitan areas and the towns along the way. Several trains, including **Metroliner** shuttle service and high-speed **Acela Express** trains, travel the Northeast Corridor from Washington, D.C., to Philadelphia, New York City, and Boston. **Empire Service** runs north from New York City to Albany, then west to Syracuse, Rochester, Buffalo, and Niagara Falls; the *Maple Leaf* runs daily, extending the same route through Toronto, Canada. The *Adirondack* travels the Hudson River Valley north to Albany (making stops in Yonkers, Croton-on-Hudson, Poughkeepsie, Rhinecliff, and Hudson), then follows along Lake Champlain to Plattsburgh and finally Montreal, Canada.

Check the website for Internet-only deals or ask your phone representative about regional and seasonal promotions before you reserve tickets. Seniors automatically receive 15% off regular fares, and membership discount programs are available to veterans and students. Families should note that for each adult ticket purchased, two kids under 15 may ride for half price, and one child under 2 comes along for free.

Amtrack Vacations (© **877/YES-RAIL;** www.amtrak.com/savings/amtrakvacations.html) can put together a complete travel package including train, hotel, car rental, and sightseeing. Through a partnership with United Airlines, Amtrak has created the **Air Rail** program, which allows travelers to explore destinations at leisure by rail, then make a speedy return home by plane.

11 Getting Around

New York State is larger than many people realize; the drive from New York City to Niagara Falls can take 7 or 8 hours, depending on your route. Before you commit to hours of drive time, you may want to weigh the alternatives.

BY CAR

A road trip is usually the most direct way to get from one place to another, and allows the freedom of traveling where you want, when you want. For an explanation of major New York State roadways and the cities they connect, see "Getting There," above.

Gas prices in New York State tend to be about 10¢ higher than the national average. Of the major cities, Albany and Binghamton have the cheapest gas. Not surprisingly, New York City's is the most expensive.

If you plan to travel from December to March, be advised that winter weather can present significant obstacles, such as wet or icy pavement, poor visibility, or routes that are just plain shut down. Make sure that your vehicle is adequately prepared with snow tires and working windshield wipers, battery, and defrosters. Most likely, though, you won't run into too many problems. Roads are well maintained in the winter, and even after a storm side streets and highways alike are cleared fairly quickly.

Highway speed limits are 55 or 65 mph. The speed limit in New York City is 30 mph unless otherwise posted. "Right on red" (making a right turn at red light after coming to a complete stop) is permitted, except in New York City. Motorcyclists must wear helmets, and goggles if helmets are not equipped with face shields. Everyone should buckle up, but at the minimum, state law requires drivers, front seat passengers, and children under 10 to wear seat belts. Children under 4 must ride in safety seats. Fines can run up to $100. Talking on a hand-held cellphone while driving is punishable by a fine of up to $100 (exceptions are made for emergency situations, such as calls to the police). Drivers can be charged with driving while intoxicated (DWI) for having a blood alcohol content of .08% or higher and sentenced to a fine or jail time upon conviction.

BY TRAIN

The train won't get you where you're going any faster, but it will cut down on the amount of time you have to spend behind the wheel. Once you get where you're going, though, you'll probably need to rent a car anyway since public transportation is not very extensive beyond New York City.

Amtrak (℡ **800/USA-RAIL;** www. amtrak.com) basically follows the same paths as the New York State Thruway and the Adirondack Northway (Rtes. 90 and 87), leaving much of the state inaccessible by rail. For more information on cities served by Amtrak, see "Getting There," above.

Visitors to Long Island can take the **Long Island Railroad** (**LIRR;** ℡ **718/217-5477;** www.mta.nyc.ny. us/lirr). With service from New York City's Penn Station, the LIRR is the main mode of transportation for commuters as well as Manhattanites weekending in the Hamptons. Since seating is normally unreserved, trains are often standing room only during the summer vacation season. New **Hamptons Reserve Service** (℡ **718/558-8070**) guarantees passengers a seat on the Friday express train for an extra fee in addition to the regular fare.

Metro-North Railroad (℡ **800/ METRO-INFO** or 212/532-4900; www.mta.nyc.ny.us/mnr/index.html) makes the Hudson Valley region easily reachable from New York City's Grand Central Station with commuter lines extending as far north as Poughkeepsie and Wassaic, and west to Port Jervis.

BY PLANE

CommutAir (www.commutair.com), a partner of **Continental Airlines** (℡ **800/525-0280;** www.continental. com), offers flights from their Albany hub to Buffalo, Rochester, Syracuse, Elmira, White Plains, Islip, Plattsburg, and Lake Placid. Reservations must be made through Continental.

JetBlue Airways (℡ **800/538-2583;** www.jetblue.com) is hard to beat, with consistently low ticket prices and daily runs from New York City (JFK Airport) to Buffalo, Rochester, and Syracuse.

US Airways (℡ **800/428-4322;** www.usair.com) and its partner **Colgan Air** (www.colganair.com) provide direct flights from New York City to Albany, Buffalo, Ithaca, Rochester, and Syracuse, as well as service from Albany to Buffalo and Islip.

12 Tips on Accommodations

New York offers a wide range of accommodations—from Manhattan's superchic luxury hotels, to the rustic mountain retreats of the Catskills, to Long Island's salty seaside motels, and everything in between.

The **New York State Hospitality and Tourism Association** (© **518/ 465-2300;** www.nyshta.org) covers the gamut of hotel and motel options and provides a free map listing the names and basic rates of their members statewide.

The perfect bed-and-breakfast can be hard to track down since few are well known outside their local areas. The **Empire State Bed & Breakfast Association** (© **800/841-2340;** www. esbba.com) makes the task easier with its free, color guide to 150 inns and B&Bs across the state. Another good bet is **Bed & Breakfast Inns Online** (www.bbonline.com), where you can view interior and exterior photos of almost every property profiled, including several listed on the National Register of Historic Places. The site offers last-minute, midweek, and seasonal specials besides a variety of other packages.

House swaps aren't for everyone— clean freaks and people with control issues may skip ahead to the next section. However, some consider staying in a private home while the owners stay in yours a comfortable and cost-effective alternative to booking a hotel. **Home Link International** (© **800/638-3841** or 813/975-9825; www.homelink.org) is an established house-swapping service. Apartment swaps in Manhattan, Brooklyn, and other New York City boroughs can be found through **Craigslist.org**. People over 50 may register their homes with **Seniors Home Exchange** (www. seniorshomeexchange.com).

SAVING ON YOUR HOTEL ROOM

The **rack rate** is the maximum rate that a hotel charges for a room. Hardly anybody pays this price, however. To lower the cost of your room:

- **Ask about special rates or other discounts.** Always ask whether a room less expensive than the first one quoted is available, or whether any special rates apply to you. You may qualify for corporate, student, military, senior, or other discounts. Mention membership in AAA, AARP, frequent-flier programs, or trade unions, which may entitle you to special deals as well. Find out the hotel policy on children— do kids stay free in the room or is there a special rate?
- **Dial direct.** When booking a room in a chain hotel, you'll often get a better deal by calling the individual hotel's reservation desk than at the chain's main number.
- **Book online.** Many hotels offer Internet-only discounts, or supply rooms to Priceline, Hotwire, or Expedia at rates much lower than the ones you can get through the hotel itself.
- **Remember the law of supply and demand.** Resort hotels are most crowded and therefore most expensive on weekends, so discounts are usually available for midweek stays. Business hotels in downtown locations are busiest during the week, so you can expect big discounts over the weekend. Many hotels have high-season and low-season prices, and booking the day after "high season" ends can mean big discounts.
- **Look into group or long-stay discounts.** If you come as part of a large group, you should be able

to negotiate a bargain rate, since the hotel can then guarantee occupancy in a number of rooms. Likewise, if you're planning a long stay (at least 5 days), you might qualify for a discount. As a general rule, expect 1 night free after a 7-night stay.

- **Avoid excess charges and hidden costs.** When you book a room, ask whether the hotel charges for parking. Use your own cellphone, pay phones, or prepaid phone cards instead of dialing direct from hotel phones, which usually have exorbitant rates. And don't be tempted by the room's minibar offerings: Most hotels charge through the nose for water, soda, and snacks. Finally, ask about local taxes and service charges, which can increase the cost of a room by 15% or more. If a hotel insists upon tacking on a surprise "energy surcharge" that wasn't mentioned at check-in or a "resort fee" for amenities you didn't use, you can often make a case for getting it removed.
- Consider the pros and cons of **all-inclusive** resorts and hotels. The term "all-inclusive" means different things at different hotels. Many all-inclusive hotels will include three meals daily, sports equipment, spa entry, and other amenities; others may include all or most drinks. In general, you'll save money going the "all-inclusive" way—as long as you use the facilities provided. The down side is that your choices are limited and you're stuck eating and playing in one place for the duration of your vacation.
- Carefully consider your hotel's meal plan. If you enjoy eating out and sampling the local cuisine, it makes sense to choose a **Continental plan (CP),** which includes breakfast only, or a **European plan (EP),** which doesn't include any meals and allows you maximum flexibility. If you're more interested in saving money, opt for a **modified American plan (MAP),** which includes breakfast and one meal, or the **American plan (AP),** which includes three meals. If you must choose a MAP, see if you can get a free lunch at your hotel if you decide to do dinner out.
- **Book an efficiency.** A room with a kitchenette allows you to shop for groceries and cook your own meals. This is a big money saver, especially for families on long stays.

LANDING THE BEST ROOM

Somebody has to get the best room in the house. It might as well be you. You can start by joining the hotel's frequent-guest program, which may make you eligible for upgrades. A hotel-branded credit card usually gives its owner "silver" or "gold" status in frequent-guest programs for free. Always ask about a corner room. They're often larger and quieter, with more windows and light, and they often cost the same as standard rooms. When you make your reservation, ask if the hotel is renovating; if it is, request a room away from the construction. Ask about nonsmoking rooms, rooms with views, rooms with twin, queen- or king-size beds. If you're a light sleeper, request a quiet room away from vending machines, elevators, restaurants, bars, and discos. Ask for one of the rooms that have been most recently renovated or redecorated.

If you aren't happy with your room when you arrive, say so. If another room is available, most lodgings will be willing to accommodate you.

13 Tips on Dining

One of the best ways to experience any destination is by taste. The food can say as much about a region as its museums and monuments, whether you're traveling abroad or in your own country.

In many parts of New York, hometown favorites are hearty, flavorful foods that no self-respecting local would be caught dead eating with a fork and knife. Western New Yorkers will insist that you try the "beef on 'weck," shorthand for sliced roast beef sandwiches on salty kimmelweck rolls, or Buffalo's famous chicken wings, blazing with hot sauce and properly served with celery stalks and blue cheese dip. Binghamton natives love the "spiedie" (pronounced, and sometimes spelled, *speedie*), a marinated lamb, pork, or chicken sandwich served on Italian bread, while former Rochester citizens miss the "white hot," a spicy white hot dog hard to come by in other parts of the country.

The amazing array of cuisine in New York City is a testament to the city's diverse cultural heritage. Jewish deli fare, Chinese dim sum, and Japanese sushi are three mainstays of the Manhattan diet, but there's much more to be found here, including Indian, Thai, Korean, Russian, and Turkish restaurants to name a few.

Once you decide what to eat and where, do pick up the phone and make a reservation. If you already know that you want to eat at the best restaurant in town during your stay, call for reservations as soon as you confirm your travel dates. This is especially important in New York City, where world-class restaurants like Daniel and Nobu book up weeks or months in advance and trendy restaurants are packed on weekends with an influx of "bridge-and-tunnel" traffic from Long Island and New Jersey in addition to city residents. This doesn't mean you'll be stuck ordering room service if you forget to make dinner reservations. The hotel concierge is likely to have relationships with several good restaurants, and will surely be able to fit you in somewhere. If you're calling the restaurant yourself, try requesting an extra-early or extra-late seating when it's likely to be less busy, or ask to be put on a waiting list in case another party cancels.

FAST FACTS: **New York State**

American Express For the location of the nearest American Express Travel office, call ℂ **800/297-3429** or log onto www.americanexpress.com. If you have questions about traveler's checks, call ℂ **800/221-7282**. For help with your credit card account, call ℂ **800/528-4800**. See "Lost & Found" below for what to do in the event of lost or stolen credit cards or traveler's checks.

Area Codes Several changes have been made to area-code dialing in New York over the last few years. New area codes have been added in Western New York, Long Island, New York City, and the Hudson Valley/Catskill region, bringing the state total to 14. In addition, callers in New York City (which includes the boroughs of Manhattan, the Bronx, Brooklyn, Queens, and Staten Island) are now required to dial the area code for both local and long distance calls. This means dialing eleven digits (1 + the area code + the seven-digit local number) whether calling another borough or calling across the street. New York City also uses multiple area codes to cover the same territory, so addresses that share the same city block don't necessarily have the same area code. To avoid confusion, be sure to confirm the area code when taking down a number. For a list of New York State area codes, consult the phone book or go to www.verizon.com.

ATMs Check the back of your bank card or credit card to find out which ATM network you belong to. To locate ATMs that participate in the **Cirrus** network call ℂ **800/424-7787** or go to www.mastercard.com. For **PLUS** call ℂ **800/843-7587** or go to www.visa.com. For cards with the **NYCE** logo, visit www.nyce.net. To locate **Star** ATMs go to www.star.com.

Business Hours Business hours in New York State don't differ much from the rest of the country, with one notable exception. It may be a tired cliché, but they don't call New York City "the city that never sleeps" for nothing. Although some stores close at 7pm, many are open until 9pm, and a few as late as 11pm. Most restaurants serve until 11pm, and later on weekends. Some diners serve breakfast all night to bar crawlers and club kids, and 24-hour convenient stores on every other block sell an assortment of items you might need during the night, such as groceries, beer, ice cream, cigarettes, and cold remedies.

Car Rentals See "Getting Around," earlier in this chapter.

Driving Rules See "Getting Around," earlier in this chapter.

Embassies & Consulates See chapter 3, "For International Visitors."

Emergencies Call ℂ **911** to report a fire, call the police, or get an ambulance anywhere in the United States. This is a toll-free call. (No coins are required at public telephones.)

Holidays See "Calendar of Events," earlier in this chapter.

Information See "Visitor Information," earlier in this chapter.

Internet Access Cybercafes in midtown Manhattan and Greenwich Village are convenient places to check e-mail and surf for information while visiting New York City. Public Internet access is harder to come by in other parts of the state, though you have a better shot in college towns like Buffalo, Albany, Syracuse, Binghamton, and Ithaca. Your best bet in a small town may be the local library. For a list of New York State public libraries go to www.nysl.nysed.gov/libdev/libs/publibs. **Kinko's** (ℂ **800/254-6567;** www.kinkos.com) copy centers are almost as ubiquitous as Starbucks and not much more expensive than cybercafes. Call or visit their website for locations. See "The 21st-Century Traveler," earlier in this chapter, for more tips on accessing the Internet.

Legal Aid If you find yourself in need of legal representation, contact the **New York State Bar Association's Lawyer Referral and Information Service** (ℂ **800/342-3661** or 518/487-5709; www.nysba.org).

Liquor Laws The drinking age is 21, and you'll probably be asked for state- or government-issued identification—such as a driver's license or passport—anytime you purchase an alcoholic beverage. Even if you feel your crow's feet betray your old age, the bartender, bouncer, or salesclerk may disagree, so bring ID to avoid a hassle.

In general, grocery and convenience stores sell beer and other products that are less than 6% alcohol by volume (like wine coolers). Many of these stores are open 24 hours, but state law forbids them to sell alcohol from 3am to noon on Sunday. Wine and spirits are sold at liquor stores, also called package stores. Hours vary, but by law they must remain closed from midnight to 8am Monday through Saturday. Some stores may be open from noon until 9pm on Sundays, but many are closed. All liquor stores are closed Christmas Day.

Restaurants and bars can't serve drinks before 8am Monday through Saturday, or before noon on Sunday. Closing time for bars, taverns, and nightclubs varies by county. Albany, Buffalo, and New York City bars close at 4am; in Rochester and Syracuse they close at 2am. In quieter areas, closing time comes as early as 1am. For die-hards who can dance until dawn, a few clubs stay open well into daytime; however, no alcohol is permitted to be sold or consumed beyond legal hours.

Lost & Found   Be sure to tell all of your credit card companies the minute you discover your wallet has been lost or stolen and file a report at the nearest police precinct. Your credit card company or insurer may require a police report number or record of the loss. Most credit card companies have an emergency toll-free number to call if your card is lost or stolen; they may be able to wire you a cash advance immediately or deliver an emergency credit card in a day or two. Visa's U.S. emergency number is © 800/847-2911 or 410/581-9994. American Express clients should call © 800/221-7282 regarding traveler's checks and © 800/528-4800 regarding credit cards. MasterCard holders should call © 800/307-7309 or 636/722-7111. For other credit cards, call the toll-free number directory at © 800/555-1212.

If you need emergency cash over the weekend when all banks and American Express offices are closed, you can have money wired to you via **Western Union** (© 800/325-6000; www.westernunion.com).

Identity theft and fraud are potential complications of losing your wallet, especially if you've lost your driver's license along with your cash and credit cards. Notify the major credit-reporting bureaus immediately; placing a fraud alert on your records may protect you against liability for criminal activity. The three major U.S. credit-reporting agencies are **Equifax** (© 800/766-0008; www.equifax.com), **Experian** (© 888/397-3742; www.experian.com), and **TransUnion** (© 800/680-7289; www.transunion.com). Finally, if you've lost all forms of photo ID call your airline and explain the situation; they might allow you to board the plane if you have a copy of your passport or birth certificate and a copy of the police report you've filed.

Maps   The **New York State Division of Tourism,** P.O. Box 2603, Albany, NY 12220-0603 (© 800/CALL-NYS or 518/474-4116; www.iloveny.com/main.asp), will mail you a free map, or you can download state and regional maps from their website. You can also find maps at state **information centers,** or ask for one at the **rental-car company** when you pick up your car. **Mapquest** (www.mapquest.com) can instantly plot your route online. Maps can also be purchased at most bookstores, gas stations, and rest stops.

Newspapers & Magazines The *New York Times,* the *Wall Street Journal,* and *USA Today* are sold at newsstands everywhere in New York City and are generally available in hotels and corner newspaper boxes throughout the state. Major cities have their own daily papers. The largest of these are the *Buffalo News, Rochester Democrat and Chronicle, Syracuse Post-Standard,* and *Albany Times Union.* In Manhattan, magazine stores carrying all kinds of domestic and international publications are located in most neighborhoods. In other cities, bookstore chains such as Barnes & Noble carry a wide selection of magazines.

Police In nonemergency situations, call the nearest police station. Local police precinct telephone numbers can be found in the blue "government" pages of the phone book.

Safety See "Health & Safety," earlier in this chapter.

Smoking The legal age to purchase cigarettes and other tobacco products in New York State is 18. But you won't find many places left to smoke them, aside from your hotel room. A state law passed in 2003 prohibits smoking in almost all public venues and in the workplace. This includes bars and restaurants, although smokers can still light up in cigar bars, designated outdoor areas of restaurants, and some private clubs. The law does not affect Native American–run casinos, and smoking is still permitted there.

Taxes Sales tax in New York State varies between 7.25% and 8.75% (the state tax is 4.25%, and counties generally tack on another 3% or 4%). On top of the sales tax, hotel occupancy taxes can add as much as 5% to hotel and motel bills; an additional 5% typically applies to car rentals as well.

Time Zone New York State is located in Eastern Standard Time (EST). So, for example, noon in New York City (EST) is 11am in Chicago (CST), 10am in Denver (MST), 9am in Los Angeles (PST), 8am in Anchorage (AST), and 7am in Honolulu (HST). **Daylight savings time** is in effect from 1am on the first Sunday in April through 1am on the last Sunday in October.

Useful Phone Numbers Contact the U.S. Dept. of State Travel Advisory at ✆ **202/647-5225** (staffed 24 hr.); the U.S. Centers for Disease Control International Traveler's Hotline at ✆ **404/332-4559**; and the New York State Thruway Authority at ✆ **800/THRUWAY** (recorded road condition updates).

3

For International Visitors

by Karen Quarles

Whether it's your first visit or your 10th, a trip to the United States may require an additional degree of planning. This chapter will provide you with essential information, helpful tips, and advice for the more common problems that some visitors encounter.

1 Preparing for Your Trip

ENTRY REQUIREMENTS

Check at any U.S. embassy or consulate for current information and requirements. You can also obtain a visa application and other information online at the **U.S. State Department**'s website, at **www.travel.state.gov**.

VISAS & PASSPORTS The U.S. State Department has a **Visa Waiver Program** allowing citizens of certain countries to enter the United States without a visa for stays of up to 90 days. At press time these included Andorra, Australia, Austria, Belgium, Brunei, Denmark, Finland, France, Germany, Iceland, Ireland, Italy, Japan, Liechtenstein, Luxembourg, Monaco, the Netherlands, New Zealand, Norway, Portugal, San Marino, Singapore, Slovenia, Spain, Sweden, Switzerland, and the United Kingdom. Citizens of these countries need only a **valid passport** and a round-trip air or cruise ticket in their possession upon arrival. If they first enter the United States, they may also visit Mexico, Canada, Bermuda, and/or the Caribbean islands and return to the United States without a visa. Further information is available from any U.S. embassy or consulate. Canadian citizens may enter the United States without visas; they need only proof of residence.

Citizens of all other countries must have (1) a valid passport that expires at least 6 months later than the scheduled end of their visit to the United States, and (2) a tourist visa, which may be obtained without charge from any U.S. consulate.

British subjects can obtain up-to-date passport and visa information by calling the **U.S. Embassy Visa Information Line** (© **0891/200-290**) or the **London Passport Office** (© **0990/210-410** for recorded information) or they can find the visa information on the U.S. Embassy Great Britain website at www.passport.gov.uk.

Irish citizens can obtain up-to-date passport and visa information through the **Embassy of USA Dublin,** 42 Elgin Rd., Dublin 4, Ireland (© **353/1-668-8777**; www.irigov.ie/iveagh/services/passports/passportforms.htm).

Australian citizens can obtain up-to-date passport and visa information from the **U.S. Embassy Canberra,** Moonah Place, Yarralumla, ACT 2600 (© **02/6214-5600**; www.usisaustralia.gov/consular/niv.html).

Citizens of **New Zealand** can obtain up-to-date passport and visa information from the **U.S. Embassy New Zealand,** 29 Fitzherbert Terrace, Thorndon, Wellington, New Zealand

(© **644/472-2068;** http://usembassy.org.nz).

MEDICAL REQUIREMENTS

Unless you're arriving from an area known to be suffering from an epidemic (particularly cholera or yellow fever), inoculations or vaccinations are not required for entry into the United States. If you have a medical condition that requires **syringe-administered medications,** carry a valid signed prescription from your physician—the Federal Aviation Administration (FAA) no longer allows airline passengers to pack syringes in their carry-on baggage without documented proof of medical need. If you have a disease that requires treatment with **narcotics,** you should also carry documented proof with you—smuggling narcotics aboard a plane is a serious offense that carries severe penalties in the U.S.

For **HIV-positive visitors,** requirements for entering the United States are somewhat vague and change frequently. According to the latest publication of *HIV and Immigrants: A Manual for AIDS Service Providers,* the Immigration and Naturalization Service (INS) doesn't require a medical exam for entry into the United States, but INS officials may stop individuals because they look sick or because they are carrying AIDS/HIV medicine.

If an HIV-positive noncitizen applies for a nonimmigrant visa, the question on the application regarding communicable diseases is tricky no matter which way it's answered. If the applicant checks "no," INS may deny the visa on the grounds that the applicant committed fraud. If the applicant checks "yes" or if INS suspects the person is HIV-positive, it will deny the visa unless the applicant asks for a special waiver for visitors. This waiver is for people visiting the United States for a short time, to attend a conference, for instance, to visit close relatives, or to receive medical treatment.

It can be a confusing situation. For further up-to-the-minute information, contact the Centers for Disease Control's **National Center for HIV** (© **404/332-4559;** www.hivatis.org) or the **Gay Men's Health Crisis** (© **212/367-1000;** www.gmhc.org).

DRIVER'S LICENSES   Foreign driver's licenses are mostly recognized in the U.S., although you may want to get an international driver's license if your home license is not written in English.

CUSTOMS

WHAT YOU CAN BRING IN

Every visitor more than 21 years of age may bring in, free of duty, the following: (1) 1 liter of wine or hard liquor; (2) 200 cigarettes, 100 cigars (but not from Cuba), or 3 pounds of smoking tobacco; and (3) $100 worth of gifts. These exemptions are offered to travelers who spend at least 72 hours in the United States and who have not claimed them within the preceding 6 months. It is altogether forbidden to bring into the country foodstuffs (particularly fruit, cooked meats, and canned goods) and plants (vegetables, seeds, tropical plants, and the like). Foreign tourists may bring in or take out up to $10,000 in U.S. or foreign currency with no formalities; larger sums must be declared to U.S. Customs on entering or leaving, which includes filing form CM 4790. For more specific information regarding U.S. Customs, contact your nearest U.S. embassy or consulate, or the **U.S. Customs** office (© **202/927-1770;** www.customs.ustreas.gov).

WHAT YOU CAN TAKE HOME

U.K. citizens have a customs allowance of: 200 cigarettes, 100 cigarillos, 50 cigars, or 250 grams of tobacco; 2 liters of still table wine; 1 liter of spirits or strong liqueurs (over 22% volume), or 2 liters of fortified wine, sparkling wine, or other liqueurs; 60 milliliters of perfume; 250 milliliters of toilet water; and £145 worth of all other goods, including gifts and souvenirs. People under 17 cannot have the tobacco or alcohol allowance. For more information, contact HM Customs & Excise at ℰ **0845/010-9000** (from outside the U.K., 0208/929-0152), or consult their website at www.hmce.gov.uk.

For a clear summary of **Canadian** rules, request the booklet *I Declare,* issued by the **Canada Customs and Revenue Agency** (ℰ **800/461-9999** in Canada, or 204/983-3500; www.ccra-adrc.gc.ca). Canada allows its citizens a C$750 exemption, and you're allowed to bring back duty-free one carton of cigarettes, one can of tobacco, 40 imperial ounces of liquor, and 50 cigars. In addition, you're allowed to mail gifts to Canada valued at less than C$60 a day, provided they're unsolicited and don't contain alcohol or tobacco (write on the package "Unsolicited gift, under $60 value"). All valuables should be declared on the Y-38 form before departure from Canada, including serial numbers of valuables you already own, such as expensive foreign cameras. *Note:* The C$750 exemption only applies to citizens who have been out of the country for 7 days or more.

The duty-free allowance in **Australia** is A$400 or, for those under 18, A$200. Citizens can bring in 250 cigarettes or 250 grams of loose tobacco, and 1,125 milliliters of alcohol. If you're returning with valuables you already own, such as foreign-made cameras, you should file form B263. A helpful brochure available from Australian consulates or Customs offices is *Know Before You Go.* For more information, call the **Australian Customs Service** at ℰ **1300/363-263,** or log on to www.customs.gov.au.

The duty-free allowance for **New Zealand** is NZ$700. Citizens over 17 can bring in 200 cigarettes, 50 cigars, or 250 grams of tobacco (or a mixture of all three if their combined weight doesn't exceed 250g); plus 4.5 liters of wine and beer, or 1.125 liters of liquor. New Zealand currency does not carry import or export restrictions. Fill out a certificate of export, listing the valuables you are taking out of the country; that way, you can bring them back without paying duty. Most questions are answered in a free pamphlet available at New Zealand consulates and Customs offices: *New Zealand Customs Guide for Travellers, Notice no. 4.* For more information, contact **New Zealand Customs,** The Customhouse, 17–21 Whitmore St., Box 2218, Wellington (ℰ **04/473-6099** or 0800/428-786; www.customs.govt.nz).

HEALTH INSURANCE

Although it's not required of travelers, health insurance is highly recommended. Unlike many European countries, the United States does not usually offer free or low-cost medical care to its citizens or visitors. Doctors and hospitals are expensive, and in most cases will require advance payment or proof of coverage before they render their services. Policies can cover everything from the loss or theft of your baggage and trip cancellation to the guarantee of bail in case you're arrested. Good policies will also cover the costs of an accident, repatriation, or death. See "Health & Safety" in chapter 2 for more information. Packages such as **Europ Assistance's "Worldwide Healthcare Plan"** are sold by European automobile clubs and travel agencies at attractive rates. **Worldwide Assistance Services, Inc.** (ℰ 800/821-2828; www.worldwideassistance.com) is the agent for Europ Assistance in the U.S.

Though lack of health insurance may prevent you from being admitted to a hospital in nonemergencies, don't worry about being left on a street corner to die: the American way is to fix you now and bill the living day-lights out of you later.

INSURANCE FOR BRITISH TRAVELERS Most big travel agents offer their own insurance and will probably try to sell you their package when you book a holiday. Think before you sign. **Britain's Consumers' Association** recommends that you insist on seeing the policy and reading the fine print before buying travel insurance. **The Association of British Insurers** (© 020/7600-3333; www.abi.org.uk) gives advice by phone and publishes *Holiday Insurance,* a free guide to policy provisions and prices. You might also shop around for better deals: Try **Columbus Direct** (© 020/7375-0011; www.columbusdirect.net).

INSURANCE FOR CANADIAN TRAVELERS Canadians should check with their provincial health plan offices or call **Health Canada** (© 613/957-2991; www.hc-sc.gc.ca) to find out the extent of their coverage and what documentation and receipts they must take home in case they are treated in the United States.

MONEY
CURRENCY The U.S. monetary system is very simple: The most common **bills** are the $1 (colloquially, a "buck"), $5, $10, and $20 denominations. There are also $2 bills (seldom encountered), $50 bills, and $100 bills (the last two are usually not welcome as payment for small purchases). All the paper money was recently redesigned, making the famous faces adorning them disproportionately large. The old-style bills are still legal tender.

There are seven denominations of coins: 1¢ (1 cent, or a penny); 5¢ (5 cents, or a nickel); 10¢ (10 cents, or a dime); 25¢ (25 cents, or a quarter); 50¢ (50 cents, or a half dollar); the new gold "Sacagawea" coin worth $1;

and, prized by collectors, the rare, older silver dollar.

Note: The "foreign-exchange bureaus" so common in Europe are rare even at airports in the United States, and nonexistent outside major cities. It's best not to change foreign money (or traveler's checks denominated in a currency other than U.S. dollars) at a small-town bank, or even a branch in a big city; in fact, leave any currency other than U.S. dollars at home—it may prove a greater nuisance to you than it's worth.

TRAVELER'S CHECKS Though traveler's checks are widely accepted, make sure that they're denominated in U.S. dollars, as foreign-currency checks are often difficult to exchange. The three traveler's checks that are most widely recognized—and least likely to be denied—are **Visa, American Express,** and **Thomas Cook.** Be sure to record the numbers of the checks, and keep that information in a separate place in case they get lost or stolen. Most businesses are pretty good about taking traveler's checks, but you're better off cashing them in at a bank (in small amounts, of course) and paying in cash. *Remember:* You'll need identification, such as a driver's license or passport, to change a traveler's check.

CREDIT CARDS & ATMs Credit cards are the most widely used form of payment in the United States: **Visa** (Barclaycard in Britain), **MasterCard** (EuroCard in Europe, Access in Britain, Chargex in Canada), **American Express, Diners Club, Discover,** and **Carte Blanche.** There are, however, a handful of stores and restaurants that do not take credit cards, so be sure to ask in advance. Most businesses display a sticker near their entrance to let you know which cards they accept. (*Note:* Businesses may require a minimum purchase, usually around $10, to use a credit card.)

In New York State, Visa, Master Card, and American Express tend to be accepted more often than Diners Club, Discover, and Carte Blanche. Certain establishments—particularly upscale hotels, restaurants, and boutiques in major destinations like New York City—can accommodate international credit cards as well.

It is strongly recommended that you bring at least one major credit card. You must have a credit or charge card to rent a car. Hotels, airlines, and rental-car companies usually require a credit card imprint as a deposit against expenses, and in an emergency a credit card can be priceless.

You'll find **automated teller machines (ATMs)** on just about every block in major cities—at least in almost every town—across the country. Some ATMs will allow you to draw U.S. currency against your bank and credit cards. Check with your bank before leaving home, and remember that you will need your personal identification number (PIN) to do so. Most accept Visa, MasterCard, and American Express, as well as ATM cards from other U.S. banks. To locate an ATM where you can use your MasterCard, go to www.mastercard.com; for Visa check www.visa.com; for American Express visit www.americanexpress. com. Expect to be charged up to $3 per transaction, however, if you're not using your own bank's ATM.

One way around these fees is to ask for cash back at grocery stores that accept ATM cards and don't charge usage fees. Of course, you'll have to purchase something first.

ATM cards with major credit card backing, known as "debit cards," are now a commonly acceptable form of payment in most stores and restaurants. Debit cards draw money directly from your checking account. Some stores enable you to receive "cash back" on your debit-card purchases as well.

SAFETY

GENERAL SUGGESTIONS Although tourist areas are generally safe, U.S. urban areas tend to be less safe than those in Europe or Japan. You should always stay alert. This is particularly true of large American cities.

The good news is that New York State is safer than ever. The crime rate has been steadily dropping for the last decade, and New York City is now considered one of the safest large cities in the country. Still, no destination is 100% crime-free. If you're in doubt about which neighborhoods are safe, don't hesitate to make inquiries with the hotel front desk staff or the local tourist office.

Avoid deserted areas, especially at night, and don't go into public parks after dark unless there's a concert or similar occasion that will attract a crowd.

Avoid carrying valuables with you on the street, and keep expensive cameras or electronic equipment bagged up or covered when not in use. If you're using a map, try to consult it inconspicuously—or better yet, study it before you leave your room. Hold onto your pocketbook, and place your billfold in an inside pocket. In theaters, restaurants, and other public places, keep your possessions in sight.

Always lock your room door—don't assume that once you're inside the hotel you are automatically safe and no longer need to be aware of your

---

Travel Tip

Be sure to keep a copy of all your travel papers separate from your wallet or purse, and leave a copy with someone at home should you need it faxed in an emergency.

Size Conversion Chart

Women's Clothing

American	4	6	8	10	12	14	16
French	34	36	38	40	42	44	46
British	6	8	10	12	14	16	18

Women's Shoes

American	5	6	7	8	9	10
French	36	37	38	39	40	41
British	4	5	6	7	8	9

Men's Suits

American	34	36	38	40	42	44	46	48
French	44	46	48	50	52	54	56	58
British	34	36	38	40	42	44	46	48

Men's Shirts

American	$14\frac{1}{2}$	15	$15\frac{1}{2}$	16	$16\frac{1}{2}$	17	$17\frac{1}{2}$
French	37	38	39	41	42	43	44
British	$14\frac{1}{2}$	15	$15\frac{1}{2}$	16	$16\frac{1}{2}$	17	$17\frac{1}{2}$

Men's Shoes

American	7	8	9	10	11	12	13
French	$39\frac{1}{2}$	41	42	43	$44\frac{1}{2}$	46	47
British	6	7	8	9	10	11	12

surroundings. Hotels are open to the public, and in a large hotel, security may not be able to screen everyone who enters.

For more tips on staying safe, see "Health & Safety" in chapter 2.

DRIVING SAFETY Driving safety is important, too, and carjacking is not unprecedented. Question your rental agency about personal safety and ask for a traveler-safety brochure when you pick up your car. Obtain written directions—or a map with the route clearly marked—from the agency showing how to get to your destination. (Many agencies now offer the option of renting a cellular phone for the duration of your car rental; check with the rental agent when you pick up the car.) And, if possible, arrive and depart during daylight hours.

If you drive off a highway and end up in a dodgy-looking neighborhood, leave the area as quickly as possible. If you have an accident, even on the highway, stay in your car with the doors locked until you assess the situation or until the police arrive. If you're bumped from behind on the street or are involved in a minor accident with no injuries, and the situation appears to be suspicious, motion to the other driver to follow you. Never get out of your car in such situations. Go directly to the nearest police precinct, well-lighted service station, or 24-hour store. You may want to look into renting a cellphone on a short-term basis. One recommended wireless rental company is **InTouch USA** (© **800/872-7626;** www.intouchusa.com).

Park in well-lighted and well-traveled areas whenever possible. Always keep your car doors locked, whether the vehicle is attended or unattended. Never leave any packages or valuables in sight. If someone attempts to rob you or steal your car, don't try to resist the thief/carjacker. Report the incident to the police department immediately by calling ℭ **911.**

2 Getting to the U.S.

BY PLANE Most international flights to New York State arrive at **John F. Kennedy International Airport** (JFK) in New York City, which is served by more that 50 international carriers, including **Aer Lingus** (ℭ 0818/365-000; www.aerlingus. com), **Air Canada** (ℭ 888/247-2262; www.aircanada.ca), **British Airways** (ℭ 0845/773-3377; www.britishair ways.com), **Qantas** (ℭ 131-313; www.qantas.com.au), **South African Airways** (ℭ 0861/359-722; www.fly saa.com), and **Virgin Atlantic** (ℭ 01293/450-150; www.virgin atlantic.com). Landing at **Newark Liberty International Airport** (EWR) just across the river in New Jersey may be another option since it's served by close to 20 international carriers.

Of the airlines listed above, only Air Canada flies direct to other major cities in New York, with service to Albany, Buffalo, Rochester, Syracuse, and White Plains.

U.S. carriers like **American Airlines** (www.aa.com), **Continental** (www.continental.com), **Delta** (www. delta.com), and **United** (www.ual. com) also have international flights in and out of New York. For more domestic airlines serving New York State, see section 10, "Getting There," in chapter 2.

The smart traveler can find numerable ways to reduce the price of a plane ticket simply by taking time to shop around. For example, overseas visitors can take advantage of the APEX (advance purchase excursion) reductions offered by all major U.S. and European carriers. For more money-saving airline advice, see section 10, "Getting There," in chapter 2. For the best rates, compare fares and be flexible with the dates and times of travel.

BY TRAIN Visitors heading down from the north can reach New York by rail on **Amtrak** (ℭ **800/USA-RAIL;** www.amtrak.com). The *Maple Leaf* runs daily from Toronto to New York City, including stops in Niagara Falls, Buffalo, Rochester, Syracuse, and Albany; the *Adirondack* makes daily stops between Montréal and New York City.

BY CAR Drivers coming from Canada to Niagara Falls and western New York can take the Queen Elizabeth Way (QEW) and then Highway 420 to Niagara Falls, or continue on the QEW into Buffalo. Traffic generated by Casino Niagara on the Canadian side of the falls often causes delays on the Rainbow Bridge. To speed your crossing from Canada to the U.S., try the Lewiston-Queenston Bridge, the Whirlpool Bridge, or the Peace Bridge.

Traveler's along Canada's Highway 401 can cross the St. Lawrence River from Cornwall, Ontario, to Massena, New York; from Prescott, Ontario, to Ogdensburg, New York; from Ivy Lea, Ontario, to Alexandria Bay, New York; and by ferry from Kingston, Ontario, to St. Vincent, New York.

Drivers approaching from Montréal can take Highway 15, which becomes I-87 in New York.

IMMIGRATION & CUSTOMS CLEARANCE Visitors arriving by air, no matter what the port of entry, should cultivate patience and resignation before setting foot on U.S. soil. Getting through immigration control can take as long as 2 hours on some days, especially on summer weekends, so be sure to carry this guidebook or something else to read. This is especially true in the aftermath of the September 11th terrorist attacks, as security clearances have been considerably beefed up at U.S. airports.

People traveling by air from Canada, Bermuda, and certain countries in the Caribbean can sometimes clear Customs and Immigration at the point of departure, which is much quicker.

3 Getting Around the U.S.

BY PLANE Some large airlines (for example, Northwest and Delta) offer travelers on their transatlantic or transpacific flights special discount tickets under the name **Visit USA,** allowing mostly one-way travel from one U.S. destination to another at very low prices. These discount tickets are not on sale in the United States and must be purchased abroad in conjunction with your international ticket. This system is the best, easiest, and fastest way to see the United States at low cost. You should obtain information well in advance from your travel agent or the office of the airline concerned, since the conditions attached to these discount tickets can be changed without advance notice.

BY TRAIN International visitors (excluding Canada) can also buy a **USA Rail Pass,** good for 5, 15, or 30 days of unlimited travel on Amtrak (© **800/USA-RAIL;** www.amtrak. com). The pass is available through many foreign travel agents. At press time, a 15-day pass cost $295 off-peak, $440 peak; a 30-day pass cost $385 off-peak, $550 peak. If you don't plan to travel extensively around the country, consider a regional pass. The Northeast Rail Pass covers travel from Virginia to Niagara Falls and Montreal. At press time, the cost of a 5-day pass was $149 peak and off-peak; a 15-day pass was $185 peak and $205 off-peak; a 30-day pass was $225 peak and $240 off-peak. With a foreign passport, you can also buy passes at some Amtrak offices in the United States, including New York City. Reservations are generally required

and should be made for each part of your trip as early as possible.

BY BUS Although bus travel is often the most economical form of public transit for short hops between U.S. cities, it can also be slow and uncomfortable—certainly not an option for everyone (particularly when Amtrak, which is far more luxurious, offers similar rates). **Greyhound/Trailways** (© **800/231-2222;** www.greyhound.com), the sole nationwide bus line, offers an **International Ameripass** that must be purchased before coming to the United States, or by phone through the Greyhound International Office at the Port Authority Bus Terminal in New York City (© **212/971-0492**). The pass can be obtained from foreign travel agents or through Greyhound's website (order at least 21 days before your departure to the U.S.) and costs less than the domestic version. At press time, pass costs were as follows: 4 days ($155), 7 days ($204), 10 days ($254), 15 days ($314), 21 days ($364), 30 days ($424), 45 days ($464), or 60 days ($574). You can get more info on the pass and check prices at the website, or by calling © **402/ 330-8552.** In addition, special rates are available for seniors and students.

BY CAR Unless you plan to spend the bulk of your vacation time in a city where walking is the best and easiest way to get around (such as New York City), the most cost-effective, convenient, and comfortable way to travel around the United States, and New York State in particular, is by car.

The interstate highway system connects cities and towns all over the country; in addition to these high-speed, limited-access roadways, there's an extensive network of federal, state, and local highways and roads. Some of the national car-rental companies include **Alamo** (© 800/327-9633; www.goalamo.com), **Avis** (© 800/331-1212; www.avis.com), **Budget** (© 800/527-0700; www.budget.com), **Dollar** (© 800/800-4000; www.dollar.com), **Hertz** (© 800/654-3131; www.hertz.com), **National** (© 800/227-7368; www.nationalcar.com), and **Thrifty** (© 800/367-2277; www.thrifty.com).

If you plan to rent a car in the United States, you probably won't need the services of an additional automobile organization. If you're planning to buy or borrow a car, automobile-association membership is recommended. **AAA,** the **American Automobile Association** (© 800/222-4357), is the country's largest auto club and supplies its members with maps, insurance, and, most important, emergency road service. The cost of joining runs from $63 for singles to $87 for two members, but if you're a member of a foreign auto club with reciprocal arrangements, you can enjoy free AAA service in America. See section 10, "Getting There," in chapter 2, for more information.

FAST FACTS: For the International Traveler

Automobile Organizations Auto clubs will supply maps, suggested routes, guidebooks, accident and bail-bond insurance, and emergency road service. The **American Automobile Association (AAA)** is the major auto club in the United States. If you belong to an auto club in your home country, inquire about AAA reciprocity before you leave. You may be able to join AAA even if you're not a member of a reciprocal club; to inquire, call AAA (© **800/222-4357**). AAA is actually an organization of regional auto clubs; so look under "AAA Automobile Club" in the White Pages of the telephone directory. AAA has a nationwide emergency road service telephone number (© **800/AAA-HELP**).

Business Hours Offices are usually open weekdays from 9am to 5pm. Banks are open weekdays from 9am to 3pm or later and sometimes Saturday mornings. Stores typically open between 9 and 10am and close between 5 and 6pm from Monday through Saturday. Stores in shopping complexes or malls tend to stay open late: until about 9pm on weekdays and weekends, and many malls and larger department stores are open on Sundays.

Currency & Currency Exchange See "Entry Requirements" and "Money" under "Preparing for Your Trip," earlier in this chapter.

Drinking Laws The legal age for purchase and consumption of alcoholic beverages is 21; proof of age is required and often requested at bars, nightclubs, and restaurants, so it's always a good idea to bring ID when you go out. Beer and wine often can be purchased in supermarkets, but liquor laws vary from state to state.

Do not carry open containers of alcohol in your car or any public area that isn't zoned for alcohol consumption. The police can fine you on the spot. And nothing will ruin your trip faster than getting a citation for DUI ("driving under the influence"), so don't even think about driving while intoxicated.

Electricity Like Canada, the United States uses 110 to 120 volts AC (60 cycles), compared to 220 to 240 volts AC (50 cycles) in most of Europe, Australia, and New Zealand. If your small appliances use 220 to 240 volts, you'll need a 110-volt transformer and a plug adapter with two flat parallel pins to operate them here. Downward converters that change 220 to 240 volts to 110 to 120 volts are difficult to find in the United States, so bring one with you.

Embassies & Consulates All embassies are located in the nation's capital, Washington, D.C. Some consulates are located in major U.S. cities, and most nations have a mission to the United Nations in New York City. If your country isn't listed below, call for directory information in Washington, D.C. (© 202/555-1212) or log on to **www.embassy.org/embassies**.

The embassy of **Australia** is at 1601 Massachusetts Ave. NW, Washington, DC 20036 (© 202/797-3000; www.austemb.org). In New York, the consulate is at 150 E. 42nd St., 34th floor, New York, NY 10017 (© 212/351-6500).

The embassy of **Canada** is at 501 Pennsylvania Ave. NW, Washington, DC 20001 (© 202/682-1740; www.canadianembassy.org). There are two Canadian consulates in New York State. One is in Buffalo at HSBC Center, Suite 3000, Buffalo, NY 14203 (© 716/858-9500); the other is in New York City at 1251 Avenue of the Americas, New York, NY 10020 (© 212/596-1628).

The embassy of **Ireland** is at 2234 Massachusetts Ave. NW, Washington, DC 20008 (© 202/462-3939; www.irelandemb.org). The Irish consulate in New York is located at 345 Park Ave., 17th floor, New York, NY 10154 (© 212/319 -2555).

The embassy of **New Zealand** is at 37 Observatory Circle NW, Washington, DC 20008 (© 202/328-4800; www.nzemb.org). In New York, the consulate is located at 222 East 41st St., Suite 2510, New York, NY 10017 (© 212/832-4038).

The embassy of the **United Kingdom** is at 3100 Massachusetts Ave. NW, Washington, DC 20008 (© 202/462-1340; www.britainusa.com). The British consulate in New York is at 845 Third Ave., New York, NY 10022 (© 212/745-0200).

Emergencies Call © 911 to report a fire, call the police, or get an ambulance anywhere in the United States. This is a toll-free call. (No coins are required at public telephones.)

If you encounter serious problems, contact the **Traveler's Aid Society International** (© 202/546-1127; www.travelersaid.org) to help direct you to a local branch. This nationwide, nonprofit, social-service organization geared to helping travelers in difficult straits offers services that might include reuniting families separated while traveling, providing food and/or shelter to people stranded without cash, or even emotional counseling. If you're in trouble, seek them out.

Gasoline (Petrol) Petrol is known as gasoline (or simply "gas") in the United States, and petrol stations are known as both gas stations and service stations. Gasoline costs about half as much here as it does in Europe (at press time, about $1.85 per gallon of unleaded gas in New

York), and taxes are already included in the printed price. One U.S. gallon equals 3.8 liters or .85 imperial gallons.

Holidays Banks, government offices, post offices, and many stores, restaurants, and museums are closed on the following legal national holidays: January 1 (New Year's Day), the third Monday in January (Martin Luther King Jr. Day), the third Monday in February (Presidents' Day, Washington's Birthday), the last Monday in May (Memorial Day), July 4 (Independence Day), the first Monday in September (Labor Day), the second Monday in October (Columbus Day), November 11 (Veterans' Day/Armistice Day), the fourth Thursday in November (Thanksgiving Day), and December 25 (Christmas). Also, the Tuesday following the first Monday in November is Election Day and is a federal government holiday in presidential-election years (held every 4 years: 2004, 2008, and so on).

Legal Aid If you are "pulled over" for a minor infraction (such as speeding), never attempt to pay the fine directly to a police officer; this could be construed as attempted bribery, a much more serious crime. Pay fines by mail, or directly into the hands of the clerk of the court. If accused of a more serious offense, say and do nothing before consulting a lawyer. Here the burden is on the state to prove a person's guilt beyond a reasonable doubt, and everyone has the right to remain silent, whether he or she is suspected of a crime or actually arrested. Once arrested, a person can make one telephone call to a party of his or her choice. Call your embassy or consulate.

Mail If you aren't sure what your address will be in the United States, mail can be sent to you, in your name, c/o General Delivery at the main post office of the city or region where you expect to be. (Call © **800/275-8777** for information on the nearest post office.) The addressee must pick up mail in person and must produce proof of identity (driver's license, passport, and so on). Most post offices will hold your mail for up to one month, and are open Monday to Friday from 8am to 6pm, and Saturday from 9am to 3pm.

Generally found at intersections, mailboxes are blue with a red-and-white stripe and carry the inscription U.S. MAIL. If your mail is addressed to a U.S. destination, don't forget to add the five-digit postal code (or zip code), after the two-letter abbreviation of the state to which the mail is addressed. This is essential to prompt delivery.

At press time, domestic postage rates were 23¢ for a postcard and 37¢ for a letter. For international mail, a first-class letter of up to 1 ounce costs 80¢ (60¢ to Canada and Mexico); a first-class postcard costs 70¢ (50¢ to Canada and Mexico); and a preprinted postal aerogramme costs 70¢.

Measurements See the chart on the inside front cover of this book for details on converting metric measurements to U.S. equivalents.

Taxes The United States has no value-added tax (VAT) or other indirect tax at the national level. Every state, county, and city has the right to levy its own local tax on all purchases, including hotel and restaurant checks, airline tickets, and so on.

Telephone, Telegraph, Telex & Fax The telephone system in the United States is run by private corporations, so rates, especially for long-distance service and operator-assisted calls, can vary widely. Generally, hotel surcharges on long-distance and local calls are astronomical, so you're usually better off using a **public pay telephone,** which you'll find clearly marked in most public buildings and private establishments as well as on the street. Convenience grocery stores and gas stations always have them. Many convenience groceries and packaging services sell **prepaid calling cards** in denominations up to $50; these can be the least expensive way to call home. Many public phones at airports now accept American Express, MasterCard, and Visa credit cards. **Local calls** made from most public pay phones in New York cost 25¢ to 50¢. Pay phones do not accept pennies, and few will take anything larger than a quarter.

You may want to look into leasing a cellphone for the duration of your trip. (See "Driving Safety," p. 57, for recommendations.)

Most long-distance and international calls can be dialed directly from any phone. **For calls within the United States and to Canada,** dial 1 followed by the area code and the seven-digit number. **For other international calls,** dial 011 followed by the country code, city code, and the telephone number of the person you are calling.

Calls to area codes **800, 888,** and **877** are toll-free. However, calls to numbers in area codes **700** and **900** (chat lines, bulletin boards, "dating" services, and so on) can be very expensive—usually a charge of 95¢ to $3 or more per minute, and they sometimes have minimum charges that can run as high as $15 or more.

For **reversed-charge or collect calls,** and for person-to-person calls, dial 0 (zero, not the letter O) followed by the area code and number you want; an operator will then come on the line, and you should specify that you are calling collect, or person-to-person, or both. If your operator-assisted call is international, ask for the overseas operator.

For **local directory assistance** ("information"), dial 411; for long-distance information, dial 1, then the appropriate area code and 555-1212.

Telegraph and telex services are provided primarily by Western Union. You can bring your telegram into the nearest Western Union office (there are hundreds across the country) or dictate it over the phone (© **800/325-6000**). You can also telegraph money, or have it telegraphed to you, very quickly over the Western Union system, but this service can cost as much as 15% to 20% of the amount sent.

Most hotels have **fax machines** available for guest use (be sure to ask about the charge to use it). Many hotel rooms are even wired for guests' fax machines. A less expensive way to send and receive faxes may be at stores such as The UPS Store (formerly Mail Boxes Etc.), a national chain of packing service shops. (Look in the Yellow Pages directory under "Packing Services.")

There are two kinds of telephone directories in the United States. The so-called **White Pages** list private households and business subscribers in alphabetical order. The inside front cover lists emergency numbers for police, fire, ambulance, the Coast Guard, poison-control center, crime-victims hot line, and so on. The first few pages will tell you how to make long-distance and international calls, complete with country codes and area codes. Government numbers are usually printed on blue paper within the White Pages. Printed on yellow paper, the so-called **Yellow Pages** list all local services, businesses, industries, and houses of worship according to activity with an index at the front or back. (Drugstores/pharmacies and restaurants are also listed by geographic location.) The Yellow Pages also include city plans or detailed area maps, postal ZIP codes, and public transportation routes.

Time The continental United States is divided into **four time zones:** Eastern Standard Time (EST), Central Standard Time (CST), Mountain Standard Time (MST), and Pacific Standard Time (PST). Alaska and Hawaii have their own zones. For example, noon in New York City (EST) is 11am in Chicago (CST), 10am in Denver (MST), 9am in Los Angeles (PST), 8am in Anchorage (AST), and 7am in Honolulu (HST).

Daylight savings time is in effect from 1am on the first Sunday in April through 1am on the last Sunday in October, except in Arizona, Hawaii, part of Indiana, and Puerto Rico. Daylight savings time moves the clock 1 hour ahead of standard time.

Tipping Tips are a very important part of certain workers' salaries, so it's necessary to leave appropriate gratuities. In hotels, tip **bellhops** at least $1 per bag ($2–$3 if you have a lot of luggage) and tip the **chamber staff** $1 to $2 per day (more if you've left a disaster area for him or her to clean up). Tip the **doorman** or **concierge** only if he or she has provided you with some specific service (for example, calling a cab for you or obtaining difficult-to-get theater tickets). Tip the **valet-parking attendant** $1 every time you get your car.

In restaurants, bars, and nightclubs, tip **service staff** 18% to 20% of the check, tip **bartenders** 10% to 15%, tip **checkroom attendants** $1 per garment, and tip **valet-parking attendants** $1 per vehicle. Tip the **doorman** only if he has provided you with some specific service (such as calling a cab for you).

As for other service personnel, tip **cab drivers** 15% of the fare; tip **skycaps** at airports at least $1 per bag ($2–$3 if you have a lot of luggage); and tip **hairdressers** and **barbers** 15% to 20%.

Toilets You won't find public toilets or "restrooms" on the streets in most U.S. cities, but they can be found in hotel lobbies, bars, restaurants, museums, department stores, railway and bus stations, and service stations. Large hotels and fast-food restaurants are probably the best bet for good, clean facilities. If possible, avoid the toilets at parks and beaches, which tend to be dirty; some may be unsafe. Restaurants and bars in resorts or heavily visited areas may reserve their restrooms for patrons. Some establishments display a notice indicating this. You can ignore this sign or, better yet, avoid arguments by paying for a cup of coffee or a soft drink, which will qualify you as a patron.

4

The Active Vacation Planner

by Neil E. Schlecht

Perhaps because New York City is—despite the green oasis of Central Park—the ultimate in asphalt adventure, New York State doesn't quite get its due as an outdoors destination. But New York is much more rural, mountainous, and crisscrossed with water than most people realize, and it's a splendid and incredibly diverse state with terrain and opportunities to satisfy the most discriminating outdoors enthusiasts. New York is, after all, where the **American Conservation Movement** began, and the state has benefited from the active presence of committed environmentalists like native son Theodore Roosevelt, the 26th president of the U.S.

Niagara Falls State Park was designated the first state park in the U.S., and state parks and forest preserves in the Adirondack and Catskill Mountains were declared "forever wild" by the State Constitution. Adirondack Park, which totals more than 6 million acres of public and private lands, ranks as the largest park in the country.

From Long Island and Great Lakes beaches to Adirondack lakes and Catskill rivers, there are myriad opportunities for water fun, including canoeing, swimming, boating, and fishing. The Catskill region is one of the fly-fishing capitals of the world. The rugged mountains and dense forests that dominate upstate beckon avid hikers, mountain bikers, and winter-sports fans. In the Catskills, 35 peaks reach 3,500 feet, while in the Adirondacks, more than 40 mountains rise above 4,000 feet. Lake Placid has hosted the Winter Olympics, and the ski mountains in the Catskills draw enthusiasts from across the northeast, as do the hundreds of miles of terrain for cross-country skiing. In warm months, New York State plays host to a number of professional championships, and the state's impressive roster of public and private courses make it one of the nation's best for golf.

The website of the **I Love New York** Travel and Tourism board—www.iloveny.com/search/recreation_index.asp—contains an exhaustive listings of parks, outfitters, facilities, and more for outdoors adventure.

1 Visiting New York's National Parks

New York State's 24 national parks include splendid natural spots like the Appalachian National Scenic Trail, the Upper Delaware Scenic and Recreational River, and Fire Island National Seashore, in addition to famous historic monuments. One is the **Upper Delaware Scenic and Recreational River,** part of the National Wild and Scenic Rivers System; it runs 73 miles along the New York–Pennsylvania border, making it the Northeast's longest free-flowing river. Perfect for boating and kayaking, the Upper Delaware is known for its Class I and II rapids, public fishing, and wintering bald eagles. An interesting fact is that nearly all the land along the Upper Delaware River is privately owned; only 30 acres belong to the U.S. government. The **Erie Canalway National Heritage Corridor,** the newest national park in New York State, comprises four navigable waterways (Erie, Champlain, Oswego, and Cayuga-Seneca) and sections of the first Erie Canal. It totals more than 500 miles in upstate New York. More than 230 trail miles along the corridor have been equipped for biking and hiking. The **Fire Island National Seashore,** located in Patchogue (1 hr. east of New York City), is the site of beautiful ocean shores, an ancient maritime forest, and historic lighthouses and estates. Outdoor activities include backpacking and birding.

Crossing New York State are two of the nation's most important scenic trails. The famous **Appalachian National Scenic Trail (A.T.),** opened as a continuous trail in 1937 and designated the first National Scenic Trail in 1968, is a 2,167-mile footpath that crosses the Appalachian Mountains, from Maine to Georgia. The trail is very popular with day, weekend, and other short-term hikers, section hikers, and through-hikers (who hike the entire length of the trail in one season). The **North Country National Scenic Trail (NST)** crosses seven northern states: New York, Pennsylvania, Ohio, Michigan, Wisconsin, Minnesota, and North Dakota.

Detailed National Park information covering travel and transportation, facilities, fees and permits, hours, wildlife and more is available through the National Park Service website at **www.nps.gov**.

NATIONAL PARK PASSES

The best way to visit National Parks not just in New York State but across the country is with the **National Parks Pass,** a $50 annual pass that provides admission to any national park that charges an entrance fee. The National Parks Pass can be purchased at national park sites, online at www.nationalparks.org, by calling ⓒ **888-GO-PARKS,** or by sending a check or money order payable to the National Park Service for $50 (plus $3.95 for shipping and handling) to National Park Foundation, P.O. Box 34108, Washington, DC 20043-4108. **Golden Eagle Passports** ($65 or $15 extra if added to a National Parks Pass) cover entrance fees at sites managed by the U. S. Fish and Wildlife Service, the U. S. Forest Service, and the Bureau of Land Management. The **Golden Age Passport** (for citizens or permanent residents of the United States age 62 or older; $10) is a lifetime entrance pass to national parks, monuments, historic sites, recreation areas, and national wildlife refuges, and it provides a 50% discount on federal use fees charged for facilities and services such as camping, swimming, parking, boat launching, and tours. A Golden Age Passport must be purchased in person at a federal area (National Park, Historic Site, Wildlife Refuge, and so on) where an entrance fee is charged. **Golden Access Passports** are for citizens or permanent residents of the United States who are blind or permanently disabled.

2 Outdoor Activities from A to Z

BICYCLING

New York State has thousands of excellent roads and mountain trails for cycling. The **Hudson Valley** features moderate hills, Hudson River views, farm landscapes, and historic estates such as those in Hyde Park. The **Finger Lakes** region is ideal for cyclists that want to circle the lakes, perhaps stopping off at wineries. Cyclists are very fond of scenic lake loops around several of the larger Finger Lakes, such as the 100-miler around **Cayuga Lake** and the 40-mile loop around **Skaneateles Lake.** In the Catskills, **Plattekill Mountain** is one of the top five mountain biking destinations in North America, and other mountains, such as **Windham** and **Hunter,** also cater to mountain bikers in summer. Easy cycling is along the **Catskill Scenic Trail** (© 607/652-2821; www.catskillscenictrail.org), 19 miles of Rails to Trails pathway. Farther upstate, **The Seaway Trail,** a scenic road route, runs 450 miles from Massena to Niagara Falls and goes along the south shore of Lake Ontario and the Saint Lawrence River. Near the shores of Lake Champlain, **Lake Champlain Bikeways** is a series of demarcated bicycling loops.

A terrific cycling option for cyclists of all abilities is along the historic **New York State Canal System,** which comprises more than 230 miles of trails across upstate New York. Multiuse trails include the 25-mile **Hudson-Mohawk Bikeway** in the Capital-Saratoga region, the 36-mile **Old Erie Canal State Park** in central New York, the 90-mile **Erie Canal Heritage Trail** in the northern Finger Lakes region, and the 8-mile Glens Falls Feeder Canal Trail in the foothills of the Adirondacks near Lake Champlain. For additional information contact the **New York State Canal Corporation,** 200 Southern Blvd., P.O. Box 189, Albany 12201-0189 (© **800/4-CANAL-4;** www.canals.state.ny.us). For information on bike tours along the Erie Canal, call © **518/434-1583** or visit www.nypca.org/canaltour.

New York City may not seem like a place to hop on a bike, but it is home to a great many dedicated cyclists. The 6¼-mile loop within **Central Park** is a classic urban cycling destination—but look out for in-line skaters, joggers, dogs, and even horses. Another favorite of locals is the ride from the city across the George Washington Bridge up to Nyack along the Hudson River, a perfect 50-mile round-trip. Each May some 25,000 intrepid cyclists take to the New York streets for the **Great Five Boro Bike Tour,** which covers 42 miles and touches all five of the city's boroughs; get more information at www.bikenewyork.org.

A great resource, with information on organizations, trails, and guided trips, is the website of **A1 Trails** (www.a1trails.com/biking/bike_ny.html). Most areas—especially the major leisure destinations, such as the Hamptons, Catskills, Adirondacks, and Finger Lakes—have bicycle shops that rent bikes. There are loads of guidebooks dealing specifically with biking in New York State. Following are some recommended titles: *25 Mountain Bike Tours in the Adirondacks* (Countryman Press); *30 Bicycle Tours in the Finger Lakes Region* (Countryman Press); *Bicycling the Canals of New York: 500 Miles of Bike Riding along the Erie, Champlain, Cayuga-Seneca & Oswego Canals* (Vitesse Press); *The Catskills: A Bicycling Guide* (Purple Mountain Press); *Cranks from Cooperstown: 50 Bike Rides in Upstate New York* (Tourmaster Publications); *Paths Along the Hudson: A Guide to Walking and Biking* (Rutgers University Press); *Ride Guide: Hudson Valley, New Paltz to Staten Island* (Anacus Press).

BOATING

New York is blessed with thousands of miles of rivers and streams, as well as 500 miles of the New York State Canal System and hundreds of lakes and the Long Island Sound. From Saratoga Lake to the Delaware River and the 11 scenic Finger Lakes, there are plenty of great opportunities for boating enthusiasts.

On the **New York State Canal System,** you can cruise the waterway's 57 locks. The Canal System stretches over 500 miles and is normally navigable from May through mid-November. There are four Canals, all easily accessible by boat. From the south, the Hudson River opens onto the Erie Canal; farther north is the Champlain Canal. The Erie Canal travels east to west, with access to the Great Lakes from the Oswego Canal or the western end of the Erie Canal, with access to Lake Erie. The Cayuga-Seneca Canal connects with the Erie Canal in central New York, allowing access to the Finger Lakes region.

You can rent an authentic, old-fashioned canal boat for a few days or a week. For more information on tour boat and cruise operators, canal passes, boats for hire, and the many sites and attractions (including state parks, canal villages, museums and urban cultural parks) along the canal system, contact the **New York State Canal Corporation,** 200 Southern Blvd., P.O. Box 189, Albany 12201-0189 (*C* **800/4-CANAL-4;** www.canals.state.ny.us). The organization puts out a "Cruising Guide to the New York State Canal System," which can be purchased by calling *C* **800/422-1825.** Individual counties also put out canal-specific tourism brochures. See chapters 11 and 13 for additional regional canal information.

Several cruises and riverboat tours are offered along the majestic **Hudson River,** passing some of the Great Estates, historic river towns and even West Point Military Academy. Another option is to rent a houseboat in the Thousand Islands and sail the St. Lawrence River, which makes its way around an estimated 1,000 to 1,800 small islands. For more information, contact the **Thousand Islands International Council** (*C* **800/8-ISLAND**).

Fans of regattas may want to check out the annual **New York YC Regatta,** coming up on its 150th year in June 2004. **Lake Champlain,** on the New York/Vermont border, plays host to a number of regattas throughout the season.

A free *New York State Boater's Guide* is available from **New York State Parks Marine and Recreational Vehicles,** Empire State Plaza, Albany NY 12238 (*C* **518/474-04545;** www.nysparks.com/boats).

CAMPING

New York State has more than 500 public and privately owned campgrounds across the state. Above all, the wilderness, forests, lakes, and rivers of the Adirondack and Catskills Mountains offer the best backwoods camping in the state. The Hudson Valley and Finger Lakes regions, while not as remote, also offer fine camping with easy access to towns and regional attractions. The **Adirondack Camping Association** (www.adirondackcampgrounds.com) is a good resource for campsite information in that region. Two good bets: **Ausable Point Campground** (*C* **518/561-7080**) sits on a stunning patch of land overlooking Lake Champlain, with 123 sites. But to really get away from everyone, reserve a spot on one of the **Saranac Lake Islands,** Saranac Lake (*C* **518/891-3170**), and prepare to canoe there. Detailed listings of campgrounds large and small are available at *C* **800/CALL-NYS** or www.iloveny.com/search/accommodations_camp.asp, www.nysparks.com, and at www.gocampingamerica.com/newyork.

The Department of Environmental Conservation (DEC) operates 52 campgrounds in the Adirondack and Catskill State Parks and publishes the free booklet "Camping in New York State Forest Preserves." For camping reservations and additional information call *C* **518/457-2500** and for reservations, contact **Reserve America** (*C* **800/456-CAMP**). Guidebooks include what some consider to be the bible of New York camping, *The Campgrounds of New York: A Guide to the State Parks and Public Campgrounds* (North Country Books); and *Adventures in Camping: An Introduction to Adirondack Backpacking* (North Country Books).

CANOEING, KAYAKING & RAFTING

From the Hudson River to the Adirondacks and rivers in the Catskills, there are thousands of miles for canoeing, kayaking, and rafting. In fact, in the Adirondacks alone, there are 1,200 miles of rivers designated Wild, Scenic and Recreational rivers—little changed since first used by Native Americans. One of the most popular routes is the **Adirondack Canoe Route,** which begins at Old Forge and flows 140 miles through the Fulton Chain of Lakes to Raquette Lake and north to the Saranac Lakes through Long Lake and then on to Tupper Lake, or east to Blue Mountain Lake. Nick's Lake is excellent for beginning paddlers, and the north branch of Moose River is more challenging. Another great spot for canoeing is the **St. Regis Canoe area** near Saranac Lake, with 57 interconnecting lakes and ponds. For information about canoeing in the Adirondacks, contact the **Department of Environmental Conservation, Preserve Protection and Management,** 50 Wolf Rd., Albany, NY 12233-4255 (© **518/457-7433**), or the **Adirondack Regional Tourism Council** (© **518/846-8016**). The **Delaware River** in the Catskills is one of the longest (73 miles) and cleanest free-flowing rivers in the Northeast, and it's excellent for tubing, rafting, kayaking, and canoeing. For more information, including access points, contact the **Upper Delaware Scenic and Recreational River** (© **570/685-4871;** www.nps.gov/upde), which maintains a 24-hour River Hotline recording from April to October: © **845/252-7100.**

Guided **white-water rafting trips** of varying difficulty, lasting a single day or even less, are available on several New York State rivers. The most challenging white water is in the spring, although some companies offer rides throughout the summer and fall. In western New York, excellent rafting is done on Cattaraugus Creek through Zoar Valley or the Genesee River in Letchworth State Park. In the Adirondacks, the Black River near Watertown is best for advanced rafters, while Indian Lake is considered "the Whitewater Capital of New York State." Moose River is another favorite of experts, while the Sacandaga River is a long and serene trip through the Adirondacks with an exciting finish.

A detailed list of canoeing, kayaking, and rafting operators is available on www.iloveny.com. You can also visit the DEC Bureau of Public Lands, www.dec.state.ny.us, or call © **518/402-9428.**

FISHING

The trout streams and rivers, such as Beaver Kill and the Delaware River, of the **southwestern Catskills** are among the best in North America—or the world, for that matter—for fly-fishing. For additional information, contact the **Delaware Country Chamber of Commerce** (© **800/642-4443;** www.delawarecounty.org) or **Sullivan County Visitors Association** (© **800/882-CATS;** www.scva.net).

The **Hudson River** is very good for striped bass from mid-March to the end of May and trout fishing. For more information, visit www.hudsonriver.com/stripers.htm.

At the eastern end of Long Island, **Montauk** is a sport-fishing capital known for its shark fishing (peaks in late June). Sport-fishing boat rentals and charters are available. Charter fishing on **Lake Ontario,** a celebrated freshwater fishery, brings in large chinook and Atlantic salmon, as well as brown, rainbow, and lake trout, walleye, and smallmouth bass. Contact the **Lake Ontario Sportfishing Promotion Council** (© **800/338-7890**).

The **1000 Islands** isn't a world-class fishing area for nothing. Grab a charter in tiny Clayton—the river serves up walleye, pike, perch, muskellunge (get your muscles ready—these grow up to 35 lb.), and bass. And in **Eastern Lake Ontario,** you'll hook onto salmon, lake trout, steelhead, and walleye.

State fishing licenses are required for anyone over the age of 16 for fishing in New York's fresh waters. Many tackle shops and fishing outfitters issue them, as do town clerk offices. Call © **518/357-2049** or visit www.dec.state.ny.us

(www.dec.state.ny.us/website/dcs/permits_level2.html) for more information on permits. Guidebooks on fishing in New York State include: *Flyfisher's Guide to New York* (Wilderness Adventures Press); *Gone Fishin: The 100 Best Spots in New York* (Rutgers University Press); and *Good Fishing in the Catskills: A Complete Angler's Guide* (Countryman Press).

GOLF

New York State has more than 600 public and private golf courses, including an outstanding number of beautiful golf courses in gorgeous natural settings. Some of the nation's most prestigious golf tournaments, including the U.S. Open and the PGA Championship, are routinely held in New York. Championship status has been awarded to James Baird and Rockland Lake North in the Hudson Valley, Saratoga Spa, Battle Island in Fulton, Chenango Valley in Binghamton; Green Lakes in Fayetteville, Beaver Island in Grand Island, and Montauk Downs and Bethpage on Long Island. New York State possesses a preponderance of the courses judged to be among the finest anywhere, routinely rated among the country's best.

But across the state, in the Catskill Region, Long Island, Finger Lakes, Hudson Valley, Adirondacks, western New York, and the area around Saratoga Springs, there are many dozens of superb courses for golfers of all abilities. Many of the large resort hotels in regions like the Catskills and Adirondacks have their own golf courses, many of them quite good.

For information about golfing in state parks, call New York State Parks (© 518/ 474-0456). For complete listings of courses across the state, visit www.iloveny.com. Golf fans and those looking to play extensively on a trip to New York would do well to consult the **New York State Golf Association** (wwwnysga.com), which maintains a ratings list of courses.

HIKING

Few places on the East Coast have the variety of mountains, forest preserves, and hiking trails that New York State does, making it a superb destination for anyone from hard-core trail hounds to casual day hikers. The wild, remote **Adirondacks** are probably the state's top location for hiking, with a great hiking trail system to high peaks, waterfalls, and secluded lakes. The trail to Avalanche Lake is extraordinary, and Phelps Mountain is a moderate climb rewarded by 360-degree views of the high peaks. Mt. Marcy, at 5,300 feet, is New York State's highest mountain, but with a heavy tree cover, there are peaks with better views to be found. One of them is **Bald Mountain,** east of Old Forge, a 2-mile (but steep) climb with gorgeous vistas. The DEC's Preserve Protection and Management (© 518/457-7433) publishes free literature on Adirondack trails. Information on the Adirondacks can also be obtained from the **Adirondack Mountain Club,** or ADK, in Lake George (© 518/668-4447; www.adk.org), New York's oldest hiking club.

Tips **When You Don't Go It Alone**

The New York State Outdoor Guides Association (NYSOGA) offers licensed guide services for guided wilderness trips—whether your interests are hunting, fishing, rock, and ice climbing, or cross-country skiing and snowshoeing. Contact NYSOGA, 211 Saranac Ave., #150, Lake Placid NY 12946 (© 866/4-NYSOGA; www.nysoga.com).

The **Catskill Region** abounds with fantastic hiking possibilities. Particularly good are trails in the Minnewaska Preserve and Mohonk Preserve. The **Hudson River Valley** is more hilly than mountainous, but there are great hikes in Bear Mountain State Park and Hudson Highlands State Park.

In terms of sheer length, nothing (save the Appalachian Trail and North Country Trail, both of which cross through New York State) is on a par with the **Finger Lakes Trail** (© 716/288-7191; www.fingerlakestrail.org), a hard-core 559-mile system of wilderness foot trails across the state. It's part of the North Country National Scenic Trail, which upon completion will extend 4,200 miles from eastern New York State all the way to North Dakota. The main Finger Lakes Trail connects the Catskill Mountains with the Allegheny Mountains. The New York State Canalway System comprises 230 miles of multiuse trails across upstate, including the 90-mile Erie Canal Heritage Trail; the 36-mile Old Erie Canal Park Trail in Central New York; the 25-mile Mohawk Hudson Bikeway in eastern New York; and the 8-mile Glens Falls Feeder Canal Trail in the foothills of the Adirondacks (near Lake Champlain). For a free map of the **Canalway Trail System,** call © 800/4-CANAL-4.

For trail information and maps, contact the conservation group (comprised of hiking clubs, environmental organizations, and individuals) **New York–New Jersey Trail Conference,** 232 Madison Ave., #802, New York, NY 10016 (© **212/685-9699;** www.nynjtc.org). The New York State Office of Parks, Recreation and Historic Preservation publishes the comprehensive *Empire State Trails;* for a free copy, contact NYS Parks, Empire State Plaza, Agency Building 1, Albany, NY 12238 (© **518/474-0456**). **New York Parks and Conservation Association** (© **518/434-1583;** www.nypca.org) has an online trail finder maps feature, with details on more than 90 trails and over 850 miles of walking, biking, in-line skating, and cross-country skiing. Another excellent resource, with information on organizations, trails, and more, is the **A1 Trails** website, **www.a1trails.com**, which has a section specifically dealing with guided hikes and adventure: www.a1trails.com/guides/gdesny.html.

The **Adirondack Mountain Club (ADK),** based in Lake George, but with chapters in all major regions in the state, has over 20,000 members and publishes guidebooks and the *Adirondack* magazine. It also manages trail maintenance and operates two lodges in the Adirondacks. For more information on specific trails, call © **800/395-8080** or visit www.adk.org. **The New York Ramblers** in New York City offers hiking and snowshoeing trips. Visit www.nyramblers.org.

Following are just a few recommended guidebooks devoted to hiking in New York State; local bookstores will have more options: *50 Hikes in Central New York: Hikes & Backpacking Trips from the Western Adirondacks to the Finger Lakes* (W.W. Norton & Co.); *50 Hikes in the Adirondacks: Short Walks, Day Trips, & Backpacks Throughout the Park* (Countryman Press); *50 Hikes in Western New York: Walks & Day Hikes from the Cattaraugus Hills to the Genessee Valley* (Countryman Press); *Hiking New York State* (Falcon Press); *Paths Less Traveled: The Adirondack Experience for Walkers, Hikers & Climbers of All Ages* (Pinto Press).

HUNTING

Hunting, especially big-game hunting, is big with New Yorkers upstate and more than a few visitors. The New York State Department of Environmental Conservation estimates that 700,000 New Yorkers and over 50,000 nonresidents hunt in the state for a large variety of wildlife, including big game, small game, game birds, and fur bearers. Small- and big-game licenses are required in New York State.

High-Flying Adventures

Elmira, in the southern Finger Lakes region, is where the first 13 national soaring contests in the U.S. were held, which is why the city is sometimes called "the Soaring Capital of America." You can hop aboard a glider or soaring plane at the **Harris Hill Soaring Corporation** (ⓒ 607/796-2988 or 607/734-0641), which offers soaring rides over the rolling countryside of Chemung County and check out the **National Soaring Museum** (ⓒ 607/734-3128; www.soaringmuseum.org) in Elmira. If you're more interested in motorized flight, you can take air in a PT-17 warplane at the **National Warplane Museum** (ⓒ 607/739-8200; www.warplane.org), in Horseheads, near Elmira. And for an amazing balloon ride over one of the state's most beautiful parks, contact **Balloons Over Letchworth** (ⓒ 585/493-3340) for a trip high above Letchworth State Park.

For information on hunting in the Adirondacks and Catskills, the two principal hunting destinations, check out the information on seasons, regulations, and more at ⓒ 518/402-8924 or www.dec.state.ny.us/website/dfwmr/wildlife/worhunt.html.

ROCK CLIMBING

The sheer white cliffs of the **Shawangunk Mountains,** colloquially called "the Gunks," near Minnewaska Preserve in the Catskill/Hudson Valley Region, offer some of the best rock climbing on the east coast—but this is probably not the place for beginners. There is also good rock climbing in and around Lake Placid and Lake George in the **Adirondacks;** contact the **Adirondack Mountain Club** in Lake George (ⓒ 518/668-4447) for locations and outfitters.

SKIING & WINTER SPORTS

New York has a surprising offer of downhill skiing—although not in the league of Vermont, it has more than respectable mountains appealing to expert skiers, novices and families. You'll find the east's only Olympic mountain (and its greatest vertical drop) at **Whiteface Mountain,** Wilmington (ⓒ 518/946-2223), just outside of Lake Placid. The top downhill area overall is the Catskill Region. **Hunter Mountain** in Hunter (ⓒ 888/HUNTER-MTN; www.huntermtn.com) and **Windham Mountain** in Windham (ⓒ 518/734-4300; www.skiwindham.com) have plenty of good trails for practiced skiers, but now also cater to beginners and families. **Belleayre Mountain** in Highmount (ⓒ 800/942-6904; www.belleayre.com) has the highest skiable peak and longest trail in the Catskills, while **Plattekill Mountain** (ⓒ 800/NEED-2-SKI; www.plattekill.com) is a small '50s-style resort. There are also good skiing mountains in the Adirondacks and near the Hudson Valley and Finger Lakes Regions. Lift tickets are in line with most ski resorts in the Northeast (that is to say, not inexpensive), though many offer very good ski packages, especially for beginners.

Cross-country trails litter the state, from the grounds of historic homesteads to state parks. Rural areas like the Adirondacks, Catskills, and Finger Lakes couldn't be better for Nordic skiing, but virtually anywhere you go in upstate NY you'll find trails. Sections of the massive 559-mile **Finger Lakes Trail** (ⓒ 716/288-7191; www.fingerlakestrail.org) are equipped for cross-country skiing.

5

New York City

by Brian Silverman

New York is the concentrate of art and commerce and sport and religion and entertainment and finance, bringing to a single compact arena the gladiator, the evangelist, the promoter, the actor, the trader and the merchant. It carries on its lapel the unexpungeable odor of the long past, so that no matter where you sit in New York you feel the vibrations of great times and tall deeds, of queer people and events and undertakings.

New York is nothing like Paris; it is nothing like London; and it is not Spokane multiplied by sixty, or Detroit multiplied by four. It is by all odds the loftiest of cities.
—E. B. White, *This Is New York*

Novelist and essayist E. B. White wrote the words above more than 50 years ago, but his characterization of New York remains accurate today. And though the grandeur and importance of New York has not changed, the city is in a constant state of flux. Restaurants and nightclubs become trendy overnight, and then die under the weight of their own popularity. But within this ebb and flow lies the answer to why we New Yorkers persist in loving our city so much, despite the high rents, the noise, the crowds, the cab drivers who don't know Lincoln Center from the Lower East Side, and the more stark realities of high-security-alert days and living in the shadow of great tragedy. Nowhere else is the challenge so tough, the pace so relentless, the stimuli so ever-changing and insistent—and the payoff so rewarding. It is why we go on; it is why we proudly persist in living our vibrant lives here.

Come witness New York's astonishing resilience for yourself—it's reason enough to visit.

1 Getting There

BY PLANE

Three major airports serve New York City: **John F. Kennedy International Airport (JFK)** (© 718/244-4444) in Queens, about 15 miles (1 hr. driving time) from Midtown Manhattan; **LaGuardia Airport** (© 718/533-3400), also in Queens, about 8 miles (30 min.) from Midtown; and **Newark International Airport** (© 973/961-6000) in nearby New Jersey, about 16 miles (45 min.) from Midtown. Information about all three airports is available online at **www.panynj.gov**; click on the "Airports" tab on the left.

Even though LaGuardia is the closest airport to Manhattan, it has a hideous reputation for flight delays and terminal chaos, in both ticket-desk lines and baggage claim. Hopefully, airport officials will have rectified the problems by the time you fly, but you may want to use JFK or Newark instead. (JFK has the best reputation for timeliness among New York–area airports.)

Almost every major domestic carrier serves at least one of the New York–area airports; most serve two or all three. Among them are **America West** (© 800/235-9292; www.americawest.com), **American** (© 800/433-7300; www.aa.com), **Continental** (© 800/525-0280; www.continental.com), **Delta** (© 800/221-1212; www.delta.com), **Northwest** (© 800/225-2525; www.nwa.com), **US Airways** (© 800/428-4322; www.usairways.com), and **United** (© 800/864-8331; www.united.com).

In recent years, there has been rapid growth in the number of start-up, no-frills airlines serving New York. You might check out Atlanta-based **AirTran** (© 800/247-8726; www.airtran.com); Chicago-based **ATA** (© 800/435-9282; www.ata.com); Denver-based **Frontier** (© 800/432-1359; www.flyfrontier.com); Raleigh/Durham-based **Midway Airlines** (© 800/446-4392; www.midwayair.com); Milwaukee- and Omaha-based **Midwest Express** (© 800/452-2022; www.midwestexpress.com); Detroit-based **Spirit Airlines** (© 800/772-7117; www.spiritair.com); and Kansas City–based **Vanguard Airlines** (© 800/VANGUARD; www.flyvanguard.com). The JFK-based cheap-chic airline **JetBlue** ✈ (© 800/JETBLUE; www.jetblue.com) has taken New York by storm with its low fares and classy service to cities throughout the nation. The nation's leading discount airline, **Southwest** (© 800/435-9792; www.iflyswa.com), flies into MacArthur (Islip) Airport on Long Island, 50 miles east of Manhattan.

TRANSPORTATION TO & FROM THE NEW YORK–AREA AIRPORTS

For complete transportation information for all three airports (JFK, LaGuardia, and Newark), call **Air-Ride** (© **800/247-7433**), which offers recorded details on bus and shuttle companies and private car services registered with the New York and New Jersey Port Authority 24 hours a day. Similar information is available at **www.panynj.gov/airports**; just click on the airport at which you'll be arriving.

The Port Authority also runs staffed Ground Transportation Information counters on the baggage claim level in each terminal at each airport, where you can get information and book on all manner of transport once you land. Most transportation companies also have courtesy phones near the baggage-claim area.

Generally, travel time between the airports and Midtown Manhattan by taxi or car is 45 to 60 minutes for JFK, 20 to 35 minutes for LaGuardia, and 35 to 50 minutes for Newark. Always allow extra time, though, especially during rush hour, peak holiday travel times, and if you're taking a bus.

BY TRAIN

Amtrak (© **800/USA-RAIL;** www.amtrak.com) runs frequent service to New York City's **Penn Station,** on Seventh Avenue between 31st and 33rd streets, where you can easily pick up a taxi, subway, or bus to your hotel. To get the best rates, book early (as much as 6 months in advance) and travel on weekends.

BY BUS

Buses arrive at the **Port Authority Terminal,** on Eighth Avenue between 40th and 42nd streets, where you can easily transfer to your hotel by taxi, subway, or bus. Call **Greyhound Bus Lines** (© **800/229-9424;** www.greyhound.com).

BY CAR

From the **New Jersey Turnpike** (I-95) and points west, there are three Hudson River crossings into the city's west side: the **Holland Tunnel** (lower Manhattan), the **Lincoln Tunnel** (Midtown), and the **George Washington Bridge** (upper Manhattan).

From **upstate New York,** take the **New York State Thruway** (I-87), which crosses the Hudson on the Tappan Zee Bridge and becomes the **Major Deegan Expressway** (I-87) through the Bronx. For the east side, continue to the Triborough Bridge and then down the FDR Drive. For the west side, take the Cross Bronx Expressway (I-95) to the Henry Hudson Parkway or the Taconic State Parkway to the Saw Mill River Parkway to the Henry Hudson Parkway south.

From **New England,** the **New England Thruway** (I-95) connects with the **Bruckner Expressway** (I-278), which leads to the Triborough Bridge and the FDR on the east side. For the west side, take the Bruckner to the Cross Bronx Expressway (I-95) to the Henry Hudson Parkway south.

Note that you'll have to pay tolls along some of these roads and at most crossings.

Once you arrive in Manhattan, park your car in a garage (expect to pay $20–$45 per day) and leave it there. Don't use your car for traveling within the city. Public transportation, taxis, and walking will easily get you where you want to go without the headaches of parking, gridlock, and dodging crazy cabbies.

VISITOR INFORMATION
INFORMATION OFFICES
- The **Times Square Visitors Center,** 1560 Broadway, between 46th and 47th streets (where Broadway meets Seventh Ave.), across from the TKTS booth on the east side of the street (© **212/768-1560;** www.timessquare-bid.org), is the city's top info stop. This pleasant and attractive center features a helpful info desk offering loads of citywide information. There's also a tour desk selling tickets for Gray Line bus tours and Circle Line boat tours; a Metropolitan Transportation Authority (MTA) desk staffed to sell Metro-Card fare cards, provide public transit maps, and answer all of your questions on the transit system; a Broadway Ticket Center providing show information and selling full-price show tickets; ATMs and currency exchange machines; and computer terminals with free Internet access courtesy of Yahoo! It's open daily from 8am to 8pm.
- The New York Convention and Visitors Bureau runs the **NYCVB Visitor Information Center** at 810 Seventh Ave., between 52nd and 53rd streets. In addition to loads of information on citywide attractions and a multilingual counselor on hand to answer questions, the center also has interactive terminals that provide free touch-screen access to visitor information via Citysearch and sells advance tickets to major attractions, which can save you from standing in long ticket lines once you arrive. There's also an ATM, a gift shop, and a bank of phones that connect you directly with American Express card member services. The center is open Monday through Friday from 8:30am to 6pm, Saturday and Sunday from 9am to 5pm. For over-the-phone assistance, call © **212/484-1222.**

CITY LAYOUT
The city comprises five boroughs: **Manhattan,** where most of the visitor action is; the **Bronx,** the only borough connected to the mainland United States; **Queens,** where Kennedy and LaGuardia airports are located and which borders the Atlantic Ocean and occupies part of Long Island; **Brooklyn,** south of Queens, which is also on Long Island and is famed for its attitude, accent, and Atlantic-front Coney Island; and **Staten Island,** the least populous borough, bordering Upper New York Bay on one side and the Atlantic Ocean on the other.

When most visitors envision New York, they think of Manhattan, the long finger-shaped island pointing southwest off the mainland—surrounded by the Harlem River to the north, the Hudson River to the west, the East River (really an estuary) to the east, and the fabulous expanse of Upper New York Bay to the south. Despite the fact that it's the city's smallest borough (13½ miles long, 2¼ miles wide, 22 sq. miles), Manhattan contains the city's most famous attractions, buildings, and cultural institutions. For that reason, almost all of the accommodations and restaurants suggested in this book are in Manhattan.

In most of Manhattan, finding your way around is a snap because of the logical, well-executed grid system by which the streets are numbered. If you can discern uptown and downtown, and East Side and West Side, you can find your way around pretty easily. In real terms, **uptown** means north of where you happen to be and **downtown** means south.

Avenues run north-south (uptown and downtown). Most are numbered. **Fifth Avenue** divides the East Side from the West Side of town, and serves as the eastern border of Central Park north of 59th Street. **First Avenue** is all the way east and **Twelfth Avenue** is all the way west. The three most important unnumbered avenues on the East Side you should know are between Third and Fifth avenues: **Madison** (east of Fifth), **Park** (east of Madison), and **Lexington** (east of Park, just west of Third). Important unnumbered avenues on the West Side are **Avenue of the Americas,** which all New Yorkers call Sixth Avenue; **Central Park West,** which is what Eighth Avenue north of 59th Street is called as it borders Central Park on the west (hence the name); **Columbus Avenue,** which is what Ninth Avenue is called north of 59th Street; and **Amsterdam Avenue,** or Tenth Avenue north of 59th.

Broadway is the exception to the rule—it's the only major avenue that doesn't run uptown–downtown. It cuts a diagonal path across the island, from the northwest tip down to the southeast corner. As it crosses most major avenues, it creates **squares** (Times Sq., Herald Sq., Madison Sq., and Union Sq., for example).

Streets run east-west (crosstown) and are numbered consecutively as they proceed uptown from Houston (pronounced *House*-ton) Street. So to go uptown, simply walk north of, or to a higher-numbered street than, where you are. Downtown is south of (or a lower-numbered street than) your current location.

As I've already mentioned, Fifth Avenue is the dividing line between the **East Side** and **West Side** of town (except below Washington Sq., where Broadway serves that function). On the East Side of Fifth Avenue, streets are numbered with the distinction "East"; on the West Side of that avenue they are numbered "West." East 51st Street, for example, begins at Fifth Avenue and runs east to the East River, while West 51st Street begins at Fifth Avenue and runs west to the Hudson River.

Unfortunately, the rules don't apply to neighborhoods in Lower Manhattan, south of 14th Street—like Wall Street, Chinatown, SoHo, TriBeCa, the Village—since they sprang up before engineers devised this brilliant grid scheme. A good map is essential when exploring these areas.

MANHATTAN'S NEIGHBORHOODS IN BRIEF

Downtown

Lower Manhattan: South Street Seaport & the Financial District Lower Manhattan constitutes everything south of Chambers Street.

Battery Park, the point of departure for the Statue of Liberty, Ellis Island, and Staten Island, is on the very south tip of the island. The **South Street Seaport,** lies a bit

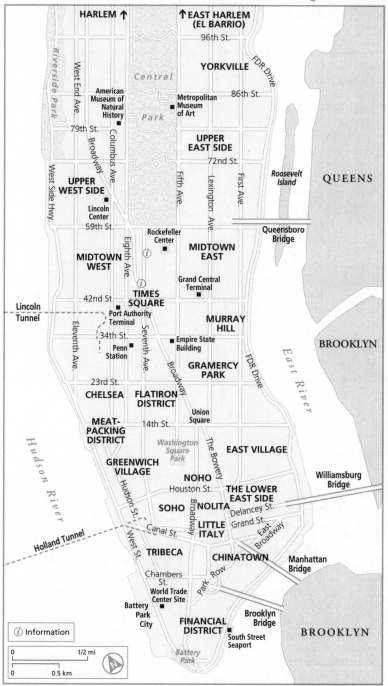

HARLEM ↑

↑EAST HARLEM
(EL BARRIO)
96th St.

Riverside Park

Central

YORKVILLE

FDR Drive

86th St.

West End Ave.

American
Museum of
Natural
History

Metropolitan
Museum
of Art

Park

79th St.

Broadway

Columbus Ave.

UPPER
EAST SIDE
72nd St.

West Side Hwy.

Fifth Ave.

Lexington Ave.

First Ave.

Roosevelt
Island

QUEENS

UPPER
WEST SIDE

Lincoln
Center
59th St.

Rockefeller
Center

Queensboro
Bridge

Eighth Ave.

MIDTOWN
WEST

ⓘ

MIDTOWN
EAST

Lincoln
Tunnel

42nd St

ⓘ

TIMES
SQUARE

Grand Central
Terminal

Port Authority
Terminal

Eleventh Ave.

34th St.

Seventh Ave.

MURRAY
HILL

Penn
Station

Empire State
Building

BROOKLYN

Broadway

GRAMERCY
PARK

FDR Drive

23rd St.

CHELSEA

FLATIRON
DISTRICT

East River

MEAT-
PACKING
DISTRICT

14th St.

Union
Square

Hudson River

GREENWICH
VILLAGE

*Washington
Square
Park*

The Bowery

EAST VILLAGE

NOHO

Houston St.

Williamsburg
Bridge

Hudson St.

SOHO

Broadway

NOLITA

THE LOWER
EAST SIDE

Delancey St.

Canal St.

West St.

LITTLE
ITALY

Grand St.

East
Broadway

Holland Tunnel

TRIBECA

CHINATOWN

Park Row

Manhattan
Bridge

Chambers
St.

World Trade
Center Site

Battery
Park
City

FINANCIAL
DISTRICT

Brooklyn
Bridge

BROOKLYN

ⓘ Information

South Street
Seaport

0   1/2 mi

*Battery
Park*

0   0.5 km

north on the east coast; it's just south of the Brooklyn Bridge.

The rest of the area is considered the **Financial District,** but may even be more famous now as **Ground Zero.** The Financial District is now anchored by the World Financial Center complex and residential Battery Park City to the west, and **Wall Street** running crosstown a little south and to the east.

Just about all of the major subway lines congregate here before they either end or head to Brooklyn.

TriBeCa Bordered by the Hudson River to the west, the area north of Chambers Street, west of Broadway, and south of Canal Street is the *Tri*angle *Be*low *Ca*nal Street, or TriBeCa. Since the 1980s, as SoHo became saturated with chic, the spillover has been quietly transforming TriBeCa into one of the city's hippest residential neighborhoods, where celebrities and families quietly coexist in cast-iron warehouses converted into spacious, expensive loft apartments. Artists' lofts and galleries as well as hip antiques and design shops pepper the area, as do some of the city's best restaurants.

Chinatown New York City's most famous ethnic enclave is bursting past its traditional boundaries and has seriously encroached on Little Italy. This booming neighborhood is now a conglomeration of Asian populations. It offers tasty cheap eats in cuisines from Szechuan to Hunan to Cantonese to Vietnamese to Thai. Exotic shops offer unique foods, herbs, and souvenirs; bargains on clothing and leather are plentiful.

The Canal Street (J, M, Z, N, R, 6, Q, W) station will get you to the heart of the action. The streets are crowded during the day and empty out after around 9pm; they remain quite safe, but the neighborhood is more enjoyable during the bustle.

Little Italy Near Chinatown is Little Italy and traditionally the area east of Broadway between Houston and north of Canal streets, the community is shrinking today, due to the encroachment of thriving Chinatown. It's now limited mainly to **Mulberry Street,** where you'll find most restaurants, and just a few offshoots. Because the Grand Street subway station is scheduled to be closed until 2005 (except for one-stop shuttle service from the Broadway–Lafayette St. station), the best way to reach Little Italy is to walk east from the Spring Street station, on the no. 6 line, to Mulberry Street; turn south for Little Italy (you can't miss the year-round red, green, and white street decorations).

The Lower East Side The Lower East Side boasts the best of both old and new New York: Witness the stretch of Houston between Forsyth and Allen streets, where Yoneh Shimmel's Knish Shop sits shoulder-to-shoulder with the city's newest art-house cinema—and both are thriving.

The neighborhood makes a fascinating itinerary stop for both nostalgists and nightlife hounds. Still, the blocks well south of Houston can be grungy in spots, so walk them with confidence and care after dark.

There are some remnants of what was once the largest Jewish population in America along **Orchard Street,** where you'll find great bargain hunting in its many old-world fabric and clothing stores still thriving between the club-clothes boutiques and trendy lounges. The exponentially expanding trendy set can be found in the blocks between Allen and Clinton streets south of Houston and north of Delancey, with more new shops, bars, and restaurants popping up in the blocks to the east every day.

This area is not well served by the subway system (one cause for its years of decline), so your best bet is to take the F train to Second Avenue and walk east on Houston; when you see Katz's Deli, you'll know you've arrived. You can also reach the neighborhood from the Delancey Street station on the F line, and the Essex Street station on the J, M, and Z lines.

SoHo & Nolita No relation to the London neighborhood of the same name, **SoHo** got its moniker as an abbreviation of "*So*uth of *Ho*uston Street." This superfashionable neighborhood extends down to Canal Street, between Sixth Avenue to the west and Lafayette Street (1 block east of Broadway) to the east. It's easily accessible by subway: Take the N or R to the Prince Street Station; the C, E, or 6 to Spring Street; or the F or V train to the Broadway-Lafayette stop (note that the B, D, and Q trains will not be serving Broadway-Lafayette during the life of this book due to construction on the Manhattan Bridge).

In the early 1960s, cutting-edge artists began occupying the drab and deteriorating buildings, soon turning it into the trendiest neighborhood in the city. SoHo is now a prime example of urban gentrification and a major New York attraction thanks to its impeccably restored buildings, fashionable restaurants, and stylish boutiques. On weekends, the cobbled streets and narrow sidewalks are packed with shoppers, with the prime action between Broadway and Sullivan Street north of Grand Street.

In recent years, SoHo has been crawling its way east, taking over Mott and Mulberry streets— and white-hot Elizabeth Street in particular—north of Kenmare Street, an area now known as **Nolita** for its *No*rth of *Li*ttle *Ita*ly location. Nolita is becoming increasingly well known for its hot shopping prospects, which include a number of pricey antiques and home design stores. Taking the 6 to Spring Street will get you closest by subway, but it's just a short walk east from SoHo proper.

The East Village & NoHo The **East Village,** which extends between 14th Street and Houston Street, from Broadway east to First Avenue and beyond to Alphabet City— avenues A, B, C, and D—is where the city's real bohemia has gone. It's a fascinating mix of affordable ethnic and trendy restaurants, upstart clothing designers and kitschy boutiques, punk-rock clubs, and folk cafes. A half-dozen Off-Broadway theaters also call this place home. The gentrification that has swept the city has made a huge impact on the East Village, but there's still a seedy element that some of you won't find appealing—and some of you will.

The East Village isn't very accessible by subway; unless you're traveling along 14th Street (the L line will drop you off at Third and First aves.), your best bet is to take the 4, 5, 6, N, Q, R, or W to 14th Street/Union Square; the N, R to 8th Street; or the 6 to Astor Place and walk east.

The southwestern section of the East Village, around Broadway and Lafayette between Bleecker and 4th streets, is called **NoHo** (for *No*rth of *Ho*uston), and has a completely different character. This area has developed much more like its neighbor to the south, SoHo. The Bleecker Street stop on the no. 6 line will land you in the heart of it, and the Broadway-Lafayette stop on the F, V line will drop you at its southern edge.

Greenwich   Village Tree-lined streets crisscross and wind, following ancient streams and cow paths.

Each block reveals yet another row of Greek Revival town houses, a well-preserved Federal-style house, or a peaceful courtyard or square. This is "the Village," from Broadway west to the Hudson River, bordered by Houston Street to the south and 14th Street to the north. It defies Manhattan's orderly grid system with streets that predate it, virtually every one chockablock with activity, and unless you live here, it may be impossible to master the lay of the land—so be sure to take a map along as you explore.

The Seventh Avenue line (1, 2, 3, 9) is the area's main subway artery, while the West 4th Street stop (where the A, C, E lines meet the F and V lines) serves as its central hub. (*Note:* Due to rail work, the B, D, and Q subway trains will not be serving W. 4th St. during the life of this book.)

The tolerant anything-goes attitude in the Village has fostered a large gay community, which is still largely in evidence around **Christopher Street** and Sheridan Square. The streets west of Seventh Avenue, an area known as the **West Village,** boasts some of the city's most charming and historic brownstones. Streets are often crowded with weekend warriors and teenagers, especially on Bleecker, West 4th, 8th, and surrounding streets. Keep an eye on your wallet when navigating the weekend throngs.

Midtown

Chelsea & the Meat-Packing District Chelsea has come on strong in recent years as a hip address, especially for the gay community. A low-rise composite of town houses, tenements, lofts, and factories, the neighborhood comprises roughly the area west of Sixth Avenue from 14th to 30th streets Its main arteries are Seventh and Eighth avenues,

and it's primarily served by the C, E and 1, 9 subway lines.

The **Chelsea Piers** sports complex to the far west and a host of shops (both unique boutiques and big names like Williams-Sonoma), well-priced bistros, and thriving bars along the main drags have contributed to the area's rebirth. Even the Hotel Chelsea—the neighborhood's most famous architectural and literary landmark, where Thomas Wolfe and Arthur Miller wrote, Bob Dylan composed "Sad-Eyed Lady of the Low Land," Viva and Edie Sedgwick of Andy Warhol fame lived, and Sid Vicious killed girlfriend Nancy Spungeon—has undergone a renovation.

The area from West 22nd to West 29th streets between Tenth and Eleventh avenues is home to the cutting edge of today's New York art scene, with West 26th serving as the unofficial "gallery row." This area is still seriously industrial and in the early stages of transition, however, and not for everyone. With galleries and bars tucked away in converted warehouses and former meat lockers, browsing can be frustrating, and the sometimes-desolate streets a tad intimidating. Have a specific destination (and an exact address) in mind, be it a restaurant, gallery, boutique, or nightclub, before you come.

The Flatiron District, Union Square & Gramercy Park These adjoining and at places overlapping neighborhoods are some of the city's most appealing. Their streets have been rediscovered by New Yorkers and visitors alike, largely thanks to the boom-to-bust dot-com revolution of the late 1990s; the Flatiron District served as its geographical heart and earned the nickname "Silicon Alley" in the process. These neighborhoods boast great shopping and dining opportunities and a central-to-everything location that's hard to beat.

The **Flatiron District** lies south of 23rd Street to 14th Street, between Broadway and Sixth Avenue, and centers around the historic Flatiron Building on 23rd (so named for its triangular shape) and Park Avenue South, which has become a sophisticated new Restaurant Row. Below 23rd Street along Sixth Avenue mass-market discounters like Filene's Basement, Bed Bath & Beyond, and others have moved in. The shopping gets classier on Fifth Avenue, where you'll find a mix of national names and hip boutiques.

Union Square is the hub of the entire area; the N, R, 4, 5, 6, and L trains stop here, as do Q and W trains (until sometime in 2004), making it easy to reach from most other city neighborhoods. Union Square is best known as the setting for New York's premier green market every Monday, Wednesday, Friday, and Saturday.

From about 16th to 23rd streets, east from Park Avenue South to about Second Avenue, is the leafy, largely residential district known as **Gramercy Park.**

Midtown West & Times Square
Midtown West, the vast area from 34th to 59th streets west of Fifth Avenue to the Hudson River is New York's tourism central, where you'll find the bright lights and bustle that draw people from all over the world.

The 1, 2, 3, 9 subway line serves the massive neon station at the heart of Times Square, at 42nd Street between Broadway and Seventh Avenue, while the F, V line runs up Sixth Avenue to Rockefeller Center (B and D lines also serve Rockefeller Center but travel no farther south than 34th St. until Manhattan

Bridge work is complete in 2005). The N, R line cuts diagonally across the neighborhood, following the path of Broadway before heading up Seventh Avenue at 42nd Street (the Q and W trains also use this line until 2004). The A, C, E line serves the west side, running along Eighth Avenue.

If you know New York but haven't been here in a few years, you'll be quite surprised by the "new" **Times Square.** Longtime New Yorkers like to kvetch nostalgic about the glory days of the old peep-show-and-porn-shop Times Square that this cleaned-up, Disney-fied version supplanted. And there really is not much here to offer the native New Yorker. The revival, however, has been nothing short of an outstanding success for tourism. Grand old theaters have come back to life as Broadway and children's playhouses. Expect dense crowds, though; it's often tough just to make your way along the sidewalks.

To the west of the Theater District, in the 40s and 50s between Eighth and Tenth avenues, is **Hell's Kitchen,** an area that is much nicer than its ghoulish name and one of my favorites in the city. Ninth Avenue, in particular, has blossomed into one of the city's finest dining avenues; just stroll along and you'll have a world of great dining to choose from, ranging from American diner to sexy Mediterranean to traditional Thai.

Unlike Times Square, gorgeous **Rockefeller Center** has needed no renovation. Situated between 46th and 50th streets from Sixth Avenue east to Fifth, this Art Deco complex contains some of the city's great architectural gems, which house hundreds of offices and a number of NBC studios.

Between Seventh and Eighth avenues and 31st and 33rd streets,

Penn Station sits beneath unsightly behemoth **Madison Square Garden,** where the Rangers and the Knicks play. Taking up all of 34th Street between Sixth and Seventh avenues is **Macy's,** the world's largest department store; exit Macy's at the southeast corner and you'll find more famous-label shopping around **Herald Square.** The blocks around 32nd Street just west of Fifth Avenue have developed into a thriving Koreatown, with midpriced hotels and bright, bustling Asian restaurants offering some of the best-value stays and eats in Midtown.

Midtown East & Murray Hill Midtown East, the area including Fifth Avenue and everything east from 34th to 59th streets, is the more upscale side of the Midtown map. This side of town is short of subway trains, served primarily by the Lexington Avenue 4, 5, 6 line.

Midtown East is where you'll find the city's finest collection of grand hotels. The stretch of **Fifth Avenue** from Saks at 49th Street extending to FAO Schwarz at 59th is home to the city's most high-profile haute shopping,

Magnificent architectural highlights include the recently repolished **Chrysler Building,** with its stylized gargoyles glaring down on passersby; the beaux-arts tour de force that is **Grand Central Terminal; St. Patrick's Cathedral;** and the glorious **Empire State Building.**

Claiming the territory east from Madison Avenue, **Murray Hill** begins somewhere north of 23rd Street (the line between it and Gramercy Park is fuzzy), and is most clearly recognizable north of 30th Street to 42nd Street. This brownstone-lined quarter is largely a quiet residential neighborhood, most notable for its handful of good budget and midpriced hotels.

Uptown

Upper West Side North of 59th Street and encompassing everything west of Central Park, the Upper West Side contains **Lincoln Center,** arguably the world's premier performing arts venue, and a growing number of midpriced hotels whose larger-than-Midtown rooms and nice residential location make them some of the best values in the entire city.

Unlike the more stratified Upper East Side, the Upper West Side is home to an egalitarian mix of middle-class yuppiedom, laid-back wealth (lots of celebs and monied media types call the grand apartments along Central Park West home), and ethnic families who were here before the gentrification.

Two major subway lines service the area: the 1, 2, 3, 9 line runs up Broadway, while the B and C trains run up glamorous Central Park West, stopping right at the historic Dakota apartment building (where John Lennon was shot and Yoko still lives) at 72nd Street, and at the Museum of Natural History at 81st Street.

Upper East Side North of 59th Street and east of Central Park is some of the city's most expensive residential real estate. This is New York at its most gentrified: Walk along Fifth and Park avenues, especially between 60th and 80th streets, and you're sure to encounter some of the wizened WASPs and Chanel-suited socialites that make up the most rarefied of the city's population. Madison Avenue from 60th Street well into the 80s is the main shopping strip—so bring your platinum card.

The main attraction of this neighborhood is **Museum Mile,** the stretch of Fifth Avenue fronting Central Park that's home to no fewer than 10 terrific cultural institutions anchored by the mind-boggling **Metropolitan Museum of Art.**

A second subway line is in the works, but it's still no more than an architect's blueprint. For now, the Upper East Side is served solely by the crowded Lexington Avenue line (4, 5, 6 trains), so wear your walking shoes (or bring taxi fare) if you're heading up here to explore.

Harlem Now that Bill Clinton has moved his postpresidential office into this uptown neighborhood, the whole world has heard the good news about Harlem, which has benefited from a dramatic image makeover in the last few years.

Harlem proper stretches from river to river, beginning at 125th Street on the West Side, 96th Street on the East Side. This area is benefiting greatly from the revitalization that has swept so much of the city, with national-brand retailers moving in, restaurants and hip nightspots opening everywhere, and visitors arriving to tour historic sites related to the golden age of African-American culture. The commercial areas are served primarily by the 2, 3, 4, 5, and A, C, D lines.

2 Getting Around

Frankly, Manhattan's transportation systems are a marvel. It's simply miraculous that so many people can gather on this little island and move around it. For the most part, you can get where you're going pretty quickly and easily using some combination of subways, buses, and cabs.

But during rush hours, you'll easily beat car traffic while on foot, as taxis and buses stop and groan at gridlocked corners (don't even *try* going crosstown in a cab or bus in Midtown at midday). You'll also just see a whole lot more by walking than you will if you ride beneath the street in the subway or fly by in a cab. So pack your most comfortable shoes and hit the pavement—it's the best, cheapest, and most appealing way to experience the city.

BY SUBWAY

Run by the **Metropolitan Transit Authority (MTA),** the much-maligned subway system is actually the fastest way to travel around New York, especially during rush hours. The subway runs 24 hours a day, 7 days a week.

PAYING YOUR WAY

The subway fare, increased in 2003, is $2, half price for seniors and people with disabilities, and free for children under 44 inches tall (up to three per adult).

Tokens were phased out in 2003 and are no longer available. People now pay fares with the **MetroCard,** a magnetically encoded card that debits the fare when swiped through the turnstile (or the fare box on any city bus). Once you're in the system, you can transfer freely to any subway line that you can reach without exiting your station. MetroCards also allow you **free transfers** between the bus and subway within a 2-hour period.

MetroCards can be purchased from each station's staffed token booth, where you can only pay with cash; at the ATM-style vending machines now located in just about every subway station in the city, which accept cash, credit cards, and debit cards; from a MetroCard merchant, such as most Rite Aid drugstores or Hudson News at Penn Station and Grand Central Terminal; or at the MTA information desk at the Times Square Visitor Center, 1560 Broadway, between 46th and 47th streets.

(Tips   Subway & Bus Information

Service is always subject to change, your best bet is to contact the **Metro-politan Transit Authority (MTA)** for the latest details; call ✆ **718/330-1234,** or visit **www.mta.nyc.ny.us**, where you'll find system updates that are thorough, timely, and clear. Once you're in town, you can also stop at the MTA desk at the **Times Square Visitors Center,** 1560 Broadway, between 46th and 47th streets (where Broadway meets Seventh Ave.) to pick up the latest subway map. (You can also ask for one at any token booth, but they might not always be stocked.)

MetroCards come in a few different configurations:

Pay-Per-Ride MetroCards, which can be used for up to four people by swiping up to four times (bring the whole family). You can put any amount from $3 (two rides) to $80 on your card. Every time you put $10 or $20 on your Pay-Per-Ride MetroCard, it's automatically credited 20%—that's one free ride for every $10, or five trips. You can buy Pay-Per-Ride MetroCards in any denomination at any subway station; an increasing number of stations now have automated MetroCard vending machines, which allow you to buy MetroCards using your major credit card. MetroCards are also available from shops and newsstands around town in $10 and $20 values. You can refill your card at any time until the expiration date on the card, usually about a year from the date of purchase, at any subway station.

Unlimited-Ride MetroCards, which can't be used for more than one person at a time or more frequently than 18-minute intervals, are available in four values: the **daily Fun Pass,** which allows you a day's worth of unlimited subway and bus rides for $7; the **7-Day MetroCard,** for $21; and the **30-Day Metro-Card,** for $70. Seven- and 30-day Unlimited-Ride MetroCards can be purchased at any subway station or a MetroCard merchant. Fun Passes, however, cannot be purchased at token booths—you can only buy them at a MetroCard vending machine; from a MetroCard merchant; or at the MTA information desk at the Times Square Visitor Center. Unlimited-Ride MetroCards go into effect not at the time you buy them but the first time you use them—so if you buy a card on Monday and don't begin to use it until Wednesday, Wednesday is when the clock starts ticking on your MetroCard. A Fun Pass is good from the first time you use it until 3am the next day, while 7- and 30-day MetroCards run out at midnight on the last day. These MetroCards cannot be refilled; throw them out once they've been used up and buy a new one.

To locate the nearest MetroCard merchant, or for any other MetroCard questions, call ✆ **800/METROCARD** or 212/METROCARD (212/638-7622) Monday through Friday between 7am and 11pm, Saturday and Sunday from 9am to 5pm. Or go online to **www.mta.nyc.ny.us/metrocard**, which can give you a full rundown of MetroCard merchants in the tristate area.

USING THE SYSTEM

The subway system basically mimics the lay of the land aboveground, with most lines in Manhattan running north and south, like the avenues, and a few lines east and west, like the streets.

Lines have assigned colors on subway maps and trains—red for the 1, 2, 3, 9 line; green for the 4, 5, 6 trains; and so on—but nobody ever refers to them by

Manhattan Subways

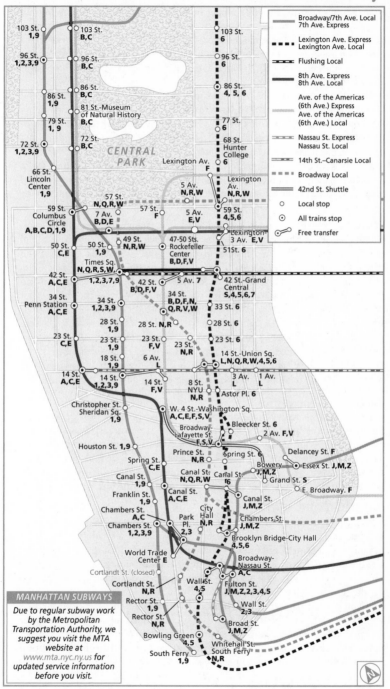

Legend:

Broadway/7th Ave. Local
7th Ave. Express

Lexington Ave. Express
Lexington Ave. Local

Flushing Local

8th Ave. Express
8th Ave. Local

Ave. of the Americas
(6th Ave.) Express
Ave. of the Americas
(6th Ave.) Local

Nassau St. Express
Nassau St. Local

14th St.–Canarsie Local

Broadway Local

42nd St. Shuttle

○ Local stop

⊙ All trains stop

⌀ Free transfer

103 St. **1,9**
103 St. **B,C**
103 St. **6**
96 St. **1,2,3,9**
96 St. **B,C**
96 St. **6**
86 St. **B,C**
86 St. **4, 5, 6**
86 St. **1,9**
81 St.-Museum of Natural History **B,C**
77 St. **6**
79 St. **1, 9**
72 St. **B,C**
68 St. Hunter College **6**
CENTRAL PARK
72 St. **1,2,3,9**
Lexington Av. **F**
66 St. Lincoln Center **1,9**
5 Av. **N,R,W**
Lexington Av. **N,R,W**
57 St. **N,Q,R,W**
57 St. **F**
5 Av. **E,V**
59 St. **4,5,6**
59 St. Columbus Circle **A,B,C,D,1,9**
7 Av. **B,D,E**
49 St. **N,R,W**
47-50 Sts. Rockefeller Center **B,D,F,V**
51St. **6**
Lexington-3 Av. **E,V**
50 St. **C,E**
50 St. **1,9**
Times Sq. **N,Q,R,S,W**
42 St. **A,C,E**
42 St. **1,2,3,7,9**
42 St. **B,D,F,V**
5 Av. **7**
42 St.-Grand Central **S,4,5,6,7**
34 St. Penn Station **A,C,E**
34 St. **1,2,3,9**
34 St. **B,D,F,N, Q,R,V,W**
33 St. **6**
28 St. **1,9**
28 St. **N,R**
28 St. **6**
23 St. **C,E**
23 St. **1,9**
23 St. **F,V**
23 St. **N,R**
23 St. **6**
18 St. **1,9**
6 Av. **L**
14 St.-Union Sq. **L,N,Q,R,W,4,5,6**
14 St. **A,C,E**
14 St. **1,2,3,9**
14 St. **F,V**
8 St. NYU **N,R**
3 Av. **L**
1 Av. **L**
Astor Pl. **6**
Christopher St. Sheridan Sq. **1,9**
W. 4 St.-Washington Sq. **A,C,E,F,S,V**
Bleecker St. **6**
Broadway-Lafayette St. **F,S,V**
2 Av. **F,V**
Houston St. **1,9**
Prince St. **N,R**
Spring St. **6**
Delancey St. **F**
Spring St. **C,E**
Canal St. **N,Q,R,W**
Canal St. **6**
Bowery **J,M,Z**
Essex St. **J,M,Z**
Canal St. **1,9**
Franklin St. **1,9**
Canal St. **A,C,E**
Canal St. **J,M,Z**
Grand St. **S**
E. Broadway. **F**
Chambers St. **A,C**
City Hall **N,R**
Chambers St. **1,2,3,9**
Park Pl. **2,3**
Chambers St. **J,M,Z**
Brooklyn Bridge-City Hall **4,5,6**
World Trade Center **E**
Broadway-Nassau St.
Cortlandt St. (closed)
Cortlandt St. **N,R**
Wall St. **4,5**
Fulton St. **A,C**
Rector St. **1,9**
Fulton St. **J,M,Z,2,3,4,5**
Rector St. **N,R**
Wall St. **2,3**
Broad St. **J,M,Z**
Bowling Green **4,5**
South Ferry **1,9**
Whitehall St. South Ferry **N,R**

MANHATTAN SUBWAYS

Due to regular subway work by the Metropolitan Transportation Authority, we suggest you visit the MTA website at www.mta.nyc.ny.us for updated service information before you visit.

color. Always refer to them by number or letter when asking questions. Within Manhattan, the distinction between different numbered trains that share the same line is usually that some are express and others are local. **Express trains** often skip about three stops for each one that they make; express stops are indicated on subway maps with a white (rather than solid) circle. Local stops usually come about 9 blocks apart.

Directions are almost always indicated using "Uptown" (northbound) and "Downtown" (southbound), so be sure to know what direction you want to head in. The outsides of some subway entrances are marked UPTOWN ONLY or DOWNTOWN ONLY; read carefully, as it's easy to head in the wrong direction. Once you're on the platform, check the signs overhead to make sure that the train you're waiting for will be traveling in the right direction. If you do make a mistake, it's a good idea to wait for an express station, like 14th Street or 42nd Street, so you can get off and change for the other direction without paying again.

SUBWAY SAFETY TIPS In general, the subways are safe, especially in Manhattan. There are panhandlers and questionable characters like anywhere else in the city, but subway crime has gone down to 1960s levels. Still, stay alert and trust your instincts. Always keep a hand on your personal belongings.

When using the subway, **don't wait for trains near the edge of the platform** or on extreme ends of a station. During nonrush hours, wait for the train in view of the token booth clerk or under the yellow DURING OFF HOURS TRAINS STOP HERE signs, and ride in the train operator's or conductor's car (usually in the center of the train; you'll see his or her head stick out of the window when the doors open). Choose crowded cars over empty ones—there's safety in numbers.

Avoid subways late at night, and splurge on a cab after about 10 or 11pm—it's money well spent to avoid a long wait on a deserted platform. Or take the bus.

BY BUS

Cheaper than taxis and more pleasant than subways (they provide a mobile sightseeing window on the city), MTA buses are a good transportation option. However, they can get stuck in traffic, sometimes making it quicker to walk. They also stop every couple of blocks, rather than the 8 or 9 blocks that local subways traverse between stops. So for long distances, the subway is your best bet; but for short distances or traveling crosstown, try the bus.

PAYING YOUR WAY

Like the subway fare, **bus fare** is $2, half price for seniors and riders with disabilities, free for children under 44 inches (up to three per adult). The fare is payable with a **MetroCard** or **exact change.** Bus drivers don't make change, and fare boxes don't accept dollar bills or pennies. You can't purchase MetroCards on the bus, so you'll have to have them before you board; for details on where to get them, see "Paying Your Way" under "By Subway," above.

If you pay with a MetroCard, you can transfer to another bus or to the subway for free within 2 hours. If you pay cash, you must request a **free transfer** slip that allows you to change to an intersecting bus route only (legal transfer points are listed on the transfer paper) within 1 hour of issue. Transfer slips cannot be used to enter the subway.

USING THE SYSTEM

You can't flag a city bus down—you have to meet it at a bus stop. **Bus stops** are located every 2 or 3 blocks on the right-side corner of the street (facing the direction of traffic flow). They're marked by a curb painted yellow and a blue-and-white sign with a bus emblem and the route number or numbers. Guide-A-Ride boxes at most stops display a route map and a hysterically optimistic schedule.

Almost every major avenue has its own **bus route.** Additionally, there are **crosstown buses** at strategic locations all around town. Some bus routes, however, are erratic: The M104, for example, starts at the East River, then turns at Eighth Avenue and goes up Broadway. The buses of the Fifth Avenue line go up Madison or Sixth and follow various routes around the city.

To make sure the bus you're boarding goes where you're going, check the maps on the sign that's at every bus stop, get your hands on a route, or **just ask.** The drivers are helpful, as long as you don't hold up the line too long.

BY TAXI

If you don't want to deal with public transportation, finding an address that might be a few blocks from the subway station, or sharing your ride with 3.5 million other people, then take a taxi. Cabs can be hailed on any street and will take you right to your destination.

Official New York City taxis, licensed by the Taxi and Limousine Commission (TLC), are yellow, with the rates printed on the door and a light with a medallion number on the roof. You can hail a taxi on any street. *Never* accept a ride from any other car except an official city yellow cab (private livery cars are not allowed to pick up fares on the street).

The base fare on entering the cab is $2. The cost is 30¢ for every ⅕ mile or 20¢ per minute in stopped or very slow-moving traffic (or for waiting time). There's no extra charge for each passenger or for luggage. However, you must pay bridge or tunnel tolls (sometimes the driver will front the toll and add it to your bill at the end; most times, however, you pay the driver before the toll). You'll also pay a 50¢ night surcharge after 8pm and before 6am. A 15% to 20% tip is customary.

Note: Taxi drivers were lobbying for a fare increase at press time, and Mayor Bloomberg was supporting it, so don't be surprised if you find higher fares when you arrive.

The TLC has posted a **Taxi Rider's Bill of Rights** sticker in every cab. Drivers are required by law to take you anywhere in the five boroughs, to Nassau or Westchester counties, or to Newark Airport. They are supposed to know how to get you to any address in Manhattan and all major points in the outer boroughs. They are also required to provide air-conditioning and turn off the radio on demand, and they cannot smoke while you're in the cab. They are required to be polite.

Tips Taxi-Hailing Tips

When you're waiting on the street for an available taxi, look at the **medallion light** on the top of the coming cabs. If the light is out, the taxi is in use. When the center part (the number) is lit, the taxi is available—this is when you raise your hand to flag the cab. If all the lights are on, the driver is off duty.

A taxi can't take more than four people, so expect to split up if your group is larger.

FAST FACTS: **New York City**

American Express Travel service offices are at many Manhattan locations, including 1185 Sixth Ave., at 47th Street (② 212/398-8585); at the New York Marriott Marquis, 1535 Broadway, in the 8th-floor lobby (② 212/575-6580); on the mezzanine level at Macy's Herald Square, 34th Street and Broadway (② 212/695-8075); and 374 Park Ave., at 53rd St. (② 212/421-8240). Call ② 800/AXP-TRIP or go online to **www.americanexpress.com** for other city locations or general information.

Area Codes There are four area codes in the city: two in Manhattan, the original **212** and the new **646,** and two in the outer boroughs, the original **718** and the new **347.** Also common is the **917** area code, which is assigned to cellphones, pagers, and the like. All calls between these area codes are local calls, but you'll have to dial 1 + the area code + the 7 digits for all calls, even ones made within your area code.

Doctors For medical emergencies requiring immediate attention, head to the nearest emergency room (see "Hospitals," below). For less urgent health problems, New York has several walk-in medical centers, like **DOCS at New York Healthcare,** 55 E. 34th St., between Park and Madison avenues (② **212/252-6001**), for nonemergency illnesses. The clinic, affiliated with Beth Israel Medical Center, is open Monday through Thursday from 8am to 8pm, Friday from 8am to 7pm, Saturday from 9am to 3pm, and Sunday from 9am to 2pm. The **NYU Downtown Hospital** offers physician referrals at ② **888/698-3362.**

Emergencies Dial ② **911** for fire, police, and ambulance. The **Poison Control Center** can be reached at ② **800/222-1222** toll-free from any phone.

Hospitals The following hospitals have 24-hour emergency rooms. Don't forget your insurance card.

Downtown: New York Downtown Hospital, 170 William St., between Beekman and Spruce streets (② 212/312-5063 or 212/312-5000); **St. Vincents Hospital and Medical Center,** 153 W. 11th St., at Seventh Avenue (② 212/604-7000); and **Beth Israel Medical Center,** First Avenue and 16th Street (② 212/420-2000).

Midtown: Bellevue Hospital Center, 462 First Ave., at 27th Street (② 212/562-4141); **New York University Medical Center,** 550 First Ave., at 33rd Street (② 212/263-5500); and **Roosevelt Hospital,** 425 W. 59th St., between Ninth and Tenth avenues (② 212/523-6800).

Upper West Side: St. Luke's Hospital Center, Amsterdam Avenue and 113th Street (② 212/523-3335); and **Columbia Presbyterian Medical Center,** 622 W. 168th St., between Broadway and Fort Washington Avenue (② 212/305-2500).

Upper East Side: New York Presbyterian Hospital, 525 E. 68th St., at York Avenue (② 212/472-5454); **Lenox Hill Hospital,** 100 E. 77th St., between Park and Lexington avenues (② 212/434-2000); and **Mount Sinai Medical Center,** Fifth Avenue at 100th Street (② 212/241-6500).

Liquor Laws The minimum legal age to purchase and consume alcoholic beverages in New York is 21. Liquor and wine are sold only in licensed stores, which are closed on Sundays, holidays, and election days while the polls are open. Beer can be purchased in grocery stores and delis 24 hours a day, except Sunday before noon. Last call in bars is at 4am, although many close earlier.

Pharmacies **Duane Reade** (www.duanereade.com) has 24-hour pharmacies in Midtown at 224 W. 57th St., at Broadway ((C) **212/541-9708**); on the Upper West Side at 2465 Broadway, at 91st Street ((C) **212/799-3172**); and on the Upper East Side at 1279 Third Ave., at 74th Street ((C) **212/744-2668**).

Police Dial (C) **911** in an emergency; otherwise, call (C) **646/610-5000** or 718/610-5000 (NYPD headquarters) for the number of the nearest precinct.

Taxes **Sales tax** is 8.625% on meals, most goods, and some services, but it is not charged on clothing and footwear items under $110. **Hotel tax** is 13.25% plus $2 per room per night (including sales tax). **Parking garage tax** is 18.25%.

Transit Information For information on getting to and from the airport, see "Getting There," in chapter 3, or call **Air-Ride** at (C) **800/247-7433**. For information on subways and buses, call the **MTA** at (C) **718/330-1234**, or see "Getting Around," earlier in this chapter.

Weather For the current temperature and next day's forecast, look in the upper-right corner of the front page of the *New York Times* or call (C) **212/ 976-1212**. If you want to know how to pack before you arrive, point your browser to **www.cnn.com/weather** or **www.weather.com**.

3 Where to Stay

After the economic boom of the late 1990s, the hotel industry in New York has come down to earth. In the year 2000, hotel occupancy was a record, 84%. But then the economy went sour, September 11 happened, and the bubble had burst. In 2001, occupancy was down around 72%, but rates remained high, hitting an astronomical average of $227. In 2002, occupancy rose slightly to 74% but rates fell to an average of $185. The downturn wasn't only economic; with all the new hotels that had opened in the past 5 years a glut had been created, meaning increased competition for your business. As a result, in 2002 and, as of press time in 2003, many hotels were offering rates they hadn't offered in almost a decade.

You might still find good rates by the time you are reading this, but you might not. And remember, this is still New York; a very expensive city, so a great deal here might mean a no-frills room at the Holiday Inn for no less than $150.

If you want to spend less than 100 bucks a night, you're probably going to have to put up with some inconveniences, such as sharing a hall bathroom with your fellow travelers. (Europeans seem to have a much easier time with this than do Americans.) If you want a room with standard amenities—like a private bathroom—plan on spending at least $150 a night or so. If you do better than that, you've landed a deal. *Note:* For hotel locations, see maps beginning on p. 91.

THE FINANCIAL DISTRICT
VERY EXPENSIVE

Regent Wall Street ★★★   Geared to traveling VPs and CEOs, this ultra-deluxe hotel sets a new standard for expense-account luxury. The mammoth and supremely comfortable rooms boast refined Italian-inspired decor in soothing natural tones and sumptuous fabrics. But the real story is the amenities, which include 34-inch TVs with DVD, large work desks with printer/fax/copier, and even minibars that the attentive staff will stock with your favorite beverages.

55 Wall St. (at William St.), New York, NY 10005. ✆ 800/545-4000 or 212/845-8600. Fax 212/845-8601. wwwregenthotels.com/wallstreet. 144 units. From $495 double; from $625 suite. Promotional rates, discounted weekend rates, and value-added packages as low as $245. Rollaway for extra adult $50. AE, DC, DISC, MC, V. Valet parking $50. Subway: 2, 3, 4, 5 to Wall St. **Amenities:** Fine-dining restaurant; lounge serving lighter fare; state-of-the-art health club; first-rate spa with signature treatments; 24-hr. concierge; well-equipped business center with secretarial services; 24-hr. room service; dry cleaning/laundry service; DVD and CD libraries. *In room:* A/C, TV w/pay movies and DVD, fax/printer/copier, dataport and high-speed connectivity, minibar/fridge, hair dryer, safe, CD player.

Ritz-Carlton New York, Battery Park ★★ This luxury hotel standing at Manhattan's south tip, Manhattan's first-ever waterfront luxury hotel, is a gem. The new glass-and-brick tower is designed such that the majority of the rooms boast views over New York Harbor. Furnishings include a generous and well-equipped work desk with desk-level inputs. Expect the full slate of Ritz-Carlton comforts and services, from Frette-dressed feather beds to the refined chain's signature Bath Butler, who will draw a scented bath for you (which you choose from an extensive menu) in your own deep soaking tub. All harbor-view rooms have views of Lady Liberty; all have sweeping views and telescopes with which to enjoy them. Service is impeccable, of course.

2 West St., New York, NY 10004. ✆ 800/241-3333 or 212/344-0800. Fax 212/344-3801. www.ritzcarlton. com. 298 units. $350–$490 double; from $450 suite. Promotional rates and weekend rates, and value-added packages as low as $209 at press time. Extra person 17 and under $40 ($100 on club level). AE, DC, DISC, MC, V. Valet parking $50. Subway: 4, 5 to Bowling Green. **Amenities:** Fine-dining restaurant; lobby lounge for afternoon tea and cocktails, outdoor seating; 14th-floor cocktail bar with light dining and outdoor seating; state-of-the-art health club with views; spa treatments; 24-hr. concierge; well-equipped business center with 24-hr. secretarial services; 24-hr. room service; dry cleaning/laundry service; shuttle service within Lower Manhattan; technology butler and bath butler services; Ritz-Carlton club level with 5 food presentations daily. *In room:* A/C, TV w/pay movies and video games, dataport and high-speed connectivity, minibar/fridge, hair dryer, safe, CD player, DVD with surround sound in suites and club rooms.

MODERATE

Holiday Inn Wall Street ★ This is Lower Manhattan's most technologically advanced hotel. The comfortable queen-bedded rooms are stocked with everything an executive might need, including an 8-foot L-shaped workstation with desk-level inputs, dual-line portable phones, and the kind of office supplies you never bring but always need, like paper clips and tape. About half of the rooms have PCs with Microsoft Word and Office applications and a CD drive. The top floor is dedicated to special SMART rooms, which feature Toshiba Satellite laptop computers (with carrying case), fax/printer/copiers, and other upgraded amenities, plus buffet breakfast. Room decor is chain standard all the way, but fresh, and perfectly comfortable. The staff prides itself on meeting the needs of its bullish guests, so expect to be well cared for.

15 Gold St. (at Platt St.), New York, NY 10038. ✆ 800/HOLIDAY, 212/232-7800, or 212/232-7700. Fax 212/ 425-0330. www.holidayinnwsd.com or www.holiday-inn.com. 138 units. $1,499–$349 double; from $389 suite. Check for discounts galore (AAA, AARP, corporate, government, military), plus deeply discounted weekend rates (as low as $109 at press time) and other specials. AE, DC, DISC, MC, V. Parking $24. Subway: 2, 3, 4, 5, A, C, J, M, Z to Fulton St./Broadway–Nassau St. Dogs up to 25 lb. accepted. **Amenities:** Restaurant; bar; exercise room and access to nearby health club; concierge; self-service business center; 24-hr. room service; dry cleaning/laundry service; executive-level rooms; CD library; delivery from 24-hr. deli. *In room:* A/C, TV w/pay movies, Internet access, and Nintendo, standard dataport and high-speed connectivity, minibar, coffeemaker, hair dryer, iron, safe, CD player.

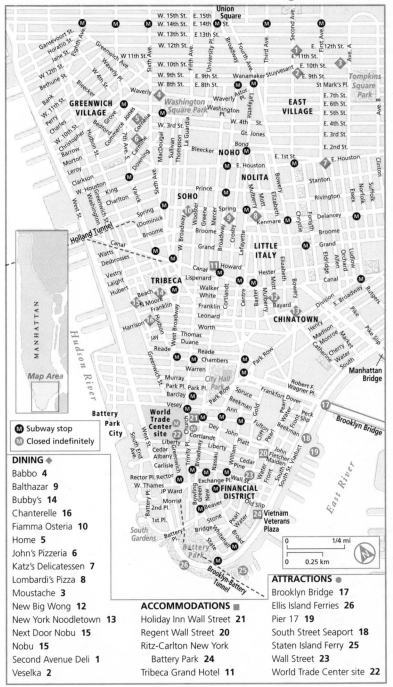

Downtown Accommodations, Dining & Attractions

Subway stop — M
Closed indefinitely — M

DINING ◆
Babbo **4**
Balthazar **9**
Bubby's **14**
Chanterelle **16**
Fiamma Osteria **10**
Home **5**
John's Pizzeria **6**
Katz's Delicatessen **7**
Lombardi's Pizza **8**
Moustache **3**
New Big Wong **12**
New York Noodletown **13**
Next Door Nobu **15**
Nobu **15**
Second Avenue Deli **1**
Veselka **2**

ACCOMMODATIONS ■
Holiday Inn Wall Street **21**
Regent Wall Street **20**
Ritz-Carlton New York
    Battery Park **24**
Tribeca Grand Hotel **11**

ATTRACTIONS ●
Brooklyn Bridge **17**
Ellis Island Ferries **26**
Pier 17 **19**
South Street Seaport **18**
Staten Island Ferry **25**
Wall Street **23**
World Trade Center site **22**

Midtown Accommodations, Dining & Attractions

ACCOMMODATIONS ■

The Algonquin **30**
Americana Inn **35**
Belvedere Hotel **6**
The Benjamin **25**
Chelsea Lodge **15**
Doubletree Times Square
  Guest Suites **9**
Gershwin Hotel **40**
Habitat Hotel **19**
Hotel Metro **37**
Le Parker Meridien **18**
The Peninsula–New York **21**
The Plaza Hotel **16**
Red Roof Inn **38**
Ritz-Carlton New York,
  Central Park **17**
The St. Regis **20**
Thirty Thirty **39**
Trump International Hotel
  & Towers **1**
W Union Square **46**
Waldorf–Astoria
  and The Waldorf Towers **29**

DINING ◆

Aquavit **23**
Carmine's **11**
Carnegie Deli **3**
Churrascaria Plataforma **7**
City Crab **45**
Dos Caminos **41**
Eleven Madison Park **42**
Jean-Georges **1**
John's Pizzeria **10**
Le Bernardin **5**
Le Cirque 2000 **28**
Le Grenouille **24**
Manhattan Chili Co. **12**
Molyvos **2**
P.J. Clarke's **22**
The Red Cat **14**
Stage Deli **4**
Veritas **44**
Virgil's Real BBQ **11**

UPPER WEST SIDE

Lincoln Center

CENTRAL

West Drive

Central Park S.

Columbus Circle

DeWitt Clinton Park

THEATER DISTRICT

MIDTOWN WEST

TIMES SQUARE

Port Authority

Lincoln Tunnel

Javits Convention Center

GARMENT DISTRICT

Penn Station/ Madison Square Garden

Tunnel Entrance

Chelsea Park

CHELSEA

Chelsea Piers

Hudson River

MEAT-PACKING DISTRICT

West End Ave.
Amsterdam Ave.
Columbus Ave.
Central Park W.
Tenth Ave.
Ninth Ave.
Eleventh Ave.
Twelfth Ave.
Broadway
Eighth Ave.
Seventh Ave.
West Side Hwy.

W. 67th St.
W. 66th St.
W. 65th St.
65th St.
W. 64th St.
W. 63rd St.
W. 62nd St.
W. 61st St.
W. 60th St.
W. 59th St.
W. 58th St.
W. 57th St.
W. 56th St.
W. 55th St.
W. 54th St.
W. 53rd St.
W. 52nd St.
W. 51st St.
W. 50th St.
W. 49th St.
W. 48th St.
W. 47th St.
W. 46th St.
W. 45th St.
W. 44th St.
W. 43rd St.
W. 42nd St.
W. 41st St.
W. 40th St.
W. 39th St.
W. 38th St.
W. 37th St.
W. 36th St.
W. 35th St.
W. 34th St.
W. 33rd St.
W 32nd St.
W. 32nd St.
W. 31st St.
W 32nd S
W. 30th St.
W. 29th St.
W. 28th St.
W. 27th St.
W. 26th St.
W. 25th St.
W. 24th St.
W. 23rd St.
W. 22nd St.
W. 21st St.
W. 20th St.
W. 19th St.
W. 18th St.
W. 17th St.
W. 16th St.
W. 15th St.
W. 14th St.
W. 13th St.

ATTRACTIONS ●

Chrysler Building **32**
Circle Line Cruise **13**
Flatiron Building **43**
Empire State Building **36**
Grand Central Terminal **33**
Intrepid Sea-Air-Space Museum **8**
New York Public Library **34**
Rockefeller Center **27**
St. Patrick's Cathedral **26**
United Nations **31**

UPPER EAST SIDE

0   1/4 mi
0   0.25 km

Transverse
East River Drive
PARK
The Pond
Central Park S.

E. 64th St.
E. 63rd St.
E. 62nd St.
E. 61st St.
From Lower Level
Roosevelt Island Tram
E. 60th St.
Queensboro Bridge
E. 59th St.
E. 58th St.
To Upper Level
E. 57th St.
E. 56th St.

York Ave.
Sutton Pl.

MIDTOWN EAST

E. 55th St.
E. 54th St.
E. 53rd St.
E. 52nd St.
E. 51st St.
E. 50th St.
Mitchell Place
E. 49th St.
E. 48th St

Sutton Pl. South
Beekman Place

Rockefeller Center

Fifth Ave.
Madison Ave.
Park Ave.
Lexington Avenue
Third Ave.
Second Ave.
First Ave.

E. 47th St.
E. 46th St.
E. 45th St.
E. 44th St.
E. 43rd St.
E. 42nd St.
E. 41st St.
E. 40th St.
E. 39th St.
E. 38th St.

United Nations

Grand Central Terminal

New York Public Library
Bryant Park

Sixth Ave. (Ave. of the Americas)

MURRAY HILL

Queens-Midtown Tunnel
FDR Drive

E 37th St.   Tunnel Exit
E 36th St.
E. 35th St.   Tunnel Entrance
E. 34th St.
E. 33rd St.
E. 32nd St.
E. 31st St.
E. 30th St.
E. 29th St.
E. 28th St.
E. 27th St.
E. 26th St.
E. 25th St.
E. 24th St.
E. 23rd St.
E. 22nd St.
E. 21st St.
E. 20th St.
E. 19th St.
E. 18th St.
E. 17th St.
E. 16th St.
E. 15th St.
E. 14th St.
E. 13th St.

Empire State Bldg.

Broadway
Fifth Ave.
Madison Ave.
Park Ave. S.
Second Ave.
First Ave.
Asser Levy Pl.

Madison Square Park

Gramercy Park

FLATIRON DISTRICT

GRAMERCY PARK

Union Square

Union Sq. W.
Union Sq. E.
Irving Pl.
N.D. Perlman Pl.

Peter Cooper Village
Stuyvesant Town

Ⓜ Subway stop

Upper Manhattan
Uptown
Midtown
Downtown

93

Uptown Accommodations, Dining & Attractions

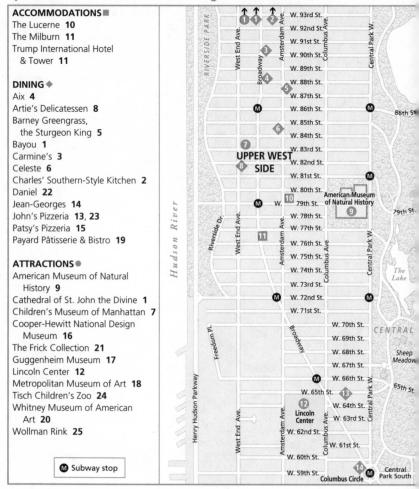

ACCOMMODATIONS ■
The Lucerne **10**
The Milburn **11**
Trump International Hotel
& Tower **11**

DINING ◆
Aix **4**
Artie's Delicatessen **8**
Barney Greengrass,
the Sturgeon King **5**
Bayou **1**
Carmine's **3**
Celeste **6**
Charles' Southern-Style Kitchen **2**
Daniel **22**
Jean-Georges **14**
John's Pizzeria **13, 23**
Patsy's Pizzeria **15**
Payard Pâtisserie & Bistro **19**

ATTRACTIONS ●
American Museum of Natural
History **9**
Cathedral of St. John the Divine **1**
Children's Museum of Manhattan **7**
Cooper-Hewitt National Design
Museum **16**
The Frick Collection **21**
Guggenheim Museum **17**
Lincoln Center **12**
Metropolitan Museum of Art **18**
Tisch Children's Zoo **24**
Whitney Museum of American
Art **20**
Wollman Rink **25**

Ⓜ Subway stop

TRIBECA
VERY EXPENSIVE

Tribeca Grand Hotel ✦✦   A triumph in merging high style, luxury comforts, and a hip downtown location. Set on a triangular plot just south of SoHo, the decidedly retro brick-and-cast-iron exterior blends perfectly with the surrounding neighborhood. Set along open atrium-facing corridors, the streamlined guest rooms boast generous built-in work space (with a Herman Miller Aeron chair) and state-of-the-art technology. A warm gold-and-red palette, interesting textures, and soft, glowing light emphasize luxury in the modern, utilitarian design.

2 Sixth Ave. (at White and Church sts.), New York, NY 10013. ✆ 877/519-6600 or 212/519-6600. Fax 212/519-6700. www.tribecagrand.com. 203 units. From $259 double or studio; from $549 suite. Internet-only rates from $239 at press time; ask about corporate rates and value-added packages. AE, DC, DISC, MC, V. Parking $42. Subway: 1, 9 to Franklin St.; A, C, E to Canal St. Pets welcomed. **Amenities:** Oh-so-hip restaurant and lounge; fitness center; well-connected 24-hr. concierge; business center with complete workstations;

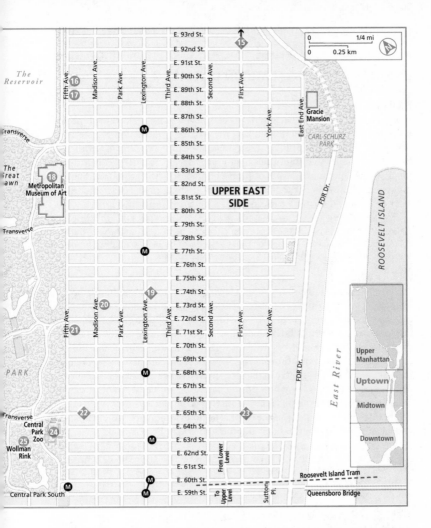

24-hr. room service; same-day laundry and dry-cleaning; video and CD libraries; screening room; coffee, tea, and cocoa bar on each floor. *In room:* A/C, TV/VCR with Internet access, minibar, hair dryer, safe, CD player, fax/printer/copier, standard dataport and high-speed connectivity.

CHELSEA
INEXPENSIVE

Chelsea Lodge ★★ *Value*   Housed in a lovely brownstone on a landmarked block, this small hotel is utterly charming and a terrific value—arguably the best in the city for budget-minded travelers. Impeccable renovations have restored original woodwork to mint condition and created a homey, country-in-the-city vibe. The beds are the finest and best outfitted I've seen in this price category. I won't kid you—rooms are petite, the open closets are small, and beds are full-size (queens wouldn't cut it). But considering the stylishness, the amenities, and the great neighborhood, you'd be hard-pressed to do better for the money. Best for couples rather than shares.

318 W. 20th St. (btwn Eighth and Ninth aves.), New York, NY 10011. ℂ 800/373-1116 or 212/243-4499. Fax 212/243-7852. www.chelsealodge.com. 22 units (all with semiprivate bathroom). $105 double. AE, DC, DISC, MC, V. Parking about $20 nearby. Subway: 1, 9 to 18th St.; C, E to 23rd St. *In room:* A/C, TV, ceiling fan.

UNION SQUARE, THE FLATIRON DISTRICT & GRAMERCY PARK

EXPENSIVE

W Union Square ⭐   Überarchitect David Rockwell has transformed the magnificent 1911 Guardian Life building overlooking leafy Union Square into a new gem. He has successfully fused original beaux arts detailing with bold, clean-lined modernism and a relaxing, grown-up air. Rooms boast distinctive touches like luminous mother-of-pearl counters in the bathrooms. Star chef Todd English's Mediterranean-accented Olives is one of the best hotel restaurants in town and Gerber's dark and sultry Underbar is just downstairs.

201 Park Ave. South (at 17th St.). New York, NY 10003. ℂ 212/253-9119. Fax 212/253-9229. www. starwood.com. $239–$550 double. Check website for specials. AE, DC, DISC, MC, V. Subway: N, R, W, 6, 5, 4 to Union Square. **Amenities:** Restaurant; bar; fitness center; concierge; 24-hr. room service; laundry/valet services; video library. *In room:* A/C, TV/DVD, fridge, dataport, Internet access.

INEXPENSIVE

Gershwin Hotel ⭐ *Kids*   If you see glowing horns protruding from a lipstick-red facade, you're in the right place. This creative-minded, Warhol-esque hotel caters to up-and-coming artistic types—and well-established names with an eye for good value—with its bold modern art collection and wild style. The standard rooms are clean and bright, with Picasso-style wall murals and Phillippe Starck–ish takes on motel furnishings. Superior rooms are best, as they're newly renovated, and well worth the extra $10; all have either a queen bed, two twins, or two doubles, plus a fairly new private bathroom with cute, colorful tile. The family room is a two-room suite that nicely accommodates four with a queen bed in one room, two twins in the other. The hotel is more service-oriented than you usually see at this price level, and the staff is very professional.

7 E. 27th St. (btwn Fifth and Madison aves.), New York, NY 10016. ℂ 212/545-8000. Fax 212/684-5546. www.gershwinhotel.com. 150 units. $99–$189 double (usually less than $150); $189–$219 family room. Check website for discounts, 3rd-night-free specials, or other value-added packages. Extra person $10. AE, MC, V. Parking $25 3 blocks away. Subway: N, R, 6 to 28th St. **Amenities:** Cafe (breakfast only); beer bar; tour desk; babysitting; dry cleaning/laundry service; Internet-access PC. *In room:* A/C, TV, dataport, hair dryer, iron.

TIMES SQUARE & MIDTOWN WEST

VERY EXPENSIVE

Le Parker Meridien ⭐⭐⭐   This formerly stuffy French luxury hotel is now decidedly more up-to-date and laid-back epitomized in its slogan: "Uptown. Not Uptight." The spacious guest rooms have been redone in a sleek yet comfortable Scandinavian style, with clean-lined, blond-wood platform beds with feather beds; built-ins that include large work desks with desk-level inputs and stylish Aeron chairs; oversized TVs with DVD/CD players; free high-speed Internet; and slate-and-limestone bathrooms.

But it's the top-notch facilities that elevate the Parker to a higher level, drawing international CEOs and celebs that could afford to stay anywhere. The excellent Gravity is a mammoth state-of-the-art health club with a full slate of classes, a jogging track, racquetball, personal trainers, a full-service spa, and a fabulous 42nd-floor pool with skyline views.

118 W. 57th St. (btwn Sixth and Seventh aves.), New York, NY 10019. ℂ 800/543-4300 or 212/245-5000. Fax 212/307-1776. www.parkermeridien.com. 731 units. $370–$680 double; from $480 suite. Excellent packages

and weekend rates often available (as low as $189 at press time). Extra person $30. AE, DC, DISC, MC, V. Parking $40. Subway: N, R, B, Q to 57th St. Pets accepted. **Amenities:** 2 restaurants; 2 bars; fantastic fitness center and spa; concierge; courtesy car to/from Wall St.; full-service business center; 24-hr. room service; dry cleaning/laundry service. *In room:* A/C, 32-in. TV w/DVD/CD player, fax, dataport, minibar, hair dryer, iron, safe.

Ritz-Carlton New York, Central Park ★★★ *Kids*   There's a lot to like about this hotel—from its enviable location overlooking Central Park to the impeccable and personable service—but what I like best is that this undoubtedly luxury hotel manages to maintain a homey elegance, and does not intimidate you with an overabundance of style. Rooms facing Central Park come with telescopes and all have flat-screen TVs with DVD. The marble bathrooms are also oversized and feature a choice of bathrobes, terry or linen, and extravagant Frederic Fekkai bath amenities. For families that can afford the very steep prices, the hotel is extremely kid-friendly. Suites have sofa beds and cribs and rollaway beds can be brought in. Children are given in-room cookies and milk, and tours to nearby FAO Schwarz can be arranged. You can even bring your dog (under 60 lb.); if it rains, the pooch gets to wear a Burberry trench coat. Now that's homey elegance.

50 Central Park South (at Sixth Ave.), New York, NY 10019. © **212/308-9100.** Fax 212/207-8831. www.ritz carlton.com. 277 units. $650–$975 double; from $1,395 suite. Package and weekend rates available. Parking $50. Subway: N, R, B, Q to 57th St. Pets accepted. **Amenities:** Fine French restaurant; bar; lobby lounge for tea and cocktails; fitness center and La Prairie spa and facial center; concierge; technology butler and bath butler services; complimentary Bentley limousine service; business center; 24-hr. room service; babysitting; overnight laundry/dry-cleaning. *In room:* A/C, TV/DVD, dataport and high-speed connectivity, minibar, hair dryer, iron, safe, telescopes in park view rooms.

EXPENSIVE

The Algonquin ★★   This 1902 hotel is one of the Theater District's best-known landmarks. This is where some of the biggest names in 1920s literati, among them Dorothy Parker, met to trade boozy quips at the celebrated Algonquin Round Table. Considering the history and comforts here, it also happens to be an excellent value.

The splendid oak-paneled lobby is the comfiest and most welcoming in the city, made to linger over afternoon tea or an elegant cocktail. While posher than ever, the small rooms are comfortable but on the cramped side. The freshened bathrooms boast short but deep soaking tubs, terry robes, and an appealing period feel. Twins are the roomiest doubles.

59 W. 44th St. (btwn Fifth and Sixth aves.), New York, NY 10036. © **888/304-2047** or 212/840-6800. Fax 212/944-1419. www.algonquinhotel.com. 174 units. $159–$299 double; from $299 suite. Check website or inquire about discounted rates or special package deals. AE, DC, DISC, MC, V. Parking $28 across street. Subway: B, D, F, V to 42nd St. **Amenities:** 2 restaurants; lounge; bar; well-outfitted exercise room; concierge; limited room service; dry cleaning/laundry service. *In room:* A/C, TV w/pay movies, dataport, hair dryer, iron, safe.

Doubletree Times Square Guest Suites ★ *Kids*   For less than the cost of a standard room in many hotels, you can have a very nice suite in this 43-story glass monolith, situated right in the heart of the bustling Times Square action. Each spacious suite has a separate bedroom, a dining/work area, and a living room with a pullout sofa, and lots of amenities. For business travelers, conference suites are large enough for small meetings and feature good workstations. What's more, this is also an exceedingly family-friendly hotel, with a floor of childproof family-size suites and special amenities for kids, such as the Kids Club featuring a playroom, an arts-and-crafts center, and computer and video games. Cribs and strollers are available, and there's even a kids' room-service menu.

1568 Broadway (at 47th St. and Seventh Ave.), New York, NY 10036. © **800/222-TREE** or 212/719-1600. Fax 212/921-5212. www.doubletree.com. 460 units. $199–$750 suite. Ask about senior, corporate, and AAA discounts and special promotions. Extra person $20. Children under 12 stay free in parent's suite. AE, DC, DISC, MC, V. Parking $35. Subway: N, R to 49th St. **Amenities:** Restaurant; lounge; fitness center; children's playroom; concierge; business center with secretarial services; 24-hr. room service; babysitting; dry cleaning/laundry service; coin-op laundry. *In room:* A/C, 2 TVs w/pay movies and video games, dataport and high-speed connectivity, minibar, fridge, wet bar with coffeemaker, hair dryer, iron, safe, microwave.

MODERATE

Belvedere Hotel ⭐ *Kids*   This is a very good, midrange Times Square option. Impressively stylish public spaces lead to sizable, comfortable, freshly renovated, and attractive rooms. Beds are nice and firm, bathrooms are smallish but very nice, and every room has a work desk and a pantry kitchenette with minifridge, sink, and microwave (BYO utensils or go plastic). Double/doubles are big enough for friends and small families who don't mind sharing, and your kids will love you for booking a room with Nintendo and on-screen Web access. Ask for a high floor (eight and above) for great views, which usually cost no more (ask when booking). Executive-level rooms have lots of extras.

319 W. 48th St. (btwn Eighth and Ninth aves.), New York, NY 10036. ℂ **888/HOTEL-58** or 212/245-7000. Fax 212/245-4455. www.newyorkhotel.com. 400 units. $145–$325 double. AAA discounts available; check website for special Internet deals (as low as $139 with breakfast at press time). AE, DC, DISC, MC, V. Parking $23 nearby. Subway: C, E to 50th St. **Amenities:** Notable Brazilian steakhouse; breakfast cafe; lounge; concierge; car-rental desk; self-service business center; dry cleaning/laundry service; coin-op laundry; executive-level rooms. *In room:* A/C, TV w/pay movies, video games, and Internet access, dataport, wet bar with microwave, fridge, and coffeemaker, hair dryer, iron, safe.

Hotel Metro ⭐⭐ *Kids*   The Metro is the choice in Midtown for those who don't want to sacrifice either style or comfort for affordability. This lovely Art Deco–style jewel has larger rooms than you'd expect for the price. They're outfitted with smart retro furnishings and smallish but beautifully appointed marble bathrooms. The family room is an ingenious invention: A two-room suite that has a second bedroom in lieu of a sitting area; families on tighter budgets can opt for a roomy double/double. The comfy, fire-lit library/lounge area off the lobby, where complimentary buffet breakfast is laid out and the coffeepot's on all day, is a popular hangout. Service is attentive, and the well-furnished rooftop terrace boasts a breathtaking view of the Empire State Building, and makes a great place to order up room service from the stylish—and very good—Metro Grill.

45 W. 35th St. (btwn Fifth and Sixth aves.), New York, NY 10001. ℂ **800/356-3870** or 212/947-2500. Fax 212/279-1310. www.hotelmetronyc.com. 179 units. $145–$250 double; $155–$300 triple or quad; $175–$350 family room; $210–$400 suite. Rates include continental breakfast. Check with airlines and other package operators for great package deals. Extra person $25. 1 child under 14 stays free in parent's room. AE, DC, MC, V. Parking $17 nearby. Subway: B, D, F, V, N, R to 34th St. **Amenities:** Restaurant; alfresco rooftop bar in summer; good fitness room; salon; limited room service; dry cleaning/laundry service. *In room:* A/C, TV, dataport, fridge, hair dryer, iron.

INEXPENSIVE

Americana Inn ⭐ *Value*   A star in the budget-basic category. The hotel is professionally run and immaculately kept. Rooms are mostly spacious and the beds are the most comfortable I've found at this price. Most rooms come with a double bed or two twins; a few can accommodate three guests in two twin beds and a pullout sofa or in three twins. One hall bathroom accommodates every three rooms or so; all are spacious and spotless. Every floor has a common kitchenette with microwave, stove, and fridge (BYO cooking tools and utensils, or go plastic). The five-story building has an elevator and four rooms are accessible for travelers with disabilities. The Garment District location is convenient for Midtown sightseeing and shopping; ask for a back-facing room away from the street noise.

69 W. 38th St. (at Sixth Ave.), New York, NY 10018. ☎ **888/HOTEL-58** or 212/840-6700. Fax 212/840-1830. www.newyorkhotel.com. 50 units (all with shared bathroom). $75–$115 double. Check website for specials (winter rates as low as $60 double). Extra person $10. AE, MC, V. Parking $25–$35 nearby. Subway: B, D, F, V to 34th St. **Amenities:** Common kitchen. *In room:* A/C, TV, hair dryer (ask reception).

Red Roof Inn *★★* (*Value*)   Manhattan's first, and only, Red Roof Inn offers welcome relief from Midtown's high-priced hotel scene. The hotel occupies a former office building that was gutted and laid out fresh, allowing for more spacious rooms and bathrooms than you'll usually find in this price category. The high-ceilinged lobby feels smarter than most in this price range, and elevators are quiet and efficient. What's more, in-room amenities are better than most competitors', and furnishings are fresh, new, and comfortable. The location—on a bright, bustling block lined with nice hotels and affordable Korean restaurants—is just a stone's throw from the Empire State Building and Herald Square.

6 W. 32nd St. (btwn Broadway and Fifth Ave.), New York, NY 10001. ☎ **800/567-7720,** 800/RED-ROOF, or 212/643-7100. Fax 212/643-7101. www.applecorehotels.com or www.redroof.com. 171 units. $100–$300 double (usually less than $159). Rates include continental breakfast. Children 13 and under stay free in parent's room. AE, DC, DISC, MC, V. Parking $22. Subway: B, D, F, V, N, R to 34th St. **Amenities:** Breakfast room; wine and beer lounge; exercise room; concierge; business center; dry cleaning/laundry service. *In room:* A/C; TV w/pay movies, video games, and Internet access, dataport, fridge, coffeemaker, hair dryer, iron.

MIDTOWN EAST & MURRAY HILL
VERY EXPENSIVE

The Peninsula–New York *★★★*   Housed in a 1905 landmark building, the Peninsula is now a state-of-the-art stunner. Inside, all that's left of the beaux arts past is the marvelous wedding-cake ceiling in the lobby. Every room boasts lots of storage and counter space, plus fabulous linens. But the real news is the technology, which includes a room-wide speaker system and mood lighting; an executive workstation with desk-level inputs, fax, and dual-line speakerphones; a bedside panel for everything, from climate controls to the DO NOT DISTURB sign; even a door-side weather display. In the huge marble bathrooms, a tub-level panel allows you to control the speaker system, answer the phone, and, if you're in any room above the lowest (superior) level, control the bathroom TV. The trilevel rooftop Peninsula Spa is one of the biggest (35,500 sq. ft.) and best spa-and-health clubs in town.

700 Fifth Ave. (at 55th St.), New York, NY 10019. ☎ **800/262-9467** or 212/956-2888. Fax 212/903-3949. www.peninsula.com. 239 units. $585–$690 double; from $800 suite. Winter weekend package rates from $395 at press time. Extra person $50. Children under 12 stay free in parent's room. AE, DC, DISC, MC, V. Valet parking $45. Subway: E, F to Fifth Ave. Pets accepted. **Amenities:** 2 restaurants; library-style lounge for afternoon tea and cocktails; spectacular rooftop bar; trilevel rooftop health club and spa with heated pool, exercise classes, whirlpool, sauna, and sun deck; 24-hr. concierge; business center; 24-hr. room service; in-room massage; babysitting; dry cleaning/laundry service. *In room:* A/C, TV w/pay movies, fax/copier/printer, dataport and T1 connectivity, minibar, hair dryer, laptop-size safe, complimentary "water bar" with 5 choices of bottled water.

St. Regis *★★★*   When John Jacob Astor built the St. Regis in 1904, he set out to create a hotel that would reflect the elegance and luxury he was used to in hotels in Europe. One hundred years later, the St. Regis, now a New York landmark, still reflects that European splendor. Located on Fifth Avenue, and close to Rockefeller Center, St. Patrick's Cathedral, and Saks, this beaux arts classic is a marvel; antique furniture, crystal chandeliers, silk wall coverings, and marble floors adorn both the public spaces and the high-ceilinged, airy guest rooms. The suites are particularly ornate, some with French doors, four-poster beds, and decorative fireplaces. The marble bathrooms are spacious and feature separate showers and bathtubs. Service is efficiently white-gloved and every guest is assigned their personal, tuxedoed butler, on call 24 hours to answer any reasonable request.

2 E. 55th St. (at Fifth Ave.), New York, NY 10022. ✆ 212/753-4500. Fax 212/787-3447. www.stregis.com. 315 units. $610–$735 double; from $1,100 suite. Check the Internet for specials as low as $400 at press time. AE, DC, DISC, MC, V. Parking $42. Subway: E, F to Fifth Ave. **Amenities:** Restaurant; historic bar; tea lounge; fitness center and spa; concierge; 24-hr. room service; babysitting; laundry/valet service; 24-hr. butler service. *In room:* A/C, TV, high-speed connectivity, minibar, hair dryer, safe, CD player.

EXPENSIVE

The Benjamin ★★★ The Benjamin boasts soothing, beautifully styled neo-classical-meets-21st-century rooms that are some of the best outfitted in town. First, the bed: a custom-designed Serta bed luxuriously dressed in Frette linens and down duvet, with a cushioned headboard. For the waking hours, you'll have one of the city's biggest and best-outfitted workstations, with desk-level inputs. The 27-inch TV has Web TV, Sony PlayStation, and front-access inputs for CD players and VCRs (available on request). The smallish white marble bathrooms are designed to maximum advantage, with good counter and shelf space, ingenious shower caddies with shaving mirrors, and even under-the-counter TV speakers. Every room has a Bose Wave radio, Frette robes, and big closets.

125 E. 50th St. (at Lexington Ave.), New York, NY 10022. ✆ 888/4-BENJAMIN, 212/320-8002, or 212/715-2500. Fax 212/715-2525. www.thebenjamin.com. 209 units. From $420 superior double; from $465 deluxe studio; from $530 suite. Call or check website for special weekend-stay offers. AE, DC, DISC, MC, V. Parking $35. Subway: 6 to 51st St.; E, F to Lexington Ave. Pets 35 lb. or less accepted. **Amenities:** Restaurant; cocktail lounge; state-of-the-art exercise room; full-service Woodstock Spa & Wellness Center; concierge; business services; 24-hr. room service; dry cleaning/valet service. *In room:* A/C, TV w/pay movies, video games, and Internet access, fax/copier/printer, dataport and high-speed connectivity, kitchenette, minibar, coffeemaker, laptop-size safe, microwave, china.

Plaza Hotel ★ There's no denying the glamour and celebrated stature of the Plaza, probably the Big Apple's most famous hotel. Remember *North by Northwest? Home Alone 2?* The 1907 landmark French Renaissance palace has been beautifully refurbished by the Fairmont chain, which recently renovated the guest rooms and lobby to the tune of $60 million and added a honey of a spa, the 8,000-square-foot Plaza Spa. Halls and rooms have been beautifully redone in an opulent traditional style in soft, elegant colors, with nice touches like pillow-top mattresses and big leather-top desks; everything is fresh and immaculately detailed. Even the smallest room is a reasonable size, and the building's U shape means that every one gets a measure of fresh air and sunlight. Some suites still boast lavish, red and gold decor; redone park-view ones feature PCs.

768 Fifth Ave. (at 59th St.), New York, NY 10019. ✆ 800/441-1414 or 212/759-3000. Fax 212/759-3167. www.fairmont.com. 805 units. $259–$584 double; from $650 suite. Some rate plans include continental breakfast. AE, DC, DISC, MC, V. Subway: N, R to Fifth Ave. **Amenities:** 4 restaurants; excellent full-service spa and health club with Jacuzzi and sauna; concierge and ticket desk; car-rental desk; business center with secretarial services; salon; 24-hr. room service; babysitting; dry cleaning/laundry service; video and CD libraries; executive-level rooms. *In room:* A/C, TV w/pay movies, fax, dataport, minibar, hair dryer, iron, safe, CD player, Internet access.

Waldorf=Astoria and the Waldorf Towers ★★★ For legendary New York glamour, there's hardly a more recognizable address in town than the Waldorf. Only the Plaza is on equal footing, but you'll get lots more space and genuine elegance here. No two rooms are exactly alike, but all are high-ceilinged and oversize, boasting attractive traditional decor, excellent quality linens and comfy beds, spacious marble bathrooms and closets, and the luxury amenities befitting an old-world hotel of this level, plus nods to the 21st century such as fax machines and dual-line phones.

Renowned for its excellent butler service and respect for privacy, the exquisite, exclusive, residential-style Waldorf Towers—managed under Hilton's ultraluxury Conrad banner—occupies floors 27 to 42 and has a separate entrance, away from the pleasant bustle of the main hotel. The hotel still boasts a notable collection of restaurants including the mahogany-paneled **Bull and Bear;** ideal for stiff drinks or a well-grilled steak in the adjoining dining room.

301 Park Ave. (btwn 49th and 50th sts.), New York, NY 10022. ℂ 800/WALDORF, 800/774-1500, or 212/355-3000. Fax 212/872-7272 (Astoria) or 212/872-4799 (Towers). www.waldorfastoria.com or www.waldorf-towers.com. 1,242 units (159 in the Towers). Waldorf=Astoria: $229–$485 double; from $349 suite. Waldorf Towers: $329–$625 double; from $515 suite. Corporate, senior, seasonal, and weekend discounts may be available (as low as $189 at press time), as well as attractive package deals. Extra person $40. Children under 18 stay free in parent's room. AE, DC, DISC, MC, V. Parking $45. Subway: 6 to 51st St. **Amenities:** 4 restaurants; 5 bars and lounges; 3,000-sq.-ft. fitness center with massage and personal training; concierge and theater desk; expansive 24-hr. business center; salon; 24-hr. room service; dry cleaning/laundry service; executive-level rooms. Tower rooms include butler service. *In room:* A/C, TV w/pay movies, fax/copier/printer, dataport (high-speed connectivity in executive-level rooms and suites), minibar, coffeemaker, hair dryer, iron; also kitchenette or wet bar with fridge, safe in Waldorf Towers.

INEXPENSIVE

Habitat Hotel 🗲   Marketed as "upscale budget," this hotel features rooms dressed to appeal to travelers who are short on funds but big on style. They're well designed in a natural palette accented with black-and-white photos. Everything is better quality and more attractive than in most hotels in this price range, from the firm mattresses to the plush towels to the pedestal sinks in every room. The bathrooms are all new; choose between shared (one for every three to four rooms), private, or a semiprivate "minisuite" (two rooms sharing an adjacent bathroom—great for friends traveling together).

A few queens are available (at the highest end of the price spectrum, of course), but most of the double rooms consist of a twin bed with a pullout trundle, which takes up most of the width of the narrow room when it's open. Despite that drawback, rates are attractive, especially for the rooms with shared bathroom, considering the *Metropolitan Home* mindset and the A-1 location.

130 E. 57th St. (at Lexington Ave.), New York, NY 10022. ℂ 800/497-6028 or 212/753-8841. Fax 212/838-4767. www.habitatny.com. 300 units (about 40 with private bathroom). $75–$115 double with shared bathroom; $135–$185 double with private bathroom; $240–$270 minisuite (2 rooms with shared bathroom); $325–$450 penthouse studio with private bathroom. Rates include continental breakfast. Inquire or check website for student rates and promotions (from $79 at press time). AE, DC, DISC, MC, V. Parking $25. Subway: 4, 5, 6 to 59th St.; E, F to Lexington Ave. **Amenities:** Restaurant/bar; tour desk. *In room:* A/C, TV, dataport.

Thirty Thirty 🗲🗲 *Value*   Thirty Thirty is just right for bargain-hunting travelers looking for a splash of style with an affordable price tag. Rooms are mostly on the smallish side, but do the trick for those who intend to spend their days out on the town rather than holed up here. Configurations are split between twin/twins (great for friends), queens, and queen/queens (great for triples, budget-minded quads, or shares that want more spreading-out room). Nice features include cushioned headboards, firm mattresses, two-line phones, nice built-in wardrobes, and spacious, nicely tiled bathrooms. A few larger units have kitchenettes, great if you're staying in town for a while.

30 E. 30th St. (btwn Madison and Park aves.), New York, NY 10016. ℂ 800/497-6028 or 212/689-1900. Fax 212/689-0023. www.thirtythirty-nyc.com. 240 units. $115–$145 double; $145–$195 double with kitchenette; $185–$245 quad. Call for last-minute deals, or check website for special promotions (as low as $99 at press

time). AE, DC, DISC, MC, V. Parking $35 1 block away. Subway: 6 to 28th St. Pets accepted with advance approval. **Amenities:** Restaurant in the works at press time (inquire when booking if it matters; concierge; dry cleaning/laundry service. *In room:* A/C, TV, dataport, hair dryer.

UPPER WEST SIDE
VERY EXPENSIVE

Trump International Hotel & Tower ★★★   Housed on 14 lower floors of a free-standing 52-story mirrored monolith at the southwest corner of Central Park, is, for a Trump venture, surprisingly cultivated. Rooms are on the small side, but high ceilings and smart design make them feel uncluttered. They're beautifully done in an understated contemporary style, with clean-lined furniture, beautiful fabrics, and soothing Tuscan tones. Floor-to-ceiling windows maximize the spectacular views, which are especially breathtaking on the park side. Each room boasts a Jacuzzi tub in the marble bathroom and a telescope for taking in the views.

The signature services and facilities are what really set the hotel apart. Each guest is assigned a Trump attaché who functions as your own personal concierge, providing comprehensive business and personal services and, following your stay, recording your preferences to have on hand for your next visit.

1 Central Park West (at 60th St.), New York, NY 10023. ☎ **888/44-TRUMP** or 212/299-1000. Fax 212/299-1150. www.trumpintl.com. 167 units. $525–$575 double; from $795 1- or 2-bedroom suite. Check website for special rates (as low as $355 at press time) and package deals; also try booking through www.travelweb.com for discounted rates. Children stay free in parent's room. AE, DC, DISC, MC, V. Parking $42. Subway: A, B, C, D, 1, 9 to 59th St./Columbus Circle. **Amenities:** Restaurant; spa and health club with steam, sauna, and pool; staffed business center with secretarial services; 24-hr. room service; in-room massage; babysitting; dry cleaning/laundry service; butler service; CD library. *In room:* A/C, TV/VCR w/pay movies and video games, fax/copier/printer, dataport and high-speed connectivity, minibar, coffeemaker, hair dryer, iron, laptop-size safe, DVD/CD player.

MODERATE

The Lucerne ★★ *Finds*   As soon as the suited doorman greets you at the entrance to the 1903 landmark building, you'll know you're getting a lot for your money. The bright marble lobby leads to comfortable guest rooms done in a tasteful Americana style. The standard rooms are big enough for a king, queen, or two doubles (great for those traveling with kids). All rooms have two-line phones with dataport (although not always near the work desk), TVs with Nintendo and on-screen Web access, and an attractive bathroom with spacious travertine counters. The suites also boast very nice kitchenettes with microwave and stocked minifridge, and sitting rooms with sofas and extra TVs. The junior suites are a great deal for couples willing to spend a few extra dollars, while the larger suites (with pullout sofas) give families the room they need.

201 W. 79th St. (at Amsterdam Ave.), New York, NY 10024. ☎ **800/492-8122** or 212/875-1000. Fax 212/579-2408. www.newyorkhotel.com. 250 units. $140–$270 double or queen; $160–$290 king or junior suite; $220–$410 1-bedroom suite. Continental breakfast an additional $5 per person. AAA discounts offered; check website for special Internet deals. Extra person $20. Children under 16 stay free in parent's room. AE, DC, DISC, MC, V. Parking $25 nearby. Subway: 1, 9 to 79th St. **Amenities:** Fitness center; business center; 24-hr. room service; dry cleaning/laundry service. *In room:* A/C, TV, Internet access, dataport, coffeemaker, hair dryer, iron.

INEXPENSIVE

The Milburn ★ *Kids*   The Milburn offers reasonably priced rooms and suites with equipped kitchenettes in a terrific neighborhood. Every studio-style suite is rife with amenities, including a dining area; a nice bathroom and kitchenette (with free coffee!); two-line phones; and more. Junior and one-bedroom suites also boast a pullout queen sofa, an extra TV, a CD player, and a work desk. The conscientious management keeps the whole place spotless and in good working order. In fact, what makes the Milburn a real find is that it's more service-oriented than most hotels in this price range.

242 W. 76th St. (btwn Broadway and West End Ave.), New York, NY 10023. © **800/833-9622** or 212/362-1006. Fax 212/721-5476. www.milburnhotel.com. 114 units. $129–$179 studio double; $149–$185 junior suite; $169–$239 1-bedroom suite. Extra person $10. Children 12 and under stay free in parent's room. AE, DC, MC, V. Parking $20–$29. Subway: 1, 9 to 79th St. **Amenities:** Exercise room; access to nearby health club and pool; business services; coin-op laundry; free video library. *In room:* A/C, TV/VCR (Sony PlayStation on request), dataport, kitchenette, fridge, coffeemaker, hair dryer, iron, safe, CD player in suites.

4 Where to Dine

Attention, foodies: Welcome to your mecca. Without a doubt, New York is the best restaurant town in the country, and one of the finest in the world. Other cities might have particular specialties, but no other culinary capital spans the globe so successfully as the Big Apple. *Note:* For restaurant locations, see maps beginning on p. 91.

RESERVATIONS   Reservations are always a good idea in New York, and a virtual necessity if your party is bigger than two. Do yourself a favor and call ahead as a rule of thumb so you won't be disappointed. If you're booking dinner on a weekend night, it's a good idea to call a few days in advance if you can; for the most popular spots you may need to book up to a month in advance.

But What If They Don't *Take* Reservations?   Lots of restaurants, especially at the affordable end of the price continuum, don't take reservations at all. One of the ways they keep prices down is by packing people in as quickly as possible. Thus, the best cheap and midpriced restaurants often have a wait. Your best bet is to go early. Often you can get in more quickly on a weeknight. Or just go knowing that you're going to have to wait if you head to a popular spot; hunker down with a cocktail at the bar and enjoy the scene around you.

TRIBECA
VERY EXPENSIVE

Chanterelle ★★★ CONTEMPORARY FRENCH   Chanterelle is one of the city's best special-occasion restaurants. There's no stuffiness here at all; everyone is encouraged to feel at home and relaxed, and the timing is always perfect. Your server will know the handwritten menu in depth and can fully describe preparations and suggest complementary combinations. The artful cuisine is based on traditional French technique, but Pacific and Pan-European notes sneak into the culinary melodies, and lots of dishes are lighter than you'd expect. The seasonal menu changes every few weeks, but one signature dish appears on almost every menu: a marvelous grilled seafood sausage. The wine list is superlative, but don't expect affordable options. Still, you don't come to Chanterelle on the cheap—you come to celebrate.

2 Harrison St. (at Hudson St.). © **212/966-6960.** Reservations recommended well in advance. Fixed-price lunch $38; a la carte lunch $20–$27; 3-course fixed-price dinner $84; tasting menu $95 ($155 with wines). AE, DC, DISC, MC, V. Mon 5:30–11pm; Tues–Sat noon–2:30pm and 5:30–11pm. Subway: 1, 9 to Franklin St.

EXPENSIVE

Nobu/Next Door Nobu ★★★ NEW JAPANESE   Unusual textures, impulsive combinations, and surprising flavors add up to a first-rate dining adventure that you won't soon forget. Virtually every creation hits its target, whether you opt for the new-style sashimi; light-as-air rock shrimp tempura; or sublime broiled black cod in sweet miso, the best dish in the house. If Kobe beef is available, try this delicacy *tataki* style (with soy, scallion, and daikon). The knowledgeable staff will be happy to guide you. However, because most dinners are structured as a series of tasting plates, be aware that the bill can soar into the "Very Expensive" category.

Can't get a reservation at Nobu? Try **Next Door Nobu,** the slightly more casual version that has a firm no-reservations policy.

105 Hudson St. (at Franklin St.). ℂ **212/219-0500** for Nobu, or 212/334-4445 for Next Door Nobu. Reservations required well in advance at Nobu; reservations accepted only for parties of 6 or more at Next Door Nobu. Main courses $8–$23 at lunch; small plates and main courses $8–$32 at dinner; sushi $3–$10 per piece; *omakase* (chef's choice) from $45 at lunch, from $70 at dinner. AE, DC, MC, V. Nobu: Mon–Fri 11:45am–2:15pm and 5:45–10:15pm; Sat–Sun 5:45–10:15pm. Next Door Nobu: Mon–Thurs 5:45pm–midnight; Fri–Sat 5:45pm–1am; Sun 5:45–11pm. Subway: 1, 9 to Franklin St.

MODERATE

Bubby's ✿ AMERICAN   How do I love Bubby's? Let me count the ways. I love Bubby's for the sublime macaroni and cheese, for the divine garlic burger and fries (accompanied by the restaurant's own "wup-ass" ketchup), for the homemade meatloaf with warm cider gravy and garlic mashies—better than Ma used to make. I love Bubby's generous portions and fresh-from-the-field greens. I love Bubby's big home-style breakfasts . . . and its coziness. And I love the candlelight that adds a touch of romance to the evening. I love the friendly waitstaff that doesn't neglect me. Best of all, I love the pies: the core of Bubby's business, baked fresh daily, a half dozen to choose from (along with another half dozen homemade cakes), and topped with fresh-made whipped cream.

120 Hudson St. (at N. Moore St.). ℂ **212/219-0666.** Reservations recommended for dinner (not accepted for brunch). Main courses $2–$7 at breakfast, brunch, and lunch, $9–$19 at dinner. AE, DC, DISC, MC, V. Mon–Thurs 8am–11pm; Fri 8am–midnight; Sat 9am–4:30pm and 6pm–midnight; Sun 9am–10pm. Subway: 1, 9 to Franklin St.

CHINATOWN
INEXPENSIVE

New Big Wong ✿ CANTONESE   There's nothing new about New Big Wong and that's a good thing. Why mess with success? For over 30 years, Big Wong has been an institution for workers from the nearby courthouses and Chinese families who come to feast on *congee* (rice porridge) and fried crullers for breakfast. Plus, they come for the superb roasted meats, pork and duck seen hanging in the window, the comforting noodle soups, and the terrific barbecued ribs. This is simple, down-home Cantonese food—lo mein, chow fun, bok choy in oyster sauce—cooked lovingly, and so very cheap. If you don't mind sharing a table, Big Wong is a must at any time of day.

67 Mott St. (btwn Canal and Bayard sts.). ℂ **212/964-1452.** Appetizers $1.50–$5; *congee* $1.50–$6; soups $3–$5; Cantonese noodles $5.25–$11. No credit cards. Daily 8:30am–9pm. Subway: N, R, 6 to Canal St.

New York Noodletown ✿✿ CHINESE/SEAFOOD   So what if the restaurant has all the ambience of a school cafeteria? The food here is fabulous. The mushroom soup could feed a small family; thick with earthy chunks of shiitakes, vegetables, and thin noodles. Another appetizer that can serve as a meal is the hacked roast duck in noodle soup. The kitchen excels at seafood preparations, so be sure to try at least one: Looking like a snow-dusted plate of meaty fish, the salt-baked squid is sublime. The quick-woked Chinese broccoli or the crisp sautéed baby bok choy make great accompaniments. Unlike most of its neighbors, New

York Noodletown keeps very long hours, which makes it one of the best late-night bets in the neighborhood, too.

28½ Bowery (at Bayard St.). © **212/349-0923.** Reservations accepted. Main courses $4–$13. No credit cards. Daily 9am–3:30am. Subway: N, R, 6 to Canal St.

SOHO & NOLITA
EXPENSIVE

Fiamma Osteria ★★ MODERN ITALIAN   High in style and quality, Fiamma Osteria is an ambitious and ultimately sumptuous modern Italian restaurant. Start with an antipasti of grilled octopus in an olive vinaigrette sprinkled with ceci beans and cooled by chopped mint leaves and then move on to a pasta or two; the *agnolini* (braised oxtail and beef shank ravioli) and the *tortelli* (buffalo milk ricotta tortelli), are both outstanding. The *orata* (grilled *daurade* with cranberry beans in a Manila clam broth), the pan-roasted cod with shrimp and broccolini, and the *nodino* (seared veal chop with sage and sweet and sour cipollini onions) are excellent entree choices. The extensive wine list features over 400 bottles, mostly Italian with a number of good offerings by the glass. Dinner is a scene so don't expect intimacy, but lunch, with a similar menu, is a much more relaxed option.

206 Spring St. (btwn Sixth Ave. and Sullivan St.). © **212/653-0100.** Reservations recommended. Pastas $21–$24; main courses $25–$32. AE, DISC, MC, V. Lunch Mon–Sat noon–3pm; dinner Sun–Tues 5pm–midnight, Wed–Sat 5pm–12:30am; Sun brunch 11am–3pm. Subway: C, E to Spring St.

MODERATE

Balthazar *Value* FRENCH BISTRO   This gorgeous space is high on the hip list. With all the trappings of an authentic Parisian brasserie, the space is gorgeous. The classic French bistro fare, ranging from steak frites and grilled calf's liver to a delightful duck shepherd's pie and a wonderful brook trout with honey mustard glaze, is surprisingly affordable and excellently prepared. The expansive raw bar offerings are beautifully displayed and make a worthy splurge. But don't expect comfort: The lofty room is so tightly packed and the tables so uncomfortably close that private conversation is a pipe dream; this is the loudest restaurant I've ever been in. The best way to enjoy Balthazar is to come in the off-hours—for breakfast, lunch, or a midday meal—to enjoy the excellent fare in a more relaxing environment.

80 Spring St. (at Crosby St., 1 block east of Broadway). © **212/965-1414.** Reservations highly recommended (some walk-ins accepted). Main courses $11–$20 at lunch (most less than $16), $12–$32 at dinner (most less than $21). AE, MC, V. Mon–Thurs 7:30am–1:30am; Fri–Sat 7:30am–2:00am; Sun 7:30am–midnight. Subway: 6 to Spring St.; N, R to Prince St.; F, V to Broadway/Lafayette St.

INEXPENSIVE

Lombardi's Pizza, 32 Spring St., between Mott and Mulberry streets (© **212/ 941-7994**), the self-described first "licensed" pizzeria, also has a pleasant garden out back.

THE LOWER EAST SIDE, EAST VILLAGE & NOHO
INEXPENSIVE

Two of the best delis in the city can be found downtown: **Katz's Delicatessen** at 205 E. Houston St., at Ludlow Street (© **212/254-2246**), New York City's best deli, and **Second Avenue Deli,** 156 Second Ave., at 10th Street (© **800/ NYC-DELI** or 212/677-0606), the best kosher choice in town.

Veselka ★ UKRAINIAN DINER   Whenever the craving hits for hearty Eastern European fare at old-world prices, Veselka fits the bill with divine *pierogi* (small doughy envelopes filled with potatoes, cheese, or sauerkraut), *kasha varnishkes* (cracked buckwheat and noodles with mushroom sauce), stuffed cabbage, grilled Polish kielbasa, freshly made potato pancakes, and classic soups like a sublime borscht. The Christmas borscht, which hits the menu in early December and stays through January, is a simple but beautiful rendering of the Eastern European classic. But if all you want is a burger, don't worry—it's a classic, too.

Regional beers from the Ukraine and Poland and a nice selection of wines from California and South America add a sophisticated touch. No wonder Veselka surpasses its status as a popular after-hours hangout with club kids and other night owls to be a favorite at any hour.

144 Second Ave. (at 9th St.). (℃ 212/228-9682. Reservations not accepted. Main courses $5–$13. AE, DC, DISC, MC, V. Open 24 hr. Subway: 6 to Astor Place.

GREENWICH VILLAGE & THE MEAT-PACKING DISTRICT
EXPENSIVE

Babbo ★★★ *Value* NORTHERN ITALIAN Chef Mario Batali's zesty, adventurous cooking has attracted a lot of attention since he began appearing on the Food Network. And justifiably so—Babbo might be the best Italian restaurant in the city. Batali has reinvented the notion of antipasti with such starters as fresh anchovies beautifully marinated in lobster oil, and warm tripe "alla parmigiana." The chef has no equal when it comes to creative pastas; ask anyone who's dined here and they'll wax poetic about the spicy lamb sausage in delicate clouds called mint love letters.

The *secondi* menu features such wonders as tender fennel-dusted sweetbreads; smoky grilled quail in a gamey but heavenly fig and duck liver vinaigrette; and spicy 2-minute calamari, a paragon of culinary simplicity. The knowledgeable sommelier can help you choose from the excellent wine list, all Italian and well priced. Last-minute diners can eat at four nonreserved cafe tables and 10 bar seats, but you should book ahead—preferably well ahead, before you leave home—to guarantee a comfortable table.

110 Waverly Place (just east of Sixth Ave.). (℃ 212/777-0303. Reservations highly recommended. Pastas $17–$21 (most under $21); meats and fish $23–$29; 7-course tasting menus $59–$65 ($45 supplement for accompanying wines, $90 for reserves). AE, MC, V. Mon–Sat 5:30–11:30pm; Sun 5–11pm. Subway: A, C, E, F, V to W. 4th St. (use 8th St. exit).

MODERATE

Home ★★ *Finds* CONTEMPORARY AMERICAN HOME COOKING This cozy restaurant with its narrow, tin-roofed dining room is always packed. The dinner menu changes regularly, but look for such signature dishes as the rich and creamy blue cheese fondue with rosemary toasts; an excellent cumin-crusted pork chop on a bed of homemade barbecue sauce; and a filleted-at-your-table brook trout accompanied by sweet potatoes, apples, and sage. Chocolate lovers should save room for the silky-smooth pudding. Breakfast and weekend brunch are great times to visit, too, with fluffy pancakes and excellent egg dishes. The wine list is lovely, boasting a large selection of local bottles from Long Island's North Fork. This is a quintessential Village restaurant, loaded with sophisticated charm. Heated year-round, the lovely garden is most charming in warm weather; book an outside table well ahead.

20 Cornelia St. (btwn Bleecker and W. 4th sts.). (℃ 212/243-9579. Reservations recommended. Main courses $8–$12 at breakfast and lunch, $14–$18 at dinner; fixed-price lunch $13; 3-course dinner $28 ($48 with wines). AE, DISC, MC, V. Mon–Fri 9am–4pm and 5–11pm; Sat 10:30am–4:30pm and 5:30–11pm; Sun 10:30am–4:30pm and 5:30–10pm. Subway: A, C, E, F, V to W. 3rd St. (use W. 3rd St. exit).

INEXPENSIVE

The original **John's Pizzeria** (there are now four of them) is at 278 Bleecker St., near Seventh Avenue (☎ **212/243-1680**); it's the most old-world romantic of the group and my favorite.

Moustache *Value* MIDDLE EASTERN   Moustache (pronounced moo-*stah*-sh) is the sort of exotic neighborhood spot that's just right. On a quiet side street in the West Village, this charming hole-in-the-wall boasts a cozy Middle Eastern vibe and authentic fare that's both palate-pleasing and wallet-friendly. Delicately seasoned dishes bear little resemblance to the food at your average falafel joint. Expect subtly flavored hummus, tabbouleh, and spinach-chickpea-tomato salad (or a large plate of all three); excellent oven-roasted "pitzas," thin, matzo-like pita crusts topped with spicy minced lamb and other savory ingredients; and—best of all—fluffy, hot-from-the-oven homemade pita bread, which puts any of those store-bought Frisbees to shame. Moustache is hugely and justifiably popular, so don't be surprised if there's a line—but it's well worth the wait.

90 Bedford St. (btwn Barrow and Grove sts.). ☎ **212/229-2220.** Reservations not accepted. Main courses $5–$12. No credit cards. Daily noon–midnight (last orders at 11pm). Subway: 1, 9 to Christopher St. Also at 265 E. 10th St., btwn First Ave. and Ave. A (☎ 212/228-2022; subway: L to First Ave.).

CHELSEA
MODERATE

The Red Cat ★ CONTEMPORARY AMERICAN   Just a few years back, New Yorkers could've never envisioned a bistro this mature and refined making a home for itself this far west. But things change quickly, and now the Red Cat is right at home in this gentrifying, gallery-rich neighborhood. Outfitted like a chic-but-cozy farmhouse with an urban flair, the long dining room is a pleasing setting for substantial Mediterranean-accented New American cooking. Witness the thick-cut, chargrilled pork chop, accompanied by a savory purée of black olives, port wine, and red onion; the simply grilled New York strip, served with Yukon golds, fennel, and aioli in a cabernet sauce; or the skate wing, pan-crisped in brown butter with capers, squash, chanterelles, and piquillo peppers. Wines are well chosen and affordable, and service is friendly and efficient.

227 Tenth Ave. (btwn 23rd and 24th sts.). ☎ **212/242-1122.** Reservations highly recommended. Main courses $18–$28 (most less than $23). AE, DC, MC, V. Mon–Thurs 5:30–11:30pm; Fri–Sat 5:30pm–midnight; Sun 5–10pm. Subway: C, E to 23rd St.

UNION SQUARE, THE FLATIRON DISTRICT & GRAMERCY PARK
EXPENSIVE

Eleven Madison Park ★★★ FRENCH CONTINENTAL   The immense, high-ceilinged restaurant located in the lobby of the Art Deco Met-Life Building is a marvel to experience, but before you have a chance to take in all that grandeur, the waitstaff, working with the efficient precision of a secret service unit, is upon you, there almost before you even have to ask. The French-infused country cooking here puts an emphasis on hearty fare, including organ meats such as the almond-crusted calf's brain; crisped pig's feet; prime-aged *cote de boeuf*, and an incredible sautéed skate wing. All the desserts are wonderful, especially the chocolate soufflé (not on the menu, but order it with your meal so it will be ready for your dessert); you might consider skipping the entrees and get right to them.

11 Madison Ave. (at 24th St.). ☎ **212/889-0905.** Reservations recommended. A la carte lunch $15–$24; 3-course prix-fixe lunch $25; dinner main courses $23–$31; tasting menu 5 to 7 courses $60–$80. AE, DC, DISC,

MC, V. Lunch Mon–Sat 11:30am–2pm; dinner Mon–Thurs 5:30–10:30pm, Fri–Sat 5:30–11pm, Sun 5:30–10pm. Subway: N, R, 6 to 23rd St.

Veritas ★★ CONTEMPORARY AMERICAN   Food takes a slight back seat to the spectacular 1,300-bottle wine list in this 65-seat restaurant. Much of the wine cellar is comprised of full-bodied reds, so a robust cuisine that is the specialty here is the perfect accompaniment. There's surprisingly little red meat on the compact menu, but even a pan-roasted monkfish, dressed with white beans, smoked bacon, roasted tomato, and picholines, bursts with flavors that can stand up to a big, bold red. The menu changes seasonally, but expect such lovely starters as citrus-cured salmon with a warm potato blini, horseradish crème fraîche and Russian Osetra caviar. Sweetbreads are crisped with glazed onions, peppercress, and black truffle. Despite the gravity of the wine list, there are many well-priced choices; the first-rate sommelier will be glad to help you choose, no matter what your budget.

43 E. 20th St. (btwn Fifth Ave. and Park Ave. South). ✆ **212/353-3700**. Reservations recommended. 3-course fixed-price dinner $68. AE, DC, MC, V. Mon–Sat 5:30–10:30pm; Sun 5–10pm. Subway: N, R, 6 to 23rd St.

MODERATE

City Crab *Kids* SEAFOOD   This big, bustling, nautical-themed bi-level restaurant is a good choice for affordable top-quality seafood. The menu is huge, and preparations are always satisfying. It's easy to eat as simply or as decadently as you like: Choices run the gamut from simple but hearty bowls of clam chowder to grilled whole Maine lobsters. Always-reliable choices include fresh-off-the-boat oysters (usually a half-dozen varieties to choose from); very good Maryland crab cakes; sautéed jumbo Gulf shrimp; whole steamed Dungeness crabs; and jumbo-size Florida stone crab claws. The desserts tend toward comfort foods: Oreo ice-cream cake, a warm brownie, New York cheesecake, Key lime pie. The service can be slow, but don't let that keep you from coming.

235 Park Ave. South (at 19th St.). ✆ **212/529-3800**. Reservations recommended. $7–$17 lunch; 3-course "express lunch" $15 (Mon–Fri 11:30am–3:30pm); $14–$30 dinner (most under $20). AE, MC, V. Mon–Fri 11:30am–11:30pm; Sat noon–11:30pm; Sun noon–11pm. Subway: 4, 5, 6, N, R, L to 14th St./Union Sq.

Dos Caminos MEXICAN   This new, upscale Mexican has become the rage of the Flatiron district. Crowds were so thick at the restaurant (and bar) when I last visited there was an assigned restroom traffic controller. The guacamole here, made fresh at your table, is a show in itself. I asked for spicy, but for my taste, it lacked the bite and citrus tang of a really great guacamole. The fish tacos, made with red snapper, in a soft taco with fresh coleslaw are outstanding as are the many ceviches, especially *pulpito* (baby octopus). The Mexican standard, chicken *mole en poblano,* is very good, though not worth the steep price (almost $20). In general, stay away from the traditional offerings and explore the more innovative dishes such as chipotle-tamarind glazed mahimahi, ancho-seared big eyed tuna, and 10-chile barbecued baby back ribs; such dishes—and some sublime tequilas—are what sets Dos Caminos apart from your local *taqueria.*

373 Park Ave. S. (btwn 26th and 27th sts.). ✆ **212/294-1000**. Reservations recommended. Appetizers $8–$12; entrees $17–$24. AE, DISC, MC, V. Sun 11:30am–11pm; Tues–Thurs 11:30am–midnight; Fri–Sat 11:30am–1am. Subway: 6 to 23rd St.

TIMES SQUARE & MIDTOWN WEST
VERY EXPENSIVE

Le Bernardin ★★★ FRENCH/SEAFOOD   You may not find a better seafood restaurant in New York, or maybe even the world. Food doesn't get better than the seared rare yellowtail, steamed bok choy, in a marinated citrus and shallot vinaigrette. Chef Eric Ripert's tuna tartare always exhilarates, its Asian seasoning a welcome exotic touch. Among main courses that shine are the steamed striped bass with roasted foie gras; pan-roasted codfish, sweet-roasted garlic, and chorizo essence; and crusted cod, served on a bed of haricots verts with potatoes and diced tomatoes. The formal service is impeccable, as is the outrageously pricey wine list, and the room is uptown gorgeous, if a little generic. The fixed-price lunch is a bargain, given the master in the kitchen. The desserts—especially the roasted pineapple ravioli and its sorbet, rum-scented caramel sauce, and lemon pineapple pound cake—end the meal with a flourish.

155 W. 51st St. (btwn Sixth and Seventh aves.). © 212/489-1515. Reservations required. Jacket required for men/tie optional. Fixed-price lunch $47; fixed-price dinner $79; tasting menus $95–$130. AE, DC, DISC, MC, V. Mon–Thurs noon–2:30pm and 5:30–10:30pm; Fri noon–2:30pm and 5:30–11pm; Sat 5:30–11pm. Subway: N, R to 49th St.; 1, 9 to 50th St.

EXPENSIVE

Aquavit 🌟 *Value* SCANDINAVIAN   When Aquavit opened in a refined pocket of Midtown nearly 16 years ago, it opened the eyes of New Yorkers to what fine Scandinavian food could be. The smorgasbord plate, an assortment of delicacies including smoky herring and zesty hot-mustard glazed salmon (which also comes as a full-size entree), and the venison meatballs, a perfect realization of this traditional Swedish dish, accompanied by parsley root purée, Brussels sprouts, and lingonberry sauce, are some of my favorites. The hot smoked Arctic char on the main a la carte menu, served with quail egg risotto and wild mushroom consommé, is another lovely choice. The bar offers a wide selection of aquavits, distilled liquors not unlike vodka flavored with fruit and spices and served Arctic cold, which have a smooth finish and are best accompanied by a full-bodied European brew like Carlsberg.

13 W. 54th St. (btwn Fifth and Sixth aves.). © 212/307-7311. Reservations recommended. Cafe: Main courses $9–$20; 3-course fixed-price meal $20 at lunch, $32 at dinner. Main dining room: Fixed-price meal $35 at lunch, $65 at dinner ($39 for vegetarians); 3-course pretheater dinner (5:30–6:15pm) $39. Tasting menus $48 at lunch, $85 at dinner ($58 for vegetarians); supplement for paired wines $25 at lunch, $35 at dinner. AE, DC, MC, V. Daily noon–2:30pm and 5:30–10:30pm. Subway: E, F to Fifth Ave.

Molyvos 🌟 GREEK   This upscale taverna is terrific. The menu boasts beautifully prepared favorites (including superb taramasalata, tzatziki, and other traditional spreads), plus a few dishes with contemporary twists. The Greek country salad is generously portioned and as fresh as can be. Among the main courses, the lemon- and garlic-seasoned roasted free-range chicken is right on the mark: juicy, tender, and dressed with oven-dried tomatoes, olives, and rustic potatoes. More traditional tastes can opt for excellent moussaka; rosemary-skewered souvlakia; or the day's catch, wood-grilled whole with lemon, oregano, and olive oil in traditional Greek style. The room is spacious and comfortable, with a warm Mediterranean appeal that doesn't go overboard on the Hellenic themes, and service that's attentive without being intrusive.

871 Seventh Ave. (btwn 55th and 56th sts.). © 212/582-7500. Reservations recommended. Main courses $13–$25 at lunch (most less than $20), $20–$30 at dinner (most less than $25); fixed-price lunch $23; pretheater 3-course dinner $35 (5:30–6:45pm). AE, DC, DISC, MC, V. Daily noon–midnight. Subway: N, R to 57th St.; B, D, E to Seventh Ave.

MODERATE

Carmine's 🌟 *Kids* FAMILY-STYLE SOUTHERN ITALIAN   Everything is B-I-G at this rollicking, family-style Times Square mainstay, sibling of the original Upper West Sider. In many cases big means bad, but not here. Carmine's, with a dining room vast enough to deserve its own zip code and massive portions, remarkably turns out better pasta and entrees than most 20-table Italian restaurants. I've never had pasta here that wasn't al dente and the marinara sauce as good as any I've had in Manhattan. For starters, the daily salads are always fresh and the fried calamari perfectly tender. Rigatoni marinara; linguine with white-clam sauce; and ziti with broccoli are pasta standouts while the best meat entrees include veal parmigiana, broiled porterhouse steak, shrimp scampi, and the remarkable chicken *scarpariello* (chicken pan broiled with a lemon-rosemary sauce). The tiramisu is pie-size, thick and creamy, bathed in Kahlúa and Marsala. Order half of what you think you'll need. Don't expect intimate conversation here; in fact, some earplugs might be in order. Unless you come early, expect to wait.

200 W. 44th St. (btwn Broadway and Eighth Ave.). © **212/221-3800.** Reservations recommended before 6pm; accepted for 6 or more after 6pm. Family-style main courses $15–$49 (most $23 or less). AE, DC, DISC, MC, V. Tues–Sat 11:30am–midnight; Sun–Mon 11:30am–11pm. Subway: A, C, E, N, R, S, 1, 2, 3, 7, 9 to 42nd St./Times Sq. Also at 2450 Broadway, btwn 90th and 91st sts. (© 212/362-2200; subway: 1, 2, 3, 9 to 96th St.).

Churrascaria Plataforma *Kids* BRAZILIAN   It's a carnival for carnivores at this colorful, upscale, all-you-can-eat Brazilian rotisserie. A large selection of teasers like octopus stew, paella, and carpaccio at the phenomenal salad bar may tempt you to fill up too quickly, but hold out for the never-ending parade of meat. Roving servers deliver beef (too many cuts to mention), ham, chicken (the chicken hearts are great, trust me), lamb, and sausage—more than 15 delectable varieties—and traditional sides like fried yucca, plantains, and rice until you cannot eat another bite. The food is excellent, the service friendly and generous, and the cavernous room *loud*—this is not the place for romance. The terrific salad bar even makes this a good choice for the vegetarians in your party. The ideal accompaniment to the meal is a pitcher of Brazil's signature cocktail, the *caipirinha* (a margarita-like blend of limes, sugar, crushed ice, and raw sugar cane liquor).

316 W. 49th St. (btwn Eighth and Ninth aves.). © **212/245-0505.** Reservations recommended. All-you-can-eat fixed-price $28 at lunch, $39 at dinner; half price for children 5–10. AE, DC, DISC, MC, V. Daily noon–midnight. Subway: C, E to 50th St.

Virgil's Real BBQ *Kids* BARBECUE/SOUTHERN   Virgil's may look like a comfy theme-park version of a down-home barbecue joint, but this place takes its barbecue seriously. The meat is house smoked with a blend of hickory, oak, and fruitwood chips, and most every regional school is represented, from Carolina pulled pork to Texas beef brisket to Memphis ribs. You may not consider this contest-winning chow if you're from barbecue country, but for New York, it's not bad. The ribs are first-rate, and the chicken is moist and tender—go for a combo if you just can't choose. Burgers, sandwiches, and other entrees (chicken-fried steak, anyone?) are also available if you can't face up to all that meat 'n' sauce. Don't worry about making a mess; when you're through eating, you get a hot towel for washing up.

152 W. 44th St. (btwn Sixth and Seventh aves.). © **212/921-9494.** Reservations recommended. Sandwiches $6–$11; main courses and barbecue platters $13–$26 (most less than $19). AE, DC, DISC, MC, V. Sun–Mon 11:30am–11pm; Tues–Sat 11:30am–midnight. Subway: 1, 2, 3, 7 to 42nd St./Times Square.

INEXPENSIVE

If you're looking for the quintessential New York Jewish deli, you have your choice between the **Stage Deli,** 834 Seventh Ave., between 53rd and 54th streets

(✆ **212/245-7850**), known for its jaw-distending celebrity sandwiches; and the **Carnegie Deli,** 854 Seventh Ave., at 55th Street (✆ **800/334-5606**), for the best pastrami, corned beef, and cheesecake in town.

There is a very nice outlet of **John's Pizzeria** in Times Square, 260 W. 44th St., between Seventh and Eighth avenues (✆ **212/391-7560**).

Manhattan Chili Co. *Kids* AMERICAN SOUTHWESTERN   This big, cartoonish, festive Theater District restaurant adjacent to Dave Letterman's Ed Sullivan Theater is a great choice for a casual and affordable meal, especially if you have the kids in tow. The big, hearty chili bowls are geared to young palates, which tend to be suspicious of anything unfamiliar. The extensive list of chili choices is clearly marked by spice level, from the traditional Abilene with ground beef, tomatoes, basil, and red wine (mild enough for tenderfeet) to the Texas Chain Gang, which adds jalapeños to the mix for those who prefer hot. In addition, expect familiar favorites like nachos, chicken wings, big salads, and generous burritos and burgers. It's really hard to go wrong here—even vegetarians have lots to choose from.

1697 Broadway (53rd and 54th sts.). ✆ **212/246-6555.** Reservations accepted. Chili bowls $10; main courses $11–$16; Sat–Sun brunch $11. AE, DISC, MC, V. Sun–Mon 11:30am–11pm; Tues–Sat 11:30am–midnight. Subway: B, D, E to Seventh Ave.; 1, 9 to 50th St. Also at 1500 Broadway, entrance on 43rd St. (✆ 212/730-8666; subway: N, R, S, 1, 2, 3, 7, 9 to 42nd St./Times Sq.).

MIDTOWN EAST & MURRAY HILL
VERY EXPENSIVE

La Grenouille ✮✮✮ CLASSIC FRENCH   They don't come more old school than this jewel of a restaurant, which has been serving New Yorkers in classic French style since 1962. La Grenouille may be classic, but it doesn't feel the least bit stuffy. The tuxedoed waitstaff is one of the warmest and most attentive in the city. There's a rare confidence here, in both the food and the service, that sets a tone of comfort and ease. Nothing comes out of the kitchen that isn't flawlessly prepared and presented. The foie gras is sautéed to perfection and boasts a delicate hint of vanilla while the port-glazed veal sweetbreads were fork-tender, not crispy, and beautifully accompanied by a chestnut and walnut cocotte. The wine list is pricey but excellent; your waiter will be happy to point you to the best values.

3 E. 52nd St. (just east of Fifth Ave.). ✆ **212/752-1495.** Reservations required (2–3 weeks in advance suggested). Jacket and tie required for men. 3-course fixed-price $45 at lunch, $85 at dinner. AE, DC, MC, V. Tues–Sat noon–2:30pm and 5:30–11:15pm. Subway: E to Fifth Ave.

Le Cirque 2000 ✮ MODERN FRENCH   Housed in a gilded-age mansion and outfitted with almost rococo interiors with jewel-toned circus colors, and outrageous furniture, fine dining goes the way of the big top at Le Cirque 2000, and it's a hit. The food is excellently prepared if not innovative: paupiette of black sea bass in crispy potatoes with braised leeks; Black Angus tenderloin in a Barolo sauce; and roasted venison chop. Dessert is Le Cirque's finest course: The crème brûlée is a perfect realization of the classic dessert, but go with the chocolate stove for a truly memorable finish. The wine list is remarkable, and there's spectacular courtyard dining in season.

In the Villard Houses, 455 Madison Ave. (at 50th St.). ✆ **212/303-7788.** Reservations required well in advance. Jacket and tie required for men. Main courses $16–$40 (most $30 or higher); 3-course fixed-price lunch $44 ($25 in lounge); 5-course fixed-price dinner $90. AE, DC, MC, V. Mon–Sat 11:45am–2:30pm and 5:30–11pm; Sun 5:30–10:30pm. Subway: E, V to Fifth Ave.; 6 to 51st St.

MODERATE

P.J. Clarke's ✮ AMERICAN   After being closed a year for renovations, which preserved most of the original detail, this 120-year-old saloon/restaurant reopened in early 2003 under new ownership (one of the owners is actor Tim Hutton). Clarke's has been a New York institution; a late-night hangout for politicians, actors, and athletes. This is where Ray Milland went on a bender in the classic 1948 movie *The Lost Weekend*. Everything has been blessedly preserved including the legendary Clarke's hamburger. Nothing more than a slab of chopped meat cooked to order, on a bun for the curious price of $8.10, the hamburger is a simple masterpiece. Try it with P.J's home fries or onion rings. Salads also are a good accompaniment to the beef, particularly the tomato, red onion, and blue cheese salad. If meat is not your thing, a new very good raw bar was added. Beer, the drink of choice here, comes in mugs but pints are available, just ask.

915 Third Ave. (at 55th St.). © 212/317-1616. Main courses $8–$21. AE, MC, V. Daily 11:30am–4am. Sidecar daily 11:30am–1am. Subway: E, V to Lexington Ave.

UPPER WEST SIDE
VERY EXPENSIVE
Jean-Georges ★★★ FRENCH   Accolades for Jean-Georges Vongerichten's immense culinary skills are so numerous they are beginning to get tedious; he's the Michael Jordan of chefs. And restaurant Jean-Georges is the perfect showcase for those skills. The menu is the best of Vongerichten's past successes (Vong, JoJo) taken one step further: French and Asian touches mingle with a new passion for offbeat harvests, like lamb's quarters, sorrel, yarrow, quince, and chicory. Young garlic soup with thyme and a plate of sautéed frogs' legs makes a great beginning. Muscovy duck steak with Asian spices and sweet-and-sour jus is carved table-side, while the lobster tartine with lemongrass, pea shoots, and a broth of fenugreek (one of Jean-Georges's signature aromatic plants) receives a final dash of spices seconds before you dig in. If the chestnut soup is on the menu, don't miss it. The wine list is also excellent, with a number of unusual choices in every price range.

In the Trump International Hotel & Tower, 1 Central Park West (at 60th St./Columbus Circle). © 212/299-3900. Reservations required well in advance. Jacket required for men; tie optional. Main courses $26–$42; 3- or 4-course fixed-price lunch $35–$45; 3- or 7-course fixed-price dinner $85–$115. AE, DC, MC, V. Dining room: Mon–Fri noon–3pm and 5:30–11pm; Sat 5:30–11:30pm. Nougatine: Mon–Sat 7am–10:30am, noon–3pm, and 5:30–11pm; Sun 8am–3pm and 5:30–10pm. Subway: A, B, C, D, 1, 9 to 59th St./Columbus Circle.

EXPENSIVE
Aix ★★ MODERN FRENCH   Not far from the smoked fish meccas of Barney Greengrass, Zabar's, and Murray's Sturgeon Shop, but seemingly worlds away comes the best new restaurant on the Upper West Side. This smartly designed, airy, and comfortable trilevel restaurant offers some surprisingly fresh twists on the traditional cuisine of Provence. A classic dish like the vegetable soup, pistou, includes fresh raw sardines and it not only works, it enhances the soup. The baked chicken with star anise, honey, mushrooms, and fingerling potatoes was cooked to perfection, while the Atlantic char, with a smoked salmon sauce so good it would make the aforementioned Barney Greengrass proud. Desserts are adventurous and may not be for everyone, but it's not often you have the chance to experience Provence salad, sugared green tomatoes and celery topped with mint sorbet. Despite the crowds, Aix's service was personable; waitresses in dowdy brown uniforms were cheerfully helpful, but the restaurant is loud, so don't expect intimacy.

2398 Broadway (at 88th St.). © 212/874-7400. Reservations highly recommended. Main courses $14–$28. AE, MC, V. Sun–Thurs 5:30–10:30pm; Fri–Sat 5:30–11pm. Subway: 1, 9 to 86th St.

MODERATE

For fun family-style Italian, there's also the original **Carmine's** (p. 109) at 2450 Broadway, between 90th and 91st streets (© **212/362-2200**), in addition to the choices below.

INEXPENSIVE

For breakfast or lunch, also consider **Barney Greengrass, the Sturgeon King,** 541 Amsterdam Ave., between 86th and 87th streets (© **212/724-4707**), one of the best Jewish delis in town.

Near Lincoln Center, **John's Pizzeria,** 48 W. 65th St., between Broadway and Central Park West (© **212/721-7001**), serves up one of the city's best pies in a nice brick-walled dining room.

Celeste ★★ *Finds* ITALIAN   Like **Aix** (see above), this is another very welcome addition to the Upper West Side dining scene. Tiny but charming Celeste features its own wood-burning pizza oven, which churns out thin-crusted, simple but delicious pizzas. But pizza is not the only attraction here; the "fritti" (fried) course is unique; the *fritto misto de pesce* (fried mixed seafood) is delectable, but the fried zucchini blossoms, usually available in the summer and fall, are amazing. The fresh pastas are better than the dried pasta; I never thought the fresh egg noodles with cabbage, shrimp, and sheep's cheese would work, but it was delicious. Not on the menu, but usually available, are plates of rare, artisanal Italian cheeses served with homemade jams. Though the main courses are also good, stick with the pizzas, antipasto, frittis, and pastas. For dessert try the gelato; the pistachio was the best I've ever had in New York. The restaurant has been "discovered," so go early or go late or expect a wait.

502 Amsterdam Ave. (btwn 84th and 85th sts). © 212/874-4559. Reservations not accepted. Pizza $10–$12; antipasto $7–$10; pasta $10; main courses $14–$16. No credit cards. Mon–Sat 5–11pm; Sun noon–3:30pm. Subway: 1,9 to 86th St.

Gabriela's ★★ *Kids* *Value* MEXICAN   Until chef/owner Garbriela Hernandez opened her restaurant almost 10 years ago, authentic Mexican food was difficult to find on the Upper West Side, not to mention most of New York City. Flavors of her native Guadalajara are prominent here; this is not your typical combination taco restaurant. Gabriela's roast chicken is the best—a blend of Yucatán spices and a slow-roasting rotisserie results in some of the tenderest, juiciest chicken in town. All of the specialties on the extensive menu are well prepared, generously portioned, and satisfying. Try one of Gabriela's delicious fruit shakes (both mango and papaya are good bets) or tall *agua frescas* (fresh fruit drinks), which come in a variety of tropical flavors; beer, wine, and margaritas are served, too.

A second location, farther downtown at 75th Street, is also quite good, but I'm partial to the original, uptown restaurant, which is large, bright, and pretty, with a pleasing south-of-the-border flair, and the service is quick and attentive.

685 Amsterdam Ave. (at 93rd St.). © 212/961-0574. Reservations accepted for parties of 6 or more. Main courses $5–$9 at lunch, $7–$20 at brunch and dinner (most less than $15); early dinner specials $9.95, includes glass of wine or frozen margarita (Mon–Fri 4–7pm; Sat–Sun 3:30–6:30pm). AE, DC, MC, V. Mon–Thurs 11:30am–11pm; Fri–Sat 11:30am–midnight; Sun 11:30am–10pm. Subway: 1, 2, 3, 9 to 96th St. Also at 315 Amsterdam Ave., at 75th St. (© 212/875-8532; subway: 1,2,3,9 to 72nd St.).

THE UPPER EAST SIDE
VERY EXPENSIVE

Daniel ★★ FRENCH COUNTRY   If Le Cirque 2000 sounds too over the top for your taste, and Jean-Georges just too modern, Daniel Boulud's *New York Times* four-star winner is the place for you.

The menu is heavy with game dishes in elegant but unfussy preparations, plus Daniel signatures like black sea bass in a crisp potato shell, with tender leeks and a light Syrah sauce. Excellent starters include foie gras terrine with fennel confit and dried apricot compote, and rosemary and blood orange glazed endive. Sublime entrees may include spit-roasted and braised organic guinea hen with black truffle butter, or chestnut-crusted venison with sweet potato purée. But you can't really go wrong with anything—the kitchen doesn't take a false turn. The wine list is terrific and, divided between seasonal fruits and chocolates; the desserts are uniformly excellent. Dining in the pleasing lounge is a great way to sample the master's marvelous cuisine without laborious advance planning or succumbing to formality, since the jacket-and-tie dress code for men is not enforced.

60 E. 65th St. (btwn Madison and Park aves.). ℂ **212/288-0033**. Reservations required. Jacket and tie required for men in main dining room. 3-course fixed-price dinner $85; tasting menus $120–$160. Main courses $34–$38 in bar and lounge. AE, MC, V. Mon–Sat 5:45–11pm.

MODERATE

Payard Pâtisserie & Bistro FRENCH BISTRO/DESSERTS/AFTERNOON TEA   Sure, the bistro fare at this grand turn-of-the-20th-century, Parisian-style cafe is good. But the decadent desserts—New York's best—are the reason to come. There's no need to indulge in a full meal to enjoy Payard; feel free to come for afternoon tea or just dessert (my preference, which is why I've classified Payard as moderately priced rather than expensive).

The biggest problem? Choosing among the fabulous, beautifully presented sweet treats. Displayed like the jewels they are, elegant cakes, tempting pastries, and handmade chocolates fill the gleaming glass cases up front. Everything is house-made, from the signature cakes, breads, and pastries to the delicate candies. Whether you go with the classic crème brûlée or something more decadent (anything chocolate is to die for), you're sure to be wowed.

1032 Lexington Ave. (btwn 73rd and 74th sts.). ℂ **212/717-5252**. Reservations recommended. Main courses $12–$25 at lunch, $24–$33 at dinner; afternoon tea $19–$24; 3-course pretheater dinner $34 (5:45–6pm seating); desserts $7–$9. AE, DC, MC, V. Mon–Thurs noon–3pm, 3:30–5pm, and 5:45–10:30pm; Fri noon–3pm, 3:30–5pm, and 5:45–11pm; Sat noon–3pm, 3:30–4:30pm, and 5:45–11pm. Subway: 6 to 77th St.

HARLEM
MODERATE

Bayou ⚜ CREOLE   This intimate, casually sophisticated Creole restaurant is a prime symbol of Harlem's renaissance. The room is stylish in a trend-defying way, with burnished yellow walls, big oak tables, a long mahogany bar, and dim lighting. The well-prepared food is pure New Orleans: shrimp and okra gumbo, cornmeal-fried oysters, sautéed chicken livers, and shrimp rémoulade with deviled eggs. Shrimp Creole or crawfish étouffée are both served in their own piquant sauces over rice. Farm-raised catfish is marinated and sliced thin, then deep-fried in cornmeal until the outside is perfectly crisp, while the inside stays moist and flaky. Salads are crisp and bounteous. Service is extremely attentive and professional. Desserts are divine; don't pass up the bread pudding, made with fresh peaches and a scrumptious bourbon sauce.

308 Lenox Ave. (btwn 125th and 126th sts.). ℂ **212/426-3800**. Reservations recommended for dinner. Main courses $8–$15 at lunch, $9–$23 at dinner (most less than $18); Sun brunch $14–$21 (includes starter and Mimosa or Bloody Mary). AE, DC, MC, V. Mon–Thurs 11:30am–4pm and 6–10pm; Fri 11:30am–4pm and 6–11pm; Sat 6–11pm; Sun noon–4pm. Subway: 2, 3 to 125th St.

INEXPENSIVE

Also consider **Patsy's Pizzeria,** 2287 First Ave. (btwn 117th and 118th streets; 🕐 **212/534-9783**), my favorite pizzeria (and Frank Sinatra's, too). **Sylvia's,** 328 Lenox Ave., between 126th and 127th streets (🕐 **212/996-0660**), once the best soul-food restaurant in Harlem, has sadly turned into a tourist trap; but if you are determined to go, make it for the Sunday gospel brunch which is still an absolute joy.

Charles' Southern-Style Kitchen 🕏 *Finds* SOUL   Nothing fancy about this place, just a brightly lit, 25-seater on a not very attractive block in upper Harlem. But you don't come here for fancy, no tourist trappings, either. You come for soul food at its simplest and freshest. And you better come hungry. The all-you-can-eat buffet features crunchy, incredibly moist pan-fried chicken, ribs in a tangy sauce with meat falling off the bone, smoky stewed oxtails in a thick brown onion gravy, macaroni and cheese, collard greens with bits of smoked turkey, black-eyed peas, and corn bread warm and not overly sweet. Desserts are constantly changing, but always fresh; I had an incredible slice of carrot cake on my last visit. The beverage choices are limited to lemonade or iced tea, so bring your own of whatever else you might want. Brave the long journey uptown, you'll not regret the experience. Hours, however, can be erratic, so call ahead before you make the trek.

2841 Eighth Ave. (btwn 151st and 152nd sts.). 🕐 **877/813-2920** or 212/926-4313. All-you-can-eat-buffet: lunch $7; dinner $10 Mon–Thurs, $12 Fri–Sun. AE, MC, V. Sun 1–8pm; Mon 4pm–midnight; Tues–Sat noon–4am. Subway: D to 115th St.

5 Exploring New York City

If this is your first trip to New York, face the facts: It will be impossible to take in the entire city. Because New York is almost unfathomably big and constantly changing, you could live your whole life here and still make fascinating daily discoveries. Don't try to tame New York—you can't. Decide on a few must-see attractions, and then let the city take you on its own ride.

THE TOP ATTRACTIONS

American Museum of Natural History 🟊🟊🟊   Founded in 1869, this 4-block museum houses the world's greatest natural science collection in a group of buildings made of towers and turrets, pink granite and red brick—a mishmash of architectural styles, but overflowing with neo-Gothic charm. The diversity of the holdings is astounding: some 36 million specimens ranging from microscopic organisms to the world's largest cut gem, the Brazilian Princess Topaz (21,005 carats). If you don't have a lot of time, you can see the best of the best on free **highlights tours** offered daily every hour at 15 minutes after the hour from 10:15am to 3:15pm. **Audio Expeditions,** high-tech audio tours that allow you to access narration in the order you choose, are also available to help you make sense of it all.

The museum excels at **special exhibitions,** so check to see what will be on while you're in town in case any advance planning is required. The magical **Butterfly Conservatory** 🕏, a walk-in enclosure housing nearly 500 free-flying tropical butterflies, has developed into a can't-miss fixture from October through May; check to see if it's in the house while you're in town.

The $210 million **Rose Center for Earth and Space** 🕏, whose four-story-tall planetarium sphere hosts the excellent Space Show, "Are We Alone?," possibly the most technologically advanced show on the planet.

Central Park West (btwn 77th and 81 sts.). ℂ **212/769-5100** for information, or 212/769-5200 for tickets (tickets can also be ordered online). www.amnh.org. Suggested admission $10 adults, $7.50 seniors and students, $6 children 2–12. Space Show and museum admission $19 adults, $14 seniors and students, $12 children under 12. Additional charges for IMAX movies and some special exhibitions. Daily 10am–5:45pm; Rose Center open Fri to 8:45pm. Subway: B, C to 81st St.; 1, 9 to 79th St.

Brooklyn Bridge ★★ *Moments*   Its Gothic-inspired stone pylons and intricate steel-cable webs have moved poets like Walt Whitman and Hart Crane to sing the praises of this great span, the first to cross the East River and connect Manhattan to Brooklyn. Completed in 1883, the beautiful Brooklyn Bridge is now the city's best-known symbol of the age of growth that seized the city during the late 19th century.

Walking the Bridge: Walking the Brooklyn Bridge is one of my all-time favorite New York activities. A wide wood-plank pedestrian walkway is elevated above the traffic, making it a relatively peaceful, and popular, walk. It's a great vantage point from which to contemplate the New York skyline and the East River.

There's a sidewalk entrance on Park Row, just across from City Hall Park (take the 4, 5, or 6 train to Brooklyn Bridge/City Hall). But why do this walk *away* from Manhattan, toward the far less impressive Brooklyn skyline? Instead, for Manhattan skyline views, take an A or C train to High Street, one stop into Brooklyn. From there, you'll be on the bridge in no time: Come aboveground, then walk through the little park to Cadman Plaza East and head downslope (left) to the stairwell that will take you up to the footpath. (Following Prospect Place under the bridge, turning right onto Cadman Plaza E., will also take you directly to the stairwell.) It's a 20- to 40-minute stroll over the bridge to Manhattan, depending on your pace, the amount of foot traffic, and the number of stops you make to behold the spectacular views (there are benches along the way). The footpath will deposit you right at City Hall Park.

Subway: A, C to High St.; 4, 5, 6 to Brooklyn Bridge–City Hall.

Ellis Island ★★   One of New York's most moving sights, the restored Ellis Island opened in 1990, slightly north of Liberty Island. Roughly 40% of Americans (myself included) can trace their heritage back to an ancestor who came through here. For the 62 years when it was America's main entry point for immigrants (1892–1954), Ellis Island processed some 12 million people. The statistics can be overwhelming, but the **Immigration Museum** skillfully relates the story of Ellis Island and immigration in America by placing the emphasis on personal experience.

It's difficult to leave the museum unmoved. Today you enter the Main Building's baggage room, just as the immigrants did, and then climb the stairs to the **Registry Room,** with its dramatic vaulted tiled ceiling, where millions waited anxiously for medical and legal processing. A step-by-step account of the immigrants' voyage is detailed in the exhibit, with haunting photos and touching oral histories. What might be the most poignant exhibit is **"Treasures from Home,"** 1,000 objects and photos donated by descendants of immigrants, including family heirlooms, religious articles, and rare clothing and jewelry. Outside, the **American Immigrant Wall of Honor** commemorates the names of more than 500,000 immigrants and their families, from Myles Standish and George Washington's great-grandfather to the forefathers of John F. Kennedy, Jay Leno, and Barbra Streisand. You can even research your own family's history at the interactive **American Family Immigration History Center.** *Touring tips:* Ferries run daily to Ellis Island and Liberty Island from Battery Park and Liberty State Park at frequent intervals; see the Statue of Liberty listing (p. 121) for details.

In New York Harbor. ✆ **212/363-3200** (general info), or 212/269-5755 (ticket/ferry info). www.nps.gov/elis or www.ellisisland.org. Free admission (ferry ticket charge). Daily 9:30am–5:15pm (last ferry departs around 3:30pm). For subway and ferry details, see the Statue of Liberty listing on p. 121 (ferry trip includes stops at both sights).

Empire State Building ★★★   It took 60,000 tons of steel, 10 million bricks, 2.5 million feet of electrical wire, 120 miles of pipe, and 7 million man-hours to build. King Kong climbed it in 1933. A plane slammed into it in 1945. The World Trade Center superseded it in 1972 as the island's tallest building. On that horrific day of September 11, 2001, it once again regained its status as New York City's tallest building, after 31 years of taking second place. And through it all, the Empire State Building has remained one of the city's favorite landmarks, and its signature high-rise. Completed in 1931, the limestone-and-stainless steel streamline deco dazzler climbs 102 stories (1,454 ft.) and now harbors the offices of fashion firms, and, in its upper reaches, a jumble of high-tech broadcast equipment.

Always a conversation piece, the Empire State Building glows every night, bathed in colored floodlights to commemorate events of significance (you can find a complete lighting schedule online). The familiar silver spire can be seen from all over the city. But the views that keep nearly three million visitors coming every year are the ones from the 86th- and 102nd-floor **observatories.** The lower one is best—you can walk out on a windy deck and look through coin-operated viewers (bring quarters!) over what, on a clear day, can be as much as an 80-mile visible radius. The citywide panorama is magnificent. Starry nights are pure magic.

350 Fifth Ave. (at 34th St.). ✆ **212/736-3100.** www.esbnyc.com. Observatory admission $10 adults, $9 seniors and children 12–17, $4 children 6–11, free for children under 5. Mon–Fri 10am–midnight; Sat–Sun 9:30am–midnight; tickets sold until 11:25pm. Subway: B, D, F, N, R, V, Q, W to 34th St.; 6 to 33rd St.

Grand Central Terminal ★★   Restored in 1998, Grand Central Station is one of the most magnificent public spaces in the country. Even if you're not catching one of the subway lines or Metro-North commuter trains that rumble through the bowels of this great place, come and visit. And even if you arrive and leave by subway, be sure to exit the station, walking a couple of blocks south, to about 40th Street, before you turn around to admire Jules-Alexis Coutan's neoclassical sculpture *Transportation* hovering over the south entrance, with a majestically buff Mercury, the Roman god of commerce and travel, as its central figure.

The greatest visual impact comes when you enter the vast **main concourse.** The high windows once again allow sunlight to penetrate the space, glinting off the half-acre Tennessee marble floor. The brass clock over the central kiosk gleams, as do the gold- and nickel-plated chandeliers piercing the side archways. The masterful **sky ceiling,** again a brilliant greenish blue, depicts the constellations of the winter sky above New York. On the east end of the main concourse is a grand **marble staircase** where there had never been one before, but as the original plans had always intended.

This dramatic beaux arts splendor serves as a hub of social activity as well. Excellent-quality retail shops and restaurants have taken over the mezzanine and lower levels. The highlight of the west mezzanine is **Michael Jordan's–The Steak House,** a gorgeous Art Deco space that allows you to dine within view of

the sky ceiling. Off the main concourse at street level, there's a nice mix of specialty shops and national retailers, as well as the truly grand **Grand Central
Market** for gourmet foods.

42nd St. at Park Ave. © 212/340-2210 (events hot line). www.grandcentralterminal.com. Subway: S, 4, 5,
6, 7 to 42nd St./Grand Central.

Metropolitan Museum of Art ★★★ Home of blockbuster after blockbuster exhibition, the Metropolitan Museum of Art attracts some five million
people a year, more than any other spot in New York City. And it's no wonder—
this place is magnificent. At 1.6 million square feet, this is the largest museum
in the western hemisphere. Nearly all the world's cultures are on display through
the ages—from Egyptian mummies to ancient Greek statuary to Islamic carvings to Renaissance paintings to Native American masks to 20th-century decorative arts—and masterpieces are the rule. You could go once a week for a
lifetime and still find something new on each visit.

So unless you plan on spending your entire vacation in the museum (some
people do), you cannot see the entire collection. One good way to get an
overview is to take advantage of the little-known **Museum Highlights Tour,**
offered every day at various times throughout the day (usually 10:15am–
3:15pm; tours also offered in Spanish, Italian, German, and Korean). Visit the
museum's website for a schedule of this and subject-specific walking tours (Old
Master Paintings, American Period Rooms, Arts of China, Islamic Art, and so
on); you can also get a schedule of the day's tours at the Visitor Services desk
when you arrive. A daily schedule of **Gallery Talks** is available as well.

Highlights include the American Wing's **Garden Court,** with its 19th-
century sculpture; the terrific ground-level **Costume Hall;** and the **Frank Lloyd
Wright room.** The beautifully renovated **Roman and Greek galleries** are overwhelming, but in a marvelous way, as is the collections of **Byzantine Art** and
later **Chinese art.** The highlight of the astounding **Egyptian collection** is the
Temple of Dendur, in a dramatic, purpose-built glass-walled gallery with Central Park views. The **Greek Galleries,** which at last fully realize McKim, Mead
& White's grand neoclassical plans of 1917, and the **Ancient Near East Galleries** are particularly of note.

Fifth Ave. at 82nd St. © 212/535-7710. www.metmuseum.org. Admission (includes same-day entrance to
the Cloisters) $12 adults, $7 seniors and students, free for children under 12 when accompanied by an adult.
Sun and Tues–Thurs 9:30am–5:30pm; Fri–Sat 9:30am–9pm. No strollers allowed Sun (back carriers available
at 81st St. entrance coat-check area). Subway: 4, 5, 6 to 86th St.

Museum of Modern Art/MoMA QNS ★ MoMA is undergoing a monster
$650 million renovation of its West 53rd Street building under the guidance of
Japanese architect Yoshio Taniguchi that will double the exhibit space when the
project is complete sometime in 2005. In the meantime, the museum has
opened temporary exhibit space called **MoMA QNS** in an old Swingline sta-
pler factory in Long Island City, Queens. This is no flimsy venture: The
45,000-square-foot gallery exhibits highlights of the museum's collection,
including some of its biggest draws, among them van Gogh's *Starry Night,*
Picasso's early *Les Demoiselles d'Avignon,* and Warhol's *Gold Marilyn Monroe.*
Workshops, a limited program schedule, and special exhibitions are also part of
the fun. Yes—it's definitely worth a short subway ride to Queens. Getting there
is quick and easy; in fact, from Midtown, you can be here quicker than you can
get to the Village.

> ### ⌒ *Tips*   Art After Hours
>
> Many of the city's top museums—including the Natural History Museum, the Met, the Guggenheim, and the Whitney—have late hours on Friday and/or Saturday nights. Take advantage of them. Most visitors run out of steam by dinnertime, so even on jam-packed weekends you'll largely have the place to yourself by 5 or 6pm—which, in most cases, leaves you hours left to explore, unfettered by crowds or screaming kids. The other option is to come early; preferably when the doors open.

45–20 33rd St., Long Island City, Queens. ⓒ 212/708-9400. www.moma.org. Admission $12 adults, $8.50 seniors and students, free for children under 16 accompanied by an adult; pay what you wish Fri 4–7:45pm. Sat–Mon, Thurs 10am–5pm; Fri 10am–7:45pm. Subway: 7 to 33rd St. (MoMA QNS is across the street).

Rockefeller Center ★★ *Moments*   A streamline Art Deco masterpiece, Rockefeller Center is one of New York's central gathering spots for visitors and New Yorkers alike. Designated a National Historic Landmark in 1988, it's now the world's largest privately owned business-and-entertainment center, with 18 buildings on 21 acres.

For a dramatic approach to the entire complex, start at Fifth Avenue between 49th and 50th streets. The builders purposely created the gentle slope of the Promenade, known here as the **Channel Gardens** because it's flanked to the south by La Maison Française and to the north by the British Building (the Channel, get it?). The Promenade leads to the **Lower Plaza,** home to the famous ice-skating rink in winter (see next paragraph) and alfresco dining in summer in the shadow of Paul Manship's freshly gilded bronze statue *Prometheus,* more notable for its setting than its magnificence as an artwork. All around, the flags of the United Nations' member countries flap in the breeze. Just behind *Prometheus,* in December and early January, towers the city's official and majestic Christmas tree.

The **Rink at Rockefeller Center** ★ (ⓒ 212/332-7654; www.rockefeller center.com) is tiny but positively romantic, especially during December, when the giant Christmas tree's multicolored lights twinkle from above. The rink is open from mid-October to mid-March.

The focal point of this "city within a city" is the **GE Building** ★, at 30 Rockefeller Plaza, a 70-story showpiece towering over the plaza. It's still one of the city's most impressive buildings; walk through for a look at the granite and marble lobby, lined with monumental sepia-toned murals by José Maria Sert.

NBC television maintains studios throughout the complex. *Saturday Night Live* and *Late Night with Conan O'Brien* originate in the GE Building. NBC's ***Today*** show is broadcast live on weekdays from 7 to 10am from the glass-enclosed studio on the southwest corner of 49th Street and Rockefeller Plaza; come early if you want a visible spot, and bring your HI MOM! sign.

The 70-minute **NBC Studio Tour** (ⓒ 212/664-3700; www.nbcsuperstore. com) will take you behind the scenes at the Peacock network. The tour changes daily, but may include the *Today* show, *NBC Nightly News, Dateline NBC,* and/or *Saturday Night Live* sets. Tickets are $18 for adults, $15 for seniors and children 6 to 16. You can reserve your tickets for either tour in advance (reservations are recommended) or buy them right up to tour time at the **NBC Experience** store, on Rockefeller Plaza at 49th Street. They also offer a 75-minute **Rockefeller Center**

Tour, which is offered hourly every day between 10am and 4pm. $10 for adults, $8 for seniors and children 6 to 16; two-tour combination packages are available for $21.

The newly restored **Radio City Music Hall** ✮, 1260 Sixth Ave., at 50th Street (© **212/247-4777;** www.radiocity.com), is perhaps the most impressive architectural feat of the complex. Designed by Donald Deskey and opened in 1932, it's one of the largest indoor theaters, with 6,200 seats. But its true grandeur derives from its magnificent Art Deco appointments. The crowning touch is the stage's great proscenium arch, which from the distant seats evokes a faraway sun setting on the horizon of the sea. The theater hosts the annual **Christmas Spectacular,** starring the Rockettes. The illuminating 1-hour **Stage Door Tour** is offered Monday through Saturday from 10am to 5pm, Sunday from 11am to 5pm; tickets are $16 for adults, $10 for children under 12.

Between 48th and 50th sts., from Fifth to Sixth aves. © 212/332-6868. www.rockefellercenter.com. Subway: B, D, F, V to 47th–50th sts./Rockefeller Center.

Solomon R. Guggenheim Museum ✮   It's been called a bun, a snail, a concrete tornado, and even a giant wedding cake; bring your kids, and they'll probably see it as New York's coolest opportunity for skateboarding. Whatever description you choose to apply, Frank Lloyd Wright's only New York building, completed in 1959, is best summed up as a brilliant work of architecture—so consistently brilliant that it competes with the art for your attention. If you're looking for the city's best modern art, head to MoMA or the Whitney first; come to the Guggenheim to see the house.

It's easy to see the bulk of what's on display in 2 to 4 hours. Inside, a spiraling rotunda circles over a slowly inclined ramp that leads you past changing exhibits that, in the past, have ranged from "The Art of the Motorcycle" to "Norman Rockwell: Pictures for the American People," said to be the most comprehensive exhibit ever of the beloved painter's works. Usually the progression is counterintuitive: from the first floor up, rather than from the sixth floor down. If you're not sure, ask a guard before you begin. Permanent exhibits of 19th- and 20th-century art, including strong holdings of Kandinsky, Klee, Picasso, and French Impressionists, occupy a stark annex called the **Tower Galleries,** an addition accessible at every level that some critics claimed made the original look like a toilet bowl backed by a water tank (judge for yourself—I think there may be something to that view).

1071 Fifth Ave. (at 88th St.). © 212/423-3500. www.guggenheim.org. Admission $12 adults, $8.50 seniors and students, free for children under 12; pay what you wish Fri 6–8pm. Sat–Wed 10am–5:45pm; Fri 10am–8pm. Subway: 4, 5, 6 to 86th St.

Staten Island Ferry ✮ *Value*   Here's New York's best freebie—especially if you just want to glimpse the Statue of Liberty and not climb her steps. You get an enthralling hour-long excursion (round-trip) into the world's biggest harbor. This is not strictly a sightseeing ride but commuter transportation to and from Staten Island. As a result, during business hours, you'll share the boat with working stiffs reading papers and drinking coffee inside, blissfully unaware of the sights outside.

You, however, should go on deck and enjoy the busy harbor traffic. The old orange-and-green boats usually have open decks along the sides or at the bow and stern; try to catch one of these boats if you can, since the newer white boats don't have decks. Grab a seat on the right side of the boat for the best view. On the way out of Manhattan, you'll pass the Statue of Liberty (the boat comes closest to

AOL Keyword: Travel

Booked aisle seat.

Reserved room with a view.

With a queen – no, make that a king-size bed.

With Travelocity, you can book your flights and hotels together, so you can get even better deals than if you booked them separately. You'll save time and money without compromising the quality of your trip. Choose your airline seat, search for alternate airports, pick your hotel room type, even choose the neighborhood you'd like to stay in

Travelocity

Visit www.travelocity.com or call 1-888-TRAVELOCITY

Plan your vacation

- flights, hotels, car rentals
- cruises & vacation packages
- destination guides
- fare alerts
- go to yahoo.com, click travel

© 2003 Yahoo! Inc.

powered by hp

DO YOU YAHOO!?

Lady Liberty on the way to Staten Island), Ellis Island, and from the left side of the boat, Governor's Island; you'll see the Verrazano Narrows Bridge spanning the distance from Brooklyn to Staten Island in the distance.

There's usually another boat waiting to depart for Manhattan. The skyline views are simply awesome on the return trip. Well worth the time spent.

Departs from the Whitehall Ferry Terminal at the southern tip of Manhattan. ℂ 718/815-BOAT. www.ci.nyc. ny.us/html/dot. Free admission ($3 for car transport on select ferries). 24 hr.; every 20–30 min. weekdays, less frequently on off-peak and weekend hours. Subway: N, R to Whitehall St.; 4, 5 to Bowling Green; 1, 9 to South Ferry (ride in the first 5 cars).

Statue of Liberty ★★★ *Kids*   For the millions who first came by ship to America between 1892 and 1954—either as privileged tourists or needy, hopeful immigrants—Lady Liberty, standing in the Upper Bay, was their first glimpse of America. No monument so embodies the nation's, and the world's, notion of political freedom and economic potential. Even if you don't make it out to Liberty Island, you can get a spine-tingling glimpse from Battery Park, from the New Jersey side of the bay, or during a free ride on the Staten Island Ferry (see above). It's always reassuring to see her torch lighting the way.

First unveiled in 1886 and after nearly 100 years of wind, rain, and exposure to the harsh sea air, Lady Liberty received a resoundingly successful $150 million face-lift (including the relandscaping of Liberty Island and the replacement of the torch's flame) in time for its centennial celebration on July 4, 1986. *Touring tips:* Ferries leave daily every half hour to 45 minutes from 9am to about 3:30pm (their clock), with more frequent ferries in the morning and extended hours in summer. Try to go early on a weekday to avoid the crowds that swarm in the afternoon, on weekends, and on holidays.

A stop at **Ellis Island** (p. 116) is included in the fare, but if you catch the last ferry, you can only visit the statue or Ellis Island, not both.

Note that you can **buy ferry tickets in advance** via **www.statueofliberty ferry.com**, which will allow you to board the boat without standing in the sometimes-long ticket line; however, there is an additional service charge attached. Even if you've already purchased tickets, arrive as much as 30 minutes before your desired ferry time to allow for increased security procedures prior to boarding the ferry. The ferry ride takes about 20 minutes.

Note: At press time, only the grounds of Liberty Island were open to the public, pending additional security arrangements. Still, the close up view from the grounds alone is breathtaking enough to make the journey worthwhile. Call or check the official website (**www.nps.gov/stli**) for the latest access information.

On Liberty Island in New York Harbor. ℂ 212/363-3200 (general info), or 212/269-5755 (ticket/ferry info). www.nps.gov/stli or www.statueoflibertyferry.com. Free admission; ferry ticket to Statue of Liberty and Ellis Island $10 adults, $8 seniors, $4 children 3–17, free for children under 3. Daily 9am–5pm (last ferry departs around 4pm); extended hours in summer. Subway: 4, 5 to Bowling Green; 1, 9 to South Ferry. Walk south through Battery Park to Castle Clinton, the fort housing the ferry ticket booth.

Wall Street & the New York Stock Exchange   Wall Street—it's an iconic name, and the world's prime hub for bulls and bears everywhere. This narrow 18th-century lane (you'll be surprised at how little it is) is appropriately monumental, lined with neoclassical towers that reach as far skyward as the dreams and greed of investors who built it into the world's most famous financial market.

At the heart of the action is the **New York Stock Exchange (NYSE),** the world's largest securities trader, where you can watch the billions change hands and get a fleeting idea of how the money merchants work. NYSE came into being in 1792, when merchants met daily under a nearby buttonwood tree to try and pass off to each other the U.S. bonds that had been sold to fund the Revolutionary War. By 1903, they were trading stocks of publicly held companies in this Corinthian-columned beaux arts "temple" designed by George Post. About 3,000 companies are now listed on the exchange, trading nearly 314 billion shares valued at about $16 trillion.

20 Broad St. (btwn Wall St. and Exchange Place). © **212/656-516** or 212/656-5168. www.nyse.com. Free admission. Mon–Fri 9am–4:30pm (ticket booth opens at 8:45am) for prearranged educational group tours. Subway: J, M, Z to Broad St.; 2, 3, 4, 5 to Wall St.

Whitney Museum of American Art ✹   What is arguably the finest collection of 20th-century American art in the world is an imposing presence on Madison Avenue—an inverted three-tiered pyramid of concrete and gray granite with seven seemingly random windows designed by Marcel Breuer, a leader of the Bauhaus movement. The rotating permanent collection consists of an intelligent selection of major works by Edward Hopper, Georgia O'Keeffe, Roy Lichtenstein, Jasper Johns, and other significant artists. A pleasing second-floor exhibit space is devoted exclusively to works from its permanent collection from 1900 to 1950, while the rest of the space is dedicated to rotating exhibits.

The springtime **Whitney Biennial** (2004, 2006, and so on) is a major event on the national museum calendar; it serve as the premier launching pad for new American artists working on the vanguard in every media. Free **gallery tours** are offered daily, and music, screenings, and lectures fill the calendar.

945 Madison Ave. (at 75th St.). © **877/WHITNEY** or 212/570-3676. www.whitney.org. Admission $12 adults, $9.50 seniors and students, free for children under 12; pay as you wish Fri 6–9pm. Tues–Thurs and Sat–Sun 11am–6pm; Fri 1–9pm. Subway: 6 to 77th St.

World Trade Center site (Ground Zero) *Moments*   The World Trade Center dominated lower Manhattan. About 50,000 people worked in its precincts, and some 70,000 others (tourists and businesspeople) visited each day. The vast complex included, in addition to two 110-story towers—one of which awarded visitors with breathtaking views from the Top of the World observation deck, more than 1,350 feet in the air—five additional buildings (including a Marriott hotel), a plaza the size of four football fields rich with outdoor sculpture, a vast underground shopping mall, and a full slate of restaurants, including the spectacular Windows on the World.

Then the first plane hit the north tower, Tower 1, at 8:45am on Tuesday, September 11, 2001. By 10:30am, it was all gone, along with nearly 3,000 innocent victims.

Clean-up and recovery efforts officially ended in May 2002. Later that summer Governor Pataki of New York, Governor McGreevy of New Jersey, and New York Mayor Bloomberg dedicated a viewing wall on the Church Street side of the site called the Wall of Heroes. On the wall are the names of those who lost their lives that day along with the history of the site including photos of the construction of the World Trade Center in the late 1960s and how, after it opened in 1972, it changed the New York skyline and downtown. More than 2 years removed from the horrific events of that September day, a walk along the Wall of Heroes remains a painfully moving experience.

The future of the site is still in question. After a heated competition where proposals by designers and architects were submitted, Daniel Libeskind's vision of a towering spire and a memorial void was chosen. When and if that vision is ever realized is still very much up in the air.

Bounded by Church, Barclay, Liberty, and West sts. ✆ 212/484-1222. www.nycvisit.com or www.southst
seaport.org for viewing information; www.downtownny.com for Lower Manhattan area information and
rebuilding updates. Subway: C, E to World Trade Center; N, R to Cortlandt St.

MORE MANHATTAN MUSEUMS

Cooper-Hewitt National Design Museum ★   Part of the Smithsonian
Institution, the Cooper-Hewitt is housed in the Carnegie Mansion, built by
steel magnate Andrew Carnegie in 1901 and renovated in 1996. Some 11,000
square feet of gallery space is devoted to changing exhibits that are invariably
well conceived, engaging, and educational. Shows are both historic and contemporary in nature, and topics range from Charles and Ray Eames to Russell
Wright to Disney theme parks. Many installations are drawn from the museum's
own vast collection of industrial design, drawings, textiles, books, and prints.

2 E. 91st St. (at Fifth Ave.). ✆ 212/849-8400. www.si.edu/ndm. Admission $8 adults, $5 seniors and students, free for children under 12; free to all Tues 5–9pm. Tues 10am–9pm; Wed–Fri 10am–5pm; Sat 10am–
6pm; Sun noon–5pm. Subway: 4, 5, 6 to 86th St.

The Frick Collection ★★   One of the most beautiful mansions remaining on
Fifth Avenue is a living testament to New York's vanished Gilded Age graced
with beautiful paintings, rather than a museum. Come here to see the classics by
some of the world's most famous painters: Titian, Bellini, Rembrandt, Turner,
Vermeer, El Greco, and Goya, to name only a few. A highlight of the collection
is the **Fragonard Room,** graced with the sensual rococo series *The Progress of
Love.* The portrait of Montesquieu by Whistler is also stunning. Sculpture, furniture, Chinese vases, and French enamels complement the paintings and round
out the collection. Included in the price of admission, the AcousticGuide audio
tour is particularly useful because it allows you to follow your own path rather
than a proscribed route. In addition to the permanent collection, the Frick regularly mounts small, well-focused temporary exhibitions.

1 E. 70th St. (at Fifth Ave.). ✆ 212/288-0700. www.frick.org. Admission $10 adults, $5 seniors and students.
Children under 10 not admitted; children under 16 must be accompanied by an adult. Tues–Sat 10am–6pm;
Sun 1–6pm. Closed all major holidays. Subway: 6 to 68th St./Hunter College.

Intrepid **Sea-Air-Space Museum** ★★ *(Kids)*   The most astonishing thing
about the aircraft carrier USS *Intrepid* is how it can be simultaneously so big and
so small. It's a few football fields long, weighs 40,000 tons, holds 40 aircraft, and
sometimes doubles as a ballroom for society functions. But stand there and
think about landing an A-12 jet on the deck and suddenly it's minuscule. Fur-
thermore, in the narrow passageways below, you'll find it isn't quite the roomiest of vessels. Now a National Historic Landmark, the exhibit also includes the
naval destroyer USS *Edson,* and the submarine USS *Growler,* the only intact
strategic missile submarine open to the public anywhere in the world, as well as
a collection of vintage and modern aircraft, including the A-12 Blackbird, the
world's fastest spy plane. Kids just love this place. They, and you, can climb
inside a replica Revolutionary War submarine, sit in an A-6 Intruder cockpit,
and follow the progress of America's astronauts as they work in space. There are
even navy flight simulators—including a "Fly with the Blue Angels" program—
for educational thrill rides in the Technologies Hall. Look for family-oriented
activities and events at least one Saturday a month. Dress warmly for a winter
visit—it's almost impossible to heat an aircraft carrier.

Pier 86 (W. 46th St. at Twelfth Ave.). ✆ 212/245-0072. www.intrepidmuseum.org. Admission $14 adults,
$10 veterans, seniors, and students, $7 children 6–11, $2 children 2–5. $5 extra for flight simulator rides.

Apr–Sept Mon–Fri 10am–5pm, Sat–Sun 10am–7pm; Oct–Mar Tues–Sun 10am–5pm. Last admission 1 hr. before closing. Subway: A, C, E to 42nd St./Port Authority. Bus: M42 crosstown.

South Street Seaport & Museum *Kids*   This landmark historic district on the East River encompasses 11 square blocks of historic buildings, a maritime museum, several piers, shops, and restaurants. The 18th- and 19th-century buildings lining the cobbled streets and alleyways are impeccably restored but nevertheless have a theme-park air about them, no doubt due to the mall-familiar shops housed within. The Seaport's biggest tourist attraction is Pier 17, a historic barge converted into a mall, complete with food court and cheap jewelry kiosks.

Despite its rampant commercialism, the Seaport is well worth a look. There's a good amount of history to be discovered here, most of it around the **South Street Seaport Museum,** a fitting tribute to the sea commerce that once thrived here.

In addition to the galleries—which house paintings and prints, ship models, scrimshaw, and nautical designs, as well as frequently changing exhibitions—there are a number of historic ships berthed at the pier to explore, including the 1911 four-masted *Peking* and the 1893 Gloucester fishing schooner *Lettie G. Howard.* A few of the boats are living museums and restoration works in progress; the 1885 cargo schooner ***Pioneer*** (© 212/748-8786) offers 2-hour public sails daily from early May through September.

Even **Pier 17** has its merits. Head up to the third-level deck overlooking the East River, where the long wooden chairs will have you thinking about what it was like to cross the Atlantic on the *Normandie.* From this level you can see south to the Statue of Liberty, north to the Gothic majesty of the Brooklyn Bridge, and Brooklyn Heights on the opposite shore.

At the gateway to the Seaport, at Fulton and Water streets, is the ***Titanic* Memorial Lighthouse,** a monument to those who lost their lives when the ocean liner sank on April 15, 1912. It was erected overlooking the East River in 1913 and moved to this spot in 1968, just after the historic district was so designated.

At Water and South sts.; museum Visitors Center is at 12 Fulton St. © **212/748-8600** or 212/SEA-PORT. www.southstseaport.org or www.southstreetseaport.com. Museum admission $5. Museum: Apr–Sept Fri–Wed 10am–6pm, Thurs 10am–8pm; Oct–Mar Wed–Mon 10am–5pm. Subway: 2, 3, 4, 5 to Fulton St. (walk east, or downslope, on Fulton St. to Water St.).

SKYSCRAPERS & OTHER ARCHITECTURAL HIGHLIGHTS

Cathedral of St. John the Divine ✦   The world's largest Gothic cathedral, St. John the Divine has been a work in progress since 1892. Its sheer size is amazing enough—a nave that stretches two football fields and a seating capacity of 5,000—but keep in mind that there is no steel structural support. The church is being built using traditional Gothic engineering; blocks of granite and limestone are carved out by master masons and their apprentices—which may explain why construction is still ongoing, more than 110 years after it began, with no end in sight.

You can explore the cathedral on your own, or on the **Public Tour,** offered 6 days a week; also inquire about periodic (usually twice-monthly) **Vertical Tours,** which takes you on a hike up the 11-flight circular staircase to the top, for spectacular views. To hear the incredible pipe organ in action, attend the weekly **Choral Evensong and Organ Meditation** service, which highlights one of the nation's most treasured pipe organs, Sundays at 6pm.

1047 Amsterdam Ave. (at 112th St.). © **212/316-7540,** 212/932-7347 for tour information and reservations, or 212/662-2133 for event information and tickets. www.stjohndivine.org. Suggested admission $2; tour $3; vertical tour $10. Mon–Sat 7am–6pm; Sun 7am–7pm. Tours offered Tues–Sat 11am; Sun 1pm. Worship services Mon–Sat 8 and 8:30am (morning prayer and holy Eucharist), 12:15pm, and 5:30pm (1st Thurs service 7:15am); Sun 8, 9, and 11am and 6pm; AIDS memorial service 4th Sat of the month at 1pm. Subway: B, C, 1, 9 to Cathedral Pkwy.

Chrysler Building ★★   Built as Chrysler Corporation headquarters in 1930 (they moved out decades ago), this is perhaps the 20th century's most romantic architectural achievement, especially at night, when the lights in its triangular openings play off its steely crown. As you admire its facade, be sure to note the gargoyles reaching out from the upper floors, looking for all the world like streamline–Gothic hood ornaments. The observation deck closed long ago, but you can visit its lavish ground-floor interior, which is Art Deco to the max. The ceiling mural depicting airplanes and other early marvels of the first decades of the 20th century evince the bright promise of technology. The elevators are works of art, masterfully covered in exotic woods (especially note the lotus-shaped marquetry on the doors).

405 Lexington Ave. (at 42nd St.). Subway: S, 4, 5, 6, 7 to 42nd St./Grand Central.

Flatiron Building   This triangular masterpiece, so called for its resemblance to the laundry appliance, was one of the first U.S. skyscrapers. Its knife-blade wedge shape is the only way the building could fill the triangular property created by the intersection of Fifth Avenue and Broadway, and that happy coincidence created one of the city's most distinctive buildings. Built in 1902 and fronted with limestone and terra cotta (not iron), the Flatiron measures only 6 feet across at its narrow end. There's no observation deck, and the building mainly houses publishing offices, but there are a few shops on the ground floor. The building's existence has served to name the neighborhood around it—the Flatiron District, home to a bevy of smart restaurants and shops.

175 Fifth Ave. (at 23rd St.). Subway: R to 23rd St.

New York Public Library ★★   The New York Public Library, designed by Carrère & Hastings (1911), is one of the country's finest examples of beaux arts architecture, a majestic structure of white Vermont marble with Corinthian columns and allegorical statues. Before climbing the broad flight of steps to the Fifth Avenue entrance, take note of the famous lion sculptures—*Fortitude* on the right, and *Patience* on the left—so dubbed by whip-smart former mayor Fiorello LaGuardia. At Christmastime they don natty wreaths to keep warm.

This library is actually the **Humanities and Social Sciences Library,** only one of the research libraries in the New York Public Library system. The interior is one of the finest in the city and features **Astor Hall,** with high arched marble ceilings and grand staircases. The stupendous **Main Reading Rooms** have now reopened after a massive restoration and modernization that both brought them back to their stately glory and moved them into the computer age. Even if you don't stop in to peruse the periodicals, you may want to check out one of the excellent rotating **exhibitions.** Call or check the site for show schedules.

Fifth Ave. and 42nd St. © **212/869-8089** (exhibits and events), or 212/661-7220 (library hours). www.nypl.org. Free admission to all exhibitions. Thurs–Sat 10am–6pm; Tues–Wed 11am–7:30pm. Subway: B, D, F, V to 42nd St.; S, 4, 5, 6, 7 to Grand Central/42nd St.

St. Patrick's Cathedral   This incredible Gothic white-marble-and-stone structure is the largest Roman Catholic cathedral in the United States, as well as the seat of the Archdiocese of New York. Designed by James Renwick, begun in 1859, and consecrated in 1879, St. Patrick's wasn't completed until 1906. Strangely, Irish Catholics picked one of the city's WASPiest neighborhoods for St. Patrick's. After the death of the beloved John Cardinal O'Connor in 2000, the pope installed Bishop Edward Egan, whom he elevated to cardinal in 2001. The vast cathedral sits a congregation of 2,200; if you don't want to come for Mass, you can pop in between services to get a look at the impressive interior.

Fifth Ave. (btwn 50th and 51st sts.). ℂ **212/753-2261.** www.ny-archdiocese.org/pastoral/cathedral_about. html. Free admission. Sun–Fri 7am–8:30pm; Sat 8am–8:30pm. Mass: Mon–Fri 7, 7:30, 8, and 8:30am, noon, and 12:30, 1, and 5:30pm; Sat 8 and 8:30am, noon, and 12:30 and 5:30pm; Sun 7, 8, 9, and 10:15am (Cardinal's mass), noon, and 1, 4, and 5:30pm; holy days 7, 7:30, 8, 8:30, 9, 11, and 11:30am, noon, and 12:30, 1, and 5:30 and 6:30pm. Subway: B, D, F, V to 47–50th sts./Rockefeller Center.

United Nations   In the midst of New York City is this working monument to world peace. Opened in 1952, the U.N. headquarters occupies 18 acres of international territory—neither the city nor the United States has jurisdiction here—along the East River from 42nd to 48th streets. The complex along the East River weds the 39-story glass slab Secretariat with the free-form General Assembly on beautifully landscaped grounds donated by John D. Rockefeller Jr. One hundred and eighty nations use the facilities to arbitrate worldwide disputes.

   Guided tours leave every half hour or so and last 45 minutes to an hour. Your guide will take you to the General Assembly Hall and the Security Council Chamber and introduce the history and activities of the United Nations and its related organizations. Along the tour you'll see donated objects and artwork, including charred artifacts that survived the atomic bombs at Hiroshima and Nagasaki, stained-glass windows by Chagall, a replica of the first *Sputnik,* and a colorful mosaic called *The Golden Rule,* based on a Norman Rockwell drawing, which was a gift from the United States in 1985.

At First Ave. and 46th St. ℂ **212/963-8687.** www.un.org/tours. Guided tours $10 adults, $7.50 seniors, $6.50 high school and college students, $5.50 children 5–14 (children under 5 not permitted). Daily tours every half-hour 9:30am–4:45pm; closed weekends Jan–Feb; a limited schedule may be in effect during the general debate (late Sept to mid-Oct). Subway: S, 4, 5, 6, 7 to 42nd St./Grand Central.

CENTRAL PARK

Without the miracle of civic planning that is **Central Park** ★★★, Manhattan would be a virtual unbroken block of buildings. Instead, smack in the middle of Gotham, an 843-acre natural retreat provides a daily escape valve and tranquilizer for millions of New Yorkers.

   On just about any day, Central Park is crowded with New Yorkers and visitors alike. On nice days, especially weekend days, it's the city's party central. The crowds are part of the appeal—folks come here to peel off their urban armor and relax, and the common goal puts a general feeling of camaraderie in the air. On these days, the people-watching is more compelling than anywhere else in the city. But even on the most crowded days, there's always somewhere to get away from it all, if you just want a little peace and quiet, and a moment to commune with nature.

ORIENTATION & GETTING THERE   Look at your map—that great green swath in the center of Manhattan is Central Park. It runs from 59th Street (also known as Central Park S.) at the south end to 110th Street at the north end, and from Fifth Avenue on the east side to Central Park West (the equivalent of Eighth Ave.) on the west side. A 6-mile rolling road, **Central Park Drive,** circles the park, and has a lane set aside for bikers, joggers, and in-line skaters.

Central Park

(i) Information

Ⓜ Subway stop

0 _____ 1/5 mile

0 _____ 200 meters

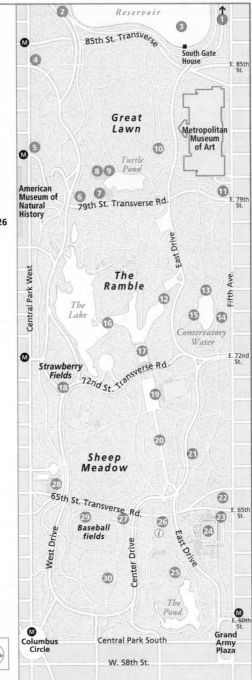

A number of subway stops and lines serve the park, and which one you take depends on where you want to go. To reach the southernmost entrance on the west side, take an A, B, C, D, 1, or 9 to 59th Street/Columbus Circle. To reach the southeast corner entrance, take the N, R to Fifth Avenue; from this stop, it's an easy walk into the park to the Information Center in the **Dairy** (℄ **212/794-6564;** open daily 11am–5pm, to 4pm in winter), midpark at about 65th Street. Here you can ask questions, pick up park information, and purchase a good park map.

If your time for exploring is limited, I suggest entering the park at 72nd or 79th streets for maximum exposure (subway: B, C to 72nd St. or 81st St./Museum of Natural History). From here, you can pick up park information at the visitor center at **Belvedere Castle** (℄ **212/772-0210;** open Tues–Sun 10am–5pm, to 4pm in winter), midpark at 79th Street. There's also a third visitor center at the **Charles A. Dana Discovery Center** (℄ **212/860-1370;** open daily 11am–5pm, to 4pm in winter), at the northeast corner of the park at Harlem Meer, at 110th Street between Fifth and Lenox avenues (subway: 2, 3 to Central Park N./110th St.). The Dana Center is also an environmental education center hosting workshops, exhibits, music programs, and park tours, and lends fishing poles for fishing in Harlem Meer (park policy is catch-and-release).

Food carts and vendors are set up at all of the park's main gathering points, selling hot dogs, pretzels, and ice cream, so finding a bite to eat is never a problem. You'll also find a fixed food counter at the **Conservatory,** on the east side of the park north of the 72nd Street entrance, and both casual snacks and more sophisticated New American dining at **The Boat House,** on the lake near 72nd Street and Park Drive North (℄ **212/517-2233**).

SAFETY   Even though the park has the lowest crime rate of any of the city's precincts, keep your wits about you, especially in the more remote northern end. It's a good idea to avoid the park entirely after dark, unless you're heading to one of the restaurants for dinner or to **Shakespeare in the Park.**

VISITOR INFORMATION   Call ℄ **212/360-3444** for recorded information, or 212/310-6600 or 212/628-1036 to speak with a live person. Call ℄ **888/NY-PARKS** for special events information. The park also has two comprehensive websites that are worth checking out before you go: The city parks department's site at **www.centralpark.org**, and the Central Park Conservancy's site at **www.centralparknyc.org**, both of which feature excellent maps and a far more complete rundown of park attractions and activities than I have room to include here. If you have an **emergency** in the park, dial ℄ **800/201-PARK,** which will link you directly to the park rangers.

EXPLORING THE PARK

The best way to see Central Park is to wander along the park's 58 miles of winding pedestrian paths, keeping in mind the following highlights.

The southern part of Central Park is more formally designed and heavily visited than the relatively rugged and remote northern end. Not far from the Dairy is the **Carousel** with 58 hand-carved horses (℄ **212/879-0244;** open daily Apr–Nov 10am–6pm, to 4:30pm in winter; rides are $1); the zoo (below); and the Wollman Rink for roller- or ice-skating.

The **Mall,** a long formal walkway lined with elms shading benches and sculptures of sometimes forgotten writers, leads to the focal point of Central Park,

Bethesda Fountain ⭐ (along the 72nd St. transverse road). **Bethesda Terrace** and its grandly sculpted entryway border a large **lake** where dogs fetch sticks, rowboaters glide by, and dedicated early morning anglers try their luck at catching carp, perch, catfish, and bass. You can rent a rowboat at or take a gondola ride from **Loeb Boathouse,** on the eastern end of the lake. Boats of another kind are at **Conservatory Water** (on the east side at 73rd St.), a stone-walled pond flanked by statues of both **Hans Christian Andersen** and **Alice in Wonderland.** On Saturday at 10am, die-hard yachtsmen race remote-controlled sailboats in fierce competitions that follow Olympic regulations.

If the action there is too intense, **Sheep Meadow** on the southwestern side of the park is a designated quiet zone, where Frisbee throwing and kite flying are as energetic as things get. Another respite is **Strawberry Fields** ⭐, at 72nd Street on the West Side. This memorial to John Lennon, who was murdered across the street at the Dakota apartment building (72nd St. and Central Park W., northwest corner), is a gorgeous garden centered around an Italian mosaic bearing the title of the lead Beatle's most famous solo song, and his lifelong message: IMAGINE. In keeping with its goal of promoting world peace, the garden has 161 varieties of plants, donated by each of the 161 nations in existence when it was designed in 1985. This is a wonderful place for peaceful contemplation.

Bow Bridge, a graceful lacework of cast iron, designed by Calvert Vaux, crosses over the lake and leads to the most bucolic area of Central Park, the **Ramble.** This dense 38-acre woodland with spiraling paths, rocky outcroppings, and a stream is the best spot for bird-watching and feeling as if you've discovered an unimaginably leafy forest right in the middle of the city.

North of the Ramble, **Belvedere Castle** is home to the **Henry Luce Nature Observatory** (℗ 212/772-0210), worth a visit if you're with children. From the castle, set on Vista Rock (the park's highest point at 135 ft.), you can look down on the **Great Lawn,** where softball players and sun worshipers compete for coveted greenery, and the **Delacorte Theater,** home to Shakespeare in the Park. The small **Shakespeare Garden** south of the theater is scruffy, but it does have plants, herbs, trees, and other bits of greenery mentioned by the playwright. Behind the Belvedere Castle is the **Swedish Cottage Marionette Theatre** ⭐ (℗ 212/988-9093), hosting various marionette plays for children throughout the year; call to see what's on.

Continue north along the east side of the Great Lawn, parallel to East Drive. Near the glass-enclosed back of the **Metropolitan Museum of Art** (p. 118) is **Cleopatra's Needle,** a 69-foot obelisk originally erected in Heliopolis around 1475 B.C. It was given to the city as a gift from the khedive of Egypt in 1880. (The khedive bestowed a similar obelisk to the city of London, which now sits on the Embankment of the Thames.)

North of the 86th Street Transverse Road is the **Jacqueline Kennedy Onassis Reservoir,** so named after the death of the beloved first lady, who lived nearby and often enjoyed a run along the 1½-mile jogging track that circles the reservoir.

North of the reservoir is my favorite part of the park. It's much less traversed and in some areas, absolutely tranquil. The **North Meadow** (at 96th St.) features 12 baseball and softball fields.

North of the North Meadow, at the northeast end of the park is the **Conservatory Garden** ⭐ (at 105th St. and Fifth Ave.), Central Park's only formal garden, with a magnificent display of flowers and trees reflected in calm pools of water. The **Lasker Rink and Pool** (© **212/534-7639**) is the only swimming pool in Central Park and in the winter its converted to a skating rink that offers a less hectic alternative to Wollman Rink. **Harlem Meer** and its boathouse were recently renovated and look beautiful. The boathouse now berths the **Charles A. Dana Discovery Center,** near 110th Street between Fifth and Lenox avenues (© **212/860-1370**), where children learn about the environment and borrow fishing poles for catch-and-release at no charge. **The Pool** (at W. 100th St.), possibly the most idyllic spot in all of Central Park, was recently renovated and features willows, grassy banks and a small pond populated by some very well-fed ducks. You might even spot an egret and a hawk or two lurking around here.

Central Park Zoo/Tisch Children's Zoo ★ *(Kids)*   It has been over a decade since the zoo in Central Park was renovated, making it in the process both more human and more humane. Lithe sea lions frolic in the central pool area with beguiling style. The gigantic but graceful polar bears (one of whom, by the way, made himself a true New Yorker when he began regular visits with a shrink) glide back and forth across a watery pool that has glass walls through which you can observe very large paws doing very smooth strokes. The monkeys seem to regard those on the other side of the fence with knowing disdain. In the hot and humid Tropic Zone, large colorful birds swoop around in freedom, sometimes landing next to nonplused visitors.

Because of its small size, the zoo is at its best with its displays of smaller animals. The indoor multilevel Tropic Zone is a real highlight, its steamy rainforest home to everything from black-and-white Colobus monkeys to Emerald tree boa constrictors to a leaf-cutter ant farm; look for the new dart poison frog exhibit, which is very cool. So is the large penguin enclosure in the Polar Circle, which is better than the one at San Diego's Sea World. In the Temperate Territory, look for the Asian red pandas (cousins to the big black-and-white ones), which look like the world's most beautiful raccoons.

The entire zoo is good for short attention spans; you can cover the whole thing in 1½ to 3 hours, depending on the size of the crowds and how long you like to linger. It's also very kid-friendly, with lots of well-written and -illustrated placards that older kids can understand. For the littlest ones, there's the **Tisch Children's Zoo.** With pigs, llamas, potbellied pigs, and more, this petting zoo and playground is a real blast for the 5-and-under set.

830 Fifth Ave. (at 64th St., just inside Central Park). © **212/861-6030.** www.wcs.org/zoos. Admission $6 adults, $1.25 seniors, $1 children 3–12, free for children under 3. Daily 10am–4:30pm. Subway: N, R to Fifth Ave.

ACTIVITIES IN THE PARK

The 6-mile rolling road circling the park, **Central Park Drive,** has a lane set aside for bikers, joggers, and in-line skaters. The best time to use it is when the park is closed to traffic: Monday to Friday 10am to 3pm (except Thanksgiving to New Year's) and 7 to 10pm. It's also closed from 7pm Friday to 6am Monday, but when the weather is nice, the crowds can be hellish.

BIKING   Off-road mountain biking isn't permitted; stay on Central Park Drive or your bike may be confiscated by park police.

You can rent 3- and 10-speed bikes as well as tandems in Central Park at the **Loeb Boathouse,** midpark near 72nd Street and Park Drive North, just in from Fifth Avenue (© **212/517-2233** or 212/517-3623), for $9 to $15 an hour, with a complete selection of kids' bikes, cruisers, tandems, and the like ($200 deposit required); at **Metro Bicycles,** 1311 Lexington Ave., at 88th Street (© **212/427-4450**). No matter where you rent, be prepared to leave a credit card deposit.

BOATING From March through November, gondola rides and rowboat rentals are available at the **Loeb Boathouse,** midpark near 74th Street and Park Drive North, just in from Fifth Avenue (© **212/517-2233** or 212/517-3623). Rowboats are $10 for the first hour, $2.50 every 15 minutes thereafter, and a $20 deposit is required; reservations are accepted. (Note that rates were not set for the summer season at press time, so these may change.)

HORSE-DRAWN CARRIAGE RIDES At the entrance to the park at 59th Street and Central Park South, you'll see a line of **horse-drawn carriages** waiting to take passengers on a ride through the park or along certain of the city's streets. Horses belong on city streets as much as chamber pots belong in our homes. You won't need me to tell you how forlorn most of these horses look; if you insist, a ride is about $50 for two for a half hour, but I suggest skipping it.

ICE SKATING Central Park's **Wollman Rink** ✪, on the east side of the park between 62nd and 63rd streets (© **212/439-6900;** www.wollmanskatingrink. com), is the city's best outdoor skating spot, more spacious than the tiny rink at Rockefeller Center. It's open for skating generally from mid-October to mid-April, depending on the weather. Rates are $8.50 for adults, $4. 50 for seniors and kids under 12, and skate rental is $4.75; lockers are available (locks are $6.75). **Lasker Rink** (© **212/534-7639**), on the east side around 106th street is a less expensive alternative to the much more crowded Wollman Rink. Open November through March. Rates are $4.50 for adults, $2.25 for kids under 12, and skate rental is $4.75.

IN-LINE SKATING Central Park is the city's most popular place for blading. See the beginning of this section for details on Central Park Drive, the main drag for skaters. On weekends, head to West Drive at 67th Street, behind Tavern on the Green, where you'll find trick skaters weaving through an NYRSA slalom course at full speed, or the Mall in front of the band shell (above Bethesda Fountain) for twirling to tunes. In summer, **Wollman Rink** converts to a hotshot roller rink, with half-pipes and lessons available (see "Ice Skating," above).

You can rent skates for $20 a day from **Blades Board and Skate,** 120 W. 72nd St., between Broadway and Columbus Avenue (© **212/787-3911;** www. blades.com). Wollman Rink (above) also rents in-line skates for park use at similar rates.

PLAYGROUNDS Nineteen Adventure Playgrounds are scattered throughout the park, perfect for jumping, sliding, tottering, swinging, and digging. At Central Park West and 81st Street is the **Diana Ross Playground** ✪, voted the city's best by *New York* magazine. Also on the west side is the **Spector Playground,** at 85th Street and Central Park West, and, a little farther north, the **Wild West Playground** at 93rd Street. On the east side is the **Rustic Playground,** at 67th Street and Fifth Avenue, a delightfully landscaped space rife with islands, bridges, and big slides; and the **Pat Hoffman Friedman Playground,** right behind the Metropolitan Museum of Art at East 79th Street, is geared toward older toddlers.

RUNNING Marathoners and wannabes regularly run in Central Park along the 6-mile **Central Park Drive,** which circles the park (please run toward traffic to avoid being mowed down by wayward cyclists and in-line skaters). The

New York Road Runners (℃ **212/860-4455;** www.nyrrc.org), organizers of the New York City Marathon, schedules group runs 7 days a week at 6am and 6pm, leaving from entrance to the Park at 90th Street and Fifth Avenue.

ORGANIZED SIGHTSEEING TOURS

Gray Line New York Tours   Gray Line offers just about every sightseeing tour option and combination you could want. There are bus tours by day and by night that run uptown, downtown, and all around the town, as well as bus combos with Circle Line cruises, helicopter flights, museum entrances, and guided visits of sights. There's no real point to purchasing some combination tours—you don't need a guide to take you to the Statue of Liberty, and you don't save any money on admission by buying the combo ticket. I've found Gray Line to put a higher premium on accuracy than the other big tour-bus operators, so this is your best bet among the biggies.

777 Eighth Ave. (btwn 47th and 48th sts.). Tours depart from additional Manhattan locations. ℃ **800/669-0051** or 212/445-0848. www.graylinenewyork.com. Hop-on, hop-off bus tours from $35 adults, $20 children 5–11.

HARBOR CRUISES

Circle Line Sightseeing Cruises ★★   Circle Line is the only tour company that circumnavigates the entire 35 miles around Manhattan, and I love this ride. The **Full Island** cruise takes 3 hours and passes by the Statue of Liberty, Ellis Island, the Brooklyn Bridge, the United Nations, Yankee Stadium, the George Washington Bridge, and more, including Manhattan's wild northern tip. The panorama is riveting, and the commentary isn't bad. The big boats are basic but fine, with lots of deck room for everybody to enjoy the view. Snacks, soft drinks, coffee, and beer are available onboard for purchase.

If 3 hours is more than you or the kids can handle, go for either the 1½-hour **Semi-Circle** or **Sunset/Harbor Lights** cruise, both of which show you the highlights of the skyline.

Departing from Pier 83, at W. 42nd St. and Twelfth Ave. Also departing from Pier 16 at South St. Seaport, 207 Front St. ℃ **212/563-3200.** www.circleline.com, www.ridethebeast.com, and www.seaportmusiccruises.com. Sightseeing cruises $16–$25 adults, $17–$20 seniors, $10–$12 children 12 and under. Subway to Pier 83: A, C, E to 42nd St. Subway to Pier 16: J, M, Z, 2, 3, 4, 5 to Fulton St.

SPECIALTY TOURS

Big Onion Walking Tours ★ (℃ **212/439-1090;** www.bigonion.com). Enthusiastic Big Onion guides (all hold an advanced degree in American history from Columbia or New York universities) peel back the layers of history to reveal the city's inner secrets. The 2-hour tours are offered mostly on weekends, and subjects include the "The Bowery," "Presidential New York," "Gangs of New York," and the ever-popular "Multiethnic Eating Tour" of the Lower East Side. Tour prices range from $12 to $18 for adults, $10 to $16 for students and seniors. No reservations are necessary, but Big Onion *strongly* recommends that you call to verify schedules.

For food lovers, **Savory Sojourns** (℃ **888/9-SAVORY** or 212/691-7314; www.savorysojourns.com), operated by Addie Tomei (Oscar-winning actress Marisa's mom) and Sally Ingraham, offer guided walking tours that are 5- to 6-hour events that give an insider's view of the culinary wonderland that is New York and hands-on experience with its bounty. The tasty adventures include Chinatown, Little Italy, Greenwich Village, and more. Tour prices are all-inclusive and range from $85 to $155. Reservations should be made 3 to 6 months in advance when possible.

Harlem Spirituals (© **800/660-2166** or 212/391-0900; www.harlemspirituals. com) specializes in gospel and jazz tours of Harlem that can be combined with a traditional soul-food meal. A variety of options are available, including a tour of Harlem sights with gospel service, and a soul-food lunch or brunch as an optional add-on. Prices start at $30, $23 for children, for a Harlem Heritage tour, and go up from there based on length and inclusions (tours that include food and entertainment are pay-one-price). All tours leave from Harlem Spirituals' Midtown office (690 Eighth Ave., btwn 43rd and 44th sts.), and transportation is included.

ESPECIALLY FOR KIDS

Some of New York's sights and attractions are designed specifically with kids in mind, and I've listed those below. But many of those I've discussed in the rest of this chapter are terrific for kids as well as adults; look for the kids icon next to the attraction.

MUSEUMS

In addition to the museums designed specifically for kids below, also consider the following, discussed elsewhere in this chapter: The **American Museum of Natural History** (p. 115), whose dinosaur displays are guaranteed to wow both you and the kids; the *Intrepid* **Sea-Air-Space Museum** (p. 123), on a real battleship with an amazing collection of vintage and high-tech airplanes; and the **South Street Seaport & Museum** (p. 124), which little ones will love for its theme park–like atmosphere and old boats bobbing in the harbor.

Children's Museum of Manhattan ★ *Kids* Here's a great place to take the kids when they're tired of being told not to touch. Designed for ages 2 to 12, this museum is strictly hands-on. Interactive exhibits and activity centers encourage self-discovery—and a recent expansion means that there's now even more to keep the kids busy and learning. The Time Warner Media Center takes children through the world of animation and helps them produce their own videos. The Body Odyssey is a zany, scientific journey through the human body. This isn't just a museum for the 5-and-up set—there are exhibits especially designed for babies and toddlers, too. The busy schedule also includes daily art classes and storytellers, and a full slate of entertainment on weekends.

212 W. 83rd St. (btwn Broadway and Amsterdam Ave.). © **212/721-1234**. www.cmom.org. Admission $6 children ages 1 and up and adults, $3 seniors. Wed–Sun and school holidays 10am–5pm. Subway: 1, 9 to 86th St.

Children's Museum of the Arts *Kids* Interactive workshop programs for children ages 1 to 12 and their families are the attraction here. Kids dabble in puppet making and computer drawing or join in singalongs and live performances. Also look for rotating exhibitions of the museum's permanent collection featuring WPA work. Call or check the website for the current exhibition and activities schedule.

182 Lafayette St. (btwn Broome and Grand sts.). © **212/941-9198** or 212/274-0986. www.cmany.org. Admission $6 for everyone 1–65; pay what you wish Thurs 4–6pm. Wed–Sun noon–5pm (Thurs to 6pm). Subway: 6 to Spring St.

New York Hall of Science ★ *Kids* Children of all ages will love this huge hands-on museum, which bills itself as "New York's Only Science Playground." Exhibits let them be engulfed by a giant soap bubble, float on air in an anti-gravity mirror, and compose music by dancing in front of light beams. There's a

Preschool Discovery Place for the really little ones. But probably best of all is the summertime Outdoor Science Playground for kids 6 and older—ostensibly lessons in physics, but really just a great excuse to laugh, jump, and play on jungle gyms, slides, seesaws, spinners, and more.

The museum is located in **Flushing Meadows–Corona Park,** where kids can enjoy even more fun beyond the Hall of Science. Not only are there more than 1,200 acres of park and playgrounds, but there's also a zoo, a carousel, an indoor ice-skating rink, an outdoor pool, and bike and boat rentals. Kids and grown-ups alike will love getting an up-close look at the Unisphere steel globe, which was not really destroyed in *Men in Black.* The park is also home to the **Queens Museum of Art** (p. 151) as well as Shea Stadium and the U.S. Open Tennis Center.

4701 111th St., in Flushing Meadows–Corona Park, Queens. © 718/699-0005. www.nyhallsci.org. Admission $7.50 adults, $5 seniors and children 4–17; preschoolers, $2.50; extra $3 for Science Playground. Free to all Fri 2–5pm. Mon–Wed 9:30am–2pm (Tues–Wed to 5pm in summer); Thurs–Sun 9:30am–5pm. Subway: 7 to 111th St.

MORE KID-FRIENDLY DIVERSIONS

ARCADES **Lazer Park,** in Times Square at 1560 Broadway (entrance around the corner at 163 W. 46th St.; © **212/398-3060;** www.lazerpark.com), has amusements ranging from good old-fashioned pinball to virtual-reality games and a full-on laser tag arena. Even better is the **Broadway City** ★, 241 W. 42nd St., between Seventh and Eighth avenues (© **212/997-9797;** www.broadway city.com), a neon-bright, multilevel interactive game center designed on a Big Apple theme where you could lose your kids (and a year's supply of quarters) for an entire day.

SHOPPING Everybody loves to shop in New York—even kids. Don't forget to take them to **Books of Wonder,** that temple of sneakerdom **Niketown,** the **NBA Store,** and **FAO Schwarz,** the best toy store in the world—just ask Tom Hanks (remember *Big?*). Actually, the brand-new **Toys "R" Us** flagship is giving it a run for its money, thanks to its very own indoor Ferris wheel. See "Shopping Highlights," below for details.

SKY-HIGH VIEWS Kids of all ages can't help but turn dizzy with delight at incredible views from atop the **Empire State Building** (p. 117). The Empire State Building also has the **New York Skyride** (© **212/279-9777;** www.skyride. com), which offers a short motion-flight simulation sightseeing tour of New York, just in case the real one isn't enough for your kids. Open daily 10am to 10pm; tickets are $17 adults, $16 kids 5 to 11, $15 for seniors and kids 4 to 12; combination Empire State observation deck/New York Skyride tickets are available at a discount.

SPECIAL EVENTS Children's eyes grow wide at the yearlong march of **parades** (especially Macy's Thanksgiving Day Parade), **circuses** (Big Apple, and Ringling Bros. and Barnum & Bailey), and **holiday shows** (the Rockettes' Christmas and Easter performances). See the "New York State Calendar of Events," in chapter 2, for details.

ZOOS & AQUARIUMS Bigger kids will love the legendary **Bronx Zoo** (p. 146), while the **Central Park Zoo** with its Tisch Children's Zoo (p. 130) is particularly suitable to younger kids. At the **New York Aquarium** at Coney Island (p. 149), kids can touch starfish and sea urchins and watch bottlenose dolphins and California sea lions stunt-swim in the outdoor aqua theater.

SPECTATOR SPORTS

BASEBALL   With two baseball teams in town, you can catch a game almost any day from opening day in April to beginning of playoffs in October. (Don't bother trying to get subway series tix, though—they're the hottest seats in town. Ditto for Opening Day or any playoff game.)

Star catcher Mike Piazza and the Amazin' **Mets** play at **Shea Stadium** in Queens (subway: 7 to Willets Point/Shea Stadium). For tickets and information, call the **Mets Ticket Office** at ☎ **718/507-TIXX,** or visit www.mets.com.

The **Yankees** play at the House That Ruth Built, otherwise known as Yankee Stadium (subway: C, D, 4 to 161st St./Yankee Stadium call **Ticketmaster** (☎ **212/307-1212** or 212/307-7171; www.ticketmaster.com) or **Yankee Stadium** (☎ **718/293-6000;** www.yankees.com). Serious baseball fans might check the schedule well in advance and try to catch **Old Timers' Day,** usually held in July, when pinstriped stars of years past return to the stadium to take a bow.

Minor-league baseball ★ made a Big Apple splash in summer 2001 when the **Brooklyn Cyclones,** the New York Mets' A-level farm team, and the **Staten Island Yankees,** the Yanks' junior leaguers, came to town. Boasting their very own waterfront stadium, the Brooklyn Cyclones have been a major factor in the revitalization of Coney Island; spanking-new Keyspan Park sits right off the legendary boardwalk (subway: F, N, Q, W to Stillwell Ave./Coney Island). The SI Yanks also have their own shiny new playing field, the Richmond County Bank Ballpark, just a 5-minute walk from the Staten Island Ferry terminal (subway: N, R to Whitehall St.; 4, 5 to Bowling Green; 1, 9 to South Ferry). What's more, with bargain-basement ticket prices at around $10, this is a great way to experience baseball in the city for a fraction of the major-league hassle and cost. Both teams have already developed a rabidly loyal fan base, so it's a good idea to buy your tickets for the summer season—which runs from June through September—in advance. For the Cyclones, call ☎ **718/449-8497** or visit www. brooklyncyclones.com; to reach the SI Yanks, call ☎ **718/720-9200** or go online to www.siyanks.com.

BASKETBALL   Two pro teams call **Madison Square Garden,** Seventh Avenue between 31st and 33rd streets (☎ **212/465-6741** or www.thegarden.com; 212/ 307-7171 or www.ticketmaster.com for tickets; subway: A, C, E, 1, 2, 3, 9 to 34th St.), home court: the **New York Knicks** (☎ **877/NYK-DUNK** or 212/465-JUMP; www.nyknicks.com); and the **New York Liberty** (☎ **212/465-6080;** www.wnba.com/liberty). Knicks tickets are hard to come by, so plan ahead if you want a front-row seat near first fan Spike Lee. *Note:* From mid-July to late August 2004, while the Garden is transformed for the Republican National Convention, New York Liberty will be playing at Radio City Music Hall.

ICE HOCKEY   The **New York Rangers** play at Madison Square Garden, Seventh Avenue between 31st and 33rd streets (☎ **212/465-6741;** www.newyork rangers.com or www.thegarden.com; subway: A, C, E, 1, 2, 3, 9 to 34th St.). The Rangers have been going through tough times, but tickets are hard to get nevertheless, so plan well ahead; call ☎ **212/307-7171,** or visit www.ticket master.com for online orders.

6 Shopping Highlights

Whether you're a bargain hunter or a high-style maven, New York is a shopper's dream. Below, I've outlined the city's main shopping districts, recommending just a few great shops by name. For a terrific Big Apple shopping guide that's loaded with store listings, I recommend *Suzy Gershman's Born to Shop New York* (Wiley Publishing, Inc.).

CHINATOWN

Don't expect to find the purchase of a lifetime on Chinatown's streets, but there's some quality browsing to be had. The fish and herbal markets along Canal, Mott, Mulberry, and Elizabeth streets are fun for their bustle and exotica. Dispersed among them (especially along **Canal St.**), you'll find a mind-boggling collection of knockoff sunglasses and watches, cheap backpacks, discount leather goods, and exotic souvenirs. It's a fun daytime browse, but don't expect quality—and be sure to bargain before you buy. (Also, skip the bootleg CDs, video, and software— these are stolen goods, and you *will* be disappointed with the product.) **Mott Street,** between Pell Street and Chatham Square, boasts the most interesting of Chinatown's off-Canal shopping, with an antiques shop or two dispersed among the tiny storefronts selling blue-and-white Chinese dinnerware. The definite highlight is the two-stop **Pearl River** Chinese emporium at two locations: 477 Broadway, at Grand Street (© **212/431-4770;** www.pearlriver.com), and 200 Grand St., between Mott and Mulberry streets (© **212/966-1010**) Subway to either location: B, D, Q to Grand Street.

THE LOWER EAST SIDE

The bargains aren't quite what they used to be in the **Historic Orchard Street Shopping District**—which basically runs from Houston to Canal along Allen, Orchard, and Ludlow streets, spreading outward along both sides of Delancey Street—but prices on leather bags, shoes, luggage, and fabrics on the bolt are still quite good. Be aware, though, that the hard sell on Orchard Street can be pretty hard to take. Still, the district is a nice place to discover a part of New York that's disappearing. Come during the week, since most stores are Jewish-owned and, therefore, close Friday afternoon and all day Saturday. Sunday tends to be a madhouse.

Before you browse, stop into the **Lower East Side Visitor Center,** 261 Broome St., between Orchard and Allen streets (© **866/825-8374** or 212/226-9010; www.lowereastsideny.com. Subway: F to Delancey St.).

SOHO

People love to complain about superfashionable SoHo—it's become too trendy, too tony, too Mall of America. True, **J. Crew** is only one of many big names that have supplanted the artists and galleries that used to inhabit its historic cast-iron buildings. But SoHo is still one of the best shopping 'hoods in the city—and few are more fun to browse. It's the epicenter of cutting-edge fashion and still boasts plenty of unique boutiques. The streets are chock-full of tempting stores, so just come and browse.

SoHo's prime shopping grid is from Broadway east to Sullivan Street, and from Houston down to Broome, although Grand Street, 1 block south of Broome, has been sprouting shops of late. **Broadway** is the most commercial strip, with such recognizable names as **Pottery Barn** and **A/X Armani Exchange.** But the real tone of the neighborhood is set by the big names in avant-garde fashion, such as **Anna Sui,** 113 Greene St., just south of Prince Street (© **212/941-8406;** www.annasui.com) and **Marc Jacobs,** 163 Mercer St., between Houston and Prince (© **212/343-1490;** www.marcjacobs.com).

NOLITA

Not so long ago, **Elizabeth Street** was a nondescript adjunct to Little Italy and the no-man's-land east of SoHo. Today it's one of the hottest shopping strips in town, the star of the neighborhood known as Nolita. Elizabeth and neighboring Mott and Mulberry streets are dotted with an increasing number of shops between Houston and Spring streets, with a few pushing 1 more block south to Kenmare. It's an easy walk from the Broadway/Lafayette stop on the F, V line to the neighborhood, since it starts just east of Lafayette Street; you can also take the 6 to Spring Street, or the N, R to Prince Street and walk east from there.

This may be a burgeoning neighborhood, but don't expect cheap—Nolita is clearly the stepchild of SoHo. Its boutiques are largely the province of sophisticated shopkeepers specializing in high-quality fashion-forward products and design. The boutique density is most intense on Elizabeth, where offerings range from whimsical milliner **Kelly Christy** at no. 235 (© 212/965-0686) to **Area . . . id,** no. 262 (© 212/219-9903), for sleek vintage Danish everything.

THE EAST VILLAGE

The East Village personifies bohemian hip. **East 9th Street** between Second Avenue and Avenue A has become one of my favorite shopping strips in the entire city. Lined with an increasingly smart collection of boutiques, it proves that the East Village isn't just for kids anymore. Up-and-coming designers, including **Jill Anderson,** 331 E. 9th St., between First and Second avenues (© 212/253-1747; www.jillanderson.com), and **Selia Yang,** across the street at 328 E. 9th St. (© 212/254-9073; www.seliayang.com), sell excellent-quality and affordably priced original fashions for women along here. It's also an excellent strip for stylish gifts and little luxuries. The surrounding blocks aren't quite as mature yet, but are on their way.

If it's strange, illegal, or funky, it's probably available on **St. Marks Place,** which takes over for 8th Street, running east from Third Avenue to Avenue A. This skanky strip is a permanent street market, with countless T-shirt and boho jewelry stands. The height of the action is between Second and Third avenues, which is prime hunting grounds for used-record collectors.

GREENWICH VILLAGE

The West Village is great for browsing and gift shopping. Specialty book and record stores, antiques and craft shops, and gourmet food markets dominate. The Village isn't much of a destination for fashion hunters, with the exception of NYU territory—8th Street between Broadway and Sixth Avenue for trendy footwear and affordable fashions, and Broadway from 8th Street south to Houston, anchored by **Urban Outfitters** at 628 Broadway, between Bleecker and Houston Street (© 212/475-0009; www.urbanoutfitters.com) and dotted with skate and sneaker shops. Clothes hounds looking for volume shopping are better off elsewhere.

The prime drag for strolling is bustling **Bleecker Street,** where you'll find lots of "discount" leather shops and record stores interspersed with a good number of interesting and artsy boutiques. Narrow **Christopher Street** is another fun strip, because it's loaded with genuine Village character. Those who really love to browse should also wander **west of Seventh Avenue** and along **Hudson Street,** where charming shops like **House of Cards and Curiosities,** 23 Eighth Ave., between Jane and 12th streets (© 212/675-6178), the Village's own funky take on an old-fashioned nickel-and-dime, are tucked among the brownstones.

THE FLATIRON DISTRICT & UNION SQUARE

When 23rd Street was the epitome of New York uptown fashion more than 100 years ago, the major department stores stretched along **Sixth Avenue** for about a mile from 14th Street up. These elegant stores stood in huge cast-iron buildings that were long ago abandoned and left to rust. In the last several years, however, the area has grown into the city's discount shopping center, with superstores and off-pricers filling up the renovated spaces: **Filene's Basement, TJ Maxx,** and **Bed Bath & Beyond** are all at 620 Sixth Ave., while **Old Navy** is next door, and **Barnes & Noble** is just a couple of blocks away at Sixth Avenue near 22nd Street.

On Broadway, just a few blocks north of Union Square, is **ABC Carpet & Home,** 881 and 888 Broadway, at 19th Street (© **212/473-3000;** www.abc carpet.com), a magnet for aspiring Martha Stewarts, if there are any of those still out there. If it's actually a rug you're looking for, a whole slew of imported carpet dealers line Broadway from ABC north to about 25th Street.

Upscale retailers who have rediscovered the architectural majesty of **lower Fifth Avenue** include **Banana Republic, Victoria's Secret,** and **Kenneth Cole.** You won't find much that's new along here, but it's a pleasing stretch nonetheless.

HERALD SQUARE & THE GARMENT DISTRICT

Herald Square—where 34th Street, Sixth Avenue, and Broadway converge—is dominated by **Macy's,** W. 34th Street and Broadway (© **212/695-4400;** www.macys.com), the self-proclaimed world's biggest department store. A few blocks north of Macy's is that dowager of department stores, **Lord & Taylor,** at 424 Fifth Ave., between 38th and 39th streets (© **212/391-3344;** www.lordand taylor.com).

TIMES SQUARE & THE THEATER DISTRICT

This neighborhood has become increasingly family oriented, hence, Richard Branson's rollicking **Virgin Megastore;** the fabulous **Toys "R" Us** flagship on Broadway and 44th Street, which even has its own full-scale Ferris wheel; and the mammoth **E-Walk** retail and entertainment complex on 42nd Street between Seventh and Eighth avenues, overflowing with mall-familiar shops like the **Museum Company.**

West 47th Street between Fifth and Sixth avenues is the city's famous **Diamond District.** The street is lined shoulder-to-shoulder with showrooms; and you'll be wheeling and dealing with the largely Hasidic dealers, who offer quite a juxtaposition to the crowds. For a complete introduction to the district, including smart buying tips, point your Web browser to **www.47th-street.com**. You'll also notice a wealth of **electronics stores** throughout the neighborhood, many suspiciously trumpeting GOING OUT OF BUSINESS sales. These guys have been going out of business since the Stone Age. That's the bait and switch; pretty soon you've spent too much money for not enough stereo. If you want to check out what they have to offer, go in knowing the going price on that PDA or digital camera you're interested in. You can make a good deal if you know exactly what the market is, but these guys will be happy to suck you dry given half a chance.

FIFTH AVENUE & 57TH STREET

The heart of Manhattan retail is the corner of Fifth Avenue and 57th Street. Time was, only the very rich could shop these sacred crossroads. Such is not the case anymore, now that **Tiffany & Co.,** 727 Fifth Ave. (© **212/755-8000;**

www.tiffany.com), which has long reigned supreme here, sits a stone's throw from **Niketown,** 6 E. 57th St. (© **212/891-6453;** http://niketown.nike.com) and the **NBA Store,** 666 Fifth Ave., at 52nd Street (© **212/515-NBA1 [6221];** www.nbastore.com). In addition, a good number of mainstream retailers, like **Banana Republic,** have flagships along Fifth, further democratizing the avenue. Still, you will find a number of big-name, big-ticket designers (including big-name jewelers) radiating from the crossroads, as well as chichi department stores like **Bergdorf Goodman,** 754 Fifth Ave., at 57th Street (© **212/753-7300**); **Henri Bendel,** 712 Fifth Ave., between 55th and 56th street (© **212/247-1100**); and **Saks Fifth Avenue,** 611 Fifth Ave., at 50th Street (© **212/753-4000;** www.saksfifthavenue.com), all of which help the avenue maintain its classy cachet.

A few blocks east on Lexington is the world's flagship Bloomingdale's 1000 Third Ave., Lexington Avenue at 59th Street (© **212/705-2000;** www.bloomingdales.com), and a great place to shop.

MADISON AVENUE

Madison Avenue from 57th to 79th streets has usurped Fifth Avenue as *the* tony shopping street in the city; in fact, it boasts the most expensive retail real estate in the world. Bring lots of plastic. This ultradeluxe strip—particularly in the high 60s—is home to *the* most luxurious designer boutiques, with **Barneys New York,** 660 Madison Ave., at 61st Street (© **212/826-8900;** www.barneys.com) as its anchor.

For those of us without unlimited budgets, the good news is that stores like **Crate & Barrel** and the fabulous **Ann Taylor** flagship make the untouchable Madison Avenue seem approachable and affordable.

Upper Madison, from about 72nd to 86th streets, has become the domain of cozy-chic home stores for the uptown set, such as **A La Maison,** no. 1078, between 81st and 82nd (© **212/396-1020**), for sophisticated country French imports.

7 New York City After Dark

For the latest, most comprehensive nightlife listings, from theater and performing arts to live rock, jazz, and dance club coverage, *Time Out New York* (www.timeoutny.com) is a very good weekly source; a new issue hits newsstands every Thursday. The free weekly *Village Voice* (www.villagevoice.com), the city's legendary alterna-paper, is available late Tuesday downtown and early Wednesday in the rest of the city. The arts and entertainment coverage couldn't be more extensive, and just about every live music venue advertises its shows here. The *New York Times* (www.nytoday.com) features terrific entertainment coverage, particularly in the two-part Friday "Weekend" section.

GETTING TICKETS   Buying tickets can be simple, if the show you want to see isn't sold out. You need only call such general numbers as **TeleCharge** (© **212/239-6200;** www.telecharge.com), which handles most Broadway and Off-Broadway shows and some concerts; or **Ticketmaster** (© **212/307-4100;** www.ticketmaster.com), which also handles Broadway and Off-Broadway shows and most concerts.

DISCOUNT TICKETS   The best deal in town on same-day tickets for both Broadway and Off-Broadway shows is at the **Times Square Theatre Centre,** better known as the **TKTS** booth run by the nonprofit Theatre Development

Fund in the heart of the Theater District at Duffy Square, 47th Street and Broadway (open 3–8pm for evening performances, 10am–2pm for Wed and Sat matinees, from 11am on Sun for all performances). Tickets for that day's performances are usually offered at half price, with a few reduced only 25%, plus a $2.50 per ticket service charge. Boards outside the ticket windows list available shows; you're unlikely to find certain perennial or outsize smashes, but most other shows turn up. Only cash and traveler's checks are accepted (no credit cards). There's often a huge line, so show up early for the best availability and be prepared to wait—but frankly, the crowd is all part of the fun. If you don't care much what you see and you'd just like to go to a show, you can walk right up to the window later in the day and something's always available.

Visit **www.tdf.org** or call **NYC/Onstage** at 🕾 **212/768-1818** and press "8" for the latest TKTS information.

THE PERFORMING ARTS

Brooklyn Academy of Music *Finds*   BAM is the city's most renowned contemporary arts institution, presenting cutting-edge theater, opera, dance, and music. Offerings have included historically informed presentations of baroque opera by William Christie and Les Arts Florissants; pop opera from Lou Reed; Marianne Faithfull singing the music of Kurt Weill; dance by Mark Morris and Mikhail Baryshnikov; the Philip Glass ensemble accompanying screenings of *Koyannisqatsi* and Lugosi's original *Dracula;* the Royal Dramatic Theater of Sweden directed by Ingmar Bergman; and many more experimental works by both renowned and lesser-known international artists as well as visiting companies from all over the world. 30 Lafayette Ave. (off Flatbush Ave.), Brooklyn. 🕾 **718/636-4100.** www.bam.org. Subway: 2, 3, 4, 5, M, N, Q, R, W to Pacific St./Atlantic Ave.

Carnegie Hall   Perhaps the world's most famous performance space, Carnegie Hall offers everything from grand classics to the music of Ravi Shankar. The **Isaac Stern Auditorium,** the 2,804-seat main hall, welcomes visiting orchestras from across the country and the world. Many of the world's premier soloists and ensembles give recitals. The legendary hall is both visually and acoustically brilliant; don't miss an opportunity to experience it if there's something on that interests you.

There's also the intimate 268-seat **Weill Recital Hall,** usually used to showcase chamber music and vocal and instrumental recitals. Carnegie Hall has also, after being occupied by a movie theater for 38 years, reclaimed the ornate underground 650-seat **Zankel Concert Hall.** 881 Seventh Ave. (at 57th St.). 🕾 **212/247-7800.** www.carnegiehall.org. Subway: B, N, Q, R to 57th St.

City Center   Modern dance usually takes center stage in this Moorish dome-topped performing arts palace. The companies of Merce Cunningham, Martha Graham, Paul Taylor, Alvin Ailey, Twyla Tharp, the Dance Theatre of Harlem, and the American Ballet Theatre are often on the calendar. Don't expect cutting edge—but do expect excellence. Sight lines are terrific from all corners, and a new acoustical shell means the sound is pitch-perfect. 131 W. 55th St. (btwn Sixth and Seventh aves.). 🕾 **877/581-1212** or 212/581-1212. www.citycenter.org. Subway: F, N, Q, R, W to 57th St.; B, D, E to Seventh Ave.

Lincoln Center for the Performing Arts   New York is the world's premier performing arts city, and Lincoln Center is its premier institution. Lincoln Center's many buildings serve as permanent homes to their own companies as well as major stops for world-class performance troupes from around the globe.

Resident companies include the following: **Metropolitan Opera** (℘ 212/ **362-6000;** www.metopera.org), with it's full production of the classic repertory and schedule packed with world-class grand sopranos and tenors, the Metropolitan Opera ranks first in the world.

The opera house also hosts the **American Ballet Theatre** (℘ 212/477-3030; www.abt.org) each spring as well as visiting companies such as the Kirov, the Royal, and the Paris Opera ballets.

The **New York State Theater** (℘ 212/870-5570) is the home of the **New York City Opera** (www.nycopera.com), a superb company that not only attempts to reach a wider audience than the Met with its more "human" scale and significantly lower prices, but it's also committed to adventurous premieres, newly composed operas, plus the occasional avant-garde work. Also based here is the **New York City Ballet** (www.nycballet.com) founded by George Balanchine and highly regarded for its unsurpassed technique. The cornerstone is the Christmastime production of *The Nutcracker.*

With regard to the symphony, you'd be hard-pressed to do better than the phenomenal **New York Philharmonic** ★ (℘ 212/875-5656; www. newyork philharmonic.org), which performs at Avery Fisher Hall. Additional resident companies: The **Chamber Music Society of Lincoln Center** (℘ 212/875- **5788;** www.chambermusicsociety.org), which performs at Alice Tully Hall or the Daniel and Joanna S. Rose Rehearsal Studio, often in the company of such high-caliber guests as Anne Sofie von Otter and Midori. The **Film Society of Lincoln Center** (℘ 212/875-5600; www.filmlinc.com) screens a daily schedule of movies at the Walter Reade Theater, and hosts a number of important annual film and video festivals. **Jazz at Lincoln Center** (℘ 212/258-9800; www.jazzatlincolncenter.org) is led by the incomparable Wynton Marsalis. In the fall of 2004, Jazz at Lincoln Center is scheduled to move into its new, $128 million, 100,000-square-foot home, the Frederick P. Rose Hall in the AOL Time Warner Center on Columbus Circle. **Lincoln Center Theater** (℘ 212/362- **7600;** www.lct.org) consists of the Vivian Beaumont Theater, a modern and comfortable venue with great sight lines that has been home to much good Broadway drama and the Mitzi E. Newhouse Theater, a well-respected Off-Broadway house that has also boasted numerous theatrical triumphs.

Tickets for all performances at Avery Fisher and Alice Tully halls can be purchased through **CenterCharge** (℘ 212/721-6500) or online at www.lincoln center.org (click on "Event Calendar"). Tickets for all Lincoln Center Theater performances can be purchased thorough **TeleCharge** (℘ 212/239-6200; www. telecharge.com). Tickets for New York State Theater productions (New York City Opera and Ballet companies) are available through **Ticketmaster** (℘ 212/307- **4100;** www.ticketmaster.com), while tickets for films showing at the Walter Reade Theater can be bought up to 7 days in advance by calling ℘ 212/496-3809. 70 Lincoln Center Plaza (at Broadway and 64th St.). ℘ **212/546-2656** or 212/875-5456. www.lincoln center.org. Subway: 1, 9 to 66th St.

LIVE ROCK, JAZZ, BLUES & MORE

Beacon Theatre   This pleasing midsize Upper West Side venue—a 1928 Art Deco movie palace with an impressive lobby, stairway, and auditorium seating about 2,700—hosts mainly pop music performances, usually for the over-30 crowd. Featured acts have ranged from street-smart pop diva Sheryl Crow to not-yet-deads the Allman Brothers. 2124 Broadway (at 74th St.). ℘ **212/496-7070.** www.livetonight.com. Subway: 1, 2, 3, 9 to 72nd St.

Blue Note   The Blue Note has attracted some of the biggest names in jazz to its intimate setting. Those who've played here include just about everyone of note: Dave Brubeck, Ray Charles, B.B. King, Manhattan Transfer, Dr. John, George Duke, Chick Corea, David Sanborn, Arturo Sandoval, Gato Barbieri, and the superb Oscar Peterson. The sound system is excellent, and every seat in the house has a sight line to the stage, however, in recent years, the hard edge that once was the Blue Note has faded. Softer, smoother jazz is the domain now so if that's your thing, enjoy. But be warned prices are astronomical. There are two shows per night, and dinner is served. 131 W. 3rd St. (at Sixth Ave.). ℂ 212/475-8592. www.bluenote.net. Subway: A, C, E, F, V to W. 4th St.

The Bottom Line   The Bottom Line built its reputation by serving as a showcase for the likes of Bruce Springsteen and the Ramones, and it remains one of the city's most well-respected venues. Shawn Colvin, Robyn Hitchcock, Lucinda Williams, Emmylou Harris, and David Johansen (and alter-ego Buster Poindexter, natch) are among the artists who make this their favored venue for area appearances. There are usually two shows nightly. 15 W. 4th St. (at Mercer St.). ℂ 212/502-3471 or 212/228-6300. www.bottomlinecabaret.com. Subway: N, R to Astor Place; A, C, E, F, V to W. 4th St.

CBGB   The original downtown rock club has seen better days, but no other spot is so rich with rock-and-roll history. This was the launching pad for New York punk and New Wave: the Ramones, Blondie, Talking Heads, the Cramps, Patti Smith—everybody got started here. These days, you've probably never heard of most acts performing here. Never mind—CB's still rocks. Expect loud and cynical, and you're unlikely to come away disappointed. 315 Bowery (at Bleecker St.). ℂ 212/982-4052, or 212/677-0455 for CB's 313 Gallery. www.cbgb.com. Subway: F to Second Ave.; 6 to Bleecker St.

Jazz Standard   Kudos to the Jazz Standard, where both the food and the music meet all expectations. Boasting a sophisticated retro-speakeasy vibe, the Jazz Standard is one of the city's largest jazz clubs, with well-spaced tables seating 150 and a reasonable $15 to $25 cover. The rule is straightforward, mainstream jazz by new and established musicians. A limited menu from Dannys Meyer's barbecue joint, Blue Smoke, located upstairs is available. 116 E. 27th St. (btwn Park Ave. S. and Lexington Ave.). ℂ 212/576-2232. www.jazzstandard.net. Subway: 6 to 28th St.

The Knitting Factory   New York's premier avant-garde music venue has four separate spaces, each showcasing performances ranging from experimental jazz and acoustic folk to spoken-word and poetry readings to out-there multimedia works. Regulars who use the Knitting Factory as their lab of choice include former Lounge Lizard John Lurie; around-the-bend experimentalist John Zorn; guitar gods Vernon Reid and David Torn; and Television's Richard Lloyd. (If these names mean nothing to you, chances are good that the Knitting Factory is not for you.) There are often two show times a night in the remarkably pleasing main performance space. 74 Leonard St. (btwn Broadway and Church St.). ℂ 212/219-3006. www.knittingfactory.com. Subway: 1, 9 to Franklin St.

S.O.B.'s   If you like your music hot, hot, hot, visit S.O.B.'s, the city's top world-music venue, specializing in Brazilian, Caribbean, and Latin sounds. The packed house dances and sings along nightly to calypso, samba, mambo, African drums, reggae, or other global grooves, united in the high-energy, feel-good vibe. Bookings include top-flight performers from around the globe; Astrud Gilberto,

Mighty Sparrow, King Sunny Ade, Eddie Palmieri, and Beausoleil, are only a few of the names who have graced this lively stage. This place is so popular that it's an excellent idea to book in advance, especially if you'd like table seating. Monday is dedicated to Latin sounds, Tuesday to reggae; Friday features a late-night French Caribbean dance party, while Saturday is reserved for samba. 204 Varick St. (at Houston St.). ✆ 212/243-4940. www.sobs.com. Subway: 1, 9 to Houston St.

Village Underground *Finds* The folks behind dearly departed Tramps have opened this intimate, comfortable, and even somewhat romantic subterranean venue. Some surprisingly big-name talent has been in the house of late, including Buckwheat Zydeco and Evan Dando. But even if you don't recognize the names, you can count on a night of quality music. You can buy advance tickets online at **www.tickeweb.com** or by calling ✆ **866/468-7619.** 130 W. 3rd St. (btwn Sixth Ave. and Macdougal St.). ✆ **212/777-7745.** www.thevillageunderground.com. Subway: A, C, E, F, V to W. 4th (use W. 3rd St. exit).

The Village Vanguard What CBGB is to rock, the Village Vanguard is to jazz. One look at the photos on the walls will show you who's been through since 1935, from Coltrane, Miles, and Monk to recent appearances by Wynton Marsalis and Chuchu Valdes. Expect a mix of established names and high-quality local talent, including the Vanguard's own jazz orchestra on Monday nights. The sound is great, but sight lines aren't, so come early for a front table. 178 Seventh Ave. South (just below 11th St.). ✆ **212/255-4037.** www.villagevanguard.net. Subway: 1, 2, 3, 9 to 14th St.

CABARET

Cafe Carlyle This is where you'll find Bobby Short—and that's all those who know cabaret need to know. Nothing evokes the essence of Manhattan more than an evening with this quintessential interpreter of Porter and the Gershwins. You might want to catch him while you still can; I've heard rumblings that he has been considering retiring soon. When he's not in residence, you'll find such rarefied talents as Eartha Kitt and Betty Buckley. The room is intimate and as swanky as they come. Expect a high tab—admission is $60 with $30 per-person minimum; dinner and two people could easily cost $300—but if you're looking for the best of the best, look no further. On most Mondays, Woody Allen joins the Eddy Davis New Orleans Jazz Band on clarinet to swing Dixie style ($75 cover). At the Carlyle hotel, 781 Madison Ave. (at 76th St.). ✆ **212/744-1600.** Closed July–Aug. Subway: 6 to 77th St.

Feinstein's at the Regency *Finds* This intimate and elegant cabaret-style nightclub is the first from Grammy-winning song impresario Michael Feinstein. Cover charges can soar, but you can count on a memorable night of first-quality dining and song, and no other cabaret merges old-school cool and hipster appeal so well. Recent high-wattage talent has included Keely Smith, Jimmy Webb, the Smothers Brothers, and the man himself. Call ahead to reserve; you can also purchase tickets through Ticketmaster. At the Regency Hotel, 540 Park Ave. (at 61st St.). ✆ **212/339-4095,** or 212/307-4100 for Ticketmaster. www.feinsteinsattheregency.com or www.ticketmaster.com. Subway: 4, 5, 6 to 59th St.

COMEDY

Carolines on Broadway Caroline Hirsch presents today's hottest headliners in her upscale Theater District showroom, which doesn't have a bad seat in the house. You're bound to recognize at least one or two of the established names and hot up-and-comers on the bill in any given week, like Dave Chapelle, Janeane Garofalo,

Colin Quinn, Lewis Black, or Kathy Griffin. Monday is usually New Talent Night. 1626 Broadway (btwn 49th and 50th sts.). ℂ **212/757-4100.** www.carolines.com. Subway: N, R to 49th St.; 1, 9 to 50th St.

Gotham Comedy Club *Finds* Here's the city's trendiest, most comfortable, and most sophisticated comedy club. The young talent—Tom Rhodes, Sue Costello, Mitch Fatel, Lewis Black of the *Daily Show*—is red hot. Look for theme nights like "Comedy Salsa" and "A Very Jewish Christmas." Tuesday is set aside for new talent. 34 W. 22nd St. (btwn Fifth and Sixth aves.). ℂ **212/367-9000.** www.gothamcomedy club.com. Subway: F, N, R to 23rd St.

BARS & COCKTAIL LOUNGES
DOWNTOWN

dba *Finds* Dba has completely bucked the loungey trend that has taken over the city, instead remaining firmly and resolutely an unpretentious neighborhood bar. It's a beer- and scotch-lover's paradise, with a massive drink menu on giant chalkboards. Excellent jukebox. 41 First Ave. (btwn 2nd and 3rd sts.). ℂ **212/475-5097.** www.drinkgoodstuff.com. Subway: F to Second Ave.

Double Happiness *Finds* The only indicator to the subterranean entrance is a vertical WATCH YOUR STEP sign. Once through the door, you'll find a beautifully designed speakeasy-ish lounge with artistic nods to the neighborhood throughout, plus a wonderfully low-key vibe. The space is large, but a low ceiling and intimate nooks add a hint of romance. Don't miss the green tea martini, an inspired house creation. 173 Mott St. (btwn Grand and Broome sts.). ℂ **212/941-1282.** Subway: 6 to Spring St.

Rise Bar Rise Bar is doing a lovely job of filling the fancy-cocktails-with-a-side-of-spectacular views bill now that the World Trade Center's glorious Greatest Bar on Earth is gone. Situated on the 14th floor of **Ritz-Carlton**'s brand-new Battery Park hotel (p. 90), this sleek and lovely bar boasts fantastic harbor views starring Lady Liberty, plus a massive waterfront terrace for enjoying warm-weather libations. Reservations are accepted, if you want to guarantee yourself a prime seat. In the Ritz-Carlton New York, Battery Park, 2 West St. (at the end of West St., just north of Battery Place). ℂ **212/344-0800.** Subway: 4, 5 to Bowling Green.

White Horse Tavern Poets and literary buffs pop into this 1880 pub to pay their respects to Dylan Thomas, who tipped his last jar here before shuffling off this mortal coil. Best enjoyed in the warm weather when there's outdoor drinking, or at happy hour for the cheap drafts that draw in a big frat-boy/yuppie crowd. 567 Hudson St. (at 11th St.). ℂ **212/243-9260.** Subway: 1, 9 to Christopher St.

MIDTOWN

Bull and Bear The Bull and Bear is like a gentlemen's pub, with brass-studded red leather chairs, a waistcoated staff, and a grand troika-shaped mahogany bar polished to a high sheen at the center of the room. Still, it's plenty comfy for casual drinkers. Ask Oscar, who's been here for more than 30 years, or one of the other accomplished bartenders to blend you a classic cocktail like The Bronx, a combination of gin, orange juice, and fresh pineapple juice. An ideal place to kick back after a hard day of sightseeing. In the Waldorf=Astoria, 301 Park Ave., between 49th and 50th sts. ℂ **212/872-4900.** Subway: 6 to 51st St.

The Campbell Apartment This swank lounge on the mezzanine level at Grand Central Terminal has been created out of the former business office of prewar businessman John W. Campbell, who transformed the space into a pre-Renaissance palace worthy of a Medici. Try to snag a seat in the little-used upstairs room if you want some quiet. Call ahead before heading over, as the space tends to be closed for private parties on a rather frequent basis. In Grand Central Terminal, 15 Vanderbilt Ave. ℭ 212/953-0409. Subway: S, 4, 5, 6, 7 to 42nd St./Grand Central.

Hudson Bar   Outfitted like a futuristic canteen, Hudson Bar, in the Hudson Hotel glows from below with an underlit floor, while the low ceiling wears a Crayola-like fresco by Francesco Clemente. In between you'll find a tony, older-than-you'd-expect crowd. The one-of-a-kind cocktail menu is terrific, too. Enter at street level, on the Ninth Avenue side of the hotel's main entrance; dress well to avoid attitude. 356 W. 58th St. (btwn Eighth and Ninth aves.). ℭ 212/554-6000. Subway: A, B, C, D, 1, 9 to 59th St./Columbus Circle.

King Cole Bar   The birthplace of the Bloody Mary, this theatrical spot may just be New York's most historic hotel bar. The Maxfield Parrish mural alone is worth the price of a classic cocktail (ask the bartender to tell you about the "hidden" meaning of the painting). The one drawback is the bar's small size; after-work hours and holiday times the bar is jammed. At the St. Regis Hotel, 2 E. 55th St. (at Fifth Ave.) ℭ 212/744-4300. Subway: E, F to 53rd St.

Mickey Mantle's   Before Mickey Mantle's officially opened some years ago I was walking past the restaurant, peered into the window, and there was my boyhood idol, the Mick, sitting at the bar by himself. Through the window I waved—and he waved back. It made my day. And though the food's not very good and the drinks are overpriced, I still have a soft spot for Mickey Mantle's and always will. With plenty of Yankee memorabilia on the walls and sports on all the televisions, it's an ideal place to watch a game but stick with the basics: beer and burgers. 42 Central Park South (btwn Fifth and Sixth aves.). ℭ 212/688-7777. www.mickeymantles.com. Subway: F to 57th St.

Pete's Tavern   The oldest continually operating establishment in the city, Pete's opened while Lincoln was still president. It reeks of genuine history—this is where O. Henry wrote the Christmas tale "Gift of the Magi." Pete's is the kind of place where you go to warm up on a cold winter's night with a dark creamy comforting Guinness. And that Guinness doesn't taste too bad in the summer when Pete's sidewalk cafe is open. 129 E. 18th St. (at Irving Place). ℭ 212/473-7676. Subway: L, N, R, 4, 5, 6 to 14th St./Union Sq.

Rainbow Room   Skip eating here, but come to this legendary bar, sip a too-expensive cocktail and soak in the ambience, views, and live piano music. No jeans or sneakers, please. 30 Rockefeller Plaza (entrance on 49th St. btwn Fifth and Sixth aves.), 64th floor. ℭ 212/632-5000. www.cipriani.com/rainbowroom.html. Subway: B, D, F, V to 47th–50th sts./Rockefeller Center.

UPTOWN

Bemelmans Bar   White-coated service, lush seating with many dark romantic corners to sink into, a nice mix of locals and guests, and incredible cocktails, like the Old Cuban, a *mojito* topped with champagne. At the Carlyle Hotel, 35 E. 76th St. (at Madison Ave.) ℭ 212/744-1600. Subway: 6 to 77th St.

Dublin House   For years, like a welcoming beacon, the Dublin House's neon harp has blinked invitingly. This very old pub is a no-frills Irish saloon and the perfect spot for a drink after visiting the nearby Museum of Natural History or Central Park. There's a long, narrow barroom up front and a bigger room in the back that's good for groups. The Guinness is cheap and drawn perfectly by the very able and sometimes crusty bartenders. Stay away on weekend nights and St. Patrick's Day when the place is overrun with amateurs; frat boys and sorority girls on pub crawls. 225 W. 79th St. (btwn Broadway and Amsterdam Ave.). ℂ **212/874-9528.** Subway: 1, 9 to 79th St.

Great Hall Balcony Bar *Moments*   One of Manhattan's best cocktail bars is only open on Friday and Saturday—and only from 4 to 8:30pm, to boot. The Metropolitan Museum of Art transforms the lobby's mezzanine level into a cocktail-and-classical music lounge twice weekly, offering a marvelous only-in-New York experience. The music is usually provided by a grand piano and string quartet. You'll have to pay the $10 admission, but the galleries are open until 9pm. At the Metropolitan Museum of Art, Fifth Ave. at 82nd St. ℂ **212/535-7710.** www.met museum.org. Subway: 4, 5, 6 to 86th St.

DANCE CLUBS

Centro-Fly   Anyone who remembers the old rock-and-roll joint Tramps won't believe the swank Op Art club that fills the space now. The place lures top-notch deejay talent ranging from Junior Sanchez to Dimitri from Paris to Grandmaster Flash. Depending on the night, look for deep house, hip-hop, or another edgy music mix. The Friday-night funky-soulful British house party GBH (www.gbh.tv), New York's longest-running house party, may be the best reason to come. 45 W. 21st St. (btwn Fifth and Sixth aves.). ℂ **212/627-7770,** or 212/539-3916 for GBH info/guest lists. www.centrofly.com. Subway: F to 23rd St.; N, R to 23rd St.

Club Shelter   House heads flock to this old-school disco. The big draw is the "Saturday Night Shelter Party" when late '80s House music takes over. The crowd is racially and sexually diverse and dress is not fancy; wear whatever is comfortable for doing some heavy sweating on the dance floor. At press time, live acts such as Patti LaBelle were set to be added. 20 W. 39th St. (btwn Fifth and Sixth aves.). ℂ **212/719-9867.** Subway: B, D, F, Q, V, 7 to 42nd St.

Nell's   If you're going to spend one night out on the town, here's the place to do it. Nell's calls itself "The Classic New York Nightclub," and it has well earned the moniker. Nell's was the first to establish a loungelike atmosphere years ago and it has been endlessly copied by restaurateurs and nightclub owners. Nell's attracts a grown-up crowd that ranges from homeboys to Wall Streeters. Although the entertainment can run the gamut from comedy and spoken word to Cuban sounds, most of the parties have a soulful edge. 246 W. 14th St. (btwn Seventh and Eighth aves.). ℂ **212/675-1567.** www.nells.com. Subway: A, C, E, 1, 2, 3, 9 to 14th St.

Shine   Shine draws a well-dressed crowd to TriBeCa with a loungey vibe and a few well-placed 21st-century twists—most notably, great cocktails, terrific deejay talent from around the globe, and a blessedly attitude-free door policy, especially for a dance scene this cool. The cavernous, high-ceilinged space and elevated center stage allows for all manner of cabaret and performance art, which can run the gamut from classic to kooky and can include risqué circus acts, burlesque, or live reggae bands. 285 W. Broadway (just south of Canal St.). ℂ **212/941-0900.** www.shinelive.com. Subway: A, C, E, 1, 9 to Canal St.

8 Highlights of the Outer Boroughs

THE BRONX

Bronx Zoo Wildlife Conservation Park ★★★ *Kids*   Founded in 1899, the Bronx Zoo is the largest metropolitan animal park in the United States, with more than 4,000 animals living on 265 acres. This is an extremely progressive zoo as zoos go—most of the old-fashioned cages have been replaced by more natural settings, ongoing improvements keep it feeling fresh and up to date, and it's far more bucolic than you might expect. In fact, I think it's one of the city's best attractions.

One of the most impressive exhibits is the **Wild Asia Complex.** This zoo-within-a-zoo comprises the **Wild Asia Plaza** education center; **Jungle World,** an indoor re-creation of Asian forests with birds, lizards, gibbons, and leopards; and the **Bengali Express Monorail** (open May–Oct), which takes you on a nar-rated ride high above free-roaming Siberian tigers, Asian elephants, Indian rhi-noceroses, and other nonnative New Yorkers (keep your eyes peeled—the animals aren't as interested in seeing you). The **Himalayan Highlands** is home to some 17 extremely rare snow leopards, as well as red pandas and white-naped cranes. The 6½-acre **Congo Gorilla Forest** is home to Western lowland goril-las, okapi, red river hogs, and other African rain-forest animals.

The **Children's Zoo** (open Apr–Oct) allows young humans to learn about their wildlife counterparts. Kids can compare their leaps to those of a bullfrog, slide into a turtle shell, climb into a heron's nest, see with the eyes of an owl, and hear with the acute ears of a fox. There's also a petting zoo.

To beat the crowds, try to visit on a weekday or on a nice winter's day. In sum-mer, come early, before the heat of the day sends the animals back into their enclosures. Expect to spend an entire day here—you'll need it.

Getting there: Liberty Lines' BxM11 express bus, which makes various stops on Madison Avenue, will take you directly to the zoo; call ✆ **718/652-8400.** By subway, take the 2 train to Pelham Parkway and then walk west to the Bronx-dale entrance.

Fordham Rd. and Bronx River Pkwy., the Bronx. ✆ 718/367-1010. www.wcs.org/zoos. Admission $9 adults, $6 seniors, $5 children 2–12; discounted admission Nov–Mar; free Wed year-round. There may be nominal additional charges for some exhibits. Nov–Mar daily 10am–4:30pm (extended hours for Holiday Lights late Nov to early Jan); Apr–Oct Mon–Fri 10am–5pm, Sat–Sun 10am–5:30pm. Transportation: See "Getting There," above.

New York Botanical Garden ⟨★⟩   A National Historic Landmark, the 250-acre New York Botanical Garden was founded in 1891 and today is one of America's foremost public gardens. The setting is spectacular—a natural terrain of rock out-croppings, a river with cascading waterfalls, hills, ponds, and wetlands.

Highlights of the Botanical Garden are the 27 **specialty gardens,** an exceptional **orchid collection,** and 40 acres of **uncut forest** as close as New York gets to its vir-gin state before the arrival of Europeans. The **Enid A. Haupt Conservatory,** a stun-ning series of Victorian glass pavilions that recall London's former Crystal Palace, shelters a rich collection of tropical, subtropical, and desert plants as well as seasonal flower shows. There are so many ways to see the garden—tram, golf cart, walking tours—that it's best to call or check the website for more information.

Getting there: Take Metro-North (✆ **800/METRO-INFO** or 212/532-4900; www.mta.nyc.ny.us/mnr) from Grand Central Terminal to the New York Botanical Garden station; the easy ride takes about 20 minutes. By subway, take the D or 4 train to Bedford Park, then take bus Bx26 or walk southeast on Bed-ford Park Boulevard for 8 long blocks. The garden operates a shuttle to and from Manhattan April through October on Fridays and weekends, Saturdays only in November and December. Round-trip shuttle and garden tickets are $15 for adults, $12 for seniors and students, $9 for children 2 to 12; call ✆ **718/817-8779** for reservations.

200th St. and Southern Blvd., the Bronx. © 718/817-8700. www.nybg.org. Admission $3 adults, $2 seniors and students, $1 children 2–12. Extra charges for Everett Children's Adventure Garden, Enid A. Haupt Conservatory, T. H. Everett Rock Garden, Native Plant Garden, and narrated tram tour; entire Garden Passport package is $10 adults, $7.50 seniors and students, $4 children 2–12. Apr–Oct Tues–Sun and Mon holidays 10am–6pm; Nov–Mar Tues–Sun and Mon holidays 10am–5pm. Transportation: See "Getting There," above.

BROOKLYN

For details on walking the **Brooklyn Bridge,** see p. 116.

It's easy to link visits to the Brooklyn Botanic Garden, the Brooklyn Museum of Art, and Prospect Park, since they're all an easy walk from one another, just off **Grand Army Plaza.** Designed by Frederick Law Olmsted and Calvert Vaux as a suitably grand entrance to their Prospect Park, it boasts a grand Civil War memorial arch designed by John H. Duncan (1892–1901) and the main **Brooklyn Public Library,** an Art Deco masterpiece completed in 1941 (the garden and museum are just on the other side of the library, down Eastern Parkway). The entire area is a half-hour subway ride from Midtown Manhattan.

Brooklyn Botanic Garden ⭐ Just down the street from the Brooklyn Museum of Art (below) is the most popular botanic garden in the city. This peaceful 52-acre sanctuary is at its most spectacular in May, when thousands of deep pink blossoms of cherry trees are abloom. Well worth seeing is the spectacular **Cranford Rose Garden,** one of the largest and finest in the country; the **Shakespeare Garden,** an English garden featuring plants mentioned in his writings; a **Children's Garden;** the **Osborne Garden,** a 3-acre formal garden; the **Fragrance Garden,** designed for the blind but appreciated by all noses; and the extraordinary **Japanese Hill-and-Pond Garden.** The renowned **C. V. Starr Bonsai Museum** is home to the world's oldest and largest collection of bonsai, while the impressive $2.5 million Steinhardt Conservatory holds the garden's extensive indoor plant collection.

1000 Washington Ave. (at Eastern Pkwy.), Brooklyn. © 718/623-7200. www.bbg.org. Admission $3 adults, $1.50 seniors and students, free for children under 16; free to all Tues and Sat 10am–noon year-round, plus Wed–Fri from mid-Nov to mid-Mar. Apr–Sept Tues–Fri 8am–6pm, Sat–Sun 10am–6pm; Oct–Mar Tues–Fri 8am–4:30pm, Sat–Sun 10am–4:30pm. Subway: Q to Prospect Park; 2, 3 to Eastern Pkwy./Brooklyn Museum.

Brooklyn Museum of Art ⭐⭐ One of the nation's premier art institutions, the Brooklyn Museum of Art rocketed back into the public consciousness in 1999 with the hugely controversial "Sensation: Young British Artists from the Saatchi Collection," which drew international media attention and record crowds who came to see just what an artist—and a few conservative politicians—could make out of a little elephant dung.

Indeed, the museum is best known for its consistently remarkable temporary exhibitions—which ranged from "The Last Expression: Art and Auschwitz" to "Pulp Art: From the Collection of Robert Lesser" in mid-2003 alone—as well as its excellent permanent collection, most notably the Egyptian, Classical, and Ancient Middle Eastern collection of sculpture, wall reliefs, and mummies. The distinguished decorative arts collection includes 28 American period rooms from 1675 to 1928. Other highlights are the African and Asian arts galleries, dozens of works by Rodin, a good costumes and textiles collection, and a diverse collection of both American and European painting and sculpture that includes works by Homer, O'Keeffe, Monet, Cézanne, and Degas.

The museum's ambitious and popular **First Saturday** program takes place on, you guessed it, the first Saturday of each month. It runs from 5 to 11pm and includes free admission and a line-up of live music, films, dancing, curator talks, and other entertainment that can get pretty esoteric—think karaoke, lesbian poetry, silent film, experimental jazz, and disco. You can always count on a full slate of cool.

200 Eastern Pkwy. (at Washington Ave.), Brooklyn. © **718/638-5000.** www.brooklynmuseum.org. Suggested admission $6 adults, $3 seniors and students, free for children under 12; free first Sat of the month 11am–11pm. Wed–Fri 10am–5pm; first Sat of the month 11am–11pm, each Sat thereafter 11am–6pm; Sun 11am–6pm. Subway: 2, 3 to Eastern Pkwy./Brooklyn Museum.

New York Aquarium *Kids*   Because of the long subway ride (about an hour from Midtown Manhattan) and its proximity to the Coney Island boardwalk, this one is really for summer. This surprisingly good aquarium is home to hundreds of sea creatures. Taking center stage are Atlantic bottle-nosed dolphins and California sea lions that perform daily during summer at the **Aquatheater.** Also basking in the spotlight are gangly Pacific octopuses, sharks, and a brand-new sea horse exhibit. Black-footed penguins, California sea otters, and a variety of seals live at the **Sea Cliffs exhibit,** a re-creation of a Pacific coastal habitat. But my absolute favorites are the beautiful white Beluga whales, which exude buckets of aquatic charm. Children love the hands-on exhibits at **Discovery Cove.** There's an indoor oceanview cafeteria and an outdoor snack bar, plus picnic tables.

If you've made the trip out, you simply must check out the human exhibits on nearby **Coney Island**'s 2¾-mile-long boardwalk. Not much is left from its heyday, and it can be a little eerie when the crowds aren't around. But you can still use the beach, drop some cash at the boardwalk arcade, and ride the famed wooden **Cyclone** roller coaster (still a terrifying ride, if only because it seems so . . . rickety). You can't leave without treating yourself to a **Nathan's Famous** hot dog, just off the boardwalk at Surf and Stillwell avenues. This is the original—where the term *hot dog* was coined back in 1906.

502 Surf Ave. (at W. 8th St.), Coney Island, Brooklyn. © **718/265-3400.** www.nyaquarium.com. Admission $11 adults, $7 seniors and children 2–12. Open 365 days 10am–4:30pm. Subway: D, F to W. 8th St., Brooklyn.

Prospect Park ★★   Designed by Frederick Law Olmsted and Calvert Vaux after their great success with Central Park, this 562 acres of woodland, meadows, bluffs, and ponds is considered by many to be their masterpiece and the pièce de résistance of Brooklyn.

The best approach is from Grand Army Plaza, presided over by the monumental **Soldiers' and Sailors' Memorial Arch** (1892) honoring Union veterans. For the best view of the lush landscape, follow the path to Meadowport Arch, and proceed through to the Long Meadow, following the path that loops around it (it's about an hour's walk). Other park highlights include the 1857 Italianate mansion **Litchfield Villa** on Prospect Park West; the **Friends' Cemetery** Quaker burial ground (where Montgomery Clift is eternally prone—sorry, it's fenced off to browsers); the wonderful 1906 beaux arts **boathouse;** the 1912 **carousel,** with white wooden horses salvaged from a famous Coney Island merry-go-round (open Apr–Oct; rides 50¢); and **Lefferts Homestead Children's Historic House Museum** (© **718/965-7777**), a 1783 Dutch farmhouse with a museum of period furniture and exhibits geared to kids (open Apr–Nov Fri–Sun 1–4pm). There's a map at the park entrance that you can use to get your bearings.

On the east side of the park is the **Prospect Park Zoo** (© **718/399-7339**). This is a thoroughly modern children's zoo where kids can walk among wallabies, explore a prairie-dog town, and much more. Admission is $2.50 for adults, $1.25 for seniors, 50¢ for children 3 to 12. April through October, open Monday through Friday 10am to 5pm, to 5:30pm weekends and holidays; November through March, open daily from 10am to 4:30pm.

At Grand Army Plaza, bounded by Prospect Park West, Parkside Ave., and Flatbush Ave., Brooklyn. ℂ **718/ 965-8951,** or 718/965-8999 for events information. www.prospectpark.org. Subway: 2, 3 to Grand Army Plaza (walk down Plaza St. W. 3 blocks to Prospect Park W. and the entrance) or Eastern Pkwy./Brooklyn Museum.

BROOKLYN HEIGHTS HISTORIC DISTRICT

Bounded by the East River, Fulton Street, Court Street, and Atlantic Avenue, the Brooklyn Heights Historic District is one of the most outstanding and easily accessible sights beyond Manhattan. The neighborhood is reachable via a number of subway trains: the A, C, F to Jay St.; the 2, 3, 4, 5 to Clark Street or Borough Hall; and the N, R to Court Street.

It's easy to link a walk around Brooklyn Heights and along its Promenade with a walk over the **Brooklyn Bridge** (p. 116), a tour that makes for a lovely afternoon on a nice day. Take a 2 or 3 train to **Clark Street** (the first stop in Brooklyn). Turn right out of the station and walk toward the water, where you'll see the start of the waterfront **Brooklyn Promenade.** Stroll along the promenade admiring both the stellar views of lower Manhattan to the left and the gorgeous multimillion-dollar brownstones to the right, or park yourself on a bench for a while to contemplate the scene.

The promenade ends at Columbia Heights and Orange Street. To head to the bridge from here, turn left and walk toward the Watchtower Building. Before heading downslope, turn right immediately after the playground onto Middagh Street. After 4 or 5 blocks, you'll reach a busy thoroughfare, Cadman Plaza West. Cross the street and follow the walkway through little **Cadman Plaza Park;** veer left at the fork in the walkway. At Cadman Plaza East, turn left (downslope) toward the underpass, where you'll find the stairwell up to the Brooklyn Bridge footpath on your left.

Note: If you need incentive to walk across the bridge, **Grimaldi's,** 19 Old Fulton St., between Front and Water streets in Brooklyn Heights (ℂ **718/858-4300)** easily provides it with delicious pizza made in a coal-oven with a rich flavorful sauce and homemade mozzarella.

QUEENS

In summer 2002, the **Museum of Modern Art** closed its main midtown Manhattan campus for a 3-year renovation project, and opened an interim exhibit space in Long Island City called **MoMA QNS** ⚘, which is well worth the easy subway ride to Queens. See p. 118 for more details.

When you head out to MoMA QNS, consider making a day of it. **Queens Artlink** (www.moma.org/qal) is a free weekend arts shuttle, running Saturday and Sunday from 11:30am to 5:30pm and linking all of the institutions listed below (except for the Queens Museum of Art). You can also catch a weekend ride on the **Long Island City Art Loop,** a free shuttle bus service between the Noguchi Museum, the Socrates Sculpture Park, and P.S. 1 Saturday and Sunday between noon and 6pm. Any participating institution can answer further questions about either shuttle.

For details on the **New York Hall of Science** and **Flushing Meadows–Corona Park** (also home to the Queens Museum of Art, below), see p. 133.

American Museum of the Moving Image ★ *Kids*   Head here if you truly love movies. It's housed in part of the Kaufman Astoria Studios, which once were host to W. C. Fields and the Marx Brothers, and more recently have been used by Martin Scorsese *(The Age of Innocence)*, Woody Allen *(Radio Days)*, Bill Cosby (his *Cosby* TV series), and *Sesame Street.*

The museum's core exhibit, **"Behind the Screen,"** is a thoroughly engaging two-floor installation that takes you step-by-step through the process of making, marketing, and exhibiting moving images. There are more than 1,000 artifacts on hand, from technological gadgetry to costumes, and interactive exhibits where you can try your own hand at sound-effects editing or create your own animated shorts, among other simulations. Also on display are sets from *Seinfeld*. Even better are the daily hands-on demonstrations, where you can watch film editors, animators, and the like at work.

35th Ave. at 36th St., Astoria, Queens. © 718/784-0077. www.ammi.org. Admission $8.50 adults, $5.50 seniors and college students, $4.50 children 5–18. Free for children under 5. Tues–Fri noon–5pm; Sat–Sun 11am–6pm (evening screenings Sat–Sun at 6:30pm). Subway: R to Steinway St.; N to Broadway.

Isamu Noguchi Garden Museum ★ *Finds*   No place in the city is more Zen than this marvelous indoor/outdoor garden museum showcasing the work of Japanese American sculptor Isamu Noguchi (1904–88). Unfortunately, the original building in Long Island City, built in 1927 and purchased by Noguchi in 1975, has been closed for renovation, but is scheduled to re-open April 2004. Until the renovations are complete, the museum has established temporary exhibition space in nearby Sunnyside, Queens. Before heading out, however, check website or call to confirm where the museum will be located. In Sunnyside, space is limited to indoor exhibitions, it's still worth visiting to see a beautifully curated collection of the artist's masterworks in stone, metal, wood, and clay; you'll even see theater sets, furniture, and models for public gardens and playgrounds that Noguchi designed. A free, guided tour is offered at 2pm. The museum shop will continue to sell Noguchi's Akari lamps as well as books, cards, posters, and the like.

Temporary site: 36-01 43rd Ave. (at 36th St.). Sunnyside, Queens. Subway: 7 to 33rd St. Walk north to 36th St., turn left and go 1 block to 43rd Ave. Original location, returning spring 2003: 32–37 Vernon Blvd. (at 33rd Rd.), Long Island City, Queens. Subway: N to Broadway. Walk west on Broadway toward Manhattan until Broadway ends at Vernon Blvd.; turn left on Vernon and go 2 blocks. © 718/204-7088. www.noguchi.org. Suggested admission $4 adults, $2 seniors and students. Wed–Fri 10am–5pm; Sat–Sun 11am–6pm.

P.S. 1 Contemporary Art Center   If you're interested in contemporary art that's too cutting-edge for most museums, don't miss this MoMA affiliate museum. Reinaugurated in 1997 after a 3-year $8.5 million renovation of the Renaissance Revival building that was originally a public school (hence the name), this is the world's largest institution exhibiting contemporary art from America and abroad. You can expect to see a kaleidoscopic array of works from artists ranging from Jack Smith to Julian Schnabel; the museum is particularly well known for large-scale exhibitions by artists such as James Turrell.

22–25 Jackson Ave. (at 46th Ave.), Long Island City, Queens. © 718/784-2084. www.ps1.org. Suggested admission $5 adults, $2 seniors and students. Thurs–Mon noon–6pm. Subway: E, V to 23rd St./Ely Ave. (walk 2 blocks south on Jackson Ave. to 46th Ave.); 7 to 45th Rd./Court House Sq. (walk 1 block south on Jackson Ave.).

Queens Museum of Art   One way to see New York in the shortest time (albeit without the street life) is to visit the Panorama, created for the 1939 World's Fair, an enormous building-for-building architectural model of New York City complete with an airplane that takes off from LaGuardia Airport. Also on permanent display is a collection of Tiffany glass manufactured at Tiffany Studios in Queens between 1893 and 1938. The *Contemporary Currents* series features rotating exhibits focusing on the works of a single artist, often with an international theme (suitable to New York's most diverse borough). History buffs should take note of the museum's NYC Building, which housed the United Nation's General Assembly from 1946 to 1952. Rotating art exhibitions, tours, lectures, films, and performances are part of the program, making this a very strong museum on all fronts.

Next to the Unisphere in Flushing Meadows–Corona Park, Queens. ℂ 718/592-9700. www.queensmuse. org. Suggested admission $5 adults, $2.50 seniors and students, free for children under 5. Tues–Fri 10am–5pm; Sat–Sun noon–5pm. Subway: 7 to Willets Point/Shea Stadium (follow the yellow signs for the 10-min. walk through the park to the museum, which sits next to the Unisphere).

6

Long Island & the Hamptons

by Rich Beattie

You've likely heard some joke about Long Island: its malls, its distinctive accent, the ungodly traffic on the Long Island Expressway (LIE). Here's the truth about the largest island adjoining the continental U.S: Yes, there are malls, yes, some people have an accent, and absolutely the traffic on the LIE can be nightmarish. Part of it is, after all, a gigantic suburb of New York City.

But look beyond that and you'll find an island ringed by some of the nation's—some would say the world's—best beaches, a thin stretch of land dotted with award-winning wineries, and an area full of some of America's earliest history.

The key to visiting is to stick close to the shoreline: Obviously that's where you'll find the beach-based recreation, along with great views of the Atlantic and the Long Island Sound. It's also where you'll find the most interesting and dramatic examples of its history, remnants from the early European residents who were whalers in seaside villages and wealthy industrialists who built homes here and insisted on co-opting those water views for themselves.

Drive east along the north shore, through the towns of Sandy Point and Oyster Bay, and you'll see where those barons built their palatial playhouses.

Continue out to the North Fork and you'll find a laid-back world that has yet to catch up with the modern era: farm stands, vineyards, antiques shops, and little towns that still bear the marks of their 17th-century whaling past.

Along the Southern Shore, Jones Beach and Long Beach make great day trips from New York City, while Fire Island is a magical, car-less beach community and a world unto itself. Go out to the Hamptons, the beachy playground for New York City-based celebs, and you may just catch an impromptu Billy Joel concert or dine next to Martha Stewart. It's just 100 miles from the New York City border to the island's easternmost tip at Montauk, but out there you'll find an entirely different culture, where playing hard is a way of life. And tucked in between the North and South forks is tiny Shelter Island, another small piece of pristine earth that completes the playground that is Long Island.

1 The North Shore ★

From Great Neck to Wading River

Drive slowly along the quiet back roads of Long Island's north shore and you just might hear it: the faint murmur of a rollicking party, with ghostly musicians stirring up hot jazz as bootleg liquor flows as freely as the wealth. The towns that line the coast have been inhabited by some of America's richest for decades, and that still holds true: Towns like Great Neck and Sea Cliff have cute "downtowns," while just outside lie homes of mammoth proportions. Drive along Route 25A into Suffolk County and the towns become even cuter: Northport, Stony Brook, and Port Jefferson give new meaning to the word "quaint."

Long Island

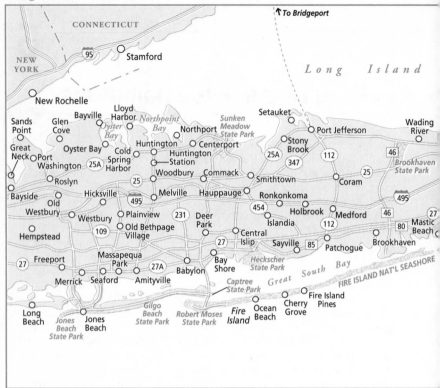

The **Gold Coast,** as it came to be known in the Roaring Twenties, was the domain of F. Scott Fitzgerald's *The Great Gatsby;* the area became famous for its glorious excesses in everything from mansions to parties. It was the place America's most powerful tycoons—bearing names like Astor and Vanderbilt—bought up to a thousand acres of land and built 100-room mansions based on English manor houses and French châteaux, designed by the world's most eminent architects.

While fox hunts are a thing of the past, and the Long Island Expressway now cuts through many of these estates, some of these homes still remain, making for a wonderful drive with some awesome stops, great views of the Long Island Sound, small beaches, and quaint towns. Start in Fitzgerald's exclusive Great Neck and drive along the main road, Route 25A; its two lanes are responsible for moving tons of traffic. But continue east and the cars start to dissipate. You'll come to Sagamore Hill, Theodore Roosevelt's summer home. You'll pass through sleepy Centerport. Keep going and the terrain becomes even more rural, with farms starting to crop up as you approach the North Fork.

A word of advice for beach lovers: Stick with the south shore. The few beaches that do exist up here tend to be on the rocky side.

ESSENTIALS
GETTING THERE
BY CAR　The **Long Island Expressway** (I-495) is your quickest way out here, when it's not packed with traffic. Avoid rush hour at all cost!

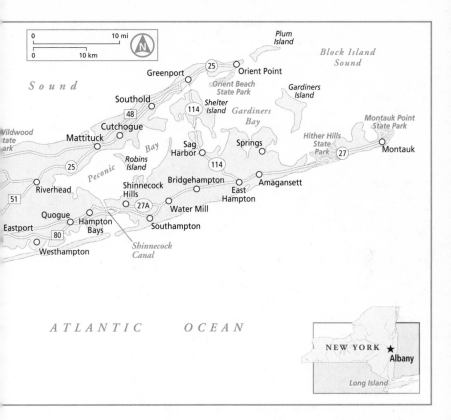

BY TRAIN In 2001, more than 85 million people rode the **Long Island Railroad** (LIRR). For schedule and fare information, call © **516/822-LIRR** or 718/217-LIRR or visit www.mta.nyc.ny.us/lirr/index.html. The LIRR services 124 Long Island stations and make more than 20 stops along the North Shore, including Great Neck, Manhasset, Port Washington, Oyster Bay, Locust Valley, Glen Cove, Sea Cliff, Roslyn, Westbury, Hicksville, Syosset, Cold Spring Harbor, Huntington, Northport, St. James, Stony Brook, and Port Jefferson. Cab service is available at all stations; you can just show up and get a cab or check the LIRR website for phone numbers.

BY PLANE LaGuardia and John F. Kennedy airports lie just over the Long Island Border in New York City (p. 73). **Long Island MacArthur Airport,** situated mid-Island in Islip (© 631/467-3210; www.macarthurairport.com), is the closest airport and is served by **Southwest** (© 800/435-9792; www.iflyswa.com), **US Airways** (© 800/428-4322; www.usairways.com), **Continental Express** (© 800/525-0280; www.continental.com), **Northwest Airlink** (© 800/225-2525; www.nwa.com), **Delta Express** (© 800/221-1212; www.delta.com), and **American Eagle** (© 800/433-7300; www.aa.com).

BY FERRY The **Bridgeport & Port Jefferson Ferry Company,** 102 W. Broadway, Port Jefferson (© **631/473-0286;** www.bpjferry.com), makes the 1¼-hour trip between Port Jeff and Bridgeport, Connecticut, every 90 minutes, from 6am to 9pm. Car and driver cost is $38; foot passengers pay $14.

VISITOR INFORMATION   The **Long Island Convention and Visitors Bureau** (© **877/FUN-ON-LI** or 631/951-3440; www.licvb.com) has an office at 330 Motor Pkwy., Ste. 30, Hauppauge. It's open Monday to Friday from 9am to 5pm; call or visit for all the info you can handle. Visit the website to print out the **Fun Card,** which will get you discounts at museums, hotels, restaurants, and activities all over the Island.

SPECIAL EVENTS   The North Shore's major events take place in summer. The **Walt Whitman Birthday Celebration** in **Huntington** (© **631/427-5240**) starts off the season, usually the first weekend in June. The **Friends of the Arts Long Island Summer Festival** runs from the end of June through early September at Planting Fields Arboretum (© **516/922-0061**), providing a summer of music on gorgeous grounds. The season winds down with the **Summer's End Weekend** in early September, with special events at Sagamore Hill, Planting Fields Arboretum, the Theodore Roosevelt Sanctuary, and more.

GETTING AROUND   A car is essential on Long Island. **Avis** (© 800/331-1212; www.avis.com) has offices in Islip, Massapequa, and Huntington Station; **Budget** (© 800/527-0700; www.budget.com) has offices in Garden City, Hicksville, and Huntington Station; **Dollar** (© 800/800-4000; www.dollar.com) has an office in Islip, and **Hertz** (© 800/654-3131; www.hertz.com) has offices in Great Neck, Huntington, and Islip.

SPORTS & OUTDOOR PURSUITS

GOLF   The Red Course at **Eisenhower Park,** 25 Melville Park Rd., Melville (© **631/753-4357**), was home to the 1926 PGA Championship and was a stop for the PGA Seniors Tour in 2003. But it's a public course—so you can go make your own history. Or bring your clubs to **Bethpage State Park,** Bethpage Road, Farmingdale (© **516/249-0700**), site of the 2002 U.S. Open.

HITTING THE BEACH   Though this shore shouldn't be your first choice for beaches—they tend to be rocky and often quite small—there are a couple nice ones that allow for swimming in the calm waters of Long Island Sound or lounging on the sand. The beach in **Governor Alfred E. Smith/Sunken Meadow State Park,** Kings Park (© **631/269-4333**), is a full 3 miles of sand that run right into tall, glacier-formed bluffs at its western end. Farther east, **Wildwood State Park,** in Wading River (© **631/929-4314**), offers 2 miles of beach.

SPECTATOR SPORTS   Long Island's only pro sports team is the NHL's **New York Islanders,** who play 40 of their 80 games from October to April at the Nassau Coliseum in Uniondale (© **800/882-ISLE;** www.newyorkislanders.com).

SHOPPING

ANTIQUES   Route 25A is dotted with lots of little antiques stores, which explode into a town full of them when you reach Port Jefferson. Along the way, there are a couple of standout towns.

   Cold Spring Harbor is a quiet little town with a couple nice places to shop. Of special note is the **Huntington Antiques Center,** 129 Main St. (© **631/549-0105**), where you'll find collections from almost 20 dealers with tons of 18th- and early-19th-century items from England, France, and America along with an excellent collection of antique Oriental rugs.

   Tiny Locust Valley, rarely even plotted on Long Island maps, is a favorite of LI antiques hunters in the know. **Le Canard Rouge,** 82 Birch Hill Rd. (© **516/671-8287**), specializes in everything early American; you'll also find an excellent

Value **Getaway Trains**

From June to October, the LIRR offers 1-day getaways from New York City that include train fare, connecting bus or ferry fees (if necessary), and entrance fees to museums. Some are specialty tours of Long Island Wine Country, for example, or the Gold Coast Mansions. Others are beach getaways to places like Fire Island. For those that aren't guided tours, just be sure you're going to return the same day or you end up paying twice for the return. Visit **www.mta.nyc.ny.us/lirr/getaways/longisland/calendar.htm** for details.

---

collection of 19th-century European and American paintings. **Cotter Krobath,** 94-96 Forest Ave. (© **516/676-5000**), boasts two large showrooms of European and Continental artwork and furniture. For a pleasant lunch break, grab one of the best burgers on Long Island at **Buckram Stables Café,** 31-33 Forest Ave. (© **516/ 671-3080**), or an ice-cream cone at the **Back Door Scoop Shoppe,** 15 Back Birch Hill Rd. (© **516/609-9103**).

In the far more touristy Port Jefferson, you'll find five dealers under one roof at **The Renaissance Room,** 1530 Main St. (© **631/331-5200**), selling everything from furniture to china to light fixtures and bric-a-brac. **Artifacts,** 1607 Main St. (© **631/331-3426**), is similarly sprawling—5,000 square feet of everything old, from large furniture to knickknacks.

RETAIL One of the most renowned shopping strips on the East Coast is the so-called "Miracle Mile." The real name is the **Americana Shopping Center,** 2060 Northern Blvd., Manhasset (© **800/818-6767** or 516/627-2277), and you'll find such high-end retailers like Barneys New York, Tiffany, Armani, Louis Vuitton, Burberry, and the ubiquitous Banana Republic as well as Barnes & Noble. Take a break for a fine lunch (salads, pasta, and more) at **Millie's Place** (© **516/365-4344**).

GOLD COAST MANSIONS

Old Westbury Gardens ☆ Worshippers of formal gardens will be in heaven, and even casual nature lovers can't help but adore the blooming buds of these 160 landscaped acres of the former Phipps estate. Stroll among the wildflower-filled nooks, lilac-laden walkways, wide-open lawns, formal rose gardens, and meticulously maintained ponds—all in a constantly changing display of seasonal colors. Step inside the property's gorgeous Charles II–style three-story mansion furnished with fine English antiques and decorative arts; it's virtually unchanged from when the Phipps family lived here in the early 20th century.

71 Old Westbury Rd., Old Westbury. © 516/333-0048. www.oldwestburygardens.org. $10 adults, 62 and over $8, 6–12 $5, free for children under 6. Wed–Mon late Apr to late Oct. Take the LIE Exit 39 (Glen Cove Rd.). Follow the service road east for 1 mile, turn right onto Old Westbury Rd. and continue ⅖ mile. The gate is on the left. LIRR to Westbury; it's just a 2½-mile taxi ride from there.

Planting Fields Arboretum/Coe Hall ☆☆ This grand expanse of historic buildings and greenhouses, the former estate of Standard Oil heiress Mai Rogers Coe and insurance king William Robertson Coe, is one of the few remaining Gold Coast properties to remain intact. As in its heyday of the 1920s, the 409 acres boast formal gardens, hiking trails, and two greenhouses with unique displays. The main building, Coe Hall, is a showy, 65-room Tudor Revival mansion that has many original pieces and furnishings, along with many wood and stone carvings, stained glass windows, and murals.

Planting Fields Rd., Oyster Bay. ☏ **516/922-8600**. www.plantingfields.com. Arboretum grounds $6 parking fee daily Memorial Day to Labor Day, other times weekends only. Coe Hall $5 adults, $3.50 seniors and students $1 children 7–12, free for children under 7. Grounds daily 9am–5pm. Coe Hall tours daily Apr–Sept noon–3:30pm. LIE to exit 41N. Take Rte. 106 north into Oyster Bay. Left on Lexington Ave., left on Mill River Rd. and follow the signs. LIRR to Oyster Bay; it's a 1½-mile taxi ride.

Sagamore Hill ★★★ Theodore Roosevelt's testosterone-laden tribute to hunting, oak, and all things manly still stands on 100 gorgeous acres overlooking Long Island Sound. His 23-room Victorian estate, the so-called summer White House between 1902 and 1908, has been preserved just the way he liked it—full of animal heads, skins, and exotic treasures—and visiting is a fun experience that also gives you some good historical insight. The home reflects his travels as a Rough Rider in Cuba, big-game hunter in East Africa, and fearless explorer in the Brazilian Amazon. You must take a guided tour, which leaves on the hour and lasts around an hour. On summer weekends, arrive early—tour tickets tend to sell out by early afternoon.

Cove Neck Rd., Oyster Bay. ☏ **516/922-4447**. www.nps.gov/sahi. $5 adults, free for children 16 and under. Daily 9:30am–4pm. Labor Day to Memorial Day Wed–Sun only. LIE to exit 41 north (NY 106 north). Take 106 north to Oyster Bay and follow signs. LIRR to Oyster Bay or Syosset; it's a 3-mile taxi ride from Oyster Bay and 6 miles from Syosset, but it's easier to find cabs at the Syosset station.

Sands Point Preserve ★ You'll think you've died and gone to medieval Europe. The castles on these grounds are a stunning display of the extravagance and wealth from a different era. Created by Howard Gould, son of railroad tycoon Jay Gould, the 100,000-square-foot 1904 castle **(Castlegould)** and 1912 Tudor style manor, Hempstead House (residence of second owner, Daniel Guggenheim) sit upon gorgeous grounds. Unfortunately, Hempstead House only offers an uninteresting Wedgwood collection and Castlegould a rotating science and history exhibit. But also on the grounds is the beautiful Falaise, a Normandy-style manor house built by Harry F. Guggenheim in 1923 that's decked out in period furnishings.

Bonus: The grounds have extensive nature trails. Pick up a picnic lunch (try the American Harvest Deli, 3 Main St., Port Washington; ☏ **516/944-5445**) and make a day of it.

95 Middleneck Rd., Sands Point (Port Washington). ☏ **516/571-7900**. www.liglobal.com/t_i/attractions/museums/sandspoint. It's $2 to visit the preserve on weekends, weekdays are free. Falaise: May–Oct Wed–Sun noon–3pm. Hempstead House and the Wedgwood exhibit open May–Oct Sat–Sun noon–3pm. Castlegould open Tues–Sun 10am–4pm year-round. Admission for each is $6. LIE to exit 36N, go straight 6 miles via Searingtown Rd., Port Washington Blvd., and Middleneck Rd. to entrance.

Vanderbilt Museum and Planetarium ★★ *Kids* I know, "planetarium" conjures up memories of horrid grade-school road trips. But before you dismiss this domed building, know that the planetarium was opened by the county merely to help sustain the amazing mansion and museum that adjoin it in the back. The real reason to come to William K. Vanderbilt II's 43-acre estate is to see the over-the-top extravagance of his 24-room Spanish Revival Mansion, built in three stages from 1910 until 1936. Rooms exemplify his eclectic taste and amazing worldwide collection of arts and science. Don't miss the Hall of Fish, a collection of fish species that were unknown in this part of the world during Vanderbilt's lifetime. But don't completely dismiss the planetarium—the shows are great for kids.

181 Little Neck Rd., Centerport. (C) **631/854-5555**. www.vanderbiltmuseum.org. Admission $8 adults, $6 students and seniors for the mansion tour; planetarium shows $7 adults, $5 students and seniors, $5 for grounds admission only. Tues–Sun Apr–June noon–5pm; July–Oct 10am–5pm; Oct–Apr noon–4pm. LIE to exit 51, go north on Deer Park Ave., bear left at the fork onto Park Ave. At 3rd light, turn right onto Broadway, continue for 5 miles to Rte. 25A. Cross 25A (to left of Shell gas station), and you're on Little Neck Rd.

MORE MUSEUMS & ATTRACTIONS

Garvies Point Museum and Preserve   Want to get a sense of what the land was like some 5,000 years ago? Head out here, an area of shoreline occupied by Matinecock Indians as early as 2500 B.C. Take a walk through the museum to see depictions of Indian life before the invasion of European settlers. But the real treasure out here is the land surrounding the museum. The preserve comprises 5 miles of nature trails that wind through 62 acres of glacial moraine, including forests, thickets, and meadows. You'll find old-growth hardwood forest, meadows, and woodland that's been allowed to return to its natural state after being used for cattle grazing in the early 1900s. You can see more than 140 species of birds, and keep an eye out for the woodchucks, raccoon, and red fox traipsing these woods as well. You'll get great harbor views along with ponds and tidal pools.

50 Barry Dr., Glen Cove, (C) **516/571-8010**. www.516web.com/museum/garvie. Admission $2 adults, $1 ages 5–14. Tues–Sun 10am–4pm. LIE to exit 39N, take Glen Cove Rd. north to the Glen Cove Arterial Hwy. Take the Arterial to the end, turn right, and follow signs. LIRR to Glen St.; it's a 2-mile taxi ride.

Heckscher Museum of Art ✮   If only we all could afford a huge collection of eclectic artwork and build a small beaux-arts museum to house them. But we all can't be like industrialist August Heckscher, who did just that in 1920. Today, this impressive and wide-ranging collection includes more than 1,800 paintings, sculptures, and other works spanning from Egyptian artifacts through the Renaissance to the noted collection of Hudson River and Long Island landscape schools.

2 Prime Ave., Huntington. (C) **631/351-3250**. www.heckscher.org. Suggested admission $5, seniors and students $3, children over 6 $1. Tues–Fri 10am–5pm; Sat–Sun 1pm–5pm; first Fri of the month until 8:30pm. LIE to exit 49N, take Rte. 110N into Huntington, turn right on 25A, make a left at the first light. LIRR to Huntington; it's a 3-mile taxi ride.

John P. Humes Japanese Stroll Garden ✮✮   Walking meditation is the goal at this extremely serene Japanese garden, set amid 4 acres of deep woodland. Step through the gate and you'll be awash in *yamazato,* or the transcendent feeling of a remote mountain hideout. Follow the trail, a symbolic path to enlightenment that takes you past a lake garden, as well as the shrubs and rocks that are essential to imperial garden design. The garden is the dream child of Ambassador Humes, who was inspired by a 1960 visit to Kyoto, Japan. Today, it's a refuge from the world. For a special treat, come to a tea ceremony held just a couple of days per month (no reservations required, but call for schedule).

347 Oyster Bay Rd., Mill Neck. (C) **516/676-4486**. Admission $5 adults, free for children under 12; $10 for tour with tea ceremony. Late Apr to Oct Sat–Sun 11:30am–4:30pm. LIE to exit 39 N to Northern Blvd., turn right and go 3 miles to Wolver Hollow Rd., turn left to end, turn right on Chicken Valley Rd.; go 1¾ miles to Dogwood Lane, turn right.

Nassau County Museum of Art ✮✮   One of the finest suburban art museums in the nation, this surprisingly notable collection sits on 145 acres in a home once owned by steel baron Henry Clay Frick. Today, there's a wide variety of art to peruse. The permanent collection includes more than 600 works of 19th- and 20th-century European and American artists like Edouard Vuillard, Roy Lichtenstein, and Robert Rauschenberg. You'll also find changing exhibits, along with formal gardens and an outdoor sculpture area that are glorious to

Sunday Driving

While some North Shore towns can't claim huge Vanderbilt mansions or sprawling gardens, they still make for great places to take a drive. **Sea Cliff** began as a Methodist summer campground in 1871 and now boasts some two dozen homes on the National Register of Historic Places (as well as 900 structures built before WWII). Come to walk the steep streets and admire the Victorian homes with their gingerbread porches and Gothic gables. Then stop off at Memorial Park for spectacular sunsets over the water. You won't even find **Locust Valley** on many maps—this very cute small town (just 1 square mile) is full of great antiques shops and boutiques and is one of the island's biggest secrets. **Cold Spring Harbor** is another antiques-filled haven right on the water; Route 25A takes you through town and past some gorgeous water-views. Stop in at the **Whaling Museum,** Main Street (© **631/367-3418**), then walk the length of Main Street (it's only ¼ mile) and admire some of the structures that date to the days when whaling was the backbone of industry here. Named after the third president, **Port Jefferson** is a bustling town on the water, full of restaurants, antiques shops, marinas, and cute storefronts. It's also a docking point for one of the Connecticut ferries, so it's constantly in motion with activity, especially in the summer.

walk through on a nice day. Making for an even bigger experience is the Tee Ridder Miniature Museum, also on the grounds.

One Museum Dr., Roslyn Harbor. © 516/484-9338. www.nassaumuseum.com. Admission $6, seniors $5, children and students $4, free for children under 5. Tues–Sun 11am–5pm. LIE to exit 39, go north 2 miles to Northern Boulevard (Rte. 25A) and turn left. At the second light turn right. LIRR to Roslyn; it's a 2-mile taxi ride.

Old Bethpage Village Restoration ★ *Kids* Yes, it's another village recreation, but this one shines a spotlight on the unique blend of cultures that made Long Island what it is today. Here you can go back to a time when the Dutch influenced the island's architecture and cider was strictly alcoholic (and drunk by the entire family). The village has been around since the 1960s, offering a representative sampling of 19th-century structures and ways of life, but its roots go back even further, to its English and Dutch settlers of the 17th and 18th century, when life was closely tied to the land. Today there are 51 buildings on 209 acres. Bring the kids and tour the blacksmith's shop, the general store, and the cider press.

Round Swamp Rd., Old Bethpage. © 516/572-8401. www.oldbethpage.org. Admission $7, children 4–14 and seniors $5, free for children under 4. Nov–Apr Wed–Sun 10am–4pm; May–Oct Wed–Sun 10am–5pm. LIE to exit 48, right on Round Swamp Rd. and left at the next light. LIRR to Hicksville; it's a 4-mile taxi ride.

Walt Whitman Birthplace You don't have to be a *Leaves of Grass* fan to enjoy this famous poet's birthplace, a tiny historic home that looks oddly out of place in the heart of strip-mall country. Though Whitman left here at an early age, Long Island was always home for him. A new interpretation center offers a good collection of his manuscripts and photographs, chronology of his career as journalist, editor, and Civil War correspondent, as well as recordings of Whitman himself reading his work. And the home is an interesting step back in time, since it looks much as it did when he was born in 1819, though outfitted with replacement furniture.

246 Old Walt Whitman Rd., South Huntington. © 631/427-5240. $3 adults; $2 seniors and students; free to children under 12. Mid-June to Labor Day Mon–Fri 11am–4pm, Sat–Sun noon–5pm; Labor Day to mid-June Wed–Fri 1–4pm, Sat–Sun 11am–4pm. LIE to exit 49N, north 1¾ miles, turn left on Old Walt Whitman Rd.

WHERE TO STAY

Many chains hotels put the Gold Coast within easy reach: **Holiday Inn Express,** 3131 Nesconset Hwy., Centereach (© **631/471-8000**); **Hampton Inn,** 680 Commack Rd., Commack (© **631/462-5700**); and the **Hilton,** 598 Broad Hollow Rd., Melville (© **631/845-1000**).

EXPENSIVE

Danford's ★★★   A sprawling resort right on the Long Island Sound, Danford's is its own Colonial New England–style village that's imbued with a nautical theme. The spacious quarters are done in deep blues and reds with furniture that's comfortable but perhaps a bit too formal for this laid-back seafaring town. Get a room with a view of the Port Jeff harbor, which gets tons of light; balcony rooms let you take in the sea air.

25 E. Broadway, Port Jefferson, NY 11777. © **800/332-6367** or 631/928-5200. Fax 631/928-9082. www. danfords.com. Weekend packages available. AE, DC, DISC, MC, V. 85 units. Apr–Oct $199–$229 double, $259–$409 suite; Nov–Mar $179–$199 double, $209–$409 suite. **Amenities:** Restaurant; lounge; exercise room; spa; salon; limited room service; in-room massage; babysitting; laundry service; same-day dry cleaning. *In room:* A/C, TV w/pay movies, dataport, some with kitchenette, coffeemaker, hair dryer, iron.

Inn At Great Neck ★★★   The Roaring Twenties live on—sort of—at this upscale hotel in exclusive Great Neck. The lobby's Art Deco decor, however, doesn't carry over into the spacious modern and extremely comfortable bedrooms. Bathrooms are similarly large, with good lighting and lots of marble. Grab a movie from the front desk's library and pop it into the VCR, or just kick back with a copy of *The Great Gatsby.*

30 Cutter Mill Rd., Great Neck, NY 11021. © **516/773-2000.** www.innatgreatneck.com. 85 units. Jan–Apr, July, Dec $189–$219 double, $259 suite; May, Aug, Nov $199–$219 double, $279 suite; June, Sept–Oct $209–$239 double, $299 suite. AE, DC, DISC, MC, V. Valet parking $10. LIE to exit 33; make a left onto Lakeville Rd. Turn left at the Fleet Bank onto Cutter Mill Rd. **Amenities:** Restaurant; lounge; exercise room; concierge; business center; limited room service; in-room massage; babysitting; laundry service; same-day dry cleaning. *In room:* A/C, TV/VCR w/pay movies, dataport, kitchenette (some units), minibar, fridge, coffeemaker, hair dryer, iron, safe.

The Three Village Inn ★★   You may have to duck to get through some of the doorways in this charming 1750s country inn, set on the harbor. That, of course, is just the point. With exposed beams, narrow hallways, and antiques, you'll feel like you're padding around in your grandmother's attic. The all-nonsmoking rooms aren't huge, but they're comfy and decked out in pastels with frilly drapes. Cottages give you a bit more space and some with extras you won't find in the inn, such as stone fireplaces and water views.

150 Main St., Stony Brook, NY 11790. © **631/751-0555.** Fax 631/751-0593. www.threevillageinn.com. 26 units. $179–$225 double. Rates include breakfast. AE, MC, V. LIE to exit 62; north 10 miles to 25A; left 1½ miles at "Historic Stony Brook" sign to Main St.; right ½ mile to the inn. **Amenities:** Restaurant; lounge. *In room:* A/C, TV, dataport, iron.

MODERATE

Swan View Manor   A converted motel right on the main road and across the street from Cold Spring Harbor, this inn's main house is a beautiful historic home. But most of the nonsmoking rooms are in the single-story motel section that looks odd done over in quasi-antiques. Though the floral and lace designs and friendly staff make it a welcoming place to stay, the traffic rolling by right outside your door means you shouldn't come searching for a quiet getaway.

45 Harbor Rd., Cold Spring Harbor, NY 11724. *©* **631/367-2070.** www.swanview.com. 19 units. May–Oct weekday $122–$177 double, weekend $137–$192 double; rest of year weekday $112–$157 double, weekend $127–$172 double. 2-night minimum on summer weekends. Rates include continental breakfast. AE, DC, DISC, MC, V. *In room:* A/C, TV, dataport.

INEXPENSIVE
Heritage Inn *Value* The heritage of this inn is more value-driven than historical, but it's still a quality place to stay in Port Jeff. Rooms are very sparsely furnished, and don't count on big bathrooms.

201 W. Broadway, Port Jefferson, NY 11777. *©* **631/928-2400.** Fax 631/474-0627. www.portjeffheritage inn.com. 30 units. Jan–Mar $79–$89 double; May–Aug weekday $99–$109 double, weekend $129–$139 double. Spring and fall rates in between high and low season are priced according to demand. AE, DISC, MC, V. *In room:* A/C, TV/VCR, dataport, some with kitchenette, coffeemaker, hair dryer, iron.

WHERE TO DINE
EXPENSIVE
La Plage ★★ NEW AMERICAN With the salty air blowing in straight from the ocean across the street, this tiny bistro boasts washed tones, a rustic wooden floor, and some tables with great views. The food is decidedly New American; weaving together flavors that work a delicate magic into hearty dishes, like the pork chop with a cabernet glaze, accompanied by a gratin of apples, onions, and goat cheese.

131 Creek Rd., Wading River. *©* **631/744-9200.** Reservations requested. Main courses $22–$32, lunch $12–$18. AE, MC, V. Memorial Day to Sept Mon–Thurs noon–3pm, 4–9pm, Fri–Sat noon–3pm, 4–10pm, Sun 2–9pm. Sept–May: Closed Mon–Tues. LIE to exit 68, go north to 25A, go east ¾ mile, turn left on Randalls Rd., turn right on North Country Rd., at stop sign turn left on Sound Ave.

Peter Luger ★★★ STEAKHOUSE "Wow" is the only word that comes to mind when you bite into Luger's porterhouse. This famous steakhouse deserves its reputation as one of America's best—they take meat seriously and they do it right. The porterhouse is what you want—dry aged, brushed with a delicious glaze, and served up straightforward, just the way you want it cooked. But they take no credit cards, so bring lots of cash.

255 Northern Blvd., Great Neck. *©* **516/487-8800.** Reservations recommended. Steak for 2, $65, other entrees $14–$32. No credit cards. Mon–Thurs 11:45am–9:45pm; Fri–Sat 11:45am–10:45pm; Sun 12:45–9:45pm.

MODERATE
Elk Street Grill ★★ CONTINENTAL This friendly oasis in Port Jefferson is a neighborhood favorite. Skip the appetizers since you'll get a salad with great homemade dressings (try the sesame); entree winners are the pan-seared tuna with a tangy ginger sauce and flaky blackened salmon with a pineapple-mango chutney, but meats score well too.

201 Main St., Port Jefferson. *©* **631/331-0960.** Main courses $13–$25. AE, DC, DISC, MC, V. Tues–Thurs noon–10pm; Fri noon–11pm; Sat 4–11pm; Sun noon–9pm.

Tupelo Honey ★★★ *Finds* AMERICAN With mosaics forming ocean-life scenes, an open kitchen shaped like a mythic castle, and chandeliers shaped like wings, this North Shore gem is fanciful, but not in a Disney way—it's actually tasteful and romantic. The food matches the unique decor, with flavor combinations that bring a Spanish influence to an otherwise American menu. Even old favorites are served with a twist. The salmon, for example, comes crusted with coriander, golden beet couscous, horseradish cucumber salad, and avocado yogurt.

39 Roslyn Ave., Sea Cliff. ℂ **516/671-8300.** Reservations strongly suggested. Main courses $22–$31. AE, DC, MC, V. Mon–Thurs 5–10pm; Sat–Sun 5pm–11pm; Sun 4 –10pm. Take Rte. 25 to Glen Cove Rd., go north for 3 miles to the sign that says Cedar Swamp Rd. to Sea Cliff, veer right to the first light, turn left onto Sea Cliff Ave., go 1 mile to Roslyn Ave.

INEXPENSIVE

Best Bagels 🐸 BAGEL SHOP   If you're going to claim to be the best, your product better live up to the boast. These bagels are not too dense, not too puffy, cooked on the outside and not too mushy inside—done just right. Endless toppings and sandwich combos are available.

40 Middle Neck Rd., Great Neck, ℂ **516/482-9860.** Bagel sandwiches $4–$9. Cash only. Mon–Sat 6:30am– 6pm; Sun 6:30am–3pm.

Renaissance Gourmet Shop ★ *Finds* CAFE   It's hard to imagine a more delightful environment to grab a morning coffee or a lunchtime sandwich. The Garden Room is bursting with color and Italianate windows painted on the walls. Breakfast options include homemade muffins; for lunch you'll find delicious sandwiches, burgers, salads, and pizzas.

35A Gerard St., Huntington Village. ℂ **631/549-2727.** AE, MC, V. Sandwiches $6–$7. Mon–Thurs 7am–9pm; Fri–Sat 7am–10pm; Sun 7am–6pm.

THE NORTH SHORE AFTER DARK

There are a couple of outstanding places for music and other live events. The **Tilles Center,** 720 Northern Blvd., Brookville (ℂ **516/299-3100**), part of the C. W. Post Campus of Long Island University, boasts a 2,242-seat hall and more than 70 events each season (Sept–May) in music, dance, and theater. Everyone from the Big Apple Circus to Wynton Marsalis has performed there. The **Westbury Music Fair,** 960 Brush Hollow Rd., Westbury (ℂ **516/334-0800**), tends to host performers of somewhat recent memory, like Tom Jones and Cyndi Lauper. The **Nassau Veteran Memorial Coliseum,** 1255 Hempstead Tpk., Uniondale (ℂ **516/794-9300**), is not only home to professional hockey's New York Islanders but it also hosts big-name concerts (such as Justin Timberlake) and family shows like *Sesame Street Live.* Huntington's smaller, but wonderful not-for-profit **Inter-Media Art Center** (IMAC), 370 New York Ave. (ℂ **631/549-ARTS;** www.imactheater.org), presents an eclectic concert mix. There are a couple of bars worth noting: **Chesterfields,** 330 New York Ave., Huntington (ℂ **631/425-1457**), serves up live music, and the **Harbor Bar & Grill,** 154 W. Broadway, Port Jefferson Village (ℂ **631/928-9595**), has nightly entertainment and dancing, but also a great happy hour.

2 The North Fork ★★

Golden beaches and the sweet nectar of fermented grapes are the sirens that lure most travelers to this slender strip of Long Island. Though close to the Hamptons, the attitude is completely un-Hamptons; in fact, South Forkers refer to this area as "upstate."

Thank goodness. Right now it's a laid-back playground that's quaint, beautiful, and completely unpretentious. Wineries took root out here just over 25

Fun Fact **What Lies Beneath**

America's first submarine base was created here, in the town of New Suffolk.

---

years ago, and Long Island wines are growing in recognition—and numbers. There are now 23 places to sample them (see tour, p. 166). But this tiny tract of flat, beachy turf is also a great place to just relax. Though it lacks the range of lodging and dining options found due south, it also lacks the Hamptons' high prices.

Just two roads slice through the North Fork: Route 25 and Route 25A. Take either of them past Riverhead and you'll trade malls for farm stands, wineries, and tiny towns brimming with antiques shops and small-town flair. The two roads come together in Greenport, where most of the area's action (such as it is) can be found. Take that road out to the tip at Orient Point for gorgeous views. You won't be alone: on summer weekends, you can expect to find huge traffic jams. Yes, the roads are narrow, but more and more people are discovering the treasures of the North Fork, all while staying in hotels right on the beach with fantastic views of the Sound and spending their days shopping and tasting great wines.

Note: For town locations, see map on inside back cover.

ESSENTIALS

GETTING THERE   The **Long Island Expressway** runs to Riverhead; from there, take Route 25 East. **The Long Island Railroad** (✆ **516/822-LIRR**) stops in Mattituck, Southold, and Greenport. **Sunrise Coach Lines** (✆ **800/ 517-7709** or 631/477-1200; www.sunrisecoach.com) offers bus service from New York City to Riverhead, Mattituck, Cutchogue, Southold, and Greenport for $16 each way. **Long Island MacArthur Airport** (✆ **631/467-3210**), situated mid–Long Island, is the closest airport and is served by several airlines mentioned above. From Connecticut, take the **Cross Sound Ferry** (✆ **631/323- 2525;** www.longislandferry.com), which sails from New London, Connecticut, to Orient Point, New York. Schedules change daily, leaving 8 to 12 times a day. Cars and passenger trucks are allowed.

VISITOR INFORMATION   Tourist information booths are located on Main Road in the towns of Laurel (✆ **631/477-1383**) and Greenport (same number), but are only open daily during July and August (scattered hours at other times). You can also contact the **Long Island Convention and Visitors Bureau** (✆ **877/ FUN-ON-LI** or 631/951-3440)

GETTING AROUND   While cars offer flexibility for, say, visiting wineries, many people don't want to brave the summer traffic. In summertime, though, calling a taxi could mean a long wait. **Hertz** (✆ **800/654-3131**) has a rental office in Riverhead. If you need a lift, try **Maria's Taxi,** Greenport (✆ **631/477- 0700**), or **Southold Taxi,** Southold (✆ **631/765-2221**).

BEACHES & OUTDOOR PURSUITS

BEACHES   There are lots of beaches out here, but check for signs—some are permit-only. For public beaches, your best bet is the more than 8 miles of beach in **Orient Point State Park,** Orient Point (✆ **631/323-2440**), where you'll also find plenty of breathing room and a maritime forest of red cedar and prickly-pear cactus. Two permit-only beaches worth checking out are **Norman Klipp Marine Park** in Greenport and **Town Beach** in Southold, which a popular family beach. Pick up your permit from the attendant at either beach (after 10am): it's $12 for a daily nonresident pass.

BOATING One of the most unique ways to check out Greenport is aboard the electric *Glory*, a 30-foot fantail launch with varnished hardwood and brass. It sails every hour; $15 for adults. Go to Preston's Dock at the foot of Main Street, Greenport, or call ✆ **631/477-2515** for details. Or go boating yourself: the inlets, creeks, and marshes make canoeing or kayaking a great way to see herons, osprey, hawks, fish, and turtles. Rent from **Eagle's Neck Paddling Company,** 49295 Main Rd., Southold (✆ **631/765-3502**). Rentals start at $20 for 2 hours.

FARM STANDS Once you pass Riverhead, Long Island becomes a collection of farms, not malls. Definitely plan to stop at one of them. From tomatoes and sweet corn in the summer to pumpkins and apples in the fall, get your produce at **Wickham's Fruit Farm,** Route 25, Cutchogue (✆ **631/734-6441**), **Harbes Family Farmstand,** Main Road, Jamesport (✆ **631/722-8546**), and **Punkin-ville USA,** Route 48, Peconic (✆ **631/734-5530**). **Briermere Farms,** 4414 Sound Avenue, Riverhead (✆ **631/722-3931**), is famous for it's divine selection of fruit-filled pies, from raspberry cherry to blueberry cream.

FISHING The tradition of fishing lives on out here, with many boats made for the novice caster. Summertime you may be after shark or tuna or fluke. Other prime catches are sea bass and flounder. Fishing season generally runs from April or May to October, and local captains will set you up with all the gear you need. Go with **Captain Bob**'s fleet in Mattituck (✆ **631/289-5727**), or the *Peconic Star II* with **Capt. Dave Brennan** in Greenport (✆ **631/289-6899**) and expect to pay around $50 for a full day. If you want to go it alone, contact the **Southold Town Clerk's** office (✆ **631/765-1800**), **Warren's Bait & Tackle** (in Aquebogue; ✆ **631/722-4898**) or **Jamesport Bait & Tackle** (in Mattituck; ✆ **631/298-5458**) for beach-fishing permits.

GOLF You're choices are limited. Try **Cherry Creek Golf Links,** 900 Reeves Ave., Riverhead (✆ **631/369-6500**), which has 18 holes and a driving range. To work on those chipping and putting skills, head to **Cedars Golf Club,** Cases Lane, Cutchogue (✆ **631/734-6363**).

WINERIES The East End's wine industry is relatively young; it turns out that with its well-drained, sandy soil, the North Fork is ideal for grapes, so the industry has taken off. See sidebar on p. 166.

SHOPPING
ANTIQUES This is an old seafaring world, full of antiques shops and galleries. Step into some of these musty old shops and start digging. Most towns have one or two stores, but Jamesport and Greenport offer some of the best selections on the North Fork. You'll find a wealth of stained-glass lamps and handmade furnishings at **Lydia's Antiques and Stained Glass,** 215 Main St., Greenport (✆ **631/477-1414**). At the **Old School House Antiques,** 68320 Main Rd., Greenport (✆ **631/477-8122**), there's a nice selection of clocks, lamps, Christmas collectibles, and jewelry. **Three Sisters Antiques,** 1550 Main Rd., Jamesport (✆ **631/722-5980**), specializes in linens, postcards, and paper,

Along the Long Island Wine Trail

Long Island sustains some 50 vineyards, ranging in size from 2 to 600 acres, with 30 wineries producing a half-million cases annually. Here on the East End, with some 3,000 acres in vines, is New York's only all-*vinifera* wine region; that is, it's the only wine-producing area that cultivates *vinifera*–a single European species of vine family, from which most of the world's wine is made—exclusively. In just 30 years, wine production has transformed a sleepy farming community into a vibrant wine district, producing wines that appear on world-renowned wine lists.

Here's why: Ever looked at the "hardiness zone" map in garden books? Eastern Long Island lies in a zone quite different from the rest of the state; a Zone 7, it shares company with Virginia, Kentucky, and northwestern Texas.

Cultivating wine grapes to perfection is a matter of climate, and Long Island's climate is often compared to that of Bordeaux. Of primary importance is the temperature: spring comes late to the East End, influenced by the surrounding bay, sound, and ocean. The chance of frost at "bud break" is gone. In the fall, the nearby waters extend the season, allowing harvest into November. Then there's the sun. The area from Riverhead to Peconic sees more sunshine than any other spot in New York—around 230 sunny days per year. Finally, soil comes into play. The North Fork is a glacial moraine—sandy, well-drained soil—again, like Bordeaux. It's good for potatoes (whose "feet" don't like being wet) and very, very good for grape vines.

Merlot, the most widely planted variety on the North Fork, ripens here beautifully, and reliably, allowing winemakers to create lush wines from ripened fruit. Chardonnay is second, considered the best white grape of the New World wine regions, partly for its adaptability, but mostly because of its great character, which allows a winemaker to craft a variety of wines. Many North Fork wineries offer two styles: one that is fruity and crisp, fermented in steel tanks, and another that's more buttery, and rich, with vanilla flavors imparted from its fermentation in oak barrels. Some wineries even produce a third style somewhere in the middle.

As the region celebrates it 30th anniversary, the North Fork is becoming a destination in itself for gastronomes. More local chefs are pairing fresh local fare with wines resulting in some matches made in heaven, such as Long Island duck and merlot, and lobster with barrel-fermented chardonnay. Top contenders include the **Frisky Oyster** in Greenport (© **631/477-4265;** see review p. 171), **The Seaford Barge** in Southold (© **631/298-4800;** reviewed p. 171), the **Red Door** in Mattituck (© **631/298-4800**), and the **Jamesport Country Kitchen,** in Jamesport (© **631/722-3537**).

But you'll want to do some tasting yourself. Most of the local wineries are open daily, and many offer tours, whether self-guided or guided by appointment. Lots of wines can be sampled free, though a modest charge may be added for pricier wines. Give some thought to tasting sequence: white wines before red; dry before sweet; simple wines before complex ones; and leave the sweetest (dessert) wines for the last. If you plan to make several stops, make sure your encounters are of the swirl-sniff-sip-spit variety, designate a driver, or schedule one of the services that you can hire for the day to take you wine-tasting. **Vintage Tours** (℮ **631/765-4689;** www.northfork.com/tours) offers wine tours that include lunch ($55 per person weekends, $48 on weekdays). **Regency Transportation** (℮ **516/933-0100;** www.regencylimos.com) provides transportation for two at a rate of $65 per hour. The height of the season is in the autumn, during pumpkin-picking season.

Start your tour at Route 25 (Main Rd.) in Paumanok. Wineries are marked with a green and white WINE TRAIL sign. Here are some highlights:

Paumanok Vineyards   A turn-of-the-20th-century barn renovated into a sun-lit tasting room with outdoor decks overlooks some 77 acres of vineyards provides this setting for this family-owned winery; it's only winery in the region to produce chenin blanc and a late-harvest sauvignon blanc. Paumanok (the original Indian name for Long Island), also offers two merlots, cabernet franc, and three chardonnays. Established in 1981, Paumanok, is known to craft two, sometimes three, styles of cabernet sauvignon (and with certain vintages, a Bordeaux-blend they named "Assemblage"); 1074 Main Rd., Aquebogue; ℮ **631/722-8800;** www.paumanok.com; 11am to 6pm daily.

Continue east on Route 25, just ³/₁₀ mile to Jamesport Vineyards

Jamesport Vineyards   This father-and-son collaboration also began in 1981, giving Jamesport Vineyard's among the North Fork's oldest vines. This "estate winery," using its 60 acres planted in vines as the sole source of fruit for the winery, specializing in sauvignon blanc and merlot, but also produces chardonnay, merlot, cabernet franc, and reisling. A charmingly rustic 150-year-old barn houses both the tasting room and the winery; 1216 Main Rd., Jamesport; ℮ **631/722-5256;** www. jamesport-vineyards.com; Monday to Saturday from 11am to 5pm, Sunday noon to 5pm.

Continue east on Main Road (Rte. 25) for 9 miles to BedellCellars, on your left.

Bedell Cellars   The Bedell Cellars group, owned by Michael Lynne, includes three vineyards (Bedell Cellars, Corey Creek Vineyards, and Wells Road Vineyards), two tasting rooms, and a winery. Founder Kip Bedell, who began the winery in 1980, continues as winemaker and oversees operations totaling over 100 acres. Known for its merlot, Bedell also produces chardonnay, cabernet sauvignon, viognier, and a late-harvest reisling; 36225 Main Rd., Cutchogue; ℮ **631/734-7537;** www.bedellcellars.com; summer Monday to Thursday, 11am to 5pm; Friday to Sunday 11am to 6pm; off- season daily 11am to 5pm.

Continue east on Rte. 25 another ¹/₂ mile to Lenz on your left.

The Lenz Winery   Founded in 1979, Lenz is one of the oldest wineries on the East End, yielding three chardonnays, three merlots, gewürztraminer, cabernet sauvignon plus a sparkling wine from pinot noir that spends

7 years *sur lie* (French for "on the lees" [or settled yeast cells]), a key element in quality in a traditional method sparkling wine, adding complexity. "Old Vines" merlot is produced here, from some of the oldest merlot vineyards found in North America; Main Road, Peconic; (✆ **631/734-6010**; www.lenzwine.com; June to December 10am to 6pm daily; January to May 10am to 5pm daily.

Continue east on Route 25 another 4 miles to The Old Field on your right.

The Old Field First growing fruit for sale, The Old Field, established in 1974, began making wines with its first pinot noir released in 1997, and then moving on to merlot, cabernet franc, chardonnay, pinot noir blush and, in the wings, a sparkling wine; 59600 Main Rd., Southold; (✆ **631/765-2465**; www.theoldfield.com; Friday to Sunday and Monday holidays, from 11:30am to 5pm; Monday to Thursday, by appointment.

Leaving Old Field, turn left on Route 25, driving west again 3 miles to Peconic Lane. Turn right (north) on Peconic Lane and proceed past the railroad tracks to The Tasting Room on your left.

The Tasting Room In May 2003, four small North Fork vineyards opened a tasting room, with a nice old-world oak bar, and retail sales outlet for their wines in a restored storefront. For sampling and sales, **Sherwood House** offers a chardonnay and merlot; **Schneider Vineyards**, its noted cabernet franc and chardonnay; **Broadfields Wine Cellars** offers its merlot and cabernet franc and **Le Clos Thérèse** offers its merlots under the label Comtesse Thérèse; 2885 Peconic Lane, Peconic; (✆ **631/765-6404**; Wednesday to Monday from 11am to 6pm; closed major holidays.

Continue north on Peconic Lane to the divided highway (Rte. 48/Sound Ave.). Turn left, heading west for 3 miles for Castello di Borghese on your left.

Castello di Borghese Vineyard & Winery The "founding" vineyard of the Long Island estate wine industry Castello di Borghese (formerly Hargrave Vineyards, est. 1973) produces three chardonnays, pinot blanc, two sauvignon blancs, cabernet franc, two merlots, pinot noir, and riesling. Don't miss the wonderful gift shop; Route 48, Alvah's Lane, Cutchogue; (✆ **631/734-5111**; www.castellodiborghese.com; Sunday to Friday 11am to 5pm; Saturday 11am to 6pm.

—*Mary Foster Morgan*

but you'll also find glass, china, kitchenware, books, and artwork. **Kapell's Antiques,** 400 Front St., Greenport (✆ **631/477-0100**), is the place for early whaling and marine items. And **Pastimes Antiques,** 56025 Main Rd., Southold (✆ **631/765-1221**), offers five rooms of porcelains, cut glass, and sterling silver.

RETAIL The last mall you'll see before you hit the fork is the **Tanger Outlet Center I & II,** 1770 West Main St., Riverhead (✆ **800/407-4894** or 631/369-2732), where you'll find upscale shops like Kenneth Cole and Barneys New York, along with Nike, Old Navy, and Bose.

MUSEUMS

Horton Point Lighthouse ⭐   It's a lighthouse. It's a museum. It's also a great place to bring a picnic lunch, since this 8-acre park provides great views of the Sound and picnic tables. The lighthouse dates from 1857, and inside, the small museum has a collection of lighthouse and other early marine artifacts.

Lighthouse Rd., Southold. © 631/765-5500. Suggested donation $2. Grounds open daily. Museum: Memorial Day to Columbus Day Sat–Sun 11:30am–4pm. From Rte. 48, make a left onto Young Ave., a right onto Old North Rd., then a left onto Lighthouse Rd.

Indian Museum ⭐   It's easy to overlook Long Island's Native American history. It's worth an hour to let this museum fill you in on the history of the area through interesting exhibits of old pots, arrowheads, pipes, wampum, toys, and fishing tools that have been dug up out here.

Main Bayview Rd., Southold. © 631/765-5577. $2 adults, 50¢ for kids. Sept–June Sun 1:30–4:30pm; July–Aug, Sat–Sun 1:30–4:30pm.

WHERE TO STAY

Accommodations here are a mix of motels and B&Bs. Don't expect to see many chains. Some motels sit on waterfront property, but they date from the 1950s and many haven't changed much since then; increased tourism, however, is pushing some owners to renovate. In the meantime, however, you can enjoy cheap rooms, even if they aren't the height of luxury.

VERY EXPENSIVE

Shady Lady ⭐⭐⭐   This over-the-top inn is bawdy, outrageous, and totally incongruous on the laid-back North Fork, but if you like dramatic, romantic rooms, this is definitely the place to find them. With fanciful (and nonsmoking) rooms decked out in red-velvet walls or a birch-bark bed—it's the most elegant place to stay. It's also one of the few places with amenities.

305 North Rd., Greenport, NY 11944. © 631/477-4500. Fax 631/477-4260. www.shadyladyinn.com. 8 units. Mid-May to mid-Oct $295–$400 double; mid-Oct to mid-May $235–$320 double. Rates include continental breakfast. Guests receive 10% off dining. AE, DC, MC, V. Children not allowed. 2-night minimum in summer. **Amenities:** 2 restaurants; lounge; limited room service. *In room:* A/C, TV, dataport, hair dryer.

EXPENSIVE

Arbor View B&B ⭐⭐   Instead of going with the regular antique look, the affable innkeepers went with a muted decor that leans more toward the elegant than the rustic. All rooms are named for grapes, with shades of colors reflecting the names (Champagne, rose, merlot). Since the inn sits on the main drag, you'll likely hear some traffic, but not enough to be a deal-breaker. The nicest room, the Zinfandel, boasts a gorgeous four-poster but is unfortunately downstairs right next to the entrance.

8900 Main Rd., East Marion, NY 11939. © 631/477-8440. Call for fax. www.arborviewhouse.com. 4 units. May–Nov Mon–Thurs $185–$235 double, Fri–Sun $205–$255 double; Mar–Apr $125–165 double midweek, $165–$205 double weekend; Dec–Feb $145–$195 double midweek, $175–$225 double weekend. 2-night minimum May–Nov. Rates include an excellent full breakfast. AE, MC, V. Inn located about 2 miles east of Greenport. *In room:* A/C, hair dryer, no phone, CD player.

Bayview Inn ⭐   This newcomer to the North Fork inn scene is a bit of a misnomer, since you have to squint past trees to get a view of the bay. Still, the rooms in the main house are cozy and plainly furnished, but with smallish bathrooms. Snag room 8, which is a bit bigger than the others. The cottage is actually a separate house next door with two units; they're nice and modern but unfortunately sparsely furnished and quite sterile.

10 Front St., South Jamesport, NY 11970. ℂ **631/722-2659.** www.northforkmotels.com. 9 units. May–Sept. $150–$170 double inn rooms, $225 double cottage rooms; Sept–May $110 double inn rooms, $175 double cottages. 2-night minimum on summer weekends. AE, DISC, MC, V. From Rte. 25, turn south on S. Jamesport Ave. to Front St. **Amenities:** Restaurant; lounge. *In room:* A/C, TV/VCR, full kitchens (cottage rooms), no phone.

MODERATE

Blue Dolphin ★★ "The Blue" is fast becoming *the* place to be on the North Fork. With the goodwill of its party-hearty owners, the pool and bar areas are crowded all summer long. Though it retains its 1950-era motel facade, the new owners have gutted everything, bringing a new-millennium feel to it, with funky lighting, some exposed beams, comfy beds and sofas, and kitchenettes in every room.

7850 Main Rd., East Marion, NY 11939. ℂ **631/477-0907.** www.bluedolphinresort.com. 29 units. Late May to late Sept $169–$199 double, $219–$299 suite; May and Oct $129–$179 double, $189–$249 suite; Nov–Apr $79–$119 double, $139–$199 suite. **Amenities:** Restaurant; lounge; game room; coin-op washers and dryers; courtesy stretch limo. *In room:* A/C, TV, kitchenettes, fridge, coffeemaker (some units), no phones.

Motel on the Bay   Across the street from the Bayview Inn (and owned by the same folks), this property harbors no pretensions of being a classy inn. Its down-at-the-heels rooms are offset by its location right on the beach. And though the rooms are all smoking (and smell like it), they have some nice touches like exposed beams and kitchenettes. Room no. 10 is a suite with great views.

67 Front St., South Jamesport, NY 11970. ℂ **631/722-3458.** www.northforkmotels.com. 18 units. May–Sept. $150–$250 double, Sept–May $75–$185 double. AE, DISC, MC, V. From Rte. 25, turn south on S. Jamesport Ave., turn left on Front St. *In room:* A/C, TV, kitchen.

Silver Sands ★   Set back from the road, this motel sits on 36 acres with a quarter-mile of private beach, *the* reason to stay here. Rooms are far from glamorous: they're clean, but they maintain their dated furniture, linoleum floors, and small bathrooms. Stay in room no. 1 or 22 and you'll get that wonderful Sound view. Cabins are similarly furnished with two bedrooms but not a lot of extra space. A huge wildlife preserve is also on the grounds.

Silvermere Rd., Greenport, NY 11944. ℂ **631/477-0011.** www.silver-sands-motel.com. 40 units. Mid-June to Labor Day motel rooms $150–$200 double, cottages only by the week, double $1,500–$2,500; Labor Day to mid-June motel rooms $80–$150, cottages $150. Motel rates include breakfast. AE, DC, DISC, MC, V. Head east on Rte. 25 out of Southold and at the first right after passing the Lutheran church you'll see the sign for the motel on the right. **Amenities:** Outdoor heated pool; game room; laundry service; same-day dry cleaning. *In room:* A/C, TV, dataport, kitchenette or microwave and fridge (motel rooms), kitchens (cottages only), coffeemaker, iron.

WHERE TO DINE

Restaurants on the North Fork operate according to their own timetable: they close when people stop coming in, their "in season" starts up whenever the traffic warrants, and they may shut down at a moment's notice for a month's vacation. Especially in the winter months, it's best to call first.

EXPENSIVE

Coeur des Vignes ★★★ FRENCH & MEDITERRANEAN   It's not every restaurant where the owners fish and hunt for menu items, cook and serve 'em, and also greet everyone with a warm welcome. But this family-run standout offers just that—and serves some of the best food on the North Fork. The service is relaxed (though not slow) in this romantic, candlelit French venture. Game is where this restaurant shines: roasted rabbit, roasted pheasant, quail, and meats like venison come seared and crusted on the outside and moist and succulent inside. Save room for the handmade chocolate liquor truffles.

57225 Main Rd. (Rte. 25), Southold. ☏ **631/765-2656**. Reservations recommended. Main courses $19–$42. AE, DC, DISC, MC, V. Mid-May to Oct Mon–Fri 5–9pm; Sat noon–9pm, Sun 2–9pm. Off season closed Tues, sometimes Mon, and for 1 month, usually Mar; Wed–Fri 5–9pm, Sat noon–9pm, Sun 2–8pm.

Frisky Oyster ★★★ ECLECTIC   The irony of this minimalist, modern restaurant is that it may not actually have oysters on the menu (it changes often). Still, its inventive cuisine—a potpourri of choices that are often tweaked with Asian, French, or Mexican touches—always gets rave reviews. Start with one of their excellent soups or salads, and continue on to entrees like the steak frites, a juicy strip steak with thin, crispy fries. A simple red snapper comes decked out with corn and fava beans, succotash, and citrus balsamic vinaigrette.

27 Front St., Greenport. ☏ **631/477-4265**. Reservations recommended. Main courses $18–$32. AE, DC, DISC, MC, V. Memorial Day to Labor Day daily 5–10pm; Labor Day to Memorial Day Thurs–Sun 5–10pm (they may be open on Wed as well starting in 2004).

The Seafood Barge ★★ SEAFOOD   This is *the* place for lobster. And crab cakes. And clam chowder. In fact, it's hard to find a seafood dish the Barge doesn't do right. Set on the water with a gorgeous view, it serves up fresh takes on lots of old-sailor dishes: Crab cakes come with a cilantro-mint vinaigrette tucked underneath, and fried shrimp are made with the lightest of batters. Stick with fish: Meat dishes are fine, but there's nothing special about them.

62980 Main Rd. (Rte. 25), Southold. ☏ **631/765-3010**. Main courses $17–$32. AE, DISC, MC, V. Memorial Day to Columbus Day Mon–Fri noon–2:45pm, Mon–Thurs 5–9pm, Fri 5–10pm, Sat noon–10pm, Sun noon–9pm; Columbus Day to Memorial Day closing is 1 hr. earlier each day.

MODERATE

Legends AMERICAN   When you're steps from the water, you better offer fresh fish, and this casual restaurant doesn't disappoint. The bar area is rowdy, with 22 TVs and a stone fireplace, but, thankfully, the dining room is quieter. In either place you'll find very good dishes like pan-fried panko-crusted fresh flounder and grilled mahimahi with ratatouille and balsamic drizzle.

835 First St., New Suffolk. ☏ **631/734-5123**. Main courses $15–$25. Reservations not accepted. AE, DC, DISC, MC, V. Sun–Thurs noon–9pm; Fri–Sat noon–10pm. From Cutchogue, turn left at the light (New Suffolk), go 1½ miles to the blinking lights, turn left onto New Suffolk Ave. then left onto First St.

Modern Snack Bar AMERICAN   When this North Fork opens for the season in early April, people flock here for the home cooking. This dinerlike restaurant has grown from an actual snack bar in 1950 to include all kinds of courses today. The standard burgers and salads are complemented by mom-knows-best dishes like meatloaf and fried chicken.

628 Main Rd., Aquebogue. ☏ **631/722-3655**. Main courses $10–$21. Reservations not accepted. AE, DISC, MC, V. Early Apr to late Dec Tues–Thurs 11am–9pm; Fri–Sat 11am–10pm; Sun noon–9pm. Closed Mon.

INEXPENSIVE

Bruce's Cheese Emporium and Café ★★ CAFE   Step into this Greenport market and you're immediately hit with the aromas of coffee and cheese commingling. Tables are set in the middle of the market and surrounded by old-time photos and antiques. It's a great place to come for a morning omelet, a lunchtime sandwich, or just to buy bread and cheese to take to the waterfront.

208 Main St., Greenport. ☏ **631/477-0023**. Omelets and sandwiches $6–$8. AE, MC, V. July–Oct Mon, Wed–Thurs, Sun 8am–5pm, Fri–Sat 8am–6pm; Jan–May Thurs–Sun 9am–4pm, scattered hours in spring and fall.

Harbourfront Deli DELI   This wide-open, light-flooded restaurant is a great place to start your morning or grab an afternoon sandwich. It's right on the main drag in charming Greenport and serves up several different kinds of burgers, grilled chicken sandwiches, and homemade salads.

48 Front St., Greenport. ℂ 631/477-1878. Sandwiches $5–$6. No credit cards. Daily 6am–6pm.

Rudy's Coffee Bar COFFEE BAR   This laid-back coffee bar/sandwich shop is has one of the most comfortable environments on the North Fork. Grab a spot on an overstuffed sofa, then get a wrap or some soup and have a beer or fill up your cup with one of eight kinds of coffee.

50 Love Ln., Mattituck. ℂ 631/298-7407. Sandwiches $4–$5. Mon–Fri 6am–5pm; Sat 8am–10pm; Sun 8am–5pm.

THE NORTH FORK AFTER DARK

While the North Fork nightlife scene is nothing like the Hamptons, summer weekend nights can get a bit crazy. If you want to stand elbow to elbow with tons of revelers on an outdoor wharf with the music blasting till all hours, head to **Claudio's,** 111 Main St., Greenport, (℗ **631/477-0627**). Since its renovation, the **Blue Dolphin,** 7850 Main Rd., East Marion (℗ **631/477-0907**), has attracted more and more revelers. And **Bay & Main,** 300 Main St., Greenport (℗ **631/477-1442**), also comes alive after dark, right in the heart of Greenport.

3 South Shore Beaches ⟨★⟨★: Long Beach, Jones Beach & Robert Moses State Park

Ah, the beaches. Standing in the heart of Manhattan, it's hard to believe that golden beaches are only an hour away. And though both Long and Jones beaches become absolute sardine factories on summer weekends, they're still great places to grab your own stretch of sand on a quick day trip from the city. People come here for one reason only: glistening, golden sand and a chance to get away from the rigors of city living—so you won't find tons of services or activities.

While Jones Beach, Long Beach, and Robert Moses State Park are the biggest stretches of sand, there are some smaller (and sometimes less crowded) beaches you may want to check out as well. Just watch out—they're also surfer havens. **Tobay Beach** is a half-mile of sand just east of Jones Beach, and **Gilgo Beach** is another gorgeous stretch 6 miles west of Robert Moses.

JONES BEACH

Jones Beach has a dual function, as both beach and concert venue. For more than 80 years it's been swimming heaven; with more than 6 miles of ocean beach and a half-mile of bay beach, it can get crowded, but the water's surprisingly clean and nice. And with a summertime stadium, the area also sees some of music's biggest names. The beach and stadium are set out over a causeway and not accessible by train. In fact when Jones Beach opened in the 1920s, it was socially exclusionary; buses couldn't negotiate the low underpasses, and less wealthy people didn't own cars. Now beach- and concertgoers travel the causeway by car and bus to walk the Jones Beach boardwalk and enjoy the ocean breezes.

Tip: To escape the crushing crowds, head to the beach's west end—there you'll find the park's most undeveloped areas that are home to a variety of migratory birds and native plants. For even fewer crowds, head to Tobay or Gilgo beaches or Robert Moses State Park.

> **Tips** **Al Fresco Dining**
>
> For something a little more formal, and far tastier, than the numerous
> hot dog and soda vendors, duck into Jones Beach's **Boardwalk Restau-
> rant** (© 516/785-2420), open May to Labor Day for lunch or dinner. The
> lobster ravioli and baked scallops béarnaise were quite good. Sure, you
> could dine indoors, but why? Grab a seat on the patio and take in the
> salt air.

ESSENTIALS

GETTING THERE   From New York City, the **Long Island Railroad** (© 516/
822-LIRR) offers a Jones Beach Package in summer that includes round-trip rail
fare to Freeport plus round-trip Long Island Bus connections to the beach. By
car, take the Long Island Expressway East or Grand Central Parkway East to
Northern State Parkway East to Wantagh Parkway South to Jones Beach State
Park or Belt/Southern State Parkway East to Wantagh Parkway South to State
Park. It's $8 to park.

VISITOR INFORMATION   The main number for **Jones Beach State Park**
is © 516/785-1600.

ACTIVITIES & ATTRACTIONS

CONCERTS   From June through August, the Jones Beach stadium (© 888/
706-7600 or 516/221-1000) hosts the hottest outdoor music events around. In
2003, for example, Counting Crows, James Taylor, Neil Young, Peter Gabriel,
and Poison played.

GOLF   A fun way to pass some time and to get a great view of the ocean is at
the **Pitch & Putt** (© 516/785-1600; Apr–Nov), a par-3 course that's right next
to the boardwalk and the Atlantic. Park in field 4 or 5. Cost is $7 per 18 holes;
club rental is $2.

NATURE   The **Theodore Roosevelt Nature Center,** at the west end of Jones
Beach Park (© 516/679-7254), houses educational exhibits, interactive activities, environmental displays, and video programs. Children can dig in a mystery
bone discovery area, explore a section of a shipwreck, and see a butterfly garden,
along with exhibits on the dunes and endangered species. Open weekends year-
round and Wednesday to Friday from Memorial Day to Labor Day.

ROBERT MOSES STATE PARK

Technically part of Fire Island since it sits at the island's western end, this gorgeous stretch of beach is in a different world because you can actually drive here.
Motor over to the eastern end of the park and you'll see the barriers that prevent
access to the car-free area of Fire Island. So park and take a stroll on the 5 sandy
miles, or take in a game of pitch and putt.

ESSENTIALS

GETTING THERE   Take the Southern State Parkway to Robert Moses
Causeway (exit 40) and go south to the western end of Fire Island. Parking fee
is $8.

VISITOR INFORMATION   The main number for **Robert Moses State Park**
is © 631/669-0470.

LONG BEACH

Long Beach is also best experienced as a day trip from the city, since it's not set up for overnighters: All the beachfront property is apartments and retirement homes, and hotels (and boardwalk restaurants) are virtually nonexistent. People come for the beaches and to walk the lengthy boardwalk. With miles of surprisingly clean beach and water, sunbathers and surfers congregate here in mass quantities. Make no mistake: The beaches get supercrowded on summer weekends, and the skies are even more crowded, with planes on their way into and out of New York.

To actually get onto the beach, you have to purchase a beach pass ($6) on the weekends from late May to late June and then daily until early September. You can buy them from the cabanas on the boardwalk or with your train ticket from New York City. When you tire of the beach, the boardwalk makes for a great bike ride with the sea breezes in your nose and the center lane reserved for bikes. For rentals, try **Buddy's,** 907 W. Beech St. (© **516/431-0804**); they'll set you up with a 3-hour rental for $15.

ESSENTIALS

GETTING THERE   The **Long Island Railroad** (© **516/822-LIRR**) goes straight to Long Beach in about 50 minutes from Penn Station. Driving? Take Route 27 to Route 878. If street parking proves difficult—and it probably will— your best bet is the train station lot, which is just a couple of blocks from the ocean.

VISITOR INFORMATION   Contact the **Long Beach Chamber of Commerce,** 350 National Blvd. (© **516/432-6000**), or the **Long Island Convention and Visitors Bureau** (© **877/FUN-ON-LI** or 631/951-3440).

WHERE TO DINE

There are a few worthwhile restaurants, congregated on Park Avenue just west of the train station or on Beech Avenue, west of where the beach ends. **Turquoise,** 50 W. Broadway (© **516/431-9600**), sits right on the boardwalk and is a great place to enjoy a lunchtime burger or salad or a late-afternoon treat of littleneck clams and cold beer. **Chesapeake Bay,** 780 West Beech St. (© **516/432-7262**), is expensive but turns out some of the town's freshest seafood. Both the cuisine and decor at **Duke Falcon's,** 46 West Park Ave. (© **516/897-7000**), span the globe, and it takes a while to sift through the zillions of entrees, which include everything from Italian to Japanese to a delicious Chilean sea bass. Don't skip the creamy gelato for dessert. With its high-backed velvet banquettes and well-spaced tables, the clubby **Josie's,** 232 West Park Ave. (© **516/897-3600**), affords tons of privacy while turning out great meals, such as honey-mustard pork medallions and grilled Montauk swordfish.

4 Fire Island ✸✸✸

A half-mile wide, 32 miles long, car- and attitude-free, Fire Island is about as emotionally far from New York City as you can get within a couple of hours. A patchwork of national seashore and private property, the island has few formal addresses; folks ride beat-up bicycles barefoot and know places only by name. Regulars talk of "the mainland" like it was a distant continent rather than right across the bay. And the word "ostentatious" hasn't even been coined yet—informality rules the day. With punishing winters, Fire Island is strictly a summertime getaway. When Memorial Day hits, the small hamlets fill with warm-weather revelers, while other parts of the island see only congregations of deer. And after September's over, most everything shuts down.

Since cars are off-limits and the water taxi is expensive, it's best to decide what kind of experience you're after before you go. Ocean Beach is the hub of island activity, where you'll find most of the island's hotels and restaurants, along with most of the party-hearty weekend visitors. The small hamlets of **Kismet** and **Ocean Bay** are mostly residential and great for crowd escape, but have few hotels or restaurants. **Cherry Grove** and **Fire Island Pines** are popular gay communities. And to get away from everyone, head to **Watch Hill** and points east—the area boasts a fantastic wildlife preserve, but no facilities besides camping. Walk the beach at night and it'll just be you, the surf, and the moonlight. Out here (and on the western end), beaches are clothing-optional, though going topless is tolerated everywhere.

ESSENTIALS
GETTING THERE   Robert Moses wanted to build a superhighway through the island, but fervent residents put up a fight, and we thank them for it. Now, ironically, you can drive to the eastern end of Robert Moses State Park and walk over. But unless you're a world-class swimmer, the ferry's your only other option for getting out here. Though some boats operate year-round, they mostly run from May to October a few times daily, with very frequent service in July and August. Take the **Long Island Railroad** (© 516/822-LIRR) to one of three stops: Bay Shore, Sayville, or Patchogue. Van taxis will be waiting to whisk you to a ferry for $3 per person. **Fire Island Ferries** (© 631/665-3600; www.pagelinx.com/fififerry/index.shtml) gets you from Bay Shore to Ocean Beach from the Fire Island Ferry Terminal; **Sayville Ferry** (© 631/589-0810; www.sayvilleferry.com) takes you from Sayville to Sunken Forest from the Sailors Haven Ferry Terminal; and **Davis Park Ferry** (© 631/475-1665; www.pagelinx.com/dpferry/index.shtml) gets you from Patchogue to Watch Hill from the Watch Hill Ferry Terminal. Most ferries are $7 for the 20- to 30-minute jaunt across the bay.

GETTING AROUND   Cars are off-limits. You can walk from town to town, but distances are deceptively long, so consider calling **South Bay Water Taxi** (© 631/665-8885) and they'll come collect you from any pier.

Outside of the expensive water taxis and hoofing it, **bikes** are the only way to get around. Rent them from **Ocean Beach Hardware,** 482 Bayberry Walk, Ocean Beach (© 631/583-5826), for $10 per day.

VISITOR INFORMATION   There's no tourist office here, but the **Long Island Convention & Visitors Bureau** (© 877/386-6654) may provide some info.

SHOPPING
While tacky T-shirt shops and home-decor stores dominate the streets of Ocean Beach, you can find real art at the **Kenny Goodman Gallery,** 325 Denhoff Walk, Ocean Beach (© 631/583-8207), open weekends only in May and June and September and October, daily July and August. Since 1968, Kenny's been making beautiful wooden walking sticks and eerily disturbing wooden heads, along with gorgeous silver jewelry.

EXPLORING FIRE ISLAND
For a little history with a killer 360-degree view of island, bay, and ocean—you can even see Manhattan on a superclear day—climb the 182 steps to the top of

Where the Boys (& Girls) Are

While all of Fire Island has a reputation as a hangout for gays and lesbians, the action is mostly in The Pines (for boys) and Cherry Grove (for girls). The biggest day of the year out here is the Invasion of the Pines on July 4, when boatloads of drag queens from Cherry Grove come and terrorize the posh Pines. In the Pines, the place to stay is **Pines Place** (© **631/597-6162**). And in Cherry Grove, try the **Cherry Grove Beach Hotel** (© **631/597-6600**), at least, as long as you don't mind dorm-style rooms. Nightclubs hop in these two towns until all hours of the night and morning. In the Pines, party at **The Pavilion** (© **631/597-6131**). In Cherry Grove, **The Ice Palace** (© **631/597-6600**) is the hottest spot, with drag shows and theme parties throughout the summer.

the **Fire Island Lighthouse** (© **631/661-4876**), near Kismet at the island's western end. The light has been guiding ships since 1825. It's open 9:30am to 5pm, daily July 1 to Labor Day, weekends only the rest of the year; admission is $4. Midisland, the **Sunken Forest** (© **631/661-4876**) is a gorgeous nature preserve and a great walkabout that's free and always open. Set behind the dunes, this 250-year-old forest is a crowded collection of American holly and sassafras that twists and tangles to create a shady canopy. The dense growth has withstood the punishment of constant salt spray better than most of the homes. The marked boardwalk trail will help you sort out what's what.

WHERE TO STAY

With demand for accommodations far outweighing supply, it's decidedly a seller's market. Even tiny, moldy rooms with bathrooms down the hall still get away with charging more than $100 a night. Buyer beware!

Clegg's Hotel ⭐   The owners of this hotel, family-run since the 1940s, actually care about cleanliness. Plus, Clegg's occupies a prime position in the middle of the Ocean Beach action. Standard rooms are closet-size and sparsely furnished with either a full bed or two twins. You'll have to share a bathroom with several other rooms. A better choice? One of the studio apartments with a bay view: You'll also get a small private bathroom and a kitchenette.

478 Bayberry Walk, Ocean Beach, Fire Island, NY 11770. © **631/583-5399**. Fax 631/583-9375. www.cleggs hotel.com. 20 units. May–Sept Sun–Thurs $110 double; $200 suite; Fri–Sat $160 double, $210 suite. 2-night minimum on weekends. AE, MC, V. *In room:* A/C, kitchenette in suites, no phone.

Ocean View Hotel ⭐⭐   The Ocean View occupies the upstairs at Tequila Jack's restaurant, a 10-minute walk from Ocean Beach, and the party below rages till the liquor stops flowing. So if you came here to sleep, look elsewhere. The rooms give you some decent space, full of light and color. They come outfitted with comfy beds and hardwood floors, and some have great water views. There's no air-conditioning (there are fans), and though bathrooms are private (a rarity out here), you'll have to limber up so you can maneuver in the tiny showers.

Robins Rest, Fire Island, NY, 11770. Mailing address: 121 Maple Ave., Bayshore, NY 11706. © **631/583-0375**. Fax 631/583-6122. www.bayshoreferry.com. 12 units. Memorial Day to Labor Day Sun-Thurs $125–$175 double; Fri-Sat $225–$275 double. 2-night weekend minimum. AE, MC, V. Hotel runs a private shuttle from Maple Ave. Marina in Bayshore, call ✆ 631/665-6001 for schedule. **Amenities:** Restaurant. *In room:* No phone.

CAMPGROUNDS

Unless you know someone, camping at **Watch Hill** is the only way to sleep for free out here, and while it's far removed from any facilities or action, it's superquiet and in the island's most beautiful area. The 26-site campground, which is not free, books up a year in advance (get a reservation request form and all the rules at www.watchhillfi.com). You can, however, get a free backcountry pass from the **Watch Hill Visitor Center** (✆ 631/597-6455) and walk a quarter-mile east on the beach into the Otis Pike Wilderness Area. Pop your tent anywhere behind the dunes.

RENTALS

Most people rent a home for their Fire Island vacations. For a place in Ocean Beach, Sea View, Robins Rest, or other points on the island's western end, call **Red Wagon Realty,** 471 Denhoff, Ocean Beach (✆ 631/583-8158). For the Pines, call **Pines Harbor Realty** (✆ 631/597-7575). In Cherry Grove, call **A Summer Place** (✆ 631/597-6140).

WHERE TO DINE

Two words: Bring money. Restaurateurs have only a couple of months to make money, so it's not cheap to eat out here.

Matthew's Seafood House ★★ SEAFOOD   Get past the hokey fishnet decor and you'll find Fire Island's best seafood. As you sit on a wooden patio overlooking the bay, the cornbread comes warm and portions are supersized, making the high prices more tolerable. Stick with the fish: Shrimp and scallops are excellent, and tuna or swordfish steaks are prepared 11 ways. Come Sunday (3–6pm) for their weekly party, which includes 75¢ clams, wings, and other bar food.

935 Bay Walk, Ocean Beach. ✆ 631/583-8016. Reservations recommended. Main courses $16–$33. AE, MC, V. Memorial Day to mid-Sept daily noon–4pm and 5:30–10pm.

Rachel's ★ *Value* DINER   This centrally located diner has been dishing up breakfast, lunch, and dinner for 32 years, and the fan-cooled, skylight-filled building is the town's closest thing to a reasonably priced diner. With breakfast served from 7am to 4pm, the blueberry pancakes are a great way to start the morning or afternoon. Dinners are fair, but your best bet is to have breakfast or lunch here. Want something to go? Hit the bakery next door.

325 Bay Walk, Ocean Beach. ✆ 631/583-5953. Breakfasts and burgers $5–$9, dinner entrees $15–$20. AE, DISC, MC, V. Mid-Apr to mid-Oct. daily 7am–11pm.

FIRE ISLAND AFTER DARK

Tequila Jack's, on the water in Robbins Rest (✆ 631/583-0375), is open daily from 11am till you leave and boasts the largest deck on Fire Island and hence the biggest party. Go for the daily "sunset shot"—a shot and a moment of silence to celebrate the spectacular sunset. Drinkers love the down-at-the-heels feel of **Housers,** Bayview Walk in Ocean Beach (✆ 631/583-8900), open 4pm to midnight; it's one of the biggest indoors scenes in town. To party on the water, head to **Casino Bar and Café,** on the ocean in Davis Park (✆ 516/597-9414), which has a huge deck where DJs spin on the weekends.

5 The South Fork: The Hamptons (★(★(★

Generally referred to as simply "The Hamptons," the South Fork is actually made up of a group of towns, not all of which actually end in "hampton," and each with its own flavor. Regardless of name, though, this is where the rich and famous spend their summers, and with good reason: Some of the most gorgeous land in New York State—and some of the best beaches in the world—are here. In fact, ever since the railroad was built out to Southampton in 1870, people have been hooked on the South Fork.

While winters are relatively quiet, the summer season brings crushing crowds and a flashy nightclub scene. A drive along Route 27 requires immense patience, so it's worthwhile figuring out what kind of experience you're after so there's not a lot of backtracking. **Eastport** is a tiny hamlet filled with antiques shops; **Westhampton** is a little more Long Beach (see above) than a true Hampton; **Southampton** boasts old money, huge estates, and chic stores; **East Hampton** is the trendy, new-money capital of Long Island—Jerry Seinfeld, Billy Joel, and Martha Stewart have homes here; **Sag Harbor** is a gorgeous town on the water where even the dry cleaner has antique irons in the window; **Amagansett** and **Bridgehampton** are cute little towns; and laid-back **Montauk** relishes its position at the island's tip; set apart from the more exclusive villages, it's also a big draw for fishermen and surfers.

To locate the towns in this section, please see the map on the inside back cover.

ESSENTIALS

GETTING THERE   The **Long Island Railroad** (© 516/822-LIRR) makes stops in Westhampton, Hampton Bays, Bridgehampton, East Hampton, Amagansett, and Montauk. By car, take the **Long Island Expressway** to Riverhead (where it ends) and head south to Route 27, which takes you all the way out to Montauk. The **Hampton Jitney** (© 800/936-0440 or 631/283-4600) buses run daily. Pickup locations include Manhattan, LaGuardia, JFK, and Islip airports and several stops in the Hamptons. The complete route takes around 3½ hours, but allow for traffic delays at peak travel times. Count on around $25 each way. The buses run by **Hampton Luxury Liner** (© 631/537-5800) offer more room than the Jitney, with just 21 reclining leather captain's seats. Peak rate is $37 each way. **MacArthur Airport** (© 631/467-3210), situated mid–Long Island, is the closest airport (see above). **Viking Ferry** (West Lake Dr., Montauk; © 631/668-5709) runs a passengers-only service between Montauk and Block Island and Newport, Rhode Island, and New London and Mystic, Connecticut.

VISITOR INFORMATION   The **Southampton Chamber of Commerce** is at 76 Main St., Southampton (© 631/283-0402), or contact **the Long Island Convention and Visitors Bureau** (© 877/FUN-ON-LI or 631/951-3440)

GETTING AROUND   Cars are your best option out here. Rent from **Hertz** (© 800/654-3131) in Riverhead or **Avis** (© 800/331-1212), which has an office in Southampton. For a taxi in Southampton, call **McRides Taxi** (© 631/744-1155). In Montauk, call **Montauk Taxi** (© 631/668-2468).

BEACHES & ACTIVE PURSUITS

BEACHES   Hamptons beaches are world-class for a reason: Not only are the grains of gold perfectly maintained, but they stretch on forever. Unlike some

Fun Fact Just Ducky

Long Island is famous for its duck, but you likely won't see any duck farms out here—in fact the only duck you may see is the landmark 20-foot-tall Big Duck statue (on Rte. 24 at the Flanders/Hampton Bays border). So what gives? Well, there used to be many farms, but the smell drove residents to have them closed. Now there are just a couple of farms, providing ducks to only a few select restaurants. Anyone else who calls it Long Island Duck is just a quack.

beaches that are interrupted by cliffs or rocks, these sandy stretches allow you to walk for hours, just getting lost in the grandness of the ocean—and if you look to the other side, the grandness of the homes. There's just one problem when it comes to enjoying these beaches: parking. Walk, ride a bike, take a taxi—do anything but drive to the beach. Nonresident park permit fees run from $125 to $225 and daily parking fees can be $25—if a spot's even available.

Your best option? Stay at a hotel that has beach rights. Hotels like Gurney's Inn are right on the water, so you'll have no problems. Some off-beach places like the Southampton Inn will shuttle you to the water for free.

So where do you go? In Southampton, **Cooper Neck Beach** is the main public beach; it's beautifully maintained and you'll find a concession stand, but it can get crowded, and parking costs as much as $25. **Old Town Beach** is much less crowded and there's no parking permit required, but it has only 30 spaces, so get there early. **Main Beach** in East Hampton is gorgeous and in view of some giant mansions. A weekday parking pass is $15, and there are no nonresident parking permits on weekends. **Westhampton Beach Village** has some of the best beaches on Long Island, but forget about parking. Even walking onto the beach requires a permit (call ✆ **631/288-1654**).

If you want to tote your lunch along, pick up sandwiches to go at **Hampton Bagels;** there are outlets in Southampton, 42 Jagger Lane (✆ **631/287-6445**), East Hampton, 74 North Main (✆ 631/324-5411), and Hampton Bays, 252 W. Montauk Hwy. (✆ 631/728-7893). For something fancier, check out the gourmet cheeses and huge salad bar at **Schmidt's Market,** 120 N. Sea Rd., Southampton (✆ **631/283-5777**).

BOATING   Go exploring on the water by kayak. The **East Coast Adventure Tour Company,** 3253 Noyac Rd., Sag Harbor (✆ 631/725-4712), will take you out for lessons ($30 per hr.) or rent you a kayak ($16 per hr.). They also offer all kinds of tours, like sunset tours, clambake tours, and children's tours (prices vary). Open April to October.

DRIVING   Wheel around Southampton and check out some of the amazing estates that line Gin Lane and Coopers Neck; unfortunately, many of them are blocked by sky-high hedges.

FISHING   Montauk is renowned as one of the nation's best places for surfcasting. Start getting your muscles ready now: 40- and 50-pound bass migrate through these waters in the fall, and gigantic bass and stripers can be caught in the summer as well. Climb aboard with **Sea Otter Fishing Fleet** (✆ 631/668-2669), where a half-day is $30. Or go with the larger **Viking Lines,** Montauk Harbor (✆ **631/668-6668**); a half-day is $32.

GOLF   Montauk Downs on Fairview Ave. east of Montauk (© 631/668-5000) has a beautiful course. It's $36 for 18 holes on the weekend; start after 4pm, however, and you'll pay just $19. A great value course is the nine-hole Barcelon Neck, off Route 114 between East Hampton and Sag Harbor (© 631/725-2503). It's just $12 on weekdays, $18 on weekends. Shinnecock Hills, 200 Tuckahoe Rd., Southampton, will be home to the U.S. Open in 2004, but it's a private course, so you'll have to make friends with a member.

HORSEBACK RIDING   Dating from the 1600s, Montauk's Deep Hollow Ranch, Montauk Highway (© 631/668-2744; www.deephollowranch.com), is the oldest cattle ranch in the U.S. (sorry Texas). Their collection of horses is available for beach and trail rides, which are usually 1½ hours long and cost $60. They take riders 8 years and older, though you can be any experience level, and the wranglers are great with kids. There's also tons of entertainment, like barbecues.

U-PICK FARMS   Have fun picking your own fruit. For strawberries, visit Osborn Farm, Main Street, Wainscott (© 631/537-0586); for apples and pumpkins, it's John Halsey Farms, Montauk Hwy, Water Mill (© 631/537-2565). Hank Kraszewski Farms has a couple of outlets: For strawberries, head out Route 39, Southampton Bypass, Southampton (© 631/726-4964), and for pumpkins take Route 27, Water Mill (same number).

SURFING   Just below the Montauk Point Lighthouse, you'll find some of the biggest waves on Long Island—along with boarders who come out for some impromptu wave-catching. The currents are very tricky where the ocean meets the Sound, but experienced riders will have a blast. Pick up your supplies at Plaza Surf & Sports, 716 Main St., Montauk (© 516/668-9300).

WINERIES   While you won't find a winery every mile like on the North Fork, the South Fork does boast three fine wineries: Wölffer Estate, 139 Sagg Rd., Sagaponack (© 631/537-5106); Duck Walk Vineyards, 231 Montauk Hwy., Watermill (© 631/726-7555); and Channing Daughters, 1927 Scuttlehole Rd., Bridgehampton (© 631/537-7224).

SHOPPING

For chic shopping, walk along Main Street in Southampton, where you'll find the country homes of upscale Manhattan shops like Saks Fifth Avenue, 50 Main St. (© 631/283-3500), and the clothing and furnishings at Edward Archer, 85 Main St. (© 631/283-2668). Gallery-wise, don't miss the collection of artists at the Chrysalis Gallery, 2 Main St. (© 631/287-1883).

East Hampton also boasts loads of upscale shops like the Coach Factory Stores, 69 Main St. (© 631/329-1777), and the Polo Country Store Ralph Lauren, 31-33 Main St. (© 631/324-1222), plus many art galleries showing the work of highly regarded artists, including the Lizan-Tops Gallery, 66 Newtown Lane (© 631/324-3424).

For antiques, two villages stand out: Eastport and Bridgehampton. In Eastport, drop by the Eastport Antique Center, 500 Montauk Hwy. (© 631/325-0388), and Ragamuffins, 486 Montauk Hwy. (© 631/325-1280). In Bridgehampton, it seems every other store sells antiques: Try Gemini Antiques, 2418 Main St. (© 631/537-4565), for American Folk Art pieces, and Hampton Briggs Antiques, 2462 Main St. (© 631/537-6286), for Asian pieces. For Native American arts and crafts, stop at the Shinnecock Trading Post, Montauk Highway, Southampton (© 631/287-3200).

MUSEUMS & ATTRACTIONS

Montauk Point Lighthouse Museum ★★   Up on a hill, overlooking the rocky coastline of Long Island's easternmost point, this museum hosts a bevy of artifacts and a chance to get a great view. Commissioned by Congress under George Washington in 1792 and completed in 1796, the first lighthouse in New York State offers old exhibits of historical documents and the lonely life of a lighthouse keeper, as well as a chance to climb the 110-foot tower to get a stunning view of ocean, coastline, and the dense scrub that lines the road from the town of Montauk out here.

Located at the very end of Rte. 27. ℂ **888/MTK-POIN** or 631/668-2544. Admission $6 adults, $3 children. Daily mid-May to mid-October, usually 10:30am–6pm, scattered hours in the off season, mostly weekends only.

Whaling Museum ★   Housed in a gorgeous 1845 Greek Revival mansion built by whaling ship magnate Benjamin Huntting, the home is as cool as the collection inside, devoted to the industry that put this part of the world on the map. Highlights include 100-year-old genuine whale jawbones, a reconstructed 18th-century kitchen, tools and weapons of whalers, and samples of whale oil.

200 Main St. at Garden St., Sag Harbor. ℂ **631/725-0770.** Admission $3. Mid-May to late Sept daily 10am–5pm and weekends in Oct (call first, the Oct schedule may change).

WHERE TO STAY

Accommodations span the range from small motels to extravagant resorts to tiny historical inns. But they all have one thing in common: in summer, they require 2- and 3-night minimums.

EXPENSIVE

Gurney's Inn ★★★   Right on a gorgeous stretch of white sand, Gurney's sprawls across several buildings with a great spa. Only some of the buildings are right on the ocean, and the range of rates reflects your view. Rooms are spacious and very modern, which translates to a bit sterile. While the marble and glass interiors may not be overly charming, they're still comfortable and generally get plenty of light.

290 Old Montauk Hwy. ℂ **631/668-2345.** Fax 631/668-3576. www.gurneys-inn.com. 109 units. May–Sept midweek $350–$435 double, weekend $370–$455 double, $395 and way up suite and cottage; Sept to mid-Oct midweek $255–$325 double, weekend $300–$365 double, $325 and way up suite and cottage; mid-Oct to Apr midweek $234–$295 double, weekend $295–$350 double, $242 and way up suite and cottage. Rates include $25 dinner credit and $13 breakfast credit per person. Packages available. 4-night weekend minimum June–Aug. AE, DC, DISC, MC, V. Free valet parking. **Amenities:** 3 restaurants; lounge; heated indoor pool; big exercise room overlooking ocean; spa; children's programs in summer; game room; concierge; courtesy bus; salon; limited room service; massage (in-room available); laundry service; same-day dry cleaning. *In room:* A/C, TV/VCR w/pay movies, dataport, kitchenette in cottages, fridge, coffeemaker, hair dryer, iron, safe.

Seatuck Cove House ★★★   If you've ever dreamed of staying in one of the enormous Victorian waterfront homes that dot the shoreline, then this inn is for you. Its country-furnished look gives it a laid-back feel, and you're just a stone's throw from the inn's small private beach. The nonsmoking rooms are painted white, and with one exception they're spacious and bright with separate sitting areas. The Dune Road room is amazing—huge with great water views, a temperature-controlled whirlpool tub, flat-screen digital TV with DVD player, stone fireplace, and high ceilings.

61 South Bay Ave., Eastport, NY 11941. ℂ **631/325-3300.** Fax 631/325-8443. www.seatuckcovehouse.com. 5 units. May–Sept weekday $250–$325 double, weekend $325–$400 double, 2-night minimum on weekends;

Oct–Apr weekday $150–$225 double, weekend $225–$300 double. Rates include full breakfast. AE, DC, DISC, MC, V. Go east through village of Eastport, turn right onto South Bay Ave., travel to end of road. **Amenities:** Heated outdoor pool. *In room:* A/C, 4 rooms w/TV/VCR, dataport, hair dryer.

1708 House ★★★   This cozy Colonial actually does date from 1708 and you can stay in the original 18th-century rooms. The inn offers just four rooms (nos. 1–4) in this style: they're not the world's largest, but have original wood floors and exposed-beam ceilings, along with beautiful four-poster beds and claw-foot tubs. The other rooms were added in 1996 and are also decked out in gorgeous furniture and wood floors, but they're much more modern. The cottages are beachy and modern.

126 Main St., Southampton, NY 11968. ☎ 631/287-1708. Fax 631/287-3593. www.1708house.com. 12 units. May–Oct weekday $195–$375 double, weekend $275–$475 double; Nov–Apr weekday $145–$225 double, weekend $150–$275 double. Rates include continental breakfast. AE, MC, V. 2-night weekend minimums apply May–June and Sept–Oct. 3-night minimum weekends apply July–Aug. Holidays are 4-night minimum. **Amenities:** Lounge. *In room:* A/C, TV (some w/VCR), dataport, kitchen in 2 of the cottages, hair dryer, iron.

MODERATE

Inn at Quogue ★★ *Finds*   A combination of quaint country inn and pool-centered resort, this 67-unit inn stretches across several different buildings off the beaten path of the eponymous town, offering cheap, small poolside rooms as well as the more formal but much nicer inn rooms. These were designed by Ralph Lauren's people and outfitted with his stuff. They're tiny but bright and gorgeously decorated. If you can, grab room no. 1 in the main house, a bright big split-level room with original floors from 1785.

47–52 Quogue St., Quogue, NY 11959. ☎ 631/653-6560. Fax 631/653-8026. www.innatquogue.com. Mid-June to Labor Day $215–$275 double, $395 and up suite, Mon–Wed half-price, $50 more on summer holidays; Labor Day to early Nov and mid-Apr to mid-June $145–$195 double, $275 and up suite; early Nov to mid-Apr $85–$100 double, $150 and up suite. AE, DC, DISC, MC, V. Pets allowed with a $50 extra charge. **Amenities:** Restaurant; lounge; outdoor pool (indoor pool being built at press time); small exercise room; Jacuzzi; bike rental; limited room service; massage (in-room available). *In room:* A/C, TV, some w/kitchenette, some w/hair dryer.

Southampton Inn ★★ *Kids*   Set on extensive grounds with a conference center, pool, tennis court, and kid's programs, this inn is more of a resort destination, but it's just around the corner from the town's chic shops and restaurants. And with the inn's free shuttle to the beach in summer, the nightmare of parking near Southampton sand vanishes. It's the kind of place that caters to everyone: families, groups, couples, even pet lovers, and does a good job making everyone happy. Standard rooms are nothing extravagant, but they are very comfortable and spacious and come loaded with amenities, making for a good value, even in the heart of summer.

91 Hill St., Southampton, NY 11968. ☎ 800/832-6500 or 631/283-6500. Fax 631/283-6559. www.southamptoninn.com. 90 units. Nov–Apr $119–$199 double, $319 and way up suite; May–Oct $149–$489 double, $319 and way way up suite. Rates include small continental breakfast in the winter months only. Packages available. AE, DC, DISC, MC, V. 2-night minimum on weekends May–Sept; 3-night minimum summer holiday weekends. Pets allowed with $29 fee. **Amenities:** Restaurant; outdoor heated pool; outdoor tennis court; exercise room; children's programs; game room; complimentary beach shuttle; limited room service; babysitting; laundry service; same-day dry cleaning. *In room:* A/C, TV w/pay movies, dataport, fridge, hair dryer.

INEXPENSIVE

Harborside Resort Motel   A solid, affordable option that's just 3 blocks from the Sound and one of its beaches, this small L-shaped motel offers decent rooms in a quiet locale. Rooms are nothing extravagant and some are a tight fit;

some are a little heavy on the wood paneling, which others are painted white. Still, when you need to get out, there's a pool and tennis court on premises—and, of course, the beach nearby.

371 West Lake Dr., Montauk, NY 11954. © **631/668-2511.** www.peconic.net/harborside. 28 units. June to Labor Day $95–$155 double, $230 apt.; Nov–Apr $58–$85 double; about $165 apt. AE, DISC, MC, V. 2-night summer minimum, 3 nights weekends; spring and fall 2-night weekend minimum. 1 mile east of Montauk, turn left on to West Lake Dr. (County Rd. 77). **Amenities:** Outdoor pool; 2 tennis courts. In room: A/C, TV, kitchenettes (apts. only).

CAMPGROUNDS

Hither Hills State Park, Montauk (© **631/688-2554**), is a gem of a beach park without the pretension of the Hamptons. It also offers a rarity: camping just steps from the 2-mile-long white-sand beach. A campground in chic East Hampton seems like an anomaly (and it is), but **Cedar Point County Park** (© **631/852-7620**) is set in a densely wooded area of East Hampton overlooking the Sound. The 190 campsites, which are a few minutes' walk from the water, can be used for tents and campers, though none have electric hookups.

WHERE TO DINE

While you'll always find the well dressed (and well heeled) in Hamptons restaurants, you won't feel out of place in casual attire unless you're dining at a very formal place like East Hampton's The Palm (an outpost of the New York City steakhouse). Even servers at hot new Almond are clad in blue jeans. Of course, under intense pressure to be the next big thing, restaurants can come and go pretty quickly. Keep up-to-date with the comings and goings by picking up the ubiquitous *Dan's Papers*.

EXPENSIVE

Almond ★★★ FRENCH BISTRO   This newcomer has quickly caught fire as the Hamptons hottest bistro, attracting celebs—Billy Joel and Joy Behar were here the night I was—and making reservations sometimes hard to come by. If you can, get a table in the back for a more relaxed atmosphere. The menu offers traditional bistro fare that is as simple as the decor, with only a few selections each night. Steak frites is a delicious (and excellent) choice, and salmon and flounder come tender and flavorful; many dishes are helped along with subtle doses of saffron.

1970 Montauk Hwy., Bridgehampton. © **631/537-8885.** Reservations recommended. Main courses $19–$32. AE, DC, MC, V. Memorial Day to Labor Day Mon–Thurs 6–11pm, Fri–Sat 6pm–midnight, Sun 6–10pm; Labor Day to Memorial Day closed 1 hr. earlier and Wed.

George Martin ★★★   Step into the dark environs of this steak-friendly restaurant and you'll know you're in a chophouse that takes meat seriously. Indeed, red meat is where they shine, but they even do fish expertly. Tempura shrimp come lightly battered with a tangy sauce, while crab cakes come crispy and fresh. Even the side dishes are good: The de rigueur creamed spinach comes dusted with Parmesan and in a sauce with just enough texture to make it creamy. Desserts are enormous—the signature brownie is not to be missed.

56 Nugent St., Southampton. © **631/204-8700.** Main courses $18–$29. AE, MC, V. Memorial Day to Labor Day Sun–Thurs 6–10pm, Fri–Sat 6–11pm; Labor Day to Memorial Day closed Mon–Tues.

Surfside Inn ★★   It's not easy to find excellent food with great ocean views, but this casual locale out in laid-back Montauk has been combining them all for almost 20 years. Overlooking the Atlantic in a striking Victorian house, the dining room, porch, and deck serve sweeping sandy vistas, while the pleasant staff serve some of the best food this far east, with straightforward American standards like prime rib, lobster, and crab cakes.

Old Montauk Hwy., 2 min. west of Montauk. © 631/668-5958. Reservations not accepted. Main courses $18–$30. June–Aug Mon–Fri 10am–11pm, Sat 8am–11pm, Sun noon–10pm; off season: dinner nightly, but call first in winter.

Tierra Mar ★★   You can get an amazing ocean view with your dinner if you don't mind eating before the sun goes down. The dining room itself is spectacular, with chandeliers and a formal yet beachy feel. Appetizers fall short, so head straight for the entrees, paired with a wine from the extensive list. Steak comes with a merlot sauce and the cedar-plank roasted Montauk lobster is served with portobello mushrooms. Other dishes have a delicious twist to them, like barbecued Saigon swordfish with ginger demiglaze, bok choy, and shiitake mushrooms.

At the Bath & Tennis Hotel, 231 Dune Rd., Westhampton Beach. © 631/288-2700. Reservations recommended. Main courses $20–$35. AE, MC, V. Sept–May Mon–Fri noon–8pm, Sat–Sun noon–10pm; June–Aug to 11pm.

MODERATE

Rowdy Hall ★ AMERICAN   The acclaimed burger at this English-pub-style restaurant is well worth the hype. Stacked high with all the fixins, it's also well worth the $10. Even if you're not a burger fan, this place, tucked back among the shops of tony East Hampton, offers a good selection of upscale pub food and beers that make it perfect for lunch or dinner.

10 Main St., East Hampton. © 516/324-8555. Reservations not accepted. Main courses $10–$25. AE, MC, V. Memorial Day to Labor Day daily noon–3:30pm and 5–11pm; Labor Day to Memorial Day daily noon–3:30pm, Sun–Thurs 5–10pm, Fri–Sat 5–11pm.

Southampton Publick House ★★ *Finds* PUB   This bustling pub is the only microbrewery out here, and is worth coming for a meal or just for the party that rages continuously. You'll find summer wheat beers and winter stouts. And their inventive formulas have won them all kinds of awards. The menu covers the basics, but they're done well—from ale-battered fish and chips to Cajun duck breast.

40 Bowden Sq., Southampton. © 631/283-2800. AE, DC, MC, V. Main courses $13–$24. Sun–Thurs noon–10pm, Fri–Sat noon–11pm; Tap Room Sun–Thurs noon–1am, Fri–Sat. noon–2am.

INEXPENSIVE

Golden Pear COFFEE SHOP   With great coffee, fresh baked muffins, and fluffy omelets, the four small Golden Pears are consistently good and quaint. They're the perfect place to grab a Sunday morning coffee with your *New York Times.* Or come by later in the day for lunch, when you'll find soups and salads.

Locations: 99 Main St., Southampton (© 631/283-8900); 34 Newtown Lane, East Hampton (© 631/329-1600); 2426 Montauk Hwy., Bridgehampton (© 631/537-1100), 103 Main St., Westhampton Beach (© 631/288-3600). Sandwiches $6–$9. AE, MC, V. 7am–5:30pm daily at all but the Westhampton Beach outlet, which is seasonal.

Provisions WHOLE FOODS ★   This natural foods market and cafe is a great quiet place to relax and tuck into a breakfast nosh like a scrambled tofu wrap or a tempeh reuben with melted soy cheese and organic sauerkraut. And don't miss the smoothies and organic juices.

Corner of Bay and Division St. Sag Harbor. © 631/725-3636. Sandwiches $5.25–$9. AE, MC, V. Daily 8:30am–4pm.

Sip 'n Soda ★★ *(Kids) (Value)* DINER   This old-fashioned soda fountain dates from 1958 and is a fun place for kids and adults alike. It also boasts prices that haven't hit the new millennium yet, making for some of the cheapest eats in Southampton.

40 Hampton St., Southampton. © 631/283-9752. Entrees from $4, burgers from $2.75. No credit cards. July–Aug 7:30am–10pm, rest of year 7:30am–5pm.

THE HAMPTONS AFTER DARK

As you might imagine, Hamptons nightlife can be quite the scene. Bars can fill up quickly and some even roll out the velvet rope to restrict their clientele to models and people with movie deals. And while the über-chichi (and now infamous) Conscience Point Inn in Southampton closed its doors, you'll never be lacking for nightlife; just wander around Southampton or East Hampton and you may well mistake it for ancient Rome, right before its decline. Grab a copy of *Dan's Papers* or pick up the *East Hampton Star* or the *Southampton Press* for listings.

NIGHTCLUBS & LIVE MUSIC

Resort ★★   East Hampton's chichi nightclub opened in 1999 and quickly became the area's hottest spot—and a 2003 renovation breathed new life into it. The über-hip club, decked out in turquoise, orange, and palm trees, is all things Miami and St. Tropez, and it fills up with an equally cool crowd. One warning: The club is used for fancy product launches and private parties and can be hard to get into; call first to see if there are any special events at which mere mortals might not be welcome. Open Thursday to Saturday 10pm to 4am. 44 Three Mile Harbor Rd., East Hampton. © 631/329-6000. Admission $15–$25. AE, MC, V.

Stephen Talkhouse ★★★   Year-round live music draws folks in droves to this small Amagansett club for events that are often standing-room only. Covers range from $5 to $100 depending on the act, which could be local blues acts or bigger names like Suzanne Vega or Todd Rundgren. The space gets a bit cramped, but the music is almost always great. And folks like Billy Joel, Paul Simon, and Paul McCartney have been known to show up unannounced and party with the band. Open nightly 7pm to 4am. 161 Main St., Amagansett. © 631/ 267-3117. AE, MC, V.

6 Shelter Island

Tiny and secluded, nestled between Long Island's two forks, Shelter Island is truly a sheltered getaway spot. Laid back and barely developed, you'll find some nice beaches, secluded coves great for boating and swimming, and a laid-back atmosphere that's unlike anything on the North or South forks. Few people make the short ferry trip across the bay; those who do tend to be family-oriented groups looking for a quiet getaway; you won't find the share scene you do in the Hamptons, or its raging party.

Part of what keeps things quiet is the obvious barrier of the water—even though it's a quick jaunt, you'll still have to ferry across the bay to get to Shelter Island. The other part is the structure of the island itself: More than one-third of Shelter Island is owned by the Nature Conservancy and maintained as a nature preserve. There's lots of lush greenery and dense woods all across the island, with very little in the way of a town. It's really the perfect place to bicycle, walk, play tennis, golf, ride horseback, sail, windsurf, kayak, and fish, or just kick back with a book and read.

Fun Fact **For the Birds**

Look up in the sky: The island is famous for its osprey. And say what you will about the telephone company, but it's built special platforms on its poles along the causeways to Little Ram and Big Ram to accommodate the birds' nests.

And it's always been like this: From the mid-17th century into the 18th, the development of the island grew slowly because the stench of fertilizer from mossbunker herring dominated the island. In the late 19th century it became a religious meeting place for clergy and laymen from Brooklyn; they did away with the fertilizer factories, and Shelter Island was developed after that. Frederick Law Olmsted helped shape the landscape here, and it soon took off as a vacation spot. Today, the town and many of its homes resemble Nantucket or Martha's Vineyard, with clapboard siding, scalloped shingles, and gorgeous, serene spots to get away from it all.

You'll only find one "townlike" area, around Shelter Island Heights on the island's northwest corner. One hotel, a couple antiques shops, a coffee shop, and a couple of restaurants are really all that's here.

ESSENTIALS

GETTING THERE   Shelter Island's only accessible by boat, but it's only about a 10-minute ferry trip from the mainland. If you're driving, the **LIE** runs out to Riverhead; then head north to Greenport or the south to Sag Harbor. From the North Fork, the **North Ferry Co.** (© **631/749-0139**) leaves every 15 to 20 minutes from 6am to 11:45pm. Price is $8 for car and driver, $1 per extra person or for walk-ons. From Sag Harbor, the **South Ferry** (© **631/749-1200**) runs every 10 to 12 minutes from 6am to 11:45pm year-round, extended hours in the summer and extended weekend hours in the spring and fall. Price is $7 for car and driver, $1 per extra person or for walk-ons. Since Shelter Island is so small, it doesn't matter which ferry you take, but if you don't want to bother with a car, you can take the **Long Island Railroad** (© **516/822-LIRR**) to Greenport; the ferry is right next to the train station.

VISITOR INFORMATION   Contact the **Long Island Convention and Visitors Bureau** at © **877/FUN-ON-LI** or 631/951-3440.

GETTING AROUND   If you just want to relax at your hotel, someone will pick you up from the ferry. But if you want to venture out, you'll need a car. Check out the North Fork or South Fork sections for information on car rentals. On the island, you can get a taxi by calling **Flying Cow Transportation** (© **631/749-3421**).

BEACHES & OUTDOOR PURSUITS

BEACHES   Beaches here tend to be narrow strips of sand, but the protected waters are perfect for swimming. Head to **Crescent Beach** and **Silver Beach,** both along the southwestern area of the island.

FISHING   Take off among the rich waters around the island in search of striped bass and bluefish (May–July) and then catch stripers, blues, and false albacore on a half or full-day charter with **Light Tackle Challenge,** 91 W. Neck Rd. (© **631/749-1906**).

HIKING The **Mashomack Preserve,** Route 114 (near the South Ferry office; © **631/749-1001**), encompasses more than 2,000 acres in southeastern Shelter Island, more than a third of the island. Ex–hunting club territory, the Nature Conservancy purchased it in 1980 and has protected its oak woodlands, marshes, freshwater ponds and tidal creeks ever since. Car-free, it's a great place to go for easy hikes and look for osprey, ibis and hummingbirds, muskrats, foxes, harbor seals, and terrapins. As many as 82 breeding species have been recorded there. It's a quiet, wilderness way to spend an afternoon. It's open daily, July to August, from 9am to 5pm; October to March, Wednesday to Monday, 9am to 4pm. Park just inside the preserve entrance and pick up a trail map and hike the four well-marked trails of varying lengths and difficulty (up to 11 miles).

KAYAKING The protected waters of Shelter Island's bays make for a scenic place to slice through on a kayak. You'll likely see the island's deer, osprey, and other wildlife. Go with **Shelter Island Kayak Tours,** Route 114 and Duvall (© **631/749-1990**). Rent a kayak or take a 2-hour tour ($45). The **Nature Conservancy** (© **631/749-1001**) also runs a few kayaking trips around Mashomack Preserve in the summer.

WHERE TO STAY

With a couple of exceptions, don't count on rooms with tons of space.

MODERATE

Olde Country Inn ★★★ *Finds* This quiet, nonsmoking home in the middle of the island boasts lots of country charm, including gorgeously ancient creaky hardwood floors. Guest rooms are outfitted with wrought-iron beds in formal antiques-filled surroundings. Some upstairs rooms have cathedral ceilings—grab one of them for more breathing room. And try for a room with a whirlpool tub—these also have the biggest bathrooms (the others are teeny).

11 Stearns Point Rd., P.O. Box 1209, Shelter Island, NY 11965. © 631/749-1633. www.oldecountryinn.com. From the North Ferry, take Rte. 114 S to West Neck Rd. Make a left onto the 2nd street after the stop sign. 9 units. Fri–Sat June–Oct. $155–$275 double, Nov–May $95–$155; Sun–Thurs rates 15% less. Rates include full breakfast. AE, MC, V. 2-night weekend minimums, 4-night weekend minimums July–Aug. **Amenities:** Restaurant. *In room:* A/C, no phone.

The Pridwin ★ *Kids* Sitting on the same stretch of beach as the Sunset Hotel (see below), this larger inn is decidedly less hip, but offers good value. With one big inn and several small cottages, the grounds are fairly extensive and many rooms offer good water views. The smallish hotel rooms have a retro look; get one with a water view, which is spectacular. Cottages have the same '70s feel and small bathrooms but offer big decks and kitchenettes.

P.O. Box 2009, Crescent Beach, Shelter Island, NY 11964. © **800/273-2497** or 631/749-0476. Fax 631/749-2071. www.pridwin.com. 49 units. Open early May to mid-Oct. Late June to early Sept Sun–Thurs $149–$189 double, $219 cottage; Fri–Sat $179–$219 double, $249 cottage, rates include full breakfast, for dinner plan, add $40 for 2 people; early May to mid-May and mid-Oct to late Oct. $114–$169 double, $144–$179 cottage; late May to late June and Sept to mid-Oct $134–$159 double, $154–$199 cottage. Outside of high season rates include continental breakfast on weekends only. 2-night weekend minimums Jun–Sept. AE, MC, V. From the North Ferry, take 114 south to West Neck Rd.; it becomes Shore Rd. and hotel is on the left. **Amenities:** Restaurant; lounge; outdoor saltwater pool; 3 tennis courts; extensive watersports rentals; bike rentals; game room; coin-op laundry. *In room:* A/C, TV, kitchenette (in cottages).

Ram's Head Inn ★★   Set on a small, private beach with extensive grounds, this inn is one of the island's most luxurious. Rooms have comfortable wicker furniture, lacy table coverings, and nice touches like pedestal sinks (though some have a shared bathroom). They're comfortable, but beware: These rooms are small, with small bathrooms to match. But you don't come here to sit in your room; the grounds are gorgeous, with Adirondack chairs, hammocks, a small beach, and free use of the hotel's boats.

108 Rams Island Dr., Shelter Island, NY 11965. © **631/749-0811.** Fax 631/749-0059. www.shelter islandinns.com. 17 units (5 with private bathroom). Apr–Oct $105–$135 double with shared bathroom, $175–$250 with private bathroom; Nov–Mar $65–$75 with shared bathroom, $175–$250 with private bathroom. Rates include continental breakfast. 2-night weekend minimums in peak season. AE, MC, V. From North Ferry take 114 north, bear right onto Cartwright Rd., turn right at stop sign to Ram Island Rd., turn right onto Ram Island Dr. **Amenities:** Restaurant; lounge; tennis court; tiny fitness room; sauna; complimentary watersports; limited room service. *In room:* A/C.

Sunset Beach ★★★   Designed by Andre Balazs of L.A.'s Chateau Marmont fame, this hotel drips all the hipness you'd expect. The minimalist rooms are done all in white, with contemporary aluminum lamps and splashes of color (like bold orange sinks). But the prize in these rooms is outside: enormous balconies on all of them, looking out onto the water, which more than makes up for the teeny bathrooms and small kitchenettes.

35 Shore Rd., Shelter Island, NY 11965. © **631/749-2001.** Fax 631/749-1843. www.sunsetbeachli.com. 20 units. Open mid-May to Sept. July–Aug weekday $205–$225 double, weekend $350–$375 double; May–June and Sept weekday $195–$215 double, weekend $295–$325 double. AE, DC, DISC, MC, V. From the North Ferry, take Rte. 114 south to W. Neck Rd., which becomes Shore Rd. Pets allowed with $100 fee. 2-night weekend minimum. **Amenities:** Restaurant; tiny aboveground pool; free use of mountain bikes; laundry service; limited room service. *In room:* A/C, TV/VCR, kitchenettes (some units), minibars (some units), hair dryer, iron.

WHERE TO DINE
EXPENSIVE
Ram's Head ★★★ AMERICAN   Shelter Island's best restaurant is in the flowery, formal, and intimate dining room of the Ram's Head Inn. New chef Alan Batson has created an eclectic menu that blends French with a dash of Brazilian. The Brazilian style empanada appetizer with sautéed spinach, roast garlic, and a light tomato cream was excellent. And the nut-crusted swordfish, cedar-roasted, and served with hibiscus glaze, lemon thyme beurre blanc, and jasmine rice was a perfect follow-up. The service and wine list are very good.

108 Rams Island Dr. © **631/749-0811.** Reservations recommended. Main courses $25–$35. AE, MC, V. Apr–Oct Sun–Thurs 5–9:30pm; Fri-Sat 5–10pm; Sat–Sun noon–3pm. From North Ferry take 114 north, bear right onto Cartwright Rd., turn right at stop sign to Ram Island Rd., turn right onto Ram Island Dr.

Vine Street Café ★★★ *Finds* AMERICAN   This brand-new entree to the Shelter Island scene is bound to cause a stir. The café's interior couldn't be more basic: wood floors, simple wooden tables and chairs, white walls, with exposed beams. But the brief menu—relying on local, organic ingredients—presents intensively complex flavors, such as the miso-glazed salmon with bok choy, mushrooms, and jasmine rice.

41 South Ferry Rd. © **631/749-3210.** Reservations preferred. Main courses $18–$28. AE, DISC, MC, V. Mid-June to Labor Day Sun–Wed 6pm–10pm, Thurs–Sat 6–11pm, Sun 11am–3pm; Labor Day to mid-June Thurs, Sun, Mon 6–10pm, Fri–Sat 6–11pm.

MODERATE
Sweet Tomato's ★★ AMERICAN   This brand-new venture in the tiny town of Shelter Island Heights is quickly catching on as a good lunch stop while

antiquing. The menu doesn't offer any surprises, but among the bright, cheery environment with classic hardwood floors, the restaurant serves up classics nicely, such as the Chicken Antonio: chicken breast chunks with sautéed onions and peas in a pink, cognac cream sauce and rigatoni.

15 Grand Ave. © 631/749-4114. Main courses $11–$20. Lunch, sandwiches $7. AE, DC, DISC, MC, V. July to Labor Day 5–10pm, Thurs–Sun noon–4pm; Labor Day to June Sat–Sun noon–4pm, Thurs–Tues 5–10pm.

INEXPENSIVE

Pat & Steve's Family Restaurant ⭐ *Kids* DINER   As you might expect from the name, this is a family favorite that clamors with patrons for its only meals of breakfast and lunch. Tuck into pancakes for just a couple bucks, or snag perhaps the only $4 burger in town.

63 N. Ferry Rd. © 631/749-1998. Sandwiches $4–$8. No credit cards. Thurs–Tues 6am–3pm.

7

The Hudson River Valley

by Neil E. Schlecht

The Mississippi is the longest and most famous river in the United States, but no river commands a larger place in American history than the Hudson. America's first great river flows from the Adirondacks down to New York City and the open sea. First sailed by Henry Hudson in 1609, it became the principal highway for the emergent colonies in 17th and 18th centuries; strategic territory during the war for American independence; and the axis along which some of America's most legendary families—among them, the Livingstons, Vanderbilts, Roosevelts, and Rockefellers—shaped the face of American industry and politics, leaving legacies of grand country estates and the towns that grew up around them. The rise of the United States from renegade colony to great nation is intrinsically linked at every stage to the mighty Hudson River.

Just over 300 miles long, the river is less mighty in size than stature. The Hudson River Valley spans eight counties along the east and west banks of the river, from Albany down to Yonkers. Divided into manageable thirds, the Lower, Middle, and Upper Hudson together comprise a National Heritage Area and one of the most beautiful regions in the eastern United States. The river valley's extraordinary landscapes gave birth to America's first art school, the Hudson River School of Painters, and writers like Edith Wharton and Washington Irving set their stories and novels along the banks of the Hudson. And though a place of immense historical importance and beauty, the river valley is also full of things to do. The Hudson is lined with impressive country manor houses open to the public, unique museums, splendid historic sites, and easygoing Victorian hamlets. You can hike, fish, boat, and even ski within easy reach of any of the towns along the Hudson. For lovers of culture, history, the arts, and the outdoors, the Hudson River Valley has few rivals anywhere.

1 Orientation

ARRIVING

BY PLANE   Most visitors traveling by air will probably fly into one of the New York City area's three major airports. For information on those, please see chapter 5. Other possibilities include **Albany International Airport,** 737 Albany-Shaker Rd. (© **518/242-2299;** www.albanyairport.com), at the north end of the Upper Hudson Valley, and **Stewart International Airport,** Route 207, New Windsor (© **845/564-2100;** www.stewartintlairport.com), near Newburgh, which handles 50 daily flights from major U.S. cities such as Atlanta, Chicago, Philadelphia, Raleigh/Durham, and Washington, D.C.

BY CAR   Most visitors embark on tours of the Hudson Valley by private automobile. Major rental car companies, including Avis, Budget, Enterprise, Hertz, National, and Thrifty, have representatives at all the major airports. The Lower

The Hudson River Valley

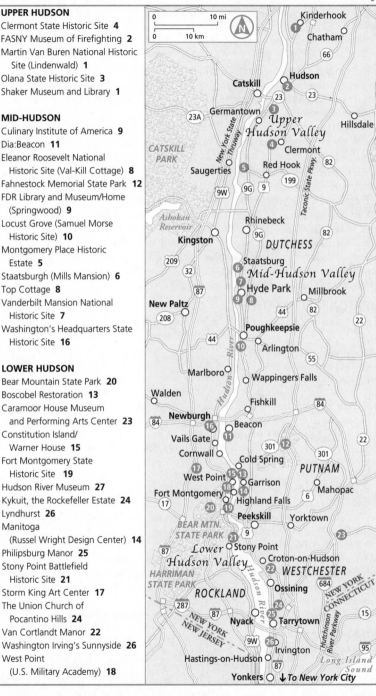

Hudson Valley begins just north of New York City, on either side of the river; take either I-87 (New York State Thruway) north or the Taconic State Parkway. From Albany south, take I-87 south to 9W or I-90 south to Route 9. Heading either east or west, the most direct route is along I-84.

BY TRAIN   **Amtrak** (© 800/USA-RAIL; www.amtrak.com) has service to the Hudson Valley from New York City, Syracuse, Buffalo, Montréal, and Boston, with stops in Albany, Rensselaer, Poughkeepsie, Rhinecliff, New Rochelle, Yonkers, Croton Harmon, and Hudson.

The **Metro-North Railroad** (© 800/638-7646; www.mta.nyc.ny.us/mnr) travels up and down the Hudson. The trip hugging the river on the east side is one of the prettier train trips in the U.S. The commuter line runs from Grand Central Station in New York City and services Westchester, Orange, Rockland, Putnam, and Dutchess counties (with stops in Beacon, Chappaqua, Cold Spring, Garrison, Katonah, Poughkeepsie, Tarrytown, and Yonkers, among others).

BY BUS   Bus service throughout the Hudson Valley is available on **Adirondack and Pine Hills Trailways** (© 800/225-6815), with service to New York City, New Paltz, Kingston, and Albany; **Greyhound Bus Lines** (© 800/231-2222; www.greyhound.com); and **Shortline Coach USA** (© 800/631-8405; www. shortlinebus.com), with local service from New York City and throughout Orange, Rockland, and Dutchess counties.

VISITOR INFORMATION

General tourist information is available by calling **Hudson Valley Tourism, Inc.** (© 800/232-4782); visit the organization's website, **www.travelhudsonvalley. org,** for links to the very informative sites maintained by each of the eight counties that touch upon the Hudson River Valley. A number of towns have tourist information offices or kiosks (and even cabooses) in town and at many historic sites, often operated in season only. Offices that provide information and other resources for travelers include: **Orange County Chamber of Commerce,** 11 Racquet Rd., Newburgh (© 845/567-6229; Mon–Fri 8:30am–5pm); **Greater Cornwall Chamber of Commerce,** 238 Main St., Cornwall (© 845/534-7826; Mon–Fri 9am–4:30pm); **Westchester County Office of Tourism,** 222 Mamaroneck Ave., Suite 100, White Plains ((© 800/833-9282); **Putnam Visitors Bureau,** 110 Old Rte. 6, Bldg. 3, Carmel (© 800/470-4854); **Dutchess County Tourism Promotion Agency,** 3 Neptune Rd., Suite M-17, Poughkeepsie (© 914/463-4000); **Rhinebeck Chamber of Commerce,** Route 9, Rhinebeck (© 914/876-4778); **Hudson Office of Tourism,** 401 State St., Hudson (© 800/727-1846; Mon–Fri 8:30am–4pm); **County Office Building,** 10 Westbrook Lane, Kingston (© 845/340-3566; Mon–Fri 9am–5pm).

Many good free publications are widely available at hotels, restaurants, and other sites; look for *Hudson Valley Guide, Hooked on the Hudson River Valley, About Town,* and *Chronogram.* These all contain information on arts, entertainment, and dining.

For fall foliage reports, visit **www.empire.state.ny.us/tourism/foliage**.

AREA LAYOUT

The Hudson Valley extends from the banks of the river to the foothills of the Catskill Mountains in the west and approaches the Connecticut border in the east (and the Massachusetts border in the Upper Hudson Valley). This chapter goes in an order contrary to the way the current of the Hudson River flows: from Lower to Upper. For the purposes of this chapter, the Lower Hudson includes the area from Yonkers and Nyack to Newburgh and Beacon (comprising Rockland, Orange, Westchester, and Putnam counties); the Mid-Hudson, from Newburgh to Rhinebeck (Ulster and Dutchess counties); and the Upper Hudson, west of the river and north to Chatham (Columbia County). These dividing lines are some-what arbitrary, with occasional county overlap; if you're intending to explore only a single section of the Hudson Valley, be aware that attractions and lodgings in one part of the valley may be only minutes by car from those categorized in another.

The Hudson River Valley is packed with sights from one end to the other, but the area is pretty manageable in size and easy to get around, especially if you have your own transportation. From the town of Hudson in the north to Yonkers, just beyond New York City, is a distance of 120 miles and just over 2 hours by car. You may wish to concentrate on one section of the valley, although picking and choosing sights carefully would allow you to cover much of the length of the river in several days (though you could also quite easily spend a couple of weeks following the river from end to end). For this reason, note that in the sections that follow, attractions are grouped geographically, rather than alphabetically, with the hopes of orienting visitors toward sites that are easily seen in tandem with others in the immediate area.

GETTING AROUND

BY CAR   By far the easiest way to get around the Hudson Valley is by car. Pub-lic transportation, especially where it concerns county bus systems, is unduly complicated. Your best bet if not traveling by private automobile is one of the major bus carriers (see above), the train or a tour operator The main roads tra-versing the length of the Hudson Valley are I-87 and Route 9W on the west, and Route 9 and the Taconic Parkway on the east.

The major rental car agencies, which have outlets at airports and at several addresses throughout the region, include: **Alamo** (© 800/327-9633); **Avis** (© 800/331-1212); **Budget** (© 800/527-0700); **Dollar** (© 800/800-4000); **Enterprise** (© 800/RENT-A-CAR); **Hertz** (© 800/654-3131); **National** (© 800/227-7368); and **Thrifty** (© 800/367-2277).

BY BUS OR TRAIN   See "Getting There," above.

BY TAXI   Local taxis are available at all the major train and bus stations, and in larger towns. Among taxi services throughout the Hudson Valley: **Rocket Cab,** in Hyde Park (© 914/456-5783); **Yellow Cab Company** in Poughkeepsie (© 845/471-1100); **Rhinebeck Taxi** (© 845/876-5466); and **Howard's Taxi** in Hudson (© 518/828-7673).

BY ORGANIZED TOUR   Shortline Coach USA (© 800/631-8405; www.shortlinebus.com) offers Hudson Valley day trips and overnight packages and

---

Tips **Closer Than You Think**

Visitors to the Mid-and Upper Hudson Valley should also refer to chapter 8, "The Catskill Mountain Region"; that region borders the Hudson Valley to the west, and several important attractions at the edges of the range—including the towns of Catskill, Saugerties, New Paltz, and High Falls, as well as the Mohonk and Minnewaska Preserves, and the legendary Mohonk Mountain House—are within easy reach and could very easily be considered part of, or be combined with a trip to, the Hudson Valley.

Tips **When to Go**

Many of the great Hudson River estates and other attractions in the region are closed during the long winter months. Above all, spring and summer—a number of the estates have extensive formal gardens and are absolutely glorious in May and June, and many have special events like concerts—and autumn, when the leaves are ablaze with color and gorgeously set off against the backdrop of the river, are the best times to visit the valley.

---

tours. **River Valley Tours** (© 800/836-2128; www.rivervalleytours.com) organizes weeklong, inn-to-inn, boat-and-bus trips along the Hudson. They're not offered often and are a little pricey (at just under two grand per head), but they allow visitors to really experience the grandeur and history of the Hudson River. **New York Waterway** (© 800/53-FERRY; www.nywaterway.com) offers tours by boat from Pier 78 in Manhattan (weekends and Monday holidays, May–Oct). Round-trip tickets include a cruise up the Hudson River to Tarrytown and transportation from the dock to Lyndhurst, Philipsburg Manor, or Kykuit. **Metro-North Railroad** (© 800/METRO-INFO; www.mta.nyc.ny.us/mnr/html/outbound.htm) offers a series of "One-Day Getaways" to such places as Cold Spring and Woodbury Common, as well as organized 1-day hiking and biking tours.

2 The Lower Hudson Valley

The Lower Hudson Valley, just north of New York City, claims some of the region's most popular sights, including the literary legends and grand estates of Sleepy Hollow, West Point Military Academy, and important Revolutionary War sites. Two of the Valley's most picturesque and enjoyable villages, Cold Spring and Nyack, cling to either side of the river, and the scenery, with the rocky Palisades framing the wide expanses of the river, is stunning.

EXPLORING THE LOWER HUDSON VALLEY

The Lower Hudson contains some of the state's biggest visitor draws, including several of the valley's finest manor houses (among them the Rockefeller Estate and Lyndhurst), on the east side of the river, and the ever-popular West Point Military Academy on the west. There are also important Revolutionary War battle sites, one of the world's greatest outdoor art collections, and a couple of absolutely charming riverfront villages. It's not a section of the valley to rush through.

THE TOP ATTRACTIONS
EAST SIDE OF THE HUDSON

Washington Irving's Sunnyside ★ Washington Irving—man of letters, diplomat, architectural historian, gentleman farmer, and first true international celebrity—designed an eclectic cottage in the country in 1835. Before he wrote *The Legend of Sleepy Hollow* and introduced the world to the Headless Horseman and Rip Van Winkle, Irving lived in England and was minister to Spain, where he rediscovered the Alhambra palace and reawakened its mystical architecture and magic aura with his *Tales of the Alhambra*. Sunnyside, with its melange of historic and architectural styles, including a Dutch stepped-gable roofline, a Spanish tower, and master bedroom modeled after a Paris apartment, was Irving's very personal Romantic retreat, a place to write and retire. Today the charming pastoral villa, swathed in vines and wisteria and nestled into the grounds along the Hudson, remains as he left it, with his books and writing papers in the study. The train rumbles by the riverfront property, as it did toward the end of Irving's life (he died here in 1859 at the age of 76). During the holidays, Sunnyside is festooned with Victorian Christmas decorations, and there are singalongs and storytelling—perfectly appropriate for a storybook house. Plan on spending at least an hour here.

West Sunnyside Lane, off Rte. 9, Tarrytown. © 914/591-8763. www.hudsonvalley.org/web/sunn-main.html. Admission $9 adults, $8 seniors, $5 students ages 5–17; grounds only pass, $4. Apr–Oct Wed–Mon 10am–5pm (last tour at 4pm); Nov–Dec Wed–Mon 10am–4pm (last tour at 3pm); Mar weekends only 10am–4pm (last tour at 3pm); closed Jan–Feb. Metro-North to Tarrytown.

Lyndhurst ★★ *Kids*   One of the most impressive estates along the Lower Hudson, this Gothic Rival mansion, the finest of its style in the U.S., was designed by A. J. Davis in 1838 for a former New York City mayor. Later purchased by the railroad magnate and financier Jay Gould, the villa features an asymmetrical structure and grand Gothic interiors (including lots of faux stone and marble and stained glass windows). The 67-acre estate, an excellent example of 19th-century landscape design, features a massive glass and steel-framed conservatory (the largest of its day), rose garden, and arboretum. Today the mansion, a National Trust Historic Site, is decorated with many original furnishings and decorative objects culled from the three families that inhabited the estate over 123 years. A number of lectures and other activities, including vintage "base ball" games staged on the front lawn and candlelight Christmas evenings, are held at Lyndhurst. The self-guided audio tour, included in the price of admission, is extremely well done, with an extended version that covers the entire property and Hudson Valley history and a children's version with entertaining features that will tune the kids in to history and architecture. Plan on at least an hour here, several if you wish to explore the grounds.

635 S. Broadway, Tarrytown. © 914/631-4481. www.lyndhurst.org. Admission $10 adults, $9 seniors, $4 students ages 12–17; free for children under 12; grounds-only pass $4. Mid-Apr to Oct Tues–Sun and holiday Mon 10am–5pm; Nov to mid-Apr, weekends and holiday Mon 10am–4pm. Guided tours at 11am, 2:30pm, and 4:15pm on weekdays, more frequently on weekends. Metro-North to Tarrytown.

Philipsburg Manor ★★ *Kids*   Just a half-hour upriver from the 21st-century pace of New York City, this eye-opening and serenely beautiful agricultural estate is a jarring retreat to the late 17th and early 18th centuries. The bridge across the millpond of this colonial farm and water-powered grist mill transports visitors to a complicated time in history, when this estate functioned as one of the largest slave plantations in the North—a shock to those who associate slavery only with the South. Organizers use that history to educate and place the estate, the entire Hudson Valley, and the influence of African culture in a historical context. Live demonstrations and scripted vignettes by interpreters in period dress bring to life the colonial agricultural and merchant activities that took place here, re-creating the lives of the single caretaker and 23 skilled slaves who lived and worked at this provision plantation. Frederick Philipse made his fortune in shipping and export to the West Indies, commerce that included the human slave trade. The large original manor houses dates from 1685; Philipse's landholdings in the area totaled more than 50,000 acres. When he died a bachelor, he left a 50-page inventory of his belongings, including the names of all his slaves, testimony to his extraordinary wealth. The site still functions as a working farm, with horses and sheep, wool spinning, milling of flour, and harvesting of rye in June and July. A great, educational outing for families; allow a couple of hours.

Rte. 9, Sleepy Hollow. (C) **914/631-3992**. www.hudsonvalley.org/web/phil-main.html. Admission $9 adults, $8 seniors, $5 students ages 5–17. Apr–Oct Wed–Mon 10am–5pm (last tour 4pm); Nov–Dec Wed–Mon 10am–4pm (last tour 3pm); Mar weekends only 10am–4pm (last tour 3pm); closed Jan–Feb. Metro-North to Tarrytown.

Kykuit, the Rockefeller Estate ★★★   The Hudson River is lined from one end to the other with grand manor houses, but none compares to Kykuit (pronounced "*kye*-cut"). It's not the oldest or even the largest of the estates, but most find it the most spectacular. When John D. Rockefeller, founder of Standard Oil, built Kykuit in its present classical Greek-Roman style in 1913, he was the richest man in the world. The estate, which became home to four generations of one of America's most famous business and philanthropic families, is architecturally grand and spectacularly sited and landscaped, with lovely stone terraces, fountains, and extensive Italianate formal gardens. Kykuit also houses Governor (and later Vice President) Nelson Rockefeller's incredible collection of 20th-century modern art, which graces the gardens and fills the entire lower level of the house. The sculpture collection includes important works by Alexander Calder, Henry Moore, Constantin Brancusi, and David Smith among its 70 works, all placed with great care to take maximum advantage of the gardens and their sweeping views of the Hudson (both of which are perhaps unequaled by any of the great river estates). Outstanding among the pieces in the very '60s art gallery in the house is a unique series of giant and shockingly vibrant tapestries commissioned from Pablo Picasso.

Visits to Kykuit begin at Philipsburgh Manor (see above); coaches shuttle visitors to Kykuit. Tours of Kykuit last 2 hours and 15 minutes; choose between House and Garden or Garden and Sculpture Tours. In high season, tours often sell out by midday, but advance reservations for individuals are not necessary.

Pocantino Hills, Sleepy Hollow. (C) **914/631-9491**. www.hudsonvalley.org/web/kyku-main.html. Admission $20 adults, $19 seniors, $17 children 17 and under; not recommended for children under 10. Late Apr to early Nov Wed–Mon House and Garden Tours 10am–3pm; Garden and Sculpture Tour 3pm on weekdays, 3:15pm on weekends. Visitor Center at Philipsburg Manor opens at 9am to sell Kykuit tickets for that day only; tickets also available online. Metro-North to Tarrytown.

Boscobel Restoration ★★   Two things about this magnificent mansion on the Hudson stand out: its splendid setting, among the finest in the entire Hudson Valley, and its incredible history. The house, an early-19th-century neoclassical Georgian mansion, was rescued from government destruction (it was sold at auction for $35 in the 1950s), moved piece-by-piece to its current location, and meticulously restored thanks to the generosity of the cofounder of *Reader's Digest*. The decorative arts of the Federal Period that fill the house are indeed impressive, but they have a difficult time competing with the extraordinary river and gorge views afforded from the lawns, gardens, and orchards. No estate site along the river is more dramatic. Many activities are held here, and should not be missed, including the Hudson Valley Shakespeare Festival (advance reservations required; www.hvshakespeare.org) in the summer, big band dancing in the fall, and pre-Victorian Christmas Candlelight tours.

1601 Rte. 9D, Garrison. (C) **845/265-3638**. www.boscobel.org. Admission $10 adults, $9 seniors, $7 students ages 6–14; grounds only, $7 adults, $5 seniors, free students ages 6–14. Apr–Oct Wed–Mon 9:30am–5pm (last tour at 4:15pm); Nov–Dec Wed–Mon 9:30am–4pm (last tour at 3:15pm). Closed Jan–Mar. Metro-North to Tarrytown.

> ### (Finds) Constitution Island/Warner House
>
> From the end of June to the beginning of October, visitors to West Point can take a ferry out to Constitution Island, nearly forgotten in the middle of the Hudson River 900 feet east of the military academy. The tiny island (287 acres) is home to the 1836 Warner mansion, the fully furnished Victorian home of the writers Susan and Anna Warner (Susan was the author of the million-selling *Wide, Wide World*), and Revolutionary War ruins of Fort Constitution (chains were floated across the Hudson here to delay advancing British troops). The sisters, who never married, lived on the island until their deaths (they are buried at West Point Cemetery). Costumed docents lead visitors on a most unexpected view of American history from the middle of one of its most historic rivers, and kids love it. Reservations are essential, as tours are limited to 40; ferries leave from the South Dock at West Point. Tours are given Wednesdays and Thursdays, June 25 to October 2, at 1pm and 2pm; www.constitutionisland.org. Admission is $10 adults, $9 seniors and children ages 6 to 16, $3 children 5 and under. Tours last 2 hours, 15 minutes. For reservations and information, call © 845/446-8676.

WEST SIDE OF THE HUDSON

West Point (U.S. Military Academy) ★   West Point, the nation's oldest and foremost military college—which celebrated its 200th anniversary in 2002 and is the oldest continually used military post in the U.S.—has produced some of the greatest generals and leaders this country has known, including Robert E. Lee, Ulysses S. Grant, Douglas MacArthur, George Patton, and Dwight D. Eisenhower. (Edgar Allan Poe, however, dropped out!) West Point is one of the nation's most esteemed and rigorous science and engineering colleges. The most popular attraction in the entire Hudson Valley, West Point is no longer as visitor-friendly as it once was, however, due to heightened security concerns. In fact, whereas visitors once were free to roam the campus among the orderly cadets in their dress blues, for the foreseeable future the only way to visit is by organized 1- or 2-hour tour on a bus that makes stops at the famous Cadet Chapel, which possesses stained-glass windows that were gifts of graduating classes and the largest church organ in the world, with more than 21,000 pipes; the Cadet Cemetery; and Trophy Point, where cannons captured from five wars are gathered in remembrance. The massive campus (home to just 4,000 student soldiers), with its Gothic Revival buildings perched on the west side above the Hudson River, is undeniably handsome, especially in fall. Tickets for all tours must be purchased at the Visitor's Center. Behind the Visitors Center, the West Point Museum is the oldest and largest collection of war memorabilia and war trophies in the U.S. See an atomic bomb, the cannon that fired the first American shot in WWI, Hitler's Lilliputian presentation pistol, and uniforms and artifacts that trace the history of warfare. For war and history buffs, it will be fascinating; for others, considerably less so. Allow 2 to 3 hours for the entire visit.

Rte. 218, Highland Falls. © 845/446-4724. www.usma.edu. www.westpointtours.com. West Point tours admission $7–$9 adults, $4–$6 children under 12; museum free. Apr–Oct Mon–Sat 10am–3:30pm, Sun 11:15am; May–Oct Mon–Sat additional 2-hr. tours at 11:15am and 1:15pm, Sun 1:15pm only; Nov–Mar

Mon–Sat 1-hr. tours 11:15am and 1:15pm only (Sun 1:15pm only). No tours on Sat of home football games. Museum Mon–Sun 10:30am–4:15pm.

Storm King Art Center ★★★ *Kids*   A most unusual museum, this fabulous collection of modern, monumental sculpture benefits from one of the most stunning outdoor settings modern art has ever seen: 500 acres of rolling hills, meadows, and woodlands that, especially in autumn, are capable of converting contemporary art doubters into passionate enthusiasts. Storm King's interplay between nature and human creativity is extraordinary. On view are nearly 100 large-scale works by some of the greatest American and European sculptors of the postwar 20th century, including Mark di Suvero, Henry Moore, Magdalena Abakanowicz, Isamu Noguchi, Alexander Calder, Richard Serra and, forming the nucleus of the collection, 13 works by David Smith (with the outdoor placement echoing Smith's studio in the Adirondacks). Every year Storm King presents a temporary exhibition of a couple dozen works by a major sculptor (in the past they have focused on Smith and Calder). Though a warm, sunny day may be nicest to enjoy Storm King, the sculptures look and feel different under different conditions and in different seasons, so there is really no bad time to visit. Storm King is a great place to spend an entire day, and perfect for introducing children to art; bring a picnic lunch, as you are encouraged to do (no food concessions are on the grounds). You'll need several hours to see Storm King and could easily spend an entire day here.

Old Pleasant Hill Rd., Mountainville. (C) **845/534-3115.** www.stormkingartcenter.org. Admission $9 adults, $7 seniors, students $5, free children under 5; Acoustiguide audio tours $5. Apr to late Oct Wed–Sun 11am–5:30pm (on Sat late May to late Aug, grounds remain open until 8pm and trams until 7pm); late Oct to mid-Nov 11am–5pm. Closed mid-Nov to Apr. Free docent-guided "Highlights of the Collection" tours at 2pm daily; free self-guided trams run daily noon–4:30pm.

MORE TO SEE & DO
EAST SIDE OF THE HUDSON

Hudson River Museum *Kids*   This large cultural complex in Yonkers, just north of New York City, covers several bases, including fine art, science, and history. It features six modern art galleries (showing the works of George Segal and Andy Warhol, among others) and a high-tech planetarium. Also on the premises is a handsome restored 19th-century Victorian mansion overlooking the Hudson River and Palisades. The museum hosts a variety of interesting temporary exhibits as well as concerts.

511 Warburton Ave., Yonkers. (C) **914/963-4550.** Admission $5 adults, $3 seniors and children. May–Sept Wed–Thurs and Sat–Sun noon–5pm, Fri noon–9pm; Oct–Apr Wed–Sun noon–5pm.

The Union Church of Pocantino Hills ★   A short jaunt from the Rockefellers' Kykuit estate is this tiny country chapel, remarkable not for its architecture per se but for its unique collection of stained-glass windows by Marc Chagall and Henri Matisse, two masters of modern art better known for their canvasses. The collection, commissioned by the Rockefeller family, features a large rose window by Matisse—the final work of his life—and a series of nine side windows by Chagall—his only cycle of church windows in the U.S.—that illustrate biblical passages. One, at the back right-hand corner is a memorial to the son of Nelson Rockefeller, who died on an expedition to New Guinea in the early 1960s. Matisse's rose window is very soothing, while Chagall's painterly images swirl with brilliant color; try to visit the church on a sunny day, when it is ablaze with dramatic light and color.

Route 448 (Bedford Rd.), Sleepy Hollow. ℂ **914/631-2069**. www.hudsonvalley.org. Admission $4. Apr–Dec Mon and Wed–Fri 11am–5pm; Sat 10am–5pm; Sun 2–5pm.

Van Cortlandt Manor   Although superficially the least spectacular of the seven Historic Hudson Valley properties, this working estate and Revolutionary War–era country manor house is a living history museum that reveals much about the life and activities of the 18th century. Guides don Federal Period dress, and the massive open-hearth kitchen and grounds play host to cooking, black-smithing, weaving, and brick-making demonstrations. The tavern on the premises served customers of a ferry business that carried people back and forth across the Croton River.

South Riverside Ave. (off Rte. 9; Croton Point Ave. exit), Croton-on-Hudson. ℂ **914/232-5035**. www.hudson valley.org. Admission adults $9, seniors $8, $5 children ages 5–17, free for children under 5; grounds-only pass, $4. Apr–Oct Wed–Mon 10am–5pm (last tour 4pm); Nov–Dec weekends only 10am–4pm (last tour 3pm).

Caramoor House Museum and Performing Arts Center *(Finds)*   Just west of the Hudson, a little off the beaten track for most Hudson Valley visitors, is this surprising mansion and performing arts center, well worth a visit for a summer concert or a view of the unusual Mediterranean villa constructed by a wealthy New York couple, Walter and Lucie Rosen. The Rosens purchased entire rooms from European palaces, churches, and country homes, brought them to the U.S., and had them reconstructed and incorporated into their sprawling mansion, built around a Spanish courtyard, designed with those exact rooms and furnishings in mind. It's hard to believe that the mansion and its bewildering array of Eastern, medieval, and Renaissance art and antiques were assembled onsite in the late 1930s. The collection contains treasures and furnishings of great value and others of highly personal taste. Caramoor is best known as a center of music and arts, and in particular for its summer outdoor Music Festival, which grew out of the Rosens' love for hosting concerts for their large circle of friends. The heart of the house is the extraordinary Music Room, a small palace unto itself and where chamber concerts are held throughout the year. Afternoon tea is served on the family's original china in the Summer Dining Room, Thursday and Friday afternoons at 3pm. Tours of the house last about an hour.

149 Girdle Ridge Rd. (off Rte. 22), Katonah. ℂ **914/232-5035**. www.caramoor.org. Admission adults $7, free for children 16 and under. May–Dec guided tours Wed–Sun 1–4pm (last tour 3pm). Metro-North to Katonah.

Manitoga (Russel Wright Design Center) *(Finds)*   Russel Wright, a preeminent midcentury American designer, tucked a unique country home into the woods and blurred the lines between interior and exterior, combining natural materials with industrial design. The only 20th-century modern home open to the public in New York, the 1962 house is very Zen-like, with abundant vegetation nearly camouflaging its simple lines. The house is sliced into a cliff above a dramatic waterfall and pond carved out of an abandoned quarry. Wright named the site Manitoga, which means "place of the great spirit," but he called the house "Dragon Rock," after his daughter's description of the massive rock that dips into the pond. In addition to the house, open for guided 90-minute tours, there are more than 4 miles of hiking trails on the property.

Rte. 9D, Garrison. ℂ **845/424-3812**. www.russelwrightcenter.org. House tour admission $15; hiking trails $5 adults, $3 seniors and children under 12. Mid-Apr to late Oct guided tours daily 11am; woodland garden paths open weekdays year-round 9am–4pm; weekends Apr–Oct 10am–6pm; reservations recommended.

Cold Spring *★★*   One of the Hudson's most adorable waterfront towns, Cold Spring, located in Putnam County, about an hour north of New York City, has inviting views of the river, a main street chock-a-block with antiques dealers, inns, cafes, and restaurants in Victorian cottages. Adorning the riverfront is a Victorian band shell and park benches with spectacular panoramic views of the Hudson. Near the dock is the Chapel of Our Lady, built in the 1930s and the oldest Catholic church along the Hudson. A couple of blocks away from Main Street is a small but interesting museum, the **Foundry School Museum** (63 Chestnut St.; © 845/265-4010; admission $5 adults, $2 seniors and children; Tues–Thurs 10am–4pm and Sat–Sun 2–5pm), housed in the 1830 West Point Foundry schoolhouse; on view are tools and equipment from the 19th-century foundry, as well as local works of art and an original schoolroom.

WEST SIDE OF THE HUDSON

Nyack ⟨⟩ One of the most charmingly "lived-in" river villages along the Lower Hudson, Nyack is a bedroom community of New York with a laid-back life all its own. The town has a smattering of antiques shops, cafes, booksellers and restaurants. The American realist painter Edward Hopper was born and went to high school in Nyack, and his mid-19th-century Queen Anne childhood home, today the **Hopper House Art Center** (82 N. Broadway; © 845/358-0774; Thurs–Sun 1–5pm) is preserved as a small museum of the artist's life and career and gallery space for temporary exhibitions. The **Runcible Spoon** (37-9 N. Broadway; © 845/358-9398) is a great little bakery and favorite rest stop for cyclists who make the 50-mile round-trip from New York City.

Stony Point Battlefield Historic Site   This site commemorates the historic 1779 Battle of Stony Point, during which American forces led by Brigadier General Anthony Wayne stormed a British stronghold at midnight and caught the enemy by surprise. The victory was the last major battle in the north, and is credited with boosting American morale. Visitors can walk the battlefield and see an audiovisual presentation at the onsite museum. Stony Point Lighthouse, built on the site in 1826, is the oldest on the Hudson; lantern walks are offered several times a year.

Battlefield Rd. (off Rte. 9W), Stony Point. © 845/786-2521. Apr 15–Oct Wed–Sat 10am–4:30pm, Sun 1–4:30pm. Grounds daily Mar–Nov 10am–4pm. Free admission; audio tours $4 adults, $3 children ages 12 and under.

Fort Montgomery State Historic Site   Fort Montgomery was the site of a brave 1777 Revolutionary War battle to control the Hudson River. Patriot troops effectively stalled the British march to aid Burgoyne's army at Saratoga—which may have made the difference in the war. Visitors can view ruins of the fortifications and listen to an audio tour that explains the battle and importance of the Hudson to the Patriot and British war plans. A visitors center and trails are slated to be fully operable by 2004.

Rte. 9G, 1¼ miles north of Bear Mountain State Park, Bear Mountain. © 845/786-2701. Free admission; audio tours $4 adults, $3 children ages 12 and under. Daily dawn–dusk; staffed mid-Apr to Oct Wed–Sun 10am–4:30pm.

ESPECIALLY FOR KIDS

The Lower Hudson Valley has a number of great activities for families and kids. Tops is **Bear Mountain State Park;** besides its zoo, swimming lake and pool, ice-skating rink, and hiking trails, it has added an incredible $3 million carousel; the carved animals aren't just horses, but bobcats, rabbits, and bears—animals found in the park. The **Hudson River Museum** in Yonkers is a favorite of kids for its state-of-the-art planetarium. Although contemporary sculpture might not sound like most kids' idea of fun, the **Storm King Art Center,** with 100 monumental pieces spread over 500 beautiful acres, is a blast for children, who may have a more intuitive understanding of the works than their parents! Several of the historic houses and estates along the river are entertaining for children. Interpreters in period dress at **Sunnyside, Van Cortland Manor,** and **Philipsburg Manor** are entertaining and educational; the latter, a working farm that aims to present history lessons through actors and demonstrations, is particularly eye-opening. Occasional activities at **Lyndhurst,** such as vintage "base ball" games, should also delight kids.

SPORTS & OUTDOOR PURSUITS

The Lower Hudson Valley abounds in outdoor sports, from hiking and biking to cross-country skiing to kayaking and sailing.

BOATING & SAILING   The **NY Waterway** (𝒞 800/53-FERRY; www.ny waterway.com) takes visitors from New York City to Sleepy Hollow to visit Sunnyside and Philipsburg Manor (adults $46, seniors $44, children $25). It also offers cruises to Lyndhurst, Kykuit, and a 2-hour North Hudson tour (adults $15, children $8) from Tarrytown. Tours operate May to November. **Hudson Maritime Services** of Cold Spring (𝒞 845/265-76212; www.hudsonriver.cjb. net) offers sailing on Newburgh Bay and scenic cruises along the river. **Hudson Highlands Cruises** (𝒞 845/534-7245; www.commanderboat.com) embarks on 3-hour narrated cruises through the Hudson Highlands (adults $15, seniors and children under 12, $13). **Hudson Valley Riverboat Tours** (𝒞 845/788-4000) offers midweek cruises on *The River Queen,* a historic paddle-wheeler, in July and August.

CYCLING & MOUNTAIN BIKING   **Red Tail Bicycle Tours** (Putnam Valley; 𝒞 845/216-8109; www.redtailbiketours.com) arranges 2-day bicycle tours in the Lower and Mid-Hudson Valley. Bike rentals are available from **Bikeway,** 692 Rte. 6 in Mahopac (𝒞 845/621-2800).

FISHING   The Hudson, which flows from the Adirondacks to the open sea, is excellent for striped bass from mid-March to the end of May. There is also good trout fishing. For more information, visit **www.hudsonriver.com/stripers.htm.**

GOLF   There are more than 150 golf courses in the Hudson River Valley; for specific information and course previews, see **www.hudsonrivergolf.com** and **www.golfhudsonvalley.com.**

HIKING   There are too many great hiking spots in state parks in the Lower Hudson Valley to mention. Near Cold Spring, **Hudson Highlands State Park** has a number of great day trails. Recommended hikes in the vicinity of Cold Spring include Breakneck Ridge and Bull Hill; in the southern highlands south of Garrison, popular trails include those to Anthony's Nose and White Rock. Pick up a map at **Hudson Valley Outfitters,** 63 Main St., Cold Spring (𝒞 845/265-0221; www.hudsonvalleyoutfitters.com), which also offers guided hikes in the area, or contact the New York–New Jersey Trail Conference (p. 71). **Bear Mountain** and **Harriman State Parks** make up the majority of the Palisades Interstate Park and offer dozens of splendid hiking opportunities, including a section of the Appalachian Trail. For trail maps and more information, visit the Palisades Interstate Park Commission at Bear Mountain (𝒞 845/786-2701).

KAYAKING & RAFTING   Hudson Valley Outfitters (see "Hiking," above), is tops in the region for kayak rentals and guided tours. Their major competitor is **Pack & Paddle Adventures,** 12 Market St., Cold Spring (✆ **845/265-2940;** www.hvpackandpaddle.com), which also handles kayak and canoe rentals and instruction.

SWIMMING　**Bear Mountain State Park** offers swimming in both the Hessian Lake and Bear Mountain pool, open in summer. There is also a public pool at Tallman State Park (Palisades Interstate Park Commission; ✆ **845/359-0544**), just south of Nyack on Route 9W.

WINTER SPORTS　For snowshoe and cross-country ski packages, contact Cold Spring's Hudson Valley Outfitters. Bear Mountain State Park has cross-country ski trails, ski jumps, and an outdoor skating rink open late October through mid-March. Croton Point Park, Route 9 in Croton-on-Hudson, is also popular with Nordic skiers.

SHOPPING

The biggest draw by far among shopaholics is **Woodbury Common,** said to be the world's largest discount complex, about an hour north of New York City. It's in Central Valley, just south of Newburgh (498 Red Apple Court; ✆ **845/928-4000;** Mon–Sat 10am–9pm and Sun 10am–8pm). There are more than 220 purveyors of clothing, home furnishing, jewelry, luggage, leather, and gift items, including Barneys New York, Burberry, Calvin Klein, Chanel, Coach, Dolce & Gabbana, Donna Karan, Giorgio Armani, Gucci, Max Mara, Neiman Marcus Last Call, Gap Outlet, Nike Factory Store, Saks Fifth Avenue, Polo Ralph Lauren Factory Store, Versace, and Williams-Sonoma. By car, take exit 16 off New York State Thruway, or I-87. You can also hop a Gray Line bus from the Port Authority Bus Terminal at 42nd Street and 8th Avenue. The bus leaves daily at 8:45am ($38 round-trip). **Cold Spring** is the best antiques center in the Lower Hudson Valley. Main Street is lined with more than a dozen small antiques dealers and cute home furnishings shops. **Taca-Tiques Antiques,** 109 Main St. (✆ **845/265-2655**), specializes in Victorian and Estate sterling silver and beveled mirrors. **Nyack** is another town with a number of antiquing possibilities. Elsewhere, **Boscobel Restoration** in Garrison has one of the best gift shops attached to a historic site.

Though it's a bit removed from the Hudson Valley per se, lots of folks make the trip west to the **Sugarloaf Art & Craft Village,** a hamlet in Orange Country (north of Warwick, off Rte. 17) that features more than 50 shops and galleries dealing in jewelry, stained glass, and metalsmithing, among others. Sugar Loaf is open Tuesday to Sunday from 11am to 5pm; call ✆ **914/469-9181** for events and more information.

WHERE TO STAY

The Lower Hudson's proximity to New York City makes it popular as a day trip, but there is so much to see and do that it fortunately has the widest and most plentiful array of accommodations in the valley. There's a good mix of historic inns, modern, hotels and small B&Bs, as well as motel and hotel chains that are hard to come by farther up the Hudson.

VERY EXPENSIVE

Castle on the Hudson ★★★　This small, exclusive hotel (formerly The Castle at Tarrytown), in a grand 45-room castle built in 1910 on a bluff overlooking the river, offers some of the most extravagant accommodations along the Hudson Valley—at least since the Vanderbilts and company opened their estate to the public. If you're willing and able to pony up to live like a prince, this is the place. Reminiscent of castles in Scotland and Wales, it comes equipped with the requisite stone walls, turrets, and heavy medieval touches, though the Relais & Châteaux property has been endowed with every possible luxury for guests. Rooms are elegant and extremely plush, with fine carpets, flowing drapes, and stylish linens on four-poster and canopied beds. The handsomely landscaped grounds don't skimp on fantastic views of the Hudson River. The Castle's fancy Equus restaurant is one of the most highly touted in the Lower Hudson Valley; even if you're not staying here, it's well worth it for a special four-course prix-fixe meal or one of the periodic wine-tasting dinners.

400 Benedict Ave., Tarrytown, NY 10591. ℂ 914/631-1980. Fax 914/631-4612. www.castleonthehudson. com 31 units. Weekdays $295 double, $335–$565 suite; weekends $315 double, $525–$650 suite. AE, DC, DISC, MC, V. Free parking. **Amenities:** Restaurant; bar; large outdoor pool; fitness center; tennis court; concierge; limited room service; massage; laundry service; same-day dry cleaning. *In room:* A/C, TV/VCR, mini-bar, hair dryer.

EXPENSIVE

The Bird & Bottle Inn ★★★   Make a detour right into the Revolutionary War era at this charming inn, one of the oldest in New York State. It began its business life on the Old Albany Post Road in 1761 as Warren's Tavern, and the wide floorboards, dark beams, and rustic flavor of the place bow very little to modernity. For anyone looking for a dose of history, though, this is it. Rooms are not fussy, as indeed they shouldn't be, but are very comfortable and inviting, with working fireplaces stocked with wood and luxurious four-poster and canopied beds; the bathrooms, though, could use a bit of updating. There's a separate cottage on the premises for those who want additional privacy. The sumptuous, formal and rather pricey restaurant, which absolutely reeks of early American flavor, has a reputation as one of the finest in upstate New York, even though some contend that it has been riding on its laurels for a couple of years. The cozy first-floor "Drinking Room" is a great place for exactly that.

1123 Old Albany Post Rd., Garrison, NY 10524. ℂ 845/424-3000. Fax 845/424-3283. www.birdbottle.com. 4 units. $210–$260 double. Rates include breakfast. Weekend 2-night minimum. AE, MC, V. Free parking. **Amenities:** Restaurant; tavern. *In room:* A/C, hair dryer, no phone.

Cromwell Manor ★★   This sophisticated inn, in an imposing, historic house with white pillars that was once owned by a descendant of Oliver Cromwell, sits on 7 acres next to a farm and is just minutes from Storm King Art Center and 5 miles from West Point. Well managed and largely successfully decorated in period style (rooms are elegant, but a few touches and bathrooms may strike some as a little modern and functional), it is one of the best B&Bs in the Hudson Valley. It faces a 4,000-acre nature preserve, which is spectacular in autumn. The 1820 manor house has nine rooms, six of which have wood-burning fireplaces. The Cromwell Suite has a private entrance and a bathroom so large that the owners have stuck a Stairmaster in it (kid you not!). The separate Chimneys Cottage, the oldest part of the house (1764), is the most charming; it has four guest rooms, one of which has an enormous sitting room. Rooms are all quite different, so visit the website or call for additional details. The hands-on owners schedule a number of special events, such as weekend chef dinners and cooking classes, so check for scheduling as well as golf and spa packages and special offers.

174 Angola Rd., Cornwall, NY 12518. ℂ 845/534-7136. Fax 845/534-0354. www.cromwellmanor.com. 13 units. $165–$370 double. Rates include full gourmet breakfast. AE, DC, DISC, MC, V. Free parking. **Amenities:** In-room massage; free wireless Internet access. *In room:* A/C, hair dryer, robes.

Dolce Tarrytown House ★★ (Kids) A sprawling hotel complex and conference estate, with one 1840s mansion and six or seven outpost buildings on the property, tucked serenely behind gates just up the road from Washington Irving's Sunnyside home on the river. Loaded with amenities and sports facilities but surprisingly easygoing and intimate, this is a perfect place for both business and leisure travelers, including families. Rooms are quite large and very comfortable; they were recently renovated in attractive contemporary style (brightly colored and flowered, but unfussy, bedcovers). The best rooms by far, though $100 more than others, are in the Georgian-style King House; they have antiques, fireplaces, and large and nicely appointed bathrooms. Some even have terrific wraparound terraces with excellent views. Ask about the Passport to Sleepy Hollow Country package, which includes 2 nights' accommodations, breakfast, and admission to three nearby historic sights (Kykuit, Lyndhurst, and so on).

East Sunnyside Lane, Tarrytown, NY 10591. © **800/553-8118** or 914/591-8200. Fax 914/591-0059. 212 units. www.dolce.com/tarrytown. Weekday $169–$269 double; weekend $129–$239 double. AE, DC, DISC, MC, V. Free parking. **Amenities:** Restaurant; bar; large indoor and outdoor pools; fitness center with sauna; 3 tennis courts; concierge; business center; executive business services; limited room service; massage; laundry service; same-day dry cleaning; basketball court; racquetball. *In room:* A/C, TV/VCR, minibar, hair dryer, complimentary wireless high-speed Internet.

MODERATE

Hotel Thayer ★ Ensconced within the grounds of the West Point campus, this is the best bet for anyone who always wanted to attend the military academy. A fine, large old hotel (built in 1926), built in a similar style to the Gothic campus and named for General Thayer, the "father of the academy," it has decent-size rooms with large, firm beds. Although one side looks over the beautiful campus and the other the Hudson River, light sleepers should know that the train rumbles by right below on the river side, both late at night and early in the morning. You'll miss the river views, but the campus side is much quieter. The medieval-style restaurant in the basement is easily the best restaurant in the immediate area; Sunday brunch is especially popular. Don't even bother trying to get a room during West Point graduation week; the hotel is booked 4 years in advance.

674 Thayer Rd., West Point, NY 10996. © **800/247-5047** or 845/446-4731. Fax 845/446-0338. www.thethayerhotel.com. 127 units. Apr–Nov $150–$200 double; Nov–Mar $135–$150. AE, DC, DISC, MC, V. Free parking. **Amenities:** Restaurant; fitness center; concierge; limited room service; salon; laundry service, dry cleaning. *In room:* A/C, TV w/pay movies, dataport, coffeemaker, minibar, hair dryer.

Hudson House River Inn ★ Facing a wide expanse of the Hudson River in one of the cutest towns in the Valley, Cold Spring, this small but adorable inn (just 12 rooms) was built in 1832 and has operated as a hotel ever since. The historic building retains many period features but has been nicely updated. Rooms are sweetly decorated in a country style, with comfortable bedding. Rooms no. 1 and 2 are equipped with riverfront balconies; the views are enviable. The attractive restaurant, which has both a river room and a cozy old tavern with a fireplace, is one of the better places to stop for a meal in Cold Spring.

2 Main St., Cold Spring, NY 10516. © **845/265-9355.** Fax 845/265-4532. www.hudsonhouseinn.com. 12 units. Mon–Thurs $140–$185 double; Fri–Sun $150–$225 double. Rates include continental breakfast on weekdays, full breakfast on weekends. See website for special packages. AE, DC, DISC, MC, V. Free parking. **Amenities:** Restaurant; laundry service. *In room:* A/C, TV w/pay movies, hair dryer.

Pig Hill Inn (Finds) Right on Cold Spring's Main Street, which is packed with antiques shops, this friendly and rustic little B&B is tucked behind a little antiques and gift shop of its own. In the cozy public rooms are plenty of decorative pigs on display, of course, while guest rooms are attractively done, with Chippendale pieces, chinoserie, and other antiques. Rooms have four-poster beds and comfortable quilts; many are equipped with fireplaces. Some rooms are very light and airy, while others are considerably darker and more masculine. A gourmet breakfast is served in the Victorian conservatory, out back in the cute terraced garden area, or in the main dining area.

73 Main St., Cold Spring, NY 10516. (C) **845/265-9247.** Fax 845/265-4614. www.pighillinn.com. 9 units (5 with private bathroom). Mon–Thurs $120 double with shared bathroom, $145 double with private bathroom; Fri–Sun $150 double with shared bathroom, $170 double with private bathroom. Rates include full breakfast. Weekend and holiday 2-night minimum in high season. AE, DC, DISC, MC, V. Free parking. **Amenities:** Tea and antiques gift shop. *In room:* A/C.

INEXPENSIVE

Bear Mountain Inn ★★ *Value Kids*   This sturdy wood-and-stone lodge hotel, opened in 1915 within the Bear Mountain State Park, is undergoing an ongoing $10 million renovation (though the inn was reopened in May 2003). This landmark of park architecture is being brought back to its rustic glory and Adirondack charm. The interior of the main lodge features original chestnut log posts and beams, massive stone fireplaces, timber framing, birch and iron light fixtures, and plenty of animal trophies. Accommodations—for now only the Overlook and Stone lodges a mile from the main inn across Hessian Lake—are simple. Those in the main inn are being given cosmetic makeovers and will be transformed into suites. But currently at under $100 for a double in such splendid surroundings, they're a real bargain. The inn's cozy Lobby Lounge, with its vaulted ceilings and handsome fireplace, is a great spot to relax after a day on the hiking trails. Kids will love all the activities just outside the door, including visiting the Trailside Museum and Wildlife Center, swimming in the lake, and hopping on the fantastic new Bear Mountain Merry-Go-Round. For weekend stays, it's advisable to make reservations at least a month in advance.

Bear Mountain State Park, Bear Mountain. (C) **845/786-2731.** Fax 845/786-2543. www.bearmountaininn. com. 60 units. $99 double. AE, DC, DISC, MC, V. Free parking. **Amenities:** Restaurant; bar; outdoor pool; skating rink. *In room:* A/C, TV.

CAMPGROUNDS

There are many campgrounds around the Valley. Among them: **Croton Point,** Route 9, Croton ((C) **914/271-3293;** open year-round; 180 sites, 48 with electricity); **Mills-Norrie State Park,** Old Post Road, Staatsburg ((C) **800/456-CAMP;** mid-May to late Oct; 55 sites); **Harriman State Park: Beaver Pond,** Route 106, Bear Mountain ((C) **800/456-CAMP;** mid-Apr to early Oct); 200 sites; and **Fahnestock State Park,** Route 301, Carmel ((C) **80/456-CAMP;** Memorial Day to Labor Day weekend; 86 sites).

WHERE TO DINE

Whether it's pizza for kids tired of touring grand estates or a romantic dinner in a historic inn or casual meal in a riverfront restaurant, dining in the Lower Hudson offers a good mix of possibilities.

EAST SIDE OF THE HUDSON
Expensive

The Bird & Bottle Inn ★★★ AMERICAN/CONTINENTAL   A tavern and inn since colonial times, when travelers stopped along the Old Post Road to Albany for fortification, this is hands-down one of the most atmospheric places to dine in the valley. The three separate dining rooms with fireplaces are models

Hudson Valley Hotels & Motels

Though some of the best places to stay in the Hudson Valley are quaint inns in small towns along the river, there are also more mainstream (and often cheaper) hotels and motels located near busier towns in the Lower and Mid-Hudson Valley, with more restaurant options and conveniences nearby. Most of these standard chain hotels offer few surprises but all the amenities you're likely to need. In Fishkill, on the east side of the Hudson near Cold Spring, Beacon and Poughkeepsie, there is a large cluster of chain hotels (and chain eateries) on two corners of the intersection of Routes 9 and 84. The hotels include **Holiday Inn** (542 Rte. 9, Fishkill; ✆ 800/Holiday or 845/896-6281; fax 845/896-5410; www.holiday inn.com; $109–$149 double); **Courtyard Fishkill** (17 Westage Dr./Rte. 9 and I-84; ✆ 800/321-2211 or 845/897-2400; fax 845/897-2274; www. courtyard.com; $99–$149 double); **Hampton Inn** (544 Rte. 9, Fishkill; ✆ 845/896-4000; fax 845/896-2799; www.hampton-inn.com; $119–$129 double); **Marriott Residence Inn** (14 Schuyler Blvd., Fishkill; ✆ 800/331-3131 or 845/896-5210; fax 845/896-9689; www.residenceinn.com; $149–$169 double); and **Hilton Garden Inn** (21 Westage Dr., Fishkill; ✆ 845/896-7100; fax 845/896-7111; www.hiltongardeninn.com; $109–$139 double).

Also worth considering on the east side of the Hudson are: **Courtyard Tarrytown Greenburgh** (475 White Plains Rd., Tarrytown; ✆ 800/589-8720 or 914/631-1122; fax 914/631-1357; www.courtyard.com; $199 double); **Courtyard Poughkeepsie** (2641 South Rd./Rte. 9, Poughkeepsie; ✆ 845/485-6336; fax 845/485-6514; www.courtyard.com; $109–$159 double); and **Hilton Tarrytown** (455 S. Broadway, Tarrytown; ✆ 914/631-5700; fax 914/631-0075; www.tarrytown.hilton.com; $114–$139 double). On the west side of the Hudson, try **Holiday Inn** (503 Washington Ave., Kingston; ✆ 800/HOLIDAY; www.holidaykingston.com).

of rustic elegance. Dinner is a four-course prix-fixe, with entree choices determining the cost. Your appetizer might be grilled tiger shrimp over sautéed spinach and mango, followed by a nice salad and an entree of venison saddle or Black Angus sirloin in sweet onion cream. The wine list has a number of surprisingly affordable choices. Jackets are requested for gentlemen at dinner. The Sunday four-course Champagne Brunch is also quite an affair, though more casual.

1123 Old Albany Post Rd. (off Rte. 9D), Garrison. ✆ **845/424-3000.** Reservations recommended weekends and holidays. Brunch prix fixe $19–$27; dinner prix fixe $40–$63. AE, MC, V. Dinner Thurs–Sat 6–10pm; Sun brunch 11am–3pm.

Moderate

Blue Dolphin Ristorante *Value* ITALIAN   In the heart of Katonah's all-American main street, the sign out front says "Diner," but this isn't your typical diner fare. In fact, though Blue Dolphin is indeed housed in a stainless steel 1950s-era diner, inside it doesn't much look the part, either. Rather, it's an adorable, intimate, and very good Italian bistro—specializing in dishes from Capri and the Amalfi Coast—that's so popular with locals that you may face a wait. The interior has been redone with home polished wood and a vaulted ceiling. The homemade pastas are a favorite of many long-time patrons, but just as good are dishes like veal caprese, chicken Marsala, and grilled swordfish. There's a good list of daily specials and a small but decent wine list.

175 Katonah Ave., Katonah. © **914/265-7676.** Reservations not accepted. Main courses $13–$19. AE, MC, V. Mon–Sat 11am–3pm and 5–10pm.

Brasserie Le Bouchon ★★ (Value FRENCH BISTRO   This new French restaurant makes quite a statement in laid-back, antiques-mad Cold Spring: It's sexy and chic, with deep bordello red walls and ceilings, red banquettes, glittering mirrors, and bistro lighting. For the most part, it emphasizes classic, rich, home-cooked French fare like mussels, slow-braised pork tenderloin, and steak frites, steak tartare, and steak au poivre. Appetizers include duck and pork pâté. Desserts, such as Grand Marnier double dark chocolate mousse, are similarly sinful. It's not the kind of place to worry about your waistline. The restaurant is very late-night cool, and it has a nice little bar at the back, a good spot to have a drink. If it's nice outside, you can dine on the patio, though it pales in comparison with the interior.

76 Main St., Cold Spring. © **845/265-7676.** Reservations recommended weekends and holidays. Main courses, $13–$24. AE, MC, V. Mon, Wed, Thurs, Sun noon–9:30pm; Fri–Sat noon–10pm.

Cold Spring Depot AMERICAN/PUB FARE   In the old train station, built in 1893 by Cornelius Vanderbilt (the train still rumbles by at all hours), this easygoing restaurant is a favorite of both locals and weekend visitors on antiquing treks. It serves comfort food, mainly, either in the popular tavern or the warmly decorated main dining room. Try Guinness potpie, Ma Ralston's meatloaf, homemade chili, or fish and chips. Sophisticates who find those too pedestrian can opt for the filet mignon or seafood paella. There's occasional live jazz on Saturday nights, and in summer an ice cream parlor operates next door. After you've had a couple of drinks, have a seat on the bench outside at 10:13pm and ask locals about "the ghost of the depot"—a woman murdered by her husband as she tried to escape on the train to Poughkeepsie in 1898.

One Depot Square, Cold Spring. © **845/353-8361.** Reservations recommended weekends and holidays. Main courses $13–$27. AE, MC, V. Mon–Thurs 11:30am–9pm; Fri–Sat 11:30am–11pm; Sun 11am–9pm. Sun brunch.

Inexpensive

Santa Fe Restaurant MEXICAN/SOUTHWESTERN   A storefront on Tarrytown's attractive Main Street, which is perched above the Hudson River and the Tappan Zee bridge, Santa Fe is a locals' Mexican restaurant that cloaks itself in the colors and kitsch of the American Southwest. The menu is more or less Mexican, with faithful takes on the standard sloppy dishes of enchiladas, tacos, fajitas (the house specialty), and some more carefully prepared fish and shellfish dishes. For lunch you can get some easy stuff like burgers and burritos. While combo plates won't satisfy a purist in search of authentic Mexican cuisine, it's a perfectly acceptable joint for a margarita and some satisfying gringo comfort food after a day touring the mansions of the Lower Hudson Valley.

5 Main St., Tarrytown. © **914/332-4452.** Main courses $8.95–$19. AE, MC, V. Mon–Tues 11:30am–9pm; Wed–Thurs 11:30am–10pm; Fri 11:30am–10:30pm; Sat noon–10:30pm; Sun 1–9pm.

WEST SIDE OF THE HUDSON

Hotel Thayer ★ (Value   Eat where the parents of West Point cadets do, in this 1920s hotel on the campus of the famous military academy. Easily the best restaurant in the immediate area, the Hotel Thayer's elegant restaurant, with its dark wood, chandeliers, and exposed stone walls, keeps pace with the dramatic architecture of the West Point campus. It has a vaguely medieval feel, like dining in the workers' mess hall in a Gothic castle. Even if you're not staying here, it's worth passing through two or three security checkpoints for a meal. Entrees included pan-seared red snapper, baked stuffed shrimp with crabmeat, and rack of lamb with mint demi-glace. The restaurant is fairly priced and has attentive service and a good wine list. Sunday's champagne brunch is very popular, as are special events like comedy and dinner and dancing on Friday and Saturday evenings.

674 Thayer Rd., West Point. ② 845/446-4731. Reservations recommended. Main courses $12–$22; Sun brunch $26. AE, DC, DISC, MC, V. Breakfast 7am–10:30am daily; lunch 11am–2pm Mon–Sat; dinner 5:30–9pm daily; Sun brunch 10am–2pm.

Lanterna Tuscan Bistro ★ TUSCAN   Nyack's a charming town, and in the new Lanterna it got what it deserved, a charming restaurant with flair but few pretensions. A small and mostly minimalist space with wood tables, white tablecloths, white walls and slow-moving ceiling fans, it features one long corridor and two small sitting areas—one upfront and the other back by the kitchen. The young chef, Rossano Gianni, turns out authentic Tuscan dishes and also offers cooking classes, demonstrations and wine tastings. Lunch might be a simple affair of homemade pasta and soup or salad, while the dinner menu features risotto, fresh fish (monkfish sautéed with white wine and herbs is a good one) and hearty meat dishes such as filet mignon topped with toasted walnut and Gorgonzola sauce. As you would hope, the wine list features some good Italian selections. On a nice day, a few tables are set up on the sidewalk for al fresco dining.

3 S. Broadway, Nyack. ② 845/353-8361. Reservations recommended weekends and holidays. Main courses $12–$27. AE, MC, V. Mon–Sat lunch 11:30am–3:30pm; Sun brunch 11am–3:30pm; dinner Sun–Thurs 4:30–9:30pm and Fri–Sat 4:30–10:30pm.

Prima Pizza (Kids) PIZZA/ITALIAN   An adorable family-owned and old-fashioned New York pizza joint, Prima has been in the same family since 1954. It's friendly and cozy, with bar stools at the counter and about 10 tables under hanging plants. The fresh dough is made daily, and sauces and meatballs are made on the premises. Besides some very creative pizzas, including lemon chicken and health-conscious no-fat and low-fat pizzas, it serves a mean meatball hot sub and more substantial dishes like lasagna and eggplant parmigiana. Cornwall, by the way, is a small town a stone's throw from West Point and Storm King Art Center in Mountainville—good to know if you're lugging kids around on art and history tours. If you find yourself back home with a hankering for Prima Pizza, you can even order it online at www.pizzaofnewyork.com and have it shipped overnight to your house.

252 Main St., Cornwall. ② 845/534-7003. Reservations not accepted. Main courses $13–$19. AE, DISC, MC, V. Tues–Thurs 10am–9pm; Fri 10am–10pm; Sat 11am–10pm and Sun noon–9pm.

THE LOWER HUDSON VALLEY AFTER DARK

The small towns along the Hudson River Valley offer just a few alternatives for evening entertainment; the biggest offering is of summertime concerts. In Katohah, **Caramoor Peforming Arts Center,** 149 Girdle Ridge Rd. (off Rte. 22; ② 914/232-5035; www.caramoor.org), features a popular Summer Music Festival, with outdoor classical music concerts, as well as indoor chamber and cabaret performances in the spring and fall. **Boscobel Restoration** in Garrison, 1601 Rte. 9D (② 845/265-3638; www.boscobel.org), is home to the Hudson Valley Shakespeare Festival (www.hvshakespeare.org) on the lawn in the summer and big band dancing in the fall. In Tarrytown, **The Music Hall Theatre,**

13 Main St. (© **914/631-1000;** www.tarrytownmusichall.org), a terrific 1885 theater and National Historic Landmark that was saved from destruction, is a great place to see a theater production or music performance. Events range from Sleeping Beauty, the ballet, to Eddy Palmieri, the Latin jazz giant. Nyack is home to a handful of bars; the one with the most going on is **91 Main,** 91 Main St. (© **845/353-9844;** www.91main.com; Tues–Sat), which plays host to funk, R&B, jazz, and blues musicians, with DJ nights and Thursday mixers.

3 The Mid-Hudson Valley

The Mid-Hudson Valley is often called the Great Estates Region. This is where families like the Vanderbilts and the Mills built truly spectacular spreads that epitomized the fantastic wealth and lofty aspirations of the Gilded Age. The region was also home to Franklin and Eleanor Roosevelt, pivotal 20th-century American figures who remained vitally connected to their roots here. Parts of the Mid-Hudson are undergoing greatly needed revitalization, with towns like Kingston and Newburgh taking advantage of their waterfront locations for development, spawning lively bar and restaurant scenes, and Beacon catapulting to life with the arrival of a stunning new contemporary art museum. Though within easy reach of many towns on the east side of the Hudson, several attractions that lie at the edge of the Catskill Mountains, including New Paltz, High Falls, and the Minnewaska Preserve (and the Mohonk Mountain House), are covered in chapter 8.

EXPLORING THE MID-HUDSON VALLEY

The great estates of the Gilded Age and the country's first presidential library combine with some of the hippest attractions in the art and culinary worlds to make the Mid-Hudson Valley a huge attraction for visitors of all stripes.

THE TOP ATTRACTIONS
EAST SIDE OF THE HUDSON

Dia:Beacon ★★★   In a 1929 Nabisco box-printing factory on the banks of the Hudson, the Dia Art Foundation, begun by Heiner Friedrich and Philippa de Menil in the 1970s, has created the world's largest contemporary art museum, an institution that sticks to the foundation's single-minded purpose. The new museum houses Dia's rarely seen permanent collection of pivotal Conceptual, Minimalist, and Earth artists, mostly men who came of age in the 1960s and 1970s. Nearly 250,000 square feet of gallery space—illuminated almost entirely by natural light that streams in through the factory's original skylights—were designed to exhibit the works of single artists. The museum's opening in

---

Take the Trolley

After your visit to Dia:Beacon, hop aboard Beacon's Main Street Trolley (Fri–Sun) for a spin through town and check out the city's self-described "Renaissance on the Hudson." The trolley makes several stops along Main Street (hop on and off all afternoon for 2 bucks), but be sure to check out the charming East End antiques district, and the contemporary galleries that dot Main Street. Highlights include Collaborative Concepts (348 Main), Concentric Gallery (174 Main), and the brand-new Hudson Beach Glass, housed in a restored firehouse at 162 Main St. *Note:* If the trolley isn't running during your visit, it's just a 1-mile drive downtown.

May 2003 represented the biggest development in the art world since the Guggenheim in Bilbao, Spain, and the new Modern in Fort Worth. As great as the space is, Dia is more about art than architecture. The museum exhibits 24 artists, including the sculptor Richard Serra (whose long gallery, the former train shed, is devoted to his massive *Torqued Ellipse* pieces), the fluorescent-light sculptures of Dan Flavin, Andy Warhol's work *Shadows* (a series of 102 brilliantly colored, silk-screened canvasses), and mixed-media installations by Joseph Beuys. Other noted artists include Gerhardt Richter, Louise Bourgeois, Sol LeWitt, Walter De Maria, and Bruce Nauman. These are ambitious and challenging artists across the board, but even visitors who aren't great fans of contemporary art are likely to find the museum space, and site on the river, with a landscape design by Robert Irwin, quite extraordinary.

Note: Metro-North Railroad is scheduled to offer a "1-day getaway fare" that will include round-trip train fare from New York City and admission to Dia:Beacon for a 25% discount on the individual prices. See www.mta.nyc.ny. us/mnr/html/outbound.htm for additional information.

3 Beekman St., Beacon. ✆ 845/440-0100. www.diabeacon.org. Admission $10 adults, $7 seniors and students, free for children under 12. Mid-Apr to mid-Oct Thurs–Mon 11am–6pm; mid-Oct to mid-Apr Fri–Mon 11am–4pm. Metro-North to Beacon.

Vanderbilt Mansion National Historic Site ★★★   One of the finest and most intact of the lavish estates built by wealthy 19th-century industrialists along the Hudson, Frederick William Vanderbilt's 54-room country palace in Hyde Park, built in 1898, is a no-holds-barred gem. One of the first steel-framed houses in the U.S., at 55,000 square feet (on 670 acres), it was the smallest and least expensive of the famed Vanderbilt mansions (others were in Newport, Bar Harbor, and Asheville), but it still epitomized the Gilded Age's nouveau riche. French in every respect, from Louise's Versailles-like bedroom to the grand dining room and Frederick's glittering master bedroom, it was decorated in impressively grand style. Yet the house, where the Vanderbilts spent only a few weeks each year in the spring and fall, functioned as a kind of spa retreat; guests were encouraged to enjoy the outdoors: the majestic views of the Hudson and Catskills in the distance and the wonderful gardens and woodlands surrounding the house.

Rte. 9, Hyde Park. ✆ 845/229-7770. www.nps.gov/vama. Admission $8 adults, free for children under 16. Mid-Apr to Oct Wed–Sat 10am–5pm and Sun 1–5pm. Guided tours daily 9am–5pm; closed Thanksgiving, Christmas, and New Year's Day. Grounds daily year-round 7am–sunset. Metro-North and Amtrak to Poughkeepsie.

Franklin Delano Roosevelt Presidential Library and Museum/FDR Home (Springwood) ★★★   Franklin Delano Roosevelt, the four-term president of the United States who was faced with not only the Great Depression and World War II but living with polio, loved the Hudson River Valley. FDR designed his own presidential library, the nation's first, while still in his second term and built it next to his lifelong home in Hyde Park. He actually used the study while president and often would be in residence while the library was open to the public; it is the only presidential library to have been used by a sitting president. See his cluttered White House desk (left as it was the last day of his presidency), exhibits on the FDR presidency and times, and FDR's beloved 1936 Ford Phaeton, with the original hand controls that allowed him to travel all over the estate. Two wings added in memory of his wife, Eleanor Roosevelt, make this the only presidential library to have a section devoted to a first lady. Springwood, the house next door, was built by FDR's father; FDR expanded the

---

(*Value* Hyde Park Discounts & National Parks Passes

The Vanderbilt and Roosevelt National Historic Sites in Hyde Park—including the FDR home, library, and museum, and the twin retreats Val-Kill and Top Cottage—are grouped for joint visits; visit the home of FDR, FDR Library and two additional sites for $22 or three additional sites for $30.

These historic sites in Hyde Park belong to the extensive network of national parks. Several discount passes are available to visitors, including: Golden Age Passports, $10 (seniors; lifetime membership); National Park Service Pass, $50 (individuals; good for 1 year); and Golden Eagle Passport, $65 (for families; good for 1 year). All park passes, good for free entry to any Vanderbilt-Roosevelt historic site tour, can be purchased at the national park sites in Hyde Park. For more information, see www.nps.gov.

---

modest farmhouse in an eclectic Dutch colonial style. The home isn't grand by the standard of the great river estates, but FDR entertained Churchill, the king and queen of England, and other dignitaries here. FDR and Eleanor are buried in the rose garden on the grounds. The Wallace Center, an impressive new visitor's center at the entrance to the library (where tickets for all FDR sites are purchased), presents a short film on FDR and Eleanor.

4079 Albany Post Rd. (off Rte. 9), Hyde Park. ⓒ 800/FDR-VISIT or 845/229-8114. www.nps.gov/hofr and www. fdrlibrary.marist.edu. Admission $8 adults; free for children under 16. Buildings open 9am–5pm daily; grounds open 7am–sunset daily. Metro-North and Amtrak to Poughkeepsie.

Eleanor Roosevelt National Historic Site (Val-Kill Cottage) & Top Cottage ⚐ Both Eleanor Roosevelt—who like her husband grew up in the Hudson River Valley—and FDR maintained serene and simple private country retreats away from Springwood. When FDR was away, and after his death, Eleanor—one of the most admired and influential women in American history—lived and worked out of Val-Kill Cottage, the only home she ever owned. A simple, rustic cabinlike home, Val-Kill is where Eleanor received world leaders and made her mark on civil rights legislation and international humanitarian issues (as a U.N. delegate, she chaired the committee that drafted the U.N. Human Rights Universal Declaration). The grounds were also the headquarters of Val-Kill Industries, which Eleanor and several other women established to teach trades to rural workers and produce colonial revival furniture and crafts.

FDR's retreat on a hilltop, which he christened Top Cottage, was more rustic still. He built it on Dutchess Hill in the 1930s as an informal place to get away from it all and think about issues confronting his presidency. FDR was at his most relaxed here, allowing himself to be photographed in his wheelchair. Restored but unfurnished, Top Cottage has recently been opened to visitors who come to see FDR's cherished views of the Catskill and Shawangunk Mountains from the famous porch, where he entertained guests such as Winston Churchill and King George VI and Queen Elizabeth of England (guests at his "scandalous" 1939 hot dog dinner). A wooded trail leads from Springwood to Val-Kill and Top Cottage. Visits to both cottages are by guided tour only (tickets are available at the Visitor's Center at the FDR Presidential Library and Museum).

Rte. 9G, Hyde Park. ⓒ 845/229-9115. www.nps.gov/elro. Admission to either $8 adults; free for children under 16. May–Oct daily 9am–5pm; Nov–Apr Thurs–Mon 9am–5pm (last tour at 4:30pm); grounds open daily year-round sunrise–sunset. Metro-North and Amtrak to Poughkeepsie.

Staatsburgh (Mills Mansion) ⭐   One of the most opulent and elegant of the Hudson River estates, Staatsburgh, an 1896, 65-room beaux-arts mansion on 1,600 acres (now the Mills Norrie State Park), was the country home of Ogden and Ruth Livingston Mills. Mrs. Mills, a member of the prominent Livingston clan, inherited the simpler original home—one of five Mills family mansions—in 1890. She and her husband renovated it in grand European style, combining her aristocratic lineage with the big new money of the era, and the result is pure Gilded Age: 18-foot ceilings, a massive Louis XIV–style dining room with green Italian marble on the walls, sumptuous library, dramatic central staircase crowned by a ceiling mural, and 14 bathrooms. The house, the first in the area to have electricity, is outfitted with all original furnishings. Staatsburgh is thought to have been the model for the Bellomont estate in Edith Wharton's *The House of Mirth*. A number of special events are held here, including summer concerts, "Celtic Day in the Park" (Sept), "Gilded Age Christmas," and an antique car show in October.

Old Post Rd. (off Rte. 9), Staatsburgh. ✆ 845/889-8851. www.staatsburgh.org. Admission $5 adults; $4 seniors and students; $3 children ages 5–12; free for children under 5. Apr to Labor Day Wed–Sat 10am–5pm, Sun noon–5pm; Labor Day to last Sun in Oct Wed–Sun noon–5pm; Dec special hours for holiday program; Feb–Mar Sun 11am–4pm. Metro-North and Amtrak to Poughkeepsie.

Montgomery Place Historic Estate ⭐⭐   One of the most lovingly sited and best preserved estates along the Hudson, this 434-acre, early-19th-century country Federal-style home enjoys splendid lawns and gardens and outstanding views overlooking the Hudson River and the distant Catskill Mountains. The most prominent designers of the day, the architect A. J. Davis and landscape designer Andrew Jackson Downing, built the home in fieldstone and stucco for Janet Livingston Montgomery, the widow of Revolutionary War hero General Richard Montgomery. Inside are family possessions from the late 1700s all the way to the second half of the 20th century. The house exhibits a very strong French influence, with hand-painted wallpaper and a formal parlor fashioned after Dolly Madison's White House parlor, though the massive kitchen in the basement and its original hearth are very Dutch in style. Many of the gardens were created in the 1930s, and they are some of the most beautiful of any estate along the Hudson. Montgomery Place is a great place to bring a picnic lunch and walk among the orchards, gardens, and woodland trails that lead to Sawkill falls.

Annandale Rd. (River Rd.), off Rte. 9G), Annandale-On-Hudson. ✆ 914/758-5461. www.staatsburgh.org. Admission $7 adults; $6 seniors; $4 children ages 5–17; grounds only pass $4. Apr–Oct Wed–Mon 10am–5pm; Nov Sat–Sun only 10am–5pm; Dec first 2 weekends only noon–5pm. Last tour 4pm. Metro-North and Amtrak to Rhinecliff.

WEST SIDE OF THE HUDSON

Washington's Headquarters State Historic Site ⭐   General George Washington established his military headquarters on the banks of the Hudson, in Newburgh, in 1782–83, during the final years of the Revolutionary War. He, his wife Martha, and his principal aides and their servants occupied a 1750 farmhouse donated to the army by a prosperous family, the Hasbroucks. Washington stayed here 16 months (and Martha 12 months), longer than any other headquarters during the war. In 1850, the property was declared the nation's first public historic site. The farmhouse displays Washington's office (where he wrote the famous "circular letter" and Newburgh addresses) and the original tables and chairs of the General's aides de camp. A museum, opened in 1910, across the lawn displays memorabilia such as medals of honor (including a 1783 original badge of military merit), locks of Washington's hair, and Martha's pocket watch from her first marriage. Revolutionary War buffs may also wish to visit the **New Windsor Cantonment** (✆ **845/561-1765**), a few miles away on Route 300. The staff at Washington's Headquarters can give directions to reach this site where Washington's 7,500 troops and their families camped during the winter of 1782–83. There are living history presentations and military demonstrations in season.

84 Liberty St., Newburgh. ✆ 914/562-1195. Admission $4 adults, $2 seniors and students. Mid-Apr to Oct Wed–Sat 10am–5pm and Sun 1–5pm.

OTHER ATTRACTIONS
EAST SIDE OF THE HUDSON

Culinary Institute of America   The nation's oldest culinary arts school and only residential college in the world dedicated to culinary training, the CIA and its lovely 150-acre riverside campus (a former Jesuit seminary) are open for tours (not to mention culinary "boot camps" for serious nonprofessionals). The institute has trained thousands of chefs and food-service industry professionals, including some of the most prominent chefs in the country, since its founding in 1946, and you'll see students on campus in their chef whites, a parallel to the West Point cadets across the river in their dress blues. You'll also smell what's cooking in the 41 kitchens and bake shops. The CIA also operates four restaurants and a bakery cafe open to the public (see "Where to Dine," below) and a culinary bookstore and gift shop.

1946 Campus Dr., Hyde Park. ✆ 845/451-1588. www.ciachef.edu. Admission $5 person. Tours Mon 10am and 4pm; Sept–Oct Mon 10am and 4pm and Thurs 4pm. Closed July. Reservations required.

Rhinebeck ⭐   A historic, gracious small town marked by the oldest inn in America, the Beekman Arms, Rhinebeck is one of the most visitor-friendly spots along the Hudson. It has an expanding number of inns, sophisticated restaurants, diverse furnishings and antiques shops, and even an art-house movie theater. It's a perfect town to walk around and enjoy at a leisurely pace. Chief among its attractions are the **Old Rhinebeck Aerodome,** a museum of antique airplanes with 30 annual air shows, and **Wilderstein,** an elegant 19th-century Queen Anne mansion, once occupied by Daisy Suckley, FDR's distant cousin and close confidant. The house, which features a five-story tower, massive veranda, and reams of family documents and belongings, is undergoing ongoing renovation, but is fascinating for the contrast it provides to the grander and somewhat more buttoned-up estates up and down the Hudson; the Suckleys' economic fortunes significantly declined during the Great Depression, and the house reflects that past. Similarly historic and easygoing small towns nearby and worth a short visit are **Red Hook** and **Tivoli,** both just a few miles north of Rhinebeck.

RHINEBECK ATTRACTIONS   Old Rhinebeck Aerodome: Stone Church Rd. and Norton Rd., Rhinebeck. ✆ 845/752-3200. www.oldrhinebeck.org. Admission Mon–Fri (museum) $6 adults, $5 seniors, $2 children 6–10; Sat–Sun (museum and air show) $12 adults, $10 seniors, $5 children 6–10. Daily mid-May to Oct 10am–5pm; air shows every Sat–Sun mid-June to mid-Oct 2pm. Wilderstein: 330 Morton Rd., Rhinebeck. ✆ 845/876-4818. www.wilderstein.org. Admission $8 adults, free for children 12 and under; May–Oct Thurs–Sun noon–4pm; formal teas offered several times a year.

Locust Grove (Samuel Morse Historic Site)   Locust Grove, a 150-acre estate and Tuscan-style villa, was purchased by Samuel Morse, painter-turned-inventor. The 19th-century artist invented the electric telegraph and Morse code and made a fortune that his paintings—though respected—never brought him. Morse purchased the 1830 Georgian estate from the Young family (today the art, furnishings and decorative arts primarily recall their stay here) and brought in the noted architect A. J. Davis (designer of Lyndhurst and Montgomery Place) to expand and remodel it. The property has a man-made lake, waterfall, and lovely gardens. A recent addition to the estate is a small but well-done museum dedicated to the life, art, and inventions of Morse and an excellent visitor's center that shows a film on the estate and Morse's life.

2683 South Rd. (Rte. 9), Poughkeepsie. ℂ 845/454-4500. www.morsehistoricsite.org. Admission $7 adults, $6 seniors, $3 students ages 6–18; free for children under 6. May–Nov daily 10am–3pm; special Dec hours. Grounds open year-round 8am–dusk.

WEST SIDE OF THE HUDSON

Kingston ⭐   New York State's first capital, the old Dutch town of Kingston, on the west bank of the Hudson, has two distinct historic areas of great interest to visitors. In uptown Kingston is the historic **Stockade District,** a pleasant commercial area marked by the presence of 21 pre-Revolutionary, Dutch-style stone houses (all four corners at the intersection of John and Cross streets are occupied by 18th-century stone houses, unique in the U.S.). Chief among the historic landmarks is the **Senate House,** which housed the first New York State Senate in 1777 after the adoption of the first constitution, until British troops burned Kingston later that same year. The Senate House Museum contains colonial artifacts and the paintings of John Vanderlyn. Along North Front and Walls streets is a pretty 2-block area of buildings with turn-of-the-20th-century-style canopied sidewalks, called the Pike Plan, home to a number of shops, galleries, restaurants, and cafes. The Old Town Stockade Farmer's Market is held Saturdays, June through September. Opposite the Old Dutch Church is the **Fred J. Johnston Museum,** an 1812 Federal-style house with an excellent collection of American decorative arts. At the other end of town, Kingston's historic waterfront area, the **Rondout,** reached its pinnacle in the days of the D&H Canal in the early 19th century but declined with the advent of the railroad. Today it's a nicely revitalized commercial area with a burgeoning number of restaurants and bars. It is also home to the **Hudson River Maritime Museum and Lighthouse** (an old boat shop with exhibits on the history of boating and ships), weekend vintage trolley rides out to the Hudson (which begin in front of the Maritime Museum), Sampson opera house, and a handsome new visitor's center. Boats leave from the Maritime Museum to go out along Rondout Creek to the 1913 Rondout Lighthouse. The Rondout is also the spot to catch the larger **Hudson River Cruises** on the Rip Van Winkle ships (for more information, see p. 215).

KINGSTON ATTRACTIONS   Senate House: 296 Fair St., Kingston. ℂ 914/338-2786. Apr 15–Oct Wed– Sat 10am–5pm and Sun 1–5pm; $3 adults, $2 seniors, $1 children ages 5–12. Fred J. Johnston Museum: 63 Main St., Kingston. ℂ 845/339-0720. May–Oct Sat–Sun 1–4pm; $3. Hudson River Maritime Museum: One Rondout Landing, Kingston. ℂ 845/338-0071. www.hrmm.org. May 4–Oct 20 museum daily 11am–5pm; boat rides July–Aug weekends and holidays noon–3pm and Mon, Thurs, and Fri noon–3pm (on the hour); May, June–Sept, and Oct weekends and holidays, noon–3pm. Admission museum only $4 adults, $3 seniors and children; museum and boat ride, $9 adults, $8 seniors and children.

ESPECIALLY FOR KIDS

Kids will love the Rhinebeck Aerodome, with its vintage airplanes and cool air shows. In Kingston, families can take a cruise on the Hudson River out to the lighthouse or hop aboard a vintage trolley car. Some of the great estates have extraordinary grounds and gardens with trails through the property; check out the Vanderbilt Mansion, Staatsburgh, and Montgomery Place. And finally, as an educational supplement to history classes, take the kids to Washington's Headquarters in Newburgh and the FDR Presidential Library and Museum in Hyde Park.

SHOPPING

In the Mid-Hudson Valley, **Beacon, Red Hook,** and **Rhinebeck** are the best towns for antiquing. Each has a couple of streets lined with good and interesting shops. In Beacon, **Relic,** 484 Main St. (© 845/440-0248), is the place for vintage housewares. **Beacon Hill Antiques** (474 Main St.; © 845/831-4577) peddles fine antiques while **Past Tense Antiques,** across the street at 457 Main (© 845/838-4255), offers well-priced antique and vintage pieces. **Hoffman's Barn Sale** in Red Hook, 19 Old Farm Rd. (© 845/758-5668), is an old barn with thousands of old, used and antique items of varying quality. A particularly fine store in Rhinebeck is **Asher House Antiques,** 6380 Mill St. (© 845/876-1796), which deals in both elegant and country-rustic English and French pieces. Behind the Beekman Arms Hotel on Mill Street is the **Beekman Arms Antique Market,** with several dealers in an old barn (© 845/876-3477). **Gold Goat,** 6119 Rte. 9 (© 845/876-1582), is a small gallery with some cool pieces of American folk art. Rhinebeck hosts the **Rhinebeck Antiques Fair,** with three big shows annually featuring more than 200 dealers at the Dutchess County Fairgrounds, Route 9 (© 845/876-1989; www.rhinebeckantiquesfair.com).

Those with a specific interest in arts and crafts should pick up the free "Explore Dutchess County Crafts and Arts Trail" brochure (available at many hotels, shops, and tourist information offices), which details more than two dozen crafts shops and galleries on the east side of the Hudson and crafts shows.

SPORTS & OUTDOOR PURSUITS

The Mid-Hudson Valley is rich in outdoors possibilities, including river cruises, hiking and biking, and cross-country skiing. Besides more traditional outdoor sports, thrill seekers may want to check out barnstorming flights on biplanes over the Hudson Valley at the Old Rhinebeck Aerodome (p. 213). Flights take off before and after air shows (15 min.; $40 per person).

BOATING & SAILING   **Hudson River Cruises,** Rondout Landing at the end of Broadway, in Kingston (© 800/843-7472; www.hudsonrivercruises.com), sets sail aboard the *Rip Van Winkle,* a modern 300-passenger vessel. The standard 2-hour cruises (adults $13, seniors $12, children ages 4–11 $6) visit the Mid Hudson Valley in spring, summer, and fall; there are also specialty cruises, some with live music, and a 90-minute Sunset Sail ($11) on Wednesdays. In Newburgh, **Hudson River Adventures** (Newburgh Landing; © 845/782-0685; www. prideofthehudson.com) operates 2-hour sightseeing cruises (adults $15, seniors $13, children ages 4–11 $13) from May to October on the *Pride of the Hudson,* a 130-passenger boat. **Scenic Hudson Sails** (© 845/546-1184; norriepointsail@ aol.com) offers weekend and sunset cruises and private charters aboard *Doxie,* a 31-foot sloop, a traditional-style yacht.

GOLF   There are more than 150 golf courses in the Hudson River Valley. **Dinsmore Golf Course,** Old Post Road (Rte. 9), Staatsburgh (© 845/889-4071; greens fees $18–$22), the second oldest golf course in the United States, is part of the 1,000-acre Mills-Norrie State Park, which includes the Mills Mansion State Historic Site. With panoramic views of the Hudson River and majestic Catskill Mountains, it was named "Best Public Golf Course in the Hudson Valley" by *Hudson Valley Magazine.* **Branton Woods,** 178 Stormville Rd., Hopewell Junction (© 845/223-1600; www.brantonwoodsgolf.com; greens fees $45–$125), has been named one of the top public courses in the nation by *Golf Digest.* Putnam County's **Centennial Golf Club,** Simpson Road, Carmel (© 845/225-5700; www.centennialgolf.com; greens fees $125), a hilly 1999 design by Larry Nelson, is one of the most picturesque in the Hudson Valley. **The Garrison,** 2015 Rte. 9, Garrison (© **845/424-3604;** www.garrisongolf club.com; greens fees $85) is a classic old 18-hole course overlooking the Hudson across from West Point. It has a yoga center and distinguished restaurant on the premises. **Mansion Ridge** (© **845/782-7888;** www.mansionridgegolf.com; greens fees $135) was the first public course designed by Jack Nicklaus in the tri-state region. The course is shorter and not as endlessly frustrating as some others designed by The Golden Bear.

Tip: If you plan to play a lot of golf, it may be worthwhile to pick up the $20 **Hudson Valley Golf** discount card, available through the website **www.hudson rivergolf.com**. It offers discounts at 15 area courses.

For additional course information and course previews, see www.hudson rivergolf.com and **www.golfhudsonvalley.com**.

HIKING   Four miles north of Cold Spring on Route 9D, an excellent trail leads to **South Beacon Mountain,** the highest point in the East Hudson Highlands (a 6-mile round-trip). **Clarence Fahnestock Memorial State Park,** a 7,000-acre park southwest of Beacon (Rte. 301, Carmel; © **914/225-7207**), is also a terrific place for hiking, with a number of trails and loops (suggested hikes include Three Lakes Trail and East Mountain–Round Hill). Less strenuous trails can also be found in **Mills-Norrie State Park** (© **914/889-4100**), the site of the Staatsburgh Mills Mansion.

SWIMMING   Canopus Lake in **Clarence Fahnestock Memorial State Park,** southwest of Beacon (Rte. 301, Carmel; © **914/225-7207**), has an attractive beach and swimming area open to the public.

WINTER SPORTS   **Fahnestock Winter Park** (Rte. 301, Carmel), part of Clarence Fahnestock Memorial State Park between Cold Spring and Beacon, is one of the best spots for Nordic skiing, snowshoeing, and sledding. Besides tons of trails, it also offers equipment rentals and lessons. For information and condition reports, call © **845/225-3998.**

WHERE TO STAY

The Mid-Hudson isn't loaded with accommodations options—there is little in the way of national chain hotels and motels—but among the few it has are quite special. Note that a good-value option is above the Raccoon Saloon, in Marlboro (see "Where to Dine," below).

EXPENSIVE

Belvedere Mansion ★★   For unrestrained luxury in a country inn, none comes close to the Belvedere. The 1900 neo-Classical mansion, with its pillared façade perched above the Hudson just south of Rhinebeck, also has a carriage house, pond, and lodge on the property. The elegant interiors aim to recreate the grandeur of the Gilded Age estates along the Hudson, and indeed the 18th-century antiques, silk fabrics, rich colors, luxurious linens, and marble baths are fit for a prince. The seven main-house rooms are the biggest and most expensive; several have fantastic river views and details like claw-foot tubs and canopied beds. The Henry Hudson Suite, in what was previously the servants' quarters, is a cool trio of rooms on the top floor, all sharing a bathroom—perfect for a genteel family or group of friends. The carriage-house rooms are smaller but also very nicely decorated; a nice bargain are the four small rooms called "cozies," which adequately describes their charm. Four additional luxury rooms with fireplaces occupy the Hunt Lodge.

Rte. 9, Staatsburgh, NY 12561. ℂ **845/889-8000**. www.belvederemansion.com. 22 units. "Cozies" $75–$95 double; Carriage House $150–$195 double; Mansion Rooms $275; Lodge $250–$300; $350–$450 suite. All rates include gourmet breakfast. 2-night minimum stay weekends; 3-night minimum some holidays. AE, DC, DISC, MC, V. Free parking. **Amenities:** Restaurant; tavern; laundry service. *In room:* A/C, hair dryer.

MODERATE

Beekman Arms/Delamater House ⭐   The Beekman Arms has the distinction of being America's oldest continually operating inn; it's been around since 1761, and very much looks the part. How's this for pedigree? George Washington, Benedict Arnold, and Alexander Hamilton all drank, ate, and slept here. And the Colonial Tap Room (tavern) and lobby look like it could still welcome them, with their wide-plank floors, stone hearth, and hand-hewn beams. Rooms in the main inn are upstairs; updated in the mid-'90s, they are nicely decorated and perfectly comfortable, if not quite as special as the public rooms might lead you to expect. The Delamater House, just up the street on Mill Street/Route 9, is the new kid on the block; the noted architect A. J. Davis built the main American Gothic house in 1844. The main house has gorgeous verandas, while the property has seven separate buildings, both old and new, with 44 guest rooms total (more than half have working fireplaces). The oldest rooms are in the main house, carriage house, and gables; courtyard rooms are more contemporary but have working fireplaces and four have kitchenettes. Most rooms are a little frilly; the carriage-house rooms are the most interesting of the lot.

6387 Mill St./Montgomery St. (Rte. 9), Rhinebeck, NY 12572. ℂ **845/876-7077** or 845/876-7080. www. beekmanarms.com or www.delamaterinn.com. 63 units. Beekman Arms $105–$160 double; motel rooms $95–$125 double; Delamater Inn $95–$180 double. Rates include breakfast. 2-night minimum stay on weekends May–Oct and all holiday weekends. AE, DC, DISC, MC, V. Free parking. **Amenities:** Restaurant; tavern; laundry service. *In room:* A/C, hair dryer, dataport; many have working fireplaces; several Delamater courtyard rooms have small kitchenettes with microwave and coffeemaker.

Journey Inn ⭐⭐   A contemporary inn run by two sisters who've named rooms after favorite sojourns and stocked them with souvenirs, this exceedingly friendly and very comfortable B&B has one exclusive advantage going for it: It is literally right across the street from the gate of the Vanderbilt mansion and just minutes from all the FDR attractions in Hyde Park (as well as the Culinary Institute of America). While the inn isn't old and decorated with period furniture, for many travelers that will be a blessing: instead, it has new, excellent bathrooms, great big comfortable beds, central air-conditioning, and no creaky floors. The sisters, Diane and Michele, just added a new breakfast wing, where they wow visitors with their gourmet breakfast creations (one's the baker, the other the cook).

One Sherwood Place, Hyde Park, NY 12538. ℂ **845/229-8972**. www.journeyinn.com. 6 units. $95–$150 double; $175 suite. Rates include full breakfast. Weekend 2-night minimum. No credit cards. Free parking. **Amenities:** Dial-up Internet access. *In room:* A/C, hair dryer.

Stockbridge Ramsdell House on Hudson ⭐⭐ *Finds*   A magnificent 1870 Queen Anne Victorian, once owned by the president of the Erie Railroad, this terrific B&B is emblematic of the revitalization going on in Newburgh. In the heart of New York's largest historic district, just a short block from the waterfront where a half-dozen restaurants have popped up, the owners in just a short time have created a wonderfully inviting inn. The house is warm and quaint, with seven fireplaces and attractive sitting rooms, without being fussy. The screened porch, where a splendid home-cooked gourmet breakfast is served, looks out over the river. Guest rooms are huge, with fantastic canopy beds, fireplaces, and nice touches like Frette robes and CD clock radios. A couple have private riverfront decks with some of the best Hudson views an inn could hope for. Join Lucinda and Howard for wine and cheese in the evening in the living room overlooking the river. Within easy reach are Washington's Headquarters as well as West Point, Storm King, and, across the river, the new Dia:Beacon art museum.

158 Montgomery St., Newburgh 12550. ℭ 845/562-9310. howardmallen1@aol.com 6 units. Nov–Mar $135–$175 double; Apr–Oct $150–$195 double (rates $20 higher for 1-night stay). Rates include full breakfast. Weekend 2-night minimum. AE, DC, DISC, MC, V. Free parking. **Amenities:** Nightly wine and cheese. *In room:* A/C, TV/VCR, hair dryer, robes, CD clock radio.

WHERE TO DINE

With the Culinary Institute of America on the east bank of the Hudson, it's not surprising that there's some great eating in this section of the valley. Chief among the options are the student-staffed restaurants on the campus of the CIA, which are professionally run in every respect and require some foresight to nab reservations.

EAST SIDE OF THE HUDSON
Expensive

Allyn's ★★ CREATIVE AMERICAN   Amid Dutchess County's horse farms and fancy-pants hunt clubs, Allyn's is a consistent winner. In winter, the best spot is next to the roaring fire in the charmingly rustic bar (for a while there my wife and I had a virtual standing snowy-night reservation); in spring and summer, get a table outside to admire the view of rolling hills. Terrific main courses include sautéed rainbow trout with sun-dried tomatoes, capers, and oyster mushrooms, served with basmati rice pilaf; and a grilled 12-ounce sirloin with fried leeks and garlic mashed potatoes. There are always excellent daily specials and lighter options (including a good burger and nice soups and salads). Allyn's is just up the road from the Millbrook Winery, and makes a good before or after visit.

4258 Rte. 44, Millbrook (4 miles east of the village). ℭ 845/677-58888. Reservations recommended weekends. Main courses $17–$24. MC, V. Wed–Sat and Mon 11:30am–3pm and 5:30–10pm; Sun 11:30am–3:30pm and 5–10pm.

Culinary Institute of America (CIA) ★★★ AMERICAN/FRENCH/ITALIAN/BAKED GOODS   The nation's foremost culinary arts college has four on-campus restaurants and a bakery cafe that are open to the public. They're staffed by students of CIA, but they hardly seem like training grounds. All are extremely professional, which is why it can be so hard to get a reservation (reservations are accepted 3 months in advance and for weekends in season, you may need that much of a cushion). The three main restaurants are the elegant Escoffier Restaurant, serving classic French fare with a lighter touch; Ristorante Caterina de Medici, a handsome villa with a regionally varied Italian menu; and American Bounty Restaurant, which focuses on regional American specialties and ingredients from the Hudson River Valley. St. Andrew's Café is contemporary and casual, offering wood-fired pizzas, vegetarian dishes and natural ingredients, while the newest addition to the roster is the Apple Pie Bakery Café, an informal place for baked goods and a nice lunch or early dinner. You'll know the nation's food-service industry is in good hands after a meal at one of the restaurants and a walk around CIA. The three main restaurants request business or "country club casual" (collared shirt and slacks or khakis) attire and no jeans, sneakers, or sandals. Reservations accepted online (often the best way to get in) at www.ciachef.edu; note that dining hours are limited.

1946 Campus Dr. (off Rte. 9), Hyde Park. ℭ 845/471-6608. www.ciachef.edu. Reservations essential. Main courses $14–$28. AE, DC, DISC, MC, V. American Bounty Tues–Sat 11:30am–1pm and 6:30–8:30pm; Apple Pie Bakery Café Mon–Fri 8am–6:30pm; Escoffier Tues–Sat 11:30am–1pm and 6:30–8:30pm; Ristorante Caterina

> ### *Tips* The Other CIA
>
> Throughout the Hudson Valley, inns and restaurants large and small count chefs and other personnel trained at the prestigious Culinary Institute of America, also known by its unfortunate acronym CIA, among their staffs. A diploma from the food-industry CIA is a real badge of distinction, and a terrific boon to the region to have so many culinary pros in the kitchens. If a local someone tells you about a new restaurant opened by a chef, in the local parlance, "from the Culinary," check it out; chances are you'll find a winner.

de Medici Mon–Fri 11:30am–1pm and 6:30–8:30pm (selected menu items available in Al Forno Room Mon–Fri 1–6pm); St. Andrew's Café Mon–Fri 11:30am-1pm and 6:30–8:30pm.

Moderate

Piggy Bank, Beacon ⭐ Beacon is definitely on the upturn, with the arrival of the new Dia:Beacon Art Center, but the formerly sleepy river town isn't yet in a position to deal with too many Manhattanite hipsters. Piggy Bank, though, has its own sense of cool. Serving authentic southern barbecue out of a former 1880 bank (complete with a Remington & Sherman bank vault-turned-wine cellar), the restaurant is great looking, with scuffed wood tables, funky lighting fixtures, and a tin ceiling. The pit barbecue cranks out chili, hickory-smoked ribs, burgers, pulled pork barbecue sandwiches, and grilled chicken breasts with cornbread and fantastic sweet potato fries. On "Rack Attack Tuesdays," you can don a napkin and settle in for an all-you-can-eat rib dinner for $18. Live bands play on Friday nights and on Beacon's newly institutionalized "Second Saturday" of each month, and during warm months the outdoor patio is open.

448 Main St., Beacon. ℂ **845/838-0028.** Reservations recommended on weekends. Main courses $7.75–$21. AE, DC, DISC, MC, V. Tues–Thurs 11am–9pm; Fri 11am–10pm; Sat noon–10pm; Sun noon–8:30pm.

Traphagen Restaurant & Colonial Tap Room (Beekman Arms) ⭐⭐ AMERICAN/CONTINENTAL   The official names of the restaurant and tavern of America's oldest continually operating inn are a bit unwieldy. But a stop here is almost obligatory. The tavern especially exudes Revolutionary War–era flavor, with its wide-plank floorboards and wood posts, paneling and beams. It's a great place for a mug of ale and hearty soup—probably just what George Washington and his fellow war planners did when they dined here in the 1780s. I always eat in the Tap Room, just for the ambience, but the connected restaurant serves the same high-quality menu. Main courses include appropriately hearty items like tournedos of veal, aged Black Angus sirloin, Dutch-style turkey potpie, and slow-roasted duck. Slightly less macho dishes, such as baked crab-meat-stuffed brook trout with goat-cheese polenta, also make appearances.

6387 Mill St. (Rte. 9), Rhinebeck. ℂ **845/876-1766.** Reservations recommended on weekends. Main courses $13–$27. AE, DC, DISC, MC, V. Lunch daily 11:30am–3pm; dinner Mon–Thurs 5:30–9pm, Fri–Sat 5:30–10pm, Sun 4–9pm; Sun brunch 10:30am–2pm.

Inexpensive

Foster's Coach House *Value* *Kids* PUB FARE   A homey, historic restaurant where prices are about as cheap as you're going to find in this part of the country, Foster's has been in operation since just after World War I. An old tavern was converted into a full-scale restaurant, with horse stalls as dining booths. It is dark and cool, but incredibly relaxed. The bar is a favorite watering hole for locals when there's a game on. On the menu nothing exceeds $14, and desserts like cheesecake and pecan pie are two measly bucks. Foster's is a perfect place to drop in for lunch or an informal dinner. Basics are best: chopped sirloin with onions and mushroom gravy, turkey with stuffing and gravy, shrimp scampi, and sandwiches and burgers for lunch. Beer is cheap, and so is wine by the glass.

22 Montgomery St., Rhinebeck. ✆ 845/876-8052. Main courses $4–$14. AE, DC, DISC, MC, V. Tues–Sat 11am–11pm; Sun noon–11pm.

WEST SIDE OF THE HUDSON

Cena 2000 ✪ NORTHERN ITALIAN   On the newly revitalized and incredibly popular waterfront district—site of about a dozen new restaurants in the past 3 years, a real beacon of hope for Newburgh—this is, according to many locals, the best of the lot. Contemporary and understated (if you don't count the wildly colored, whimsical bar), the upscale restaurant (pronounced "chay-nah") has a waterfront patio and riverfront terrace with dining under tall umbrellas. The menu is especially strong on fresh seafood dishes, and it offers excellent Italian specialties like *caccuicco toscano* (a traditional Tuscan fish stew) and grilled scaloppine of veal with grilled mushrooms and spinach, as well as a daunting array of daily specials. There's always a *risotto del giorno* (risotto of the day). The wine list has some interesting Italian options, and desserts are worth saving room for (although the tiramisu is a little lackluster).

50 Front St., Newburgh. ✆ 845/561-7676. Reservations recommended. Main courses $14–$26. AE, DISC, MC, V. Daily noon–3pm and Sun–Thurs 5–10pm; Fri–Sat 5–11pm.

Raccoon Saloon ✪✪ CREATIVE AMERICAN   In a classic pre-Revolutionary saloon, this unassuming, family-owned and -operated restaurant and bar is hands-down one of the most charming spots along the Hudson. A mother, daughter, and (CIA-trained) chef son run the place, a relaxed but great-looking bar with a couple of separate, vintage dining rooms and a small terrace with tables that sits high above a rushing waterfall and the mighty Hudson River. The Raccoon is the annual winner of a poll naming the Hudson Valley's best burgers (and they are truly fantastic, large and juicy, served with homemade ketchup and extras like guacamole, mushrooms, and bacon), and you might think it's just a bar if you peek in, but the menu offers many other, more sophisticated delights. Try the black truffle chicken liver pâté, seared filet of salmon with mandarin orange sauce, or rib-eye steak au poivre with cracked peppercorn and cognac. Desserts are all homemade, and ice creams are imaginative and delicious: flavors include basil, lavender, and honey. The homemade ginger ale is out of this world.

Upstairs, the Raccoon Saloon also operates a small inn, with four very nice rooms, two with fantastic waterfall and river views. Room no. 3, lemon yellow with a black-and-white tile floor and large bathroom, is my personal favorite ($85 double).

Rte. 9W, Marlboro-on-Hudson. ✆ 845/236-7872. Reservations recommended weekends. Main courses $10–$24. AE, DISC, MC, V. Mon–Thurs 11am–9:30pm; Fri–Sat 11am–10pm; Sun noon–9:30pm.

Ship to Shore ✪ AMERICAN/STEAKHOUSE   This cool, jazzy spot, one of the new arrivals in the revitalized Kingston waterfront district, known as the Rondout, is a hip take on the classic New York steakhouse. The chef, a graduate of the Culinary Institute of America (always a good thing in these parts) prepares an extensive menu of steaks and chops as well as seafood and pastas, always augmented by a long list of fresh daily specials. Meat eaters can dive into broiled rib eye with Portobello mushroom sauce or double-cut boneless pork loin, while seafood lovers can try dishes like semolina-crusted red snapper with linguini or seared ahi tuna with sticky rice and seaweed salad. For lunch there are some great, creative sandwiches and an array of salads. Back past the bar are a couple of more intimate dining areas if the front gets too loud. There's live jazz on Friday and Saturday nights, and Wednesdays are half-price wine nights.

15 West Strand (Rondout District), Kingston. © 845/334-8887. Reservations recommended on weekends. Main courses $13–$27. AE, DISC, MC, V. Daily 11am–11pm.

THE MID-HUDSON VALLEY AFTER DARK

The spectacular new **Richard B. Fisher Center for the Performing Arts** ★★, on the campus of Bard College in Annandale-on-Hudson (© 845/758-7900; www.bard.edu/fishercenter), is the latest building by the innovative architect Frank Gehry (designer of the Guggenheim Bilbao). This distinctive and intimate theater, which opened in 2003 and seats just 900 in the main hall, featured performances by Elvis Costello and the Mingus Orchestra, Merce Cunningham, and Ballet Hispánico in its inaugural year; it's still a bit uncertain how many and what kind of public events will take place here in the coming years, as the center is also, or primarily, a teaching space. But if anything is scheduled, it's very much worth the trek. Poughkeepsie's legendary **Bardavon Opera House,** 35 Market St. (© 845/473-2072; www.bardavon.org), which has hosted a variety of classical music, opera and other musical and theatrical performances since 1869, is one of the top spots in the Valley. Programs include music, dance, film, and theater; the schedule ranges from the Hudson Valley Philharmonic and Itzhak Perlman to Lily Tomlin and screenings of *King Kong.*

Beacon, basking in the attention of the new Dia:Beacon Art Center, has initiated a program called **"2nd Saturdays";** trolleys pick up passengers at the train station and ferry them down Main Street, where art galleries and shops stay open until 9pm on the second Saturday of every month and a number of bars and restaurants feature live music. For more information on scheduling, call © 845/838-4243 or visit www.nynarts.com. Newburgh and Kingston's **revitalized waterfronts** are loaded with bars and restaurants. Both have become real scenes in the last couple of years. A Newburgh-Beacon commuter ferry is in the works, which will make it very easy to cross the Hudson and check out the restaurants and bars of either side. Rhinebeck has a number of congenial local bars, but its cool local art-house theater, **Upstate Films,** 6415 Montgomery St. (© 845/876-2515; www.upstatefilms.org), is unique in these parts.

4 The Upper Hudson Valley

The great estates continue in the Upper Hudson Valley, one of the most pastoral segments of the region. The simple beauty of the landscape was a perfect complement to the Shakers, who established one of their largest communities in the area east of the Hudson, near Chatham. Today there's an excellent museum and library dedicated to the Shaker legacy. The Upper Hudson is perhaps best known for the town of Hudson, which has exploded as an art and antiques center. The east side of the Hudson, including the towns of Catskill and Saugerties, is covered in chapter 8.

EXPLORING THE UPPER HUDSON VALLEY
THE TOP ATTRACTION

Though the predominantly rural Upper Hudson Valley isn't as loaded with the must-see attractions that are in the Mid- and Lower Hudson, it does have two splendid estates and the area's best antiquing center, as well as the fascinating tra-ditions of the Shaker community.

East Side of the Hudson

Clermont State Historic Site ⚑★   The oldest of the great estates on the Hud-son, this 1750 Georgian manor house was home to seven successive generations of one of New York State's most prominent families, the Livingstons. Philip Liv-ingston was one of the signatories of the Declaration of Independence, and Robert Livingston possessed one of the largest private libraries in the U.S., a large portion of which survives at Clermont. The family's important role in Rev-olutionary activities led the British to burn Clermont in 1777. The nearly 500-acre estate, on a 45-foot-high bluff with great views of the river below and Catskills Mountains in the distance, has excellent woodland hiking trails out past the formal gardens, bar and gardener's cottages. The house today for the most part evokes the 1920s, when the house was remodeled as a colonial revival, though it contains furnishings and belongings from more than 200 years of Liv-ingstons at Clermont. The visitor's center plays a short film that interviews the last resident of the house, Alice Livingston.

One Clermont Ave. (off Rte. 9G), Germantown. ℂ 518/537-4240. www.friendsofclermont.org. Admission $5 adults, $4 seniors and students, $1 children ages 5–12, free for children under 5. Apr–Oct Tues–Sun 10:30am–5pm, Mon holidays 11am–4:30pm; Nov to mid-Dec Sat–Sun 11am–4pm. Grounds open year-round 8:30am–sunset.

Olana State Historic Site ⚑★★★   Olana, though not as massively grand as some of the homes built by the 19th-century industrialists, is surely the most unique of all the great Hudson Valley estates. A Persian fantasy perched on a hill high above the river, with stunning panoramic views, it was the home of the accomplished Hudson River School painter Frederick Church (1826–1900). Well traveled in the Middle East, Europe, and South America, Church made his home perhaps his most important work of art, an indoor and outdoor museum incor-porating artifacts, design elements, and furnishings of his favorite places. He was particularly taken with Moorish-style architecture and design, which is reflected in the mansion's windows, courtyards, thick carpets, and decorative tile motifs; sumptuous parlors look like opium dens. The dark and heavy dining room, how-ever, was meant to evoke a medieval castle. The landscaping on the 336-acre estate grew out of Church's romantic, painterly affection for the Hudson Valley. Inside are not only Church's collection of exotic treasures from around the world, but a few of his most important paintings, such as his landscape of Petra in Jordan, as well as other works by Hudson River School painters like Thomas Cole. Guided tours last 45 minutes; in high season, tours (maximum 12 people) often sell out early in the day, and reservations are suggested on weekends.

Rte. 9G, Hudson. ℂ 518/828-0135. www.olana.org. Admission $3 adults, $2 seniors and students, $1 children ages 5–12, free for children under 5. First Wed in Apr to Memorial Day Wed–Sun 10am–5pm; June 1–Oct 1 Wed–Sun 10am–6pm; Oct 1 to last weekend in Oct Wed–Sun 10am–5pm; Nov Wed–Sun 10am–4pm; Dec spe-cial hours for holiday programs and tours; late Dec to Mar, tours by reservation. Last tour 1 hr. before closing.

Hudson ⚑★★   Only a decade or so ago, Hudson was just a small upstate town with very little going for it save some beautiful countryside and rundown archi-tecture. However, an influx of antiques dealers and part-time residents from the city has given it a remarkable makeover. Today it is *the* antiquing destination of the Hudson Valley and full of enjoyable shops and cafes. Most of its development and refurbishing is restricted to a single street, the long and charming **Warren Street,** which is packed end-to-end with antiques shops. Also worth checking out in Hudson is the surprisingly engaging **FASNY Museum of Firefighting** ★. Hudson, home to the oldest volunteer fire department in the U.S., is also the site of this large and very well-organized museum, which has been around since 1925. It contains more than 80 fire apparatuses, ranging from a 1725 Newsham wooden cart, the first fire "engine" in New York City, to wonderfully ornate mid-19th-century carriages. A small 9/11 exhibit in the front reminds visitors of the importance and bravery of firefighters. For current information on gallery exhibits and other Hudson happenings, visit **www.warrenstreet.com**.

FASNY Museum of Firefighting. 117 Harry Howard Ave. © **518/828-7695**. Donation suggested. Daily 9am–4:30pm.

Shaker Museum and Library ★ *Finds*   The Shakers, the early American religious group known not only for their religious devotion and sexual abstinence but their exquisite craftsmanship and ingenious architectural simplicity that have influenced legions of designers, established communities in upstate New York and New England at the end of the 18th century. The Shakers believed that every living act was an act of devotion, and they pursued their work like prayer. This rustic museum of nearly 20,000 objects and repository of books, journals, photographs, and papers—established in 1950 as the first public museum concerning the life, work, art, and religion of the United Society of Believers in Christ's Second Appearing, commonly known as the Shakers—contains one of the largest collections of the community's heavenly round baskets, furniture, textiles, kitchen implements, spinning wheels, farm tools, and machinery. The museum and library will eventually relocate to a state-of-the-art facility in the Shakers' Great Stone Barn (a stunning building and the largest stone barn in America) in nearby New Lebanon, New York, very close to the historic Mount Lebanon Shaker Village, from which more than three-quarters of the collection comes. When that happens, the Shaker site will become one of the top attractions in the Upper Hudson Valley.

88 Shaker Museum Rd., Old Chatham. © **518/794-9100**. www.shakermuseumandlibrary.org. Admission $8 adults, $6 seniors, $4 children ages 8–17. Late May to late Oct Wed–Mon 10am–5pm.

OTHER ATTRACTIONS

Martin Van Buren National Historic Site (Lindenwald)   The eighth president of the U.S.—admittedly, not one of the best-remembered presidents in American history—Martin Van Buren (1782–1862), grew up in the Upper Hudson Valley in the town of Kinderhook (it's said that "okay" comes from his references to Old Kinderhook by its initials). Van Buren bought the estate in 1839 during his presidency as a place to retire. He named the 226-acre farm Lindenwald and built a Georgian-style mansion here, where he lived out the final 21 years of his life.

Old Post Rd. (Rte. 9H), Kinderhook. © **518/758-9689**. www.nps.gov/mava. Admission $8 adults, $6 seniors, $4 children ages 8–17; free for children under 8. May 20–Oct 31 daily 9am–4:30pm; Nov 1–Dec 7 Sat–Sun only 9am–4:30pm.

ESPECIALLY FOR KIDS

The **Museum of Firefighting** in Hudson is sure to delight kids—especially little boys—with its fantastic collection of vintage firetrucks. The grounds at the **Clermont** and **Olana** estates are great for exploring, with plenty of beautiful trails, and having a picnic.

SPORTS & OUTDOOR PURSUITS

HIKING   Nice and easy hiking trails can be found at the state historic sites **Clermont** (Clermont; ℂ **518/537-4240**), **Olana** (Greenport; ℂ **518/828-0135**), and **Martin Van Buren Park** (Kinderhook; ℂ **800/724-1846**).

WINTER SPORTS   For downhill skiing, try **Catamount,** Route 23, Hillsdale (ℂ **800/342-1840;** www.catamountski.com), on the Massachusetts border in the southern Berkshires. There are good cross-country ski trails at the state historic sites **Clermont** (Clermont; ℂ **518/537-4240**), **Olana** (Greenport; ℂ **518/828-0135**), and **Martin Van Buren Park** (Kinderhook; ℂ **800/724-1846**).

SHOPPING

Antiquing is a huge business and pastime in the Upper Hudson Valley. In the last decade, **Hudson** has been transformed from a sleepy and fairly run-down upstate town into one of the premier antiques destinations in New York State, with more than 70 shops and galleries spread out along 5 blocks of Warren Street and a few streets that fan out from there. It has many slick, high-end shops (though most shoppers find the prices a bit more accessible than in New York City) and a few stores for the rest of us. Pieces range from Egyptian to fine French and midcentury modern. There are too many to mention, but among the nicest shops are **Eustace & Zamus,** 422½ Warren St. (ℂ **518/822-9200**); **Van den Akker,** 547 Warren St. (ℂ **518/822-1177**); **Vince Mulford,** 417-419 Warren St. (ℂ **518/828-5489**); **Historical Materialism,** 601 Warren St. (ℂ **518/671-6151**); and **Gottlieb Gallery,** 524 Warren St. (ℂ **518/822-1761**). If those are too pricey, check out **Fern,** 554 Warren St. (ℂ **518/828-2886**); **Cottage & Camp,** 521 Warren St. (ℂ **518/822-9175**); and above all, **The Armory Art & Antique Gallery,** State Street at North 5th (ℂ **518/822-1477**), an eclectic and lower-priced assembly of some 60 dealers. Other non-antiques shops of interest, selling mostly housewares and gift items, include: **Shop Naked,** 608 Warren St. (ℂ **518/671-6336**); **Pieces,** 609 Warren St. (ℂ **518/822-8131**); **Rural Residence,** 316 Warren St. (ℂ **518/822-1061**); and the unique jewelry store **Ornamentum,** 506½ Warren St. (ℂ **518/671-6770**). For a full list of stores and galleries, visit www.warrenstreet.com.

The Shaker Museum & Library, in Old Chatham (88 Shaker Museum Rd.; ℂ **518/794-9100**), has a gift shop with an excellent selection of high-quality crafts based on Shaker traditions (such as oval boxes, furniture, and baskets), as well as books about the Shakers and other gift items.

WHERE TO STAY

Options in the Upper Hudson are largely limited to small but charming and intimate bed-and-breakfasts. The area is near enough other sections of the valley that you might also consider basing yourself farther downriver.

MODERATE

Hudson City B&B   This nicely restored three-story 1865 Victorian is in the heart of Hudson, just two blocks from Warren Street and its roster of antiques shops. In keeping with the town's newfound forte, this B&B is filled to the brim with pictures, antiques and knickknacks. The house has a lovely, large front porch and a sweet little "meditation" garden out back. Guest rooms are spacious and furnished largely with period pieces and original art, though those who have a fear of flowery bedspreads may have to look elsewhere. The top-floor suites are huge and have brass showers and soaking tubs. In one part of the house, next to the computer room, the owner operates an unobtrusive hair salon.

326 Allen St., Hudson, NY 12534. (C) **518/822-8044**. www.hudsoncitybnb.com. 5 units. Nov–Apr $99–$189 double, $235–$245 suite; May–Oct $155–$209 double, $295–$315 suite. Rates include breakfast. AE, DISC, MC, V. Free parking on street. **Amenities:** Garden; video library; Internet access. *In room:* A/C, TV/VCR.

Inn at Silver Maple Farm   A large converted barn complex on the outskirts of Chatham, not far from the Shaker Museum and Library and on the New York side of the Berkshire foothills, this 10-acre estate nestled into a hillside is a relaxing retreat. Rooms are varied, with a number of different views and designs. In all you'll find comfortable beds, handsome linens, and down comforters, with other touches like antique trunks and hand-painted murals. The Pines suite has a downstairs living room, fireplace, and upstairs loft. The Lodge rooms are rustic and sedately decorated, without the frills of a few others. Breakfast is generous and includes items like French toast, apple pie pancakes, and fresh-baked muffins.

Rte. 295, Canaan, NY 12029. (C) **518/781-3600**. Fax 518/781-3883. www.silvermaplefarm.com. 11 units. May–Oct and holidays $95–$150 double; $190–$290 suite; Nov–Apr $80–$120 double, $165–$245 suite. Rates include full breakfast. AE, DISC, MC, V. Free parking. *In room:* A/C, TV.

INEXPENSIVE

Inn at Shaker Mill Farm   About as unpretentious as a rustic upstate inn can get, this 1824 erstwhile Shaker gristmill, transformed into an inn over 30 years ago, isn't the most luxurious place you could stay. Though the downstairs reading room, with an open circular central fireplace and deck overlooking a rushing creek and waterfall, is splendid, the rooms are fashioned inexpensively out of the upstairs, with rather makeshift bathrooms and furnishings. However, the inn is ideally located if you want to explore both the Upper Hudson Valley and the Berkshires Hills of Massachusetts, and if you're an outdoors type or avid reader who's going to be spending most of your time perusing the many hundreds of books (most are for serious readers) in the public room, the austere rooms may matter little. The rates are per person, which is meant to appeal to singles and not to foster a couples-only atmosphere. The place is not for everyone, but there are those who love it.

Cherry Lane (off Rte. 22), Canaan, NY 12029. (C) **800/365-9345** or 518/794-9345. Fax 518/794-9344. www. shakermillfarminn.com. 20 units. May 31–July 1 and Oct 15–July 1 midweek $50 per person; weekends $110 per person per weekend; July 1–Oct 15 midweek $55 per person; weekends, $135 per person per weekend; Sat only $75 per person. All rates include breakfast. MC, V. Free parking. **Amenities:** Reading room and library.

WHERE TO DINE

You may have to search out a restaurant a bit more in the northern section of the valley, since its best dining is quite spread out, but the restaurants below are every bit as good a bet as those in the Mid- and Lower Hudson.

EXPENSIVE

Aubergine ★★ AMERICAN/HAUTE COUNTRY   A longtime favorite, this restaurant in a late-18th-century Dutch Colonial house about 15 miles east of Hudson, is worth the drive for an elegant and delicious meal. The chef, David Lawson, creates French-inspired country cuisine in a surprisingly formal environment. The restaurant consists of four dining rooms and a tavern with a copper bar. Most main courses are hearty and traditional, though a few dishes have real flair. The menu changes seasonally, but past favorites have included monkfish medallions with green lentils and mashed potatoes; skillet-seared New York sirloin steak with black-olive tapenade and caramelized onions; and fennel and pepper-crusted Atlantic salmon with sautéed zucchini and white bean sauce.

Wine Trails & Farmer's Markets

The Hudson Valley, the nation's oldest winemaking region, is today home to about three dozen wineries. Though few of the area's wineries yet attained national followings, a number of them offer tours and tastings, and several are blessed with outstandingly scenic locations. If you'd like to visit a winery or two during your stay, all you have to do is follow the trail—either the **Dutchess Wine Trail** (© **845/266-5372;** www.dutchesswinetrail.com) or the **Shawangunk Wine Trail** (© **845/255-2494;** www.shawangunkwinetrail.com). More than a dozen are open to regular visits; the following is merely a selection of my favorites: The Dutchess (Country) Trail consists of **Cascade Mountain Winery,** 835 Cascade Mountain Rd., Amenia (© **845/373-9021**), which has a lovely setting and a very nice little restaurant with outdoor seating; **Clinton Vineyards,** Schultzville Road, Clinton Corners (© 845/266-5372), makers of a pretty nice white, a Seyval blanc; **Alison Wines & Vineyards,** 231 Pitcher Lane, Red Hook (© **845/758-6335**), the newest of the bunch, with a garden shop, baked goods, and cut-your-own Christmas trees on the premises; and **Millbrook Vineyards & Winery,** 26 Wing Rd., Millbrook (© **800/662-WINE**), the largest and certainly one of the best of the lot. Millbrook makes an excellent pinot noir reserve, offers a full tour, features art exhibits and live music on Saturday nights in summer, and is worth the visit for the views over the rolling hillsides and horse farms alone. Several of the nine family-owned wineries of the Shawangunk Trail, all sandwiched between the Shawangunk Mountains and the Hudson River in Ulster County, are easily visited on a Hudson Valley trip. Among them are **Brotherhood Winery,** 35 North St., Washingtonville (© **845/496-9101**), the oldest winery in the United States, in operation

---

Desserts are rich and uniformly excellent. If you get too full to leave, Aubergine offers four nicely outfitted guest rooms upstairs.

Intersection of Rtes. 22 and 23, Hillsdale. © **518/325-3412.** Reservations recommended weekends. Main courses $24–$27. AE, MC, V. Wed–Sun 5:30–9:30pm.

MODERATE

Carolina House *(Finds* AMERICAN   For those poking around off the beaten track in the Upper Hudson Valley, this cozy, congenial, and very popular restaurant is a find. It doesn't look like all that much from the outside—perhaps because it's usually obscured by cars—but inside is a warm, wood-paneled restaurant with nice small booths and table lamps, and a comfortable separate tavern. Among the main courses are Louisiana trout, baby back ribs, and casual fare like burgers and pulled-pork barbecue sandwiches. Unusual to find up here, but a local favorite, is southern-fried chicken.

Rte. 9, Kinderhook. © **518/758-1669.** Reservations recommended weekends. Main courses $11–$24. AE, MC, V. Mon, Wed–Thurs 5–9:30pm; Fri–Sat 5–10:30pm; Sun 4–9:30pm.

INEXPENSIVE

Historic Village Diner *(Value (Kids* DINER   Some of the best midcentury American diners are up in this part of the country, and this one is one of the best. It's

since 1839. Though the winery doesn't grow its own grapes (instead importing them from Long Island, the Finger Lakes, and California), its grounds constitute a well-stocked campus, with vast underground vaulted cellars and a whole host of shops and activities on-site. Claiming to be the oldest continuously operating vineyard in the U.S. is **Benmarl Wine Company,** 156 Highland Ave., Marlboro-on-Hudson (© 845/236-4265; www.benmarl.com), a small, family-owned independent with awe-inspiring views from a hilltop location on the west side of the Hudson (between Newburgh and New Paltz). It also offers a small gallery of the owner's illustrations and artwork; Mark Miller was one of the best-known magazine illustrators in the world in the 1940s and 1950s. Other Shawangunk Trail wineries are covered in the Catskills region chapter (see chapter 8). Schedules for winery tours and tastings vary, though most are open to visitors throughout the Memorial Day to Labor Day season; for current hours and events, check the Trail websites or pick up a brochure at any tourism information outlet.

Farmer's markets and **pick-your-own farm stands** are everywhere in this beautiful, bucolic region. There are dozens and dozens, so here are just a few: **Mead Orchards and Farm Stand,** 25 Scism Rd., Tivoli (9 miles north of Rhinebeck; © 914/756-5641), with pick-your-own apples and pumpkins; **Greig Farm,** Pitcher Lane, Red Hook (© 914/758-1234), which has pick-your-own fruit and vegetables and a farm market; **Millbrook Farmers Market,** Franklin Avenue at Front Street, Millbrook village, every Saturday from 9am to 1pm; and **Tarrytown Farmers Market,** Patriot's Park, Route 9, Tarrytown (© 914/923-4837). Ask around and locals will come up with many more.

known as a "silk road dining car," and though it was moved around a bit earlier in its life, it's exceedingly popular and at home in Red Hook. Breakfasts are great, as are reliable lunch and dinner standards like the half-pound Black Angus burger, Silk City Special (grilled turkey with bacon), meatloaf, and roast turkey with stuffing (entrees are served with potato or salad bar). Everything is cheap and well prepared, and the staff is friendly.

7550 North Broadway, Red Hook. © 845/758-6232. Reservations not accepted. Main courses $4–$11. MC, V. Daily 6am–9pm.

THE UPPER HUDSON VALLEY AFTER DARK

The nightlife is pretty quiet in the Upper Hudson Valley. When you tire from all the antiques shops and galleries in Hudson, pay a visit to the **Hudson Opera House,** housed in the Old City Hall, 27 Warren St. (© 518/822-1438; www.hudsonoperahouse.org). It hosts concerts, theater productions, workshops, lectures, and readings. Hudson is also home to a handful of cafes and bar/restaurants. My favorite watering hole and restaurant on Warren Street is **Red Dot,** 321 Warren (© 518/828-3657).

8

The Catskill Mountain Region

by Neil E. Schlecht

The historic American conservation movement originated in the Catskill Mountains, 6,000 square miles of mountains, rivers, forests, and parkland that were considered **America's First Wilderness.** Though just 100 miles north of New York City, the region's natural state has been remarkably preserved; the state constitution designated a quarter of a million acres "forever wild" forest, and the region is the watershed for New York City and almost half the state. Yet natural beauty is not what many people know the region for; mention "The Catskills" and most Americans of a certain age conjure either nostalgic or dreaded notions of resort vacations from another era.

Infamous to many Americans through Hollywood movies like *A Walk on the Moon* and *Dirty Dancing,* the Catskill region is an area in transition, if not a full-blown identity crisis. For most of a century it was *the* vacation area for New Yorkers, beginning in the late 19th century, when steam trains deposited elegantly dressed vacationers at stations for their horse-drawn carriage rides to massive mountain lodges and boarding houses, and continuing through the 1960s, when it became famous for the kind of resorts, many of them ethnic enclaves where family men from the city joined their wives, kids, and neighbors on weekends in the mountains and engaged in 9-to-5 schedules of planned activities, that earned it the sobriquet the "borscht belt."

Today, that type of vacationing has fallen out of favor. The Catskill region, still boldly beautiful and remote, is addressing its fall from grace in the latter half of the 20th century and is busy repositioning itself as a new kind of Catskills, open to new types of visitors and new forms of leisure activities. The new Catskill region has not only renamed itself but set about recapturing its essence, the Great Outdoors, and holding on to an easygoing, rural lifestyle.

And so it should. The spiritual and natural heart of the region is the 700,000-acre Catskill Park and Forest Preserve, a dense area with 35 peaks soaring to elevations of 3,500 feet. This scenic area overflows with lush hills and valleys, forests, farmland, waterfalls, trout streams, reservoirs, and six major river systems. It is regarded as one of the world's greatest fly-fishing areas, and anglers make pilgrimages from across the globe to wade in its trout streams. The Catskill Mountains practically beg for outdoors enthusiasts to sample the incredible variety of hiking and biking trails, sheer cliffs for rock climbing, and peaks for skiing. But you don't have to be a fleece-clad extreme sports fan to enjoy the region, which is also home to a great number of historic homesteads, out-of-the-way antiques shops, and nostalgic attractions like old trains, vintage "base ball" (yes, it was two words originally) teams, and pick-your-own co-ops and dairy farms.

Locals are anxious for visitors to know that this is no longer your

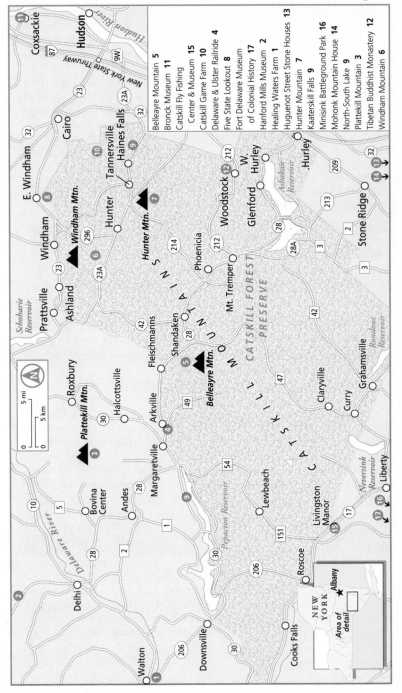

Catskill Mountain Region

Belleayre Mountain **5**
Bronck Museum **11**
Catskill Fly Fishing
  Center & Museum **15**
Catskill Game Farm **10**
Delaware & Ulster Railride **4**
Five State Lookout **8**
Fort Delaware Museum
  of Colonial History **17**
Hanford Mills Museum **2**
Healing Waters Farm **1**
Huguenot Street Stone Houses **13**
Hunter Mountain **7**
Kaaterskill Falls **9**
Minisink Battleground Park **16**
Mohonk Mountain House **14**
North-South Lake **9**
Plattekill Mountain **3**
Tibetan Buddhist Monastery **12**
Windham Mountain **6**

Grandad's Catskills. Today mountain bikers plunge down Plattekill Mountain caked in mud, and luxury inns and spas have sprouted, offering individual, rather than massified, service. Refugees from New York City and elsewhere are being newly awakened to the natural beauty, small towns, and tranquil pleasures of the Catskill region. Young couples are moving in and starting up small businesses, restaurants, bars, inns. Individuals and families weary of the Hamptons and other chic destinations are finding second-home bargains in the area.

Of course, this remains the Catskills, and a handful of old-school resorts still exist in what can only be described as a nostalgic time warp, charmingly resistant to change. If you want a trip down memory lane, you can still find megaresorts where you can play shuffleboard at 11:30am, attend pool games at 1pm, and get your hair done before a bland buffet dinner and the night's entertainment of Rocco singing Italian love songs. But those places are quickly being outnumbered in the new Catskill region—one that is returning to its roots.

1 Orientation

ARRIVING

By Plane   Most visitors traveling by air will probably fly into one of the New York City area's three major airports. For information on those, please see chapter 5. Other visitors traveling by air will arrive via **Albany International Airport,** 737 Albany-Shaker Rd. (© **518/242-2299;** www.albanyairport.com), and **Stewart International Airport,** Route 207, New Windsor (© **845/564-2100;** www.stewartintlairport.com), near Newburgh, which handles 50 daily flights from major U.S. cities such as Atlanta, Chicago, Philadelphia, Raleigh/Durham, and Washington, D.C.

BY CAR   Most visitors tour the Catskill Mountain Region by private automobile. The region begins about 90 miles, or about 2 hours, north of New York City; there is easy access via exits 16 through 21B of the New York State Thruway (I-87). From the south, Route I-81 and Route 17 (future I-86) also provide direct access. From New England, I-84 and I-90 connect with Route I-88, I-87 and Route 17 (future I-86).

Major rental car companies, including Avis, Budget, Enterprise, Hertz, National, and Thrifty, have representatives at all the major airports.

BY TRAIN   **Amtrak** will get you as close as Poughkeepsie, Schenectady, Albany, or Syracuse. For more information and reservations, contact Amtrak at © **800/ USA-RAIL** or visit www.amtrak.com.

BY BUS   **Greyhound** (© **518/434-8095;** www.greyhound.com) travels to Arkville, Andes, Bearsville, Catskill, Fleischmanns, Hensonville, Highmount, Kerhonkson, Kiamesha, Liberty, Livingston Manor, Monticello, Mountainville, New Paltz, Phoenicia, Rock Hill, Roscoe, Stone Ridge, Tannersville, Windham, and Woodstock. **Adirondack Trailways** (© **800/858-8555;** www.trailways.com/ members/adirondack.html) serves the eastern part of the Catskill Region, and **Shortline Coach USA** (© **800/631-8405;** www.shortlinebus.com) the western section (from New York City to Monticello).

VISITOR INFORMATION

Get additional information before you go from the **Catskill Association for Tourism Services** in Catskill (© **800/NYS-CATS;** www.catskillregiontoday or www.catskillvacation.net) or one of the four counties that make up the Catskill

Mountain region: **Ulster County Tourism Office,** 10 Westbrook Lane, Kingston (© **800/342-5826;** www.co.ulster.ny.us); **Green County Promotion Department,** P.O. Box 527, Catskill (© **800/355-CATS;** www.greene-ny.com); **Delaware Country Chamber of Commerce,** 114 Main St., Delhi (© **800/ 642-4443;** www.delawarecounty.org); and **Sullivan County Visitors Association,** 100 North St., Monticello (© **800/882-CATS;** www.scva.net).

2 Southeastern Catskill Region (Ulster County)

The southeastern section of the Catskill Mountains, centered in Ulster County and the closest to New York City (many parts are just 2 hr. by car), is one of the most historic, sophisticated, and beautiful parts of the Catskill region. It is an area of bucolic farmlands and original settlers' homes belonging to French, Dutch, and English immigrants. The area straddles the easily blurred divide between the Catskill Mountains and the Mid-Hudson Valley, and is thus easy to combine with tours of the river valley. Some of the most legendary names are contained in this section that skirts the southern edge of the Catskill Forest Preserve: Mohonk Mountain House, Woodstock, and New Paltz, as well as up-and-comers like small but increasingly sophisticated towns like Saugerties and Phoenicia.

ESSENTIALS
GETTING THERE   From north and south, direct access by car is from I-87.

VISITOR INFORMATION   **Ulster County Tourism Office,** 10 Westbrook Lane, Kingston (© **800/342-5826;** www.co.ulster.ny.us); the **Woodstock Chamber of Commerce** operates an information kiosk, 10 Rock City Rd., Woodstock (© **845/679-6234;** Thurs–Sun 11am–6pm), which dispenses town and area maps.

NEW PALTZ & ENVIRONS
The largest historical attraction in the southeastern Catskills is in New Paltz, a likable college town founded in 1678. The **Huguenot Street Stone Houses** ✦✦, 18 Broadhead Ave. (© **845/255-1660;** www.hhs-newpaltz.net; standard tour $10 adults, $9 seniors, $5 students ages 6–17, $24 family; abbreviated tour, tour $7 adults, $6 seniors, $3 students ages 6–17, free for children under 6, $17 family; tours May 1–Oct 31 Tues–Fri hourly 10am–4pm, Sat–Sun every half-hour 10am–4pm), represent some of the oldest remaining architecture in the region: a collection of a half-dozen colonial-era stone houses built by a small group of French religious refugees, the Protestant Huguenots. A National Historic Landmark, the Huguenot district once occupied 40,000 acres at the edge of the Walkill River. The original stone houses, earliest built in 1692, have been restored with period furnishing and heirlooms and operate as house museums. Also on the site are the **1705 DuBois Fort** (now a visitor's center and museum shop) and the **French Church,** a reconstruction of the 1717 original. Visits are by guided tour only; the standard tour (90 min.) visits three of the houses and the church; the abbreviated tour last 50 minutes and goes to one Colonial-period house and the church. The street is open year-round, though the actual houses are closed.

In the tiny, charming village of **High Falls,** which backs up to the waters that flowed through what was once the Delaware and Hudson Canal, the **D&H Canal Museum,** in an 1885 church on Mohonk Road (© **845/687-9311;** www.canal museum.org; $2 adults, $1 children, $5 families; May 30 to Labor Day Thurs–Sat and Mon 11am–5pm; Sun 1–5pm; weekends only May, Sept–Oct) displays original locks and vignettes relating life along the 19th-century canal. A great spot for easy hikes is the **D&H Canal Heritage Corridor** (Rosendale; ℂ **845/331-2100**), which runs 35 miles along the D&H towpaths and the Ontario & Western railway from Ellenville to Kingston. The **Five Locks Walk** covers the ground between locks 16 and 20 alongside the canal.

The **Mohonk Preserve** ★★ is more than 6,000 acres of fabulously wild forest, fields, ponds, and streams, all part of the northern Shawangunk Mountains, with more than 60 miles of fantastic trails through dense woodlands and up bleached-white mountain crags. It is the largest privately held preserve (it's owned by a nonprofit environmental organization) in New York State. Not to be missed are the unmatched, breathtaking views from the climb to tower at **Skytop**—at this spot, 1,500 feet above sea level, you can see into six states on a clear day. Day passes and more information are available at the Mohonk Preserve Visitor Center, Route 44/55 (ℂ **845/255-0919;** www.mohonkpreserve.org). The legendary **Mohonk Mountain House** ★★★, a fantasy-like Victorian castle perched on a ridge within the preserve, is worth a visit even if you're not staying there—and it really has to be seen to be believed (see "Where to Stay," below). Day guests can hike the trails ($13), eat at the imposing lodge restaurant, and ice skate at the beautiful outdoor pavilion.

Minnewaska State Park Preserve, Route 44/55 in Gardiner (ℂ **845/255-0752**), is 12,000 acres ripe for hiking, biking, cross-country skiing, and lake swimming. There are 30 miles of footpaths and carriage-ways, as well as two lakes, waterfalls and great mountain viewpoints. The panoramic views of the **Roundout Valley** from an overlook off Route 44/55, just beyond the Minnewaska Preserve, are breathtaking. The incredibly sheer white cliffs of the **Shawangunk Mountains** offer some of the best rock climbing on the east coast. The Eastern Mountain Sports shop next door to the Minnewaska Lodge, offers guides and equipment. The **Wallkill Valley Rail Trail** (www.gorailtrail.org), which extends from New Paltz to Gardiner, is 12 miles of linear park, perfect for low-impact cycling, hiking and skiing.

An excellent boutique winery, with gorgeous views of the Shawangunk cliffs, is **Whitecliff Vineyard and Winery,** a member of the Shawangunk Wine Trail (www.shawangunkwinetrail.com). Run by a husband-and-wife team, Whitecliff, 331 McKinstry Rd., Gardiner (ℂ **845/255-4613;** May–Oct Thurs–Sun noon–5pm), produces very nice, European-style reds and whites. Other area wineries open for visits are **Adair Vineyards,** 52 Allhusen Rd., New Paltz (ℂ **845/255-1377**), set in a 200-year-old dairy barn, and **Rivendell Winery,** 714 Albany Post Rd., New Paltz (ℂ **845/255-2494**), with a Vintage New York store featuring artisanal wines from across the state on-site.

Though perhaps not pristine as Huguenot Street in New Paltz, the two dozen stone houses that populate the downtown area of **Hurley,** off Route 209, are among the oldest and largest grouping of lived-in stone houses in the country. Main Street is lined with them, dating from the first half of the 18th century. Your only real opportunity to peek inside some of them is on Hurley Stone House Day is held the second Saturday in July, when guided tours are held. For more information, call ℂ **845/331-4121.**

WOODSTOCK ★ & SAUGERTIES ★

Saugerties has been officially discovered. A blindingly cute little town upriver from Kingston and just 7 miles northeast of Woodstock, it has a sweet main drag, Partition Street, lined with good restaurants and suddenly teeming with art galleries, antiques dealers, and shops. Still a peaceful and charming place, it makes quite a good base for exploring both the Catskills and the Upper and Mid-Hudson Valley. Not to be missed is the enjoyable mile-long woodland walking trail out to the river and **Saugerties Lighthouse** (off Rte. 9W), built in 1838 (here's the kicker: you can actually sleep here; see "Where to Stay," below).

Southeast of Saugerties, **Woodstock** has a name recognition any tourist town would die for. The watershed 1969 rock concert that defined a generation didn't actually take place here, but in an open field some 50 miles west of here, in Bethel. Woodstock, a longtime artists' community (beginning with the Byrdcliffe arts colony in 1902) with a vibe and creativity that fueled the '60s counterculture, has in recent years become essentially a boutique shopping mall living off of people's hippie expectations. That said, it's still a pretty and enjoyable place, perfect for strolling, and *the* shopping destination in this part of the Catskill Mountains. The long main street, stuffed with shops and galleries, is Mill Hill Road, which becomes Tinker Street. **Byrdcliffe Arts Colony,** 34 Tinker St. (✆ 845/ 679-2079; www.woodstockguild.org), offers guided walking tours of the Arts & Crafts colony (the largest surviving colony of its kind) as well as artists-in-residence programs. The **Woodstock Artists Association,** 28 Tinker St. (✆ 845/ 679-2940), is a long-standing cooperative with a large gallery space exhibiting local members. The **Center for Photography at Woodstock,** 59 Tinker St. (✆ 845/679-6337), has excellent photography exhibits by well-known artists and workshops. Other galleries worth a look include **Fletcher Gallery,** 40 Mill Hill Rd. (✆ 845/679-4411); **Art Forms,** 40 Mill Hill Rd. (✆ 845/679-1100); **Fleur de Lis Gallery,** 34 Tinker St. (✆ 845/679-2688); and **Clouds Gallery,** 1 Mill Hill Rd. (✆ 845/679-8155). Cool quilting classes are available at **Woodstock Quilt Supply,** 79 Tinker St. (✆ 845/679-0733; www.quiltstock.com).

Woodstock may not have been the site of the big concert, but it features plenty of year-round live-music concerts, poetry readings, and theater performances. The **Maverick concert series,** founded in 1916, is the oldest summer chamber music series in the U.S. Check the events schedule at **www.woodstock-online.com.**

A worthwhile detour is to the **Tibetan Buddhist Monastery,** Meads Mountain Road (which begins as Rock City Rd.; ✆ 845/679-5906), high above Woodstock, a must not just for Buddhists, but for anyone with an interest in eclectic architecture. Tours are held for individuals on weekends.

MOUNT TREMPER & PHOENICIA

The road to Mount Tremper, Route 28, skirts the northern shore of **Ashokan Reservoir,** a beautiful 12-square-mile lake. Follow Route 28A around the 40 miles of shoreline for spectacular views of mountains rising in all directions; it's especially scenic in the fall. A little farther on, **Catskill Corners** ✫, Route 28 in Mount Tremper, is a surprising empire of refined goods and services at the southern edge of Catskill Forest Preserve that's become a purpose-built tourist destination. **The Marketplace,** inhabiting a mid-19th-century dairy barn, is an outstanding array of upscale shops; see "Shopping," below. But the major attraction in these parts is the **Kaatskill Kaleidoscope Theatre** ✫. Like a planetarium, only trippier, the 60-foot kaleidoscope inside the old barn silo—according to the *Guinness Book of World Records* the world's largest—gives visitors an opportunity to climb inside the tube of a superhuman kaleidoscope. The psychedelic shows ($5 adults; $8 two shows; $7 seniors two shows, free for children under 12) are a blast, with different programs seasonally. Also at Catskill Corners are a lodge hotel, cafe, Spotted Dog Firehouse Restaurant, and the swank Emerson Inn and Spa (see "Where to Stay," below).

Phoenicia is perhaps the epitome of the new Catskills. Only a few years ago, this was just another forgotten, miniscule town with gorgeous mountain views. At the end of the 1990s, a small handful of restaurateurs and young people moved in and revamped the place. Its perfectly unassuming Main Street now has a couple of creative, stylish shops and an excellent restaurant, all of which cohabit nicely with the long-time locals bars. The town is surrounded in all directions by the big peaks of the Catskill Forest Preserve. **The Town Tinker,** Bridge Street (© **845/688-5553;** www.towntinker.com), in a barn at the edge of town, rents inner tubes for floating down a 5-mile stretch of the Esopus River, something no kid could refuse. There are two river courses, one for novices and the other, which covers rapids and flumes, for expert floaters. Tubes are $10 to $12 per day, and the Tinker even offers tube taxi transportation.

The **Catskill Mountain Railroad,** Route 28, Mount Pleasant (© **845/688-7400;** www.catskillmtrailroad.com; adults one-way $5, round-trip $8; children 4–11, $5 round-trip; children under 4 free), operates an Esopus Creek Shuttle, a 6-mile (40-min.) round-trip along the river from Mount Pleasant depot (where tickets can be purchased) to Phoenicia's 1910 station. The trip is beautiful, and an added bonus is that you can tube down the river from Phoenicia to Mount Pleasant and then take the train back. Special 1-day-only teddy bear and Halloween theme train trips are also scheduled.

SPORTS & OUTDOOR ACTIVITIES

BIKING & HIKING For the best hiking, see the text on the Mohonk and Minnewaska Preserves, above. Bike rentals are available from **Cycle Path,** 138 Main St., New Paltz (© **845/255-8723**), **Table Rock Tours and Bicycle Shop,** 292 Main St., Rosendale (© **845/658-7832;** www.tablerocktours.com); and **Overlook Mountain Bikes,** 93 Tinker St., Woodstock (© **845/679-2122**).

KAYAKING **Atlantic Kayak Tours,** 320 W. Saugerties Rd., Saugerties (© **845/246-2187;** www.atlantickayaktours.com), guides experts and novices on 40 different tours along the Hudson.

ROCK CLIMBING **EMS,** 3124 Rte. 44-55, Gardiner (© **800/310-4504**), has equipment and climbing lessons.

SKIING Northwest of Phoenicia, **Belleayre Mountain,** Route 28, Highmount (© **800/942-6904;** www.belleayre.com), has the highest skiable peak and longest trail in the Catskills, with 36 other trails and eight lifts, but also a lower mountain that's perfect for beginners and intermediates.

SHOPPING

On the other side of the river, **New Paltz** is, apart from Woodstock, probably the best shopping town. It has a preponderance of Woodstock-like shops overflowing with tie-dye and incense, but it also has a couple of good antiques shops. One is **Medusa,** 2 Church St. (© **845/255-6000**). Also take a look at **Water Street Market,** 10 Main St. (www.waterstreetmarket.com), which contains several specialty crafts shops, art galleries and The Antique Barn.

Saugerties is on the upswing, and its main drag, Partition Street, is a smaller cousin of Hudson's Warren Street across the river. Worth a look are **Saugerties Antiques Gallery,** 104 Partition St. (© **845/246-2323**); **Partition Street Antiques,** 114 Partition St. (© **845/247-0932**), full of antique wicker and Stickley and Arts and Crafts furniture; **Central Hotel Antiques,** 83 Partition St., Saugerties (© **845/246-6874**); and **Dust and Rust Antiques,** Route 32,

Saugerties (© **845/246-7728**). **Arcadia,** 78 Partition St. (© **845/246-7321**), is a cute housewares shop with nice ceramic pieces.

Woodstock ☆ is the pinnacle among shopper's destinations in the Catskill Mountains. It has everything from antiques and mod clothing to Tibetan crafts and tribal rugs. **Woodstock Glassworks,** 70 Rock City Rd., creates handblown glass on the premises. A neat little antiques shop is **Treasure Chest Antiques,** a tiny cottage down Waterfall Way (off Tinker St.). **The Golden Notebook,** 25-29 Tinker St. (© **845/679-8000**), is a great little bookshop, a real reader's hangout.

Don't miss the bevy of polished, upscale specialty shops at **The Marketplace** ☆ in Catskill Corners, 5340 Rte. 28 (© **845/688-5800;** www.themarketplaceshops. com), Mount Tremper. From fine women's apparel and a bath and spa emporium to country furnishing and gardening shops and the amazing Kaleidostore, specializing in hundreds of fine-art kaleidoscopes, this is one shopping experience that will entertain you before making off with your wallet. Tiny **Phoenicia** just down the road has a handful of interesting home furnishings and gifts shops, including **The Tender Land,** 45 Main St. (© **845/688-2001**); **The Nest Egg,** 84 Main Street (© **845/688-5851**); and **Tender Land Home,** 64 Main St. (© **845/688-7213**).

WHERE TO STAY
VERY EXPENSIVE

Emerson Inn & Spa ★★★   About as far removed from the clichéd Catskills resort of yesteryear as one can imagine, this swank inn and soothing spa hotel, opened in 2000, caters to the sybarite with refined tastes and a wish for total pampering. Quality and service of this level don't come cheap, of course, but several value packages are available, and the Emerson is definitely the place to splurge in the Catskills. The magnificently restored 1874 Victorian mansion is not shyly decorated; it features sumptuous common rooms and meticulously designed rooms that evoke distant lands, exotic journeys, and the romance of the Orient Express. The Asian-inspired spa is one of the most sophisticated and relaxing I've seen. The elegant, tapestry-clad dining room continues the jet-set extraordinaire theme, tempting the epicure with delightful menus of food and wine (including a 5,000-bottle wine room with a floor-to-ceiling humidor). The Emerson is simply a place where no detail has been overlooked, a place to indulge oneself and return to the world, at least temporarily, relaxed and utterly refreshed.

146 Mt. Pleasant Rd., Mount Tremper, NY 12457. © 845/688-7900. Fax 845/688-2789. www.theemerson. com. $24 units. $500–$675 double; $700–$1,050 suite. Modified American plan (MAP) rates include 2 meals and afternoon tea daily as well as use of spa facilities. AE, DC, DISC, MC, V. Free valet parking. **Amenities:** Restaurant; bar; full-service spa; concierge; conference center; complimentary mountain bikes. *In room:* A/C, TV (upon request), dataport, hair dryer, safe.

Mohonk Mountain House ★★★ *Kids*   This National Historic Landmark, a mammoth mountaintop Victorian castle, is one of the country's great old hotel resorts. Like a mountain lodge in the great West, it commands huge views of the serene Shawangunk Mountains. The resort was built in 1869 by two brothers on a 2,200-acre rocky ridge overlooking a large glacial lake, pristine gardens, and the 6,400-acre Mohonk Forest Preserve, and its setting is incomparable. Still owned by the Smiley family, the fanciful, seven-story lodge is loaded with turrets, towers, porches, and parlors, as well as cozy sitting rooms with fireplaces. Rooms vary considerably as to size and views, which may be of the gardens, mountains, or lake, but all are warmly decorated with period Edwardian, Victorian, and Arts and Crafts furnishings. Many have fireplaces and balconies. Activities abound: ice skating in the beautiful new open-air pavilion, snowshoeing, and cross-country skiing in winter; hiking, boating, tennis, and golf in warm-weather seasons; and plenty of children's programs and entertainment, including theme weeks and weekends. It's a hiker's paradise, with more than 85 miles of woodland trails. However, Mohonk is also a fabulous place to relax with a book in a rocker on the veranda, taking in the views. In high season, though, it's packed with everyone from young families to groups of seniors.

1000 Mountain Rest Rd., Lake Mohonk, New Paltz 12561. ✆ 800/772-6646 or 845/255-1000. Fax 845/256-2100. www.mohonk.com. 251 units. $335–$515 double; $520–$670 suite. Children over age 12 $125; ages 4–12 $75; free for children under 4. Rates include 3 meals plus afternoon tea and many complimentary activities and entertainment. Jackets are required for men at dinner. 2-night minimum stay most weekends. AE, DC, DISC, MC, V. Free valet parking. **Amenities:** Restaurant; swimming and boating lake; 9-hole golf course; 6 clay and Har-Tru tennis courts; fitness center, concierge; business center; massage and spa services; laundry service; ice-cream parlor/soda fountain; ice-skating pavilion; library. *In room:* A/C, hair dryer.

EXPENSIVE

Minnewaska Lodge Outdoor enthusiasts especially will appreciate this 2-year-old small lodge built at the base of the 1,200-foot Shawangunk cliffs on 17 acres. The area, adjacent to the Mohonk Preserve and a short distance from Minnewaska State Park (and just 6 miles from New Paltz), is a favorite of hikers and rock climbers. The lodge is woodsy and rustic, like a comfortable mountain inn. It has a great outdoor deck with cliff views, and some rooms have private decks (the suite has a private patio). Rooms on the second floor are very handsomely decorated in a contemporary style and have cathedral ceilings and either cliff or forest views.

3116 Rte. 44/55, Gardiner (outside New Paltz) 12525. ✆ 845/255-1110. Fax 845/255-5069. 27 units. www.minnewaskalodge.com Nov–Apr $125–$165 double, $235–$245 suite; May–Oct $155–$209 double; $295–$315 suite. Rates include continental breakfast. 2-night minimum stay on weekends, 3-night minimum stay on holiday weekends. AE, DC, DISC, MC, V. Free parking. **Amenities:** Restaurant; fitness center; gift shop. *In room:* A/C, TV, dataport.

Pinegrove Dude Ranch *(Kids)* Among all the idiosyncratic Catskills resorts, this is one of the oddest—a full-blown family-oriented dude ranch, with horse trail rides (there are 125 horses), cattle drives, line dancing, and all kinds of outdoor activities for kids. The strange thing is that it works. The resort is very lodge-like: Rooms aren't especially luxurious, but they're pretty large and comfortable. The Western theme is carried throughout, from the Chuck Wagon Snack Bar and the saloon to the Old West stable and giant carved animal and Indian figures dotting the 600-acre property. There are enough activities to exhaust any young cowpokes and their parents. It's not what most people expect from the Catskills, granted, but what the hay! Check the website for special packages.

30 Cherrytown Rd., Kerhonkson, NY 12446. ✆ 800/346-4626 or 845/626-7345. Fax 845/726-7365. www.pinegroveranch.com. $310–$380 double; $430–$480 cottage suite. Rates include 3 meals daily, all activities, parties, and entertainment but no beverages. AE, DC, DISC, MC, V. Free parking. **Amenities:** Restaurant; bar; 24-hr. snack bar; nightclub; indoor and outdoor swimming pools; indoor and outdoor tennis and basketball courts; stables; gift shop; game room. *In room:* A/C, TV.

MODERATE

Locktender Cottage (Depuy Canal House) *(Finds)* Along the banks of the old Delaware & Hudson Canal, hovering between the Hudson Valley and the Catskills Mountains, is this surprising retreat attached to one of the finest restaurants in the region. A cute and cozy Victorian cottage that backs right up to the canal houses two charming, if not overly large, rooms; the upstairs "chef's quarters" are larger, with a low-peaked ceiling, kitchenette, and Jacuzzi, but without some of the flavor of the other two. Across the street, where you'll find the famed and atmospheric Depuy Canal House restaurant, two more rooms have been created; they are larger suites and one has an outdoor garden patio and screened sitting area, but I prefer the rooms in the original cottage. For both dining and outdoors enthusiasts, this is a small slice of heaven: there are great trails for hiking, and the Mohonk Nature Preserve, with 90 miles of trails, is nearby.

Rte. 213, High Falls, NY 12440. ℂ 845/687-7700. www.depuycanalhouse.net. 5 units. Wed–Sun and holidays $120–$145 cottage double, $175–$225 suite; Mon–Tues $75–$95 cottage double, $150–$200 suite. Rates include $15 meal voucher (1 per room). 3-night minimum on holiday weekends and 2-night minimum May–Nov. Rates include full breakfast. Weekend 2-night minimum. AE, DC, DISC, MC, V. Free parking. **Amenities:** 2 restaurants. *In room:* A/C, 2 suites have kitchenettes and dinettes, suites have TV.

Sparrow Hawk B&B ★★   This handsome 1770 brick Colonial, originally a farmhouse, is a very professionally run inn that's both elegant and relaxed. It has a nice library, sitting room, fireplaces, and pretty grounds. The rooms are very large and nicely appointed, with modern wicker furniture, plush bedding, towels, and robes. The Grand Room features a 100-year-old Bechstein grand piano. Howard's excellent gourmet breakfasts are something to look forward to. The only problem is that it's an old house on a main road, so there's some early morning traffic noise; if that will spoil your stay, you should ask for one of the rooms facing the back of the property.

4496 Rte. 209, Stone Ridge, NY 12484. ℂ 845/687-4492. www.sparrowhawkbandb.com. 5 units. $115–$170 double. Rates include full breakfast. AE, DISC, MC, V. Free parking. **Amenities:** TV lounge, library. *In room:* A/C.

The Villa at Saugerties ★ *Value*   A uniquely stylish and chic take on a country inn—modern boutique hotel rather than Victorian B&B—this new venture, opened by a couple of young Manhattan refugees in 2002, is one of the coolest and least expected spots in the valley. A 1929 Mediterranean villa on 4 acres of woodland bordering on two brooks, it turns the notion of country rustic on its head, substituting a hip mid-century modern aesthetic. Rooms are enlivened with bold colors and original art, yet they don't sacrifice comfort for style. Each room is uniquely decorated and inviting; beds and linens are top of the line. Two rooms have private entrances. Gourmet breakfasts are served on the outdoor patio in season, and a 40-foot outdoor pool beckons. Saugerties is on the upswing, with new hip restaurants and a wealth of antiques shops and art galleries, and Woodstock and the Catskills (including Hunter Mountain) are only minutes away.

159 Fawn Rd., Saugerties 12477. ℂ 845/246-0682. 4 units. www.thevillaatsaugerties.com. June–Oct $110–$160 double; Nov–May $95–$140 double. All rates include full breakfast. AE, MC, V. Free parking. **Amenities:** Outdoor swimming pool; sauna; *In room:* A/C, TV.

INEXPENSIVE

Twin Gables *Value*   A former boarding house for artists, this charming and easygoing old guesthouse on Woodstock's main drag has the perfect feel for the town. Rooms are colorful, clean, and very sweetly decorated; most feature pretty quilts and hooked rugs. There is quite a variety of accommodations available. Some have shared bathrooms, others large private ones, a couple have twin beds, and there's even a single, which is becoming harder and harder to find. My favorite would have to be room no. 11, which is lavender with a large private bathroom. The young couple that owns and operates Twin Gables has ensured that it maintains a very high quality-to-price ratio.

73 Tinker St., Woodstock, NY 12498. ℂ 845/679-9479. Fax 845/679-5638. www.twingableswoodstockny.com. 9 units. $69–$115 double. Rates include full breakfast. AE, DISC, MC, V. Free parking. *In room:* A/C.

Unique Lodging in Saugerties

Saugerties, fast becoming one of the hippest little spots between the Upper Hudson and the Catskill Mountains, is still being discovered. Two "inns" offer unique and "in-the-know" small-scale accommodations possibilities. **Café Tamayo,** 89 Partition St., Saugerties, NY 12477 (**©** **845/246-9371;** three units; www.cafetamayo.com; $75 double; $120 suite; rates include full breakfast), is a great value and one of the best restaurants in the region, is housed in an 1864 building on the main drag; upstairs are two simple but very affordable rooms and one suite with queen-size brass beds, comfortable reading chairs, and TVs. One of the regular rooms has a claw-foot tub, while the suite has two separate bedrooms and a sitting room. What could be better than having a terrific dinner and then stumbling upstairs to bed?

Even more unexpected is **Saugerties Lighthouse,** off 9W and Mynderse Street, Saugerties, NY 12477 (**©** **845/247-0656;** two units; www. saugertieslighthouse.com; Apr 1–Oct 31 $160 double; Nov 1–Mar 31 $135; rates include breakfast). Not just a poetic name for an inn, it's an actual B&B within an 1869 lighthouse at water's edge. It may not be the most conveniently located B&B you'll ever stay at—access is by a mile-long trail through wood- and wetlands, but how often do you get to sleep in the upstairs of a historic lighthouse overlooking the Hudson River? Inside the lighthouse are a small museum, keeper's quarters, two bedrooms, a kitchen, and a living room. Rooms are nicely, if simply furnished. The smaller one has windows facing both south down the Hudson and west up the Esopus Creek toward town, while the larger room has two windows looking out on the river. Linens, towels, and soap are provided, but it's suggested that you take only a few belongings in a backpack. A single downstairs bathroom, with a sink, shower with hot water, and composting toilet, is shared by everyone staying in the lighthouse. Area restaurants will deliver to the lighthouse; guests can also make use of the kitchen, refrigerator, and gas grill.

The Lodge at Catskill Corners ★ *Kids* If Emerson Inn & Spa, with the same owners, is just a tad too indulgent for your tastes, you may be more comfortable in this contemporary Western-style lodge hotel across the road. Casually luxurious and cozy, it features log-cabin beams, plaid woolen blankets, and many rooms have fireplaces and private decks overlooking the Esopus trout stream; you can almost fish off your balcony. The "upscale rustic" accommodations are large and handsome, perfect for families and people who just want to kick back in jeans and Tevas. The lodge is next door to Catamount Café restaurant, all the shops, and the world's largest kaleidoscope at Catskill Corners and within minutes of biking, hiking, fishing, skiing, and plenty more outdoors activities. Check the website for special package deals.

5368 Rte. 28, Mount Tremper, NY 12457. **©** **877/688-2828** or 845/688-2828. Fax 845/688-5191. 27 units. www.thelodgeusa.com. $125–$220 double; $199–$370 suite. Minimum 2-night stay most weekends. Pets allowed. Rates include continental breakfast. AE, DC, DISC, MC, V. Free parking. **Amenities:** Concierge. *In room:* A/C, TV, dataport, hair dryer.

CAMPGROUNDS

Blue Mountain Campground, 3783 Rte. 32, Saugerties (© **845/246-7564**), has 50 sites with electricity.

WHERE TO DINE

Bear Café ★★ CREATIVE AMERICAN   In a theater complex that was the original playground of the founder of Bearsville Records (and manager of Dylan, Joplin, and The Band), this restaurant with a rock 'n' roll pedigree is a sophisticated but casual eatery a couple of miles from Woodstock. The decor is charmingly rustic and warm, with peaked old-wood ceilings overlooking a flowing brook. Although you could opt for something simple like a half-pound burger, this is a place to indulge; meat eaters should try the signature dish, filet mignon with port garlic sauce and Stilton blue cheese, a French classic of sweet and sharp tastes. There is a long list of specials daily, and an extensive regular menu. At the front there's a nice and lively bar with a good mix of locals, weekenders, and visitors. Service is excellent, as are the delectable homemade desserts.

Rte. 212 (The Bearsville Theatre Complex), Bearsville. © 845/679-5555. Reservations recommended. Main courses $17–$27. AE, MC, V. Wed–Sun 5–10pm.

Café Tamayo ★★ CREATIVE AMERICAN   A saloonlike, romantic, and even modestly sexy spot in an original 1864 tavern with several spectacular features—including a gorgeous old carved mahogany bar with antique mirrors and slow-moving ceiling fans powered by a cool original pulley system—this is one of the most attractive restaurants in the region. Run by a husband-and-wife team, the restaurant focuses on local produce and organic meats and poultry, and the chef, a Culinary Institute of America (CIA) grad, puts a creative twist on American fare. There are good daily specials and dishes such as braised beef brisket, shell steak au poivre with Madeira sauce, but very little to tempt a committed vegetarian. The wine list is remarkably affordable and includes a large number of New York State wines. The owners have opened a new casual spot, Mediterranean Kitchen, next door (at 91 Partition St., open daily for lunch and dinner), serving vegetarian dishes, seafood, and grilled pizzas.

89 Partition St., Saugerties. © 845/246-9371. Reservations recommended weekends. Main courses $14–$26. MC, V. Wed–Sat 5–10pm; Sun 11:30am–3pm and 5–10pm.

Depuy Canal House ★★★ NOUVELLE AMERICAN/CONTINENTAL An evocative 200-year old stone tavern is home to one of the most creative and pleasurable restaurants in the entire Hudson Valley. Perched on the edge of the Catskills, the restaurant is the work of Executive Chef John Novi, who for more than 30 years has used fresh local products to fire his imagination. The restaurant couldn't be better looking; it rambles throughout a series of intimate and sumptuous dining rooms with roaring fires and elegant place settings. The menu, which changes daily, is either a la carte or by four- or seven-course prix fixe; entrees are on the order of sea bass fillet with roasted red pepper cellophane noodles, or goat-meat barbecued with black bean Polish prosciutto strudel. For an incredible experience, reserve a table on the balcony and watch the kitchen from above. Downstairs in the wine cellar is a more informal, but also excellent, bistro and bakery, called Chefs on Fire (it features a large wood-fired brick oven). It's open for lunch and dinner (Wed–Thurs) and breakfast, lunch, and dinner (Fri–Sun). If you want to stay for another meal, ask about the charming cottage rooms across the street and next door.

Rte. 213, High Falls. ✆ **845/687-7700.** Reservations essential. Main courses $23–$44; prix-fixe menus $60–$75. AE, DISC, MC, V. Depuy Canal House dinner Thurs–Sun 5–10pm, Sun 11:30am–2pm and 4–9pm; Chefs on Fire Wed–Thurs 11am–9pm, Fri–Sun 8am–10pm.

Heaven ⭐ HEALTH FOOD/CAFE   A cool, laid-back cafe serving the best coffee in town, this is also a great spot for breakfast or lunch (it's not open for dinner). A chef trained at the Culinary Institute of America creates healthy and organic-based meals such as "world curries" (Caribbean black bean and Thai green), great salads (including one that automatically donates two bucks to the Village Green Revitalization Program), and brilliant breakfasts. There are also incredible—er, heavenly—home-baked pastries and desserts. I think I bought three megacookies to go, after I'd already had dessert with my lunch.

17 Tinker St., Woodstock. ✆ **845/679-0011.** Reservations not accepted. Main courses $6–$18. MC, V. Daily 9am–4pm.

Sweet Sue's ⭐⭐ *Finds* BISTRO/BREAKFAST CAFE   Plenty of locals will tell you that Sue's, which suffered a devastating fire in 2003, is the stuff of legend. That's big praise for an informal breakfast and lunch place, but Sue's, recently restored and reopened, is the real deal, a terrific neighborhood cafe. Breakfast is extraordinary, with pecan-crusted French toast, a dozen kinds of pancakes (including pumpkin), and amazing home fries. The lunch menu changes weekly, but always makes use of the finest handpicked produce and locals meats. You'll surely have to wait for a table, but you will be happy you did.

Main St., Phoenicia. ✆ **845/688-7852.** Reservations recommended. Main courses $7–$12. MC, V. Thurs–Mon 7am–3pm.

3 Northeastern Catskill Region (Greene County)

The upper reaches of Ulster County extend along the Upper Hudson Valley. In the glory days of train travel from New York City in the late 19th century, steam trains brought thousands of people seeking country refuge at grand hotels like the Catskill Mountain House and Mohonk Mountain House to the station at Catskill, where they were met by horse-drawn carriages for their rides up into the mountains. But most of the northeastern section of the Catskills is rural Greene County, the biggest ski destination in the Catskill region. A few of the sleepy little towns in Greene Country are receiving new injections of life in the form of inns, restaurants and cultural organizations.

ESSENTIALS
GETTING THERE   By car, there is easy access via exits 16 through 21B of the New York State Thruway (I-87).

VISITOR INFORMATION   The **Green County Promotion Department,** P.O. Box 527, Catskill (✆ **800/355-CATS;** www.greene-ny.com), operates a visitors center at exit 21 of the New York State Thruway (I-87) on the right after the tollbooth.

EXPLORING THE NORTHEASTERN CATSKILL REGION
Catskill, an historic town across of the river from Hudson, frankly has seen better days, though it is pinning its hopes on a rebound. Its riverfront zone and marina are slowly being developed, and in addition to a restaurant and public boat dock, there's a small museum and interpretation center of the area's history in the old freight master's building on **The Point** overlooking Catskill Creek and the Hudson River. A Saturday farmer's market and concerts are held here in summer,

including the Catskill Jazz Festival the first week of August. The most important historic sight in Catskill is the **Thomas Cole National Historic Site (Cedar Grove),** 218 Spring St. (© 518/943-7465; www.thomascole.org; admission $5; May–Oct Fri–Sat 10am–4pm and Sun 1–5pm; Memorial Day, Labor Day, and Columbus Day 1–5pm; Independence Day 10am–4pm), a large yellow 1815 Federal-style home, which once sat on 88 prime acres with unimpeded Catskills views and was the home of Thomas Cole, founder of the Hudson River School of Painting. A painter, poet, musician, and architect, Cole lived in the house for 12 years after his marriage and died here in 1848; it was in this house that he tutored Frederick Church. Until the 1970s, Cole's descendants lived in the house. Cedar Grove was recently restored with surprising alacrity; it has some of Cole's personal effects and original family items, but the period furnishings aren't original to the house. The house is worth a visit mostly for fans of Cole's romantic American landscape painting. Worth a brief peek in downtown Catskill is the **Greene County Council on the Arts,** 398 Main St., with two floors of exhibit area for local artists.

Farther north along Route 9W in Coxsackie, the **Bronck Museum** ★★, 90 County Rte. 42 (© 518/731-6490; www.gchistory.org; admission $5 adults, $3.50 seniors, $2 students ages 12–15, $1 children ages 5–11, free for children under 5; Memorial Day to Oct 15 Tues–Sat and Mon holidays 10am–4pm, Sun 1–5pm), is distinguished by a real rarity, the oldest surviving home in upstate New York, a beautifully solid stone Dutch medieval built in 1663 by the cousin of the man who would settle the Bronx. How old is that? Enough to predate the Constitution by 113 years. The museum is actually an entire complex of architecturally significant buildings. The homestead was a working farm and home to eight generations of Broncks, original Dutch settlers, until 1939. The original house has massive beams, wide floorboards, a cellar hatchway, and an early Dutch door; rooms feature Federal, Empire, and Victorian furniture. Also on the premises are a 1785 Federal brick house and three barns (including the unique 1835 "13-Sided Barn," the oldest multisided barn in New York). Coxsackie is a small but attractive town, a good place to grab a bite (see "Where to Dine," below).

If want to get your Irish up, you might pop in to see a couple of sights in East Durham. The **Our Lady of Knock Shrine,** Route 145, features stained-glass and mahogany carvings from County Mayo, Ireland. The **Irish American Heritage Museum,** 2267 Rte. 145 (© 518/634-7497; www.irishamericanheritage museum.org), has exhibits and educational programs about the Irish experience in America. On the agenda in East Durham is a future Irish Village. More interesting for most is the **Five State Lookout,** an overlook on Route 23 (The Mohican Trail) in East Windham. On Route 23A in Jewett is another ethnic contribution to the area, one of interest to architects. **St. John the Baptist Ukrainian Catholic Church and Grazhda** (© 518/734-5330; www.brama.com/stjohn) is a small, wonderfully crafted, rustic wooden basilica, built without nails or cement. You may have to get the non-English-speaking priest to open it up so you can see the wooden chandelier, but it's worth a look.

Several of the small towns in this region get their biggest jolt from winter downhill skiing and snowboarding at **Windham** and **Hunter Mountains** (see "Sports & Outdoor Activities," below), though the areas, with their golf courses and summer music and arts festivals, are also good year-round destinations. The village of **Hunter** has a newly thriving arts scene due to the efforts of the **Catskill Mountain Foundation,** Rte. 23A (© 518/263-4908), which operates an arts center, farm market, excellent book store and cool movie theater. In Tannersville, next door to Hunter, is a sight for naturalists: the **Mountain Top Arboretum,**

Route 23C (© **518/589-3903;** www.mtarbor.org), a pretty 10-acre spot surrounded by mountains and containing nice woodland walking trails, and flowering trees, evergreens, wildflowers, and shrubs; it's especially beautiful in summer.

Tip: The **Kaaterskill Trolley** (© **518/589-6150;** $1 (children under 5 free) runs from the village of Hunter to Tannersville and South and North Lake beaches, between noon and 9:30pm; weekend schedule beginning Fridays at 5:30pm.

The natural highlight of the area, though, is **Kaaterskill Falls** ★★, Route 23A, Haines Falls (© **518/589-5058**), the highest waterfall in New York State (higher even than Niagara). There's a beautiful and easy half-mile hike along a path from the bottom that wends along the creek, though you have to park in a small lot on Route 23A, cross the road, and walk along it to the beginning of the path. You can also see the falls from the top by taking Route 23A to North Lake Road and turning right on Laurel House Lane. A short path there takes you right to the edge of the precipitous drop; some folks are brave enough to sit on the flat rocks dangling the feet over the edge of the falls. Nearby is **North-South Lake,** the former site of the famed Catskill Mountain House, the first great mountain resort in the U.S. If you have time, I suggest you take both paths to see the falls from both ends.

The northeastern section of the Catskill Mountains is home to a number of the classic old resorts and attractions that have been here for years. The area around Cairo and Round Top, tucked in the fold of the Catskill Forest Preserve, has a number of small, family-run resorts. **Catskill Game Farm,** Game Farm Road, off Route 32 (© **518/678-9595;** www.catskillgamefarm.com; adults $17, seniors $15, children 4–11 $13; May–Oct 9am–5pm), has been in the same family since 1933. It began as one man's small collection of exotic animals and in the 1960s, at the height of the Catskills as a vacation destination, saw more than 10,000 visitors each day. It's nowhere near those heights today, but it keeps adding to its stock of 2,000 animals imported from Africa and other parts, including wallabies, emu, alpacas, Arabian camels, Watusi cattle, and more. Two small trams ferry people about, and there are animal shows. The highlight is certainly the feeding ground and animal nursery/petting zoo, where children can get up close and personal with baby lambs, pygmy goats, and pot-bellied pigs. Some visitors who aren't really fans of zoos may find that animal pens, while in accordance with regulations, seem a little bit cramped for such large animals.

SHOPPING

Ann Stewart, 384 Main St., Catskill (© **518/943-0975;** www.kiltshop.com), is a maker of authentic Scottish kilts, one of only a handful in the U.S. Her shop could easily be called "All Things Scottish." The **Bookstore,** run by the Catskill Mountain Foundation, Main Street, Hunter (© **518/263-5157**), is the only—yes, only—new-edition bookstore in Greene County. **The Barn,** Route 23 West at Jewett Road, Windham (© **888/883-0444**), is a restored barn full of antique furnishings, clothing, toys, and other collectibles. **Ulla Darni at the Blue Pearl,** 7751 Rte. 23, East Windham (© **518/734-6525;** www.ulladarni.net), features the fanciful lamps, sconces, and chandeliers of renowned lighting artist Ulla Darni. Her colorful, handcrafted lamps fetch huge prices. A nice traditional gallery is **Windham Fine Arts,** in a 19th-century house at 5380 Main St., Windham (© **518/734-6850;** www.windhamfinearts.com); it focuses mostly on regional painters and sculptors. The **Windham Mini Mall,** 5359 Main St., Windham (© **518/734-5050**), is a general store with gourmet foods, a dangerous candy display, books, jewelry, and camping and fishing supplies. **Village Candle Pottery**

and Gifts, Main Street, Tannersville (© **518/589-6002**), has an outstanding collection of scented candles and outdoors goods. **The Snowy Owl,** Main Street, Tannersville (© **518/589-9939**), is a cool home furnishings and gifts store with a decided mountain look.

SPORTS & OUTDOOR ACTIVITIES

GOLF   There are nearly a dozen golf courses in the northeastern Catskills. Call © **866/840-GOLF** or check out the website www.greenecountygolf.com for additional information. The finest is **Windham Country Club,** South Street, Windham (© **518/734-9910;** www.windhamcountryclub.com), a championship course highly rated by *Golf Digest.*

WINTER SPORTS   Skiing is the big draw. **Hunter Mountain,** Route 23A West, Hunter (© **888/HUNTER-MTN;** www.huntermtn.com), is a skier's (and boarder's) mountain—the closest "Big Mountain" to New York City, it likes to say—that's long been popular with hard-core, rowdy singles who party it up afterwards at the bars in Tannersville. In 2002, the mountain added The Learning Center, a huge and superb beginner's ski facility that's doing much to attract families. It features excellent learner's packages. The resort itself has some great black runs and a nostalgic clubhouse where the drinking cranks up. In off season, there are a host of festivals, such as Oktoberfest and Celtic, German Alps, and Microbrew festivals. **Mountain Trails Cross-Country Ski Center,** Route 23A, Tannersville (© **518/589-5361**), offers 20 miles of groomed trails, instruction, rentals, and a warming hut. Bike rentals are available at **Twilight Mountain Sports,** North Lake Road and Rte. 23A, Haines Falls (© **518/589-6480**).

   Windham Mountain, C.D. Lane Road, Windham (© **518/734-4300;** www.skiwindham.com), has a nice variety of trails and facilities. If you're not into the singles scene and, perhaps, less of a hard-core skier, Windham is an excellent choice. Both Windham and Hunter Mountains feature mountain biking on trails in the off season and chairlifts up for the views (a great idea in fall foliage season). Check out **Windham Mountain Outfitters,** Route 296 and South Street, Windham (© **518/734-4700**), for ski and snowboard rentals and other equipment, including bicycle and kayak rentals.

WHERE TO STAY

Albergo Allegria ★★ *Value*   This family-owned and -operated midsize inn is top of the line all the way, and it couldn't be any friendlier. It strikes a great balance of comfort, cleanliness, and character. The building has 19th-century heritage, though it's been nicely updated. Rooms in the main house are all uniquely decorated and different in size; many have excellent mountain views. Even the cheapest, called the "cozy rooms," are pretty spacious. The large "requested rooms," named for months of the year, are probably the best value. Carriage House Suites are new construction within the old carriage house; they have cathedral ceilings and separate entrances, perfect for skiers and anyone wanting a bit of privacy. For a splurge, but at prices that are still somewhat reasonable, indulge in the Master or Millennium Suite, both of which are humongous and very well appointed. The inn, a Triple A Four-Diamond property, is immaculate and provides lots of luxury details for the price, like free beverages in the kitchen 24 hours a day, luxurious linens and towels, and excellent, comfortable beds.

Rte. 296, Windham, NY 12442. © **518/734-5560**. Fax 518/734-5570. www.albergousa.com. 21 units. $73–$189 double; $169–$269 suite. Rates include full breakfast. AE, DC, DISC, MC, V. Free parking. *In room:* A/C, TV, dataport, hair dryer.

Crystal Brook Resort *(Value)* This small and proud "German-American resort" looks like an authentic German outpost, a slice of Bavaria. It has been in the same family since 1960 (though it's been around for 55 years). It's well known for its Mountain Brauhaus restaurant and bar, where Oktoberfest and other German dance parties get the beer and German music flowing, and has a crew of regulars. Rooms are pretty large and comfortable, mostly in a motel style. Many have private balconies. The restaurant prepares hearty German and Austrian specialties. Weekends in season are themed, such as Schlactfest, Bauernball, and Bavarian weekends. Crystal Brook may be from another era when the Catskills were *the* destination, but it has a lot of stubborn charm. If you catch the right weekend, you might want to bring your lederhosen.

Winter Clove Rd., Round Top, NY 12473. (C) **800/999-7376** or 518/622-3751. Fax 518/622-9610. www.crystal brook.com. 33 units. $116–$136 double. Weekend/weekly rates and packages available. Rates include 3 meals daily. MC, V. Free parking. **Amenities:** Restaurant; bar; tennis court; outdoor swimming pool; Jacuzzi. *In room:* A/C, TV.

Fairlawn Inn *★ (Value)* Right on the main drag in the village of Hunter, facing Hunter Mountain, this impressively restored, gorgeous 1904 Queen Anne Victorian inn is the top place to stay right in town. Though the inn appears massive, it has just nine cozy and romantic rooms, which feature queen-size Victorian reproduction beds. Some rooms have claw-foot tubs, perfect after a day at the slopes, while others have private porch entrances. Perhaps the most coveted room is the Gazebo Room, in the fantastic three-story turret.

Main St., Hunter, NY 12442. (C) **518/263-5025.** www.fairlawninn.com. 9 units. $99–$179 double. Rates include full breakfast. AE, MC, V. Free parking. **Amenities:** Bar; TV lounge. *In room:* A/C, TV.

Stewart House *(Finds)* This funky old place, formerly the late Victorian 1883 Athens Hotel, is a slightly bohemian inn and restaurant on the west bank of the Hudson. It's got lots of artsy character, but feels a bit like a work in progress. One room, called the Ironweed Room, is where the death scene with Meryl Streep was filmed in the movie version of William Kennedy's Pulitzer Prize–winning book. Actors in town for the summer Shakespeare on the Hudson Festival (run by the inn's owners) often stay up on the top floor. On the river are a nice gazebo and a bar at the boat dock. The stylish bistro restaurant serves Northern Italian fare and has all the makings of a hipster bar, though it's a little tough to imagine in this out-of-the-way spot.

2 North Water St., Athens, NY 12015. (C) **518/945-1357.** www.stewarthouse.com. 5 units. $110–$125 double. Rates include continental breakfast. MC, V. Free parking. **Amenities:** Restaurant; bar. *In room:* A/C.

Washington Irving Lodge *★★* A charming Victorian ambience pervades this lovely 1890 house, outfitted with nice antiques, modern bathrooms, a fantastic reading room and parlor, fully equipped cocktail lounge, and large dining room. Some rooms on the third floor are very large, while those in the original tower (my favorite) are very cozy and rustic, with paneled walls and tower windows. All are very warmly decorated with a 19th-century feel. The house sits on 8 acres and has an outdoor pool and tennis court, rarities for an inn of this size. The friendly owner, Stephanie, is sometimes helped out by her equally gregarious son Nick, whom you may find tending bar. Midweek ski packages are available.

Route 23A, Hunter, NY 12442. (C) **518/589-5560.** Fax 518/589-5775. www.washingtonirving.com. 15 units. $125–$225 double. Rates include full breakfast. 2-night minimum stay on weekends in season. AE, DC, DISC, MC, V. Free parking. **Amenities:** Bar; outdoor pool; tennis court. *In room:* A/C, TV, dataport, hair dryer.

Winter Clove Inn ⭐ *Value*   Tucked into 400 beautiful acres in the foothills of North Mountain, one of the highest peaks of the northern Catskills, this old-school resort, amazingly in the same family since 1838, is like a great old boarding house from another era. Rooms are pretty spacious and have quite a bit of charm, with hooked rugs, hardwood floors, and four-poster beds, as well as modern bathrooms. In the old carriage house is a great six-lane bowling alley that looks ripped from a movie set.

Winter Clove Rd., Round Top, NY 12473. ✆ 518/622-3751. Fax 518/622-3267. www.winterclove.com. 49 units. $160–$180 double. Weekend and weekly rates and packages available. Rates include 3 meals daily. 2-night minimum stay on weekends. MC, V. Free parking. **Amenities:** Restaurant; bar; indoor and outdoor swimming pools; 9-hole golf course; tennis court; TV lounge. *In room:* A/C, no phone.

WHERE TO DINE

The Catskill Mountain Country Store and Restaurant ⭐ *Kids* BREAKFAST/CAFE   This cute and casual gourmet country store hides one of the best places for breakfast in the Catskills. The morning menu is as impressively creative as it is long, and portions are gigantic. The eight kinds of signature pancakes are outstanding, as are items like banana pecan French toast and the slightly spicy Italian wrap. Breakfast is served all day. Lunch menu features mostly healthy and organic-based items, using their own farm-fresh produce, such as spicy arugula salad, homemade soups, great wraps, chili, and burgers, with a few Tex-Mex offerings as well. Children will love the mini zoo and gardens out back, where they'll find the pigs Priscilla and Daisy, as well as chickens, roosters, and more.

5510 Rte. 23, Windham. ✆ 518/734-3387. Reservations not accepted. Main courses $6–$8. DISC, MC, V. Mon–Fri 9am–6pm; Sat 8am–6pm; Sun 8am–5pm.

Last Chance Cheese & Antiques AMERICAN   The name doesn't lie: This casual spot, with a country-store ambience, is part restaurant, part antiques, gifts, and gourmet foods shop. It's decorated with hanging musical instruments and antiques, and it has a deli with a few tables and an enclosed patio dining area. The menu is surprisingly diverse. Start with a homemade soup, or perhaps cheese fondue or a nice, large salad, followed by specialty sandwiches, light fare like quiches, or go whole hog with substantial entrees, such as St. Louis ribs, meatloaf, or stuffed filet of sole. An even bigger surprise is that this little place has a phenomenal beer list to go with 100 imported cheeses: Choose from among 300 imported beers, including several very select Belgians.

Main St., Tannersville. ✆ 518/589-5424. Reservations not accepted. Main courses $6.95–$16. AE, MC, V. Daily 11am–7pm.

Maggie's Krooked Café & Juice Bar *Finds* BREAKFAST/CAFE   A cool little two-room bohemian cafe done up in funky colors, Maggie's does an amazing breakfast, with a long list of egg dishes and omelets and great buckwheat and potato pancakes. Lunch is mainly burgers and simple items like veggie melts, salads, and grilled chicken sandwiches. The home-baked muffins and cakes are incredible.

Main St., Tannersville. ✆ 518/589-6101. Reservations not accepted. Main courses $6.95–$16. AE, MC, V. Daily 7am–5pm.

Mountain Brook Dining and Spirits ⭐⭐ *Kids* CREATIVE AMERICAN   A lodgelike space with views of Hunter Mountain, an outdoor deck overlooking Schoharie Creek, and a popular bar at the front, this casually elegant restaurant is one of the top spots in Hunter. Chef-owner Wendy Cappello creates main courses like pan-seared Maine salmon with apricot couscous, Black Angus grilled strip steak with grilled tomatoes and mushrooms, and a longtime favorite, meat-loaf with onion rings and chive mashed potatoes. Daily specials might be oven-roasted rack of lamb, or grilled Jumbo Gulf shrimp with miso-sake glaze. A nice bonus at a fine dining spot like this is the kid's menu.

Main St. (Rte. 23A), Hunter. ✆ 518/263-5351. Reservations recommended. Main courses $14–$9. MC, V. Thurs–Tues 5–10pm.

Reed's Landing ⭐ AMERICAN   In an old brick mercantile building on Coxsackie's historic main street, across from the town bank, this friendly, good-looking bistro is the best restaurant in the area. It has a nice bar area and high-backed booths, with live music on Saturday nights. For lunch, choose among a selection of good wraps, hot sandwiches, and pastas. Entrees include shrimp Parmesan, surf and turf (prime rib or New York strip with shrimp or scallops), and veal *cordon bleu.*

10 Reed St., Coxsackie. ✆ 518/731-2000. Reservations recommended weekends. Main courses $9–$18. AE, MC, V. Wed–Thurs noon–4pm and 5–9pm; Fri noon–4pm and 5–10pm; Sat 4:30–10pm; Sun–Mon 4:30–9pm.

Ruby's Hotel & Restaurant ⭐⭐ *(Finds)* CREATIVE AMERICAN   A con-verted 19th-century hotel in the village of Freehold, Ruby's is a funky venture by a dynamic New York City chef, Ana Sporer, who's inhabited the cool space with a light hand but tons of vigor. Unassuming from the street, the restaurant features an amazing Deco bar, a classic 1938 soda fountain, hand-blocked Vic-torian wallpaper, and the original tables and chairs found in the place. Fortu-nately, the menu and execution are anything but afterthoughts. Though the menu changes frequently according to the whims of the chef and seasonal ingre-dients, standards are coq au vin, braised lamb shank with saffron Israeli cous-cous, and homey favorites like turkey chili, chicken potpie, and a Cuban sandwich. At press time, a few rooms upstairs were in the process of being ren-ovated for overnight stays.

3689 Rte. 67, Freehold. ✆ 518/634-7790. Reservations recommended. Main courses $8.95–$19. AE, MC, V. Winter Fri–Sat 5–10pm; summer (June–Aug) Thurs–Sat 5–10pm.

Vesuvio ⭐⭐ *(Kids)* NORTHERN ITALIAN   This romantic and surprisingly formal, family-owned restaurant—with the same chef, Joseph Baglio, for more than 25 years—has two large dining rooms and an outdoor space. Pastas, such as fettuccine matriciana (with prosciutto, pancetta, and more) are excellent, as are traditional items like veal chops, rack of lamb, and filet mignon. The children's menu (cheese ravioli or penne with meatballs, followed by ice cream) should keep the kids happy. Vesuvio's features a nice wine list and superb service.

Goshen Rd., Hensonville. ✆ 518/734-3663. Reservations recommended. Main courses $16–$24. AE, DC, DISC, MC, V. Mon–Thurs 4–10pm; Fri–Sat 4–11pm; Sun 3–10pm.

SPECIAL EVENTS & HUNTER/WINDHAM AFTER DARK

The summertime **Shakespeare on the Hudson Festival** (✆ 877/2-MCDUFF; www.shakespeareonthehudson.com), with actors from New York City and else-where, is held at a great space along the river in Athens, 1 mile north of the Rip Van Winkle Bridge on Route 385. The **Windham Chamber Music Festival,** 740 Rte. 32C, Windham (✆ 518/738-3852; www.windhammusic.com), fea-tures a sophisticated lineup of chamber-music concerts from January to Labor Day at the Historic Windham Civic Center on Main Street. The renovated **Catskill Mountain Foundation Movie Theater,** Main Street, Hunter (✆ 518/ 263-4702), features first-run Hollywood and foreign and independent films in two great theaters. A wide array of classical music, theater, dance, and popular music performances are held across the street at the foundation's red-barn **Performing Arts Center and Gallery,** Main Street, Hunter (© **518/263-4908;** www.catskillmtn.org). A handful of clubs on Main Street in Tannersville cater to après-skiers in search of singles and dance action.

4 Northwestern Catskill Region (Delaware County)

The intensely rural Catskill Region gets even more remote and more rural in Delaware County, home to just 25,000 New Yorkers—but to 700 miles of fishing streams and 11,000 acres of reservoirs and other waterways. This is a land of long uninterrupted vistas, deeply green valleys, rivers, streams, and isolated dairy farms, with a handful of covered bridges and historic towns tossed in. Though just over 3 hours from New York City, it's one of the best places in the state to get away from it all and get outdoors to hike, mountain bike, kayak, or ski. The region is so rural that one can pick up a brochure from the **Catskill Center for Conservation and Development** in Arkville (© **845/586-2611;** www.catskill center.org) and spend days doing a self-guided tour of the Barns of Delaware County. Hmm. Sounds like a movie.

ESSENTIALS

GETTING THERE   Route 28 is a 110-mile corridor running west from Kingston to Cooperstown, bisecting Delaware County and providing easy access to the entire county.

VISITOR INFORMATION   **Delaware Country Chamber of Commerce,** 114 Main St., Delhi (© **800/642-4443;** www.delawarecounty.org).

EXPLORING THE NORTHWESTERN CATSKILL REGION

Roxbury today is a fairly somnolent rural burg, but it wasn't always that way. Its Main Street is lined with impressive Tudor and Victorian homes and maple shade trees. Helen Gould Shepard, daughter of the famous financier and railroad magnate—and Roxbury native—Jay Gould was the town benefactor in the late 1800s. She was responsible for the **Gould Memorial Church** (Main St./Rte. 30), built in 1894 by the same architect who designed the state capitol and the famous Dakota apartment building in New York City. Inside are four Tiffany stained-glass windows and a monumental pipe organ. Behind the church is **Kirkside Park,** formerly Helen Gould's estate. The site has been cleaned up and restored in recent years, with rustic bridges built over the stream and trails and walkways added. A **vintage "base ball"** team, the Roxbury Nine, plays its games (according to 1864 rules and uniforms) here. On Labor Day, the town celebrates "Turn of the Century Day," and locals dress in period costume, while the opposing team is brought in by vintage train. The **John Burroughs Homestead and Woodchuck Lodge,** John Burroughs Memorial Road (© **607/ 326-372;** www.roxburyny.com; open occasionally in summer), was the rustic summer retreat of the renowned naturalist and essayist. The 1860s farmhouse, a National Historic Landmark, remains as it was when Burroughs lived and wrote here. To get to it, turn west off of Route 30 heading north to Grand Gorge from Roxbury; the house is several miles up on the right.

The **Hanford Mills Museum,** Routes 10 and 12, East Meredith (© **800/ 295-4992;** www.handfordmills.org; May–Oct 10am–5pm), is a restored farmstead with 16 historic buildings, including a working, water-powered sawmill, an antique boxcar, woodworking shop, and special events like an Old-Fashioned 4th of July, Quilt Show, and Lumberjack Festival. One of the most enjoyable

Take Me Out to the Last Century

Vintage "base ball"—America's pastime as it was played pre-Ruth, when it was spelled "base ball"—has taken off as the ultimate in retro sporting style. Players wear thick period woolen uniforms and for the most part use no gloves; balls and bats are constructed strictly according to regulations of the day. There are about 100 teams in the U.S., and quite a number in New York State and the Northeast. Roxbury's opponents are the New York Gothams, Brooklyn Atlantics, Providence Grays, and Hartford Senators, among others. What no one seems able to agree on is which era should be faithfully reproduced. Some teams play by 1860 rules, while others adopt 1864 rules, and still others prefer to live in 1872, 1887, or 1898. Roxbury's team—which counts Mrs. Gould Shepard's grandson among its roster—is one of the most active in the Northeast, playing 16 to 20 games every summer and drawing as many as 3,000 people in attendance. For more information on the vintage "base ball," visit www.vbba.org.

attractions in this section of the Catskills Region is **Healing Waters Farm** ✷✷, Route 206, Walton (✆ **607/865-4420;** www.healingwatersfarm.com; Apr–Dec Thurs–Fri 11am–6pm, Sat 10am–4pm, Sun 11am–4pm; admission $5 adults, $4 children), a splendid all-in-one agrotourism attraction for families. Kids will be delighted by Little Boy Blue Animal Land, the petting zoo with amazingly friendly (and rotating) roster of exotic and barnyard animals like a camel, llamas, emus, and baby goats, and hayrides across the rolling acres of farmland. Also onsite, in a 19th-century dairy barn, are the Walton Carriage Museum (a collection of antique horse-drawn carriages), a country antique shop and cool Western clothing and gift shop. The two dynamo guys behind this ever-expanding project plan all sorts of special events and seasonal programs.

The Penn Central Railroad arrived in these parts in 1872. The **Delaware & Ulster Railride** ✷, 43510 Rte. 28 in Arkville (✆ **800/225-4132;** www.durr.org), south of Roxbury is a tourist excursion train that takes visitors through the Catskill Mountains in an historic train or open-air flat car, departing from the old depot, a must for train fans. The Ulster & Delaware Railroad was one of the most scenic of the day, traversing dramatic mountain scenery from the Hudson to Oneonta. Special events include train runs with staging of a "Great Train Robbery" and "Twilight on the Rails," a slow-moving party excursion with live music and food onboard. Trains also travel to Halcottsville, Roxbury, and Highmount on weekends May through October, and Wednesday to Friday as well during July and August. For the most part, trains depart at 11am and 2pm for the trip to Roxbury; admission is $10 adults, $8 seniors, $6 children ages 3 to 12. A 2:30pm departs to Halcottsville; admission is $8 adults, $7 seniors, $5 children age 3 to 12. On summer and fall weekends, visitors can also take the train to Belleayre Mountain and ride the trolley to the chair lift "sky ride." Check the website or call for current schedules and special-event trains.

Margaretville is the most commercially developed of the small rural towns in Delaware County, with a cute Main Street (where *You Can Count On Me,* with Laura Linney and Matthew Broderick, was filmed) lined with several antiques shops, a village pub, and a couple of restaurants. **Andes** (www.andesny.org) is a similar historic village with an interesting past. During the Anti-Rent War of the 1840s in New York, the local sheriff and his deputies, arrived at the Moses Earle farm to collect overdue rents. Locals disguised themselves as Indians, killing the sheriff and resulting in the arrest of 100 men and two death sentences. Today, though, it's much more peaceful, and definitely on the upswing, with the arrival of several new restaurants, shops and, likely, accommodations. The **Hunting Tavern Museum,** Main Street (*C* 845/676-3775; Memorial Day to Columbus Day Sat 10am–3pm) is housed in one of the oldest buildings in Andes and tells the story of life in the village in the 19th century.

SHOPPING

As rural as Delaware County is, it's not exactly a shopper's mecca. However, a number of tourist-oriented shops are in old barns, which makes it fun. Besides the shops of Healing Waters Farm in Walton, described above, **Pakatakan Farmer's Market** is held Saturdays from May to October in a fantastic 1899 Round Barn, one of the oldest such structures, on Route 30 in Halcottsville. In season, you'll see dozens of farms selling produce across the region.

If you must shop for man-made things, Margaretville is your place. The **Margaretville Antique Center,** Main Street (*C* 845/586-2424), has several dealers under one room, while **The Commons in Margaretville,** Main Street (www.shop thecommons.com), has antiques, clothing, kitchenware, flowers, and Internet hookups. Walton's **Country Emporium,** 134 Delaware St. (*C* 607/865-8440; www.countryemporiumltd.com), is a marketplace in a historic building with lots of gourmet foods, antiques, and crafts. A funky flea market is held Saturdays and Sundays in summer, along Route 28 in Arkville. In Fleischmanns, **Robert's Auction House,** Main Street, holds court every Saturday night from 7:30pm to midnight, providing entertainment and shopping excuses to locals and visitors to the area. It's low-rent but a lot of fun, like a yard sale, except with an auctioneer at the helm. The folding chairs have locals' names on them.

SPORTS & OUTDOOR ACTIVITIES

CANOEING & KAYAKING   With all the water around, **canoeing** and **kayaking** are big, especially along the East and West branches of the Delaware River. Rentals and in some cases, canoe and kayak tours, are available from: **Al's Sport Store,** Routes 30 and 206 in Downsville (*C* 607/363-7740; www.alssportstore. com); **Catskill Outfitters,** Delaware and North Street, Walton (*C* 800/631-0105; www.catskilloutfitters.com); and **Susan's Pleasant Pheasant Farm,** 1 Bragg Hollow Rd., Halcottsville (*C* 607/326-4266; www.pleasantpheasantfarm.com).

FISHING   The western Catskills are one of North America's top fishing destinations. You'll find great tailwater, still water, and freestone fishing. Fly-fishing is huge in the east and west branches of the Delaware River, Beaverkill River, and Willowemoc. The junction pool at Hancock, where the East and West branches join to form the main stem of the Delaware River, is legendary for large brown and rainbow trout. **Pepacton Reservoir** is a great open-water brown trout fishery. **Al's Sport Store,** Routes 30 and 206 in Downsville (*C* 607/363-7740; www.alssportstore.com), is the best resource in the area for equipment and knowledge. Al knows everything about fishing the Catskills. For more information on fishing in the northern Catskills, request a **Delaware County Chamber Fishing Guide** (*C* 800/642-4443; www.delawarecounty.org) or **I Love NY Fishing Map** (*C* 607/652-7366). The **West Branch Angler & Sportsman's**

Resort in Deposit is a terrific upscale cabin resort targeting anglers (see "Where to Stay," below).

Remember, state licenses are required for fishing (p. 69).

GOLF   For golf, check out the sweet and hilly **Shepard Hills Golf & Tennis Club,** Golf Course Road (1 mile off Rte. 30), Roxbury (© **607/326-7121;** www. shepardhills.com) The nine-hole course dates from 1916.

HIKING & BIKING   The **Catskill Scenic Trail** (© 607/652-2821; www. catskillscenictrail.org) is 19 gentle miles of Rails to Trails (hard-packed rail path) that run from Grand Gorge to Bloomville; it's terrific for hiking, biking, and cross-country skiing (in winter, watch out for snowmobiles roaring by). The best spot to pick up the trail is Railroad Avenue in Stamford. Within 15 miles of Margaretville, there are 12 peaks above 3,000 feet; **Balsam Lake Mountain** has nice marked trails. **Dry Brook Trail** begins at a trailhead in Margaretville and passes Pakatakan Mountain, Dry Brook Ridge, and Balsam Lake Mountain. In **Andes,** a nice hike is around the Pepacton Reservoir to Big Pond and Little Pond; from the trail heads, you can hike to the summits of **Cabot** or **Touch-menot Mountain.** The **Catskill Center for Conservation and Development,** Route 28, Arkville (© **845/586-2611;** www.catskillcenter.org), offers guided hikes, snowshoe excursions, and bird walks. Birders and naturalists may be interested in "Talons: A Birds of Prey Experience" (Andes; © **845/676-4885;** www.talonsbirdsofprey.com) guided hawk walks with a licensed falconer.

Mountain bikers have lots to choose from, but **Plattekill Mountain** (© **800/ GOTTA BIKE;** www.plattekill.com) is one of the top five mountain-biking destinations in North America; it's very popular with extreme downhill crazies in head-to-toe gear and caked in mud, but there are also trails for novices and intermediates.

WINTER SPORTS   Skiers and boarders have two good options. **Belleayre Mountain** (p. 234) and **Plattekill Mountain** (© **800/NEED-2-SKI;** www. plattekill.com) is a small, laid-back 1950s-era resort that's good for families and novice-to-intermediate skiers.

SPECIAL EVENTS

One of the big annual events in the area is the **Great County Fair** (© **607/865-4763;** www.delawarecountyfair.org), held in mid-August in Walton (closing in on 120 years of tradition). You'll find live music, tractor pulls, midway rides, goat shows, livestock auctions, and more. The **Belleayre Music Festival** (© **800/942-6904;** www.belleayremusic.org) in July and August brings big-name musicians, such as Wynton Marsalis and Ray Charles, to the mountain in Highmount.

WHERE TO STAY

Chestnut Inn at Oquaga Lake   On the shore of sterling Oquaga Lake, this 1929 inn, with all original chestnut inside, is a homey and comfortable place to stay, good if you want a lake location but not all the sign-up schedules and activities of the Scott family inn (and this one is open year-round). Rooms are narrow and a little frilly, though they're pretty nice. About half of them have lake views; the other half look out back to the woods. Bathrooms, some of which are shared, are a bit dated and 1960s-looking. The hotel has a very respected, though relatively pricey restaurant with great lake views.

498 Oquaga Lake Rd., Deposit, NY 13754. © **866/467-0002** or 607/467-3094. www.chestnutinn.net. 30 units. $129–$219 double with private bathroom, $159–$259 suite; $99–$149 double with shared bathroom.

AE, DISC, MC, V. Free parking. **Amenities:** Restaurant; bar; 9-hole golf course; 3 outdoor and 1 indoor tennis court; sail and rowboats, cabaret shows. *In room:* A/C, TV.

Margaretville Mountain Inn *(Value)*

An 1866 Queen Anne, slate-roofed Victorian, up a long road from downtown Margaretville, this comfortable, informal inn has stupendous mountain views on its side. The panoramic view from the porch, overlooking Catskill Mountain State Park, is worth the price of a night's stay. Rooms have some period antiques and modern bathrooms; the Emerald Room inhabits the turret, but I may prefer the cozy Birch room. The owners also have a property in the village of Margaretville, with two, two-bedroom suites with full kitchens, fireplaces, and a private yard (each sleeps as many as six—a real bargain for close-knit families).

Margaretville Mountain Rd., Margaretville, NY 12455. ℃ **845/586-3933.** Fax 845/586-1699. www. margaretvilleinn.com. 4 units. $75–$98 double; $110–$130 suite; $125–$150 2-bedroom village suite. AE, DISC, MC, V. Free parking. *In room:* A/C, TV, VCR (in village suites), kitchen (in village suites).

River Run *(Value)*

A large 1887 Victorian on the main drag in Fleischmanns, just down the street from the locally famous Roberts Auction House, this inn is run by a very friendly young married couple. The house is simply decorated, not overdone like so many B&Bs with Victorian pretensions. The nice backyard runs to the creek flowing behind Main Street. The private, basement-level Retro Suite, a two-bedroom kitschy apartment, is a good value and perfect for two couples or families (rooms upstairs with shared bathrooms would also work well for families with kids). The inn is very gay, family, and dog friendly (apologies for the juxtaposition).

882 Main St., Fleischmanns NY 12430. ℃ **845/254-4884.** www.catskill.net/riverrun. 9 units. $95–$145 double with private bathroom, $70–$85 double with shared bathroom; suite $165. Rates include full breakfast. 2-night minimum stay on weekends (3 on major holidays). AE, DC, DISC, MC, V. Free parking. *In room:* A/C, TV, no phone.

Scott's Oquaga Lake House *(Kids)*

This family-owned resort has, incredibly, been in the same family since 1869! But that's not even the most notable fact about it; what's really unique is that several generations of the "singing Scott family" continue to perform in nightly cabaret revues for their guests all summer. The shows have to be seen to be believed. For some guests, it will be like time travel to another, gentler planet: planet 1940s Americana. Their literature says it best: "the excitement of a cruise; the friendliness of a bed & breakfast." Actually, the marketing tag line I like better is "Be our guest, be our guest, put our service to the test." The resort's accommodations are pretty modest, but the place is ensconced on 1,100 lakefront acres, and spring-fed Oquaga Lake is stunning. All recreational activities, meals, and best of all, cabaret shows are included in the price, and the family is strict about enforcing a "no tipping" policy. You can take free ballroom or square dance lessons, water-ski, play tennis, golf, or volleyball; the possibilities for fun, one imagines, are endless. The Scott house is popular with families, who, like the Scotts, return year after year.

Oquaga Lake Rd., Deposit 13754. ℃ **607/467-3094.** www.scottsfamilyresort.com. 135 units. $208–$260 double; $298–$330 2-bedroom suite. Rates include 3 meals daily and all activities and entertainment. Weekly rates available. AE, MC, V. Free parking. **Amenities:** Restaurant; bar; 9-hole golf course; 3 outdoor and 1 indoor tennis court; sail- and rowboats cabaret shows. *In room:* A/C, TV.

Susan's Pleasant Pheasant Farm

I challenge you to say the name of this cozy B&B and 1810 mill house perched right on the edge of a dam and waterfall with great river and mountain views, three times fast. Rustic and relaxed, it has the feel of an antiques shop. The downstairs sitting room has nice water views, a roaring fire, and, occasionally, five Great Pyrenees dogs roaming through

---

Tips Gone Fishin'

Anglers who really just want to concentrate on the fish and don't want anything fancy or expensive should check out the **Downsville Motel,** Routes 30 and 206, Downsville (© **607/363-7575;** www.downsvillemotel.com; $60 double). The eight rooms are standard motel rooms, but they have private balconies overlooking the east branch of the Delaware River, and they're just paces from Al's Sports Store, which dispenses just about anything a fisherman could need.

---

it. There are a nice upstairs deck and an outdoor fireplace. Rooms are simple but comfortably furnished. The lake-view suite, with large picture windows, is the best and largest option. The owners have a kayak sales and rental service, and use of kayaks is complimentary for guests.

1 Bragg Hollow Rd., Halcottsville, NY 12438. © 607/326-4266. www.pleasantpheasantfarm.com. 4 units. $75–$100 double; $150 suite. Rates include full breakfast. AE, MC, V. Free parking. *In room:* A/C, TV.

West Branch Angler & Sportsman's Resort ★★ *(Kids)*   Though this great setup of near-luxury cabins on the banks of the west branch of the Delaware River—one of the world's most famous tailwater trout fisheries—is all about fly-fishing, you don't have to come with your waders and rods to enjoy the place. Far from it. If you want something out of the ordinary, with good amenities and services but lots of contact with nature, this is the place. It sits on 200 acres of mountain forests, with lots of hiking and biking trails, and has a very nice restaurant and bar, swings, and a playground overlooking the river, as well as miniature golf and a large outdoor pool. The one- and two-bedroom cabins are upscale rustic, with porches facing the river, picnic areas, and nice kitchens; some have fireplaces. If fishing is what your stay in the Catskills is all about, this is really your kind of place. There's a full-service fly shop, expert instruction, and guides. The resort is dog-friendly.

Faulkner Rd., Deposit 13754. © 800/201-2557. Fax 607/467-2215. www.westbranchangler.com. 24 units. $125–$195 studio and 1-bedroom double; $225 2-bedroom cabin (double occupancy). Rates include breakfast. 2-night minimum stay on weekends in season. AE, DC, DISC, MC, V. Free parking. **Amenities:** Restaurant; bar; swimming pool; exercise room; miniature golf. *In room:* A/C, TV, hair dryer.

WHERE TO DINE

The Andes Hotel ★★ *(Value)* CREATIVE AMERICAN   Sally and Ed O'Neill, bought and restored this classic 1850 inn, with a massive front porch, in the center of Andes. Ed is a Culinary Institute grad, and the restaurant strikes a nice balance between creative impulses and down-to-earth good food and good value. The decor is simple, with reddish brown paneling and simple white tablecloths and drop ceilings. Appetizers include an excellent warm wild mushroom salad. A nightly special (on Monday it's baby back ribs) complements the unpretentious but consistently well-prepared menu, which features items like a double-cut pork chop, roasted brook trout, and herb-crusted leg of lamb. The tavern next door serves bar comfort foods, like popcorn chicken and buffalo wings, so that folks of all stripes and means feel comfortable. The owners are in the process of sprucing up the hotel's 10 accommodations, which at this point are still pretty basic, but not bad and certainly not expensive (just $60 double).

110 Main St., Andes. © 845/676-3980. Reservations recommended. Main courses $13–$18. AE, MC, V. Daily noon–3pm and 5–10pm.

Café on Main ★ Kids AMERICAN BISTRO   This attractive little cafe restaurant in the middle of Margaretville's Main Street is open for breakfast, lunch, and dinner. The lunch menu is mostly soups, salads, and a long list of sandwiches and burgers. For dinner, it's hard to go wrong with the fresh pastas, chicken cacciatore, or marinated and grilled flank steak. Check out the seasonal specials, such as crayfish, clam and sausage gumbo, or filet mignon stuffed with portobello mushrooms and Asiago cheese. The good-value children's menu will keep the little ones happy, and the inexpensive breakfasts are a good way to start off the day.

Main St., Margaretville. © 845/5862343. Reservations recommended. Main courses $9.95–$19. AE, MC, V. Wed–Mon 8am–9pm.

The Old Schoolhouse Inn & Restaurant AMERICAN   A hunter's paradise, this restaurant, although in a 1903 schoolhouse, looks more like a hunting lodge. It is crammed to the rafters with taxidermy and hunting trophies of all shapes, sizes, and species. The Sunday brunch is a big local affair, with a huge spread under the watchful eyes of moose and elk in the front room and a shrimp and salad bar. Entrees are upscale and sophisticated, with a large array of fresh trout preparations, steaks, and pastas. The Saturday Special is roast prime rib au jus. Vegetarians and animals rights activists: This may not be your kind of place!

Main St., Downsville. © 607/363-7814. Reservations recommended on weekends. Main courses $12–$29. AE, MC, V. Wed–Sun noon–3pm and 5–10pm; Sun brunch 10am–2pm.

River Run Restaurant AMERICAN/GRILL   Tucked into the riverfront acreage of the West Branch Angler & Sportsman's Resort, this nice restaurant is a perfect place to unwind (and, if you're staying in one of the cabins, easy to get to) after a long day of—what else?—fishing. It's got the requisite, masculine lodge feel, and the tavern downstairs has a fancy, huge plasma TV behind the bar, so you can kick back with a beer and watch big-screen sports. The restaurant features a number of nice pastas, including spinach ravioli, and shrimp and scallop carbonara; entrees are pretty evenly divided between meat and fish, with a grilled burgundy filet, veal tenderloin, and grilled scarlet red snapper among the well-prepared options. The tavern menu includes items like club sandwiches and big, juicy burgers.

At the West Branch Angler & Sportsman's Resort, Faulkner Rd., Deposit. © 800/201-2557. Reservations recommended. Main courses $8.95–$23. AE, MC, V. Tues–Thurs 5–10pm; Fri-Sat 5–11pm; Sun brunch 10am–3pm; bar menu only in Trout Skellar lounge 5–10pm.

5 Southwestern Catskill Region (Sullivan County)

The Upper Delaware River paints the southwestern border of Sullivan County, separating New York State from Pennsylvania and running about 75 miles from Hancock to Sparrowbush. The Delaware River is considered one of the top 10 fishing rivers in the world, and, along with Beaverkill and Willowemoc Creeks, defines the southwestern section of the Catskills every bit as much as the mountains do. The area is one of the most important destinations in North America for trout fly-fishing, and river sports like canoeing and kayaking are also huge. Beyond the area's natural bounty, Sullivan County is a picturesque region of covered bridges, scattered historic sights, and towns positioned to take advantage of growing tourism, like Narrowsburg and Roscoe.

ESSENTIALS

GETTING THERE   Route 17 (future I-86 "Quickway") cuts northwest across Sullivan County, running from the New York State Thruway (I-87) and passing through Rock Hill on the way west to Deposit.

VISITOR INFORMATION   Contact **Sullivan County Visitors Association,** 100 North St., Monticello (✆ **800/882-CATS** or 845/794-3000; www.scva.net), or **National Park Service Upper Delaware Scenic and Recreational River** information center, Narrowsburg (✆ **570/685-4871;** www.nps.gov/upde) for more information.

EXPLORING THE SOUTHWESTERN CATSKILL REGION

Roscoe, which likes to tout itself as "Trout Town USA," is a pleasant, laid-back town with an attractive downtown that's lined with shops set up to capitalize on the tourist trade, which is almost wholly outdoors enthusiasts and fishermen. Roscoe is one of the primary base camps in the Catskill Region for anglers; it's perched at the edge of one of the most famous fishing spots in the country, **Junction Pool**—the confluence of the renowned trout-fishing streams, Beaverkill and Willowemoc Creek. The kickoff of fly-fishing season is celebrated here every April 1. Legend holds that the fish are detained long enough at this crossroads, unsure in which direction to swim, that they grow exponentially in size and offer themselves up as catch-and-release trophies. The **Roscoe O&W Railway Museum,** Railroad Avenue (✆ **607/498-5500;** Memorial Day to Columbus Day Sat–Sun 11am–3pm; free admission), across from the red NY O&W car, is a minor museum that contains artifacts and memorabilia from the old O&W railway line, a scale model railroad, and exhibits on the area's major attractions and industry.

Anglers have their own cultural institution to celebrate: the **Catskill Fly Fishing Center & Museum** ★★, 1031 Old Rte. 17 (between exits 94 and 96 off Rte. 17), Livingston Manor (✆ **845/439-4810;** Apr–Oct daily 10am–4pm; Nov–Mar Tues–Fri 10am–1pm, Sat 10am–4pm; $3 adults and students, $1 children under 12), is a handsomely built and displayed exhibit touting the achievements, art, science, and folklore of fly-fishing. Especially interesting are the numerous displays of wet, dry, nymph, and streamer flies and the actual tying tables of several of the most renowned tiers in the business. A stuffed doll of a 6-pound fish gives kids an idea what it would be like to catch a big one. Expert fly-fishers conduct demonstrations on Saturdays April to October.

Fans of historic covered bridges have a number to choose from in Sullivan Country, including ones in **Willowemoc** (built in 1860, 2 miles west of town); **Beaverkill** (1865, in Beaverkill State Campground); and **Livingston Manor** (1860, just north of town). All are signed. A different type of bridge, but well worth seeking out, is the centerpiece of the **Stone Arch Bridge Historical Park,** Route 52 near Kenoza Lake. The three-arched stone bridge was built in 1880 by Swiss-German immigrants.

Down Route 17 from Livingston Manor, the town of **Liberty** is distinguished by an attractive historic district with Gothic Revival, Romanesque, and Greek Revival buildings. The **Apple Pond Farming Center** (✆ **845/482-4674;** www. applepondfarm.com; Tues–Sun 10am–5pm), Hahn Road, in Callicoon Center, is a traditional horse-powered organic farm that offers demonstrations of milking, work and sport horses and border collies, as well as goat-cheese-making classes and horse-drawn wagon rides. It's a great spot for kids. **Bethel,** on Route 178 west of Route 17, is the site of the 1969 Woodstock Festival, the famous rock 'n' roll party where Jimi Hendrix, Janis Joplin, and others jammed for a seriously mind-altered audience. There's a small **Bethel Woodstock Museum,** Route 55 (✆ **845/583-4300;** Mon–Sat 10am–5pm, Sun 10am–3pm; free admission) with photos and exhibits from the festival and events since.

Tips   Out & About

Sullivan County is one of the few predominantly rural counties around that openly courts gay visitors and promotes gay-friendly establishments. Look for the "Out in the Catskills" rack card that highlights certain gay-friendly businesses and other informational brochures with a gay and lesbian rainbow symbol on them.

The surprising village of **Narrowsburg,** perched on the Pennsylvania border, is on the upswing, with a number of galleries and restaurants now populating its main street and a rich cultural life for such a small town, with an opera company in summer residence at the Tusten Theater, a film series, and chamber music concerts. Its biggest attraction, aside from its picturesque location at the edge of Big Eddy, is the **Fort Delaware Museum of Colonial History** ✦, 6615 Rte. 97 (© **845/252-6660;** www.fortdelaware.org; Memorial Day to Labor Day, Wed–Sun 10am–5:30pm; admission $4 adults, $3.25 seniors, $2.25 children ages 6–16, $11 families), a fascinating living-history museum. Originally established as a museum in 1959, Fort Delaware was a stockaded settlement of the Connecticut Yankees who settled in the Delaware Valley in the mid–18th century. Interpreters in 18th-century period dress reenact the work habits and traditions of the day, including candle making, spinning and weaving, woodworking, blacksmithing, and cooking over open fire pits. Interactive exhibits and children's workshops are intelligently designed and really involve kids in history; they can even be a part of day-long apprentice programs, craft days, and 3-day camps in which they learn an 18th-century skill. The **Delaware Arts Center,** 37 Main St. (© **845/252-7576**), is an active cultural center with art exhibits and concerts held in the historic Arlington Hotel.

Minisink Battleground Park (daily 8am–dusk; free admission), County Road 168 near Route 97 in Minisink Ford, is a 57-acre park on the site of a 1779 Revolutionary War battle, the only one that took place along the Upper Delaware. A tiny colonial militia took on Tories and Native Americans that were aligned with the British. Onsite are self-guided trails and an interpretive history center.

SHOPPING

There are a number of good antiques stores in Sullivan County; pick up a copy of the "Antiques Trail Map," available at many hotels and restaurants, as well as antiques shops. Among the best are: **Ferndale Marketplace,** 52 Ferndale Rd., Ferndale (© **845/292-8701**), a very large, 120-year-old country general store with seven dealers; **Antiques of Callicoon,** 26 Upper Main St., Callicoon (© **845/887-5918**), in a 19th-century building across from the train station; **Artisans Gallery,** 110 Mill St., Liberty (© **845/295-9278**); **Memories,** Route 17 Quickway, Parksville (© **845/292-4270**), a massive gallery between Livingston Manor and Liberty; and **Hamilton's Antique Shoppe,** Route 55/Main Street, Neversink (© **845/985-2671**). Roscoe has a number of cute shops (in addition to all the fishing gear and tackle stores), including **Annie's Place,** Stewart Avenue, Roscoe (© **607/498-4139**), with contemporary country gifts; and the perfectly named **The Fisherman's Wife,** Stewart Avenue, Roscoe (© **607/498-6055**), a purveyor of antiques and collectibles.

Narrowsburg has a nice art gallery, **River Gallery,** Main Street (© **845/252-3230**), showing contemporary artists and photographers, while its **Delaware Arts Alliance,** 37 Main St. (© **845/252-7576**), shows local artists.

SPORTS & OUTDOOR ACTIVITIES

FISHING　Anglers will be in heaven in this part of the Catskill Mountains. Sullivan County possess several of the best trout streams in North America; the Delaware River and Beaverkill and Willowemoc Creeks are among the most storied trout-fishing rivers in the world, and the famed fly-fisher Lee Wulff established a fly-fishing school here. The fishing season, which attracts anglers from across the globe, begins in April. Pick up a copy of the *Sullivan County Visitors Guide* for a full listing of lakes, streams, and fishing preserves in the county. The **New York State Fish Hatchery,** 402 Mongaup Rd., Livingston Manor (© **845/ 439-4328**), open year-round, is the site of more than one million brown trout raised annually. For instruction and guided incursions into the world of fly-fishing, try **Catskill Flies & Fishing Adventures,** Roscoe (© **607/498-6146**); **Baxter House River Outfitters & Guide Services,** Old Route 17, Roscoe (© **800/ 905-5095** or 607/498-5811); or **Tite-Line Fly Fishing School,** 563 Gulf Rd., Roscoe (© **607/498-5866**). **Gone Fishing Guide Service,** 20 Lake St., Narrowsburg (© **845/252-3657**), also offers half- and full-day float fishing trips. Among the many providers of equipment and tackle are **Beaverkill Angler,** Stewart Avenue, Roscoe (© **607/498-5194**), and **The Little Store,** 26 Broad St., Roscoe (© **607/498-5553**).

GOLF　Golf fans can tee it up at some fine courses in scenic locales. Try the championship courses at: **Grossinger Country Club,** 26 Rte. 52 E., Liberty (© **888/448-9686;** www.grossingergolf.net; greens fees $45–$65), whose "Big G," which features an island green on hole 13, is considered one of the most beautiful and difficult in the Northeast; **Concord Resort & Golf Club,** Route 17/Concord Road, Kiamesha Lake (© **845/794-4000;** www.concordresort.com; greens fees $35–$95), which has two championship courses, one called "the Monster," a *Golf Digest* top 100 course for more than 25 years; and **Villa Roma Country Club,** 356 Villa Roma Rd., Callicoon (© **800/533-6767;** www.villa roma.com; greens fees $55–$65).

HIKING　In Sullivan County, there's very good hiking along the **Tusten Mountain Trail,** a moderately difficult but immensely scenic 3-mile round-trip trail maintained by the National Park Service. The trailhead near the Ten Mile River access site off Route 97 between Barryville and Narrowsburg, and the trail climbs to an elevation of more than 1,100 feet. For more information, call © **570/ 685-4871** or visit www.nps.gov/upde.

RAFTING & KAYAKING　The rivers of Sullivan County, lacing the foothills of the Catskills and Pocono Mountains, are ideal for rafting, canoeing, tubing, and kayaking. The most experienced operator for boat rentals of all sorts is **Lander's River Trips** in Narrowsburg (© **800/252-3925** or 845/557-8783; www. landersrivertrips.com). The company also operates campgrounds along the Delaware River and rents mountain bikes (and offers combined canoeing or rafting plus camping trips).

WILDLIFE　Sullivan County plays host to more **bald eagles** than any other spot on the East Coast, and the state set aside more than 1,200 acres specifically for the protection of the migrant eagle population of about 100 that return every winter. **The Eagle Institute,** Barryville (© **845/557-6162;** www.eagleinstitute. org; weekends Dec–Mar), offers interpretative programs and guided eagle watches on weekends during the winter migrating season. Along Route 55A is a bald eagle observation site on the **Neversink Reservoir,** just outside the village of Neversink. Guided bald-eagle habitat trails are found in **Pond Eddy,** with the

Upper Delaware Scenic and Recreational River National Park Services; the best times to see bald eagles are December and early March (call ℂ **570/729-8251** for additional information).

WHERE TO STAY
EXPENSIVE

The Inn at Lake Joseph ★★★   Although pricey, this professionally run luxury country inn, secluded on a 20-acre estate and surrounded by forest and down a wooded path from beautiful Lake Joseph, may be just the place for a very relaxing and pampering getaway. Formerly a summer residence and then a retreat for two Catholic Cardinals, the 135-year-old Victorian estate exudes elegance and tranquillity. Rooms are divided among the main house, carriage house, and cottage, the last two nicely secluded and though more modern and rustic than the manor house, I think they're more special. Several of those rooms are gigantic, with cathedral ceilings; many have private sun decks and a couple, full kitchens. All but one room has a gas fireplace, and a guest kitchen is open around the clock. Pets are welcome in the outbuildings. The inn overflows with relaxing spots, from the lovely pool to hammocks and swings strewn in the woods.

400 Saint Joseph Rd., Forestburgh, NY 12777. ℂ **845/791-9506.** Fax 845/794-1948. www.lakejoseph.com. 15 units. $170–$280 double; $270–$385 suite. Rates include full breakfast. AE, DC, DISC, MC, V. Free parking. **Amenities:** Outdoor swimming pool; tennis court; boating facilities; bicycles; *In room:* A/C, TV/VCR, (some rooms have fridge, coffeemaker, hair dryer, microwave, Jacuzzi).

New Age Health Spa ★ *Finds*   A country-style, intimate destination spa tucked away in the hills at the edge of the Catskills State Forest Preserve, this is the perfect place for a relaxing retreat without the factory feel of some larger, more institutional spas. All kinds of treatments and classes, including tai chi, aqua aerobics, yoga, and meditation, are available; classes are included in the price. Guest rooms are located in five lodges and are very comfortable but not overly fancy; healthful spa-cuisine meals are served in the rustic dining room, which has a nice deck area for eating outdoors. Beautiful hiking trails wind through the 280-acre property (guided hikes are scheduled), and horses roam down by the stable. Lots of outdoor activities are programmed, as are frequent mind-and-body lectures. Guests are not allowed nicotine, caffeine, or alcohol, and guests caught smoking or drinking will be asked to leave. Check the website for specials.

658 Rte. 55, Neversink, NY 12765. ℂ **800/682-4348** or 845/985-7600. Fax 845/985-2467. www.newage healthspa.com. 37 units. $348–$608 double. Rates include 3 meals daily, classes and activities (spa treatments extra). AE, DC, DISC, MC, V. Free parking. **Amenities:** Restaurant; 2 outdoor tennis courts; full spa facilities; TV and computer lounge with Internet access. *In room:* A/C.

Villa Roma   A massive, all-inclusive resort huddled on hundreds of acres near Callicoon, Villa Roma is one of those old-school Catskills Resorts that provides as many round-the-clock activities as you can sign up for. From golf, tennis, and horseback riding to shuffle board, bowling, line dancing, and massages—as well as things like psychics, gala dinners, and talent shows—you won't be bored here, unless group activities aren't your bag. If that's the case, you're in trouble. The hotel property itself is a bit dated, even though there's been some recent remodeling. Rooms are standard hotel style, but this is the kind of place that's more about the public facilities, which are endless; the swimming pools and golf course, in particular, are first rate. Villa Roma is to some visitors like home away from home; many come back year after year, and a good number of them end up buying time shares here.

356 Villa Roma Rd., Callicoon, NY 12723. © **800/727-8455** or 845/887-4880. Fax 845/985-2467. www.villa roma.com. 270 units (including 50 suites). $170–$295 double; $298–$399 suite. Rates include 3 meals daily, classes, and activities (spa treatments extra). Special packages for golf and seniors available, as well as theme weekends and weekly stays. AE, DC, DISC, MC, V. Free valet parking. **Amenities:** Restaurant; 18-hole golf course; 5 outdoor swimming pools, 1 indoor pool; 2 indoor and 2 outdoor tennis courts; fitness center; massages and spa services; horseback riding; racquetball courts, snowmobiling. *In room:* A/C, TV, coffeemaker, hair dryer.

MODERATE

The Lodge at Rock Hill ★ *Value* This surprising hotel, on 65 acres facing a major road, was an old Howard Johnsons, but you'd never know it once inside. It was completely and handsomely redone in 2001 with sedate colors, warm tones, and excellent furnishings. Rooms are very large and impeccably clean. Out back, there are hiking trails through 65 acres of property. Take my word for it: behind a boring facade, which reveals its Ho Jo origins, is an excellent and very good-value hotel. The indoor pool with a deck and a nice big Jacuzzi is a huge bonus, as is the fact that the hotel is pet-friendly.

283 Rock Hill Dr., Rock Hill, NY 12775. © **866/RHLODGE** or 845/796-3100. Fax 845/796-3130. www. lodgeatrockhill.com. 73 units. $89–$179 double; $159–$239 suite. Rates include continental breakfast. AE, DC, DISC, MC, V. Free parking. **Amenities:** Indoor swimming pool; Jacuzzi; business center; video game room. *In room:* A/C, TV, dataport, coffeemaker, hair dryer.

The Reynolds House Inn and Motel ★ *Value* The oldest operational B&B in the county, this welcoming inn was built in 1902 as a "tourist home," or boarding house. John D. Rockefeller, a fishing fanatic, used to stay here, and "his" room, the largest and with a claw-foot tub, retains his name. The rooms are cozy and very attractively decorated, though bathrooms are on the small side. Today a charming Irishman and his wife run the inn, which also has inexpensive motel rooms and a cottage out back—perfect for long-term fishermen.

1934 Old Rte. 17 South, Roscoe, NY 12776. © **607/498-4422.** www.reynoldshouseinn.com. 7 units (in main house); 11 motel rooms. Main house $75–$110 double; motel rooms $55–$75 double. Rates include full breakfast. 2-night minimum on weekends May–Oct. AE, DC, DISC, MC, V. Free parking. *In room:* A/C, TV.

WHERE TO DINE
EXPENSIVE

Manny's Steakhouse & Seafood ★★ *Finds* STEAKHOUSE Hiding behind an undistinguished exterior that would seem appropriate for a strip mall chain restaurant, Manny's surprises with a spacious and nice, even elegant interior of warm tones and lots of wood. For lunch, there are good wraps (like the filet mignon) and sandwiches, while the classic steakhouse dinner menu emphasizes steaks and seafood (the name pretty much tells it like it is). Meat eaters can't go wrong with the prime porterhouse, prime rib, and baby back ribs; among fish and seafood, try the king crab legs or broiled flounder. There are also a number of good pastas, as well as a pretty decent and affordable wine list.

79 Sullivan Ave., Liberty. © **845/295-3170.** Reservations recommended. Main courses $12–$29. AE, MC, V. Daily 11:30am–10pm.

The 1906 Restaurant ★★ AMERICAN ECLECTIC/GRILL This 15-year-old upscale restaurant, a favorite of visitors and second-home owners in the area, has one of the best reputations in Sullivan County. The interior is almost homey, featuring lots of pine, tin ceilings, and ceiling fans, as well as an odd overdose of pink tablecloths. The menu is also a bit of a surprise, featuring anything but comfort food; it includes several exotic meats, such as ostrich and buffalo. Other signature dishes include steak au poivre, baby rack of lamb, and the 1906 burger, prepared with sautéed onions and mushrooms, Swiss cheese, and bourbon or

Tips **A Fine Catch**

Folks with fishing on their minds, but who prefer stocked ponds to world-class trout streams, might check out **Eldred Preserve,** Route 55, Eldred, NY 12732 (© **800/557-FISH; $75–$95 double**). The motel complex—rooms are simple but large—is built around a fishing preserve and ponds stocked with trout and catfish for either catch-and-release, or catch-and-keep. An outdoor pool and restaurant are on the premises.

chili corn sauce (it tries hard to prove its worth at $14). Specials exhibit some flair: They include Cajun shrimp over fettucine with jalapeño sauce, and veal rollatini with mushrooms and Marsala sauce. The wine list, with more than 175 selections, is one of the most extensive you'll find in the Catskills, and it's been continually recognized by *Wine Spectator.*

41 Lower Main St., Callicoon. © 845/887-1906. Reservations not accepted. Main courses $16–$32. AE, MC, V. Daily 7am–9pm.

INEXPENSIVE

Dave's Big Eddy Diner *(Value* AMERICAN   This adorable little restaurant with a retro feel and green paneled walls has a great location: on Narrowsburg's rapidly developing historic Main Street, with an awesome deck suspended over the Big Eddy of the Delaware River. The very solid and creative chef-owner playfully calls it a diner, but that's really a disservice. Though he offers some polished (but still inexpensive) diner foods at breakfast and lunch, the quality of the food and the surroundings outdistance pretty much any diner you've ever visited. The Cobb salad, Narrowsburg Cheese Steak, and Dave's signature Big Eddy burger are all delicious, as are the stir-fries. The chalkboard holds a list of daily specials; for dessert, don't miss the handmade deep-dish fruit pies.

40 Main St., Narrowsburg. © 845/252-3817. Reservations recommended weekends. Main courses $4.95–$14. MC, V. Wed–Fri 7am–4pm; Sat–Sun 7am–3pm and 6–9pm.

Roscoe Diner *(Kids* DINER   This large, classic American diner in the center of Roscoe, has a massive and diverse menu. It serves everything from expected diner fare like club sandwiches, burgers, and meatloaf to prime rib, stuffed filet of sole, and broiled lobster tails, plus Greek and Italian specialties. No matter what you're in the mood for, the Roscoe Diner should be able to satisfy just about any food urge. Kids should be happy with the children's menu, which offers nine choices. All baking is done on the premises, and you know what that means: Save room for the pie (or any of the very long list of pastries and cakes).

Rte. 17 (exit 94), Roscoe. © 607/498-4405. Reservations not accepted. Main courses $5.45–$30. AE, DC, DISC, MC, V. Daily 7am–9pm.

AFTER DARK

Callicoon Theater, 30 Olympia St., Callicoon (© **845/887-4460**), is a cool single-screen 1948 "post Deco" theater still in use, showing first-run and art and independent films. **Tunsten Theater,** 210 Bridge St., Narrowsburg (© **845/252-7576**), is a fantastic, nicely renovated Deco-styled theater that seats 160 for live music, including blues, jazz, chamber, and theater performances; the Delaware Valley Opera is in residence at the theater during the summer. The annual summer **Jazzfest** at the theater produces a great lineup of bands in May and June; call © **845/252-7576** for schedules.

9

The Capital Region: Saratoga Springs & Albany

by Neil E. Schlecht

Sandwiched between the gentility of the Upper Hudson River Valley and the wilds of the Adirondack Mountains are two towns at polar opposites. The capital city of the Empire State, Albany is an everyman's working city, home to state legislators, lobbyists, and banking and insurance industry workers. Just a half-hour away, Saratoga Springs is all about leisure: Its relaxed pace and cultural refinement override such prosaic matters as work.

Virtually equidistant from New York City, Boston, and Montreal, Albany is ideally placed for a state capital. On the banks of the Upper Hudson, Albany, now 350 years old, lays claim to being the oldest chartered city in the United States. The original Dutch settlement Beverwyck is today a city dominated by government business, one much more accustomed to lobbyists than tourists, but it has a surprisingly full slate of

culture and architecture to entertain anyone visiting without a government or business agenda.

Saratoga Springs, a graceful and historic resort town, lies just north of the capital. The site of the tide-turning 1777 Battle of Saratoga, the town later transformed itself into one of the country's most popular vacation destinations, renowned for its therapeutic mineral springs, expansive urban parks, and beautiful downtown dominated by Victorian architecture. By the mid–19th century, Saratoga had earned the moniker "Queen of the Spas." Saratoga Springs especially thrives in warm months, when its elegant Race Course hosts one of the nation's most prestigious thoroughbred racing seasons and the city simmers with a rich platter of cultural events, including prestigious ballet and music companies in residence.

1 Orientation

ARRIVING

BY PLANE Most visitors traveling by air will arrive via **Albany International Airport,** 737 Albany-Shaker Rd. (© **518/242-2299;** www.albanyairport.com), located about 10 minutes from downtown Albany and about a half-hour from Saratoga Springs. The airport is served by most major domestic and several international airlines. The information desk can provide details on getting to either Albany or Saratoga Springs, as well as basic lodging and tourist information. The significantly smaller **Saratoga County Airport** (© **518/885-5354)** handles small charter flights.

Ground transportation to Albany or Saratoga Springs is by bus, airport shuttle, private car, charter limo, courtesy car, or taxi. To Albany, the Capital District Transit Authority (CDTA) operates **ShuttleFly** buses that depart the airport Monday through Friday several times each hour between 6am and 11pm (on weekends service begins about a half-hour earlier). For additional information, call CDTA at ✆ **518/482-8822.** Taxis are also on hand at airport arrival gates. You can make airport transportation reservations by calling **Albany Yellow Taxi** (✆ **518/869-2258**), **Saratoga Taxi** (✆ **518/584-2700**), or **Saratoga Capitaland Taxi** (✆ **518/583-3131**), among taxis, and **Premiere Limo** (✆ **800/515-6123** or 518/459-6123) or **A Destiny Limousine of Saratoga** (✆ **518/587-5221**), among limousine services. From the airport, taxi fares to Albany and Saratoga Springs are about $15 and $40, respectively; a limo should cost about $50 to Albany and $90 to Saratoga.

Driving from Albany International Airport   To downtown Albany, you can either take Albany-Shaker Road south, which will put you close to the visitor's center and Broadway, or take I-87 south to I-90 west. The highways that ring Albany are notoriously confusing, though, and if you go the wrong way, you may end up circling around for a seemingly interminable amount of time.

The fastest way to reach Saratoga Springs is to take I-87 north, and exit 13N. Follow Route 9 north about 5 miles to downtown Saratoga Springs.

BY CAR   Most major rental car companies, including **Avis** (✆ 800/331-1212), **Budget** (✆ 800/527-0700), Enterprise (✆ 800/Rent-A-Car), **Hertz** (✆ 800/654-3131), **National** (✆ 800/227-7368), and **Thrifty** (✆ 800/THRIFTY), have representatives at Albany International Airport.

To get to Albany from points north, take the Adirondack Northway (I-87) south to I-90 east to I-787 south. From points south, take the New York State Thruway (I-87) to exit 23 to I-787 north. From the western part of the state, take the New York State Thruway (I-87) to exit 24 and follow I-90 to I-787 south.

To Saratoga Springs from points south, take I-87 to exit 13 south and Route 9 right into town; from the north, take I-87 south to exit 15 and Route 50 south. Saratoga Springs is about 3 hours by car from New York City. From Albany, the drive to Saratoga Springs is about a half-hour.

BY TRAIN   The new **Albany-Rensselaer Rail Station,** 525 East St., Rensselaer (✆ **518/462-5763**), receives Amtrak trains from western New York (Empire Service), the midwestern U.S., and Massachusetts (Lake Shore Limited), Canada (Maple Leaf), and points north and south of the capital (Adirondack and Ethan Allen Express Lines). Taxis are available for travel to downtown Albany.

To Saratoga Springs, there is daily service on Amtrak's Adirondack (originating in New York City and Montreal) and Ethan Allen Express (traveling from New York City to Vermont) Lines. The Saratoga station is located at West Avenue and Station Lane; there are taxis as well as Enterprise and Thrifty rental car agencies at the station. For more information and reservations, contact Amtrak at ✆ **800/USA-RAIL** or visit www.amtrak.com.

BY BUS   Greyhound (✆ **518/434-8095;** www.greyhound.com) and **Adirondack Trailways** (✆ **800/858-8555;** www.escapemaker.com/ny/capitalsaratoga.html) travel to both Albany and Saratoga Springs. The **Upstate Transit Albany-Saratoga Bus Service** (✆ **518/584-5252**) travels between Albany and Saratoga.

2 Saratoga Springs ✶✶✶

35 miles north of Albany; 190 miles north of New York City; 290 miles east of Buffalo; 200 miles northwest of Boston

Saratogians proudly call their town a city in the country, one that offers the sophistication and culture of a major metropolis but the greenery and unhurried pace of a rural area. A historic and stately town that saw its fortunes rise with the explosion of casino and thoroughbred racing tourism in the mid– to late 19th century, Saratoga has bounced back from postwar malaise and is again becoming a hot resort spot in upstate New York. Saratoga hits high stride with the advent of 6 weeks of horse racing at one of the world's prettiest tracks, public parks in full bloom, and an enviable offering of culture, both the New York City Ballet and Philadelphia Orchestra in summer residence. Horse-mad, cigar-smoking track bettors mingle with urban sophisticates in designer outfits at outdoor cocktail parties, while families hit the trails in Saratoga State Spa Park and soak up classical music concerts and outdoor picnics.

Saratoga today is indistinguishable from horse racing and its attendant galas, but its historic importance is well established. Nearby is the site of the most famous battle of the Revolutionary War, the 1777 Battle of Saratoga, which marked the turning point in favor of Washington's American forces. At the end of the 1800s, Saratoga was touted for the healing properties of its naturally carbonated mineral springs; at its apex, the small town counted two of the largest hotels in the world, each with more than 1,000 rooms. Saratoga lost many of its famous hotels to postwar razing, but this graceful small town retains an outstanding collection of predominantly Victorian architecture. Saratoga Springs has remained very popular with the horse set and culture vultures, but over the past decade or so has begun to welcome droves of new visitors who discover that this delightful town's elegant, time-honored traditions live on.

VISITOR INFORMATION
Saratoga has some of New York's finest tourism information. The **Urban Heritage Area Visitors Center,** 297 Broadway (© **518/587-3241**), has a wealth of helpful information not only on Saratoga Springs, but much of upstate New York. It also has regional displays, videos, and memorabilia, and offers walking tours in season. From April through November, it's open daily, 9am to 4pm; from December through March, it's open Monday through Saturday, 9am to 4pm. The Saratoga County Chamber of Commerce also operates an **Information Booth** (no phone), Broadway at Congress Park, open July and August from 9am to 5pm daily. You can also visit the chamber's website at **www.saratoga.org**. Free area maps are available at both the visitor's center and the information both.

CITY LAYOUT
Saratoga Springs is relatively small and very easy to navigate. Everything revolves around the main axis, Broadway, which is Route 9 once you come in to town. Most restaurants and shops are located on the small streets off of Broadway (though there are plenty on Broadway, too), such as Phila, Caroline, and Spring streets. Saratoga Spa State Park is just a mile southwest of downtown down Broadway, while Union Avenue, site of grand Victorian homes and the Saratoga Race Course, is a couple of blocks due west of Broadway. Skidmore College is a couple of miles straight up North Broadway.

GETTING AROUND
BY PUBLIC TRANSPORTATION Most of Saratoga is easily walked, but in summer (late June to Labor Day) a **Saratoga Springs Visitor Trolley** operates a Broadway loop ($1 round-trip).

BY CAR Car rental agencies in and around Saratoga Springs include **Enterprise Rent-A-Car,** 180 So. Broadway (© **518/587-0687**); **Morris Ford-Mercury,** Route 50 (© **518/399-9188**); **New Country Saratoga Auto Park,** Route 50

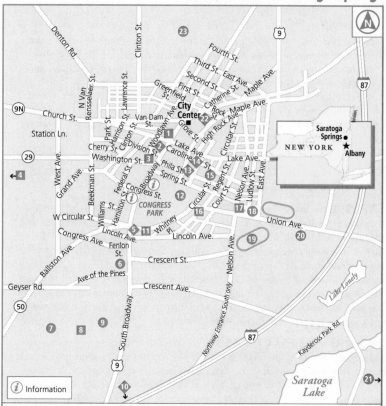

ACCOMMODATIONS ■
Adelphi Hotel **3**
Batcheller Mansion Inn **11**
Circular Manor B&B **16**
Gideon Putnam Hotel
  and Conference Center **8**
The Mansion Inn **4**
Saratoga Arms **1**
Union Gables B&B **17**

DINING ◆
Beverly's **13**
Chez Sophie Bistro **10**
Chianti Il Ristorante **5**
Sperry's Restaurant **14**
The Olde Bryan Inn **22**
The Wine Bar **2**

ATTRACTIONS ●
The Children's Museum
  at Saratoga **15**
The Gardens at Yaddo **20**
Historical Society of Saratoga
  Springs and Canfield Casino **12**
National Museum of Dance
  & Hall of Fame **6**
National Museum of Racing
  and Hall of Fame **18**
Saratoga Automobile Museum **9**
Saratoga National Historical Park **21**
Saratoga Race Course **19**
Saratoga Spa State Park **7**
The Tang Teaching
  Museum and Art Gallery **23**

Moments **Rewards for Early Risers**

Early morning before races is a great time to come out to the track; expert commentary accompanies the thoroughbreds as they go through their morning workouts, and a buffet breakfast is served each racing day on the Clubhouse Porch from 7 to 9:30am.

(© 518/584-7272); and **Saratoga Car Rental, Inc.,** 360 Maple Ave. (© 518/583-4448).

BY TAXI   Taxi services include **Saratoga Taxi,** 15 West Harrison St. (© 518/584-2700); **A Destiny Limousine,** 80 Church Ave., Ballston Spa (© 518/587-5221); and **Saratoga Capitaland Taxi,** 285 Broadway (© 518/583-3131).

EXPLORING SARATOGA SPRINGS

Saratoga is a delight to explore on foot, whether through its plentiful parks and gardens or its historic streets that are graced with fine examples of late-19th and early-20th-century architecture. But exploring Saratoga also means doing what visitors have come to this resort town to do for many decades: see a horse race at the internationally renowned Saratoga Race Course; walk or ski in Saratoga State Spa Park; and take advantage of some of the best summer cultural life any city has to offer. Saratoga Springs may be at its most enjoyable in summer, but the shoulder seasons reveal a pleasant, slower pace.

THE MANE ATTRACTIONS

Saratogians like to say that their town isn't just about horses, but during the race season, everything else definitely takes a back seat to the track. Saratoga's race season lasts 6 weeks, from the end of July to Labor Day. The Saratoga Race Course, built in 1864, is the oldest thoroughbred track in the nation, acclaimed as perhaps the most beautiful in the country; its fans are legion. If you're in Saratoga during the meet, it's an obligatory visit to join the socialites and the hard-core race fans and bettors. Races are held every day but Tuesday, with the first race post time at 1pm. The Saratoga Race Course, a 350-acre, 1⅛-mile track, is located at 267 Union Ave. General admission is $3 and Clubhouse admission, $5. Reserved seats in the Clubhouse are $8; grandstand, $5. For advanced ticket purchase, contact the **New York Racing Association** at © **718/641-4700,** or during race season, © 518/584-6200, ext. 360. You can also visit their website, **www.nyra.com/saratoga,** for tickets, schedules, and additional information.

Race fans may also enjoy a bit of harness racing, which you can witness year-round at the **Saratoga Equine Sports Center,** Nelson Avenue (© **518/584-2110**). Races generally start at 7:40pm, but see **www.saratogaraceway.com** for the exact schedule. Polo anyone? From June through September, **Saratoga Polo** organizes matches played at Lodge Field (corner of Crescent and Nelson aves.) and Whitney Field (corner of Bloomfield and Denton roads), usually 4 nights a week at 5:30pm. For more information, call © **518/584-8108.**

THE TOP SITES

Historical Society of Saratoga Springs and Canfield Casino   In its heyday in the late 19th century, Saratoga was the elegant refuge of high-society high rollers. The Canfield Casino, built in 1870 in Congress Park, is a stately red brick Victorian that today is home only to the ghosts of gamblers past and a museum and historical collection that chronicles Saratoga Springs's era as a resort known the world over. The original casino was built by John Morrissey, a heavyweight champion boxer turned entrepreneur, and later made over in haute style by a wealthy gambler, Richard Canfield, at the turn of the 20th century. Canfield's lavish decor included marble tables, massive mirrors, grand chandeliers, and the world's largest seamless rug. In the casino's parlors, Amelia Earhart was feted and grand balls and teas attracted the Gilded Age's fabulous wealthy. The Historical Society's exhibitions of photography depict Saratoga Springs in all its splendor, and on the second floor is a re-creation of the high-stakes room and parlors with an original collection of handcrafted John Henry Belter furnishings. On the top floor, eight rooms re-create Pine Grove, the prominent Walworth family's Victorian home that was demolished in the 1950s. Allow about an hour.

Congress Park (off Broadway). (℃) **518/584-6920**. www.saratogahistory.org. Admission $4 adults, $3 seniors and children ages 12–17, free for children under 12. Memorial Day to Labor Day daily 10am–4pm; winter Wed–Sat 10am–4pm and Sun 1–4pm. Free guided casino tours, summer Tues 1pm and Wed–Thurs 11am.

National Museum of Racing and Hall of Fame   Across the road from the famous Saratoga Race Course, this midsized museum pays tribute to three centuries of thoroughbred racing in the U.S. Trophies, memorabilia, artworks, and film tell the story of the sport that grips the attention of so many in Saratoga during summer race season. The Hall of Fame celebrates the greatest names, both jockeys and horses, in the sport's history. Uniforms and artifacts are on display, and interactive screens allow visitors to relive great moments in racing. The museum is mostly for true fans, though even those without much interest in horse racing can pick up some interesting tidbits. For example, did you know that the average racehorse weighs 1,000 pounds? And whereas a Ferrari can go from zero to 60 mph in 5.5 seconds, a racehorse can accelerate to 42 mph in just 2.5 seconds. The museum is unlikely to detain you for more than 45 minutes.

191 Union Ave. (℃) **518/584-0400**. www.racingmuseum.org. Admission $7 adults, $5 seniors and students, free for children under 5. Mon–Sat 10am–4:30-pm; Sun noon–4:30pm (during the Saratoga racing meet, the museum is open daily 9am–5pm).

Saratoga National Historical Park (★)   Saratoga was no less than the turning point in the American Revolution. In 1777, American troops defeated the British army—considered to be one of the most significant military victories in history—and forced its surrender on October 17, prompting France to recognize American independence and sign on as its ally. Today this historical area is a National Park, which comprises the 4-square-mile battlefield in Stillwater, the General Philip Schuyler House, and the Saratoga Monument in the nearby village of Victory. A 9½-mile battlefield tour road traces American defensive positions, battle sites, and British defensive positions, with a series of 10 interpretive stops along the way. Also on the grounds is the 4-mile Wilkinson Trail for hiking and cross-country skiing. Living history demonstrations are presented in summer months.

The Schuyler House, located 8 miles north in Schuylerville, was the residence of General Philip Schuyler; burned by the British, the present reconstruction was built after the American victory. The Saratoga Monument is a 155-foot memorial that marks Burgoyne's surrender. Plan on several hours if you go to all the sites.

648 Rte. 32, Stillwater (15 miles southeast of Saratoga Springs). (℃) **518/664-9821**. www.nps.gov/sara. Admission $5 private vehicle, $3 individual (on foot, bike, or horse) or by National Parks Pass or Golden Pass (p. 66 for details). Visitor Center, year-round 9am–5pm; Tour Road Apr 1 to mid-Nov, daily 9am–5pm; The Schuyler House, May 25 to Labor Day, guided tours Wed–Sun 9:30am–4:30pm.

Finds **Hyde Collection Art Museum**

Saratoga Springs's charms can make the resort town difficult to leave, but art fans may be pried loose by the presence of a splendid collection of Old and Modern Masters just 20 minutes north of town in Glens Falls. The Hyde Collection Art Museum, housed in a gorgeous renovated mansion, is reminiscent of New York City's Frick Collection in its breadth and beautiful setting. Among the treasures assembled in the 1912, neo-Renaissance Florentine-style villa are works by Raphael, da Vinci, Van Dyck, Tiepolo, El Greco, Reubens, Tintoretto, Homer, Whistler, Turner, Degas, Seurat, Renoir, Picasso, and van Gogh. The most remarkable works are Rembrandt's unusual *Portrait of Christ* (1655–57), purchased from the Russian government in 1934, and Botticelli's small *Annunciation* (1492), the first piece collected by the Hydes. Louis and Charlotte Hyde were a wealthy industrialist couple who began collecting European art in the 1920s; their mansion is furnished as they maintained it, with French and Italian 17th- and 18th-century pieces and massive tropical plants in the skylit central courtyard. A new wing hosts temporary exhibits and a gift shop. The museum was closed in summer 2003 for a year-long renovation project; it's expected to reopen mid-July 2004. You'll need at least an hour here. The museum is located about 8 miles north of Saratoga Springs at 16 Warren St. in Glens Falls (© **518/792-1761;** www.hydeartmuseum.org). Admission is free, but donations are accepted. It's open Tuesday through Saturday from 10am to 5pm; Thursday until 7pm; and Sunday from noon to 5pm.

Saratoga Spa State Park ★ *Kids*   Saratoga Springs rose to prominence in the mid–19th century as a spa town, on the strengths of mineral springs and baths that drew wealthy patrons to exercise and "take the waters." Now a National Historic Landmark—and certainly one of the prettiest urban parks in the country—Saratoga Spa State Park is still a relaxing place to escape from daily pressures. The 2,200-acre park is a pine forest with natural geysers; it's home to a swimming pool complex, two golf courses, endless trails for walking and cross-country skiing in winter, picnic pavilions, a skating rink, tennis courts, and two restored bathhouses, designed in the classical European spa tradition. Also tucked into the park are a large historic hotel, three restaurants, the renowned Saratoga Performing Arts Center and two small museums. You could easily spend all day in the park, depending on the diversions you choose.

19 Roosevelt Dr. © **518/584-2535.** www.saratogaspastatepark.org. Admission for some activities. Open year-round dawn to dusk.

MORE TO SEE & DO

The Children's Museum at Saratoga *Kids*   Less of a museum than a terrific playground, the space includes adorable areas meant to create a little person's main street circa 1920: there's a bank, a general store, a diner, a schoolhouse, and a fire station (complete with a sliding pole). Kids will be entertained for at least an hour or two.

69 Caroline Street. © 518/584-5540. www.childrensmuseumatsaratoga.org. Admission $4, free for children under 1. July to Labor Day Mon–Sat 9:30am–4:30pm; Labor Day to June Tues–Sat 9:30am–4:30pm and Sun noon–4:30pm.

National Museum of Dance & Hall of Fame ★ *Kids* Housed in the old Washington Bath House, a handsome European-style mineral spa built in 1918, this is the only museum in the country dedicated to American professional dance. Its archives, photographs, and exhibits of sets and costumes chronicle a century of dance. The museum is also a place that makes new contributions to the field; on-site are three full-size dance studios modeled after those of the New York City Ballet, which not coincidentally takes up residence in Saratoga Springs every July. Visitors have the opportunity to view rehearsals as well as participate in workshops, classes, and lectures. For children or adults interested in dance, the museum's programs are excellent learning tools. Plan on about a half-hour, unless there are rehearsals or workshops.

99 South Broadway (Rte. 9). © 518/584-2225. www.dancemuseum.org. Admission $6.50 adults, $5 seniors and students, $3 children under 12. Apr–Oct Tues–Sun 10am–5pm; Nov–Mar Sat–Sun 10am–5pm.

Saratoga Automobile Museum *Kids* Housed in an old bottling plant in the middle of Saratoga Springs Spa State Park, this surprising museum will delight car lovers. On view are some interesting classic automobiles representing the once-vital New York State auto industry, such as Charles A. Lindbergh's 1928 Franklin, made in Syracuse, and an extraordinary 1931 Pierce Arrow, manufactured in Buffalo. The top floor is devoted to race cars, and there are curiosities like the 1957 BMW Isetta 300, called the "Rolling Egg." Kids into cars will love the tables set up with pads of paper and crayons and an invitation to draw and display their "Dream Car." A spin through should take about 45 minutes.

Saratoga Springs Spa State Park. © 518/587-1935. www.saratogaautomobilemuseum.org. Admission $7 adults, $5 seniors, $3.50 children ages 6–16, free for children 5 and under. May–Nov daily 10am–5pm; Nov–Apr Tues–Sun 10am–5pm.

The Tang Teaching Museum and Art Gallery *Finds* The first art museum in Saratoga Springs, on the campus of Skidmore College, the Tang is most notable for its striking modern architecture. The stunning building in stone, concrete, and stainless steel by Antoine Predock slopes gently out of the ground and is surrounded by white pines, tucked neatly into the landscape; two large exterior staircases ascend and effectively create a short cut across campus that goes over the top of the building. The irregularly shaped galleries inside the 39,000-foot museum host often challenging contemporary art and cross-disciplinary exhibits (highlighting its role as a teaching institution). Allow about an hour to explore.

815 North Broadway. © 518/580-8080. www.skidmore.edu/tang. Free admission. Tues–Sun 11am–5pm.

ESPECIALLY FOR KIDS

Saratoga Springs is a nice and relaxed place for families, with plenty of parks and a handful of sights that should entertain children of all ages. Most kids would love to attend a thoroughbred horse race at the **Saratoga Springs Race Course,** one of the most famous and beautiful tracks in the world. There are great features for kids at the track, including free walking tours of the stable area, a tram ride, and starting gate demonstration. An interactive exhibit, the Discovery Paddock, teaches children how horses and jockeys prepare for races, and kids can even ride the "Equipony" and dress up like a jockey, "weigh in" on a scale, and hammer a shoe on a mock-horse hoof. Open every racing day from 8am to 9am in season.

Taking the Waters

Native Americans believed the waters of Saratoga Springs had natural therapeutic properties, and so did early Americans such as George Washington and Alexander Hamilton. Saratoga Springs became a famous spa town in the 19th century, and was known as "Queen of the Spas," with hotels hosting visitors seeking the local mineral waters for drinking and mineral baths. A geological fault line runs through Saratoga Springs and a solid layer of shale, producing naturally carbonated waters from deep limestone beds. Saratoga Springs's heritage as a mineral spa resort town lives on, if on a smaller scale. **Lincoln Mineral Baths,** South Broadway (at the entrance to Saratoga Spa State Park; ✆ **518/583-2880;** www.gideonputnam.com), makes the most of the town's heritage with a full-service spa in one of the old classic spa buildings, built in the 1930s. Charmingly low-tech and reminiscent of old-world European spas, it even retains old steam cubicles and instruments. Services include mineral baths, massages, reflexology, body wraps, and hot stone therapy. Look for the Lincoln Baths to move into the **Roosevelt Bath House,** also a historic building, in the Saratoga Spa State Park in the near future. More modern is **The Crystal Spa,** 120 South Broadway (✆ **518/584-2556;** www.thecrystalspa.com), also offering clay and mud wraps, facials, and "pamper packages." Credit cards are not accepted.

You can also take a **self-guided tour** of Saratoga's mineral springs. There are 16 spots in and around the city, in Congress Park, Saratoga Spa State Park, and High Rock Park. Pick up the tour brochure, "Tasting Tour of Saratoga's Springs," at the Saratoga Springs Visitor Center.

The **Saratoga Children's Museum,** with its cute play areas, is a no-brainer for tots, and the **Saratoga Automobile Museum** (p. 267) is also a fun outing. **Saratoga Springs Spa State Park** is a delightful urban park with miles of hiking trails, two swimming pools and a skating rink, fun in any season. The Saratoga Visitor's Center publishes a brochure called "Things to Do with Kids!"

ORGANIZED TOURS

Saratoga Race Course, Union Ave. (✆ **518/584-6200;** www.nyra.com), offers free walking tours of the stable area and a tram ride and starting gate demonstration, daily, from 8am to 9am in season. The **Upper Hudson River Railroad,** 3 Railroad Place, North Creek (✆ **518/241-5334;** www.upperhudsonriverr. com), is a scenic passenger train ride that departs from the North Creek depot and runs along the Hudson into the Adirondacks (spring, summer, and fall; $12 adults, $11 seniors, $8 children ages 3-11). For guided hiking, cycling, rock climbing, and snowshoeing adventures, as well as equipment rentals, contact **All Outdoors,** 35 Van Dam St. (✆ **518/587-0455;** www.all-outdoors.com).

OUTDOOR PURSUITS

For additional information on all outdoor activities in Saratoga Springs, consult the website **http://guides.saratoga.org/web/attractions/outdoorfun/index. htm.**

BIKING, IN-LINE SKATING & JOGGING The 2,200-acre Saratoga Spa State Park is by far the best place in town, with tons of trails in a gorgeous park just minutes from downtown—in fact, within walking or jogging distance.

BOATING & FISHING Saratoga Lake, on the outskirts of town, is the place for boating and fishing enthusiasts. **Lake Lonely Boat Livery,** 378 Crescent Ave., Saratoga Springs (✆ **518/587-1721**), has a tackle shop and rowboat and canoe rentals; there are largemouth bass, northern pike, and pan fish in the lake. **Point Breeze Marina,** 1459 Rte. 9P, Saratoga Lake (✆ **518/587-3397**), is the largest marina in town and rents boats, canoes, and pontoons. **Saratoga Boatworks,** 549 Union Ave., Rte. 9P, Saratoga Lake (✆ **518/584-2628**), rents ski boats, pontoons, and fishing boats. **Saratoga Rowing Center,** 251 County Rte. 67, Saratoga Springs (✆ **518/584-7844**), is a sports shop dedicated solely to rowing, with rentals and instruction.

GARDENS Garden and horticultural enthusiasts should visit **The Gardens at Yaddo,** handsome turn-of-the-20th-century gardens and a working artists' community created by a philanthropist couple. A Rose Garden with a fountain, terraces and pergola was inspired by Italian Renaissance gardens, while the Rock Garden features ponds and fountains. The Yaddo Gardens, on Union Avenue (near exit 14 of I-87), are open to the public free of charge, with guided tours on weekends at 11am, from mid-June to Labor Day and also Tuesdays during racing season. **Congress Park,** off Broadway, was developed beginning in 1826; it has nature walks and ponds, and a wealth of tree species; the Visitor Center even publishes a free guide for easy identification. **Saratoga Spa State Park** is 2,200 acres of woodlands and trails featuring naturally carbonated mineral springs.

GOLF **Saratoga Lake Golf Club,** 35 Grace Moore Rd. (off Lake Rd.), Saratoga Springs (✆ **518/581-6616;** www.saratogalakegolf.com), is a public 18-hole course, opened in 2001 on 200 acres near the lake. Greens fees are $18 to $30. **Saratoga Spa Golf,** 60 Roosevelt Dr. (✆ **518/584-2006;** www.saratogaspagolf.com), is an 18-hole in the pine forests of Saratoga Spa State Park. Greens fees are $11 to $25. **Saratoga National Golf Club,** 458 Union Ave., Saratoga Springs (✆ **518/583-4653;** www.golfsaratoga.com), sits on 400 acres of rolling hills in wetlands within pitching range of the Race Course. *Golf Digest* ranked it

---

Architectural Tours

Saratoga Springs is awash in splendid examples of Victorian and other diverse styles of architecture, from Queen Anne and Colonial Revival to Early Federal, Greek Revival, and English Gothic. To get a feel for the array of styles, simply stroll down Union Avenue, Circular Street, and others in the historic district, or take a more systematic approach by following the self-guided walking tours laid out in brochures of Saratoga's Historic West and East Sides, available at the Visitor Center. Each highlights about two dozen buildings in a manageable walking area.

The small town **Ballston Spa,** about 5 miles south of Saratoga Springs off Church Avenue (Route 50), is a Victorian village with about 20 or so notable houses and churches. Pamphlets for self-guided tours of Ballston Spa are also available at the Visitor Center.

#5 among "Best New Upscale Public Courses in the U.S." in 2001. You'll pay for the privilege: Greens fees are $85 to $100.

See **www.saratoga.org/specials/golf/index.asp** for golf special packages.

HORSE RACING   see "The Mane Attractions," above.

TENNIS   Use of the eight hard court and clay tennis courts in Saratoga Spa State Park is free to park visitors.

WINTER SPORTS   Saratoga Spa State Park (✆ **518/584-2535;** www.saratoga spastatepark.org) is the place for ice-skating, snowshoeing, and cross-country skiing, for which there are several miles of groomed and ungroomed trails used for both sports. Winter use trail maps are available at the Park Office.

SHOPPING

Until recently, Saratoga Springs had no chain stores in its historic downtown. Today, inevitably, local independent shops mingle with a small number of national chains, such as Gap, Eddie Bauer, and Banana Republic. In the heart of downtown, there are also about a half-dozen antiques dealers, mostly on Broadway and Regent Street, including **Mark Lawson Antiques,** 444 Broadway (✆ **518/587-8787**), and **Regent Street Antique Center,** 153 Regent St. (✆ **518/584-0107**), with 30 dealers under its historic roof. A good antiquarian bookseller is **Lyrical Ballad Bookstore,** 7-9 Phila St. (✆ **518/584-8779**). Jewelry, clothing, home furnishings and accessories, and gift shops line Broadway and dot other streets in historic downtown Saratoga Springs. A particularly interesting shop, specializing in contemporary American glass, is **Symmetry Gallery,** 348 Broadway (✆ **518/584-5090**). Check out **deJonghe Original Jewelry,** 470 Broadway (✆ **518/587-2435**), for, well, it's all in the name.

SARATOGA'S FARMS

The Saratoga area is blessed with a surfeit of farms, including dairy and horse farms, orchards, and farm stands. **Saratoga Apple,** 1174 Rte. 29, Schuylerville (✆ **518/695-3131**), is a year-round farmer's market and pick-your-own apple orchard with wagon rides in the autumn. **Weber's Farm,** 115 King Rd., Saratoga Springs, has a pick-your-own vegetable operation from May to December. **Hanehan's Pumpkins,** 223 County Rte. 67, Saratoga Springs is a farm stand that sells pumpkins, squash, and corn in season. Clark **Dahlia Garden & Greenhouses,** 139 Hop City Rd., Ballston Spa (✆ **518/885-7356**), has homemade jams, seasonal produce, and fruit and flowers. **Bliss Glad Farm,** 129 Hop City Rd., Ballston Spa (✆ **518/885-9314**), specializes in gladiolus bulbs and has cut flowers and perennials. There are many others in easy reach of Saratoga Springs; pick up a brochure of "Saratoga Farms" at the Visitor Center.

WHERE TO STAY

Hotel rates rise meteorically (doubling or even tripling) when most in demand: during racing season. But they also climb considerably during Skidmore College's graduation in May, the Jazz Festival in late June, and during other special events. Be sure to confirm rates when booking. Many of the city's most charming Victorian homes have been converted into welcoming bed-and-breakfast inns. For race season, depending on the type of accommodations you want, I'd recommend booking 6 months to 1 year in advance. The Saratoga Chamber of Commerce and the Visitor's Center (see "Visitor Information," above) can help with reservations in high season; their website, **www.saratoga.org**, may be useful for finding additional hotels. Also, see "More Places to Stay," below.

EXPENSIVE

Batcheller Mansion Inn   This fanciful, fairy-tale Victorian castle, built in 1873, is extraordinary from the outside. A riot of turrets and minarets, it looks like something hatched from the fertile imagination of Walt Disney or Antoni Gaudí. Inside, the grand home—the first to be patented in the U.S.—is quirky and rambling, with loads of interesting parlors and Victorian furnishings. That said, some of the accommodations are a bit disappointing, with heavy executive-style desks and older-style furnishings that aren't quite period or as nice as the common rooms. The raspberry-colored Trask Room, though, has its own grand balcony, and the Brady Room, for those of you looking for something out-of-the-ordinary, has a regulation-size pool table within the room, as well as a massive Jacuzzi tub.

20 Circular St. (at Whitney), Saratoga Springs, NY 12866. (800/616-7012 or 518/585-6595. Fax 518/581-7746. www.batchellermansioninn.com. 9 units. Late Nov to Mar Sun–Thurs $120–$200 and Fri–Sat $150–$235 double; Apr–July and Sept–Oct Sun–Thurs $135–$230 and Fri–Sat $180–$270 double; racing season $260–$395 double. Rates include breakfast. 2-night minimum stay on weekends. AE, MC, V. Free parking. *In room:* A/C.

Gideon Putnam Hotel and Conference Center   Tucked into a quiet location among the tall trees of the Saratoga Springs Spa State Park, this stately old 1930s hotel is popular with conventions and conferences, but would also be good for families. It has stately grounds, an impressive exterior, and elegant common areas, though accommodations have low ceilings and bathrooms especially are a bit old-style, in need of some serious updating. The standard rooms leave a lot to be desired. Sports enthusiasts, though, will appreciate the adjacent 18-hole and 9-hole golf courses, 8 tennis courts, swimming-pool complex in the park, and miles of nearby walking and cross-country skiing trails.

24 Gideon Putnam Rd. (Saratoga Springs Spa State Park), Saratoga Springs, NY 12866. (800/732-1560 or 518/584-3000. Fax 518/584-1354. www.gideonputnam.com. 120 units. May–July and Sept–Oct $190–$265 double; racing season $335–$535 double; Jan–Apr and Nov–Dec $155–$215. AE, DC, DISC, MC, V. Free parking. **Amenities:** 3 restaurants; bar; 3 outdoor pools; fitness center; 8 tennis courts; 18- and 9-hole golf courses; concierge; limited room service; massage; laundry service; same-day dry cleaning. *In room:* A/C, TV, minibar, hair dryer.

Saratoga Arms ★★   Perfectly situated on the main drag in the heart of the historic district, this family-owned small hotel is like a grown-up B&B, elegant but very relaxed. A one-time boarding house converted to a luxury inn in 1999, it's in a beautiful 1870 "Second Empire" red brick building with a terrific wrap-around porch; from its antique wicker chairs, you can watch the world go by. Rooms are good sized and nicely appointed, with period antiques, handsome ornamental moldings, and nice details like luxury robes and towels. Several rooms have electric fireplaces, and a number have claw-foot bathtubs. Prices vary not only according to season but bed and room characteristics; highest prices are for kings with fireplaces and whirlpool tubs.

495-497 Broadway, Saratoga Springs, NY 12866. (518/587-1775. Fax 518/581-4064. www.saratoga-lodging.com. 16 units. Nov 1–May 15 $150–$275 double; May 16–Oct 31 $175–$300 double; racing season $295–$465 double. Rates include breakfast. AE, DC, DISC, MC, V. Free parking. *In room:* A/C, TV, dataport, minibar, hair dryer, CD player.

MODERATE

Adelphi Hotel ★★★   In a world of increasingly homogenized hotels, it's a treat to discover the Adelphi, an eclectic and eccentric midsized hotel that wears its exuberant personality on its sleeve. Behind a brown-and-yellow, 1877 brick façade is one of the funkier places you're likely to stay, with just the right touch of High Victorian decadence. The Adelphi survived the demolitions of most of Saratoga Springs's great old hotels from the town's tourism heyday, and this classic hotel has undergone a recent renovation to again take its place as one of the coolest spots in town (though the lobby, with no air-conditioning, can get pretty hot in the summer). Its atmosphere is born of interesting old-world touches and Victorian clutter. Period antiques, old engravings and photographs, lacy curtains, and charming print wallpaper adorn rooms, which are all uniquely decorated; styles range from English country house, French provincial, and High Victorian to Adirondack, Arts and Crafts, and folk art. Yet it all works. The second-floor piazza is ideal for people-watching, outfitted with antique wicker and Adirondack furniture, and there's a charming pool with leafy landscaping and a lovely pergola out back.

365 Broadway, Saratoga Springs, NY 12866. © **518/587-4688.** Fax 518/587-0851. www.adelphihotel.com. 39 units. May–July and Sept–Oct weekdays $115–$150 double, $175–$185 suite; May–June and Sept–Oct weekends $135–$175 double, $205–$220 suite; July weekends, Jazz Fest, and Skidmore week $160–$220 double, $250–$270 suite; race meet weekdays $190–$275 double, $355–$375 suite; weekends $245–$350, $440–$470 suite. Some weekends 2-night minimum stay; during race weekends 3-night minimum stay. Rates include continental breakfast. AE, DC, DISC, MC, V. Free parking. **Amenities:** 2 cafes; outdoor swimming pool. *In room:* A/C, TV.

Circular Manor B&B ★★ *Value*   A warm and stately 1903 Colonial Revival, on a quiet street in the historic district within walking distance of both downtown and the Race Course, this small, couple-owned B&B is gracious and friendly. The large and marvelously restored home has a welcoming Queen Anne circular porch and quarter sawn oak staircase banisters, floors, and pocket doors. All the rooms are handsomely decorated; most bathrooms have marble floors and antique fixtures, including claw-foot tubs and deco sinks. The sun-filled Hydrangea Suite, with a sitting room and French doors, is one of the better rooms you'll find at a B&B. Breakfast is a gourmet repast. Open seasonally only.

120 Circular St., Saratoga Springs, NY 12866. © **518/585-6595.** www.circularmanor.com. 5 units. Late Apr to July $105–$155 double; racing season $205–$295 double. Rates include full breakfast. MC, V. Free parking on street. *In room:* A/C.

The Mansion Inn ★★★ *Value*   Seven miles west of downtown Saratoga Springs is one of the finest places to stay in the area, a magnificently restored 1866 Victorian on 4 acres. The period details in the house—impressively carved wood and marble mantelpieces, Tiffany chandelier, etched glass doors, and gracious parlor with a grand piano—make this a very romantic and sophisticated place for a luxury getaway. Each unique room is sumptuously decorated with bold colors and inviting large beds dressed with top-of-the-line linens. The gourmet breakfast is taken in the handsome dining room in front of a massive fireplace. In the early evening wine and cocktails are served in the parlor. The new owners have done a remarkable job of renovating the inn in a very short time, and they have big plans for the place, including the addition of a terrace for sipping cocktails off the porch and a renovation of the barn for cabaret performances or other functions. For the ultimate in pampering, there's a house Bentley to ferry you to town in true robber-baron style.

801 Rte. 29, Rock City Falls, NY 12863. © **888/996-9977** or 518/885-1607. www.themansionsaratoga.com. 9 units. May–Oct (excluding racing season) $90–$160 double, $200–$250 suite; racing season $160–$275 double, $350 suite; Nov–Apr $90–$145 double, $160–$180 suite. Rates include breakfast. AE, DISC, MC, V. Free parking. *In room:* A/C, TV.

More Places to Stay

Reflecting its past as a prime resort town, Saratoga Springs has a surfeit of hotels, motels, and inns for a small town (many more are located within 10 miles). In prime horse-racing and culture season, July and August, even though prices rise (nearly doubling at some spots), places can really fill up. Try one of the following hotels and inns, or contact the **Saratoga Chamber of Commerce** (28 Clinton St.; ℂ **518/584-3255;** www.saratoga.org) for a list of available accommodations.

Longfellows Inn & Restaurant (500 Union Ave., Rte. 9P South; ℂ **518/ 587-0108;** www.longfellows.com; 112 units; $95–$295 double), owned by the same folks who operate the Olde Bryan Inn restaurant, is a large, modern place a few miles east of downtown; it occupies a converted 1915 dairy barn.

Six Sisters B&B (149 Union Ave.; ℂ **518/583-1173;** www.sixsistersbandb. com; 8 units; $75–$175 double, much higher during racing season), an 1880 Victorian across from the Race Course. Its handsome porch sits under a striped awning, and some rooms have private balconies.

Brunswick B&B (143 Union Ave.; ℂ **800/585-6751** or 518/584-6741; www.brunswickbb.com; 10 units; $75–$175 double, higher during racing season), an 1886 Victorian Gothic home.

The Inn at Saratoga (231 Broadway; ℂ **518/583-1890;** www.theinnat saratoga.com; 38 units; $99–$175 double), a modern hotel housed in an 1880 Victorian right on the main drag (Broadway).

Lewis House B&B (38 East High St., in Ballston Spa (5 miles south of Saratoga Springs; ℂ **518/583-1173;** www.lewishouse.com; 6 units; $95– $125 double, $150–$250 racing season), an Italianate Victorian dating from 1865.

Hilton Garden Inn (125 S. Broadway; ℂ **518/587-1500;** www.saratoga springs.gardeninn.com; 112 units; $99–$300 double), a well-placed standard hotel with high-speed Internet access.

Holiday Inn (232 Broadway; ℂ **800/465-4329;** www.spa-hi.com; 168 units; $150–$195 double, racing season $279–$319 double), very large but conveniently located and with new indoor and outdoor pools.

Union Gables B&B ★ *Value*   A rambling 1901 Queen Anne Victorian— marked by distinctive turrets and gables—across the street from the Saratoga Race Course, this comfortable, easygoing B&B is lived in and not too perfect or fussy. For the most part, rooms are quite large, and named for the siblings of two families. The rooms facing Union Avenue are the best; "Linda" is full of pastel pinks and light green, while "Annie" is huge and very light, decorated in lilac and purple. "Bruce," a more masculine room, has a peaked attic ceiling. The handsome common areas include a massive wraparound porch and large living room. Unusual for a B&B, there are plenty of body-conscious amenities, including a tennis court, exercise room, and outdoor hot tub.

55 Union Ave., Saratoga Springs, NY 12866. ℂ **800/398-1558** or 518/584-1558. Fax 518/583-0649. www. uniongables.com. 10 units. Nov–Apr $120–$135 double; May–Oct $150–$165 double; racing season

$270–$295 double. Rates include breakfast. AE, MC, V. Free parking. **Amenities:** Tennis court; exercise room; outdoor hot tub. *In room:* A/C, TV.

CAMPGROUNDS

Whispering Pines Campsites & RV Park, 560 Sand Hill Rd, Greenfield Center (© **518/893-0416;** www.saratogacamping.com), is 8 miles northwest of Saratoga Springs and set on 75 acres of pines with a new outdoor pool and restroom facility. For additional grounds in the area, visit **www.saratoga.org/accommodations** and click on "Campground."

WHERE TO DINE

Saratoga Springs has a very nice little roster of fine dining and laid-back eateries, with something to appeal to picky gourmands and fussy families. Like the majority of inns, almost all are independently and locally owned.

EXPENSIVE

Chez Sophie Bistro ★★★ FRENCH BISTRO   Inhabiting a gleaming 1950s stainless steel diner, a unique setting for simple but sophisticated French bistro fare, Sophie's is a legendary restaurant on the outskirts of Saratoga Springs. The young chef is the son of Sophie, who began her eponymous restaurant up this way in 1969; now Paul, with his wife, Cheryl, continued the tradition but have added some new wrinkles, including an elegant backroom addition with just six tables (but you can also sit up front for the full diner effect). The menu is creative without being fussy, focusing on fresh ingredients and the best organic produce, meats, and fish from local suppliers. The menu changes daily, but mains have included a yummy roast loin of pork with cranberry-pear chutney, and veal scaloppine with cream and lemon. There's a fantastic wine list, with many moderately priced bottles and a surprisingly well-chosen beer list. In "honor of the restaurant's diner heritage," it offers a terrific midweek bargain, the "pink plate special," a prix-fixe, three-course meal for $25.

2853 Rte. 9, Malta Ridge (5 miles south of Saratoga Springs). © **518/583-3436.** Reservations recommended. Main courses $24–$32. "Pink plate special" prix-fixe (Tues–Thurs) $25. AE, MC, V. Dinner Tues–Sat 5:30–10pm.

MODERATE

Chianti Il Ristorante ★★★ *Value* NORTHERN ITALIAN   Ask Saratogians for their favorite restaurant in town, and they're almost sure to tell you Chianti. Charmingly Mediterranean, with deep-red curtains, flickering candlelight, a main dining room lined with racks of wine bottles, and a warm and inviting Italian host (the owner, who greets you at the door), the restaurant sets the stage for a delightful meal. And the kitchen doesn't disappoint, with items such as porcini risotto in a light cream sauce, *filetto al Gorgonzola* (beef filet prepared with Gorgonzola cheese), dry-aged filet mignon, and grilled homemade sausage. There are also many good-value pastas such as *costa ligure* (linguine with scampi, olives, and capers in a spicy tomato sauce), and the salads are huge and excellently prepared (the *misticanza toscano* is a winner, with mixed greens, Tuscan white beans, Gorgonzola, walnuts, and roasted tomatoes). The extensive and impressive wine list includes many well-chosen Brunellos and Super Tuscans, but not too many at the lower end. You'd never know it, but Chianti is in a former Long John Silver's fast-food restaurant; talk about a transformation!

208 South Broadway. © **518/580-0025.** Reservations recommended. Main courses $12–$25. AE, MC, V. Daily 5:30–11pm.

The Olde Bryan Inn AMERICAN/PUB FARE   This convivial place, an inn since 1773 (and named for a Revolutionary War hero and first permanent local settler, who purchased it in 1787), is a local favorite and is jam-packed during lunch. Cozy, with several brick-lined dining rooms, stone walls, and wood-beamed ceilings, it's a good spot for a serviceable meal: certainly not the town's finest dining experience, but consistently well-prepared and friendly. The menu includes both hearty items like old-fashioned turkey dinner and lighter meals, such as citrus-encrusted haddock. A number of daily specials at lunch are a particularly good deal for under $8.

123 Maple Ave. (at Rock St.). *©* 518/587-2990. Reservations recommended on weekends. Main courses $14–$21. AE, MC, V. Daily 11am–9pm.

Sperry's Restaurant *Value* AMERICAN BISTRO   Sperry's is a dependable local favorite that's been around since the thirties, and rarely disappoints. It's an attractive bistro with black-and-white tile floors, a few high-backed booths, and a welcoming bar on one of Saratoga Springs's cutest streets. The restaurant has a long list of daily specials, with entrees such as chicken Dijon, 14-ounce steak au poivre, and Maryland crab cakes; lunch specialties include jambalaya and a Cuban sandwich.

30½ Caroline St. *©* **518/584-9618.** Reservations recommended weekends for dinner. Main courses $13–$25. AE, MC, V. Mon–Sat 11:30am–3pm; daily 5:30–10pm.

The Wine Bar CREATIVE AMERICAN   With more than 50 wines by the glass and a ventilated smoking lounge where cigars are welcomed, this is the joint for would-be high rollers to celebrate their winnings at the track (or drown their sorrows in a good glass of wine and a nice meal). Trendy but moderately priced, with an upstairs bar and attractively modern and clean decor, it features a menu that will appeal both to wine-and-cigar guys and fashionable sorts. Dishes are available in both small-plate and entree portions, and they change seasonally; among recent offerings were lobster poached in truffle butter with roasted beet and citrus salad; rare ahi crusted with Asian spices and served with a calamari stir-fry; and a beef filet with braised vegetables, forest mushrooms, and a foie gras demi sauce. For dessert, the best idea is a good dessert wine and one of the many cheese plates. Friday nights there are usually DJs spinning tunes downstairs.

417 Broadway. *©* 518/584-8777. Reservations recommended. Main courses $14–$22. AE, MC, V. Tues–Sat 4–10pm (July–Aug Tues–Sun 4–10pm).

INEXPENSIVE

Beverly's *★ Value* BREAKFAST/CREATIVE AMERICAN   This small, slender cafe should be your first stop in the morning if your hotel doesn't include breakfast. The morning menu is extraordinary, with both creative dishes and traditional fresh-baked comfort foods and great coffee. The standard menu includes baguette French toast, eggs Benedict, and pancakes with a touch of wheat germ. Daily breakfast specials include whimsical dishes like poached eggs on roasted eggplant with dill hollandaise, or banana and walnut pancakes. Beverly's is also open for lunch, which might be a chicken teriyaki salad, grilled chicken breast with roasted peppers and pesto, or the quiche of the day.

47 Phila St. *©* 518/583-2755. Reservations not accepted. Main courses $3.75–$8.95. AE, MC, V. Daily 7am–3pm.

SARATOGA SPRINGS AFTER DARK

The **Saratoga Performing Arts Center,** or SPAC, is in a class by itself. From June to September, this is *the* place to be in Saratoga Springs (after you've already been to the Race Course, of course) to see the amazing roster of high-culture talent that takes up summer residence, including the New York City Ballet and the Philadelphia Orchestra. SPAC is also the host of the Saratoga Chamber Music Festival, Freihofer's Jazz Festival in late June (with top-flight jazz talent, 26 years and counting), the Lake George Opera, and the 3-day Saratoga Wine & Food Festival. Set within the Saratoga Spa State Park grounds, perfect for walks and picnics, the center has a sheltered amphitheater and an intimate Spa Little Theatre. The box office opens May 11, but preseason discounts are available (up to 50% off ticket prices). Other discounts are SPACWIRE Internet specials and season lawn passes. Call ℂ **518/587-3330** or check the website, **www.spac.org**, for schedules and tickets.

Caffé Lena, 47 Phila St. (ℂ **518/583-0022**), is a legendary upstairs folk-music coffeehouse that's a little tattered but still reeks of all the folkies that have played there since 1960. There's mostly live acoustic music (and some blues, jazz, and poetry) Wednesday to Sunday nights, and some relatively big names, like Tish Hinojosa, still drop by. Reservations are recommended; covers are generally $10 to $15. The **Tin & Lint,** 2 Caroline St. (ℂ **518/587-5897**), is a pub popular with Skidmore students; it's where Don McLean, a former waiter, wrote the '70s pop anthem "American Pie" on a cocktail napkin. **Luna Lounge,** 17 Maple Ave. (ℂ **518/583-6955**), is a new upscale late-night lounge with a New York City industrial look, owned by the proprietor of Chianti Il Ristorante. **The Wine Bar,** 417 Broadway (ℂ **518/584-8777**) has a cigar lounge, upstairs bar, and loads of wine by the glass, with DJs in-house on Friday nights. The local movie theater, **Saratoga Film Forum,** 320 Broadway (ℂ **518/584-FILM**), shows first-run films. For a romantic end to the evening (or a nice afternoon activity), **Saratoga Horse & Carriage Company** (ℂ **518/584-8820**) offers horse-drawn carriage rides through Saratoga Springs. For contracted private rides, they'll pick you up at your hotel or inn in Saratoga.

3 Albany

The local author William Kennedy has famously chronicled the state capital with his cycle of Albany novels, including *Legs* and *Ironweed,* which summoned not only the politics and grime of the city, but also its ghosts. Kennedy's depiction is of a city that's a little raw and rough around the edges, a reality Albany struggles to escape. The much-maligned capital of New York State, Albany is a manageable, medium-size city dominated by government and banking—and a firm wish for greater respect. Albanians are proud of their city's great history on the upper Hudson, its culture and continued efforts at urban renewal, but the city has had a somewhat difficult time convincing many from around the state of its charms. Beyond school groups on civics-class field trips, Albany attracts many more government and business than leisure travelers. The latter, though, are likely to find a fascinating dose of history, full roster of summer festivals, user-friendly public spaces and a few surprises that may just win the city some newfound respect.

Two monumental building projects have distinguished the city's physical evolution. The New York State Capitol, a stunning pile of native stone, took more than 30 years and the efforts of five architects to build, finally exhausting the patience of the governor, Theodore Roosevelt, in 1899. In the 1970s, another governor, Nelson Rockefeller, left his imprint on the capital by building the dramatic Empire State Plaza and remaking downtown as one of the most starkly modern government headquarters this side of Brasilia. Rockefeller's ambition was

Downtown Albany

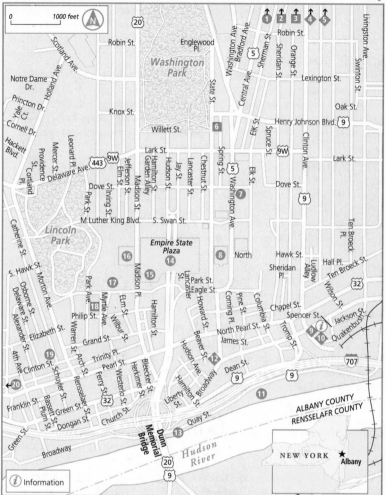

to make Albany the country's most beautiful capital city; whether that was accomplished or not is a matter of debate, but the modern art collection he amassed in the name of the capital is the largest publicly owned and displayed in the country.

VISITOR INFORMATION

The **Albany Heritage Area Visitors Center,** 25 Quackenbush Sq. (✆ **518/434-0405;** www.albany.org), is open Monday through Friday, from 9am to 4pm and weekends from 10am to 4pm. In addition to the tourist information center, there are a small history gallery, a planetarium, and a gift shop. Trolley tours leave from here in summer (see "Organized Tours," below). For pretrip information, consult the website www.albany.org.

CITY LAYOUT

Downtown Albany is relatively small and easy enough to get around, either by foot, by bus, or by trolley. However, much of the city's hotel accommodations and dining lie beyond the major highways that ring the city, I-787 and I-90, in suburbs like Colonie (north of Albany). Central Avenue is the main thoroughfare that leads all the way from downtown to Colonie, and is often referred to as "Restaurant Row." The major highways around Albany are notoriously difficult for newcomers to navigate; one frequently circles and circles, unable to determine which way one actually wants to go. Map out destinations in advance if you're staying on the outskirts of town and ask locals for directions.

GETTING AROUND

BY PUBLIC TRANSPORTATION The Downtown Albany Circulator (buses 16 and 20; $1) runs between Empire State Plaza and Broadway on weekdays from 6:30am to 6pm; there is also a "Downtown Circulator" trolley. For schedules and additional route information, contact the Capital District Authority (✆ **518/482-3371;** www.cdta.org).

BY CAR Car-rental agencies in Albany include **Enterprise Rent-A-Car,** Pepsi Arena, 51 South Pearl St. (✆ **518/472-1111**), and **Hertz Rent-A-Car** in the Crowne Plaza Hotel (✆ **518/434-6911**). You'll find representatives of Avis, Budget, Enterprise, Hertz, National, and Thrifty at Albany International Airport (see "Arriving," p. 261).

BY TAXI Taxi services include: **Yellow Cab,** 137 Lark St. (✆ **518/434-2222**); **Advantage Limousine & Car Service** (✆ **518/433-0100**); and **Premiere Transportation,** 456 North Pearl St. (✆ **800/515-6123** or 518/459-6123).

BY TRAIN See "Arriving," p. 261.

BY BUS **Adirondack Trailways,** 34 Hamilton St. (✆ **518/436-9651**), and **Greyhound Bus,** 34 Hamilton St. (✆ **518/434-8095**), travel to Saratoga Springs and other destinations in upstate New York.

EXPLORING ALBANY

Albany has just a handful of must-see sights, including two excellent museums and the State Capitol building, almost all conveniently located downtown. The best idea is probably to start at the unmistakable Empire State Plaza, where several of the top sights are located.

THE TOP ATTRACTIONS

Albany Institute of History & Art ★ *Kids* Albany's best art museum is the second-oldest museum in the United States—older even than the Smithsonian and Louvre. Restored and sensitively expanded in 2001—two turn-of-the-20th-century buildings were linked by a modern glass lobby—the museum presents the history of the Hudson River and Albany through the works of local artists and artisans. The permanent collection includes decorative arts, furniture, and nearly five centuries of paintings and sculpture. Among the most important are paintings by artists, such as Thomas Cole, from the Hudson River School, the first American school of art. In the colonial Albany gallery are furnishings, paintings, and artifacts that tell the story of the ancient Dutch settlement in this area 350 years ago. Ancient Egypt galleries feature a pair of mummies, a priest and priestess, from 304 B.C. and 966 B.C. The museum presents special exhibits that are among the best in upstate New York, and there are plenty of lectures and activities geared toward children. An hour or two should be sufficient here.

125 Washington Ave. (*C*) **518/463-4478**. www.albanyinstitute.org. Admission $7 adults, $5 seniors and students, $3 children ages 6–12, free for children under 6. Wed–Sat 10am–5pm; Sun noon–5pm.

Empire State Plaza ★ *Kids*   A dramatic public plaza, named for Gov. Nelson A. Rockefeller, who undertook the massive project in 1962 (it wasn't finished until 1978), is Albany's most distinctive urban feature. Rockefeller envisioned a kind of starkly modern Brasilia in upstate New York. Fiercely controversial at the time, not only for its daring aesthetics but the fact that an entire residential neighborhood was wiped out to install it, the plaza and its unique buildings have since grown on most locals and visitors. The centerpiece of the plaza is the spherical Performing Arts Center, known to all as "The Egg." One glance and you'll know why. The plaza is flanked by the New York State Museum, the Capitol (alongside legislative and justice buildings), four tall state agency buildings, and the tallest structure in Albany, the 42-story Corning Tower. War and other memorials share the open air with an important 92-piece collection of large-scale modern sculpture, most by artists associated with the New York School, including Tony Smith, Alexander Calder, David Smith, and Claes Oldenburg. The Empire Plaza might be cold and off-putting, but the city schedules concerts, festivals, ice-skating, fireworks, and other activities that draw Albanians in rather than keep them away.

Bordered by State St., South St., and Madison Ave. (*C*) **518/473-7521**. www.ogs.state.ny.us/plaza. Free admission (hours vary for individual components).

New York State Capitol ★   This impressive building, seat of New York State government since the 1880s and so jarring a contrast with the stark modern Empire Plaza and agency buildings that rise around it, was the first massive and problematic project in the area. It took more than 3 decades (beginning at the end of the 19th century) and five architects to build, and cost more than $25 million (making it relatively one of the most expensive buildings ever erected in the U.S). One of the last load-bearing structures to be built, with no steel reinforcements until the top floor, and constructed of solid granite masonry, it was to have been crowned by a cupola, but the governor at the time, Theodore Roosevelt, had had enough and proclaimed it finished in 1899. Its grandest features are the Great Western Staircase—the so-called "$1 million staircase," a riot of elaborate stonework that contains over 1,000 carved small faces (most are anonymous, but there are 77 "famous" visages, such as Andrew Jackson and Henry Hudson)—and the vibrant William de Leftwich Dodge ceiling murals of battle depictions in the Governor's Reception Room. Tours last about 45 minutes.

Plaza Visitor Center, Rm. 106 Concourse, Empire State Plaza. (*C*) **518/474-2418**. www.ogs.state.ny.us. Free admission. Guided tours daily 10am, noon, 2pm, and 3pm (by appointment). No parking (paid parking on the street or next to the New York State Museum).

(*Kids*) **Albany's Highs & Lows**

It takes just 28 seconds to reach the **Corning Tower Observation Deck** on the 42nd floor (which makes this the tallest building between New York City and Montréal). On a clear day, you can see the Catskills, the Green Mountains of Vermont, and the Hudson River. The observation deck is open Monday through Saturday, from 10am to 2:30pm; admission is free. At the other extreme, underground in the Concourse passageway that travels beneath the Empire State Plaza, is a most unexpected art gallery—the largest publicly owned and displayed **art collection** in the U.S., purchased at the behest of Gov. Nelson A. Rockefeller, who strongly believed that art was a fundamental component of a capital city. Mixed in with fast-food shops and government offices are dozens of works by some of the most important artists of the 20th century, almost all of whom were identified with the New York School, including Isamu Noguchi, Robert Motherwell, Ellsworth Kelly, Franz Kline, Mark Rothko and Donald Judd, among many others. Note that many large sculptures are also placed outside on and around the plaza. The Concourse is open Monday through Friday from 6am to 11pm and on weekends from 10am to 2:30pm; free admission.

New York State Museum ★★ *(Kids)*   This massive museum, which from the exterior looks like a giant monolith, is the largest museum of its kind in the country. It aims to tell the story of New York State, both natural and cultural. Several new galleries have really enlivened this war horse. The newest permanent gallery, "The World Trade Center: Rescue, Recovery Response," was the first major museum exhibit of artifacts from the September 11, 2001, terrorist attacks. It documents the 24-hour aftermath of the disaster; on view are giant fragments of the towers, a destroyed fire engine (one of the first on the scene), and the stunning video shot by two French brothers. Elsewhere, New York City is traced from early port to metropolis, with a recent gallery addition devoted to Harlem. A large and accurate depiction of a Mohawk Iroquois village longhouse is a visitor favorite. Of great interest to visitors who can't visit NYC is the hall of rotating great art from the city's major museums (including the Metropolitan, Guggenheim, and MoMA). On the top floor is the new Café Terrace, with great views of the Empire State Plaza and creative regional displays, along with something that kids run screaming toward: a historic, functioning 36-horse carousel, hand-carved in the 1890s in Brooklyn. Allow a couple of hours.

Madison Ave. (between Eagle and Swan sts.). ℂ **518/474-5877.** www.nysm.nysed.gov. Free admission (donation suggested). Daily 10am–5pm. Paid parking on the street or next to the Museum.

MORE TO SEE & DO

Historic Cherry Hill   This stately home, a big yellow clapboard Georgian Colonial that once looked over gentle lands to the edge of the Hudson River, is today in the middle of a bad neighborhood and the din of the highway. But no matter, it still presents an interesting history lesson, told through the story of Catherine Putnam and the Van Rensselaer family, whose descendants occupied the house for 200 years, until 1963. The house is overflowing with original furnishings, documents, and artifacts, and is most interesting for the way organizers present the house as a reflection of Albany history.

523½ S. Pearl St. (off I-787). ℂ 518/434-4791. www.historiccherryhill.org. Admission $4 adults, $3 seniors, $2 college students, $1 children 6–17. Apr–June and Oct–Dec Tues–Fri, guided tours on the hour noon–3pm; Sat 10am–3pm, Sun 1pm–3pm; July–Sept Tues–Sat, guided tours on the hour 10am–3pm, Sun 1pm–3pm.

Hudson River Way *Finds* *Kids*   The newest addition to the Albany landscape is this cool new pedestrian bridge, opened in 2002, which connects downtown to Corning Preserve Park on the banks of the Hudson. It is lined with 30 trompe l'oeil paintings on lampposts that depict the city's history and heritage, from pre-historic times and early Dutch merchants to the present. There are also two large murals on staircase landings.

Maiden Lane/Corning Preserve Park. ℂ 518/434-2032. Free admission.

New York State Executive Mansion   The Governor's Mansion, built in 1856 as a banker's home, was totally remodeled in the 1860s. The first governor to live (and rent) here was in 1875; in 1877, the state purchased it, and it was given its third major makeover in 1885, to its current Queen Anne style. Famous inhabitants include Theodore Roosevelt and Franklin Delano Roosevelt (whose wheelchair you can see in the exhibit space on the second floor). The house, which isn't overly large or grand, is still the official residence of the current governor, George Pataki, and his family (at least when he's in Albany). Tours last about an hour.

138 Eagle St. ℂ 518/473-7521. www.ogs.state.ny.us. Free admission. Guided tours Sept–June Thurs at noon, 1pm, and 2pm (by appointment). Wed–Sat 10am–5pm; Sun noon–5pm. No parking (paid parking on the street or next to the New York State Museum).

Schuyler Mansion State Historic Site   This large English-style 1762 estate, the home of Philip Schuyler, one of the first four generals under Washington during the first 2 years of the Revolutionary War, is more interesting for what it represents than what there actually is to see. The house is only partially restored, but it was essentially a military outpost during the war, with visits by George Washington, Benedict Arnold, and Alexander Hamilton, who married Schulyer's daughter at the mansion. Incredibly, Schuyler had the British general John Burgoyne and his retinue under house arrest here after their defeat at the Battle of Saratoga, and Loyalists raided the house in an attempt to kidnap Burgoyne in 1781.

32 Catherine St. ℂ 518/434-0834. Admission $3 adults, $2 students, $1 New York State seniors. mid-Apr to Oct Wed–Sun 10am–4pm.

Shaker Heritage Society   America's first Shaker settlement, the 1776 Watervliet Church Community, retains its 1848 Meeting House and seven other buildings, where modern life has now encroached. The Shakers (the United Society of Believers), the early American religious group, were known for their remarkable craftsmanship as well as their religious devotion. Work was a way of devoting oneself to God, and they sought to create heaven on earth with communitarian social structure and celibacy; they adopted needy children and brought them into the "family," to work on the estate; on Sundays outsiders came to see their mesmerizing church services. The Shakers, who at their peak numbered about 350 here, abandoned the site in 1924. Mother Ann Lee and more than 400 other Shakers are buried on the grounds. Craft workshops are held on the premises, where there is a small gift shop. Allow about a half-hour.

875 Watervliet-Shaker Rd., Colonie. ℂ 518/456-7890. Free admission. Guided tours: $3 per person, 12 and under free. Tues–Sat 9:30am–4pm.

USS *Slater* (Kids)   A WWI destroyer escort ship, one of three remaining, sits docked on the banks of the Hudson, open to tours of the crew's quarters, galley, and main guns. The ship is currently being restored.

Snow Dock, south of Dunn Memorial Bridge (off I-787). 📞 518/431-1943. www.ussslater.org. Admission $5 adults, $4 students 12–16, $3 students 6–11, free under 5. Apr–Dec Wed–Sun 10am–4pm.

ESPECIALLY FOR KIDS

Albany, as the state capital, gets tons of school visits, of course, but at first glance it might not appear the best place to travel with kids. Actually, it's got plenty for children of all ages. Starting with the Albany Visitor's Center, the **Henry Hudson Planetarium** has shows every Saturday at 11:30am and 12:30pm. The **Albany Institute of History & Art** schedules a bevy of special children's programs. The **New York State Museum** has interesting exhibits that will appeal to both younger and older children, including one on 9/11, another on the Adirondacks, plus a Native American longhouse that kids can enter and play around with using a nifty interactive feature. But best of all is the antique carousel on the museum's top floor. The **Hudson River Way** is a pedestrian bridge with lampposts marked by paintings that trick the eye and tell the story of Albany's history. And young soldiers will surely find it cool to board a World War I destroyer, the **USS *Slater*,** docked on the Hudson.

ORGANIZED TOURS

Albany Trolley Tours—guided trolley tours of downtown tours, historic homes, and historic churches—are offered from July to the end of August. They begin at the Visitor Center at Quackenbush Square (corner of Clinton and Broadway). Downtown tours (Fri 11am; Sat 10:30am) cost $10 for adults, $9 for seniors, and $5 for children 14 and under; Church and Homes tours (alternating Wed July–Aug) cost $12 for adults, $10 for seniors, and $6 for children 14 and under. For more information, call 📞 518/434-0405; advance reservations are recommended. **Albany Remembered Tours,** 100 State St. (📞 518/427-0401) offers guided walking tours of historic sights. The **Upper Hudson River Railroad,** 3 Railroad Place, North Creek, NY (📞 518/241-5334; www.upperhudsonriverrr.com), runs seasonal 2-hour train trips along a gorgeous section of the Upper Hudson River; spring, summer, and fall; $12 adults, $11 seniors, $8 children ages 3 to 11. **Dutch Apple Cruises,** corner of Quay and Madison avenues (📞 518/463-0220; www.dutchapplecruises.com), cruises the Hudson with narrated lunch and dinner trips with entertainment. **Canal Pilot,** Waterford (📞 518/928-1863), does custom boat tours of the Hudson River as well as Lake Erie and Champlain canals. **Hart Tours,** 1 Becker Terrace, Delmar (📞 800/724-4225 or 518/439-6095), is a tour operator that has 1-, 2-, and 3-day area itineraries, including tours of the Adirondacks and Capital District.

OUTDOOR PURSUITS

BIKING, IN-LINE SKATING & JOGGING   The **Hudson-Mohawk Bikeway** is a 41-mile path along the Hudson and Mohawk rivers, connecting Albany with Schenectady and Troy, with smaller, more manageable paths. It begins in Island Creek Park and continues through Corning Preserve Park (at the end of the Hudson River Way bridge). **State Bike Route 9** runs to Hudson Shores Park, near Watervliet. For more information, call 📞 518/458-2161 or pick up a copy of "Capital District Regional Bike-Hike Map" at the Visitor's Center.

> **Fun Fact Rack 'em Up**
>
> The modern billiard ball was created in Albany in 1868, using celluloid as a substitute for ivory (of which there was a shortage), by John Wesley Hyatt. The Albany Billiard Ball Company on Delaware Avenue produced billiard balls until it went out of business in 1986.

FESTIVALS   Especially in summer, Albany thrives with public outdoor festivals, many held at the Empire State Plaza. Here's a sampling:

- The **Tulip Festival.** Washington Park (May 9–11; © **518/434-2032;** www. albanyevents.org). The city and park bloom with tens of thousands of tulips, a 50-year-old clear indicator of Dutch ancestry.
- **Albany Alive at Five.** Thursday-night free outdoor summer concerts in Tricentennial Park on Broadway (June–Aug; © **518/434-2032;** www.albany events.org).
- **Price Chopper Fourth of July.** Empire State Plaza: fireworks, music, and more.
- **Classic Rock, Swing, and Oldies concerts.** Empire State Plaza (Wed July–Aug; © **518/473-0559;** www.ogs.state.ny.us).
- **Fleet BluesFest.** Empire State Plaza (July 12–13; © **518/473-0559;** www. ogs.state.ny.us).
- **African-American Arts and Culture Festival.** Empire State Plaza (Aug 3; © **518/473-0559;** www.ogs.state.ny.us).
- **Food Festival.** Empire State Plaza (Aug 14; © **518/473-0559;** www.ogs. state.ny.us).
- **Latin Festival.** Washington Park (Aug 24; © **518/434-2032;** www.albany events.org).
- **Columbus Parade and Italian Festival.** Washington Park (Oct 13; © **518/ 434-2032;** www.albanyevents.org).
- **Capital Holiday Lights in the Park.** Washington Park (Nov 29–Jan 1; © **518/434-0392;** www.albanyevents.org).

GOLF   **Orchard Creek Golf Club,** 6700 Dunnsville Rd., Altamont (© **518/ 861-5000;** www.orchardcreek.com), an 18-hole public course, was rated America's #1 Best New Bargain by *Golf Digest* in 2001 (greens fees $14–$19). **Stadium Golf Club,** 333 Jackson Ave., Schenectady (© **518/374-9104;** www.stadiumgolfclub. com), is another 18-hole course just north of Albany. Greens fees are $13 to $26.

PARKS & GARDENS   **Washington Park,** at State and Willett streets, is where the annual springtime Tulip Festival is held. **Corning Riverfront Park** is at the west bank of the Hudson, at the end of the Hudson River Way pedestrian bridge.

WINTER SPORTS   You can **ice skate** outdoors at Empire State Plaza (© **518/ 474-2418**) and Swinburn Rink (© **518/438-2406**). The closest downhill skiing is at **Ski Windham,** Windham (© **800/729-7549;** www.skiwindham.com), and **Catamount,** Rte. 23, Hillsdale (© **800/342-1840;** www.catamountski.com), on the Massachusetts border in the southern Berkshires.

SPECTATOR SPORTS
The **Albany Conquest** (© **518/487-2222;** www.albanyconquest.com) is the local Arena football team, and it plays its eight home games at the Pepsi Arena

from April through July. The **Albany River Rats** (𝄐 **518/487-2244;** www.
albanyriverrats.com), an affiliate of the American Hockey League's New Jersey
Devils, also plays at Pepsi Arena, October through May. The **Albany Attack**
(𝄐 **518/427-8145;** www.albanyattack.com) has the same home field for its
National Lacrosse League games from January through April. A Class A minor-
league baseball team, the **Tri-City Valley Cats,** an affiliate of the Houston
Astros (𝄐 **518/629-2287;** www.tcvalleycats.com) plays on the Hudson Valley
Campus in Troy.

SHOPPING

The biggest mall in the Albany area is **Crossgates Mall,** exit 24 of I-87 (at the
base of the Adirondack Northway; 𝄐 **800/439-2001**), which gained a bit of
national notoriety when a couple of antiwar protesters got thrown out for wearing T-shirts with peace messages before the war in Iraq in early 2003. It has more
than 250 shops and big department stores. **Stuyvesant Plaza,** Western Avenue
and Fuller Road (𝄐 **518/482-8986**), is an enjoyable open-air mall with a couple
of dozen shops, including jewelry, home furnishings, clothing, gifts, bakery, and
chocolate. **Lark Street** in downtown Albany is a bit of an open-air gallery itself,
with more than 60 shops, galleries, and restaurants. It's good for strolling and
snacking. **Ten Thousand Villages,** Stuyvesant Plaza, 1475 Western Ave. (𝄐 **518/
435-9307**), is a small mall of handcrafts created by artisans from some 30 countries; purchases directly benefit the craftspeople's families.

FARMER'S MARKETS

A good farmer's market, south of Albany on Route 9J along the Hudson, is
Goold Orchards, 1297 Brookview Station Rd., Castleton (𝄐 **518/732-7317**),
which features an apple orchard, farm store, cider mill, and bake shop. It offers
pick-your-own apples, strawberries, and pumpkins in season as well as an apple
festival in October and a corn maze. City versions of farmer's markets in town are
Wallenberg Park, Clinton Avenue and North Pearl (Mon 10am–1pm); SUNY
Plaza, corner of Broadway and State (Thurs 11am–2pm); and Empire State Plaza
(Wed and Fri 11am–2pm).

WHERE TO STAY

The supply of good downtown hotels in Albany is extremely limited. By far the
best choice is a small B&B/boutique hotel (The Morgan State House, see below),
which is not only the best place to stay in Albany, it's one of the finest inns in
upstate New York. Most decent hotels of any size, which tend to be standard
hotel and motel chains, are on the outskirts of town, in a suburb called Colonie.

Comfort Inn & Suites *Value* *Kids*   In a town with few good upscale options,
this is an excellent standard choice; you know what you get with Comfort Inn,
good services and nicely appointed rooms for the price. Located just 10 minutes
from the airport and along the main drag of restaurants and shops, 6 miles from
downtown Albany, it's well located. It has a small exercise room and good indoor
pool. For families, it's perfect: Kids under 18 stay free. A recommended restaurant, The Hungry Horseman, is located in a separate building on the premises,
though it's not associated with the hotel.

1606 Central Ave., Albany, NY 12205 (in Colonie; I-87, exit 4). 𝄐 800/233-9444 or 518/869-5327. Fax 518/
456-8971. www.choicehotels.com. 109 units. $89 double; $134–$240 suite. Rates include continental break-
fast. AE, DC, DISC, MC, V. Free parking. **Amenities:** Restaurant; fitness center; indoor pool; business center;
laundry service; airport shuttle service. *In room:* A/C, TV, coffeemaker, hair dryer.

The Desmond *Value*   This large, 30-year-old hotel and conference center is designed to look like a village of sorts, which I guess it does in that faux-Disney way. It looks a little bit more like a food court at the mall. Bellboys are even dressed in faux-colonial getups. But it's actually a pretty good place to stay, with good-size and comfortable rooms overlooking the courtyard that feature four-poster canopy beds, 18th-century replica furnishings, and lots of floral prints. The hotel is close to the airport and has all the facilities you're likely to need.

660 Albany-Shaker Rd., Albany, NY 12211 (in Colonie; I-87, exit 4). © **800/448-3500** or 518/869-8100. Fax 518/869-7659. www.desmondhotelsalbany.com. 324 units. $159–$169 double. AE, DC, DISC, MC, V. Free parking. **Amenities:** 2 restaurants; indoor pool; outdoor pool; fitness center; business center; limited room service. *In room:* A/C, TV, coffeemaker, hair dryer.

Mansion Hill Inn   This small inn tucked in a corner of downtown Albany is a pretty good choice, though it pales in comparison to the State House, which is, remarkably, similarly priced. The Mansion Hill Inn has a good location, just a few blocks from the Empire State Plaza, and its eight rooms are decent-size, but the decor could use an updating. They look and feel more like that of a small chain motel than a B&B. The attached restaurant, which plays to small groups, is probably the inn's best feature.

115 Philip St. (at Park Ave), Albany, NY 12202. © **518/465-2038.** Fax 518/434-2313. www.mansionhill.com. 8 units. $175–$195 double. Rates include breakfast. AE, MC, V. Free parking. **Amenities:** Restaurant. *In room:* A/C.

The Morgan State House ★★★ *Value*   One of the finest urban B&Bs you're likely to stumble upon, the elegant and professionally run Morgan State House is really a European-style boutique hotel. Its rooms are nothing short of extraordinary: huge and gorgeously (and uniquely) decorated, with great 19th-century period detailing and furnishings, and tile bathrooms with claw-foot tubs, and some of the best down and feather bedding and linens you'll ever rest your head on. A couple of rooms even have working fireplaces. The beautiful town house, on "Mansion Row" just a few blocks from the Empire State Plaza, and across the street from peaceful Washington Park, was built in 1888 by the same architect who designed the cathedral in Albany. It remained a single-family house until 1975. The B&B's six rooms are in high demand; if none are available, perhaps you can land one of the 10 apartments with kitchenettes at The Washington Park State House, in a condo building a couple of doors down at 399 State St. They have the owner's same unmistakable good taste, though are a touch more modern, and are ideal for business travelers. Guests at Washington Park also have breakfast at the Morgan State House (on a nice day, sip your coffee in the charming interior garden courtyard). No children under 16 are accepted at either place.

393 State St., Albany, NY 12210. © **888/427-6063** or 518/427-6063. Fax 518/463-1316. www.state house.com. 16 units. Morgan State House $160–$200 double, 2-bedroom suite $260; Washington Park State House $135–$150 apt. Rates include full breakfast. AE, DISC, MC, V. Free parking. *In room:* A/C, TV, kitch-enettes in Washington Park State House rooms.

WHERE TO DINE

Lark Street downtown is home to a number of small neighborhood eateries with cuisines from around the world. The majority of chain and fast-food restaurants are located on Central Avenue, also known as "restaurant row."

EXPENSIVE

Nicole's Bistro ★★ *Value*   FRENCH BISTRO   In what is in all probability the oldest standing home in Albany, an original Quackenbush (early Dutch, ca. 1730) structure, this handsome, upscale two-story French is one of Albany's

Hotel & Motel Chains in the Albany Area

If none of the recommended hotels are available—and Albany can get crowded during large conventions and when lobbyists are swarming the capital—try one of the following international hotel chains, which are mostly located on the outskirts of downtown, near the airport: **Best Western Albany Airport Inn** (200 Wolf Rd., Albany, NY 12205; ℂ 800/ 310-6143 or 518/458-100; www.bestwestern.com; $89–$99 double); **Holiday Inn Albany** (205 Wolf Rd., Albany, NY 12205; www.sixcontinents hotels.com; ℂ 518/458-7250; $105–$149 double); **Quality Inn Hotel Albany** (Everett Rd., Albany, NY 12206; ℂ 518/438-8431; www.quality inn.com; $85–$95 double); **Red Roof Albany Inn** (188 Wolf Rd., Albany, NY 12205; ℂ 518/459-1971; www.redroof.com $63–$73 double); **Courtyard by Marriott** (168 Wolf Rd., Albany, NY 12205; ℂ 800/321-2211 or 518/482-8800; www.courtyard.com; $89–$159); **Days Inn Wolf Road** (16 Wolf Rd., Albany, NY 12205; ℂ 800/329-7466; www.thedaysinn.com; $60–$80 double).

For additional chain hotels and motels (of which there are many in the greater metro area), see **www.albany.org**.

best. Charming and elegant, it's surely the best place in town for a celebratory or romantic dinner. The seafood cassoulet is a standard in southern France, a hearty fish stew of shellfish, scallops, mussels, crab claws, and seafood sausage in a spicy tomato-fennel broth. Classic meat dishes include rack of lamb with garlic mashed potatoes and steak au poivre. The lunch menu is considerably lighter and cheaper. A truly excellent deal is the nightly three-course prix-fixe dinner special for $25 ($34 with two glasses of wine). Bread fanatics take note: The basket of assorted home-baked breads delivered to your table is irresistible. A cute little cocktail bar at the entrance is a good spot for a before- or after-dinner drink (you can also eat there).

Quackenbush House, 633 Broadway (corner of Clinton Ave). ℂ **518/465-1111.** Reservations recommended. Main courses $18–$25. AE, MC, V. Mon–Fri 11:30am–2:30pm and 5–9pm.

Yono's ★★★ *Finds* CONTINENTAL/ASIAN/INDONESIAN A true surprise in Albany: Not only is this white-gloved haute Indonesian cooking, it's located in the midst of car dealers and a garage. A wackier location you couldn't dream up. You enter the Armory Center, home to a low-rent theme restaurant, a tire store, and a bar; you'd never guess that behind a door on the second floor is one of the city's most distinguished restaurants, an exercise in fine, and exotic, dining. The acclaimed chef Yono, who's appeared on NBC *Today* and picked up numerous awards, moved from downtown a couple of years ago and hasn't looked back. The sophisticated menu focuses on delicious Indonesian specialties, though another page is a full roster of well-prepared Continental dishes "if you're feeling less adventurous." Yono's signature dish is a Balinese specialty, Babi Kecap Singa Raja, a mouthful that translates into pork tenderloin in sweet soy, ginger, and orange rind. If you're unfamiliar with Indonesian cuisine, your best bet is the Nasi Rames, a tasting menu of five dishes. The wine list is outstanding, with more than 500 bottles (though pairing wines with spicy Indonesian dishes is a bit of an art; try a Riesling or even a Belgian-style beer).

64 Colvin Ave. (in the Armory Center, off Central Ave.). © 518/482-0100. Reservations recommended. Main courses $17–$43. AE, DISC, MC, V. Wed–Sat 5:30–11pm.

MODERATE

Albany Pump Station *Kids* *Value* AMERICAN/PUB FARE   Housed in a cavernous 19th-century former pump station, this is part microbrewery and part restaurant. It gets crowded at happy hour with downtown office workers, but then begins to fill up with individual and family diners. The menu is surprisingly diverse, with plenty of salads, pastas, burgers, sandwiches, and other pub grub, but also good entrees such as old-fashioned meatloaf, French Quarter gumbo, and eggplant lasagna. The house beers are quite good; check out the award-winning Kick-Ass Brown and the Quackenbush Blonde. A late-night menu of pub food kicks in after 10pm (11pm Fri–Sat), and there's a special (and cheap) kids' menu, as well as "Sunday Family-Style Dining," a complete meal for just $13.

19 Quackenbush Sq. © 518/447-9000. Reservations recommended on weekends. Main courses $6.95–$19. AE, DISC, MC, V. Daily 11am–10pm.

The Hungry Horseman Grill *Value* *Kids* AMERICAN/COMFORT FOOD In the heart of "restaurant row," in the parking lot of a Comfort Inn hotel, this congenial place falls somewhere between roadside diner and neighborhood eatery. The kitchen serves up lots of pastas, steaks, and seafood; the Hungry Horseman favorites are hearty comfort food like Yankee pot roast, roast turkey dinner, and pork chops. The bar at one end effectively becomes a small sports bar when there's a good game on the tube. Brunch is served on Sundays.

1610 Central Ave. © 518/464-5050. Reservations recommended on weekends. Main courses $9.95–$18. AE, MC, V. Daily 11am–10pm.

Jack's Oyster House ★ CLASSIC AMERICAN   Known as just "Jack's," this Albany classic has been around since 1913, and it still serves up the kind of clubby insider ambience we tend to associate with another era. It's the kind of place where lobbyists and politicos come to hammer out government contracts. Waiters are nattily attired in black jackets and bow ties with white aprons; the restaurant has black-and-white tile floors, dark wood paneling, deep booths, and photos of old Albany. The menu for the most part stubbornly resists trendiness. Classic appetizers include Jack's Famous 1913 Manhattan clam chowder, clams casino, shrimp cocktail, and oysters Rockefeller. Main courses include steak Diane, calves liver, and jumbo lobster tail. In mid-2003 the last page of the menu listed a 2002 dinner menu—so it's a bit behind the times, but that's what people love about Jack's.

42-44 State St. © 518/465-8854. Reservations recommended. Main courses $6.95–$26. AE, DISC, MC, V. Daily 11am–3pm and 5–9pm.

ALBANY AFTER DARK

The Egg, Empire State Plaza Concourse Level (© **518/473-1845;** www.theegg. org), is the funky spherical half-egg on the plaza; its two theaters inside are nearly as cool as the exterior. It hosts a diverse range of entertainment, from modern dance of Mark Morris and classical music to comedy, theater, and the guitar riffs of rock bands like Cheap Trick. **The Palace Theatre,** 19 Clinton Ave. (© **518/465-4663;** www.palacealbany.com), is a gorgeously restored grand 1931 movie theater that now hosts top level talent, including pop concerts (such as Billy Joel and Ray Charles), comedy (Jerry Seinfeld), and the Albany Symphony Orchestra and the Albany Berkshire Ballet. It also handles a number of children's theater performances during the school year. The **Pepsi Arena,** 51 South Pearl St. (© **518/487-2000;** www.pepsiarena.com), is the big place in town for large rock and country-music concerts in addition to sporting events. The **Capital Repertory Theatre,** 111 North Pearl St. (© **518/462-4531;** www. capitalrep.org), features Broadway and Off-Broadway touring musicals and dramatic theater. Outside of town, the **Troy Savings Bank Music Hall,** 7 State St., Troy (© **518/273-0038;** www.troymusichall.org), a wonderfully preserved concert hall in a former 1823 bank, hosts some of the area's best jazz concerts as well as chamber music and other performances; there's almost always something interesting scheduled, and it's just 8 miles from downtown Albany. Past performers have included Ella Fitzgerald and Yo-Yo Ma.

Bars and pubs worth dropping in on include **Albany Pump Station,** 19 Quackenbush Sq. (© **518/447-9000**), a brewpub within a historic pump station; **Riverfront Bar & Grill,** Corning Riverfront Park (© **518/426-4738**), which you can get to by crossing the Hudson River Way pedestrian bridge; and the **Waterworks Pub,** 76 Central Ave. (© **518/465-9079**), which has a large dance floor and DJs spinning tunes. Movie theaters include **Hoyt's** at Crossgates Mall (© **518/452-6440**) and **Spectrum 7 Theaters,** 290 Delaware Ave. (© **518/449-8995**).

10

Central New York

by Rich Beattie

Sandwiched in between the bustling Albany area, the subtle Catskills, the gorgeous Adirondacks, and the pretty Finger Lakes, central New York may not immediately spring to mind as a destination hot spot. To be honest, there are only a few must-sees and -dos here, but those few "musts" warrant passing through.

The area has certainly seen better days—in the 19th century and into the 20th this region of the state produced more hops than elsewhere in the country. As always, some people profited mightily. But ultimately the Depression, agricultural disease, and the discovery that hops could be grown cheaper in the Pacific Northwest ruined this economic outlet.

Today, the centerpiece of this region—and the main reason people go—is the amazing village of **Cooperstown,** the former home of legendary author James Fenimore Cooper and current home to the Baseball Hall of Fame. You could easily spend a couple of days here wandering around the charming town, its gorgeous lake, and variety of attractions.

Though Cooperstown is the area's main draw, it isn't the only hall of fame you'll find: Oddly, soccer and boxing have theirs in these parts as well. Look closer and you'll find that you're in cavern country, and the show cave Howe Caverns makes for an interesting journey underground. The city of Utica has a couple surprises to offer, and recreation abounds on the beautiful Oneida Lake.

And of course once you're done scoping out the scene here, you'll be perfectly positioned on the doorstep to the Adirondacks, the 1000 Islands, the Finger Lakes, and the Catskills.

1 Cooperstown ★★★

77 miles west of Albany, 141 miles east of Rochester, 213 miles northwest of New York City

Set on gorgeous (and mostly undeveloped) Lake Otsego, this tiny village feels frozen in an era where gracious mansions lined the streets, folks greet you by name, and people played a stick-and-ball game that didn't even have a name yet. The town of 2,400 people swells to 50,000 on summer weekends, but despite the crush of visitors, Cooperstown hasn't outgrown its small-town roots. With a couple of exceptions, you won't find chain stores here (the horror! no Starbucks!): Coffeehouses, bookstores, and restaurants are, for the most part, independently run. That personalized, hands-on ownership shows: People are friendly and excited to turn you on to their town.

Though once home to author James Fenimore Cooper—who named Lake Otsego "Glimmerglass" in his Leatherstocking Tales—the town was actually named for his father, William Cooper, in 1786. Today, most people come to see the **Baseball Hall of Fame,** but that's not the only game in town. There are several worthwhile sites, and Lake Otsego harbors a magic all its own. *Just a warning:* The town shuts down early—there are no movie theaters and restaurants close as early as 9pm in the winter months.

ESSENTIALS

GETTING THERE   Off on its own, Cooperstown is easiest to get to by car. From the New York State Thruway, take exit 30 at Herkimer and go south on State Highway 28 or State Highway 80—both will take you to Cooperstown. By bus, **Pine Hills Trailways** (© 800/225-6815 or 845/339-4230; www.trailways. com/members/pinehill.html) provides twice-a-day round-trip service between Cooperstown and New York City. The closest airport, **Albany International Airport** (© 518/242-2200; www.albanyairport.com) is about 75 miles east. See chapter 9 for more details.

VISITOR INFORMATION   The helpful **Cooperstown Chamber of Commerce,** 31 Chestnut St. (© 888/875-2969 or 607/547-9983; www.cooperstown chamber.org), is open daily May through October, 9am to 5pm; from November to April it's open Monday to Saturday, 9am to 5pm.

GETTING AROUND   With thousands of people converging on Cooperstown during the summer, you're best off leaving your car outside town and taking the **trolley** (unless you're staying in town, of course). Look for the blue PARK AND TAKE THE TROLLEY signs as you approach Cooperstown. Parking is free in the outer lots, in the following locations: off Route 28 just south of Cooperstown (traveling north from Oneonta); off Route 28 (Glen Ave.) at Maple Street (traveling south on Rte. 28 from Rte. 20); on Route 80 at upper parking lot of Fenimore House Museum (traveling south on Rte. 80 from Rte. 20). An unlimited daily trolley pass is $2 for adults, $1 for kids. The trolley stops at the museums, Main Street shopping, and other points of interest. From Memorial Day to the last week in June, it runs weekends only, 8:30am to 9pm; from last week in June to Labor Day, it runs daily, 8:30am to 9pm; from Labor Day to Columbus Day, weekends only, 8:30am to 9pm.

EXPLORING COOPERSTOWN

Baseball Hall of Fame ★★★   Yes, you'll find plenty of statistics-spouting baseball fanatics walking around the Hall. But this museum isn't just for passionate lovers of the game or its coveted collectibles. After all, this is America's pastime, and a walk through the 30,000 exhibits shows just how important this sport has been to America's past and present. The hall collected its first artifact in 1937, and now you can find baseballs, bats, uniforms, ballpark artifacts, priceless trading cards, and a microcosm of American history. You'll learn about the Negro Leagues and the integration of baseball, find out the president who established the tradition of throwing out the first pitch on opening day, and, of course, see some of the greatest moments of the greatest players ever. Depending on how big a fan you are, you could spend anywhere from an hour to more than a half day browsing, learning, and loving the game.

25 Main St. © 888/HALL-OF-FAME or 607/547-7200. Admission $9.50 adults, $4 ages 7–12, free for children under 7. Memorial Day to Labor Day daily 9am–9pm; Labor Day to Memorial Day daily 9am–5pm.

Brewery Ommegang ★★   Forget microbrews—Belgian beers blow most of them away with their hoppy taste and high alcohol content. And even though this farmland brewery is some 3,600 miles from Belgium, the brewers are absolutely passionate about the very specialized science of creating the European beverage. Using their own strain of yeast, high-temperature open fermentation, and warm cellaring, they've created small batches of award-winning beers that are strong, hoppy, and worth the trip out of town. Tours are interesting and, of course, you'll get some free samples.

656 County Hwy. 33. ℂ 800/544-1809. 25-min. tours are $4 and include beer tasting; fee is redeemable against any purchase. Memorial Day to Labor Day daily 11am–6pm; Labor Day to Memorial Day daily noon–5pm. From Main St. in Cooperstown turn onto Pioneer St., continue to the T and turn right. Then turn left on Susquehanna Ave. Continue ½ mile. Turn right on County Hwy. 33.

Farmers Market ★ Don't let the name throw you: This walk-through-the-buildings museum is an interesting look at rural village life circa 1845. The 25 historic buildings were moved to this site, a working farm since 1790, to re-create a 19th-century village. Workers staff some of the buildings dressed in period costumes and fully acting the part: the blacksmith is banging out horseshoes, the printer is creating a poster, and the pharmacist is passing out information on the herbal remedies of the time. They bring the museum to life and make it worth spending an hour or so here.

Lake Rd., 1 mile north of Cooperstown. (C) 888/547-1450 or 607/547-1450. Admission $9 adults, $4 children 7–12. Apr to mid-May Tues–Sat 10am–4pm; mid-May to mid-Oct daily 10am–5pm.

Fenimore Art Museum ⭐   Built on the site of James Fenimore Cooper's home, a visit to this elegant 1930s mansion overlooking Otsego Lake is a great way to spend an hour. Inside you'll find a revolving collection depicting local life, portraits of Cooper, a great collection of folk art, and examples of Hudson River School paintings. The real treasure is in the collection of Native American art, a section of the museum added in 1995. You'll see masks, sculptures, bows and arrows, headdresses, moccasins, and gorgeous beadwork from tribes all over America.

Lake Road. (C) 888/547-1450 or 607/547-1400. Admission $9 adults, $4 ages 7–12. June–Sept daily 10am–4pm; Oct–Dec and Apr–May Tues–Sun 10am–4pm.

Hyde Hall ⭐   This enormous neoclassic mansion museum is quite the anomaly here in the land of small towns. Built by George Clarke, the 50-room home was built between 1817 and 1834 to be a showplace at the center of his agricultural empire. It's considered one of the nation's major private architectural undertakings in the years between the Revolutionary and the Civil wars, and it offers a stunning contrast to the Farmer's Museum in showing how the other half lived. Today, you'll explore great rooms, a wine cellar, chapel, and of course servants quarters. With four structures on the property, 50 rooms, and a gorgeous view of Lake Otsego, you'll want to spend some time beyond the hourlong tour. Bring a picnic lunch!

1 Mill Rd. (C) 607/547-5098. Admission $7 adults, $4 children. Mid-May to late Oct. Thurs–Tues 10am–5pm; last tour is at 4pm. From Cooperstown, go east on Main St. over the bridge and up E. Lake Rd. (Rte. 31) about 8 miles, past Glimmerglass State Park. Turn left on Mill Rd. and follow it for about ½ mile. Turn left.

OUTDOOR ACTIVITIES

BOATING   Take a 1-hour narrated historic tour of gorgeous Lake Otsego aboard a classic 1912 mahogany yacht with **Lake Otsego Boat Tours,** 1 Fair St. ((C) **607/547-5295**). Or do it yourself without the chattering by renting a canoe or kayak from **Sam Smith's Boat Yard,** State Hwy. 28 ((C) **607/547-2543**), for $20 an hour.

GOLF   The Otesaga, 60 Lake St. ((C) **800/348-6222** or 607/547-9931; www.otesaga.com), has a renowned course that consistently rates among the nation's top resort courses. Even if you're not a duffer it's worth checking out the intimidating 18th tee, which sits on an island; you have to hit back over the water toward the hotel. Greens fees are $70 for guests, $85 nonguests.

SHOPPING

As you can imagine, baseball memorabilia and all kinds of accessories are the heart of the shopping world here. From autographed baseball cards to inscribed bats and old-time photos, you'll find it all along Main Street. You'll find good

---

Tips Value Pass

If you're planning on visiting the Hall of Fame, the Farmer's Museum, and the Fenimore Art Museum, buy a pass at the first one you visit. Entrance to all three costs $22 for adults, $9.50 for kids. Entry to the Hall of Fame plus one other museum costs $15 for adults, $6.50 for kids.

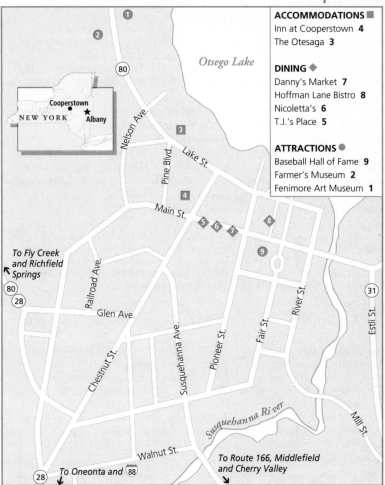

ACCOMMODATIONS ■
Inn at Cooperstown **4**
The Otesaga **3**

DINING ◆
Danny's Market **7**
Hoffman Lane Bistro **8**
Nicoletta's **6**
T.J.'s Place **5**

ATTRACTIONS ●
Baseball Hall of Fame **9**
Farmer's Museum **2**
Fenimore Art Museum **1**

selections at **Pioneer Sports Cards,** 106 Main St. (© **607/547-2323**); **Extra Innings,** 54 Main St. (© **607/547-2292**), and **Cooperstown Sports,** 69 Main St. (© **607/547-4477**). Get your wooden bat personalized at **Cooperstown Bat Co.,** 118 Main St. (© **888/547-2415**). Outside of the baseball realm and just outside of town, **Fly Creek Cider Mill & Orchard,** 288 Goose St., Fly Creek (© **607/547-9692;** May–Dec 25), squeezes out some outstanding cider and is the home of all things apple, even salsa and fudge.

WHERE TO STAY
With a limited supply of rooms and tons of visitors in the summertime, even hotels of dubious quality jack up their rates to near the level of some of the inns in the "expensive" category. In other words, you're better off paying $20 more per night and getting accommodations you can count on. One chain in the city limits is the **Best Western,** 50 Commons Dr. (© **607/547-9439**). In Oneonta, 25 miles away, you'll find a **Holiday Inn,** Route 23 (© **607/433-2250**).

VERY EXPENSIVE

The Otesaga ★★★   Since 1909, the Otesaga has been the grande dame of the area, offering luxurious digs on the shores of the gloriously undeveloped Lake Otsego—and today you can only experience it from mid-April to the end of November. A recent renovation has updated the Otesaga's infrastructure, but fortunately hasn't changed its formal country look too much. It maintains heavy wooden doors, high ceilings, and spacious rooms that come luxuriously furnished and very comfortable, not stuffed full of useless amenities; some of them, like no. 245, are huge. Done in creamy tones and floral patterns, there's a refined elegance about the place; step out onto one of the numerous verandas and you'll find a refined serenity as well (along with some great views of the lake and the challenging golf course). A couple of drawbacks: The service is spotty—some staffers at this old-time hotel are used to doing things in a particular way and special requests may be greeted coolly. Also, you must stay on the Modified American Plan (MAP), which includes breakfast and dinner.

60 Lake St., Cooperstown, NY 13326. ② **800/348-6222** or 607/547-9931. Fax 607/547-9645. www.otesaga. com. 136 units. Late May to mid-Oct $340–$485; late Apr to late May and mid-Oct to mid-Nov $315–$460. Rates include breakfast buffet and 4-course dinner. AE, MC, V. Free valet parking. 2-night minimum on weekends. **Amenities:** 3 restaurants; 2 lounges; heated outdoor pool; 2 tennis courts; exercise room; complimentary canoe and boat use; game room, concierge; small business center; limited room service; babysitting; laundry service; dry cleaning. *In room:* A/C, TV, dataport, hair dryer, iron, safe.

EXPENSIVE

Blue Mingo B&B ★   This tiny inn, set in a gorgeous home just outside the bustle of town, is one of the few places to stay right on Lake Otsego. The inn's furnished in a rather formal style, but still maintains a relaxed air about it. The nonsmoking rooms are generally spacious (but a bit on the flowery side); there's no A/C, but ceiling fans usually get the job done, even in the middle of summer. Stay away from the ground-floor room, which is too close to the public area. My favorite is the Empire Room, outfitted with period antiques including a king sleigh bed and lake views. Guests can use the inn's canoes to take out and explore the lake. *Bonus:* The breakfast is one of the best I've ever had at a B&B.

6088 State Hwy. 80, W. Lake Rd., Cooperstown, NY 13326. ② **607/547-9414.** www.bluemingoinn.com. 5 units, 3 with private bathroom. $185–$225 double (Memorial Day to Labor Day); $165–$200 double (rest of May, Sept, Oct). Closed Nov–Apr. Rates include full breakfast. 2-night weekend minimums June–Aug. MC, V. **Amenities:** Restaurant; heated outdoor pool; complimentary use of canoes. *In room:* TV.

Inn at Cooperstown ★★   This gorgeous, yellow Victorian inn dates from 1874, and with no TVs or phones in the rooms it remains a great place to get away from it all. A classic inn without a trace of pretension and amazingly affable innkeepers, it's located right off of Main Street and just a short walk from the Hall of Fame. The hotel was the first designed by Henry J. Hardenbergh, who went on to design New York City's Plaza Hotel; the grand dreams he had show up more on the outside, with the inn's extravagant facade and sweeping veranda. The inside has a very cozy feel: Rooms are by no means enormous but they're quite comfortable, even though some rooms have quite a small shower. People congregate downstairs in the sitting room—the kind of place people curl up on the sofa to watch TV—or sit out on the veranda in a rocking chair with a book.

16 Chestnut St., Cooperstown, NY 13326. ② **607/547-5756.** Fax 607/547-8779. www.innatcooperstown. com. 17 units. Mid-June to Labor Day $185 double, $295 suite; Sept–Oct midweek $140 double, weekend

$185 double, midweek $225 suite, weekend $295 suite; Oct–Dec $118 double, $190 suite; Jan–Mar $120 double, $200 suite; Apr to mid-June $160 double, $225 suite. Rates include continental breakfast. 2-night minimum on holiday weekends. AE, DC, DISC, MC, V. *In room:* A/C, hair dryer, iron, no phone, CD player.

Inn at Fly Creek ★   Bright, cheery, modern, and peacefully removed from the hubbub of the town (but just a 5-min. drive away), this tiny inn boasts the amenities of a much larger hotel. You'll find an indoor pool, tennis court, a stocked fishing pond, and hiking trails that wander all over this wooded countryside property that doubles as a stable (you can take a riding lesson, too, though it's extra). Public areas are big and bright with gorgeous wood floors and the nonsmoking rooms and bathrooms are enormous and decorated in bright tones. The Master Suite is nothing less than completely indulgent, with heated wooden floors, a working fireplace, enormous whirlpool tub, and a huge bay window and screened-in porch overlooking the lake and the countryside.

434 Bed Bug Hill Rd., Fly Creek, NY 13337. © 607/547-9311. www.flycreekstables.com. 5 units. Memorial Day to Labor Day $165–$250 double; Labor Day to Memorial Day $132–$200 double. Rates include full breakfast. MC, V. **Amenities:** Indoor pool; tennis court lighted for night play; small exercise area; Jacuzzi. *In room:* A/C, TV/VCR, dataport, fridge.

MODERATE

American Hotel ★★   Just 25 miles from Cooperstown, the 1847 building that houses the American was saved from complete ruin by its affable owners and opened in 2002. They've done such an amazing job restoring it, actually that they're brave enough to put the "before" photos on their website. Today the pillars of this inn stand tall outside, while the interior bursts forth with good taste. Though the rooms are on the small side, their simple, subtle colors and eclectic decor keep them bright, airy, and cheery. There's no TV, just the quiet rustle of the breeze. A couple rooms have two twin beds, so be sure to specify if you want one bed.

192 Main St., P.O. Box 121, Sharon Springs, NY 13459. © 518/284-2105. www.americanhotelny.com. 9 units. June–Aug $150 double; Sept–Oct and Apr–May $120 double; Nov–Mar $100 double. Rates include full breakfast. 2-night minimum on weekends July–Aug. AE, DC, DISC, MC, V. Between I-88 and I-90 at the crossroads of rtes. 10 and 20. The hotel is on the east side of Main St./Rte. 10, 3 blocks north of Rte. 20. **Amenities:** Restaurant; lounge. *In room:* A/C, dataport, hair dryer.

CAMPGROUNDS

Cooperstown Shadow Brook Campground, 2149 County Rd. 31 (© 607/ 264-8431), has a pool, playground, stocked fishing pond, and theme weekends and is great for families. **Glimmerglass State Park,** 1527 County Hwy. 31 (© 607/547-8662), 8 miles outside of Cooperstown, overlooks Lake Otsego.

WHERE TO DINE
EXPENSIVE

Alex & Ika ★★★ *Finds* CONTINENTAL   Drive past this former bowling alley in the tiny town of Cherry Valley and you'd never guess that there's a culinary magic show happening inside. The menu—now featuring smaller, tapas-style dishes—changes weekly. But whatever you choose, you will remember the inventive combinations of flavors long after the meal has ended. Dishes may include spicy habañero shrimp, delicately fried and served with passion fruit cream. You'll just be recovering as more plates arrive: shredded duck served with chile-carrot-cherry salsa, Thai coconut curry, cilantro cream, shiitake mushrooms, and basmati rice. Even standards like lamb come with a creation of spinach and pine nuts, slow-roasted tomato, fried polenta, and balsamic glaze.

It all happens in a tiny, homey space that's intimate and romantic, and even the wine and beer lists are excellent. The only drawback is that they're only open on weekends.

11 Main St., Cherry Valley. © 607/264-9315. Reservations not accepted. Tapas $6–$11. No credit cards. Fri–Sat noon–10pm. Closed 2 weeks in fall and winter.

MODERATE

Hoffman Lane Bistro ★★ CONTEMPORARY AMERICAN   Cooperstown's hippest locale sits just off the mayhem of Main Street. People crowd into the lively downstairs bar to hear the occasional musician or just relax. The noise doesn't disrupt a quiet dinner, but for extra privacy, head upstairs. Entrees include tasty pastas, such as linguine with salmon sautéed with Roma tomatoes, onions, and mushrooms in a pesto-wine sauce; inventive takes on home cooking, like the meatloaf made with lamb, pork, and beef; or more complex dishes like pan-seared tuna au poivre in a brandy cream sauce.

2 Hoffman Lane © 607/547-7055. Reservations recommended. Main courses and pastas $11–$20; lunch $6–$7. AE, MC, V. June–Sept daily 11:30am–2pm and 5–10pm; Oct–May Wed–Sun 11:30am–2pm and 5–9pm.

Nicoletta's Italian Café ★ ECLECTIC ITALIAN   Step into this small Main Street restaurant and the delightful aroma of roasted garlic and Italian spices practically knocks you off your feet. You'll find paintings of Italy on the wall and will likely hear Sinatra playing. But even when it gets crowded in this intimate restaurant, it's never too loud for conversation. And once your meal arrives, you may not want to talk anyway. Nicoletta's covers all the basics and does them well—one house favorite is the frutti di mare, a full platter of shrimp, scallops, mussels, and clams sautéed in a light roma tomato sauce served over capellini.

96 Main St. © 607/547-7499. Reservations recommended. Main courses and pastas $11–$20. MC, V. Daily 4–9pm.

INEXPENSIVE

Danny's Market ★★ *Value* DELI   This bustling deli is Main Street's busiest, and there's a good reason: great sandwiches served on excellent fresh baked bread. The best ones: "Aged in Caves," paper-thin slices of prosciutto with smoked Gouda, tomato, and honey mustard; and the "Chicken Dilemma," which comes with homemade mozzarella and marinated red peppers. Or design your own sandwich. My suggestion? Take it to go and enjoy it lakeside.

92 Main St. © 607/547-4053. Sandwiches $6–$6.50. MC, V. Mon–Sat 7:30am–8pm; Sun 7:30am–5pm. Closed Feb.

T.J.'s Place *Kids* AMERICAN   With a life-size hot dog statue, old Coca-Cola signs, and signed photos of old ball players lining the walls—all of it for sale—this is a great place to bring the kids and look for memorabilia. And if you're in the market for lunch or dinner, you'll find all the burger basics, plus down-home cookin' like barbecued spare ribs, ham steak with pineapple, lasagna, and even liver and onions.

124 Main St. © 800/860-5670 or 607/547-4040. Reservations not accepted. Main courses $10–$17; lunch $6–$10. Daily June to Columbus Day 7:30am–8pm; Columbus Day to June 7:30am–8pm.

COOPERSTOWN AFTER DARK

PERFORMING ARTS   Glimmerglass Opera, north of Cooperstown on Route 80 (© 607/547-5704), has evolved from performances in the auditorium of Cooperstown High School in 1975 to an internationally acclaimed summer opera house. With four operas in July and August, they produce new, little-known, and familiar operas, among other works of music theater—all of which performed in the original language with projected English titles. The 900-seat theater, open since 1987, sits on 43 acres of farmland with unusual sliding walls that allow everyone to enjoy fresh air and views of the countryside before per-formances and during intermissions.

2 Utica & Environs

96 miles northeast of Albany, 203 miles east of Buffalo.

Utica had its heyday in the era of the Erie Canal, when manufacturing was boom-ing. It attracted business, travelers, even the founders of a Utopian society—one that went on to create some of the country's finest flatware. The Oneida Com-pany is still around, but the Utica/Rome area is hardly the same. Those cities are trying to stage something of a comeback, but it's an uphill struggle: The biggest success story has been the reopening of the gorgeous Hotel Utica.

You won't want to spend much time in the cities—there's just not much there—but the countryside is very pretty. For nature exploration and outdoor fun try Howe Caverns and gorgeous Oneida Lake.

ESSENTIALS

GETTING THERE   The New York State Thruway (I-90) passes through the heart of it all. **Amtrak** and **Greyhound** both arrive into Utica at Union Station, 321 Main St. (© **315/797-8962**). The major airport in the area is **Syracuse Hancock International** (p. 352), but **Continental Connection** (© **800/525-0280**) flies into **Oneida County Airport** (© **315/736-9404**), just 10 minutes from downtown Utica; Avis and Hertz both have rental counters at Oneida.

VISITOR INFORMATION   For the most detailed info, visit or call the **Oneida County Convention & Visitors Bureau,** exit 31 off I-90 (© **800/426-3132;** Mon–Fri 9am–5pm, Sat–Sun 10am–6pm). For general information, con-tact the **Central–Leatherstocking Region** tourist office (© **800/233-8778**).

GETTING AROUND   Not the place to be without a car—I-90 will be your quickest (if most boring) way of getting around; just be aware that it's a toll road. If you need a taxi, call **Utica Area Black & White** (© **315/732-3121**) or **City Comb** (© **315/724-5454**).

AREA ATTRACTIONS

Erie Canal Village ★★ *Kids*   This reconstructed 18th-century settlement makes for a fun and interesting half-day experience for the family. Built on the site where the first shovelful of earth was turned for the Erie Canal on July 4, 1817, there's now an entire village full of Colonial buildings staffed by costumed players. Sound like the Farmer's Museum in Cooperstown? They're very similar—don't do both. Walk around at your own pace: in this self-guided tour, you'll see a tavern, ice house, church, blacksmith shop, train station, school, print shop, and three homes. There's also a nice collection of horse-drawn carriages, sleighs, and farm equipment.

5789 New London Rd., rtes. 46 and 49, Rome. (© **888/374-3226** or 315/337-3999. Village admission $5 adults, $4 seniors, $3 age 5–17, free for children under 4. Boat ride is extra $5, train ride an extra $1.50. Memorial Day to Labor Day Wed–Sat, 10am–5pm, Sun noon–5pm; Sept Sat–Sun noon–5pm. Take I-90 to exit 32, turn right on 233N to 49W.

Fort Stanwix ⭐ *Kids*   The wooden posts that now guard this 18th-century fort may look out of place today in the middle of downtown Rome, but this fort makes for a fun brief stopover. It's hard to imagine that at one time this area was an essential portage that helped bridge the waterways between the Atlantic Ocean and the Great Lakes, but protecting the strategic position was exactly why this fort was built in 1758. It went on to be an important base of protection during the French and Indian and the Revolutionary wars, and today the fort's been almost completely reconstructed. Take a walk or a guided tour through its grounds and get a glimpse of how fort-bound pioneers once lived.

112 E. Park St., Rome. © **315/336-2090.** Free admission. Apr–Dec daily 9am–5pm; late June to late Aug daily 9am–7pm. New York State Thruway to exit 32 to Rte. 233 north to Rte. 365 west, following the signs to downtown Rome.

Howe Caverns ⭐   Discovered in 1842 when farmer Lester Howe found a passage to central New York's underworld in his field, Howe Caverns has become the area's biggest attraction—you'll see billboards for miles around. And since 1929, when walkways, lighting, and elevators were installed, people have flocked to take the journey. While it's hardly in the same league as big holes like Mammoth Cave in Kentucky, there's a certain charm to this relatively small underground space, and kids think it's pretty cool. The 80-minute tours are guided and include a quarter-mile boat ride on the underground Lake of Venus.

255 Discovery Dr., Howes Cave. © **518/296-8900.** www.howecaverns.com. Admission $15 adults, $12 seniors, $7 ages 7–12, free for children under 7. July to Labor Day 8am–8pm daily; Labor Day to June 9am–6pm daily. I -90 to exit 25A; I-88 west to exit 22.

Matt Brewing Company ⭐   They've garnered awards for their excellent Saranac Beer, but the Matt Brewing Company, now run by the fourth generation of the Matt family, also produces Utica Club and some fun specialty brews, like Three Stooges Ale, out of their Utica headquarters. Their 1-hour tour takes you through the entire beer-making process. And of course what brewery tour would be complete without a tasting?

Brewhouse Sq., Utica. © **800/765-6288** or 315/732-0022. Tours $3 adults, $1 age 6–12, free for children under 6. June–Aug tours are on the hour Mon–Sat 1–4pm and Sun 1–3pm; Sept–May tours Fri–Sat at 1 and 3pm. Tours run 1 hr., call in advance to make reservations. New York State Thruway exit 31, take Genesee St. south through downtown Utica to Court St. and take a right.

BEACHES & OUTDOOR ACTIVITIES
HITTING THE BEACH   On the eastern shore of Oneida Lake lies a nice stretch of sand—**Sylvan Beach.** Lined with restaurants and an amusement park, the slender beach gets absolutely packed with sunbathers in the summertime and parking is tight. If you're planning to soak up the sun, come early or stay here (see below). Farther north on the shores of Lake Ontario, **Sandy Island Beach,** off Route 3 on County Route 15 in Sandy Creek (© **800/596-3200,** ext. 3451, or 315/349-3451) is part of the Eastern Lake Ontario Dune and Wetland Area, a 17-mile stretch of shoreline. The area is the only significant freshwater dune site in the northeastern U.S., which means not only can you relax on the beach but you can also go hiking among the dunes to see several species of migratory birds and waterfowl, including sandpipers, plovers, killdeer, gulls, and terns. You may also see fox, deer, beaver, and turtles moving among the wetland and shore areas.

GOLF   In between Utica and Rome, hit the links at the 7,000-yard par-72 **Crestwood Golf Club,** Route 291, Marcy (② **315/736-0478;** green fees $17). In Rome, try the **Golf Knolls Golf Course,** 5219 Rome–Taberg Rd. (② **315/337-0920;** call for green fees). And in Utica, line up your shots at the **Valley View Golf Course,** 620 Memorial Pkwy., Utica (② **315/732-8755;** green fees $18).

ESPECIALLY FOR KIDS

Right on the shores of Oneida Lake is **Sylvan Beach Amusement Park,** on Route 13 in Sylvan Beach (② **315/762-5212**), which boasts central New York's largest roller coaster. Granted, that's not saying much, but this is a fun little amusement park, especially for younger kids, with bumper cars and boats, a slide, and plenty of games. Best of all, admission is free—you just pay for your activities. A smaller spot for summertime family fun is the **Peterpaul Recreation Park,** Route 49 West, Rome (② **315/339-2666**). And the **Fort Rickey Children's Discovery Zoo,** 5135 Rome–New London Rd. (② **315/336-1930**), is a petting zoo where kids can touch a python or a porcupine.

SHOPPING

The tradition of the Oneida Community lives on—you can purchase all sorts of housewares where the original utopian society was founded: the **Oneida Factory Store,** 606 Sherrill Rd., Sherrill (② **315/361-3661**). You can get the famous flatware, along with crystal, china, and tableware.

WHERE TO STAY

There are some chains in the area. The nicest is the **Radisson,** 200 Genesee St., Utica (② **800/333-3333** or 315/797-8010).

MODERATE

Governor's House B&B ★★ *Finds*   This B&B came oh-so-close to becoming the governor's mansion the mid-19th century: Lawmakers wanted the state leader to live here because the living room is said to be the exact geographical center of the state. But by one vote, the capitol was placed in Albany, leaving the Federal brick mansion to fend for itself—and today it looks great. Unlike many historic properties, its gorgeous wood floors and furniture haven't been gutted, just renovated. Now its five nonsmoking guest rooms boast private bathrooms, high ceilings, and canopy beds.

50 Seneca Ave, Oneida Castle, NY 13421. ② **800/437-8177** or 315/363-5643. 5 units. Sun–Thurs $115–$134 double; Fri–Sat $135–$161 double. MC, V. No children under 12. Full breakfast on weekends, continental breakfast weekdays. Take I-90 exit 33, turn left on Rte. 365 west, drive 4 miles to intersection with Rte. 5. *In room:* A/C, TV/VCR.

Hotel Utica ★★★ *Finds*   One of central New York's success stories was the reopening of this grand historic hotel that opened its doors in 1912, shut them in 1972, and reopened in 2001. It's dripping with history; FDR campaigned here in the '20s, jazz great Lionel Hampton played here in 1939, Judy Garland sang here around 1950, and Bobby Kennedy stayed here on a campaign trip. Now it's been totally gutted and redone in grand style, with pillars and chandeliers gracing the elegant lobby. Rooms are huge and outfitted with very comfortable furniture. Decorated in mahogany, royal blues, and deep reds, you'll find sizable workstations and big bathrooms. In fact, the rooms are big enough that suites aren't worth the extra price unless you need meeting space. Get one on the eighth or ninth floor (future renovations will open up floors 10–14) and you'll get a view out over the city, which is always nice, even when the city is Utica.

102 Lafayette St., Utica, NY 13502. © **877/906-1912** or 315/724-7829. Fax 315/733-7621. www.hotel uticany.com. 112 units. Apr–Oct $119 double, $149–$169 suite; Nov–Mar $109 double, $139–$159 suite. AE, DC, DISC, MC, V. **Amenities:** Restaurant; lounge; access to nearby health club; 24-hr. small business center; limited room service; laundry service; same-day dry cleaning. *In room:* TV w/pay movies (suites have VCRs), fridge in most rooms, dataport, coffeemaker, hair dryer.

Sunset Cottages ✶   This collection of cottages sits right on the beach at the edge of Lake Oneida. Its location means that there's always a party going on, but inside the rooms it's surprisingly quiet. The cottages themselves are nothing fancy, though they are spacious, with full kitchens, and nicer than any of the lakefront motels. Oddly, though, linens aren't provided, so you must bring your own sheets and towels. Newer, renovated cottages are bright and airy, while the older ones still have dark wood paneling.

P.O. Box 134, Park Ave., Sylvan Beach, NY 13157. © **315/762-4093.** www.sylvanbeach.com. 28 units. Apr–Sept $125–$150 double. 2-night minimum stay. MC, V. From I-90 take exit 34 at Canastota. Turn right on Rte. 13 North for 7 miles. Turn right after crossing the bridge; it loops around to become Park Ave. *In room:* A/C, TV, kitchen.

CAMPGROUNDS

To pitch your tent with a great view of Lake Oneida, set up at **Verona Beach State Park,** 6541 Lake Shore Rd. South, Verona Beach (© **315/762-4463**). For another water-view campground, check out **Delta Lake State Park,** 8797 State Rd. 46, Rome (© **315/337-4670**).

WHERE TO DINE
MODERATE

Savoy ✶ AMERICAN   The Savoy is a friendly neighborhood spot that starts filling up fast the moment it opens. Everyone's rushing in for the menu that features a good selection of soups, salads, and starters, along with heaping portions of chicken, steak, and fish. You'll also find some good barbecue, like a St. Louis–style rib rack that comes hot out of the smoker. Or opt for a burger—it's just $5.

225 E. Dominick St., Rome. © **315/339-3166.** Main courses $7–$15. AE, DC, DISC, MC, V. Mon–Thurs 11:30am–10pm; Fri 11:30am–11pm; Sat 5–11pm; Sun 4–9pm.

Sea Shell Inn ✶ AMERICAN   A good alternative to the party-hearty beachfront bars that line Lake Oneida. This laid-back restaurant has knotty pine walls and ceiling fans, while the unique tables are filled with sand and shells and covered with glass. For the most relaxation, head to the tables on the back patio, on a lawn overlooking the lake. Outside of the fried frog legs, you won't find anything wildly different on the menu, but it's mostly done well, with emphasis on seafood. Don't fixate on the apps: Dinners come with plenty of extras.

Lake Shore Rd., Verona Beach. © **315/762-4606.** Main courses $9–$16. Sun from 3pm; Tues–Sat from 4pm. AE, DISC, MC, V.

INEXPENSIVE

Harpoon Eddie's ✶ AMERICAN   Set right on the beach, there's always a party happening here. In fact, it's the area's best place to sit outside and have a cold drink while checking out all the beach activity. If you want a bite, there are the basic hot dogs, burgers, and wings plus some nice fish dishes like mahimahi and grilled tuna sandwiches.

611 Park Ave., Sylvan Beach. © 315/762-5238. Main courses $5–$10. MC, V. Spring 4–11:30pm; summer noon–11:30pm (the season changes when the owner says it does).

UTICA & ENVIRONS AFTER DARK

Gamblers may want to check out **Turning Stone Casino,** just off I-90's exit 33 (© **800/771-7711**). Run by the Oneida Nation, you'll find a wealth of slots and table games, as well as live shows. And if you're in the mood for more live entertainment, check out **Beck's Grove Dinner Theater,** 4286 Oswego Rd., Blossvale (© **315/336-7038**), which dates from Prohibition.

11

The Finger Lakes Region

by Neil E. Schlecht

On a map of New York, 11 narrow blue streaks snake across the middle of the state. These curious parallel formations, the result of glaciers receding at the end of the last Ice Age, are the Finger Lakes, so named for their obvious resemblance to the slender, crooked digits of a human hand. But what those deep cobalt, glossy-surfaced lakes look like on a map is nothing compared to their appearance in person. The vast region is a pastoral patchwork of storybook waterfront villages, grand Victorian homes, dairy farms, forests, waterfalls, and sloped vineyards. And throughout, the lakes run through it.

The "fingers" are the five major lakes (there are actually 11) that stripe the region. These unique bodies of water, which range in length from 3 to 40 miles and are as narrow as one-third of a mile across, are framed by a gentle rise of vineyard-covered banks and rolling hills. The region is like a dream marriage of Scotland and Napa Valley. The lakes have given rise to unique conditions and microclimates that are ideal for grape-growing, and the region is home to one of the most notable winemaking concentrations in the country; an ever-growing roster of some 75 wineries dot the lakes. Several are boutique wineries that have made great strides in challenging the accepted supremacy of California and Oregon winemakers. Three large, official wine trails—comprising the wineries along Cayuga, Seneca, and Keuka lakes—can be followed, making it easy to visit Finger Lakes wineries and taste their wines.

Quite amazingly, the Finger Lakes region remains unknown to many Americans—and even many New Yorkers. Anchored by medium-size cities on either side, Syracuse and Rochester, the Finger Lakes are mostly largely about outdoor recreation, relaxed wine tours and small-town life, though the area packs a few surprises, such as the astounding Corning Museum of Glass; the summer haunts of Mark Twain; the legacy of the underground railroad that carried slaves to freedom; and the origins of the women's suffrage and civil rights movements, American aviation, and the modern Mormon Church.

In warm months, the Finger Lakes Region comes alive with cyclists, wine tourists, and theater and music fans. Though the region is most often thought of as a summer destination, it is really a year-round place. It is gorgeous in winter—which is actually much milder than most parts of upstate New York—and perhaps most stunning in autumn, when the brilliant blue waters are framed by an earthy array of reds and yellows, sun-kissed vineyards.

1 Orientation

ARRIVING

BY PLANE Most visitors traveling by air will fly into either the **Greater Rochester International Airport,** 1200 Brooks Ave., Rochester (© **716/464-6000;** www.rocairport.com), or Syracuse's **Hancock International Airport,** 1000

The Finger Lakes Region

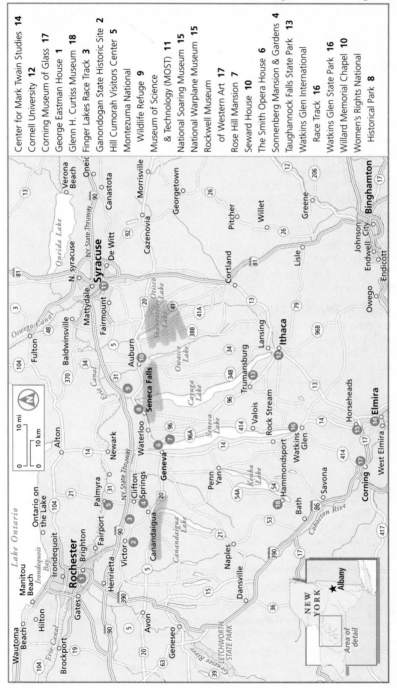

Colonel Eileen Collins Blvd., Syracuse (© **315/454-4330;** www.syrairport.org); both are serviced by most major airlines. Smaller regional airports are **Elmira/ Corning Regional Airport,** 276 Sing Sing Rd., Horseheads (© **607/795-0402;** www.elmiracorningairport.com), and **Tompkins County Airport,** 72 Brown Rd., Ithaca (© **607/257-0456**).

BY CAR   The Finger Lakes Region is within a day's drive of most major metropolitan areas in the northeastern U.S. and eastern Canada; Seneca Lake is about 300 miles from New York City, 400 miles from Boston, 230 miles from Toronto, and 275 miles from Philadelphia. The New York State Thruway **(I-90),** travels across the top of the region, from Albany all the way to Rochester and beyond. From Binghamton and Pennsylvania, **I-81** travels north to Syracuse, and **Route 17** west to Corning.

The major rental car agencies have outlets at the two largest airports.

BY TRAIN   Amtrak (© **800/USA-RAIL;** www.amtrak.com) has service to the Finger Lakes Region to Syracuse and Rochester from New York City, Buffalo, Boston, and other cities.

BY BUS   Bus service to the Finger Lakes is available on **Greyhound Bus Lines** (© **800/231-2222;** www.greyhound.com), with stations in Ithaca, Syracuse, Geneva, and Rochester, and **Trailways** (© **800/343-9999;** www.trailways.com), which travels to Elmira, Geneva, Rochester, and Syracuse.

VISITOR INFORMATION

For general tourist information before your trip, contact **Finger Lakes Association,** 309 Lake St., Penn Yan, NY 14527 (© **800/548-4386;** www.fingerlakes. org). Their web page has contact information and links to each of the region's individual county websites.

Many, many good free publications are widely available across the region, at hotels, restaurants, and other sites, with tons of information on wine routes, outdoor activities, accommodations, festivals, and more.

AREA LAYOUT

Stretching from Lake Ontario in the north almost to the Pennsylvania border, about midway between New York City and Niagara Falls, the Finger Lakes Region covers some 9,000 square miles and touches upon 14 counties, occupying a huge chunk of central-western New York. The region is roughly equidistant between Albany and Buffalo and extends from Lake Ontario in the north and almost to the Pennsylvania border in the south.

The region is covered below in a clockwise direction, beginning with the southeast region around Ithaca. Since many of the major towns and attractions

---

Fun Fact **Say What?**

The Finger Lakes take their names from Native American languages of the original inhabitants of the region. Lake and place names can work a real number on your tongue; here's a guide to meanings and pronunciations:

Skaneateles	Long Lake	skinny-atlas
Cayuga	Boat Landing	*kyoo*-gah
Seneca	Place of the Stone	*sen*-uh-kah
Keuka	Canoe Landing	*kyoo*-kah
Canandaigua	Chosen Place	can-uhn-*day*-gwuh

Moments The Finger Lakes Wine Trails

The Finger Lakes Region, with more than 75 bonded wineries and some 10,000 acres of vineyards, is one of the nation's great wine-producing regions. A cool-climate viticultural region—comparable to the Burgundy and Champagne regions in France—the Finger Lakes are ideal for growing vinifera, or noble, grapes. The lakes themselves, products of glacial receding, produce unique microclimates that make the region such a propitious grape-growing and winemaking region. The lakes act as natural forces of air-conditioning, cooling the regions in summer and warming them in winter (which is why the brutal winters of Buffalo and other parts of upstate New York are unknown in the Finger Lakes), thus protecting grapes from extreme temperature conditions. The sloping hillsides accentuate natural air drainage. The Finger Lakes Region produces excellent riesling, pinot noir, chardonnay, sparkling, and rare ice wines.

Grape growing and wine production are fundamental to the region's economy and tourism. The wine country is centered around four main lakes: Canandaigua, Keuka, Seneca, and Cayuga. Three major (and one minor) wine trails have been organized to facilitate touring and tastings at the wineries that dot them. They are: Cayuga Wine Trail, Seneca Lake Wine Trail, Keuka Lake Wine Trail, and the smallest, Canandaigua Wine Trail. Pick up brochures on the individual trails in the region as well as the "Free Map & Guide" of all the wineries in the Finger Lakes, and see the sidebars on each wine trail below.

Hitting the wine trails is a blast: scenic, educational, and fun. The worst thing to do, though, is to drink and drive as you go from winery to winery. Fortunately, there are other options. For organized wine tours in limousines and other multipassenger vehicles, contact one of the following wine transportation and tour specialists: **Finger Lakes Winery Tours & Transportation** (✆ 585/329-0858; www.fingerlakeswinerytours. com); **Quality Winery Tours** (✆ 877/424-7004; www.qualitytran.com); **VRA Imperial Limousine, Inc.** (✆ 800/303-6100; www.implimo.com); **Park Place Limousine and Transportation Services** (✆ 585/223-7780; www. rochesterlimousine.com); and **Grapevine Country Tours** (✆ 877/557-6769; www.grapevinecountrytours.com).

in the area tend to be clustered at the top or bottom ends of lakes, when traveling by car it's probably easiest to move in one direction from east to west or west to east, rather than circling entire lakes, which although not wide are certainly long.

GETTING AROUND

BY CAR A car is virtually indispensable for any kind of traveling in the Finger Lakes Region; there is very little public transportation in the area, except between major cities. As I've mentioned, the major car-rental companies have outlets at both Rochester International Airport and Syracuse's Hancock International Airport.

BY ORGANIZED TOUR   Finger Lakes Tours, Ltd., Drawer 9, Jasper, NY 14855 (℡ 607/792-3663; www.finger-lakes-tours.com), offers all-inclusive family, hunting, fishing, biking and hiking, wine festival, and even "women only" organized tours of the region, in a variety of price ranges. New World Tour Company (℡ 607/387-6292; www.newworldtour.com) and Grapevine Country Tours (℡ 877/557-6769; www.grapevinecountrytours.com) organize Finger Lakes Wine Trail tours.

2 Ithaca ⭐⭐ & Southern Cayuga Lake

240 miles northeast of New York City; 40 miles east of Corning

Ithaca, home to Cornell University and Ithaca College, may be best known as a college town, but given its stunning setting on the south shore of 40-mile-long Cayuga Lake, and sandwiched between two incredible gorges, it perhaps deserves to be even better known for its natural beauty. Certainly that's not lost on residents, most of whom seem to cruise around town with T-shirts or bumper stickers that read "Ithaca is Gorges." Ithaca is a cosmopolitan town with many of the amenities of a bigger city, such as good restaurants, bars, and theaters, but few of the hassles. The city and surrounding Tompkins County abound in beautiful natural areas ripe for hiking, biking, and other outdoor activities, while wine fans can follow the Cayuga Wine Trail. About a dozen wineries line the lake, many of them in the southern half, where they are easily accessible from Ithaca.

ESSENTIALS
GETTING THERE
BY AIR   The regional Tompkins County Airport, 72 Brown Rd., Ithaca (℡ 607/257-0456) is serviced by US Airways.

BY CAR   Ithaca is about a 4-hour drive from New York City. The nearest major highways are I-81, which travels north to Syracuse, and Route 17, which heads west to Corning. Routes 13 and 96B head directly into Ithaca.

BY BUS   Greyhound stops in Ithaca at the Brenda Wallace Bus Terminal, 710 W. State St. (℡ 607/272-7930); Shortline Bus (℡ 800/631-8405; www.shortlinebus.com) travels to Ithaca, also stopping at 710 W. State St., as well as Elmira, from New York City.

VISITOR INFORMATION   The Ithaca/Tompkins County Convention & Visitors Bureau is located at 904 East Shore Dr., Ithaca (℡ 800/284-8422 or 607/272-1313; www.visitithaca.com).

EXPLORING ITHACA & SOUTHERN CAYUGA LAKE
The top attraction in town is probably Cornell University, a handsome Ivy League school on 745 acres that sits high on a hill in so-called "Collegetown," from which it surveys the rest of Ithaca and the splendid stripe of Cayuga Lake that stretches northward. On campus the top public draw is the Herbert F. Johnson Museum of Art ⭐ (University Ave.; ℡ 607/255-6464; www.museum.cornell.edu; Tues–Sun 10am–5pm; free admission), a modern cement structure designed by I. M. Pei (1973). The museum counts more than 30,000 pieces in its collection, with particular strengths in Asian art (ranging from antiquity to contemporary artists from Japan, China, India, and the Himalayas and Middle East) as well as prints and photographs. The museum hosts interesting itinerant exhibitions, but even visitors without strong interests in art shouldn't miss the unsurpassed fifth-floor views of Cayuga Lake and the gentle

hillsides surrounding Ithaca. Across the street from the museum is a path that leads to down to a suspension bridge over **Fall Creek Gorge,** one of two beautiful and deep gorges that frame the Cornell campus, and Beebe Lake. The trails around the gorge and lake are popular with sunbathing students who make their way down to the water; find your way to **Ithaca Falls** and stand near the cascading falls that rush down tiers of stone 100 feet high and 175 feet wide. The most visible building on campus, McGraw Tower, is known for the **Cornell Chimes,** an old school tradition played daily by students and alumni (for information about chimes concerts, call ✆ **607/255-5330**). **Cornell campus tours** are available by calling ✆ **670/254-INFO.**

East of Beebe Lake is the university's museum of living plants, **Cornell Plantations** ★ (One Plantations Rd., Cornell University; ✆ **607/255-3020**; www. plantations.cornell.edu; daily 9am–6pm), is a real find, and well worth a visit for garden lovers or anyone seeking a bit of solace. The public is welcome to visit the botanical garden, wildflower garden, and Newman Arboretum, which specializes in New York State trees and shrubs, as well as any of the 3,000 acres of natural areas in and around the campus (which contains more than 9 miles of walking trails). Of particular interest are the orderly herb garden with raised theme beds (herbs are grouped according to usage) and a quiet knoll area, which contains more than 300 species of rhododendrons. Free "drop-in tours" are offered on Wednesday and Sunday at 10am. Also associated with Cornell is the **Johnson Center for Birds and Biodiversity** (159 Sapsucker Woods Rd., Ithaca; ✆ **800/ 843-BIRD;** http://birds.cornell.edu; Mon–Thurs 8am–5pm, Fri 8am–4pm and Sat 10am–4pm; trails open daily; free admission) housed in a fabulous new building within the Sapsucker Woods Sanctuary, home to many different bird species. An observatory, bird-feeding garden, trails and multimedia theater that allows visitors to hear birds in surround sound will appeal to hard-core birders.

Just 7 miles north of Ithaca, in Trumansburg along the west side of Cayuga Lake, is one of the region's most beautiful sights. Tucked in **Taughannock Falls State Park** ★★ (Taughannock Park Rd./Rte. 89 North; ✆ **607/387-6739**) is the highest free-falling waterfall in the eastern U.S.; at 215 feet, it is higher even than Niagara Falls. You can drive up to a lookout or hike in from the entrance to the park (the hike is an easy, flat ¾-mile walk). The falls are best viewed in spring and fall; in summer, there is often very little water and visitors are inevitably disappointed. Summer concerts are held in the park.

ESPECIALLY FOR KIDS

Families will enjoy a visit to **Sciencenter,** 601 First St. (✆ **607/272-0600;** www. sciencenter.org), a hands-on science museum with a walk-in camera, outdoor playground, and other exhibits that will entertain children. It's open Tuesday to Saturday from 10am to 5pm, Sunday from noon to 5pm; admission is $4.50 for adults and teens, $4 for seniors, and $3.50 for children ages 3 to 12. The museum's **Sagan Planet Walk** is an outdoor scale model of the sun and nine planets, built as a memorial to Cornell astronomer Carl Sagan. The walk starts at The Commons in downtown, goes along Willow Avenue and Cayuga Street, and ends at Sciencenter, about ¾ mile away; kids can get a passport to the solar system stamped at stations along the way and earn free admission to Sciencenter.

The falls, trails, and swimming at **Taughannock Falls State Park** are also popular with kids of all ages.

Note: The **Museum of the Earth,** 1259 Trumansburg Rd., an 18,000-square foot exhibit and education facility dedicated to the 3.5 billion year history of life

Cayuga Wine Trail

The **Cayuga Wine Trail** (© 800/684-5217; www.cayugawinetrail.com), a grouping of 15 small wineries clustered around Cayuga Lake and the first wine trail in New York State, is the model for the three other Finger Lakes wine trails. Among those welcoming visitors for tours and tastings are:

- **King Ferry Winery,** 658 Lake Rd., King Ferry (© 800/439-5271 or 315/364-5100; www.treleavenwines.com). On the east side of Cayuga Lake, King Ferry makes nice Treleaven wines from vinifera grapes, especially chardonnays and rieslings (Apr–Dec Mon–Sat 10am–5pm, Sun noon-5pm; Feb–Mar weekends only; tastings of six wines $1).
- **Swedish Hill Vineyard,** 4565 Rte. 414, Romulus (© 888/549-WINE or 315/549-8326; www.swedishhill.com) offers a large selection of wines, including chardonnays and rieslings (year-round daily 9am–6pm; guided tours May–Oct weekdays 1pm and 3pm, weekends noon, 2, and 4pm).
- **Lakeshore Winery,** 5132 Rte. 89, Romulus (© 315/549-7075; www.lakeshorewinery.com) has a neat tasting room in an 1825 barn, with a fireplace and rocking chairs, as well as picnic tables and a boat dock (May–Dec Mon–Sat 10:30am–5pm, Sun noon–5pm; Jan–Mar Sat–Sun noon–5pm; Apr Fri–Sun noon–5pm).
- **Goose Watch Winery,** 5480 Rte. 89, Romulus (© 315/549-2599; www.goosewatch.com) has a tasting room in an old barn and excellent views of the lake, and a picnic area and boat docking—not to mention an interesting selection of premium wines including pinot gris, Traminette, Viognier, merlot, and white port (daily 10am–6pm).

Other wineries worth visiting include **Knapp Vineyards,** 2770 County Rd. 128 (Ernsberger Rd.), Romulus (© 800/869-9271; www.knappwine.com), which has a restaurant open for lunch and dinner; and **Six Mile Creek Vineyard,** 1551 Slaterville Rd. (Rte. 79 E.), Ithaca (© 607/272-WINE; www.sixmilecreek.com).

on Earth, was scheduled to open at press time. For more information, contact the museum at © 607/273-6623 or www.museumoftheearth.org.

SPORTS & OUTDOOR PURSUITS

Tompkins County, and specifically the area around Ithaca and Cayuga Lake, replete with gorges, glens, and state parks, is one of the best in the Finger Lakes for all manner of outdoor sports, from hiking and biking to golf and sailing. Locals are a very outdoorsy lot, so you'll have plenty of company.

Outdoors outfitters, with backpacking, canoeing, and skiing equipment, include: **Cornell Outdoor Education,** Bartels Hall, Cornell University, Campus Road (© 607/255-1807); **Wildware Outfitters,** 171 The Commons (© 607/273-5158); and **Eastern Mountain Sports,** 722 Meadow St. (© 607/272-1935).

BOATING & SAILING The **MV** *Manhattan* **Dinner Cruise,** a great way to see Cayuga Lake, sets sail May to October from the Bistro Q restaurant, 708 West Buffalo St. (© 607/256-0898; www.cayugalakecruises.com). It also offers lunch and brunch cruises. Lake charters for sightseeing and fishing on Cayuga Lake are available from **Alcyone Charters,** on a 36-foot sloop (℗ **607/272-7963**); **Tiohero Tours** (℗ **866/846-4376;** www.tioherotours.com), which offers 1- and 2-hour narrated lake tours; and **Loon-A-Sea Charters** (℗ **607/387-5474**).

Private boat rentals are available from **Taughannock Boat Rentals,** Taughannock Park Road (Rte. 89) (℗ **607/387-3311**); and **Puddledockers,** 704½ N. Buffalo St. (℗ **607/273-0096;** www.puddledockers.com), for nonmotorized boat rentals.

CAMPING   Taughannock Falls State Park, Taughannock Park Road/Route 89 in Trumansburg, allows camping; call ℗ **800/456-CAMP** or visit www. reserveamerica.com for more information. For private campgrounds, check out **Spruce Row Campsite & RV Resort,** 2271 Kraft Rd. (℗ **607/387-9225**), near Taughannock Falls State Park, which has a swimming pool and plenty of family recreation.

HIKING & BIKING   Excellent trails for hiking and biking exist all over the Ithaca area. On the Cornell University campus, there are more than 9 miles of trails operated by **Cornell Plantations**. **Six Mile Creek Gorge,** on Hudson Street across from the South Hill School, is an old Native American trail that passes an old mill and a wildflower preserve. The **South Hill Recreation Way,** off Hudson Street, is a gravel trail built on a railroad track that's very popular with local joggers, cyclists, and cross-country skiers. You can enter near Crescent Place, where there's a self-guided interpretative nature tour. Trails in and around **Ithaca Falls,** off Lake Street, are among the most scenic in the area, as are those that lead to the falls in **Taughannock Falls State Park,** off Route 89 in Trumansburg. The **Cascadilla Creek Gorge,** at University Avenue and Court Street, is a greenway connecting downtown Ithaca to the colleges on the hills (Cornell and Ithaca College). The gorge walk is just over a mile with plenty of stairs for a good workout.

The **Cayuga Nature Center,** 1420 Taughannock Blvd. (Rte. 89; ℗ **607/273-6260**) has 5 miles of hiking trails and the Treetops observation tower. The Circle Greenway, 108 E. Green St. (℗ **607/274-6570**), is a 10-mile walk that passes the waterfront, gorges, the Cornell campus, and The Commons downtown.

Trail maps for many of these hikes are available at the tourism information office or local sports shops.

Bike rentals are available from **The Outdoor Store,** 206 The Commons (℗ **607/273-3891**) and **Cayuga Mountain Bike Shop,** 138 West State St. (℗ **607/277-6821**). Check with these outfitters to see which trails allow mountain bikers.

FISHING   Fishing is, logically, focused on Cayuga Lake and its tributaries. Salmon, lake trout, brown trout, rainbow trout, northern pike, and bass can all be found in these waters. For more information on fishing and licenses, contact the New York State Dept. of Conservation (℗ **607/753-3095;** www.dec.state.ny.us).

GOLF   There are half a dozen golf courses in the area; one of the best is **Hillendale Golf Course,** 218 N. Applegate Rd. (℗ **607/273-2363;** www.hillendale. com). Greens fees are $16 during the week, $18 on weekends; discounts for seniors and juniors (under 18).

SWIMMING   Buttermilk Falls State Park, Route 13 South (℗ **670/273-5761**), has a natural pool at the base of the falls. There is also swimming in **Taughannock Falls State Park,** off Route 89 in Trumansburg, though areas close to the falls are off-limits. **Cass Park,** 701 Taughannock Blvd. (Rte. 89N; ℂ **607/ 273-1090**), has an Olympic-size swimming pool that's open to the public.

WINTER SPORTS   Cross-country skiers should head to **Taughannock Falls State Park,** off Route 89 in Trumansburg, or the terrifically named **Podunk Cross Country Ski Center,** Podunk Road, Trumansburg (ℂ **607/387-6716**), which has 7 miles of trails, rental and instruction available. Most of the state parks in the area allow Nordic skiing. The closest downhill skiing is in Cortland, at **Greek Peak Mountain,** 200 Rte. 392 (ℂ **800/955-2-SKI**; www.greekpeak. net). Ice skating is found at **Cass Park Rink & Pool,** 701 Taughannock Blvd., Rte. 89 (ℂ **607/273-9211**).

SHOPPING

Downtown Ithaca Commons, or simply "The Commons," at the corner of West State and Cayuga streets, is a pleasant area of shops and restaurants along a wide pedestrian boulevard. It's packed with gift shops, clothing stores, bookstores, and art galleries. For a good sense of the region's agricultural and artsy roots, visit the **Ithaca Farmers' Market,** Route 13 at Steamboat Landing (Third St.); it's open April through December, Saturday 9am to 2pm and June through October, Sunday 10am to 2pm (ℂ **607/273-7109**). A cooperative with more than 100 local members, the market, in a covered pavilion on the waterfront, delivers a fabulous and entertaining array of produce, food vendors, music, art, and crafts. If you're interested in touring art studios and galleries, pick up a copy of *Greater Ithaca Art Trail,* a guide to the studios of 49 local artists. Open Studio Weekends are held in October.

WHERE TO STAY

Hotel rooms are at a premium during Cornell and Ithaca College graduations (end of May) and Finger Lakes festivals and events (including NASCAR); high season lasts from April through November. Rates at inns are generally also higher on weekends.

EXPENSIVE

Rose Inn ★★★   In a rural setting about 10 miles north of downtown Ithaca, this well-known country inn, a magnificent 1851 mansion with a stunning circular mahogany staircase and formal parlors and gardens, pampers guests with true luxury. It's little wonder that the inn, a Mobil four-star property, is so popular for weddings. Rooms contain a mix of antiques and reproduction furniture; most rooms are categorized as either deluxe or suites and impressively large and extremely elegant, with great views of the gardens; a few more affordable rooms are a tad more modern and smaller. Luxury amenities, such as feather beds and fine robes, linens, and towels, abound. Rooms facing the garden are quieter than those facing the road. Seven rooms have fireplaces and Jacuzzi tubs; only a few have TVs and VCRs. The restaurant in the old carriage house, which features live jazz, is one of the best in the region; see "Where to Dine," below.

813 Auburn Rd. (Rte. 34 N.), Lansing, NY 14851. ℂ 607/533-7905. Fax 607/533-7908. www.roseinn.com. 19 units. $125–$200 double; $230–$320 suite. Rates include full breakfast. MC, V. Free parking. **Amenities:** Restaurant. *In room:* A/C, TV, dataport, hair dryer.

The Statler Hotel   On the campus of Cornell, this large and well-run hotel is associated with the university's Hotel Management School and indeed the staff includes part-time student workers. Rooms are good-size, standard modern hotel rooms, though they have Four Seasons pillow-top bedding and nice linens;

bathrooms are small but have nice marble countertops. Many rooms have excellent views of the campus extending all the way to Cayuga Lake.

11 East Ave., Cornell University, Ithaca, NY 14853. © **800/541-2501** or 607/257-2500. Fax 607/254-2504. www.statlerhotel.cornell.edu. 150 units. $125–$199 double; $175–$475 suite. AE, DC, MC, V. Free parking. **Amenities:** 3 restaurants; limited room service; laundry service. *In room:* A/C, TV w/pay movies, dataport, coffeemaker, hair dryer, high-speed Internet access.

MODERATE

Courtyard by Marriott (*Value*)   This new corporate hotel just 3 miles from downtown Ithaca is an excellent option for those who can't do the B&B thing. It's very popular with business travelers to the area. Rooms are large, immaculate, and nicely outfitted. The location allows easy road access to both Ithaca and other sites along Cayuga Lake.

29 Thornwood Dr., Ithaca NY 14850. © **800/321-2211** or 607/330-1000. Fax 607/300-1500. www.courtyard.com/ithcy. 106 units. $99–$179 double. AE, DC, MC, V. Free parking. **Amenities:** Fitness center; indoor pool; indoor Jacuzzi; laundry service. *In room:* A/C, TV w/pay movies, dataport, coffeemaker, hair dryer, high-speed Internet access.

La Tourelle ⊛   Another fine country inn in a peaceful location on the outskirts of Ithaca, this small hotel is a good choice for those who like the amenities of large hotels and some of the intimacies of smaller inns. The lobby is very handsome, done in Mexican tiles, and the 70-acre grounds, with four tennis courts, are lovely. Rooms are large and sedately decorated, with either light wood furnishings and salmon-colored floral designs or darker Mexican, hand-crafted furniture and more masculine decor. The feather beds are plush and the bathrooms quite large. Though their appeal may be limited, two incongruous tower rooms are circular and have kitschy sunken round beds, mirror-paneled ceiling, and even a disco ball—perfect for that retro anniversary weekend! Tennis fans can stay at the tennis cottage near by the courts. The John Thomas Steakhouse on the property is a fine country restaurant specializing in dry-aged beef.

1150 Danby Rd. (Rte. 96B), Ithaca, NY 14850. © **607/273-2734.** Fax 607/300-1500. www.latourelleinn.com. 35 units. $99–$199 double. AE, DC, MC, V. Free parking. **Amenities:** Restaurant; 4 tennis courts (2 lighted for night play). *In room:* A/C, TV w/pay movies, dataport, coffeemaker, hair dryer, high-speed Internet access.

Taughannock Farms Inn ⊛⊛   Well known for its restaurant, which has served deluxe four-course meals for more than 60 years, this large inn occupies an exquisite 1873 mansion and three more modern guesthouses on a beautiful location at the edge of Taughannock State Park, overlooking Cayuga Lake. The main house has but five rooms, with either lake or forest views; though guests have to contend with the restaurant's popularity, those rooms have a bit more character than the more private and generally more modern guesthouse rooms. Accommodations are nicely decorated with some Victorian antiques and bold wallpapers and floral decor. The guesthouses are particularly good for families and friends traveling together; one guesthouse is the former early 1900s ice-house, and a few rooms are in the innkeeper's residence. The inn, a member of the Select Registry of Distinguished Inns, is open seasonally only, from May to November. The owners are in the process of adding another 10-room guesthouse with great lake views.

2030 Gorge Rd. (Rte. 89 at Taughannock State Park), Trumansburg, NY 14886. © **888/387-7711** or 607/387-7711. www.t-farms.com. 13 units. $105–$145 main inn double; $95–$185 guesthouse double. Rates include full breakfast. AE, DC, MC, V. Free parking. **Amenities:** Restaurant; small bar. *In room:* A/C, TV (in guesthouse rooms only), dataport, coffeemaker, hair dryer, high-speed Internet access.

William Henry Miller Inn ★★ The top B&B in Ithaca has an enviable downtown location: just paces from The Commons. An exceedingly handsome 1880 Victorian built by Cornell's first architecture student (he of the inn's name), and owned by just two families before becoming an inn, the house combines rich details like stained-glass windows and custom chestnut woodwork. Seven rooms are in two floors of the main house, and there's a two-room suite and another room in the carriage house. Rooms are lovingly decorated, but without the clichéd crush of Victoriana one often finds. Bathrooms are uncluttered and modern (several have Jacuzzi tubs). The very friendly and considerate owner has added ramps and a wheelchair elevator, making a couple of rooms completely accessible, a real rarity at a B&B.

303 North Aurora St., Ithaca, NY 14850. © **607/256-4553.** Fax 607/256-0092. www.millerinn.com. 9 units. $95–$155 double; $155–$175 suite. Rates include full breakfast and evening dessert. AE, DC, MC, V. Free parking. **Amenities:** Wheelchair elevator. *In room:* A/C, TV, Jacuzzi (some rooms), dataport, hair dryer.

WHERE TO DINE

Ithaca is quite cosmopolitan for a small city, and its roster of diverse restaurants of various nationalities and persuasions, everything from Greek to barbecue and cutting-edge vegetarian, reflects its widespread tastes and personality. You can choose to dine on the waterfront, at a college hangout, or out in the country at an elegant inn.

EXPENSIVE

The Carriage House at Rose Inn ★★★ CONTINENTAL/CREATIVE AMERICAN The restaurant at the celebrated Rose Inn occupies the gorgeously rustic 1842 carriage house, complete with dark-wood paneling, hand-hewn beams, and elegant place settings. Dining here, especially when live jazz plays Friday and Saturday nights, is an atmospheric treat. The food is also a pleasure, with creative appetizers like the smoked tomato and artichoke tart or sautéed chicken livers with baby spinach, and entrees such as grilled ostrich and stuffed pheasant breast. Service is attentive but relaxed. Prix-fixe three- and four-course dinners are available, as well as a la carte dining. The Carriage House is the perfect spot for a romantic dinner.

813 Auburn Rd. (Rte. 34 N.), Lansing. © **607/533-7905.** Reservations recommended weekends and holidays. Main courses $22–$30; prix-fixe dinners $42 and $50. AE, MC, V. Tues–Sun 5–10pm.

Taughannock Farms Inn ★★ *Value* AMERICAN This large Victorian inn and estate has an elegant dining room overlooking Cayuga Lake. It has been an inn since 1945, and its four-course meals—for which diners pay a single entree price—are a local favorite. Diners start with an appetizer, which might be roasted almond-and-mushroom pâté, move on to a salad, and then tuck into a timeless entree: New York Strip, rack of lamb, prime rib, or the catch of the day. Vegetarians have a single choice: Portobello Wellington. Save room for dessert; the menu lists more than a dozen homemade options.

2030 Gorge Rd., Trumansburg © **607/387-7711.** Reservations recommended. Main courses $20–$40. AE, MC, V. May–Oct Mon–Sat 5–9pm; Sun 3–8pm (hours vary in Nov).

MODERATE

Bistro Q ★ BARBECUE/ECLECTIC This informal, offhandedly cool restaurant in downtown Ithaca, right on the inlet off of Cayuga Lake—where boats can pull up and dock—has outdoor dining, live music in summer, and a relaxed and eclectic menu. The focus is on mesquite-wood barbecue dishes, including ribs and pulled pork, but you'll also find grilled steaks and fresh fish, and plenty of healthy salads. The homemade sauces are a specialty, and all sides and desserts are homemade. Indoor diners can choose between "fire" (fireplace room) and "water" (dining room facing the inlet).

708 W. Buffalo St., Ithaca. *C* **607/277-3287.** Reservations recommended weekends and holidays. Main courses $8–$26. AE, DISC, MC, V. Lunch Mon–Fri 11am–3pm; dinner daily 5–11pm.

Maxie's Supper Club and Raw Oyster Bar ★ SOUTHERN/SEAFOOD   A local late-night favorite, with live music on Sunday nights, this New Orleans–style restaurant is a great place to kick back and enjoy some jambalaya, po' boy sandwiches, "mighty mighty gumbo," and fresh seafood from the raw bar. The feel-good menu, microbrew beers, and wide-ranging list of boutique wines (though woefully short on Finger Lakes wines) make it popular with all sorts of folks, from profs and students to young professionals and families. Maxie's informal Tavern, serving sandwiches, pizzettes, and desserts, is a good place to pick up a quick lunch or have brunch on weekends. Oyster junkies should check out the half-priced raw oysters every day from 4 to 6pm. On Sundays, live music ranges from jazz, blues, and bluegrass to neohippie jams.

635 W. State St. (corner of State St. and Rte. 13S), Ithaca. *C* **607/272-4136.** Reservations not accepted. Main courses $12–$24. AE, MC, V. Daily 4pm–1am (Tavern Sun–Thurs 11:30am–11:30pm and Fri–Sat 11:30am–1am).

INEXPENSIVE
Moosewood Restaurant ★ *Value* GOURMET VEGETARIAN/INTERNATIONAL   Vegetarians and innovative chefs around the world know the Moosewood cookbooks—and here is where it all began. This informal, 30-year-old restaurant, located in a converted school building-turned alternative mall, is run by a cooperative (or "collective," as they call it) that delivers imaginative vegetarian and healthy cooking. *Bon Appétit* magazine named the Moosewood one of the 13 most influential restaurants of the 20th century. The menu is forever changing, but always features fresh, locally grown (and usually organic) produce and whole grains, beans, and soy. The creative soups, salads and side dishes are enough to make a hearty meal out of, but the homemade pasta dishes are also excellent and filling. Sunday night dinners are ethnic menus. Nonvegetarians will be delighted to find fresh fish on the menu.

215 N. Cayuga St. (in the DeWitt Mall), Ithaca. *C* **607/273-9610.** Reservations not accepted. Main courses $6–$15. AE, DISC, MC, V. Lunch Mon–Sat 11:30am–3pm; dinner summer Sun–Thurs 5:30–9pm, Fri–Sat 6–9:30pm; winter Sun–Thurs 5:30–8:30pm, Fri–Sat 5:30–9pm. Bar and cafe year-round Sun–Thurs 11am–11pm and Fri–Sat 11am–midnight.

ITHACA AFTER DARK
Ithaca has quite a lot of theater and music programmed, especially in summer. The **Kitchen Theater,** 116 North Cayuga St. (*C* **607/273-4497**), in the historic Greek-Revival Clinton House, is a top spot for year-round classic and contemporary theater. In summer, the **Hangar Theatre,** Taughannock Boulevard/Route 89 (*C* **607/273-8588**), offers professional, children's, and experimental theater, in a renovated municipal airport hangar near Lake Cayuga. The **State Theatre,** 111 West State St. (*C* **607/277-6633**), is a historic theater in the process of being fully refurbished; it hosts a wide array of programs from rock (Ani DiFranco) to plays like *The Vagina Monologues.* **Summer outdoor concert series** are held at The Commons, Taughannock Falls State Park, and the Cornell University quad. For more information on music and performing arts, see **www. ithacaevents.com**. The annual 4-day **Ithaca Festival,** held in late May, features

several stages and performances by musicians, painters, dance groups, and more. Visit **www.ithacafestival.org** for more information or call © **607/273-4646.**

Just a Taste Wine and Tapas Bar, 116 N. Aurora St. (© **607/277-9463**) is a good stop for flights of wine and appetizers before moving on for dinner or a show. **Chanticleer,** 101 West State St. (© **607/272-9678**), is a low-key watering hole, and **Stella's Martini Bar,** 403 College Ave. (© **607/277-1490**), is one of the coolest spots in Collegetown, near Cornell, with live music on weekends.

CORTLAND

At the extreme eastern edge of the region, just off I-91 midway between Binghamton and Syracuse, the small and pleasant but easy-to-overlook city of **Cortland** positions itself as a gateway to the southeastern Finger Lakes, but it has little of the natural draws—namely, lakes and other natural areas—that entice visitors to the region. As a stopover, it won't deter most for long. If you do stop over for a while, have a look at the **1890 House Museum,** 37 Tompkins St. (Rte. 13), an impressively ornate Victorian mansion with castlelike turrets and towers (© **607/756-7551**). It's open Tuesday to Sunday from 1 to 4pm; admission is $3.50 for adults, $2.50 for seniors and students. Also of interest is the attractive village of **Homer,** with a lovely town green that gives itself over to a Bluegrass Festival and other musical events in summer. The **Cortland Repertory Theatre** (© **800/427-6160;** www.cortlandrep.org) puts on fan-friendly musicals that draw New York City actors (Holly Hunter got her start here) at an old theater right on pretty Little York Lake, a few miles north of Homer.

3 Watkins Glen ⋆ & Southern Seneca Lake

28 miles west of Ithaca; 21 miles north of Corning

At the southern tip of Seneca Lake, the deepest and second-longest of the Finger Lakes, Watkins Glen is a small town that looms large on the tourism landscape in summer. It is home to Watkins Glen State Park, site of a spectacular gorge and thundering waterfalls—perhaps the single most beautiful natural area in the entire region—as well as the annual NASCAR rally and Finger Lakes Wine Festival. But even those heavily attended events have a hard time competing with the town's peaceful, picturesque location on the waterfront of Seneca Lake.

ESSENTIALS

GETTING THERE   From the north, take exit 42 off the New York State Thruway (I-90); from the south, take Route 17 (I-86) to Route 14 North.

VISITOR INFORMATION   The **Schuyler County Chamber of Commerce Visitors Center** is located at 100 North Franklin St. in Watkins Glen (© **800/ 607-4552;** www.schuylerny.com).

EXPLORING WATKINS GLEN & SOUTHERN SENECA LAKE

Lovely **Seneca Harbor** ⋆⋆ is a perfect picture composed of a marina full of bobbing sailing and fishing boats, a New England–style red schoolhouse at the end of the public fishing pier, and vineyard-laced hillsides rising from the lake. The boardwalk provides some of the most beautiful views of any vantage point in the Finger Lakes. This part of Seneca Lake is the perfect place to get out on the water on a yacht or sailboat. Most chartered boats sets sail May through the end of October. Check out the *Malabar X,* a vintage schooner yacht from 1930; scheduled cruises are daily 10am, 1pm, and 5:30pm ($27–$37). Call © **607/535-5253** or visit www.senecadaysails.com for more information. The larger *Columbia,* at Capt. Bill's, offers dinner, lunch, and moonlight cocktail cruises (lunch or dinner: $24–$37 adults, $15–$24 children; cocktail cruise: $9.95 adults). A smaller vintage motor vessel, the *Stroller IV,* is also available. Call ℂ **607/535-4541** for reservations.

Watkins Glen State Park ★★★, off Route 14 at the south end of the village, is one of the certain highlights of the Finger Lakes. Opened in 1863, the 776-acre park contains a spectacular gorge sculpted in slate, formed more than 12,000 years ago at the end of the last Ice Age, and carved by the flow of Glen Creek ever since, and 19 separate waterfalls. The walking trails in and around the gorge are splendid and accessible to almost all walkers; you can walk right in behind the 60-foot drop of Central Cascade. The gorge is a spectacle in itself, but in summer months a sound and light show depicting prehistoric times and the evolution of the gorge, **"Timespell,"** is projected into the chasm—quite a sight for the kids. Showtimes are daily July 1 to Labor Day and weekends in May, June, September, and October (9pm May–Aug and 8pm Sept–Oct; admission $4 adults, $3 children). Call ℂ **607/535-8888** for more information.

The **Watkins Glen International Race Track,** 2790 County Rte. 16 (ℂ **607/535-2481;** www.theglen.com), heats up at the end of the first week of August with the NASCAR Nextel Cup series, a race that draws many thousands and fills every hotel and inn and campsite for hundreds of miles in New York State's largest sporting weekend. Other racing events are held in summer, including the Vintage Gran Prix in September, but none comes close to NASCAR. The other huge event in town, also held at the WGI, is the annual **Finger Lakes Wine Festival** ★★ (ℂ **607/535-2481;** www.flwinefest.com), held in mid-July. Most of the local 70-plus wineries are on hand, along with music, crafts vendors, exhibits from the Corning Museum of Glass, food and wine seminars, even a toga party. As you can imagine, plenty of wine is consumed and people can get pretty festive. Advance tickets (and accommodations) are a must for most of the events at WGI, so plan in advance (way in advance for NASCAR, as much as a year or more). Tickets for the Wine Festival are available at many of the local wineries. The largest concentration of wineries in the region is clustered about Seneca Lake, and many of the wineries on the **Seneca Lake Wine Trail,** are just a cork's throw from Watkins Glen; for more on that collective and wine tours, see the sidebar on p. 316.

The village of Watkins Glen has a nice, walkable downtown area with several antiques shops, a wine shop focusing on local wines, called **NYStateWine.com** (29 North Franklin St.; ℂ **607/535-2944**), and a studio featuring original glass art, **Glassart Gallery & Studio,** 215 S. Madison Ave. (ℂ **607/535-0535**).

WHERE TO STAY & DINE

One of the best places to stay in the area is at a winery. **The Inn at Glenora Wine Cellars** ★★, 5435 Rte. 14, Dundee, NY 14837 (ℂ **800/243-5513;** www. glenora.com/inn), a new and modern hostelry, is right on the banks of Seneca Lake and just 8 miles north of Watkins Glen, set amid acres of vineyards and only steps from the winery. All the rooms have expansive, unimpeded views of the water from private terraces or patios. Rooms are large and equipped with Stickley furniture. "Vintner's select" rooms have king-size beds, Jacuzzi tubs, and electric fireplaces. It's a great value, with doubles going for $99 to $149, and luxury doubles costing $175 to $235. Check the website for special getaway packages. The finest B&B in the area is **Idlwilde Inn** ★★, One Lakeview Ave., Watkins Glen 14891

Seneca Lake Wine Trail

The **Seneca Lake Wine Trail** (☎ 877/536-2717; www.seneclakewine.com) includes some two dozen wineries dotting the shores of Seneca Lake—the largest concentration of wineries in the Finger Lakes. They are easily accessible from Watkins Glen, Corning, and Geneva in the north. Among the wineries worth visiting for a tasting and/or touring are:

- **Lakewood Vineyards,** 4024 Rte. 14, Watkins Glen (☎ 607/535-9252; www.lakewoodvineyards.com), on the west shore of the lake, has beautiful views and very good Rieslings and chardonnays, as well as a nice pinot noir. Open year-round, Monday through Saturday from 10am to 5pm and Sunday from noon to 5pm.
- **Glenora Wine Cellars,** 5435 Rte. 14, Dundee (☎ 607/243-5511; www.glenora.com), has great views of Seneca Lake and vineyards as well as a picnic area and gift shop. The winery operates an excellent restaurant and inn right on the shores of the lake. Open year-round, Monday through Saturday from 10am to 5pm and Sunday from noon to 5pm (open later in summer).
- **Hazlitt 1852 Vineyards,** 5712 Rte. 414, Hector (☎ 607/546-9463; www.hazlitt1852.com), on the east side of the lake, is best known for its party atmosphere, rock 'n' roll music, and mass-market "Red Cat" wines. If you're not much of a connoisseur and just want to have fun and taste some wines (and occasionally, see folks get a little rowdy, with sexual innuendoes and chants), this is the place. Open November to May, Monday through Saturday from 10am to 5pm and Sunday from noon to 5pm; June through October, Monday to Saturday 10am to 5:30pm and Sunday from 11am to 5:30pm.
- **Wagner Vineyards,** 9322 Rte. 414, Lodi (☎ 607/582-6450; www.wagnervineyards.com), operates an unusual octagonal winery producing 30 wines and a full slate of microbrew beers, a gift shop, and offers nice guided tours and full tastings. Open daily 10am to 5pm. There's a pleasant restaurant, Ginny Lee Café, that serves lunch daily from 11am to 4pm; on Friday nights in the summer live music plays on the terrace overlooking Seneca Lake and dinner (fish fry or barbecued chicken) is served from 7 to 9pm.
- **Lamoreaux Landing Wine Cellars,** 9224 Rte. 414 Lodi (☎ 607/582-6011; www.lamoreauxwine.com), is housed in a swank, Napa-style building with floor-to-ceiling windows and views of surrounding vineyards. Open year-round for tastings, Monday to Saturday 10am to 5pm and Sunday noon to 5pm.

(☎ 607/535-3081; www.bbhost.com/idlwildeinn), a sprawling Victorian mansion with 15 guest rooms, a great veranda, pretty gardens, and stupendous lake views. There's quite a mix of rooms, from the impressively grand to small and affordable and simply furnished (the cheapest share a bathroom). The master bedroom, no. 6, is stunningly large, with its own deck and two fireplaces, while no. 10 has a sitting room in a circular turret and a private deck. Two new rooms have been added in the carriage house. The inn, run by a European couple, is open seasonally from the end of April to November. Rates range from $85 to $225 and include a full breakfast.

If you're arriving for NASCAR or the Finger Lakes Wine Festival, you may have to look far and wide for accommodations, so be sure to look at hotels and inns listed in other sections of this chapter; those in and near Geneva, Corning, Elmira, Ithaca, and Hammondsport are all easy drives from Watkins Glen. Call ℰ 800/607-4552 or see www.schuylerny.com for assistance in getting a room. If you want to camp, check out the sites at **Watkins Glen State Park** (ℰ 607/ 535-4511), **Clute Memorial Park** (ℰ 607/535-4438), or the **KOA Kampground & Kabins** (which I hope they never abbreviate by its initials), located on Route 414 (ℰ 800/562-7430; www.watkinsglenkoa.com), which has a heated pool and good bathrooms.

Among area restaurants, **Veraisons Restaurant** ⭑⭑ at The Inn at Glenora Wine Cellars, 5435 Rte. 14, Dundee (ℰ 607/243-9500), is my favorite. The handsome, modern space has cathedral ceilings, a large stone fireplace and panoramic views of Seneca Lake. The menu combines traditional French cooking with regional ingredients. On my most recent visit, I had wonderful veal tenderloin medallions in a brandy cream sauce infused with black trumpet mushrooms. Most of the dishes are, appropriately, prepared with wine; entrees range from $17 to $27. **Seneca Harbor Station,** 3 N. Franklin St., Watkins Glen (ℰ 607/535-6101), has the advantage of fantastic views of the marina at the southern end of Seneca Lake. A casual bar and restaurant (main courses $10–$35), it's a good stop for an informal lunch like chicken Florentine and dinner items such as seafood pastas, grilled meats, and fresh fish platters. Nothing fancy, but reliable and, with those views, it's a place to linger.

4 Corning ⭑⭑ & Elmira

250 miles northeast of New York City; 150 miles east of Niagara Falls; 90 miles southeast of Rochester.

Corning may be a town of only 12,000 people, but in the Finger Lakes, as the headquarters of the Fortune 500 Corning Inc., it's a big deal. Quite literally, it's the town that Corning built; the company, the original makers of Corningware, Pyrex, and now high-tech materials like fiber optics, has employed as many as half the town's population. Corning was once known as "crystal city" for it concentration of glassworks and today glass is at the center of the town's attractions, at the world-renowned Corning Museum of Glass.

Elmira, a largely blue-collar town and southern gateway to the Finger Lakes, may not be a major stop on most itineraries, but it does offer a handful of nice surprises. The town, home to Elmira College, is known in select circles as the "soaring capital of the United States," a reference to its place in aviation history, and it also makes much of its association with the legendary writer and humorist Mark Twain, who wrote many of his most-famous works while summering in Elmira. Fans of architecture will also delight in the surprising concentration of Victorian homes; Elmira is said to have more than any other area per capita in North America.

ESSENTIALS
GETTING THERE
BY AIR   Elmira-Corning Regional Airport, 276 Sing Sing Rd., Horseheads (ℰ 607/795-0402; www.elmiracorningairport.com), serviced by Northwest and US Airways, is 12 miles from downtown Corning.

BY CAR   Corning is directly off Route 17/I-86 and a straight shot along Route 414 south of Watkins Glen; from the south, take Route 15. Elmira is off Route17/I-86, just 20 minutes east of Corning.

BY BUS   Trailways (© **607/734-2001**) travels to Elmira and its terminal at 100 E. Church St.

VISITOR INFORMATION   The **Steuben County Conference & Visitors Bureau** is located at 5 West Market St. (Baron Steuben Building, 2nd floor), Corning (© **607/936-6544;** www.corningfingerlakes.com). The **Chemung County Chamber of Commerce** is located at 400 East Church St., Elmira (© **800/ MARK-TWAIN;** www.chemungchamber.org).

GETTING AROUND   The Corning Museum of Glass operates a **free shuttle service,** daily from 8am to 6pm, from the museum along Cedar Street to Market Street and back.

EXPLORING CORNING

Corning Inc.'s major gift to the city, the **Corning Museum of Glass** ★★★ (I-86, exit 46; © **607/937-5371;** www.cmog.org), is the premier and most comprehensive collection of historic and art glass in the world. Anyone with an interest in glass (even if you think you are not one, you are almost certain to be surprised), could spend many hours or even days here; it is quite literally dazzling. On view are 35,000 glass pieces representing 35 centuries of glass craftsmanship, beginning with a piece dating from 1411 B.C. There is also a gallery of glass sculpture and a glass innovation center, with ingeniously designed exhibits that depict the use of glass in technology. The museum, now entering its sixth decade, is anything but static; it offers hot-glass demonstrations, glass-making workshops, and some of the best shopping to be found, with a sprawling array of shops dealing in glass, crystal, and jewelry. Crystal fans familiar with Steuben glass (which originated in Corning), and particularly the work of glass artist Frederick Carder, will delight in finding a huge gallery of his works. The museum is especially well designed for children, who usually can't get enough of the interactive science exhibits and opportunities to handle telescopes and peer out a periscope that "sees" out the roof of the building. A walk-in glass workshop allows visitors to make their very own glass souvenirs. The museum is open day daily from 9am to 5pm; July through Labor Day it's open daily until 8pm. Admission is $12 for adults, $6 for children ages 6 to 17, free for children under 6, and free for all kids in summer. A $16 combination ticket for adults includes admission to CMoG and the Rockwell Museum (see below). The museum also operates a free shuttle service from the museum to Market Street, downtown.

The **Rockwell Museum of Western Art** ★★, 111 Cedar St. (© **607/937-5386;** www.rockwellmuseum.org), which occupies the former City Hall, maintains an excellent collection of both historic and contemporary Western and Native American art, as well as one of the best-designed small museums in the northeast. An inviting design of bold colors and gorgeous woods inside the shell of a neo-Romanesque building, the museum features daring juxtapositions that work surprisingly well, including a number of fantastic pieces by Native Americans. The second-floor features a lodge room with a fireplace, couches, and chairs, and feels ripped from a classic Western lodge inn. A neat idea for children is the color-coded "art backpacks," which come equipped with games and lesson and drawing books, making the museum an especially interactive place.

Museum hours are as follows: July through Labor Day, Monday to Saturday from 9am to 8pm and Sunday 11am to 5pm; September through June, Monday to Saturday 9am to 5pm and Sunday 11am to 5pm. Admission is $6.50 for adults, $5.50 for seniors and students, $4.50 children ages 6 to 17, and free for children under 6. Allow an hour or two.

Those hungry to get outdoors can do so on water on in the air. **Today's Tom Sawyer,** 56 Golden Glow Dr., Elmira (© **607/734-3804**), offers raft and inflatable kayak rentals on the Chemung River for river trips from Corning to Elmira.

Balloons Over Corning, 352 Brewster St., Painted Post (© **607/937-3910**), organizes hot-air balloons with beautiful views over Corning and the Finger Lakes area. Flights take off 2 hours before sunset in summer.

SHOPPING

Corning, devastated by flood in 1972, rebuilt the picturesque centerpiece of its downtown, Market Street, which today retains a 19th-century appearance and is alive with glass galleries, gift shops, and restaurants and bars. **Vitrix Hot Glass Studio,** 77 W. Market St. (© **607/936-2488**), **Lost Angel Glass,** 79 W. Market St. (© **607/937-3578**), and **West End Gallery,** 12 W. Market St. (© **607/936-2011**) are three of the best galleries representing the American studio glass movement, though there are a number of others that are easily discovered walking about town. The two major museums in town, the Rockwell Museum of Western Art and Corning Museum of Glass, both have excellent on-site shops; the latter's is a must for anyone with the slightest interest in glass; items range from inexpensive glass souvenirs to one-of-a-kind glass art and Steuben crystal pieces.

WHERE TO STAY

Corning can get pretty crowded, both with business travelers and when big events occur, such the Corning Classic LPGA golf tournament, the NASCAR race, and Finger Lakes Wine Festival in nearby Watkins Glen, even Cornell's graduation. In addition to those below, you might check out one of the chain motels in town: **Comfort Inn** (66 West Pulteney St.; © **607/962-1515;** www.visionhotels.com), **Days Inn** (23 Riverside Dr.; © **607/936-9370;** www.corningny.com/daysinn), and **Staybridge Suites** (201 Townley Ave; © **607/936-7800;** www.staybridge.com/sbscorningny). For campers, there is the **Hickory Hill Family Camping Resort,** Route 17/I-86, exit 38; (© **800/760-0947;** www.hickoryhillcampresort.com).

Hillcrest Manor ★★★ (Value   One of the finest B&Bs I've seen anywhere, this impressively grand 1890 Greek Revival mansion, with massive pillars, porches, and terraces, sits in a quiet residential neighborhood up the hill from downtown Corning. Rooms are huge and impeccably decorated with great, luxurious taste by the two owners, art and antique collectors who recently moved to Corning from Seattle. The house features stately parlors, an elegant candlelit dining room, and a palatial cedar stairway. Two of the rooms, the Master Bedroom and the Honeymoon Suite, are almost ridiculously large; they, as well as the normal rooms, qualify as excellent values given the level of quality exhibited throughout the house. I could envision myself relaxing here for days on end. The inn's website, unfortunately, doesn't come close to reflecting the house's true elegance and sophistication, trust me.

227 Cedar St., Corning, NY 14830. © **607/936-4548.** www.corninghillcrestmanor.com. 4 units. $125–$195 double; $225 suite. Rates include full breakfast. No credit cards. Free parking. *In room:* A/C, TV, dataport, hair dryer.

Radisson Hotel Corning *Value*   This large and well-run hotel has an excellent location: tucked into a small campus of sorts at the east end of Market Street, just steps from all the restaurants, bars, and shops. It is the only full-service hotel in downtown Corning, a reason for its popularity with business travelers, though with its pool and on-site restaurant, is also a good place for families and other leisure travelers. Rooms are spacious and attractively appointed, with large work desks and high-speed Internet access.

125 Denison Pkwy. E., Corning, NY 14830. © 800/333-3333 or 607/962-5000. Fax 607/962-4166. www. radisson.com/corningny. 173 units. $89–$130 double. AE, DC, DISC, MC, V. Free parking. **Amenities:** Restaurant; bar; indoor heated pool; fitness center; outdoor Jacuzzi. *In room:* A/C, TV, minibar, coffeemaker, hair dryer, wireless high-speed Internet access.

Rosewood Inn   An 1855 Victorian home in a leafy neighborhood and walking distance from Market Street, this inn takes Victoriana all the way; rooms have themes, like the Elizabeth Royal Room and Lewis Carroll Room, and Suzanne, the theatrical owner, is even known to style herself in elegant period shawls. If you welcome a romantic, intimate B&B experience and love Victorian clutter, you will be over the moon here. The good-size accommodations on two floors are all uniquely decorated with lots of antiques and books. Guests tend to mingle and share travel tales over breakfast, a gourmet delight, served in a candlelit dining room.

227 Cedar St., Corning, NY 14830. © 607/962-3253. www.rosewoodinn.com. 7 units. $99–$145 double; $185 suite. Rates include full breakfast. AE, MC, V. Free parking. *In room:* A/C.

WHERE TO DINE

Virtually all the places to eat out in town are on Market Street, which makes it easy to stroll up and down the blocks while shopping and choose one of about a half-dozen restaurants.

The Gaffer Grille and Taproom INTERNATIONAL/GRILLED MEATS This causal eatery and bar, with some nice and cozy booths set against exposed brick walls, is one of the most popular among Corning residents. It features a pretty standard menu, with lots of steaks, ribs and chicken, along with other items like crushed peppercorn yellowfin tuna and cheese tortellini with vodka sauce, but dishes are consistently well prepared, and the ambience is very agreeable. The tap room, with a more casual menu, serves dinner until 11pm.

58 W. Market St. © 607/962-4649. Reservations recommended on weekends. Main courses $11–$24. AE, DISC, MC, V. Lunch Mon–Fri 11:30am–4:30pm; dinner Mon–Sat, 4:30–10pm; tap room Mon–Sat 11:30am–11pm.

London Underground ✮ AMERICAN   For fine dining in Corning, this three-level, family-owned restaurant on Market Street is your best bet. Elegant but not stuffy, it features a sophisticated menu and very attentive service, with a pianist on Saturday evenings. Dishes are classic, like roasted rack of lamb, prime pork loin stuffed with cranberry, apple, and raisin chutney, and filet mignon finished with a Finger Lakes red wine reduction. More casual dishes include fish and chips with peas (served every Fri) and a daily pasta. Desserts are all homemade, and the pies (pecan, deep-dish apple) are to die for. For lunch, there are plenty of fine salads and nicely prepared sandwiches. If you're in the mood for a late-afternoon snack, stop in for tea and scones or soup and salad, from 3 to 5pm.

69 E. Market St. © 607/962-2345. Reservations recommended. Main courses $13–$26. AE, DISC, MC, V. Open daily: lunch 11:30am–3pm; dinner 5–9pm; tap room Mon–Sat 11:30am–11pm.

> *Fun Fact* **Women Make the Grade**
>
> Elmira College, founded in 1855, was the first exclusive women's college and the first institution of higher learning to grant degrees to women that were equal in stature to those awarded men.

CORNING AFTER DARK

There's not a whole lot going on in Corning after dark, though a couple of bars on Market Street—once a long lineup of bars in the blue-collar, pre-great flood of 1972—draw locals and visitors alike. **Market Street Brewing Co.,** 63 Market St. (© 607/936-2337) and **Glory Hole Pub,** 74 Market St. (© 607/962-1474), are both watering hole-cum-restaurants.

EXPLORING ELMIRA

Mark Twain, born Samuel Clemens, met and married his wife, Olivia Langdon, in Elmira, and he spent 20 summers in the area. From his study at Quarry Farm, he composed some of his most famous works, including *The Adventures of Huckleberry Finn* and *The Adventures of Tom Sawyer.* On the pretty campus of **Elmira College,** One Park Place (between Fifth St. and Washington Ave.), is the Center for Mark Twain Studies (closed to the public) as well as **Twain's original study** from 1874, now a literary landmark, with several original artifacts, including his chair, photographs taken at the farm, and several documents. The study, located next to the pond, is open to visitors mid-June through August, Monday to Saturday from 9am to 5pm (© 607/735-1941; free admission). Twain, his wife, and their children are buried at Elmira's **Woodlawn Cemetery** (Walnut St.; © 607/ 732-0151; daily 8am–9pm). Twain himself wrote many of the epitaphs on the tombstones. Nearby, **Woodlawn National Cemetery** hides a little-known secret: the graves of some 3,000 Confederate soldiers, making it the northernmost Confederate grave site (at one time, there were about 12,000 POWs in Elmira, which earned it the sobriquet "Hellmira," at least down south).

Architecture buffs may be amazed by the collection of Victorian, Greek, Tudor, and Georgian Revival houses, built in the mid- to late-19th and early 20th centuries. Pick up a copy of **"A Walking Tour of the History Near Westside,"** (available at the Tourism Information Office and several inns and hotels) which spotlights and describes a few dozen homes along West Church and West Water streets, and to a lesser degree, Gray, Walnut, and Grove streets, all just north of the Chemung River. Elmira's major museum, the **Arnot Art Museum,** 235 Lake St. (© 607/734-3697), is housed in an 1833 neoclassical mansion. The museum contains 17th- to 19th-century European paintings, 19th- and 20th-century American art, and some Egyptian works on loan from the Met. The museum is open Tuesday through Saturday from 10am to 5pm and Sunday from 1 to 5pm; admission is $5 for adults, $4.50 for seniors and college students, and $2.50 for children ages 6 to 12.

About 5 miles north of Elmira, the **National Warplane Museum** ⭐, 17 Aviation Dr., Horseheads (© 607/739-8200; www.warplane.org), is the place to see 37 original military flying machines from WWI to the Gulf War. Even better than seeing the planes up close, though, is the opportunity to go up in one—whether a PT-17 or a B-17 bomber, known as "Fuddy Duddy." Flights aren't cheap (ranging from $150–$400 per person; Apr–Nov only; reservations required), but it could be the thrill of a lifetime. The museum is open Monday through Friday, from 10am to 4pm, Saturday from 9am to 5pm, Sunday from 11am to 5pm; admission is $7 for adults, $5.50 for seniors, $4 children ages 6 to 17.

The **National Soaring Museum,** Harris Hill, 51 Soaring Hill Dr. (just south of Rte. 17, exit 49, 50, or 51) (✆ **607/734-3128;** www.soaringmuseum.org), has the country's largest collection of gliders and sailplanes that takes visitors through the history of motorless flight, but also offers graceful sailplane rides in either a Schleicher 21 or Schweizer 233 ($55–$65; spring through fall; reservations recommended), a unique and mesmerizing experience. Flights soar some 2,000 feet after takeoff from Harris Hill, providing stunning views of the valley. The museum is open daily from 10am to 5pm.

Shoppers shouldn't miss **The Christmas House,** 361 Maple Ave. (✆ **607/734-9547**), a gift shop housed in a Queen Anne mansion that stocks all manner of Christmas and other items and has become a bit of a destination all its own. The top spot in town for performing arts is the **Clemens Center,** 207 Clemens Center Pkwy. (✆ **800/724-0159;** www.clemenscenter.com), which hosts orchestra, dance, and theater, which has included *Rent* and *La Bohème.*

Tip: One of the best ways to see a lot of Elmira in a short time is to hop aboard **The Elmiran,** a green trolley car that makes daily runs July and August, with a narrated history of the town, Mark Twain, and more. Catch it at the Holiday Inn Riverview, 760 E. Water St. (✆ **607/734-4211;** $2 adults, free children under 12).

WHERE TO STAY & DINE

By far the best place to stay in Elmira is **The Painted Lady B&B** ★★★, 520 W. Water St., Elmira, NY 14905 (✆ **607/732-7515;** fax 607/732-7515; www.thepaintedlady.net), a very large and meticulously decorated Victorian mansion in the heart of the historic district. Accommodations are massive and have luxurious bedding and bathrooms for $165 to $195 for a double or $225 for a two-bedroom suite. Breakfasts are home-cooked and delicious, and there's a fantastic billiards room. The inn, with just five units, is operated by a very friendly and informal young couple. If you prefer hotels, try **Holiday Inn Riverview,** 760 E. Water St., Elmira, NY 14901 (✆ **607/734-4211;** 150 units; $79–$109 double); **Hilton Garden Inn,** 35 Arnot Rd., Horseheads, NY 14845 (✆ **607/795-1111;** www.elmiracorning.gardeninn.com; 119 units; $99–$139 double); or **Econo Lodge,** 871 County Rte. 64/Rte. 17 (exit 51), Elmira, NY 14903 (✆ **607/739-2000;** 48 units; $69–$119 double).

The finest restaurant in town, and one of the best in the southeast region, is **Pierce's 1894 Restaurant** ★★, 228 Oakwood Ave. at West 14th Street (✆ **607/734-2022;** www.pierces1894.com). This family-run AAA Four-Diamond restaurant is fairly nondescript from the outside, but the four unique, supper club–like rooms inside are elegant and understated. The wine list is outstanding, with a nice selection of wines from the Finger Lakes. Service, led by the owner himself, is impeccable. The American and Continental menu features standouts like pan-seared salmon, chateaubriand, and rack of lamb (main courses $16–$26), and the dessert cart overflows with terrific homemade desserts. Reservations recommended.

5 Keuka Lake ★★★

30 miles northwest of Corning, 40 miles southwest of Geneva

The southwest quadrant of the Finger Lakes Region contains but a single Finger Lake, the small Y-shaped Keuka Lake. To many locals, Keuka is the most beautiful of all the Finger Lakes—an assessment I'd have to agree with. It's something about the deep blue of the water and the way the narrow lake splits in two and how vineyards blanket the gentle rise of the banks. Two of the more charming small villages in the Finger Lakes, Hammondsport and Naples, are located near the lake, and the Keuka Lake Wine Trail includes some of the best, most interesting, and best-sited wineries in the Finger Lakes region.

ESSENTIALS
GETTING THERE
BY CAR   Hammondsport, at the southern end of Keuka Lake, is off Route 54, which intersects with Route 17/I-86. Routes 54 and 54A travel north along the east and west sides of Keuka Lake toward Geneva.

VISITOR INFORMATION   The **Finger Lakes Association,** which oversees promotion for the entire region, is located at 309 Lake St. in Penn Yan (© **800/ 530-7488;** www.fingerlakes.org). There are also tourist information offices relatively nearby in Watkins Glen and Corning (see above).

THE FINEST OF THE FINGER LAKES
Keuka Lake is probably the prettiest and most pristine of the all Finger Lakes, plus it is uniquely shaped into its curious Y-shape (the name "keuka" in the original Native American language was thought to mean "crooked"). Keuka Lake State Park has a nice public beach for swimming, a boat launch, fishing, picnic facilities, and a children's playground. The park is located along the north shore of the West Branch of Keuka Lake, 6 miles south of Penn Yan on Route 54A.

For further exploration, **North Country Kayak & Canoe,** 665 W. Lake Rd., Hammondsport (© **607/868-7456;** amsailing02@yahoo.com), offers kayak and canoe rentals from June to September. If fishing is your thing, serene Keuka Lake offers rainbow trout, lake trout, largemouth bass, and more. Check **http:// FishSteubenCounty.com** for details on fishing and lodging packages and equipment and tackle shops.

Another way to enjoy the water is to take a cruise aboard the *Keuka Maid* **Dinner Cruise,** Route 54 (Champlin Beach), Hammondsport (© **607/569-2628;** www.keukamaid.com). Despite the company name, you can also take evening cruises, lunch and Sunday brunch cruises (Apr–Nov), as well as moonlight cruises most Saturday nights and special daylong cruises in August and September.

Another spectacular way to see Keuka Lake is to drive (or cycle) around its 20-mile perimeter. **Route 54A** is a mesmerizing scenic drive, hands-down one of the prettiest in the entire state. If you're planning to visit some wineries, you can take Route 54A to High Road.

EXPLORING HAMMONDSPORT
Tiny **Hammondsport** ⋩, at the southern end of Keuka Lake, is a postcard-perfect small town built around a village square. There are antiques and gifts shops, an ice cream parlor, and a couple of restaurants and inns. If you'd like a bit of small-town life to complement your Finger Lakes experience, it makes a good base.

Besides the lake and wineries (see box, "Keuka Lake Wine Trail," below) the biggest attraction in the immediate area is the **Glenn H. Curtiss Museum** ⋩, 8419 Rte. 54, Hammondsport (© **607/569-2160;** www.linkny.com/curtissmuseum; May–Oct Mon–Sat 9am–5pm and Sun 11am–5pm; Nov–Dec Mon–Sat 10am–4pm and Sun noon–5pm; Jan–Apr Thurs–Sat 10am–4pm and Sun, noon–5pm; $6 adults, $4.50 seniors, $3.50 students 7–18, free children 6 and under), devoted to one of the true pioneers of American aviation, who was also

Keuka Lake Wine Trail

Keuka Lake has one of the largest concentrations of wineries in the Finger Lakes, with more than a dozen dotting the banks of the lake. The **Keuka Lake Wine Trail** (© 800/440-4898; www.keukawinetrail.com; brochure widely available in the area) comprises eight independent wineries located on or near the lake. Check the trail's website for special scheduled events throughout the year. **Pleasant Valley Wine Company** ✲, Route 88, Hammondsport (© 607/569-6111; www.pleasant valleywine.com), established in 1860, is the oldest bonded winery in the Finger Lakes Region, holder of U.S. Bond No. 1, in fact. Physically it is the most atmospheric winery in the whole of the region; it retains original buildings carved out of the rocky hillside. Closed for a couple years, new ownership is working to restore it to its former stature. Full tours include an introductory film. It's open year-round: April to December, daily from 10am to 5pm and January to March, Tuesday through Saturday from 10am to 4pm.

The most distinguished winery in the entire region and a favorite of connoisseurs is **Dr. Konstantin Frank's Vinifera Wine Cellars,** 9749 Middle Rd., Hammondsport (© 800/320-0735; www.drfrankwines.com). Dr. Frank, as it's known, produces outstanding, international award-winning wines, including a splendid Johannisberg riesling and semidry riesling. Though the Finger Lakes aren't yet well known for their reds, Dr. Frank's cabernet sauvignon and pinot noir are quite excellent, and the rare Rkatsiteli and sparkling wines surprisingly good. No tours are offered, but the setting on the slopes of Keuka Lake is lovely and the

a Hammondsport native. In the early 20th century Curtiss began designing motorcycles and moved on to dirigibles, airplanes, and hydroaeroplanes ("flying boats"). His first flight, in 1908, was the first advertised public flight of aircraft (the Wright Brothers had already been aloft, but in total secrecy). The museum displays a fine collection of historical aircraft, and antique Curtiss motorcycles (including a reproduction of the one he used to achieve the world speed record, 136 mph). The museum also presents dioramas on turn-of-the-20th-century life and winemaking, as well as an interactive children's gallery.

Shoppers in Hammondsport should check out **Opera House Antiques,** 61–63 Shethar St. (© 607/569-3525), a multidealer shop featuring silver, linens, and period furniture. Across the street is **Scandia House,** 64 Shethar St. (© 607/569-2667), a shop specializing in thick Scandinavian sweaters. **Mud Lust Pottery,** 59 Shethar St. (© 607/569-3068), features locally crafted fine pottery.

WHERE TO STAY & DINE

Elm Croft Manor Bed & Breakfast ✲✲, 8361 Pleasant Valley Rd., Hammondsport, NY 14840 (© 607/569-3071; fax 607/569-2399; www.elmcroft manor.com), is an elegant 1832 Greek Revival mansion, handsomely restored with period antiques and an outdoor pool and canopied deck. The inn is walking distance from the Hammondsport Village Square and Keuka Lake. The four units, which carry girls' names, are exquisitely decorated with four-poster or full tasting is conducted by a lively group of folks who make it fun, not stuffy. Dr. Frank was a Ukrainian viticulturalist who almost single-handedly brought noble European varietals to the Finger Lakes when he began making wine in 1962. It remains a family-owned operation, run by Franks's son and grandson. It's open Monday through Saturday from 9am to 5pm and Sunday from noon to 5pm. **Heron Hill Winery,** 9249 County Rte. 76, Hammondsport (℃ **800/441-4241;** www.heronhill.com), has a gorgeous setting high above Keuka Lake, nice wines (including an excellent Meritage called "Eclipse"), frequent music events, and a good gift shop. It's open Monday through Saturday from 10am to 5pm and Sunday from noon to 5pm. Not officially part of the Keuka Lake Wine Trail, but very near the others that are, **Bully Hill Vineyards,** 8843 Greyton H. Taylor Memorial Dr., Hammondsport (℃ **607/868-3610;** www.bullyhill.com), has a reputation as the one of the zaniest wineries in the region, a reflection of its original owner, a gadfly who left the Taylor winery and repeatedly battled Coca-Cola (for the rights to use the Taylor name) after it purchased his family's business. Tours and tastings aim to inject fun into the sometimes formal wine world. Also on the premises are a quite fine restaurant and the **Greyton H. Taylor Wine Museum,** with antique winemaking implements and artwork (much of which found its way onto Bully Hill labels) of the owner. Open Monday to Saturday from 9am to 5pm and Sunday from 11am to 5pm; restaurant and wine museum open daily mid-May through October (restaurant for lunch daily, dinner Fri–Sat).

wrought-iron beds and lovely fabrics and quality linens and bedding. The Mary Belle, has its own private porch with swing. Prices range from $125 to $150 and include a full gourmet country breakfast.

The **Village Tavern Restaurant & Inn,** 30 Mechanic St., Hammondsport, NY 14840 (℃ **607/569-2528;** www.villagetaverninn.com), right on the Village Square and just a block from Keuka Lake, is a good value with four nicely equipped and comfortable, though not overly fancy, rooms above the restaurant and another four in a newly renovated old house a couple of blocks away. The latter four units are larger, quieter, and more private; they all have fireplaces, private entrances and sparkling hardwood floors. Rates range from $69 to $159 per double. The **Village Tavern Restaurant** ★★, serving American and Continental fare accompanied by fantastic wine and beer lists (with dozens of Finger Lakes wines, including many by the glass, and 130 beers), is easily the best place in town to eat. The menu features many good seafood specialties, such as crayfish étouffée, catfish creole, and fried seafood platters; there are also homemade soups, nice salads, and roast prime rib and New York Strip steak. The family-owned restaurant, a cozy and comfortable tavern, is quite popular and occasionally features live music.

The seasonal restaurant at the **Three Birds Restaurant & Inn,** 144 W. Lake Rd., Hammondsport, NY 14840 (℃ **607/868-7684;** www.threebirdsrestaurant.com), features a creative American menu and nicely prepared dishes such as pancetta-wrapped beef tenderloin, crispy Chesapeake crab and corn cakes, and honey-roasted, pecan-crusted pork tenderloin. Lots of Finger Lakes wines make the nice but manageable list. Lunch is served only in summer; dinner is served in spring, beginning in late April, Wednesday to Sunday; from mid-May to Labor Day, they serve lunch (Mon–Sat), dinner (daily), and Sunday brunch. In addition to the casually upscale restaurant, a two-bedroom suite, which was completely renovated in 2003, can accommodate up to six people. Amenities include a full kitchen, private third-floor deck, and wraparound porch with views of Keuka Lake ($135–$175).

6 Rochester ⊘

85 miles west of Niagara Falls; 45 miles west of Geneva; 105 miles northwest of Corning; 330 miles north-east of New York City

Rochester, at the southern edge of Lake Ontario, is where the Finger Lakes meet the Great Lakes. Though cities are perhaps not what most visitors associate with the Finger Lakes Region, Rochester, one of the northern gateways to the lakes, is a surprisingly agreeable city with a distinguished history that's well worth a visit for its trio of excellent museums, fine restaurants, and enjoyable festivals. The third-largest city in New York State, Rochester was an early boomtown and industrial giant in the early 19th century when it ranked as the flour-milling epicenter of the U.S. and the Erie Canal permitted the large-scale shipping of grain and flour to New York City. The city today is perhaps best known for the modern corporate success stories that got their start here, including Eastman Kodak, Xerox, and Bausch & Lomb. An extremely livable, family-friendly and attractive small city, which many contend feels more Midwestern than East Coast, Rochester has an enviable surfeit of gardens and parks but is predominantly characterized by its residents' modesty and industry.

ESSENTIALS
GETTING THERE
BY AIR   Greater Rochester International Airport, 1200 Brooks Ave. (© 716/464-6000; www.rocairport.com), is 4 miles southwest of Rochester. The airport is serviced by American, AirTran, Continental, Delta, Jet Blue, Northwest, United, and US Airways.

BY CAR   Rochester is north of I-90 (New York State Thruway), reached by either Route 490 or 590.

BY BUS   Greyhound and **Trailways** travel to the terminal at 187 Midtown Plaza (© 585/232-5121).

BY FERRY   Beginning in May 2004, a new Rochester-Toronto high-speed ferry will cross Lake Ontario in 2 hours, 15 minutes. Call the **Greater Rochester Visitors Association** (© 800/677-7282) for more information.

VISITOR INFORMATION   The **Center City Visitor Information Center** is located at 45 East Ave., Suite 400 (© 800/677-7282; www.visitrochester.com). There are also tourism information centers on the first floor of the Greater Rochester International Airport and at the rest stop of the New York State Thruway (westbound lane) near exit 45.

GETTING AROUND   Regional Transit System (RTS) buses traverse the major routes downtown. An All-Day City Pass ($4) is good for unlimited rides and can be purchased on buses. Call © 800/288-3777 for information.

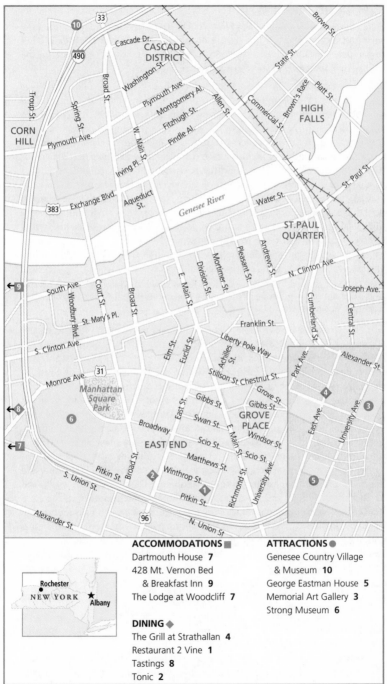

CASCADE DISTRICT

HIGH FALLS

CORN HILL

Genesee River

ST. PAUL QUARTER

GROVE PLACE

EAST END

Manhattan Square Park

ACCOMMODATIONS ■
Dartmouth House **7**
428 Mt. Vernon Bed
  & Breakfast Inn **9**
The Lodge at Woodcliff **7**

DINING ◆
The Grill at Strathallan **4**
Restaurant 2 Vine **1**
Tastings **8**
Tonic **2**

ATTRACTIONS ●
Genesee Country Village
  & Museum **10**
George Eastman House **5**
Memorial Art Gallery **3**
Strong Museum **6**

Rochester
NEW YORK
Albany

EXPLORING ROCHESTER

Start your visit in the **High Falls Historic District,** the one-time mill area at the edge of the Genesee River and a 96-foot urban waterfall. The **High Falls Visitors Center,** 60 Browns Race (℃ **585/325-3020**), has a small museum on the history of Rochester and some great views of the falls.

Genesee Country Village & Museum ★★ *Kids*   About 20 miles southwest of Rochester, this assembly of 58 historic buildings gathered from around upstate New York re-creates a working 19th-century village. Interpreters in period costume bring the 1800s to life with demonstrations of pottery making, blacksmithing, basket and cheese making, quilting, spinning, and cooking over an open hearth. Buildings include a tavern, general store, an Italianate villa mansion, an octagon-shaped home, and the boyhood home of George Eastman (of Kodak fame). The buildings are further enlivened by period gardens, roaming animals, and even a baseball diamond, where New York State's vintage teams in period dress play games according to 19th-century rules. Year-round, there is a full calendar of activities, such as a Civil War candlelight tour or country yuletide celebrations; check the website for schedule. Finally, there's an extensive gallery of wildlife and sporting art and nature center with walking trails. Allow at least a full morning or afternoon here.

1410 Flint Hill Rd., Mumford. ℃ 585/538-6822. www.gvc.org. Admission $13 adults, $9.50 seniors and students, $7 children ages 4–16, free for children under 4; Thurs, admission $2. Tues noon–4pm; Wed and Fri 10am–4pm; Thurs 10am–9pm; Sat 10am–5pm; Sun noon–5pm.

George Eastman House ★★   George Eastman, the founder of the legendary company Kodak and known as the father of popular photography, was born in upstate New York and reared in Rochester. An innovator, philanthropist, and consummate businessman, Eastman endowed the Eastman School of Music at the University of Rochester—just one of many civic-minded projects—and he left his magnificent mansion, now a National Historic Landmark and the oldest photography museum in the world, also to the University (in fact, for a time, university presidents lived there). Visitors can tour several rooms and the wonderful formal gardens of his magnificent 1905 Colonial Revival mansion. Every bit as interesting, if not more so, are the extraordinary itinerant exhibitions and permanent photography collections, which include more than 400,000 prints and negatives, one of the most important collections of silent film in the world, and a superb collection of antique cameras and photographic technology. The Eastman House, which possesses some of the most extensive motion picture and photography archives in the world, is a treasure trove for researchers. Guided tours and audio tours of the house are available. Most children love the "Discovery Room" (open Tues–Sun 1–4pm), which allows them to inspect antique cameras and make filmstrips and sun prints. Onsite are a terrific gift shop and nice cafe.

900 East Ave. ℃ 585/271-3362. www.eastman.org. Admission $8 adults, $6 seniors, $5 students $3 children ages 5–12, free for children under 5; grounds only pass $4. Tues–Sat 10am–4:30pm (Thurs until 8pm); Sun 1–4:30pm; May daily 10am–5pm.

Memorial Art Gallery ★   One of the country's best regional museums, the Memorial Art Gallery (MAG), part of the University of Rochester, covers the gamut from medieval to contemporary art, and occasionally hosts excellent traveling shows. Very good galleries of 17th- to 19th-century European art include paintings by Reubens, Rembrandt, Monet, Cézanne, and Matisse. The beautiful central gallery with a skylight over the museum's collection of 20th-century sculpture is a pleasant place to relax among works by Henry Moore and others.

The gallery's restaurant, **Cutler's,** is a great place for lunch (Tues–Sun) or dinner (Thurs–Sat).

500 University Ave. Ⓒ 585/473-7720. http://mag.rochester.edu. Admission $7 adults, $5 seniors and college students, $2 children ages 6–18, free for children under 6; Thurs admission $2. Tues noon–4pm; Wed and Fri 10am–4pm; Thurs 10am–9pm; Sat 10am–5pm; Sun noon–5pm.

Strong Museum ★★★ *(Kids)*   This imaginative place is a splendid interactive museum for children and almost certain to entertain adults, too. It is, simply, one of the finest children's museums in the country. There's a re-creation of Sesame Street, a miniature grocery store, where kids can shop and even scan their own groceries, and a fantastic dance lab and radio station where kids make their own sound effects—a real wonderland. Plenty of local families buy annual passes to make it their own personal playground and theme park. The museum even operates its own mini branch of the local library system, and there are books at every turn. The museum began as an outgrowth of a local woman's 20,000-strong collection of dolls, dollhouses, and toys (one of the largest collections in the world, it is impressive but comparatively static given all the activity going on elsewhere in the building). Adults will surely feel a tinge of nostalgia viewing the National Toy Hall of Fame. Plan on a visit of several hours if you're in the presence of curious children; also on-site are a great gift shop and an actual 1950s Skyliner diner, a great place to take a break and refuel for more playing.

One Manhattan Sq. Ⓒ 585/263-2700. www.strongmuseum.org. Admission $7 adults, $6 seniors and students, $5 children ages 2–17, free for children under 2. Mon–Thurs and Sat 10am–5pm; Sun 10am–5pm.

SPORTS & OUTDOOR PURSUITS
Beaches on the Lake Ontario shoreline, north of the city, are very popular with locals. At **Ontario Beach Park,** often called "the Port of Rochester," at the mouth of the Genessee River, has piers, a boardwalk and an antique carousel in addition to a pleasant lake beach.

The farm team of baseball's Minnesota Twins, the **Rochester Red Wings** (Ⓒ 585/454-1001; www.redwingsbaseball.com), play at Frontier Field, downtown, across from High Falls. The PGA Championship and the Ryder Cup have been held at Oak Hill Country Club, and the women play the LPGA Wegmans Rochester International at Locust Hill Country Club (www.rochesterlpga.com).

Since 1892, the annual **Lilac Festival,** held in early May at the 150-acre Highland Park, is a magnet for nature lovers: some 1,200 lilac bushes in Highland Park burst with spring color. The festival also draws musical entertainment and a commercial, carnival-like atmosphere (Ⓒ 585/256-4960; www.lilacfestival.com). Highland Park, designed in 1888 by Frederick Law Olmsted (who also created New York City's Central Park) and full of beautiful gardens and plantings, is a lovely place for a stroll.

Erie Canal and Genesee River cruises are offered aboard the *Sam Patch,* a 19th-century replica packet boat, daily from May to October. Call Ⓒ 585/262-5661 for schedules.

A Final Resting Place
More people are buried in sprawling Victorian **Mt. Hope Cemetery,** Mt. Hope and Elmwood avenues (Ⓒ 585/428-7999), than currently live in the city of Rochester, including a handful of its most notable citizens, such as Frederick Douglass and Susan B. Anthony.

The Erie Canal

Lauded as the most important engineering feat of its day, the Erie Canal, completed in 1825, created an international highway from the Great Lakes to the Atlantic Ocean. Shipping costs of flour and other raw materials and manufactured goods were reduced by as much as 90%. The canal stretched 360 miles from the Niagara River and Lake Erie in the west to the Hudson River in the east. It turned Rochester into a boomtown and was instrumental in transforming New York City into a major port, in the process opening up parts of the West for commercial expansion.

The canal diminished in importance as the railroad quickly began to crisscross the country, but it is being rediscovered as a tourism waterway. In addition to boating and cruises on the canal, the New York State Erie Canal Heritage trail follows the original towpath along the canal and is ideal for walking, biking, and skiing in winter. Anyone interested in following the canal, either by boat or car and seeing sights along it should request a copy of "Canal Connections" from any of the country tourism offices. See also www.canals.state.ny.us.

ESPECIALLY FOR KIDS

The outstanding Strong children's museum and the 19th-century Genessee Country Village & Museum (see above) are musts for kids visiting Rochester. Also of interest is the **Seneca Park Zoo,** 222 St. Paul Blvd. (© **585/467-WILD;** www.senecaparkzoo.org), which features polar bears, rare African elephants, and Eurasian Arctic wolves. **High Falls** is also a good place for families. Kids will enjoy the urban waterfall and laser-light show, shown there on weekend nights in the summer; the High Falls Visitors Center also has an educational exhibit aimed at youngsters. Lake Ontario's beaches and the nearby **Seabreeze Amusement Park,** 4600 Culver Rd. (© **800/395-2500;** www.seabreeze.com), open mid-June to Labor Day, are great spots in the heat of summer.

SHOPPING

The biggest mall in the area is **EastView Mall,** 7979 Pittsford-Victor Rd., Victor (© **585/223-3693**), about 20 minutes south of Rochester. **Craft Antique Co-op,** 3200 West Ridge Rd. (© **888/711-3463** or 585/368-0670), is one of the state's largest craft and antique co-ops, with 210 shops. Antiques hounds will want to visit the **Bloomfield Antique Country Mile** corridor along Routes 5 and 20 in Bloomfield, on the way to Canandaigua, where a few dozen antiques shops are located. **Craft Company No. 6,** 785 University Ave. (© **585/473-3413**), which deals in all manner of contemporary American crafts, including jewelry, art glass, and home decor, occupies a Victorian firehouse 1 block from the George Eastman House. One of the best strolling and shopping areas downtown is along **Park Avenue and Alexander Street,** with lots of food and drink pit stops along the way. And don't forget the excellent gift shops at the Strong Museum and George Eastman House.

WHERE TO STAY

Rochester has two very nice B&Bs in residential neighborhoods as well as a handful of large chain hotels downtown, including the **Hyatt Regency Rochester,** 125

East Main St. (© **585/546-1234;** fax 585/546-6777; http://rochester.hyatt.com; $150 double), probably the best of the lot; the **Crowne Plaza,** 70 State St. (© **585-5463450;** www.crowneplaza.com; $109–$149 double); and the massive **Clarion,** 120 Main St. East (© **585/546-6400;** www2.choicehotels.com; $139–$154 double). The independent **Strathallan Hotel,** 550 East Ave. (© **800/678-7248;** www.strathallan.com; 156 units), in a former apartment building is worth a look; it's very well located, has a terrific restaurant (see below), and most rooms have kitchenettes—but it could use some updating.

Dartmouth House ★ This ideally located 1905 English Tudor inn, nestled in a residential area near the East Avenue entertainment district and Park Avenue, is a fine place to stay. Rooms are elegantly decorated, with period antiques. The public rooms in this 15-year-old inn feature a grand piano, fireplace, and window seats, as well as handsome Arts and Crafts details.

215 Dartmouth St., Rochester, NY 14607. © **800/724-6298** or 585/271-7872. www.dartmouthhouse.com. 7 units. $120–$150 double. Rates include full breakfast. AE, MC, V. Free parking. *In room:* A/C, TV/VCR.

428 Mt. Vernon Bed & Breakfast Inn ★ A stately 1917 home on a nice wooded lot just off Highland Park, south of downtown, this relaxed and comfortable place, popular with visiting professors and business travelers, is one of the best places to stay in town. The house has Victorian-style furnishings, but is understated and not fussy. Its biggest advantages are a countrylike atmosphere and location that offer travelers a sanctuary in the midst of the city. Breakfasts are hearty.

428 Mt. Vernon, Rochester, NY 14620. © **800/836-3159** or 585/271-0792. www.428mtvernon.com. 7 units. $125 double. Rates include full breakfast. AE, MC, V. Free parking. *In room:* A/C, TV.

The Lodge at Woodcliff *Kids* A large resort hotel south of Rochester, this is a good place to stay if you're more interested in golf or exploring some of the small towns closer to the Finger Lakes than you are in getting to know Rochester; it's not at all convenient to downtown though access to I-90 is a snap. However, it has a nice little nine-hole golf course, an indoor-outdoor heated pool, and is loaded with amenities and activities. The best thing about most rooms is the excellent distant views of the countryside south of Rochester.

199 Woodcliff Dr., Rochester, NY 14692. © **800/365-3065** or 585/381-4000. www.woodclifflodge.com. 250 units. $175 double, $195–$350 suite. AE, DISC, MC, V. Free parking. **Amenities:** Restaurant; bar; golf course; fitness center; heated swimming pool; sauna *In room:* A/C, TV w/pay movies, minibar, coffeemaker, hair dryer.

WHERE TO DINE

Rochester has a surprisingly lively dining scene. Much of it is clustered around two areas, East Avenue, or the so-called "East End Entertainment District," and Park Avenue and Alexander Street. Two restaurants worth visiting, especially when you're out sightseeing, are actually located in museums: **Cutler's** (© **585/473-6380**) is an upscale option just off the modern sculpture gallery at the Memorial Art Gallery (p. 328), and **Bill Gray's Skyliner Diner** (© **585/232-5284**) is the Strong Museum's authentic 1950s diner, with food that kids will love (p. 329).

The Grill at Strathallan ★★ AMERICAN The only Mobil four-diamond restaurant in the state west of New York City, in a somewhat underwhelming hotel location, this is nonetheless the place in Rochester for haute cuisine and fine wine. Entrees are classic, like dry-aged strip steak, veal chop, and slow-roasted salmon, with just a few twists (such as the peach-lacquered duck breast with squash gnocchi, seared spinach, and foie gras). Gourmands and oenophiles should check into the periodic six-course wine dinners, with pairings for each course.

3195 Monroe Ave. 𝒞 **585/381-1881.** Reservations required. Main courses $21–$30. AE, DISC, MC, V. Daily 5:30–10pm.

Restaurant 2 Vine ★★ *Value* BISTRO/SEAFOOD   In a renovated 1890s ambulance garage, this cheery and casual, often-crowded restaurant and lively bar is a great place for dinner before or after a show at Little Theatre, which the restaurant is located behind. The space is large, handsome and warm, with subdued lighting and a beautiful long bar. The menu features fresh seasonal ingredients, organic produce, and fresh seafood delivered daily from Boston. Choose from elegant entrees like roasted halibut with mushroom-watercress risotto or classic bistro dishes such as mussels steamed in white wine with *pommes frites.* Big appetites and wallets can be steered toward towering iced platters of seafood. Service is good, if occasionally a bit harried. In keeping with its name, 2 Vine has an excellent wine list, even though it features only a couple of Finger Lakes wines.

4 Winthrop St. 𝒞 **585/454-6020.** Reservations recommended. Main courses $12–$22. AE, DISC, MC, V. Mon–Fri 11:30am–2pm and 5–9pm; Sat–Sun 5–8pm.

Tastings *Finds* AMERICAN   Next to, but more properly a part of the Wegmans grocery store—a seemingly odd place to find a good restaurant—this hopping, dimly lit place with brick vaulted ceilings and crowded tables has been a huge hit with locals, who know well the fresh ingredients and meats and fish that Wegmans supplies. Entrees include braised beef short ribs with "smashed potatoes" and homemade potato gnocchi. A great option is the tasting menu, with or without wine. For dessert, cheese lovers will faint at the sight of the cheese flights, served with a baguette, sourdough bread, and fruit.

3195 Monroe Ave. 𝒞 **585/381-1881.** Reservations recommended. Main courses $11–$26; tasting menu $40 ($58–$68 with wine). AE, DISC, MC, V. Tues–Sat lunch 11:30am–2:30pm, dinner 5:30–10pm.

Tonic ★ CREATIVE AMERICAN   This hip, upstairs loftlike bar and restaurant are very *downtown,* a real surprise in Rochester. Despite the cool look, it draws a mix of youths in black and older folks and families. You can eat at the large U-shaped bar or the wide-open restaurant space. Main courses offer no surprises, but they are well crafted and nicely prepared. I recently enjoy Hudson Valley foie gras and lobster ravioli; other interesting mains include Milanese-style braised monkfish. Tonic's sister restaurant across the street, **Pearl** (𝒞 **585/ 325-5660**), makes an even more serious, minimalist fashion statement, focusing on Asian flavors and fresh fish.

336 East Ave. 𝒞 **585/325-2923.** Reservations recommended. Main courses $16–$28. AE, DISC, MC, V. Restaurant Wed–Sat 5:30pm-9:30pm and 5–9pm; bar Wed-Sat 4:30pm-2am.

ROCHESTER AFTER DARK

The **Eastman School of Music** ★ presents more than 700 concerts a year, including jazz, classical, chamber, and opera, among others, at the Eastman Theatre and other venues in Rochester. For concert information, call 𝒞 **585/274-1100** or visit http://rochester.edu/Eastman. The **Rochester Philharmonic Orchestra** also plays at the Eastman Theatre. Call the box office at (𝒞 **585/ 454-2100** or see the schedule at www.rpo.org). The **Rochester International Jazz Festival** (first 2 weeks of June), one of the city's biggest festival and music draws, features more than 50 concerts at 15 venues by major players. Contact the hot line at 𝒞 **585/234-2002** or visit www.rochesterjazz.com.

The **Geva Theatre Center,** 75 Woodbury Blvd. (𝒞 **585/232-4382;** www. gevatheatre.org), is the major venue in town for theater productions, and the most-attended regional theater in New York State.

[handwritten annotations: "both on Man J – 332 –" "Bus District, City Hall, Court House" — and in right margin: "first light 2-3 Howell St right turn turn"]

Free laser-light shows are projected in the gorge at High Falls Friday and Saturday nights from Memorial Day to Labor Day; families and couples on dates hang out on the Rennes bridge that spans the river. The High Falls district is on the way up, with a number of new pubs and restaurants moving in. Expect more on the way. The **East End** "entertainment district" ★, along East Avenue, is one of the best spots to hang out on weekends. The cool Art Deco **Little Theatre,** 240 East Ave. (© **585/232-3906**), shows independent and foreign films, and often has live music in its cafe. Nearby East Avenue bars include the chic **Tonic** and minimalist **Pearl.** The **St. Paul Quarter,** along St. Paul and Main streets, is also replete with bars and restaurants. Among its hot nightspots is **Club Industry,** 155 St. Paul St. (© **585/262-4570**). **Dinosaur Bar-B-Q,** 99 Court St. (© **585/325-7090**), a biker bar and lively ribs joint in the old Lehigh Valley Train Station downtown, has live blues bands on weekends and can get pretty raucous.

7 Canandaigua Lake

30 miles southeast of Rochester; 19 miles west of Geneva

Canandaigua, at the northern end of the lake of the same name, is the kind of laid-back small town that epitomizes the Finger Lakes Region. Canandaigua Lake, the birthplace of the Seneca Nation that ruled this area in precolonial days, is the area's principal attraction, but there are a number of unique sights and experiences in what is rather redundantly called Lake Country. (Ontario County is home to 5 of the 11 Finger Lakes.)

ESSENTIALS
GETTING THERE
BY CAR   Canandaigua is reached along either Route 21 or 332 south from I-90.

VISITOR INFORMATION   The **Finger Lakes Visitors Connection** can be contacted at (© **585/394-3915;** www.visitfingerlakes.com).

EXPLORING CANANDAIGUA LAKE
Naturalists and garden enthusiasts should not miss the **Sonnenberg Mansion & Gardens** ★★, 151 Charlotte St. (© **585/394-4922;** www.sonnenberg.org). The 50-acre estate and 1887 Queen Anne Victorian mansion, which once belonged to the founder of what is today Citibank, possesses some of the loveliest formal gardens and landscaping you're likely to encounter, including Italian, Japanese and rock gardens. The grounds also maintain an impressive conservatory and Finger Lakes Wine Center, which conducts tastings on the premises. Special events, such as the "Haunted Gardens" in October and "Festival of Lights," in November and December, are truly special. The Sonnenberg is open daily mid-May to mid-October, from 9:30am to 5:30pm; admission is $8.50 for adults, $7.50 for seniors, $3.50 for children ages 5 to 14.

CANANDAIGUA WINE TRAIL   The collection of small vineyards and wineries clustered around Canandaigua Lake have joined forces to form the Canandaigua Wine Trail (© **800/554-7553;** www.canandaiguawinetrailonline. com), making it easy for visitors to group them together for tours and tastings. They include: **Arbor Hill Grapery,** 6461 Rte. 64, Bristol Springs, Naples (© **800/554-2406;** open May–Dec, Mon–Sat 10am–5pm, Sun 11am–5pm; Jan–April, Sat–Sun 11am–5pm), which features a shop selling a large selection of wine, food, and gift items (including grape pies), and a great little bakery/cafe—excellent for breakfast or lunch; **Casa Larga Vineyards,** 2287 Turk Hill Rd.,

Fairport (© **585/223-4210;** open year-round Mon–Sat 10am–6pm, Sun noon–6pm); and **Widmer Wine Cellars,** 1 Lake Niagara Lane, Naples (© **800/836-LAKE;** open year round, daily 10am–4pm), a century-old winery. Also of interest is the **Finger Lakes Wine Center** at Sonnenberg Gardens, 151 Charlotte St., Canandaigua (© **585/394-9016;** open daily mid-May to mid-Oct noon–5pm), which offers samples and the sales of more than 30 Finger Lakes wineries.

NEARBY ATTRACTIONS   The Church of Jesus Christ of Latter-Day Saints, better known to the rest of the world as the Mormon religion, got its start in the northwest region of the Finger Lakes before moving out west to Utah. Near Palmyra (17 miles northeast of Canandaigua), according to Mormon texts, Joseph Smith received golden plates, later translated into the Book of Mormon, from an angel in 1827. North of Canandaigua, along Route 21, is the **Hill Cumorah Visitors Center** (603 State Rte. 21, Palmyra; © **315/597-5851**); anyone who wants to learn more about the Mormon faith can drop in for some low-pressure information about the church and find out about Mormon-related sights in the area, such as Smith's log cabin. However, the big event in these parts is the annual **Hill Cumorah Pageant,** an incredible spectacle and the largest outdoor theatrical production in the U.S., with a costumed cast of 700, a nine-level stage and music by the Mormon Tabernacle Choir. Every July, its seven productions draw many thousands of believers and curious. For more information, call © **315/597-5851** or visit **www.hillcumorah.com**. Performances are free.

Not far from the Mormons, but on an altogether different spiritual plane is the **Finger Lakes Race Track** (© **585/935-5252;** www.fingerlakesracetrack.com), in Farmington, also north of Canandaigua (1 mile south of I-90, exit 44 on Rte. 332). Thoroughbred horses race there from April to November.

Clifton Springs, north and about equidistant between Canandaigua and Geneva, is a small village that smells of sulfur, which is not surprising given the natural sulfur springs that drew visitors in the 19th century seeking the Clifton Springs Water Cure. The town's Main Street, near the original sulfur brook, has a pleasant turn-of-the-20th-century feel to it, with restored period architecture now housing a variety of cute gift shops and restaurants. The best place to eat in town is **Warfield's,** 7 West Main St. (© **315/462-7184**).

Visitors interested in the region's Native American roots should head to the **Ganondogan State Historic Site,** 1488 State Rte. 444, Victor (© **585/742-1690;** www.ganondagan.org), a real find located northeast of Canandaigua. A former center of the democratically inclined Seneca people, one of the six nations comprising the Iroquois Confederacy, the site today features a replica 17th-century Seneca bark longhouse and marked ethnobotanical, Native American–themed trails that aim to teach visitors about Seneca customs and beliefs. Trails are open year-round, from 8am to sunset; the Visitor Center is open mid-May to October, Tuesday to Sunday from 9am to 5pm. Interpreted trail walks are offered year-round, Saturday at 10am and 2pm, Sunday at noon and 2pm.

ESPECIALLY FOR KIDS

Roseland Water Park, 250 Eastern Blvd. (© **585/396-2000;** www.roseland waterpark.com), with its giant wave pool and splash factory, is a good place for kids to cool off if they're not into the lake.

SPORTS & OUTDOORS ACTIVITIES

Public-access beaches on Canandaigua Lake include **Butler Beach,** West Lake Road (© **585/396-2752;** free admission), on the west side of the lake; **Deep**

Run Park, East Lake Road (☎ **585/396-4000**), on the east side of the lake; and **Kershaw Park,** Lakeshore Drive (☎ **585/396-5060; fee charged**), which has a sandy beach and an 8-acre park.

If you'd rather see the lake from a boat, the *Canandaigua Lady* (☎ **866/ 9-ANCHOR;** www.steamboatlandingonline.com) is a replica 19th-century paddlewheel steamboat, available for meal and nonmeal lake cruises. From May to mid-September, they depart from Steamboat Landing, 205 Lakeshore Dr. (at the north end of Canandaigua Lake). Fall foliage cruises (mid-Sept to Oct) board at Woodville dock, Route 21 South (south end of Canandaigua Lake). Cruise prices range from $12 to $40. Scuba diving, windsurfing, kayaking, and sailboarding rentals and instruction are available from **Canandaigua Sailboarding,** 11 Lakeshore Dr. (☎ **585/394-8150**).

Golfers will not want to miss the **Bristol Harbour Resort Golf Course** (☎ **800/288-8248;** www.bristolharbour.com), a beautiful 18-hole Robert Trent Jones–designed course right on Lake Canandaigua. Greens fees are $25 to $55.

Good hiking and cycling are available on **Ontario Pathways,** 200 Ontario St., Canandaigua (☎ **585/394-7968;** www.ontariopathways.com), 23 miles of rails-to-trails. In winter months, you can ski at **Bristol Mountain Winter Resort,** 5662 Rte. 64, Canandaigua (☎ **585/374-6000;** www.bristolmountain.com).

SHOPPING

Along Canandaigua's Main Street, an "artwalk" takes you to **Gallery on Main Street** (131 S. Main St.; ☎ **585/394-2780**), **The Christopher Wheat Gallery** (92 S. Main St.; ☎ **585/399-1180**), and **Nadal Glass** (20 Phoenix St.; ☎ **585/ 374-7850**), which features hand-blown glass in an old firehouse. The top shopping destination in the area, however, is the **Bloomfield Antique Country Mile,** a cluster of seven antiques dealers along Routes 5 and 20 in Bloomfield (just west of Canandaigua). Several are multidealer shops, such as **Alan's Antique Alley,** 6925 Routes 5 and 20 (☎ **585/657-6776**). **Wizard of Clay,** 7851 Rte. 20A, Bristol (☎ **585/229-2980**), is a cool stoneware pottery shop. A couple of very large antique malls are located in Farmington (Rochester Rd., or Rte. 332): **Ontario Mall Antiques** (1740 Rochester Rd.; ☎ **585/398-3030**), with more than 600 dealers, and **Antique Emporium of Farmington** (1780 Rochester Rd.; ☎ **585/398–3997**), with some 60 dealers.

WHERE TO STAY

Acorn Inn ★★   A charming, meticulously kept B&B—enough to earn a four-diamond rating from AAA—this 1795 Federal Stagecoach Inn west of Canandaigua Lake is one of the nicer small country inns in the Finger Lakes. The common room is cozy and lined with several thousand books and warmed by a roaring fire in cold months. In addition to the large and very handsomely appointed rooms on the second floor, all with romantic canopied beds and a couple with fireplaces, guests can luxuriate under the stars in a splendid outdoor hot tub set among the gardens near the carriage house. Among the guest rooms, the Bristol has a large sitting area, and all the rooms are equipped with spacious modern bathrooms. The candlelit breakfast is a lovely affair, served on antique English china and heirloom silver.

4508 Rte. 64 South, Bristol Center, Canandaigua, NY 14424. ☎ **888/245-4134** or 585/229-2834. http://acorninnbnb.com. 4 units. $135–$215 double (2-night minimum May–Nov). Rates include full breakfast. AE, MC, V. Free parking. **Amenities:** Jacuzzi. *In room:* A/C, TV/VCR, CD player.

Bristol Harbour Resort ★ *Kids* This small resort hotel, right on Canandaigua Lake, features some excellent outdoors amenities, such as an excellent golf course (ask about special golf packages), a private beach, and an outdoor swimming pool. The 31 cozy Adirondack-style rooms aren't merely an afterthought; they all have fireplaces and balconies, many with superb panoramic views of the lake. The Lodge restaurant, recommended below, is quite good, and the Tavern's a great place to unwind after a round of golf or touring the area.

5410 Seneca Point Rd., Canandaigua, NY 14424. ✆ 800/288-8248. www.bristolharbour.com. 31 units. $89–$169 double; $139–$209 suite. AE, DISC, MC, V. Free parking. **Amenities:** Restaurant; bar; outdoor pool; outdoor Jacuzzi; 18-hole golf course; private beach. *In room:* A/C, TV/VCR, CD player.

Canandaigua Inn on the Lake *Kids* This midsize, low-rise hotel is distinguished by its enviable lakefront location. The accommodations are good-size and comfortable, even homey, though fairly standard hotel fare. Ask for one of the few room with lake views. The restaurant, Nicole's Lakeside, is quite good, and the patio lounge overlooking the lake a great spot for a relaxing drink; there's often live weekend music under the tent. The hotel has excellent outdoor and indoor pools, the latter with a Jacuzzi, that are very popular with families.

770 S. Main St., Canandaigua, NY 14424. ✆ 800/228-2801 or 585/394-7800. Fax 585/394-5003. www.hudsonhotels.com/canandaigua. 134 units. $94–$144 double; $124–$184 suite. AE, DISC, MC, V. Free parking. **Amenities:** Restaurant; wine bar and lounge; indoor pool; Jacuzzi; fitness center. *In room:* A/C, TV w/pay movies, dataport, fridge, coffeemaker, hair dryer.

Morgan Samuels B&B Inn ★★ On 46 sylvan acres, this private, and rather prim and proper inn occupying an 1810 English-style mansion, is a nice retreat if you're looking for tranquillity. Guest rooms are pretty and romantic, and each is uniquely decorated, with such touches as Oriental rugs and antiques, French doors, and fireplaces. An awful lot of care is put into the inn's ambience, especially at breakfast, which is served fireside by candlelight in the formal dining room. The enclosed garden porch is a lovely spot to sip afternoon tea, and the library is a private nook to plunge into a good book. The elegance and old-world refinement will not suit everyone, while others will be in heaven.

2920 Smith Rd., Canandaigua 14424. ✆ 585/394-9232. Fax 585/394-8044. www.morgansamuelsinn.com. 5 units. $159–$225 double; $199–$395 suite. Rates include full breakfast. AE, MC, V. Free parking. **Amenities:** Tennis court. *In room:* A/C.

WHERE TO DINE

In addition to the restaurants below, the hotel Canandaigua Inn on the Lake (see above) has a nice restaurant, **Nicole's Lakeside,** with good views and an outdoor terrace.

Bristol Harbour's Lodge Restaurant ★ GRILL With gorgeous views of southern Lake Canandaigua, this woodsy, Adirondack-style restaurant on the grounds of an upscale golf resort is a fine place to linger over a cocktail and ease into dinner. It's the kind of masculine-looking place that cries out for an order of grilled meats, such as the filet medley, with crab cake rémoulade sauce, or New York Strip Steak with a brandy peppercorn sauce. There are plenty of less macho entrees, however, including grilled sea bass and grilled vegetables wrapped in phyllo. Even if you're not staying here, the Lodge is perfect to drop in for a hearty breakfast or lunch before hitting the links or getting out on the lake. Eat in the main restaurant or the tavern; in nice weather, there's seating on one of two outdoor patios. A grill menu is also offered daily in the Tavern from 11am to 10pm.

5410 Seneca Point Rd., Bristol Harbor. © **585/396-2200.** Reservations recommended. Main courses $11–$22. AE, DISC, MC, V. Sun–Thurs 7:30–10:30am, 11am–2pm, and 5–9pm; Fri–Sat 7:30–10:30am, 11am–2pm, and 5–10pm.

Kellogg's Pan-Tree Inn *Value* HOME COOKING   At the northern edge of the lake, this homey joint, family-owned since 1924, is a great spot for an excellent, inexpensive breakfast or lunch, when there are great views of the water across the road. (There's a nice deck with outdoor dining, open in season). It's also good for an informal dinner, with entrees ranging from charbroiled burgers and gourmet pizzas to chicken pie and filet mignon. The menu features homemade, fresh-baked breads and desserts, as well as a nice selection of Finger Lakes wines. The owners also operate an inexpensive motel out back ($54–$74 double).

130 Lakeshore Dr., Canandaigua. © **585/394-3909.** Main courses $6.75–$16. MC, V. Spring and fall Sun–Thurs 7:30am–7:30pm; Fri–Sat 7:30am–8:30pm; July–Aug daily 7:30am–8:30pm.

CANANDAIGUA AFTER DARK

The **Finger Lakes Performing Arts Center,** 4355 Lakeshore Dr., Lincoln Hill, Canandaigua (on the campus of Finger Lakes Community College), a very attractive open-air theater, hosts the Rochester Philharmonic Orchestra and popular musical events throughout the summer. For more information, visit **www.rbtl.org/html/flpac.htm** or call © **716/325-7760;** tickets are available through **Ticket Express** (© **716/222-500**). The Rochester Broadway Theatre League hosts the annual summertime **Finger Lakes Elegant Picnic** in Canandaigua, with concerts at the shell featuring such big-name acts as Diana Krall and Tony Bennett.

NAPLES

At the southern end of Canandaigua Lake, the picturesque village of Naples *★* is a quintessential small Finger Lakes town with a number of well-preserved 18th-century buildings. It's a peaceful place primarily known for its arts community until autumn and the last weekend in September, when the unique **Naples Grape Festival** takes over.

EXPLORING NAPLES

Area wineries worth a visit include **Widmer's Wine Cellars** and **Arbor Hill Grapery & Winery;** see Canandaigua Wine Trail, p. 333, for details.

Trout **fishing** is good on Canandaigua Lake, and small and shallow Honeoye Lake is known for Walleye, Largemouth and Smallmouth Bass. **Reel Magic Charters,** 8 Cohocton St., Naples (© **585/374-5197**), runs fishing charters on Canandaigua Lake.

Duffers should check out the scenic **Reservoir Creek Golf Club,** 8613 Cohocton St. (© **585/374-6828;** www.rcgolf.com). Greens fees are $39 Monday to Thursday, $43 weekends and holidays; reduced rates for seniors, juniors, "sunset" play (after 2pm), and fall season (after Oct 10).

The **Bristol Valley Theater,** 151 South Main St. (© **585/374-6318;** www.bvtnaples.org), schedules professional summer theater in a handsome outdoor amphitheater.

Tips Joyride

For a lovely, scenic drive, take the High Road—County Route 12 at Bristol Springs—to Naples.

The **Naples Grape Festival** (last weekend of Sept) is a fun-filled weekend built around the town's tradition of making grape pies. The festival has been held in Naples for more than 40 years and draws an bumper-to-bumper pilgrimage along Routes 64 and 21; as many as 50,000 grape pies are sold in that single weekend. For more information, call © **585/374-2240** or visit www.naplesvalleyny.com/ GrapeFestivalPage.htm. Grape pies, of course, are notoriously labor intensive to make (you have to peel the grapes first), perhaps the reason why they haven't exactly taken off outside Naples. They are available, however, year-round at the Arbor Hill Grapery & Winery.

Those with time to explore the region a bit more should venture west to the far edge of Livingston County and about the westernmost point of what is generally considered the Finger Lakes Region. About equidistant between Corning and Rochester is one of upstate New York's most spectacular parks, **Letchworth State Park,** in Castile, New York (© **585/493-3600;** www.nysparks.state.ny.us), a real find. The park contains what is frequently called the "Grand Canyon of the East," a dramatic 600-foot gorge that spans the Genessee River. Elsewhere nestled in more than 14,000 acres are other scenic cliffs, thick forest, natural swimming holes, and three waterfalls. It's fabulous for fall foliage fans. For outdoor enthusiasts, there are cabins and camping, and activities including hiking, rafting and cross-country skiing. For cabin and camping reservations, call © **877/444-6777.** For an extraordinary experience, why not soar over the gorge in a hot-air balloon? Contact **Balloons Over Letchworth** (© **585/493-3340;** www.balloons overletchworth.com).

WHERE TO STAY & DINE

A neat place to stay in Naples is **The Vagabond Inn** ★★, 3300 Slitor Rd., Naples, NY 14512 (© **585/554-6271;** www.thevagabondinn.com; five units; $115–$225). Secluded high on a hilltop amid 65 acres of forest, this very large contemporary house has spectacular views and unusual amenities for an inn, such as a beautiful outdoor pool and hot tub. Rooms are all unique; three of them are very large with cool features (private garden porch and patio, river-stone fireplace, private hot tub). Rates included a large full breakfast. Another good B&B in town, and a great value for the money, is **Grapevine Inn Bed & Breakfast** ★, 182 North Main St., Naples, NY 14512 (© **585/374-9298;** fax 585/374-9298; www.grapevineinnbb.com; $85–$125), a romantic 1923 English Victorian Tudor with three pretty and nicely appointed rooms. There's a swimming pool and private Jacuzzi, and a full candlelit breakfast is served.

For dining, check out the **Naples Diner,** a long-time fixture at 139 S. Main St. (© **585/374-5420**), or the **Naples Hotel,** 111 S. Main St. (© **585/374-9298**), an 1895 Federal-style hotel with a great old lounge bar.

8 Geneva ★★ & Northern Seneca Lake

10 miles east of Seneca Falls; 54 miles east of Syracuse; 19 miles west of Canandaigua; 45 miles southeast of Rochester

Geneva, tucked midway between the region's two largest cities, Rochester and Syracuse, is a gracious and historic small city at the north end of Seneca Lake. With about 15,000 residents, it's one of the larger towns in the region, an eminently livable small city and classic college town (it's home to Hobart and William Smith colleges). During the 19th century, Geneva was the major commercial hub of central New York; today its revitalized downtown boasts an architecture fan's cornucopia of restored and stately century-old row houses and

---

Tips **All Aboard!**

The **Finger Lakes Railway,** with trains operated by the Central New York chapter of the National Railway Historical Society, offers occasional scenic trips through Cayuga and Seneca counties, including nine different Memorial Weekend excursions (for example, between Cayuga and Waterloo, and between Skaneateles and Solvay). Round-trips generally range between $15 and $30. For more information, call ℂ **315/488-8208** or visit the "unofficial" website at http://fglk.railfan.net.

Victorian mansions. Seneca Lake, the deepest of the Finger Lakes at 632 feet and more than 200 feet below sea level, is a huge draw for outdoors activities.

ESSENTIALS
GETTING THERE
BY CAR   Geneva is south of I-90 along Route 14 and right on Routes 5 and 20, coming either west from Seneca Falls or east from Canandaigua.

BY BUS   **Greyhound** and **Trailways** deposit and pick up passengers at the Chalet Coffee Pot, 48 Lake St., Geneva (ℂ **315/789-2582**).

VISITOR INFORMATION   The **Finger Lakes Visitors Connection** can be contacted at (ℂ **585/394-3915;** www.visitfingerlakes.com). The nearest walk-in information center is in Seneca Falls at the **Seneca Falls Heritage Area Visitor Center,** 115 Fall St. (ℂ **315/568-2703**); it's open Monday to Saturday from 10am to 4pm and Sun noon to 4pm.

EXPLORING GENEVA
Geneva, which grew up at the end of the 18th century on the banks of Seneca Lake, has an amazing and eclectic collection of well-preserved mansions ★★ of historic and architectural significance, including examples of Greek Revival, Federal, Victorian Gothic, and Jeffersonian styles ★★, most from the first 3 decades of the 19th century. **South Main Street** is lined with row houses, resembling those of Georgetown in Washington, D.C., and grand mansions overlooking Seneca Lake. Besides the "south Main Street" walking tour brochure, pick up another one called "Architectural Landmarks" (available at the Prouty-Chew House & Museum, see below). Have a look at **Pulteney Park,** the original village green, and Washington, Genesee, Castle, and Jay streets to survey Geneva's architectural feast.

    The **Rose Hill Mansion** ★, Route 96A, 1 mile south of Routes 5 and 20 (ℂ **315/789-3848**), just east of Geneva and Seneca Lake, is an architectural landmark, an excellent example of the Greek Revival style, that was built in 1839 and reflects the grandeur of Geneva's early development. Once part of a sprawling lakefront farm, today it is a handsomely restored mansion with Empire furnishings; note the historically accurate and bold wallpaper. On the premises are a good information center, a short film about the house, and two antiques dealers in old carriage houses. The museum is open May through October, Monday to Saturday, from 10am to 4:30pm, and Sun, 1pm to 5pm; admission is $3 adults, $2 seniors and students ages 10 to 18.

    The **Prouty-Chew House & Museum,** 543 South Main St. (ℂ **315/789-5151**), is run by and headquarters of the Geneva Historical Society. The building is an 1829 Federal-style home with significant late-19th-century modifications.

Visitors are welcome to have a look around the house's two floors. You can also pick up **a self-guided architectural walking tour** map with details on about 50 buildings in Geneva. The Prouty-Chew House is open May through October, Tuesday to Friday from 9:30am to 4:30pm and Saturday (and Sun in July–Aug), from 1:30 to 4:30pm; admission is free.

A $2 million renovation has returned **The Smith Opera House** ★★★, 82 Seneca St. (© **315/781-5483;** www.thesmith.org), to its original glory as a grand movie palace. Built in 1894 but given a whimsical Deco-Baroque makeover in the 1930s, with fantastic murals and Moorish touches, the 1,400-seat theater was first an opera house and later vaudeville theater. Today it has carved out a niche showing independent and foreign art films and hosting rock and other concerts. Try to take in a movie or show; otherwise, if the box office is open and nothing's going on, ask for a peek inside.

Many of the two dozen wineries on the **Seneca Lake Wine Trail** are within easy reach of Geneva; see the sidebar on p. 316.

SPORTS & OUTDOOR ACTIVITIES

Seneca Lake is one of the two largest of the 11 Finger Lakes. Pontoon and fishing boat rentals are available from **Roy's Marina,** West Lake Road (Rte. 14; © **315/ 789-3094**). **Seneca Lake State Park,** Routes 5 and 20, is on the north end of the lake; it's a good spot for strolls, and small kids will love the new playground and water sprays to cool off in the summer heat. Seneca Lake is known for its **lake trout fishing,** and catches at the annual National Lake Trout Derby (www.flsor.com) sometimes almost top the 100-pound mark.

SHOPPING

Waterloo Premium Outlets, 655 Rte. 318, Waterloo (© **315/539-1100**), near I-90, has dozens of outlet stores, including Polo Ralph Lauren, Coach, and Mikasa. Two antiques shops operate on the premises of the **Rose Hill Mansion** (see above), selling furniture and antique collectibles on consignment. **Red Jacket Orchards,** 957 Routes 5 and 20 (© **315/781-2749**), has a nice array of fresh-picked apples and food items, including salsas, Amish cheeses, and cider from Mennonite farmers. There are several pick-your-own orchards along Routes 5 and 20.

WHERE TO STAY

Geneva has some of the grandest places to stay in the Finger Lakes, making it a good place to splurge. Although I'm not a fan of its bulky, suburban yellow-and-blue presence right on the north end of Seneca Lake, marring the beauty of the lakefront, the **Ramada Geneva Lakefront,** 41 Lakeshore Blvd., Geneva, NY 14456 (© **800/990-0907;** www.ramada.com; 148 units; $99–$149 double), does have good views, an indoor pool, and more affordable prices than some of the chic, historic inns in town.

Belhurst Castle ★★ *Value*   A late-19th-century castle facing Seneca Lake, this is one of the most extraordinary places to stay in the Finger Lakes Region. It truly is a castle, with incredible old-world style and massive proportions. Some of the rooms—especially the Tower and Dwyer suites—are among the largest hotel accommodations I've ever seen. With carved cherry and mahogany, cathedral ceilings, antique furnishings, Oriental carpets, and huge fireplaces, the inn is fit for kings and queens. All of the rooms are very different, so it's worthwhile taking a look at the website before deciding. The Study Room is cozy and cool, with a landing above the bed; the Butler's Suite has a separate sitting room but is the price of a regular room. More private, but more modern and not nearly as nice, rooms are available in the Ice, Carriage, and Dwyer houses apart from the main building. Apart from the massive suites, many of the rooms are surprisingly affordable for such a vintage property. A sumptuous restaurant—the site of many a wedding—is on-site, and complimentary wine is always available from a second-floor spigot.

Rte. 14 S., Geneva, NY 14456. (℃) 315/781-0201. www.belhurstcastle.com. 16 units. $65–$175 double; $150–$290 suite. Rates include continental breakfast. AE, DISC, MC, V. Free parking. **Amenities:** Restaurant; bar; private beach. *In room:* A/C, TV.

Geneva On The Lake ★   This exclusive, elegant lakeside hotel, a longtime AAA four-diamond property, is one of the most distinguished in the Finger Lakes. In my opinion, though, it's way overpriced, especially in high season (when some suites close in on 1,000 bucks). However, plenty of well-heeled folks don't seem to mind shelling out what it takes to stay at a phenomenal mansion with beautiful manicured gardens and views of Seneca Lake. Accommodations are handsomely appointed with Stickley or Chippendale furnishings, if a tad fussy, and all have kitchenettes. Oddly, some of the rooms have Murphy beds. The 70-foot pool perched at the end of the gardens and with lake views is positively Gatsby-like. The restaurant dining room is particularly romantic, with wall tapestries and candlelight. Check the website for package deals.

1001 Lochland Rd., Rte. 14, Geneva, NY 14456. (℃) 800/3-GENEVA or 315/789-7190. Fax 315/789-0322. www.genevaonthelake.com. 30 units. $212–$890 double (as part of package with dinner). Rates include full breakfast. AE, DISC, MC, V. Free parking. **Amenities:** Restaurant; bar; large outdoor pool; formal gardens; fishing dock; sailboats; paddleboats; canoes; Windsurfer. *In room:* A/C, TV.

White Springs Manor ★★ *Value*   Owned by the same people behind Belhurst Castle, this grand Greek Revival Farm Mansion, a mile or so up the road away from the lake, has incredibly large rooms, like its sister inn. It may not have the lake, but it has splendid distant views of the Geneva area. Rooms are equipped with antiques and many have Jacuzzis. The Lewis Suite is almost ridiculously spacious, and the Dining Room, also giant, has gorgeous views. For privacy, rent the Playhouse, a freestanding little house with a stone fireplace and Jacuzzi in the front sitting room for those romantic evenings (you might want to close the curtains on the front door); it's a very good value. Breakfast is served down at Belhurst Castle (where you'll also check in).

White Springs Lane, Geneva 14456. (℃) 315/781-0201. www.belhurstcastle.com. 16 units. $65–$225 double; $145–$295 suite. Rates include continental breakfast. AE, DISC, MC, V. Free parking. *In room:* A/C, TV, minibar.

Yale Manor Bed & Breakfast ★ *Value*   A peaceful B&B on the east side of Seneca Lake (7 miles south of Geneva), this early 1900s manor house on 10 acres with lake views is a very nice place to stay. Visitors can trek down to the lakefront, where there's a little A-frame house with a deck, a nice spot to relax or swim. Rooms are elegant and understated; particularly nice is the Monticello Room. The two simplest rooms share a bathroom (good for families).

563 Yale Farm Rd., Romulus, NY 14541. (℃) 315/585-2208. www.yalemanor.com. 6 units (4 with private bathrooms). $80–$120 double. Rates include full breakfast. AE, MC, V. Free parking. **Amenities:** Lakefront swimming area. *In room:* A/C.

WHERE TO DINE

In addition to the restaurants below, **Belhurst Castle** (see "Where to Stay," above), has a sumptuous dining room overlooking the lake. For romantic dining ambience, it can't be beat.

Cobblestone Restaurant ✦ NORTHERN ITALIAN/CONTINENTAL
An elegant restaurant in an attractive house (inhabiting the original tavern of a
1790 gentleman's farm), this is one of the best dining spots in town. There's an
atmospheric small dining room downstairs and several others upstairs, where
there's a deck with nice long views over Geneva. The menu focuses on classic
dishes, such as wood-grilled steaks and chops, chicken parmigiana, fresh lobster,
and veal scaloppine. The small and affordably priced wine list includes a number of the Finger Lakes' best. Note that locals may still refer to the restaurant by
its former moniker, "Pasta Only's."

Hamilton St. at Pre-Emption Rd. (Rtes. 5 and 20). € **315/789-8498.** Reservations recommended. Main
courses $11–$21. AE, DISC, MC, V. Lunch Tues–Fri 11:30am–3pm; dinner daily 5–10pm.

Kyo Asian Bistro ASIAN FUSION   A funky little spot with a sushi bar and
interesting Eurasian menu, this is the place to go in Geneva if you're in the mood
for something different. Choose from a large selection of "small plates and hand
bowls"—such as chicken satay, calamari salad, or shrimp salad—perfect for cob-
bling together a meal or share. The few "big plates" include curried linguine
with shiitake mushrooms and miso sea bass. And of course, it does the expected,
offering good sushi and sashimi.

486 Exchange St. € **315/719-0333.** Reservations recommended. Main courses $11–$18. AE, MC, V. Tues–Fri
11:30am–2pm and Tues–Sat 5–9pm.

Parker's Grille & Tap House GRILL/PUB FARE   Down the street from the
Smith Opera House, this is a good, casual place for a meal before or after the
show, and it's also a fine spot for a drink. The pub fare of burgers, finger foods,
hot sandwiches, and Tex-Mex isn't surprising, but it's inexpensive and solidly
prepared. A nice selection of beers and a number of local wines are good accompaniment for anything on the menu.

100 Seneca St. € **315/789-4656.** Reservations recommended. Main courses $11–$21. AE, DISC, MC, V.
Tues–Sun 11:30am–11pm.

GENEVA AFTER DARK

The Smith Opera House, 82 Seneca St. (€ **315/781-5483;** www.thesmith.
org), is the coolest after-dark spot in town. Whether you catch a concert, such as
Blues Traveler or the Dave Matthews Band, or see a movie on its huge screen, this
1930s gem is just a fantastic place to be. There's a neat little bar downstairs, but
it doesn't serve alcohol during film sessions. The **Geneva Summer Arts Festival**
(July–Aug) features dance, theater, music, and art exhibits. Among the performances, held at several venues including the Smith Opera House, are Lakefront
Gazebo concerts, featuring jazz to choral music. For a schedule of events, ask at
the Visitor Information Center or contact € 866/355-LIVE or www.genevarts.
com. The restaurant **Hamilton 258,** 258 Hamilton St. (€ **315/781-5323**), has
a cool martini bar.

9 Seneca Falls ✦✦ & Northern Cayuga Lake

10 miles east of Geneva; 48 miles east of Syracuse; 42 miles north of Ithaca

Perched on the falls of the Seneca River and a section of the Erie Canal, and cra-
dled between the two largest of the Finger Lakes, Seneca Falls was such a quintessential American small town that Frank Capra apparently used it as the model
for Bedford Falls in his classic movie *It's a Wonderful Life.* Yet the town is more
significantly known for its rabble-rousing past. In the mid–19th century, Seneca

Falls was home to political activists who fought for women's suffrage and civil rights for African Americans.

Cayuga Lake is the longest of the Finger Lakes, 42 miles from end to end.

ESSENTIALS
GETTING THERE
BY CAR   Seneca Falls is south of I-90 along Route 414 and equidistant on Routes 5 and 20 between Geneva and Auburn.

VISITOR INFORMATION   Seneca Falls Heritage Area Visitor Center, 115 Fall St. (© **315/568-2703**), is open Monday to Saturday from 10am to 4pm and Sunday from noon to 4pm. **Cayuga County Office of Tourism,** 131 Genesee St., Auburn (© **800/499-9615** or 315/255-1658; www.tourcayuga.com), is open Monday to Friday from 9am to 5pm, Saturday 9am to 2pm.

EXPLORING SENECA FALLS
The first Women's Rights Convention, the foundation for the modern struggle for civil rights, was held at the Wesleyan Methodist Chapel in Seneca Falls in 1848. The **Women's Rights National Historical Park** ★★, 136 Fall St. (© **315/ 568-2991;** wwwnps.gov/wori), which is run by the National Park Service, commemorates the struggle initiated by Elizabeth Cady Stanton, Lucretia Mott, Susan B. Anthony, Frederick Douglass, and others (the abolitionist and women's rights movements were linked from early on); such happenings at Seneca Falls expanded the definition of liberty in the United States. The extant remains of the original chapel, where 300 people gathered on July 19, 1848, and the landmark "Declaration of Sentiments" was drafted, is next to a museum that's jam-packed with information about women's and civil rights history. The museum does an excellent job raising issues to think about for visitors of both sexes and all ages, which is why it's also a great place for kids, who can also be made "Junior Rangers." The museum is open daily from 9am to 5pm; admission is $3 adults, free for students and children under 17.

Seneca Falls has, understandably, become a place of pilgrimage for people with a specific interest in women's and civil rights. A host of related sights, including the **Elizabeth Cady Stanton House,** 32 Washington St. (© **315/568-2991;** guided tours $1; sign-up at Park Visitor Center), are located in and around Seneca Falls; pick up a booklet, "Women's Rights Trail," at the museum gift shop. Down the street from the Historical Park is the **National Women's Hall of Fame,** 76 Fall St. (© **315/568-8060;** www.greatwomen.org), which is a good place to see, in name and achievement, how far women have come since the days of that legendary convention. It honors the achievements of American women in diverse fields. Worth a brief look, across the street, is the **Seneca Museum of Waterways and Industry,** 89 Fall St. (© **315/568-1510**), which tells the story of transportation and industrialization in the region.

Today Seneca Falls is relatively quiet and unassuming compared to its momentous past. **Van Cleef Lake,** forged as an expansion of the New York State Barge Canal, is one of the prettiest (and most photographed) spots in the Finger Lakes. The banks of the Cayuga-Seneca Canal are being prettified with benches and paths. The downtown area, essentially a main street with two bridges over the canal (one of which distinctly recalls that pivotal scene in *It's a Wonderful Life*), is charming, and Fall Street is lined with nice shops, including the very appropriate **WomanMade Products** (91 Fall St.; © **315/568-9364**) a very enjoyable place to while away an afternoon.

At the north end of Cayuga Lake and 5 miles east of Seneca Falls, **Montezuma National Wildlife Refuge** 🐦🐦, 395 Routes 5 and 20 East, Seneca Falls (© **315/ 568-5987;** www.fws.gov/r5mnwr; daily 8am–5pm; Visitor's Center Mon–Fri 10am–3pm, Sat–Sun 10am–4pm), established in 1938, is a magnificent spot for birding and a fantastic spot for families to get up close and personal with wildlife. The marshes in this part of the Finger Lakes is a preferred rest stop along the Atlantic Migratory Flyway, and the 7,000 acres of wetlands attract thousands of waterfowl and other water birds—including Canada geese, blue herons, egrets, and wood ducks—on their long journeys from nesting areas in Canada (at the height of migration, as many as two million birds occupy the area). During the fall migration, the peak for geese and ducks is mid- to late November; for shore-birds and wading birds, mid-August to mid-September. During the spring migra-tion, less flashy than fall, waterfowl peak in late February through April, while the peak of warbler migration is mid-May. In addition to walking trails, there's a self-guided Wildlife Drive (in winter, there's cross-country skiing and snowshoeing). Ask in the Visitor's Center for the location of the bald eagle's nest.

For more information on visiting the area's wineries, particularly those around Cayuga Lake, see the sidebar on the **Cayuga Wine Trail,** on p. 308.

SPORTS & OUTDOOR ACTIVITIES

The Cayuga branch of the Erie Canal system leads directly to Cayuga Lake and flows directly through Seneca Falls. Outdoors enthusiasts could hardly have a bet-ter or more historic place to hike or bike than the **Erie Canal Trail,** which runs along the historic canal towpath from the village of Jordan to Montezuma and the Seneca River. For more information, call © **315/252-2791. Liberty Boat Tours** (© **877/472-6688**) in Seneca Falls does canal and lake tours, and the **River Otter Boat Tour,** Riverforest Park, 9439 Riverforest Rd., off Route 34 in Weedsport, operates 2-hour tours (Mon and Sat at 10am and 2pm) of the Seneca River and Erie Canal (for reservations, call © **315/252-4171**). **Cayuga Lake State Park** (© **315/568-5163**), 2678 Lower Lake Rd., on the west side of the lake, has campgrounds (© **315/568-0919**), nature trails, playgrounds, a launch site, and docking. Cayuga Lake is known for its bass fishing, while Seneca Lake has superb trout fishing. On the shores of the two lakes are four state parks and numerous sites for swimming, boating, and picnicking. For fishing charters on Cayuga Lake, try **Eagle Rock Charters** (© **315/889-5925;** www.ctbw.com/ eaglerock). *Note:* If you want to sail your own boat along the Erie Canal, get a brochure with more information about docking and attractions from Rochester to Syracuse by calling © **800/499-9615.**

For bird-watching, don't miss the Montezuma National Wildlife Refuge (see above). And if you want to fly like a bird, check out **Sunset Adventures Bal-loon Rides,** Beach Tree Road, Auburn (© **315/252-9474;** www.fingerlakes ballooning.com).

WHERE TO STAY

There are a couple of good B&Bs in Seneca Falls, as well as a large and clean, inexpensive chain motel (the Microtel) on the outskirts of town.

Barrister's B&B 🐦   This attractive small inn on one of Seneca Falls's loveliest streets (within walking distance of downtown and the canal), is an 1888 Colo-nial Revival that has been very nicely restored and converted into a B&B. The house, run by a local couple, retains handsome details like carved fireplaces and original stained-glass windows, and the comfortable rooms, many of which get great light, have been attractively decorated. Grandmother's Room has a very large bathroom, the Grace Yawger room is nice and quiet, and Erin's Retreat is a large suite with an adjoining sitting room.

56 Cayuga St., Seneca Falls, NY 13148. © **800/914-0145** or 315/568-0145. www.sleepbarristers.com. 5 units. $95–$155 double; $235 suite (2-bedroom). Rates include full breakfast. AE, MC, V. Free parking. *In room:* A/C.

Hubbell House ⭐ A charming 1855 Gothic Revival meticulously decorated and chock full of Victorian goodies, including dolls, pictures, and books, this professionally run inn is a very nice place to stay, not least of which is due to its location on Van Cleef Lake. The house has a walkway down to gardens and a sweet little pier on the lake; some rooms, as well as the dining room and screen porch, have picturesque lake views. Breakfast is excellent, served on china with fresh-squeezed orange juice and items like "Victorian French toast." The Laura Hoskins Hubbell room is over-the-top Victoriana, while other rooms are more sedate and very cozy.

42 Cayuga St., Seneca Falls, NY 13148. © **315/568-9690**. www.hubbellhousebb.com. 4 units. $105–$125 double. Rates include full breakfast. No credit cards. Free parking. *In room:* A/C.

Microtel Inn *(Value)* Not chic, certainly not quaint, nor well located, either (it's in a strip mall on a main drag), the Microtel is new, clean, efficiently run, and a real bargain. Rooms are comfortable, standard hotel rooms.

1966 Rtes. 5 and 20, Seneca Falls, NY 13148. © **888/771-7171** or 315/539-8438. Fax 315/539-4780. www.microtelinn.com. 4 units. $55–$76 double; $79 suite. Rates include breakfast. AE, DISC, MC, V. Free parking. *In room:* A/C, TV w/pay movies (suites), fridge (suites), coffeemaker (suites), microwave (suites).

WHERE TO DINE

Downtown Deli, 53 Fall St. (© **315/568-9943**), sporting a deck facing the canal, is a good stop for New York–style sandwiches, salads, and soups. **Bailey's,** 95 Fall St. (© **315/568-0929**), is an ice-cream parlor and sandwich shop named, of course, for the character of the same name in *It's a Wonderful Life.*

Henry B's ITALIAN Henry B's is a clubby, upscale restaurant with exposed brick walls and subdued lighting; it looks something like a New York supper club. It features a good wine list and tempting desserts. Food is family-style, meaning huge portions meant to be shared (a typical main course feeds two). Salads and antipasti are great; for entrees, choose from "Pasta Unica" (one-dish meals of fettucine rustica or pappardelle with hot Italian sausage, for example), or traditional Florentine T-bone steak or grilled prime veal chops. Henry B's may not be the cheapest spot in town, but it's easily the best.

84 Falls St. © **315/568-1600**. Reservations recommended. Main courses $22–$29. AE, DISC, MC, V. Tues–Sat 4:30–10pm.

SENECA FALLS AFTER DARK

Seneca Falls has a surprisingly bustling little cluster of bars on Fall Street. The liveliest is usually **Tavern on the Flats,** 6-8 Bulls Run (© **315/568-6755**), with its canal-side entrance it can get very crowded with college students and folks who've pulled up in their boats along the canal. Part of a dying breed, the **Finger Lakes Drive-In,** Routes 5 and 20, Auburn (© **315/252-3969**), shows first-run movies from April to October, and is a popular spot in summer months.

AUBURN

East of Montezuma and midway to Skaneateles, the town of **Auburn,** though larger than Seneca Falls, doesn't have quite the charms of its neighbor, though it does possess a handful of historic sights. Chief among them is the **Willard Memorial Chapel,** 17 Nelson St. (© **315/252-0339**), the surviving piece of the once-grand Auburn Theological Seminary, built in 1818. But this Romanesque chapel holds a treasure: an interior designed by Louis Comfort Tiffany, apparently the only existing example of a complete and unaltered Tiffany interior. The series of stained-glass windows, including a nine-paneled Rose Window, and leaded-glass chandeliers are stunning. The chapel is open Tuesday to Friday from 10am to 4pm; admission is $2.

The **Seward House** ⚓, 33 South St. (© **315/252-1283;** www.sewardhouse. org), is a National Historic Landmark, and former home of the 19th-century statesman who served as U.S. secretary of state, U.S. senator, and New York governor. The handsome 19th-century home is very nearly a national library, so extensive is its collection of family artifacts, historical documents, and items collected from the life and travels of William H. Seward. Seward was known principally for negotiating the purchase of Alaska, derided in the press at the time as "Seward's Folly," and as Abraham Lincoln's secretary of state, attacked and seriously stabbed by a would-be murderer as part of the conspiracy that felled Lincoln. The museum is open mid-October to December and February through June Tuesday to Saturday from 1 to 4pm; from July to mid-October, it's open Tuesday to Saturday from 10am to 4pm and Sunday from 1 to 4pm. Admission is $4 adults, $3.50 seniors, $2 students (12–17).

Harriet Tubman, a pivotal figure in the abolitionist struggle—a former slave, she helped 300 people reach freedom via the Underground Railroad and was called the "Moses of her People"—lived and died in Auburn. The **Harriet Tubman Home,** 180 South St. (© **315/252-2081**), one of three houses owned by Tubman, is open for visitors, but truth be told, there's not a lot to see. It's furnished with period, not original, furniture, and doesn't do much to illuminate her important life. Perhaps if assumed by the National Park Service, it will become more of an educational touchstone in an area so indelibly linked with the struggle for freedom and civil rights. The Tubman Home is open February through October, Tuesday to Friday, from 10am to 4pm and Saturday from 10am to 3pm; admission is $5 adults, $3 seniors and students, $2 children.

The Underground Railroad

After passages of the Fugitive Slave Law in 1850, even the free states of the North were considered unsafe for runaway slaves. The Underground Railroad, the secretive lines of communication and safe houses that carried many slaves along a very dangerous path from the South to freedom in Canada, was active throughout the central New York State. Many stops were in the Finger Lakes Region. Auburn was home of Harriet Tubman, a former slave who conducted more than 300 people to freedom. The Seward House in Auburn was also an important stop on the Underground Railroad. Frederick Douglass, abolitionist and publisher of the newspaper *The North Star,* lived in Rochester and is buried in Mt. Hope Cemetery there. For more information on the Underground Railroad in New York and principal abolitionist activists, see **www.nyhistory.com/ugrr/links.htm**.

Aurora's Amazing Makeover

Until recently, the diminutive village of **Aurora** ✿ was just a little-known town speck in the Finger Lakes, albeit one with million-dollar views from the east shore of Cayuga Lake. It basically consisted of a main street, a tiny women's college, and an idiosyncratic ceramics factory. Lately, though, it has been awash in rumor and controversy—as well as construction. Whispers could be heard all over the Finger Lakes: "Did you hear about the town that rich woman bought?" As it turns out, Pleasant Rowland, who attended Wells College in Aurora and made a fortune with her American Girl dolls, decided to endow the college and town with a series of gifts, many of which are multimillion-dollar restorations of historic buildings owned by the college. She also purchased and is on the road to resurrecting MacKenzie-Childs, a whimsical but previously bankrupt ceramics maker. Rowland's Aurora Foundation has gutted and redone the 1833 **Aurora Inn** ✿✿✿, 391 Main St., Aurora, NY 13026 (✆ **315/364-8888;** fax 315/364-8887; www.aurora-inn.com), owned by the college and overlooking the lake, completely transforming it in grand style; it is now one of the most exquisite country inns in the Finger Lakes Region, though preservationists are alarmed at the remaking of historic buildings. Also new to the previously under-endowed town, which didn't even have a gas station, are a grocery store, pizza restaurant, and ice cream parlor. Aurora is still tiny, but it's sudden transformation has some historians and residents, unsurprisingly, worried.

   MacKenzie-Childs, 3260 Rte. 90 (✆ **800/640-0546** or 315/364-7123; www.mackenzie-childs.com), makes fanciful and brightly colored, handmade ceramics, glassware, and furniture that might be called modern baroque. You either love it or you hate it—it's almost too unique to be indifferent (I happen to love most of the stuff). Factory tours are given October to May, Monday to Friday at 1:15pm and May through September Monday to Friday at 9:30am and 1:15pm; tour costs $10 adults, $6 seniors and children under 12. New on the campus is an utterly incredible, dreamlike **Farmhouse Inn** ✿✿✿, done up in high MacKenzie-Childs Victorian camp, with four rooms. (The inn is rented in its entirety, $1,500 per night.) Equally spectacular, but more mind-bendingly so, **The Restaurant MacKenzie-Childs** ✿✿✿ (✆ **315/364-9688;** Tues–Sat 11:30am–2pm, Fri–Sat, 5:30–8:30pm, Sun brunch 11am–2pm) looks as though it were decorated by someone dreaming of Alice in Wonderland while on acid.

   For lunch in town, check out **Dorie's,** 283 Main St. (✆ **315/364-8818**), the ice cream and soda fountain of your dreams, or **Pizza Aurora** across the street.

10 Skaneateles Lake ✿✿✿

23 miles west of Syracuse; 32 miles east of Geneva

Hard to pronounce and harder to spell, Skaneateles is one of the most beautiful and photogenic towns in the Finger Lakes region, the only one whose main street backs right up to the curved shore of a sinewy Finger Lake. A small village surprisingly well endowed with creature comforts for visitors, it is one of the most popular stops in the region. Long favored by those in the know, in recent years it gained a considerable amount of attention when President and Mrs. Clinton vacationed here at the home of a wealthy friend. At Christmastime, when costumed carolers parade around the streets with good cheer and good harmony, the village becomes a Dickensian postcard.

ESSENTIALS
GETTING THERE
BY CAR   Skaneateles is on Route 20 west of Syracuse; from the south, take Route 41 North, which traces the east side of Skaneateles Lake, off I-81.

VISITOR INFORMATION   The **Skaneateles Chamber of Commerce** is located at 22 Jordan St. (✆ **315/685-0552;** www.skaneateles.com).

EXPLORING SKANEATELES

Skaneateles's **historic downtown,** which lovingly cradles the northern shore of Skaneateles Lake, is the prettiest in the Finger Lakes Region. A graceful collection of 19th-century Greek Revival and Victorian homes and charming shops, it looks and feels more like a classic New England village than one in upstate New York. But Skaneateles is endowed with incredible natural gifts as well: transparent Skaneateles Lake—one of the cleanest lakes in North America—cuts a gorgeous, 16-mile-long, gently curved swath through low hills and dense green forest. New York State Governor and former Secretary of State William Seward called it "the most beautiful body of water in the world." On the lakefront are a picturesque gazebo and a long pier that juts out over the water. The best way to enjoy the lake is to plunge into it. Lake activities abound, from swimming and boating to fishing.

East Genesee Street, the main drag in town, is lined with quaint boutiques and antiques shops as well as restaurants and inns. Inside the impressive gray stone town library, at 49 East Genesee St., is the **John D. Barrow Art Gallery** (✆ **315/ 685-5135;** open mid-June to mid-Sept daily 1–4pm; May–Dec Sat 2–4pm; free admission), where you'll find a nice collection of paintings by the Skaneateles-born artist and painter of Hudson Valley landscapes. **The Creamery,** 28 Hannum St., off West Genesee Street (✆ **315/685-1360;** June–Sept Thurs–Sat 1–4pm; Oct– May Fri 10am–4pm; free admission), is a restored creamery dating from 1899 and home to the Skaneateles Historical Society and Museum and its small collection of town historical artifacts. **Walking tours** of Skaneateles are conducted by Historical Society members during summer months; call ✆ **315/685-1360** or 315/ 485-6841 for information.

Skaneateles's emphasis on culture and the arts is disproportionate to its small size. The town hosts festivals throughout the summer, including free band concerts at the gazebo in Clift Park on Skaneateles Lake on Friday and Saturday evenings in summer; the Finger Lakes **Antique and Classic Boat Show** the last week of July; and the **Skaneateles Festival,** 97 Genesee St. (✆ **315/685-7418;** www.skanfest.org), which features chamber music as many as 5 nights a week throughout August. However, the biggest event in Skaneateles doesn't take place in summer. The **Dickens Christmas** celebration revels in old-world Victoriana, with costumed Dickens characters parading about the streets, interacting with visitors and singing Christmas carols. There are free carriage rides around Skaneateles and free roasted chestnuts and hot chocolate. The celebration, a great family event, begins the day after Thanksgiving and is held every Saturday and Sunday, from noon to 4pm, through December 22.

SPORTS & OUTDOORS ACTIVITIES

Clift Park on Skaneateles Lake has open public swimming. **Thayer Park,** east of the shops is a quiet, beautiful park for relaxing and enjoying the view. **Austin Park,** 1 Austin St. (between Jordan and State sts.), has a playground, basketball, and tennis courts, and a track for walking, biking, or skating. The **Charlie Major Nature Trail,** along the Old Short line, between Old Seneca Turnpike and Crow Hill Road, is good for hiking. **Biking** the 32-mile perimeter around the Skaneateles Lake is big with cycling clubs (and, of course, with motorcyclists).

But the best outdoors activity in Skaneateles is getting out on the lake, and a great way to do so is by cruise boat. **Mid-Lakes Navigation Co.** ★★ (© 315/685-8500; www.midlakesnav.com), a longtime local, family-run business, organizes cruises on Skaneateles Lake, including 1-hour sightseeing, Sunday brunch, champagne dinner, and luncheon cruises; if that's too typical, try boarding a U.S. mail boat as it delivers mail to old-fashioned camps on the lake. Call for more information. They also do cruises along the Erie Canal. Most cruises are July and August. For kayaking instruction and rentals, try **Northwind Expedition Kayaks,** 2825 W. Lake Rd. (© 315/685-4808; www.northwindkayaks.com); for pontoon, sailboat, canoe, and kayak rentals, see **The Sailboat Shop,** 1322 E. Genesee St. (© 315/685-7558).

The Sherwood Inn owns an antique Chris Craft, the *Stephanie,* on which it offers sunset cruises and sightseeing tours; call © 800/3-SHERWOOD for more information. For fishing charters on the lake, contact **Lakeview Charters,** 2478 E. Lake Rd. (© 315/685-8176; www.lakeviewcharters.com). If you'd rather see the lake from a distance, **Fingerlakes Aeroplane Tours,** Skaneateles Aerodome (© 315/685-6382), takes people up over the lakes in a vintage 1942 open cockpit biplane, from mid-May to October.

SHOPPING

The compact downtown area of Skaneateles, with just a couple of streets intersecting Genesee Street, is full of unique shops. **Skaneateles Antique Center,** 12 E. Genesee St. (© 315/685-0752), has several dealers and lots of china, mission furniture, and pottery. **Pomodoro,** 61 E. Genesee St. (© 315/685-8658), is a very feminine, sweet little shop in an adorable house that's packed to the rafters with home furnishings, candles, and all manner of gift items. **Rhubarb Kitchen & Garden,** 59 E. Genesee St. (© 315/685-5803), carries a nice selection of cookbooks, kitchen and garden items, and even gourmet foods.

WHERE TO STAY

Skaneateles has an excellent supply of B&Bs, inns, and small hotels around the lake and downtown, including a couple of the best inns in the entire region. More inexpensive lodging is available in motels on the outskirts of town on the way to either Syracuse or Auburn, such as **Whispering Winds Motel,** Route 20 (© 315/685-6056; www.skaneateles.com/whisperingwinds; $49–$99 double), and the **Colonial Motel,** Route 20 (© 315/685-5751; $49–$85 double), both of which have pools.

VERY EXPENSIVE

Hobbit Hollow Farm B&B ★★★   One of the most exquisite small inns in the Finger Lakes, this serene and princely estate with luxuriously appointed rooms is a place to pamper yourself. The house, a 100-year-old Colonial Revival, sits on 400 acres about 3 miles from town, next to a large horse barn, with panoramic lake views. The house is first class in every detail, from the antique furnishings to the crisp linens and beautiful bathrooms. Breakfast is served with silver and Waterford crystal. All the accommodations are different in decor and size; my favorite is the Lake View room, with a four-poster bed and a massive bathroom and Jacuzzi. The Master Suite has a private veranda and fireplace, while the Chanticleer room is sunny and charming, with a funky "pencil" bed. Less expensive rooms are smaller, but cozy and also quite charming.

3061 W. Lake Rd., Skaneateles NY 13152. (© 315/685-2791. Fax 315/685-3426. www.hobbithollow.com. 5 units. $100–$230 double; $250–$270 suite. Rates include full breakfast. AE, DISC, MC, V. Free parking. *In room:* A/C, TV.

Mirbeau Inn & Spa ★★★   This new addition to Skaneateles, about 2 blocks west of downtown, strikes out on a bold direction all its own. Designed to echo a French country château retreat, it is a stylish full-service spa and small hotel. Accommodations, decorated in a modern French country style with relaxing, rich fabrics, fireplaces and huge bathrooms, are set around a Monet-like garden and pond and 12 acres of woodlands. The spa facilities, which feature a sumptuous palazzo of a relaxation room, are extraordinary; the massage rooms are some of the most inviting I've seen. The inn's restaurant stands very much on its own merits; though not inexpensive, it offers one of the finest dining experiences in the region. For a splurge for both body and soul, Mirbeau is among the best. A number of packages, with spa treatments and dinner included, are available; check the Web site for current offers. The spa is also open to the public as a day spa, though advance booking is essential, as most times are reserved for hotel guests.

851 W. Genesee St., Skaneateles, NY 13152. (© **877/MIRBEAU** or 315/685-5006. Fax 315/685-3426. www.mirbeau.com. 34 units. $199–$325 double. AE, DISC, MC, V. Free parking. **Amenities:** Restaurant; bar; spa with exercise room; steam room and sauna. *In room:* A/C, TV/VCR, high-speed Internet access.

EXPENSIVE

Village Inn of Skaneateles ★   Just a block off Genesee Street, this tiny inn, like a cross between a European boutique hotel and a B&B, is a smart place to stay. Wholly renovated, it is very well equipped and has a modern feel, though the building dates from 1830. All rooms have gas fireplaces, whirlpool baths, and Stickley furniture. The Cottage Room has exposed brick walls, while the Terrace Room has a private balcony overlooking Skaneateles Lake. If you choose, you can take breakfast on the porch at the Sherwood Inn.

25 Jordan St., Skaneateles, NY 13152. (© **800/374-3796** or 315/685-3405. www.villageinn-ny.com. 4 units. $80–$190 double. Rates include continental breakfast. AE, DISC, MC, V. Free parking. *In room:* A/C, TV, high-speed Internet access.

MODERATE

Sherwood Inn ★★ (Value)   Once a stagecoach stop in the early 1800s, this cozy inn on the main drag, with wide-open lake views from its porch, is the top place to stay if you want to be right in the heart of Skaneateles. Recently renovated, this elegant but relaxed inn has loads of character, with hardwood floors in the hallways, four-poster and canopy beds in rooms, and a genteel, lived-in, old-money feel. Accommodations are all uniquely decorated; some are very feminine in toile, some English country, while others are library-like and masculine. My favorite is the swank and romantic Red Room, with a fireplace, Jacuzzi, and a funky light fixture. The elegant restaurant has a beautiful porch, with unequaled lake views, and a cozy tavern, a Euro-style pub with wooden booths and green leather chairs. The prices, for such a centrally located, eminently comfortable small hotel, are more than reasonable.

26 W. Genesee St., Skaneateles, NY 13152. ✆ 800/3-SHERWOOD or 315/685-3405. Fax 315/685-8983. 24 units. www.thesherwoodinn.com. $90–$175 double. AE, DISC, MC, V. Free parking. **Amenities:** Restaurant; bar. *In room:* A/C, TV.

WHERE TO DINE

In addition to those below, the **Sherwood Inn,** which has a large formal dining room and inexpensive tavern, offers a large and varied menu and is a popular dining spot—so popular, in fact, that in high season you'll definitely have to wait.

EXPENSIVE

The Dining Room at Mirbeau Inn & Spa ★★★ HAUTE COUNTRY The young chef at this innovative small spa hotel has created an equally inventive and inviting menu. The Mirbeau restaurant has quickly garnered quite a bit of attention, with a number of national magazines calling it one of the top new places in the country. The dining room is elegant French provincial, with a serene terrace for outdoor dining. Though refined and sophisticated, patrons are as likely to wear jeans as jackets. Among the excellent entrees are Dijon-braised suckling pig with potato purée and sauerkraut, Hudson Valley duck breast with sweet potato purée and sun-dried cherry sauce, and Szechuan peppercorn-crusted venison with wild mushroom ragout and a Burgundy poached pear salad. You can order a la carte, but choosing one of the tasting menus is, for my money, the best way to experience the interesting array of flavors concocted by the chef, who claims an impressionistic approach to cooking. The wine list is extensive and superbly chosen, with some nice Finger Lakes selections, and the desserts—particularly the cheese courses—are worth blowing your diet for (you can always go to the spa the next day).

851 W. Genesee St. ✆ 877/MIRBEAU or 315/685-5006. Reservations required. Main courses $27. Tasting menus $42–$58. AE, DISC, MC, V. Daily 7:30–10:30am, 11:30am–2pm, and 5–10pm.

The Kreb's 1899 ★★ *Value* TRADITIONAL AMERICAN At this seasonal restaurant, open May to Halloween, every dinner is like Thanksgiving. The Kreb's has been serving "traditional meals," or seven-course "soup-to-nuts" dinners, for more than 100 years. In an old house a long block from the waterfront, the restaurant defines classic fine dining in Skaneateles. The downstairs dining room is formal, with crisp white linen tablecloths and fresh-cut flowers, but not stuffy. The seven-course dinner, for just under 40 bucks, is an excellent value for a meal with Lobster Newburgh and English prime rib, family-style vegetables and sides, dessert, and homemade breads. You can also order a seafood menu or beef or chicken dinner for $35. Sunday brunch is perhaps the best deal of all at $15. Upstairs in the tavern, there's an informal dining menu. A very nice wine list is available.

53 W. Genesee St. ✆ 315/685-5714. Reservations recommended. Fixed-price dinners $35–$40. MC, V. Mon–Sat 6–10pm; Sun brunch 10:30am–2pm.

MODERATE

Bluewater Grill *Kids* AMERICAN Backing right up to Skaneateles Lake, just steps from the pier, this fun and casual eatery, with the look and noise level of a well-worn bar, is a favorite of locals and a great spot for a beer or margarita and easy-eating specialties like barbecued pork, Black Angus burgers, fajitas, and jambalaya. You can also go upscale with Maryland lump crab cakes or filet mignon, and there's a good selection of soups and salads. There's an "under 12" menu that few children could turn their noses up at.

11 W. Genesee St. (✆ **315/685-6600**. Reservations recommended on weekends. Main courses $10–$17. AE, MC, V. Daily 11:30am–10pm.

KaBuki ⭐ SUSHI/ASIAN   The newest hot spot in town, this cute, hip, and colorful sushi and Asian restaurant isn't a typical restaurant in this traditional town, but locals have come around to embrace this casual little joint. Start with Thai lettuce wraps and move on to a Szechuan tangerine stir-fry or sake-steamed salmon. Or sit at the bar and down sushi and cut rolls to your heart's content.

12 W. Genesee St. (✆ **315/685-7234**. Reservations recommended. Main courses $10–$17. No credit cards. Daily 5:30–10pm.

SKANEATELES AFTER DARK

Morris's Grill, 6 W. Genesee St. ((✆ **315/685-7761**), a laid-back bar next to KaBuki, is the local hangout. The tavern at the **Sherwood Inn,** which has a cozy bar and a fireplace, as well as fantastic lake views, is also a popular spot for a drink. In summer, evening activities tend to center around the music festivals in town; on Friday and Saturday nights, there's live music at the gazebo in **Clift Park** on the north shore of Skaneateles Lake.

11 Syracuse

145 west of Albany; 245 miles northeast of New York City; 58 miles northeast of Ithaca

It may not have the romantic ring to it that many villages in the Finger Lakes do, and as a modern, rather industrial upstate city, Syracuse may not appear vitally connected to the natural beauty of the region, but the second-largest city in the area is the principal eastern gateway to the Finger Lakes. Syracuse may be best known as the home of the NCAA National Champion Orangemen, but this city grew up on the Erie Canal and was once known as "Salt City, " when its role was to supply the U.S. with salt. Today Syracuse is staking its future on the largest mall in the U.S., DestiNY USA, the current Carousel Center that developers are remaking into a resortlike shopping experience. Beyond those outsized shopping opportunities—I mean, experiences—Syracuse is a city that appeals mostly to passers-by and business travelers. However, it is also a good, brief gateway stop for families.

ESSENTIALS

BY AIR   Syracuse Hancock International Airport, 2001 Airport Blvd., Syracuse ((✆ **315/454-4330;** www.syrairport.org), 10 minutes from downtown, is serviced by American, Air Canada, Continental, Delta, JetBlue, Northwest, United, and US Airways. **Century Transportation** ((✆ **315/455-5151**) provides taxi and van service at Syracuse Hancock International Airport. There are five major car-rental agencies at the airport.

BY CAR   Syracuse is located at the intersection of two major highways: Interstate 81, running north-south, and the New York State Thruway, I-90, running east-west.

BY BUS   Greyhound and **Trailways** stop in Syracuse at the Regional Transportation Center, 130 P and C Pkwy., Syracuse ((✆ **315/472-4421** or 315/472-5338).

BY TRAIN   Amtrak ((✆ **800/USA-RAIL;** www.amtrak.com) travels to Syracuse from New York City, Buffalo, Boston, and other cities. The Regional Transportation Center is located at 130 P and C Pkwy.

VISITOR INFORMATION   The principal font of tourism information is the **Syracuse Convention and Visitors Bureau,** 572 S. Salina St. (✆ **800/234-4797** or 315/470-1910; www.visitsyracuse.org). The **Syracuse Urban Cultural Park Visitor Center,** 318 Erie Blvd. E (within Erie Canal Museum; ✆ **315/471-0593**), offers guided tours of downtown for $2.

GETTING AROUND

OnTrack City Express trains (✆ **315/424-1212**) run from Syracuse University to the main station at Armory Square, 269 W. Jefferson St., and Carousel Mall. Trains operate Wednesday to Sunday, 11:25am to 6:20pm (in summer Fri–Sun); tickets are $1.50 one-way (pay as you board).

   CENTRO buses (✆ **315/685-7075;** www.centro.org; $1) travel to Skaneateles and Auburn.

EXPLORING SYRACUSE

Principal among Syracuse's attractions is the **Museum of Science & Technology (MOST)** ⭐, 500 S. Franklin St. (✆ **315/425-0747;** www.most.org;), which is located in an old armory and filled on three levels with terrific interactive science exhibits, science demonstrations, simulator rides that will entertain both youngsters and their parents, a cool domed IMAX Theater, and a planetarium. It's open Tuesday to Sunday from 11am to 5pm. Museum-only admission is $5 adults, $4 seniors and children under 12; planetarium admission $1 extra; combination IMAX/museum ticket, $9.75 adults, $7.75 seniors and children under 12. For IMAX show times and tickets, call ✆ **315/473-IMAX.**

   The **Erie Canal Museum,** 318 Erie Blvd. East (Rte. 5) at Montgomery Street (✆ **315/471-0593;** www.eriecanalmuseum.org; Tues–Sat 10am–5pm and Sun 10am–3pm; free admission) is in the original 1850 weighlock building designed to determine tolls for boats on the canal. It may not be the most exciting museum you've ever visited, but it makes for an interesting historical stop, depicting as it does six vignettes of 19th-century life along the canal. The **Everson Museum of Art,** 401 Harrison St. (✆ **315/474-6064;** www.everson.org; Tues–Fri noon–5pm, Sat–Sun 10am–5pm), was the first building designed by noted architect I. M. Pei. It contains a superb collection of American ceramics. Architecture buffs may want to go from Everson to one of the finest Art Deco buildings in Syracuse, the **Niagara-Mohawk building** on N. Franklin Street, a miniature Chrysler building that's illuminated at night.

   Visiting a bakery might not like much of an attraction, but the **Columbus Baking Company,** 502 Pearl St. (✆ **315/422-2913**), is an old-style, family-owned and -operated Italian bakery that makes only four types of artisanal, traditional Italian bread (with no preservatives), as it has for over a century. The deep, old-school ovens are right out of *Moonstruck.*

SHOPPING

The most enjoyable part of downtown for shopping and strolling is **Armory Square,** a delightfully renovated district of old buildings now given over to dozens of shops, cafes, restaurants, and bars. Walton, W. Fayette, and Franklin streets, all just paces from MOST and the OnTrack Train station, are the main arteries. Northeast of downtown Syracuse (I-81 exit 23), the **Carousel Center,** 9090 Carousel Center Dr. (✆ **315/466-7000;** www.carouselscenter.com), is destined to become, in 2006, the nation's largest shopping mall—that is, if someone else doesn't get there first. Called DestiNY USA, it will boast a golf course, five-story rock-climbing wall, and more, approximating Disneyland more than your standard mall; for advance information, visit www.aboutdestiny usa.com.

Syracuse China Company, which has been producing china and ceramics for 125 years, has a factory outlet at 2900 Court St. (℗ **315/455-4581**), with as much as 70% off retail. **Stickley, Audi & Co.** (℗ **315/637-7770**), producers of quality Arts and Crafts Stickley furniture since 1900 (Gustav Stickley had a home in Syracuse, and the original factory was in Fayetteville, New York), have a shop in the strip mall across from the Craftsman Inn on East Genesee Street. Furniture's not the easiest thing to take back, but if you catch a big sale, you just may want to ship something.

WHERE TO STAY

Bed & Breakfast Wellington ✦   This large and very lovely house, a 1914 brick-and-stucco Tudor named for its architect, is a National Historic Landmark. It is embellished with fine Arts and Crafts details, such as rich woods and fireplaces with Mercer tiles. The guest rooms are spacious and pleasant if not overly fancy (that may be a good thing), though they are decorated with nice antique and Stickley furniture and carpets. For a small B&B, it's equipped with lots of amenities, such as high-speed Internet access and central air. Downstairs is a huge apartment with a dining room and efficiency kitchen. The sunny Stickley and Lakeview rooms are my favorites.

707 Danforth St., Syracuse, NY 13208. ℗ **800/724-5006** or 315/474-3641. Fax 315/472-4976. www. bbwellington.com. 5 units. $99–$150 double. Rates include continental breakfast on weekdays, full gourmet breakfast on weekends. AE, DC, DISC, MC, V. Free parking. *In room:* A/C, TV/VCR/DVD, dataport, high-speed Internet access.

The Craftsman Inn ✦ (Value)   This Arts and Crafts hotel, located just a few miles east of downtown Syracuse, has the amenities of a large hotel but some of the intimacy of a smaller inn. Rooms are spacious and nicely decorated, with understated color schemes and full sets of handsome Stickley furniture (in either mission, colonial, or Shaker style)—a pretty extraordinary look. The Frank Baum room, named for the author of the *Wizard of Oz* who was born nearby, has nice Oz artwork on the walls. About a quarter of the rooms are in the new, adjoining Craftsman Lodge. The Craftsman House restaurant, next door, is also decorated with the same wonderful Stickley furniture.

7300 E. Genesee St., Syracuse, NY 13266. ℗ **800/797-4464** or 315/474-3641. Fax 315/637-2440. www. craftsmaninn.com. 90 units. $93–$109 double; $135–$150 suite. Rates include continental breakfast. AE, DC, DISC, MC, V. Free parking. **Amenities:** Restaurant; bar; business center. *In room:* A/C, TV/VCR, kitchen, dataport, high-speed Internet access.

Hawthorn Suites ✦   Across from the MOST museum, in the historic center of Syracuse, this new hotel in a nicely renovated historic building has a great location and large, comfortable suites (some are one-bedrooms and others studios, all with fully equipped kitchen) that are perfect for business travelers and other visitors who want to be in the midst of the restaurant and bar action of Armory Square.

416 S. Clinton St., Syracuse, NY 13202. ℗ **800/527-1133** or 315/425-0500. Fax 315/472-4976. www.hawthorn syracuse.com. 60 units. $139–$149 studio; $169–$189 1-bedroom suite. AE, DISC, MC, V. Free parking. **Amenities:** Bar; 24-hr. fitness center. *In room:* A/C, TV/DVD, kitchen, dataport, high-speed Internet access.

WHERE TO DINE

The Craftsman Inn (above), operates a nice restaurant, **The Craftsman House** (℗ **315/637-9999**), which serves items like New York strip steak, prime rib, and brook trout; like the hotel it is decorated with Stickley furniture.

Coleman's IRISH/PUB FARE A sprawling, handsome Irish pub and restaurant in the heart of the very Irish neighborhood Tipperary, Coleman's has been around since 1933. The menu is a comfortable mix of simple bar food and Irish specialties, such as, Guinness beef stew, Irish roast chicken, and homemade chili as well as pastas and fresh seafood. For dessert, if you want to stick with the Irish theme, try Bailey's cheesecake or the Irish crème bash. There's live music, from pop to traditional Irish tunes and Celtic rock, from Thursday to Saturday.

110 S. Lowell Ave. ℭ **315/476-1933.** Reservations recommended on weekends. Main courses $12–$19. AE, MC, V. Mon–Sat 11:30am–3pm; Mon–Thurs 5–10pm; Fri–Sat 5–11pm; Sun noon–9pm.

Dinosaur Bar-B-Que ★★ BARBECUE A ribs and juke joint slash biker bar, Dinosaur BBQ is a local legend that looks ripped straight out of Memphis. Don't let the tough-girl waitresses and Harley fanatics intimidate you; at mealtimes the place is a pretty even mix of suits, families, and leather-clad bikers. On weekends when there's live blues until late, the environment is rowdy and fun. The best menu items are classic barbecue: the "Big Ass" pulled pork plate, pit platters of ribs, and "ass-kickin'" chili, as well as the ⅓-pound barbecued burgers and spicy mojito chicken. Live music rocks every night but Sunday.

246 Willow St. ℭ **315/476-4937.** No reservations accepted. Main courses $5.50–$20. AE, DC, DISC, MC, V. Mon–Thurs 11am–midnight; Fri–Sat 11am–1am; Sun 2–9pm.

SYRACUSE AFTER DARK

The **Landmark Theatre,** 362 S. Salina St. (ℭ **315/475-7979;** www.landmark theatre.org), the last-remaining Depression-era movie palace in central New York and listed on the National Register of Historic Places, is a great place to take in a concert. The streets in **Armory Square** are lined with hopping bars and nearby the **IMAX Theater** at the MOST has Friday and Saturday evening showings until 9pm. **Coleman's,** 110 S. Lowell Ave. (ℭ **315/476-1933**), is a classic Irish pub.

Syracuse is host to the **New York State Fair** at the 375-acre Empire Expo Center, 581 State Fair Blvd. (ℭ **800/475-FAIR;** www.nysfair.org; adjacent to Rte. 690 just west of downtown) the last 2 weeks of August. The fair, which hosts all kinds of big-name musical acts and other exhibitions and entertainment, draws more than a million visitors annually. If you're in town during basketball season, try to catch a **Syracuse Orangemen** game (national champions in 2003) at the Carrier Dome; call ℭ **315/443-2121** or see www.suathletics.cin for schedules and information.

12

The North Country

by Rich Beattie

The Adirondack Park and 1000 Islands together make up New York's largest playground. Covering a full 20% of the state, the North Country's mountains, forests, lakes, rivers, and islands, offer endless opportunities to get out in the wilderness, explore, and have fun, whether it's hiking, skiing, canoeing, or just kicking back in an Adirondack chair overlooking a glass lake.

Drive into the Adirondack Park from almost any road and chances are you'll pass a rustic, wooden sign that welcomes you. When you cross that boundary the smell of fresh air and pine envelops you and won't let you go. It's a distinctive scent, one that can only be described as very, well, Adirondack.

I've been coming here since I was a kid, mostly summertime getaways with my family, and I can't imagine a more beautiful place to visit. The 'dacks, specifically, is an area you simply can't ignore. Its 600 million acres hold some 2,000 peaks, 100 of them taller than 3,000 feet. Nearly half of the park is forest preserve, vast forests of pine, maple, and birch. The park supports 500,000 acres of old-growth forest, 200,000 acres of which have never been logged. And water? You'll find some 2,500 lakes and ponds, along with more than 30,000 miles of rivers and streams.

Ralph Waldo Emerson and other thinkers found refuge here in the mid–19th century, forming philosopher's camps and using the woods for inspiration. And the park formed the exploratory dreams of Theodore Roosevelt, who canoed in the St. Regis Wilderness Canoe Area at the age of 12 and often returned to seek refuge.

Make no mistake: Though the peaks of the Adirondacks don't have the rugged, jagged look of, say, the Rockies, this can be harsh territory. But if you prepare well, it can be some of the most beautiful land to travel in. Well stocked with hotels, restaurants, and campsites, you can get as much or as little civilization as you please.

Drive west of the park and you'll run right into Canada—but you'll have to hop over the 1000 Islands first. A collection of tiny plots of land that sit in the middle of the St. Lawrence River, this is some of New York State's most scenic territory, which makes for terrific boating and some of the country's best fishing.

You won't find as many active pursuits as in the 'dacks, though—with no mountains and with most of the islands privately owned, you'll have to enjoy it all either from the decks of boats or from the shoreline.

Unfortunately, this area falls into the once-great category that is the fate of places like Buffalo and the Adirondack Great Camps. When New York's wealthy industrialists vacationed here 100 years ago, there were impressive hotels and more impressive architecture. Much of that is gone, now, and what's left is a hodgepodge of motels and only decent resorts that draw mostly boaters and fishermen.

1 Southern Adirondacks ⭐⭐⭐

From Lake George to Old Forge

The southern 'dacks landscape is mostly characterized by lakes. And at the center of it all is Lake George, both the 32-mile-long lake and the village. The area is hopping with tourists in the summer and fall foliage season, but most everything shuts down for the winter. Route 28, the only east-west road in the region, takes you past tiny villages, the Gore Mountain ski resort (New York's second largest), the magnificent Fulton Chain of Lakes, and over into Inlet and Old Forge, which also bustle with activity. It's about 90 miles from Lake George to Old Forge, but it's a beautiful drive (as are all the drives in the park) and it's worth spending some time cruising west from Lake George. The southwestern side section of the park is stays partially open in the winter to accommodate the thousands of snowmobilers who power through here each year. Enter the park via Route 30 and you'll pass the huge Great Sacandaga Lake, along with even more tiny villages and lakes.

ESSENTIALS

GETTING THERE

BY CAR   You'll likely drive here; I-87 becomes the Northway north of Albany and speeds you south to north along the eastern edge of the park. **Enterprise** (℀ **800/325-8007**) and **Hertz** (℀ **800/654-3131**) operate out of Glens Falls and Utica. Enterprise's Glens Falls location will pick you up and deliver you to the office in Lake George or Warrensburg without charge. Pick up and drop off service to Old Forge is available from the Utica location for a charge. Hertz has a rental desk at the Adirondack Regional Airport (see below) with very limited hours.

BY AIR   **Continental Connections** (℀ **800/523-3273**) flies into the Adirondack Regional Airport in Saranac Lake (℀ **518/891-4600**) in the northern part of the park, and into Oneida County Airport (℀ **315/736-9404**), a 45-minute drive from Old Forge. Other nearby airports include Burlington, Vermont (1 hr. from eastern section of the region), Albany (1 hr. from southern border), and Montreal (1 hr. from Plattsburg).

BY BUS   **Adirondack Trailways** (℀ **800/858-8555;** www.trailways.com/members/adirondack.html) serve Lake George, Saranac Lake, Lake Placid, Keene, Keene Valley, North Hudson, Schroon Lake, Pottersville, Chestertown, and Warrensburg, Malone, Massena, Potsdam, and Canton. In the summer, the itinerary also includes Ticonderoga and Tupper Lake. The daily service from Albany to Lake Placid takes 4 hours.

BY TRAIN   **Amtrak** (℀ **800/872-7245;** www.amtrak.com) stops in Glens Falls, Whitehall, Ticonderoga, Port Henry, Westport, Port Kent, Plattsburgh, and Rouses Point.

Fun Fact   **The Adirondack Chair**

Those ubiquitous wooden chairs with wide armrests were first designed in Westport, New York, by Thomas Lee, who simply wanted a comfortable lawn chair for his summer home. He called it the "Westport plank chair" and offered the design to carpenter friend Harry Bunnell, who patented it in 1904 and made them for the next 20 years. Originally they cost less than $4, but originals today can fetch more than $1,250.

⌒ *Moments* Bowling with the Vanderbilts

"Roughing it" means different things to different people. To the Vanderbilts and their contemporaries it meant staying in the woods . . . in luxurious Great Camps. These sprawling camps—many built in the late 19th and early 20th century—covered acres of prime forest real estate, with lots of beautifully crafted buildings to accommodate them (hot water and indoor plumbing included, of course!). Several still stand today, and there are remnants of still others. Some you can even stay in: The Wawbeek resort, for example, has remnants of a Great Camp.

One Great Camp you can visit is the rustic, deserted **Camp Santanoni** in Newcomb, just north of Route 28N (ⓒ **518/834-9328**); its 45 buildings are spread out over 12,900 acres. The main lodge was constructed from 1,500 native spruce trees in 1893; there's also a boathouse, lakeside studio, and a farm that once supplied the camp with milk, meat, and eggs. There are no furnishings anymore, and the buildings are closed to the public, but you come here to enjoy the beautiful architecture from the outside in this serene, mysterious setting. The camp's open year-round, but there's a catch: You have to hike or ski 5 miles to get here. Guided tours are offered once a month from June to September, and interpreters are on-site only in July and August.

Great Camp Sagamore, 4 miles south of Raquette Lake (ⓒ **315/354-5311**), lets you see how the Vanderbilts went camping. Their 27-building summer retreat for more than 50 years even included a bowling alley. Tours are daily in summer tours at 10am or 1:30pm; daily in fall at 1:30pm.

The two camps are about 40 miles apart; on these winding roads that could take some time to drive, so don't expect to see both in the same day, especially with the hiking involved to see Santanoni. Great Camp Sagamore is about 17 miles west of the Adirondack Museum in Blue Mountain Lake, and Santanoni about 25 miles east.

BY FERRY   Lake Champlain ferries (ⓒ 802/864-9804), all departing from Vermont, go from Grand Isle, Vermont, to Plattsburgh, New York; Burlington, Vermont, to Port Kent, New York; and Charlotte, Vermont, to Essex, New York. Schedule depends on season.

VISITOR INFORMATION   The **Adirondack Regional Tourism Council** (ⓒ **518/846-8016;** www.adirondack.org) has an information center on I-87 southbound between exits 41 and 40 that's open end of June to Labor Day from 8am to 8pm. For information on Lake George you can also contact **Warren County Tourism,** 908 Municipal Center, Lake George (ⓒ **800/365-1050** or 518/761-6366; http://visitlakegeorge.com). Farther west, contact **Inlet Information** (ⓒ 315/357-5501; www.inletny.com) or **Old Forge Tourism** (ⓒ 315/369-6983; www.oldforgeny.com).

SPORTS & OUTDOOR PURSUITS

BOAT TOURS   Explore Lake George on one of the **sightseeing cruises** that ply the lake, generally from May through October. With the **Lake George**

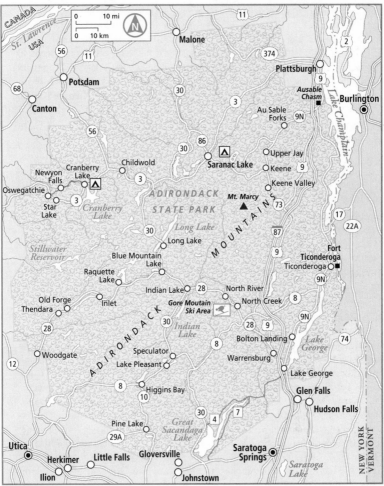

Steamboat Company, Steel Pier, Lake George (© **800/553-BOAT** or 518/668-5777; www.lakegeorgesteamboat.com), you can choose from 1- to 4-hour narrated cruises on one of three early-20th-century steamboats. Or cruise the lake on **The Sagamore** hotel's 72-foot replica of a 19th-century wooden vessel in June and July (© **518/644-9400**). To cruise the Fulton Chain of Lakes, take a sightseeing or meal cruise with **Old Forge Lake Cruises** (© **315/369-6473;** www.oldforge cruises.com/cruises.htm), or ply Raquette Lake's waters with the **Raquette Lake Navigation Co.** (© **315/354-5532;** www.raquettelakenavigation.com).

CANOEING   With lakes at every turn, canoeing is the logical method of transportation—a quiet way to explore the waters that are such an essential part of this park. Keep an eye out for white-tailed deer, red fox, beaver, and numerous bird species. More reclusive are the black bear, coyote, and moose. The Fulton Chain of Lakes (which begins east of Old Forge) is a popular and heavily trafficked route, with eight lakes spanning 16 miles. From First through Fifth lakes you'll find a continuous waterway lined with summer cottages. But you'll have to carry your boat to reach to the remaining lakes, which are less developed. Lake George is also a gorgeous place to paddle, with crystal clear spring-fed waters and a wealth of islands and small bays; at 32 miles long, you'd be better off in a sea kayak if you want to do some serious exploring. Get your canoe or kayak from **Mountain Man Outdoor Supply Company,** Route 28, Inlet (© 315/357-6672; www. mountainmanoutdoors.com). In the Lake George area, try **Lake George Kayak,** Main Street, Bolton Landing (© 518/644-9366; www.lakegeorgekayak.com).

DOWNHILL SKIING   Whiteface (Lake Placid) it ain't, but **Gore Mountain** (© 518/251-2411; www.goremountain.com) isn't exactly the ugly stepsister, either. It boasts some serious expert trails and a gondola of its own, making for a fun day on a 3,600-foot summit and 62 trails. Bonus: Since the folks up in Whiteface run this place, too, multiday tickets are good at both mountains, if you must get your Olympic fix.

GOLF   **The Sagamore** has the area's most renowned course; it dates to 1929 and was designed by the famous course designer Donald Ross. The first tee starts off with a spectacular view of Lake George, but the lake disappears after that, as did most of my golf balls. Over on the western side, **Thendara Golf Course** (© 315/ 369-3136) is also well known and also a Donald Ross creation from 1921 (the back nine were added in 1959). Greens fees are $30, or $15 if you tee off after 4pm; just beware—the course can get mosquito-ridden at dusk.

HIKING   **Bald Mountain,** east of Old Forge, is a steep but short (2 mile round-trip) climb that nabs you several open vistas and a fantastic open rocky summit. **Cascade Lake,** just north of Eagle Bay, is a 5½-mile easy loop that takes you to a scenic lake with a beautiful narrow waterfall at its eastern end. Around Lake George, the climb up **Black Mountain** is 8½ miles round-trip with a 1,100-foot vertical rise. The payoff? A rocky summit and amazing views. For more hikes, check out Barbara McMartin's *50 Hikes in the Adirondacks: Short Walks, Day Trips, and Backpacks Throughout the Park,* 4th edition (Countryman Press). For more hiking info (and other general outdoors info), contact the **Adirondack Mountain Club,** 814 Goggins Rd., Lake George (© 800/395-8080 or 518/668-4447; www.adk.org). The club also does group outings several times a year. For maps and supplies try **Mountainman Outdoor Supply Company,** Route 28 in both Inlet and Old Forge (© 315/369-6672).

RAFTING   The **Lower Moose River,** near Old Forge, is serious white water— April and early May bring Class IV and V rapids (on a scale of 1–5). The **Middle Moose River** is more mellow, perfect for families and inexperienced rafters, and runable from May to October. You can do either with **Whitewater Challengers** in Old Forge (© 800/443-RAFT). Or go with **Wild Waters Outdoor Center,** 1123 Rte. 28, Warrensburg (© 800/867-2335).

SCUBA DIVING   While diving may not be the first activity that comes to mind (the 'dacks are hardly the Caribbean, after all), diving is a popular sport thanks to the sunken ships that lie at the bottom of Lake George. Some 50 ships lie scattered around the lake's floor, several of them casualties of the French and Indian War in the mid–18th century. These historic ships are managed by a partnership between the Department of Environmental Conservation and a not-for-profit group called **Bateaux Below.** You can make a reservation by calling © 518/668-3352 and take yourself out to dive the wrecks (there are mooring chains and underwater signage). Or you can go with **Rich Morin's Scuba Center,** 20 Warren St., Glens Falls

(© **518/761-0533**). The center takes certified and uncertified divers alike; it's $129 for two 45-minute dives, though you have to be certified to go deep enough to see the historic ships.

SNOWMOBILING With some 15 feet of snow each year, the **Old Forge** area often makes national news. When that happens, adventurers on motorized horseback race up here to plow through it in the backwoods of the Inlet/Old Forge area. The most popular route connects Old Forge and Inlet to the Sargent Ponds area, the Moose River Recreation area and the Jessup River Wild Forest. For information on licenses, registrations, and trail fees, contact the **Adirondack Snowmobile Association** (© **800/648-5239**).

ESPECIALLY FOR KIDS

Lake George provides indoor and outdoor amusement for kids. As a child, I loved Old Forge's **Enchanted Forest,** 3183 Rte. 28 (© **315/369-6145**), and now it's even bigger, with amusement park rides as well as New York's largest water park (open June-Aug). In Lake George, there's **Dr. Morbid's Haunted House,** 115 Canada St. (© **518/668-3077**), open from spring through Halloween, and the **House of Frankenstein Wax Museum,** 213 Canada St. (© **518/668-3377**). Lovers of kitschy minigolf shouldn't miss **Around the World Golf,** Route 9 (© **518/668-3223**), where you can choose to putt around the U.S. (complete with graffiti under the Brooklyn Bridge) or the world (with the Egyptian pyramids and a Japanese garden). Outside Lake George, the **Wild West Ranch and Western Town,** Bloody Pond Road (© **518/668-2121**), offers trail rides, gold panning, and a petting zoo.

SEEING THE SIGHTS

Adirondack Museum ★ If you'd rather be out kayaking, skip this museum: the collection is dryly curated. But history buffs will eat up the extensive collection that traces the transportation, tourism, and personal past of this massive park, as well as a rundown of its flora and fauna. A couple odd items—a canoe big enough to camp in, a bark-covered outhouse—will appeal to everyone, and the setting, overlooking the lovely **Blue Mountain Lake,** is spectacular. Allow 3 hours to see the exhibits and grounds, and bring a picnic lunch to enjoy the view. Can't get enough? Admission is good for two consecutive days.

Rte. 30 on Blue Mountain Lake, NY 12812-0099. © 518/352-7311. www.adirondackmuseum.org. Admission $14 adults, $7 children 7–17, free children 6 and under. Memorial Day to mid-October only, daily 10am–5pm. From I-87, take exit 23, turn left and then right onto Rte. 9 N. Drive through Warrensburg to Rte. 28 and drive west for an hour until Blue Mountain Lake. At the T-intersection, follow Rte. 30 North for 1 mile.

Fort Ticonderoga ★★ Military history buffs will be in heaven at this fort set right on Lake Champlain. Built by the French beginning in 1755, the fort protected this narrow strip of water from its high perch, and since 1909 it's been open to the public, detailing the military history of the Lake Champlain and Lake George Valleys. The collection is anything but dry; on view are nearly 1,000 muskets, bayonets, pistols, and swords from the 18th century, as well as a

---

Fun Fact Parking Space

You could add the acreage from Yellowstone, Grand Canyon, Yosemite, the Everglades, and Great Smoky Mountains National Park and it still wouldn't equal the acreage in the Adirondack Park.

unique collection of uniforms. Not interested in the military stuff? There are gorgeous gardens for wandering.

On Lake Champlain, Ticonderoga. ℂ **518/585-2821.** Admission $12 adults, $11 seniors, $6 children 7–12, free children under 7. Mid-May to mid-Oct only daily 9am–5pm. King's Garden open early June to mid-Sept only daily 10am–4pm. From I-87, take exit 28, then Rte. 74 east 18 miles to Ticonderoga. Continue straight on Rte. 74 for 1½ miles. Turn left continuing on Rte. 74. Proceed straight ⅔sth mile to Fort entrance.

WHERE TO STAY

When I was growing up, many of the lakeside retreats were grand inns and lodges, complete resorts that offered everything. Unfortunately, many of them have disappeared, the beautiful old buildings knocked down in favor of sterile condos. But it's still possible to find everything from a full resort action to a quiet retreat.

You'll find many chains, especially in and around Lake George. The **Quality Inn,** 57 Canada St. (ℂ **800/4-CHOICE**), offers decent rooms, and the **Super 8,** 2159 Canada St. (ℂ **518/668-2470**), gives you a microwave and fridge in some rooms. The **Holiday Inn,** Route 9 (ℂ **518/668-5781**), has a beautiful outdoor pool and is a short walk from downtown.

Farther east, the **Best Western Sunset Inn,** Route 28, Old Forge (ℂ **800/ 418-8977**), has 59 basic rooms.

EXPENSIVE

The Sagamore ★★★   Drive onto the Sagamore's personal 72-acre island and up to its Colonial-style main building and you'll immediately see what's drawn well-heeled vacationers here since 1883: peace, quiet, and luxury. Jutting out into Lake George, this private getaway serves up a wealth of water activities or just lakeside lounging. It's mostly vacationers here—who come for the great golf course and spa, as well as the water activities—though a convention center means plenty of name-tag-wearing guests as well. The common-area decor is more formal than comfy; luckily, that stuffiness doesn't carry over to the helpful staff. The restored main-building rooms—done in flowery patterns and muted tones—have the same formal furniture, but bathrooms give you plenty of room to navigate. Suites, with two full rooms and some with views in two directions, are well worth the extra money. There are several buildings and price options. The contemporary "lodge" rooms are not actually in the lodge, but with balconies and fireplaces, offer the best bang for the buck. An eye-popping, privately owned castle is also for rent. All rooms are nonsmoking.

110 Sagamore Rd., Bolton Landing, NY, 12814. ℂ **800/358-3585** or 518/644-9400. Fax 518/743-6036. www.thesagamore.com. 351 units. May–Oct $369–$415 double, $439 and way up suite; Nov–Apr $169–$189 double, $259 and way up suite. Nov–Mar Thurs–Sun only—unless there is a group staying there. Call first. Packages available. AE, DC, DISC, MC, V. Free valet parking. From I-87, get off at exit 22 and take Rte. 9N north for 10 miles to the town of Bolton Landing. At the second traffic light turn right onto Sagamore Rd. **Amenities:** 6 restaurants; large indoor pool; off-premises golf course; indoor tennis court, 5 lighted outdoor tennis courts; large exercise room; spa; Jacuzzi; watersports rentals; bike rental; game room; children's programs; courtesy van; small business center; 24-hr room service (July–Aug), limited rest of the year; in-room massage; babysitting; laundry service, same-day dry cleaning. *In room:* A/C, TV/VCR w/pay movies, dataport, some with kitchenette, some with coffeemaker, iron.

MODERATE

The Georgian Resort ★ (Kids)   Busy, colorful, and right smack in the heart of the Lake George madness, The Georgian is the kind of place where you'd expect to find dinner theater—and you'd be right. Still, sitting right on the lake with 100 feet of private beach, the property does offer some rooms that takes advantage of the gorgeous views at its lakeside locale. It needs to, since the standard rooms are without a trace of charm. You'll find two rows of motel-style rooms, many of which face the oh-so-lovely parking lot. Of course you'll want to stay in the *other* building, closer to the lake, and preferably in rooms 191 to 198, where nothing will be in front of you but shimmering water. Suites have slightly nicer furniture and generally lots more space. Some suites are huge and have *(ack!)* heart-shaped Jacuzzis. And you thought you had escaped the Poconos.

384 Canada St., Lake George, NY 12845. © 800/525-3436 or 518/668-5401. www.georgianresort.com. 164 units. Late May to mid-Oct. $99–$279 double; $199–$369 suite. Jan to mid-May and mid-Oct to late Dec $69–$199 double; $139–$299 suite. AE, DC, DISC, MC, V. Some weekends have 2- or 3-night minimums. **Amenities:** Restaurant; outdoor heated pool; limited room service. *In room:* A/C, TV, fridge (suites only), coffeemaker, hair dryer, iron.

North Woods Inn and Resort ★   Don't expect a sprawling resort like the Sagamore, but this smallish hotel is still recommended in its price range. Some rooms are in the main building, and others are motel-style along the shores of gorgeous Fourth Lake. All of them are good sized and adequately comfortable, but decked out in unfortunately drab colors. Your best bet is to stay in the lake-front rooms, preferably one on the end, so you actually have a lake view. Jacuzzi suites have the same sad decor but offer the incentive of more space, a Jacuzzi tucked into a corner, and a wood-burning fireplace. All rooms are nonsmoking.

Rte. 28, P.O. Box 1146, Old Forge, NY 13420. © 315/369-6777. Fax 315/369-2575. www.northwoodsinn resort.com. 33 units. $120–$185 doubles; $170 and up suites. AE, DISC, MC, V. 3-night minimum on holiday weekends. **Amenities:** 2 restaurants; lounge; outdoor heated pool; exercise room; Jacuzzi in some suites; game room, limited room service to suites; limited complimentary boat use. *In room:* A/C, TV (suites have VCR), some with dataport, some with fridge, some with coffeemaker, CD player in suites.

INEXPENSIVE

The Lake Champlain Inn ★★ *Finds*   This gorgeous 1870 Victorian home has a prime location right on Lake Champlain, and its rooms offer views of the lake, the Adirondacks, and even Vermont's Green Mountains. You're also just 2 miles from the northern end of Lake George. The affable owners have maintained much of the original woodwork and red maple floors, along with period antiques, quilts, and big bathrooms. While rooms aren't the biggest, their views are among the best in the park. And they boast nice touches like wrought-iron beds or claw-foot tubs. The one suite gives you two adjoining rooms. There's also a house with two rooms, called the Schoolhouse (but isn't); it's a large modern Victorian-style house that's very modern inside and sits on 130 acres. The adjacent state land is perfect for hiking or cross-country skiing. No smoking.

428 County Rte. 3, Ticonderoga, NY 12861. © 518/547-9942. www.tlcinn.com. 6 units. $85–$135 double. Rates include full breakfast. 2-night weekend minimums apply. AE, MC, V. **Amenities:** Free use of bikes. *In room:* A/C, hair dryer, iron, no phone. Take I-87 to exit 20, turn left onto Rte. 9. At light, turn right onto Rte. 149 for 12 miles, left on Rte. 4 for 10 miles. Go straight through intersection on Rte. 22 for 15 miles. Turn right (there will be a TLC road sign) onto Lake Rd., go 2 miles, bear right, go ½ mile.

CAMPGROUNDS

Glen Hudson Campsite in Warrensburg (© **518/623-9871**) is a nice riverside campground with wooded river or open sites that's close to Lake George; it's open mid-May through mid-October. Get away—far away—from the crowds and the RVs on **Lake George Islands** (© **518/623-1200**). Accessible by boat only, the 387 isolated shoreline campsites are located on 44 state-owned islands. It's an amazing back-to-nature experience. Camping fee is $16 and is available mid-May through Columbus Day. **Golden Beach Campground** (© **315/354-4230**) has a prime perch on the southeast shore of Raquette Lake, and its 205 tent and trailer sites accommodate everyone from backpackers to 40-foot RVs. The fee is $15 for everyone and it's open mid-May to Labor Day.

WHERE TO DINE

You can walk through the village of Lake George and find all sorts of eateries, many of them of dubious quality. Fortunately, you have plenty of options.

EXPENSIVE

Seventh Lake House ★★★ *Finds* CONTEMPORARY AMERICAN   You might drive right by this unassuming house sitting between Inlet and Raquette Lake. But don't: Two brothers are inside preparing the best food in the southern Adirondacks. The quiet dining room faces a lake and is decorated in warm tones with a stone fireplace; or, you could choose to sit out on the canopied deck. The ever-changing seasonal menu combines "comfortable old favorites" with more cutting-edge "contemporary creations." You might start with paper-wrapped shrimp served with mango marmalade sauce and follow up with something similarly inventive, like the triple meatloaf—veal, beef, and pork baked with herbs and spices wrapped in pastry and served with an onion sherry sauce.

Rte. 28, Inlet (between Inlet and Raquette Lake). ✆ 315/357-6028. Reservations recommended. Main courses $14–$24. AE, DISC, MC, V. June–Sept daily 5–10pm; Oct–May Thurs–Sun 5–9pm.

Trillium ★★★ CONTEMPORARY AMERICAN   This extremely proper and formal restaurant in The Sagamore is also one of the most romantic settings in the Adirondacks. Decked out in pinks and chandeliers with a view of Lake George, the very attentive, black-tied servers present well-prepared traditional meals and an extensive wine list. The seasonal menu is limited, but fortunately most every dish works. Meats, such as the minted Gremolata rack of lamb served with cabernet mashed potatoes, are excellent, but fish is really where the kitchen shines. You find options such as pan-seared striped bass with zucchini and a jumbo lump crab cake or crisp, seared wild king salmon that practically melts in your mouth.

In The Sagamore, 110 Sagamore Rd., Bolton Landing. ✆ 800/358-3585 or 518/644-9400, ext. 6110. Reservations required. Jackets required for men during summer season (Memorial Day to Labor Day); collared shirts required in the off season. No denim or sneakers allowed. Main courses $27–$30. AE, DC, DISC, MC, V. Summer season Sun–Thurs 6–9pm, Fri–Sat 6–9:30pm, Sun 10am–2pm; off season Fri–Sat 6–9pm.

MODERATE

East Cove ★ AMERICAN   This local favorite is thankfully off Lake George's beaten path. Like many area restaurants, it's a small Adirondack-style log cabin, but this interior is fairly charming, with exposed posts and beams and historic photos lining the walls. The food, though, is what keeps them coming back. The menu spans the meat/fish/pasta realms, and includes the delicious sea scallops casino, baked with green and red peppers in garlic butter with crumb topping. On the lighter side, burgers, fish and chips, and chicken sandwiches are also available.

3873 Rte. 9L, Lake George. ✆ 518/668-5265. Main courses $10–$25. AE, DC, DISC, MC, V. Daily 5–10pm Mother's Day to Columbus Day; rest of the year Wed–Sun only.

Lanzi's Great Sacandaga Lake ★★ AMERICAN   Yes, the lake lives up to its boast of a name, and this great restaurant—run by the five Lanzi brothers—takes full advantage of its lakefront setting (a rarity on Sacandaga) with floor-to-ceiling windows in the restaurant, and a massive outdoor deck. Not only is there a great view outside, but usually a big party as well: crowds of up to 4,000 have been known to gather for themed parties, such as reggae festivals or chili cook-offs. The kitchen turns out homemade everything, from the salad dressing to the pasta. The portions are huge and very rich. Consider the Lake Chicken, grilled breast topped with sautéed lobster meat, baked under smoked mozzarella and topped with hollandaise sauce. You may need to join the dance party to work it all off.

Rte. 30, Mayfield. (✆ **518/661-7711.** May–Oct daily 11:30am–10pm (or later, depending on the crowd); Nov–Apr Mon–Thurs 4–10pm, Fri–Sun 11:30am–10pm.

2 Northern Adirondacks ★★★

Keene Valley and Plattsburgh to Cranberry Lake

Separated from the southern Adirondacks by a range of mountains known as the **High Peaks,** the northern area of this park is a different entity, where life operates at full-speed 365 days a year. Summer brings hikers, bikers, and paddlers, while wintertime beckons skiers and boarders to the state's best mountains.

Cut west from I-87 along Route 73 and you'll come to the center of activity: the village of **Lake Placid,** home to two winter Olympics and the birthplace of winter sports in America. Call it one of the ironies of geography that this town actually sits on **Mirror Lake**—the actual Lake Placid is a few miles outside of town. There's some kitsch to the town as it clings to its Olympic heritage—sure, it's cool to ski and skate where the athletes did, but 1980 was a long time ago, and 1932 a *really* long time ago. Nevertheless, the town's a beehive of activity all year-round, as it has been since the Games put the Adirondacks on America's recreation map.

West of Lake Placid, Route 73 becomes Route 86. Along Route 86, you'll pass through the village of **Saranac Lake,** which may not have the quality of restaurants Placid does, but it doesn't have the crowds, either. Cut north up Route 30 and you'll be in one of the most remote and gorgeous canoeing areas in America: the **St. Regis Canoe Wilderness Area.** Back on 86, the road takes you past two more huge lakes and countless opportunities for fishing, hiking, camping, and canoeing. Head east from Lake Placid and you'll run right into Lake Champlain; though not heavily developed for recreation or tourism, it's a gorgeous sight.

ESSENTIALS

GETTING HERE   I-87 cuts right through the forest, making it easily accessible. Cut over Route 73 and you'll be headed toward Lake Placid. **Amtrak** stops in Westport and Plattsburgh, both 50 miles from Saranac Lake. Westport is the closest stop to Placid; from there, **Majestic Limousine & Transportation,** 2 Main St., Lake Placid (✆ **866/226-1152** or 518/523-0294), can shuttle you to Lake Placid year-round (Mon–Thurs it's $25 per person, Fri–Sun it's $15). For bus and plane information see "The Southern Adirondacks," earlier in this chapter.

GETTING AROUND   You'll need a car. **Rent-A-Wreck** (✆ **800/698-1777;** www.rentawreck.com) in Lake Placid offers free pick-up/drop-off service to customers in the local vicinity. **Enterprise** in Plattsburgh (✆ **800/325-8007;** www.enterprise.com) charges a fee to pick up or return renters in Saranac Lake, Port Henry, Lake Placid, Malone, and Westport. From late December through March a **free shuttle** links Whiteface with Lake Placid. The shuttle runs every 2 hours during the week and hourly on the weekend and picks up at a few hotels in town: Howard Johnson, Mirror Lake Inn, Best Western, and Art Devlin's, but if you flag them down on Main St. they'll stop. From town, the shuttle runs direct to Whiteface.

VISITOR INFORMATION   The **Adirondack Regional Tourism Council** (✆ **518/846-8016;** www.adirondacks.org) operates an information center on I-87 southbound between exits 41 and 40; it's open daily from 8am to 5pm; from June until Labor Day, it's open until 8pm. The **Lake Placid/Essex County Visitors Bureau,** Olympic Center, 216 Main St., Lake Placid (© **800/447-5224** or 518/523-2605; www.lakeplacid.com), is open year-round Monday to Friday from 8am to 5pm and Saturday and Sunday from 9am to 4pm. The office is closed on Sunday in April and November.

SEEING THE OLYMPIC SIGHTS

The 1932 Winter Olympics put Lake Placid in the international spotlight; hosting the Games again in 1980 cemented its legacy. You can see some of the sites where legends were made, including the "Miracle on Ice" hockey victory of the Americans over the Russians. **The Olympic Regional Development Authority** (© **518/523-1655;** www.orda.org) handles it all.

Skip the Olympic Training Center (421 Old Military Rd.); there's not much open to the public. For downhill skiing on **Whiteface,** see "Outdoor Pursuits," below. You can see all of the following in one day. Start off at the **Verizon Sports Complex** ★★, Route 73 (© **518/523-2811**), 20 minutes west of Lake Placid, for cross-country skiing (see "Outdoor Pursuits," below). In the same complex—and definitely something you should not miss—is the **bobsled/luge/skeleton track,** where you'll watch athletes bomb down on and in crazy machinery. You can even strap yourself into a bobsled and race down the half-mile track with a guide and brakeman ($40)—you'll never watch the Olympics the same way. The sleds are on wheels in summer, but they go much faster on the winter ice. Then drive 10 minutes back toward town and you'll see the towering presence of the ski jump towers at the **MacKenzie-Intervale Ski Jumping Complex** ★, Route 73 (© **518/523-2202**). From December through March and June through October, watch athletes soar off these ramps. Ride the lift alongside it and take the 26-story elevator to the top of the 394-foot tower to get the skiers' terrifying perspective ($8). From June to October you can watch them jump, too—into a 750,000-gallon pool at the adjacent **Kodak Sports Park.** Drive back into town and spend a half hour in the **Winter Olympic Museum** (© **518/523-1655**) at the **Olympic Center;** it's $4 to check out a good history of the Games in Placid and tons of memorabilia. While there, go skating on the rinks where legends like Sonja Henie and Eric Heiden made history (see below).

SPORTS & OUTDOOR PURSUITS

CANOEING It's rare to find a stretch of water reserved solely for non-motorized boats, but the St. Regis Canoe Wilderness beckons with the promise of quiet. In fact, the only sounds you'll hear in this remote part of the park are birdcalls and the sound of your paddle as it slices through the glassy water. Just be prepared to carry your canoe: there are lots of portages here. But whether you're just interested in a 1-day outing or a weeklong trip, you can get outfitted, with or without a guide. **St. Regis Canoe Outfitters,** 9 Dorsey St., Saranac Lake (© **518/891-1838;** www.canoeoutfitters.com), can set you up with canoe and kayak rentals,

---

(*Value* **Savings Passport**

You can get into most Lake Placid attractions for about $40 by purchasing the **Lake Placid Passport,** available from the Olympic Regional Development Authority (© **518/523-1655;** www.orda.org). Different options are available seasonally.

guided trips, and camping gear rentals. **Adirondack Lakes and Trails Outfitters,** 168 Lake Flower Ave., Saranac Lake (© **518/891-7450;** www.adirondack outfitters.com), is another great place for canoeing advice and/or rentals; they offer a wealth self-guided and guided trips.

CROSS-COUNTRY SKIING   Just outside Lake Placid, Mount Van **Hoevenberg X-C Center** at the Verizon Sports Complex, Route 73 (© **518/523-2811**), is where Olympic athletes train; trail fees are $12 per day and equipment rental is $16. **Dewey Mountain Ski Center,** Route 3, Saranac Lake (© **518/891-2697**), is another fun place to explore. Hard-core skiers up for a challenge can head into the backcountry and take on the **Jackrabbit Trail,** a 44-mile wilderness trail that runs between Paul Smiths and Lake Clear Junction. Pick up the trail (and any equipment you need) at the **Cascade Cross Country Center,** on Route 73, 5 miles east of Lake Placid (© **518/523-9605**). This is also a great place to come on nights of a full moon from January to March, when the trails are set with bonfires, and hot chocolate, beer, and hot dogs are served.

DOWNHILL SKIING   **Whiteface,** Route 86, Wilmington (© **518/946-2223;** www.whiteface.com), is the east's only Olympic mountain (elevation 4,400 ft.), and the best skiing in the state. With the greatest vertical drop in the east (3,430 ft.), there's a variety of terrain that will appeal to all levels. In fact, 35% of the trails are rated for novices. There are 65 trails and 11 lifts in all. A 1-day lift ticket costs $59. **Mt. Pisgah,** Mt. Pisgah Road, Saranac Lake (© **518/891-4150;** www.saranaclake.com/pisgah.shtml), is decidedly less Olympic, and good skiers will get bored here, but with only five trails, it's a good hill for beginners and families. It also boasts a fun tubing hill. Lift tickets cost just $15 to $18.

FLYING   Soar high over the treetops and look down on the mountaintops during a scenic flight any time of year with **Adirondack Flying Service,** Lake Placid Airport, Route 73, Lake Placid (© **518/523-2473;** www.flyanywhere. com). A 20-minute flight is $25 per person, with family discounts available (up to 5 people; 2-adult maximum).

FLY-FISHING   The Ausable River offers tumbles and flows, twists and turns, and a pristine environment to cast your line. The village of Wilmington, about a 20-minute drive northeast from Lake Placid, is your headquarters. World-renowned fisherman Francis Betters and the guides at his **Adirondack Sport Shop,** Route 86, Wilmington (© **518/946-2605;** http://adirondackfly fishing.com), know the waters as well as anyone; a day out with the guides will run you $195 per day, including lunch and a box of his flies.

GOLF   There are lots of places to tee it up in this part of the park. The **Whiteface Club & Resort,** Whiteface Inn Road, Lake Placid (© **800/422-6757** or 518/ 523-2551; www.whitefaceclub.com), was rated four stars (out of five) by *Golf Digest;* greens fees are $39 during the summer season and club rental is available. Or hit the links at a municipal par-72 course, the **Craig Wood Golf and Country Club,** Route 73, Lake Placid (© **877/999-9473** or 518/523-9811; www. craigwoodgolfclub.com). Green fees are $27.

HIKING   Everyone wants to climb the Adirondacks' highest peak, Mt. Marcy, and its 5,344 feet of rock. And on summer weekends the paths can seem more like Midtown Manhattan than wilderness. The most popular (and crowded) approach is from the north, but the most scenic and less-crowded trail (don't tell) is the **Range Trail.** You only use your feet to scramble the last bit to the top of Whiteface; it's actually accessed by a highway, which costs $9 to drive up and is open only from May to Columbus Day (weather permitting). Then it's a short climb via a nature trail in the rocky ridge of a glacial cirque. **High Falls Gorge,** 8 miles east of Lake Placid on Route 86 (© **518/946-2278**), offers a beautiful stroll along the Au Sable River, past 700 feet of waterfalls in summer or winter. You'll cross bridges and follow trails as the water spills over ancient granite cliffs. Admission is $10. To take a guided hiking tour, talk to the folks at **High Peaks Mountain Adventures Guide Service,** 331 Main St., Lake Placid (© **518/523-3764**).

ICE SKATING   Skate on the same rink where Eric Heiden won his record five golf medals in 1980. Lake Placid's Olympic Center on Main Street (© **518/ 523-1655**) gets you out on the outdoor rink in winter nightly from 7 to 9pm for $5. On summer weeknights, you can skate indoors at the 1932 arena where Sonja Henie won Olympic Gold ($4). Rentals are $3.

RAFTING   Nothing quite beats the rush of white-water rafting, especially when the water's high from snow runoff in the spring. **Lake Placid Rafting** (© **800/510-RAFT** or 518/523-16350; www.lakeplacidrafting.com) provides everything your need for a guided run of the Hudson River Gorge. The water runs Class IV and V in April and May, when trips run on weekends only, and Class III from June through August, when trips run Tuesday, Thursday, Saturday, and Sunday. Fall foliage runs are in September and October. For a low-key raft ride, plus a walk along nature trails through primeval Adirondack forest, check out the **Ausable Chasm,** on Route 9, 12 miles south of Plattsburgh (© **518/834-7454;** www.ausablechasm.com). The entrance fee is $16 for adults, $14 for seniors and teens, $12 for kids 5 to 11; the raft ride (weather permitting) is $8 for everyone. Check the website for a coupon worth $2 off.

TOURING LAKE CHAMPLAIN   Lake Champlain doesn't offer much in the way of hotels or recreation, but it may be too large to ignore. If you want to explore the lake, consider taking a cruise aboard the **Spirit of Plattsburgh,** 2 Dock St., Plattsburgh (© **518/566-7447;** http://soea.com/SOPL_home.html). Choose from scenic and sunset cruises, or meal cruises for lunch, brunch, barbeque, and more; prices vary per cruise. You can also paddle the lake yourself in search of eagles. Rent kayaks (and power boats) from **Westport Marina,** 20 Washington St., Westport (© **800/626-0342;** www.westportmarina.com).

TRAIN   Climb aboard for a 1-hour rail journey through the forest (between Lake Placid and Saranac Lake) on the **Adirondack Scenic Railroad** (© **518/891-3238;** www.adirondackrr.com). Trains depart May through October from Saranac Lake (19 Depot St.) or Lake Placid (Union Station); themed rides take place throughout the summer. Round-trip tickets are $12 adults, $11 seniors, and $5 kids 9; one-way tickets are $8 adults and seniors; $4 kids. Visit their website for a $1-off coupon.

ESPECIALLY FOR KIDS

In winter, there's nothing in town that's as much fun as screaming down onto the ice of Mirror Lake, holding onto your toboggan for dear life. Right in Lake Placid, you'll slide down a converted ski jump (© **518/523-2591**); $5 gets you a four-person toboggan and a 40 mph rush. The slide is near the Olympic Center and the Best Western. Go mushing around the lake with **Thunder Mountain Dog Sled Tours** (© **518/891-6239**), located across from the Lake Placid Hilton ($5 per person). For a true Christmas experience (about half the year), take the kids to **Santa's Workshop,** Whiteface Mountain Memorial Highway (Rte. 431), 1½ miles northwest of Route 86 in Wilmington (© **800/806-0215**), where they can hop on rides, pet reindeer, and see Santa's house. The place is geared toward the wee ones; older kids will get bored quickly. Open daily 9:30am to 4:30pm from the end of June until Labor Day; weekends only (9:30am–4pm) Labor Day to Columbus Day and 5 weekends prior to Christmas (10am–3:30pm). Admission is $16 adults, $13 for kids 2 to 16.

SHOPPING

For outdoor gear, try **Lake Placid Mountaineering,** 132 Main St., Lake Placid (© **518/523-7586**), and **EMS,** 51 Main St., Lake Placid (© **518/523-2505**). For unique Adirondack crafts, visit the **Adirondack Craft Center,** 93 Saranac Ave., Lake Placid (© **518/523-2062**), where you'll find works from over 300 artisans. Another good bet is **Adirondack Reflections,** Main Street (Rte. 73), Keene (© **518/576-9549**).

WHERE TO STAY

Accommodations range from tiny lakeside motels of varying and dubious quality to chains to exclusive getaways and secluded campsites. In Lake Placid, know that rates are not set in stone. The village hosts many events, such as major hockey tournaments, so even in the off season, you could find rates some days that rival the summer season. Chains offer a good value for families. The **Best Western,** 148 Lake Flower Ave., Saranac Lake (© **800/780-7234** or 518/891-1970), offers clean spacious rooms with an indoor pool for $75 to $90 in the summer season.

VERY EXPENSIVE

Lake Placid Lodge ★★★   This exclusive inn, a Relais & Châteaux member, is set right on Lake Placid outside of town, with an upscale rustic look (*very* Adirondack) and lots of privacy. It's the kind of place that could get away with an air of snootiness, but there's none—you're in the woods, after all—and the service is helpful and friendly, and staffers will bend over backwards to make your stay perfect. The lodge brings the outdoors in, with birch branches everywhere from the hallway ceilings to the cozy bar to the funky, woodsy furnishings in the (nonsmoking) guest rooms. In fact, all the furniture, made by local artists, is for sale—if you like your bed (and you will!), you can buy it. Rooms and bathrooms are large, luxurious, and comfortable, but the cabins afford the ultimate in privacy—most are set right on the lake's shore, with stone fireplaces, sitting areas, and picture windows. They're the perfect place to sit in an over-stuffed sofa and watch the moon rise and reflect off the lake.

Whiteface Inn Rd., P.O. Box 550, Lake Placid, NY 12946. © **877/523-2700** or 518/523-2700. www.lake placidlodge.com. 34 units. $375–$450 double; $625–$850 suite; $600–$950 cabin. Rates include breakfast. Packages available. AE, DC, DISC, MC, V. Dogs allowed. No children under 12. From Main St. Lake Placid, turn left on Rte. 86, turn right at the Lake Placid Lodge sign (Whiteface Rd.). **Amenities:** Restaurant; lounge; access to health club; complimentary watersports and bike rentals; courtesy car; limited room service; laundry; dry cleaning. *In room:* A/C, dataport, fridge and coffeemaker in some rooms, iron, hair dryer, safe.

EXPENSIVE

Mirror Lake Inn ★★★   Just beyond Lake Placid's busy Main Street, on a hill overlooking Mirror Lake, sits this classy and gorgeous inn. Dating from 1883, it maintains a very traditional upscale feel—rustic it's not. Mahogany walls, walnut floors, and chandeliers fill the lobby and its cozy nooks. With the exception of the smallish "Cobble Hill" accommodations, standard rooms are extremely comfortable and very spacious, though there's nothing overly grand or unique about them; many, however, boast gorgeous views of the lake and mountains—some even have balconies. Suites are huge with graceful furnishing and touches like four-poster beds in some; they're the most elegant rooms in the town. Two major pluses: The

Averil Conwell Dining Room (reviewed below) is outstanding, as it the state-of-the-art spa.

5 Mirror Lake Dr., Lake Placid, NY 12946. (✆ **518/523-2544.** Fax 518/523-2871. www.mirrorlakeinn.com. 128 units. Mid-June to mid-Oct, some holiday weeks, and weekends all year $190–$325 double; $425 and way up suite; Jan–June, excluding some holiday weeks, mid-Oct to mid-Dec weekday rates $170–$240 double, $370 and way up suite. Modified American plans available as well as many packages. AE, DISC, MC, V. 2-night weekend minimum in summer. **Amenities:** 2 restaurants; lounge; 2 pools (1 indoor, 1 heated outdoor); tennis court; spa; exercise room; Jacuzzi; sauna; free use of canoes, kayaks, rowboats, and paddleboats; concierge; salon; limited room service; in-room massage; laundry service; same-day dry cleaning. *In room:* A/C, TV, dataport, fridge, hair dryer, iron.

The Wawbeek ★★★   Far from the madness of Lake Placid and set back in the woods on the shores of Saranac Lake, the Wawbeek is a dying breed—a homey, secluded, luxurious camp on the water. In its earlier manifestations as a great camp, Rockefellers and Duponts stayed here, and it's easy to see what drew them: walk the 40 acres, the 1,500 feet of shoreline, and the nature trail and you'll find your own private slice of the 'dacks. Or just sit in the gorgeous main lodge with its original knotty pine paneling and cozy corners and read. The non-smoking rooms and cottages are spread out and tucked deep in the woods, with several rooms overlooking the mountains. Rooms are generally large (though with smallish bathrooms) and come decked out in Adirondack-style furniture and some of the world's most comfortable beds. For more privacy, grab one of the log cabins, which boast decks and views.

Panther Mountain Rd., Rte. 30, Tupper Lake, NY 12986. (✆ **800/953-2656** or 518/359-2656. Fax 518/359-2475. www.wawbeek.com. 29 units. Nov 25 to late Mar and May to mid-June $125–$350 double; mid-June to early Sept $170–$440 double; early Sept to early Nov $150–$380 double. Rates include breakfast (in bed if you like). Closed Apr and 3 weeks in Nov. AE, DC, MC, V. Pets allowed in cabins. Children under 12 not allowed in some rooms. Mid-June to late Aug 3-night minimum on weekends, 1-week minimum in cabins; Sept to mid-June 2-night minimum weekends. Take Rte. 86 West to Saranac Lake, where it runs into Rte. 3. Take that West for 15 miles to Rte. 30 north. Turn right, lodge is 1 mile up on the right. **Amenities:** Restaurant; lounge; 2 tennis courts; free and extensive watersports and bikes; children's programs on summer weekdays; game room; limited room service. *In room:* Full kitchens in cabins, fridge, coffeemaker, no phone.

MODERATE

Best Western Golden Arrow Hotel ★★ *(Kids)*   It's rare to find a Best Western with this kind of setting—right in the heart of Lake Placid and directly on the shore of Mirror Lake—and such great views: boating in the summer, dogsledding in the winter. But here it is. You can even grab a complimentary canoe or kayak and head out on the water yourself. But the nonsmoking rooms are precisely what you'd expect from the chain: plain and drab, but mostly comfortable. Suites aren't worth the extra money; though they have nice extras like fireplaces and fridges and whirlpool tubs, a wall creates two cramped rooms instead of one large one.

150 Main St., Lake Placid, NY 12946. (✆ **518/523-3353.** www.golden-arrow.com. 142 units. Mid-June to Columbus Day $129–$189 double, $249–$369 suite; Columbus Day to mid-June weekdays $79–$129 double, $109–$209 suite; weekends high-season rates apply. Packages available. AE, DC, DISC, MC, V. **Amenities:** Restaurant; indoor pool; elaborate health club; Jacuzzi; sauna; complimentary watersports equipment; children's programs; game room; salon; limited room service; in-room massage; laundry service; same-day dry cleaning. *In room:* A/C, TV w/pay movies, dataport, some with kitchenette, fridge, coffeemaker, hair dryer, iron, some with safe.

Hilton Lake Placid Resort ★★ *(Kids)*   Located right in the village, this resort sprawls across two streets in three different buildings, one of which is right on the water. Offering loads of amenities, from four (!) pools to complimentary boats for use on the lake, you'll never be lacking for activity on the hotel grounds. And since about half the guests are here with a group, the place constantly buzzes. Rooms are uniformly outfitted in what the hotel calls Modern Adirondack style, one that bears a striking resemblance to standard Hilton style. That's okay, though, since they provide lots of space and are comfortable. My suggestion: Upgrade to the Lakeview Building, where guest rooms have balconies or patios. And for super-huge rooms that look straight down on the water, grab a room in the Waterfront Building. Just be aware that these rooms can book up a year in advance.

One Mirror Lake Dr., Lake Placid, NY 12946. (C) 800/755-5598 or 518/523-4411. Fax 518/523-1120. www. lphilton.com. 179 units. Mid-June to mid-Oct $129–$269 double; rest of year $59–$189 double unless there's an event or holiday, when high-season rates apply. Packages available. AE, DC, DISC, MC, V. Pets allowed with $25 fee. **Amenities:** Restaurant; lounge; 4 pools (2 indoor, 2 heated outdoor); small exercise room; Jacuzzi; complimentary canoe and kayak use; children's programs; game room; concierge; tour desk; salon; limited room service; babysitting; laundry service; same-day dry cleaning. *In room:* A/C, TV w/pay movies, dataport, fridge, coffeemaker, hair dryer, iron.

Hotel Saranac (★) Located in downtown Saranac Lake, this 1927 hotel has a unique concept; it's owned by Paul Smith's College, and the staff comprises students training in the hospitality industry. Are they trying to impress you or their professors with their attentive service? Who cares? Opened in 1927 as a unique "fireproof" hotel, the all-brick building boasts grand public spaces (the Grand Hall was modeled after the Davanzati Palace in Florence) befitting the American royalty that visited here generations ago. Rooms are a tight fit, but modern and bright. Request a corner room: You'll get feather mattresses and more space and light, though bathrooms are small.

101 Main St., Saranac Lake, NY 12983. (C) 800/937-0211 or 518/891-2200. Fax 518/891-5664. www.hotel saranac.com. 88 units. Jul–Sept $99–$195 double; Sept–July $55–$195 double. Packages available. 2-night minimum July–Aug may apply. AE, DC, DISC, MC, V. Dogs permitted. **Amenities:** Restaurant; lounge; limited room service; laundry service; dry cleaning. *In room:* A/C, TV, dataport, fridge, coffeemaker, hair dryer.

INEXPENSIVE

Art Devlin's Olympic Motor Inn (★) (*Value*) If you enjoy the kitsch value of Lake Placid, you'll adore this small hotel just 3 blocks from the Olympic Center—in the lobby you'll find some 450 trophies and medals from ski jumper extraordinaire Art Devlin. Now run by Art's son, this hotel is a little less than extraordinaire, but a good value option. Rooms are simple but spacious and painted nice bright colors. Some give you a glimpse of some high peaks, even from a balcony, while others look out onto the less-romantic parking lot. Get a room in the back building—though they don't have whirlpool tubs, they're bigger.

350 Main St., Lake Placid, NY 12946. (C) 518/523-3700. Fax 518/523-3893. http://artdevlins.com. 41 units. Mid-June to mid-Sept weekday $68–$88 double, weekend $88–$138 double; rest of year weekday $58–$68 double, weekend $78–$128 double. Rates include continental breakfast. 2-night minimum most weekends. AE, DC, DISC, MC, V. Dogs allowed. **Amenities:** Heated outdoor pool. *In room:* A/C, TV, fridge.

CAMPGROUNDS

For a truly unique experience, canoe out to one of the solitary sites on **Saranac Lake Islands,** Saranac Lake ((C) **518/891-3170;** www.dec.state.ny.us/website/do/ camping/campgrounds/saranac.html), and pitch your tent away from the crush of car campers. Sites cost $14. Open mid-May to Labor Day. **Whispering Pines Campground,** Route 73, Lake Placid ((C) **518/523-9322;** www.adirondacks.com/ whisperingpines), is a sprawling campground right on the outskirts of Lake Placid. You can set up deep inside the woods, but be prepared for loud partyers in RVs. If you're one of them, you'll love it here. Tent campers in search of a back-to-nature experience will want to look elsewhere. Tent sites are $17; water and electric hookups are $20. **Ausable Point Campground** ((C) **518/561-7080;** www.dec. state.ny.us/website/do/camping/campgrounds/ausable.html) sits on a stunning patch of land overlooking Lake Champlain with 123 sites. There's a shoreline of natural sand, and the campground borders a wildlife management area with a hiking trail. Open mid-May to mid-October, **Cranberry Lake Campground,** off Route 30 in Lake Cranberry (🕐 **315/848-2315;** www.dec.state.ny.us/website/do/ camping/campgrounds/cranberry.html), sits on a lake in one of the most undeveloped parts of the park, yet the campground is easily accessible.

WHERE TO DINE

Restaurants span the globe between romantic lakeside hideaways and busy food feasts in Lake Placid. In these parts, dining after dark isn't chic, it's just silly— with all this lakefront property, you'll want to make the most of the views.

EXPENSIVE

Averil Conwell Dining Room ★★★ AMERICAN   Like the Mirror Lake Inn it's attached to, this restaurant is upscale, traditional, classic, and unfailingly excellent. As black-tied servers scurry about, you'll be calmly ensconced in your surroundings of great lake and mountain views, a classic marble fireplace, and mahogany-paneled walls. With the spa just downstairs, a whole section of the menu is devoted to spa dining—healthy items like five-spice tofu with Oriental noodles. They're fine, but to really experience the dining room, dig into the meats, such as venison loin or filet mignon, which are fall-off-the-bone tender. You'll also find an excellent wine list.

5 Mirror Lake Dr. (inside the Mirror Lake Inn). 🕐 **518/523-2544.** Reservations recommended. Causal dress, but no blue jeans. Main courses $19–$32. AE, DISC, MC, V. Daily 5:30–9pm.

Nicola's Over Main ★★ MEDITERRANEAN   This Italian and Greek eatery not only boasts Lake Placid's best pasta, but it's *the* town scene as well. Well-dressed crowds gather around the bar in front, while the contemporary dining room bustles with a noisy gathering of locals and tourists. An open kitchen adds to the hectic pace. For some quiet, ask for a table near the window, where you'll be away from the kitchen and bar. Skip the disappointing antipasto and focus on the entrees. The tender lamb kabob is marinated and served on bruschetta with potatoes and tzatziki, but it's the pastas that are the real stars. The fresh seafood pastas are excellent: Try the calamari, sautéed with prosciutto, red onion, and tomato, in a marinara sauce and tossed with linguine. Pasta comes in three sizes; most people don't finish the large.

90 Main St., Lake Placid. 🕐 **518/523-4430.** Reservations strongly recommended in summer. Main courses $9.95–$24. AE, MC, V. Daily 5–11pm.

Richard's Freestyle Cuisine ★★★ *Finds* AMERICAN   Set right on Mirror Lake, this place is still a relative newcomer, but Richard has made his mark as one of the park's top contenders. Saying he's "twigged out," Richard sloughed off the woodsy Adirondack style of his neighbors in favor of a cleaner, more contemporary design. It's simple and understated, just like the food. Identified simply as The Soup, The Venison, The Lasagna, and so on, dishes are in reality inventive combinations of flavors that are elegantly presented. Get a table outside in the summer and enjoy the delicacies: meats are seared on the outside, tender on the inside; fish is always fresh and delicious. The oversized desserts are worth sticking around for, especially with a full moon over Mirror Lake. The Apple Charlotte, for instance, is baked buttered bread stuffed with apple compote in a pool of ginger crème anglaise.

51 Main St., Lake Placid. 🕐 **518/523-5900.** Reservations recommended. Main courses $18–$26. AE, DC, DISC, MC, V. Daily in summer 5–9:30pm; off season Wed–Mon 5–9:30pm.

The Wawbeek ★★ AMERICAN   This serene hideaway on Saranac Lake has a well-deserved reputation for outstanding food. The dining room is in the "eating cabin" of the original Great Camp, and it's heavy, rustic look includes a wooden floor and ceiling, stone fireplace, and leaded windows looking out onto the lake and mountains beyond. The food is similarly inspiring. The seasonal menu might include lamb chops Rondeau—marinated racks of lamb rolled in chopped hazelnuts and served in a pool of raspberry beurre blanc—or the Northwoods rainbow trout, brushed with infused olive oil and served in a lemon-caper butter sauce.

Panther Mountain Road, Rte. 30, Tupper Lake. ✆ **518/359-2678**. Reservations required. Main courses $19–$32. AE, DC, MC, V. Daily June–Oct 5–9pm; Nov–May Wed–Sun 5–9pm. Take Rte. 3 West to Tupper Lake until Rte. 30 and make a right. The winding driveway is on your right.

MODERATE

Great Adirondack Steak & Seafood Company ★★ STEAKHOUSE   A steakhouse and microbrewery in one—a winning combination. Right on Main Street in Lake Placid, this recently renovated restaurant comes complete with Adirondack antiques, a fireplace, large bay windows overlooking Mirror Lake, and some of the best food in town. There's nothing shocking or inventive on the menu, just very good pastas, meats, and fish. Try the rack of ribs, which comes basted with the house amber ale barbecue sauce, or the shrimp and scallops, which are simmered in a garlic cream sauce with mushrooms and shallots, topped with puff pastry. You won't be able to ignore the wonderful ales: each dish is matched with one of their house brews. The Ausable Wulff Red Ale is great.

34 Main St., Lake Placid. ✆ **518/523-1629**. Reservations not accepted. Main courses $14–$24. AE, DC, DISC, MC, V. July 4 to late Aug 8am–10pm; Sept to early July 11am–10pm.

Jimmy's 21 ★ ITALIAN   The restaurant's namesake isn't around anymore, but locals will always know this place simply as Jimmy's. The Italian food is a cut above most places in town, and the place had the bonus factor of sitting right on Lake Placid's Main Street with a view of the lake. Inside the small space, you'll find a menu that covers Italian basics well, with a special emphasis on seafood, which is often combined with the excellent pasta, such as mussels simmered in spicy marinara served over linguine.

21 Main St., Lake Placid. ✆ **518/523-2353**. Reservations not accepted. Main courses $12–$20. AE, DC, MC, V. Daily 11:30am–10pm.

INEXPENSIVE

Blue Moon Cafe ★★ *Finds* *Value* DINER   This small cafe has a loyal following that borders on the cultish. The Blue Moon is a gathering place and breakfast palace in one, patronized by locals and out-of-towners alike, who return here every time they visit the 'dacks. The reason? It may not hit you why until you start digging into the big, fluffy omelets or huge stacks of moist pancakes. Oh yes, and the coffee is amazing. Just be warned—it's easy to get hooked on this place.

46 Main St., Saranac Lake. ✆ **518/891-1310**. Omelets and sandwiches $4–$8. AE, DISC, MC, V. Mon–Fri 7am–3pm; Sat–Sun 8am–2pm.

Players Sports Bar & Grill ★ *Kids* AMERICAN   Very simply, the cheapest eats-with-a-view in Lake Placid. Set downstairs from Main Street right at water level, Players is a simply decorated place that serves up the basics as you gaze out at the water. Come here to chow on burgers, ribs, sandwiches, and salads. You'll find everything from barbecued chicken to pulled pork to hot wings and nachos.

1 Main St., Lake Placid. ✆ **518/523-9902**. Sandwiches $6–$8. AE, MC, V. Daily 11am–1am.

Backcountry Blunders

Play in the woods, but play nice. Here's how to do it:

- Don't camp within 150 feet of roads, trails, or bodies of water.
- Lean-tos are for everyone; yes, you must share!
- No outhouse? No problem: dig a hole 6 to 8 inches deep and at least 150 feet from water or campsites. Cover with leaves and soil.
- We like you smelling fresh, but no soap within 150 feet of water.
- Giardia is one bug you can avoid: Boil, filter, or treat water.
- Use only dead and down wood for fires.
- Carry out what you carry in.
- Leave wildlife and plants undisturbed—it's not nice *and* it's illegal.

LAKE PLACID AFTER DARK

There are a few fun places to grab a drink in Lake Placid. **The Dancing Bear** in the Lake Placid Hilton (© **518/523-4411**) offers live music nightly. The **Lake Placid Pub and Brewery,** 14 Mirror Lake Dr. (© **518/523-3813**), brews up some good ales (try the Ubu Ale) and offers two floors of partying. *Hint:* It's quieter downstairs. **Zig-Zags,** 134 Main St., Lake Placid (© **518/523-8221**), is a fun place to drink for the under-30 crowd. And **Rumors,** 137 Main St. (© **518/523-3611**), is the town's nightclub, where dancing lasts till the wee hours.

3 Thousand Islands

30 miles from Watertown; 90 miles from Syracuse

While everyone's heard of the 'dacks, even longtime Empire State dwellers may well stare blankly at the mention of the Thousand Islands and ask, "Is that where the salad dressing came from?" (The answer is yes.)

Salad dressing notwithstanding, there's also another group of folks—people who are absolutely passionate about the region. At first glance it's easy to see why: With hundreds of islands dotting the miles-wide St. Lawrence River, it makes for one of the most beautiful backdrops in the state. How many islands are there? Depends on whom you ask, and how they define "island." Is an island a rocky outcropping that sticks out of the water? Is it visible 365 days a year? Does there have to be vegetation on it? There's some debate; everyone agrees there are at least almost 1,000 islands; some say as many as almost 1,800. However, everyone agrees that two-thirds of these land masses belong to Canada, so there shouldn't be any international incidents. Should you cross the border to enjoy the islands? You can, but it's not necessary like at Niagara Falls—you'll find essentially the same things on either side.

The islands were carved out some 10,000 years ago, when an ancient river was forced to change course and a new channel was carved out, allowing water into area where mounds of granite had been left by a retreating glacier. Ancient people called it "The Garden of the Great Spirit," but it was those extraordinary explorers, the French, who called it the Thousand Islands.

While the region is beautiful, frankly it's not as much fun as its park neighbor to the east. First, most of the islands are privately owned—so look, but don't touch. Also, the river completely freezes over in winter as temperatures drop to

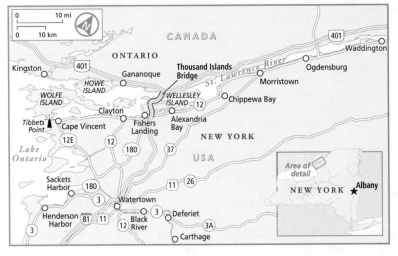

below zero, making this area essentially a summertime-only destination; most hotels and restaurants don't fully open until Memorial Day, and the season lasts just through mid-October. After that, most places close their doors and locals head to Watertown or Syracuse to work; one village on the Canadian side drops to a population of three.

You won't find mountains to climb or many trails to hike; there are no natural beaches, and few swim in the river. But the boating and fishing are unbeatable; in fact, this area offers some of the country's best fishing, with record-sized salmon and muskie just waiting to be caught.

Like the Great Camps of the Adirondacks and the heyday of Buffalo, the Thousand Islands saw its most glamorous time 100 years ago, when the Industrial Revolution created New York State millionaires who discovered the concept of leisure travel. Wealthy city dwellers would come by private rail car and be swept off by private water taxi to large, glamorous hotels. Europeans called it the Venice of the New World: People named Kellogg and Dodge owned islands, as did the founders of Neiman-Marcus and the inventor of the Lifesaver candy. They've left behind gorgeous mansions, oddly referred to as "cottages." Unfortunately, all of the classic grand hotels burned to the ground years ago and the area is now dominated by motels. The Thousand Islands current claim to fame is being the busiest freshwater shipping lane in the world.

While the Seaway Trail stretches all the way up the St. Lawrence, the heart of the Thousand Islands region is in the "tri-cities": the small towns of Cape Vincent, Clayton, and Alexandria Bay, with Alex Bay being the heart of it all.

ESSENTIALS
GETTING THERE
BY CAR I-81 shoots you north from the New York State Thruway very quickly, passing through Watertown straight up to the 1000 Islands Bridge which crosses to Canada. Watertown, 30 miles south, is the closest city to the region but is only served by **Greyhound** (✆ 800/231-2222). The terminal is at 540 State St. Otherwise, Syracuse is the closest big city, so the major airport in the area is **Syracuse**

Fun Fact   The Skinny on Salad Dressing

Yes, Thousand Island dressing did indeed originate in these here parts—to be specific, in the town of Clayton. A fishing guide named George LaLonde offered this new and unusual dressing as part of his shore dinners served after a long day of fishing. The dressing went public at the hotel that's now called the 1000 Islands Inn, and the recipe ended up in the hands of George Boldt, 1000 Islands resident and owner of New York City's Waldorf=Astoria Hotel, who put it on his hotel's menu. You can still get "original recipe" dressing at the 1000 Islands Inn: Only 5,000 bottles are produced each season and sold between mid-May and the end of September for $4.95 each.

Hancock International (① 315/454-4330), about 90 miles south, and serviced by **American Eagle** (① 800/433-7300), **Continental Express** (① 800/525-0280), **Delta** (① 800/221-1212), **JetBlue** (① 800/538-2583), **Northwest** (① 800/225-2525), **United Express** (① 800/241-6522) and **US Airways** (① 800/428-4322). Grab a rental car from **Avis** (① 800/331-1212), **Budget** (① 800/527-0700), **Enterprise** (① 800/325-8007), **Hertz** (① 800/654-3131), or **National** (① 800/227-7368).

VISITOR INFORMATION   The **1000 Islands Welcome Center,** 43373 Collins Landing, Alexandria Bay (① **800/847-5263** or 315/482-2520; www.visit1000islands.com), is your informational hub, conveniently located next to the 1000 Islands Bridge. It's open from May to mid-October, daily, from 8am to 6pm and mid-October to April, Monday to Friday, from 8am to 4:30pm.

GETTING AROUND   I-81 takes passes right through the heart of the region, and is the road to be on to cross into Canada over the 1000 Islands Bridge. Otherwise, cut off on Route 12, the road that passes through the Alexandria Bay and Clayton, becoming 12E as it follows the water down to Cape Vincent.

MUSEUMS & OTHER ATTRACTIONS

Antique Boat Museum ★★★   Boating enthusiasts simply cannot skip this museum, which contains the largest collection of inland freshwater boats in the U.S. Even people with just a passing interest in boats, or those who appreciate gorgeous woodwork will like this place. More than 200 boats grace the property, including a Chippewa dugout canoe dating from 1860 and the world's largest runabout. There are Chris Crafts and Gar Woods, 1920s racing boats, and other rare breeds. Show up in August and you can catch the antique boat show, the town's biggest event and the oldest wooden boat show in the U.S.

750 Mary St., Clayton. ① **315/686-4104.** Admission $8 adults, $4 children. Mid-May to mid-Oct 9am–5pm.

Boldt Castle ★   One of the last remaining symbols of true American grandeur in the 1000 Islands, this sprawling stone mansion built by Waldorf=Astoria Hotel owner George C. Boldt casts a regal presence over Heart Island and the shoreline of Alexandria Bay. With turrets, 365 windows, a Gaudi-like kid's playhouse, its own power house, and formal gardens, the castle and all its pieces are gorgeous—and look entirely out of place today. The home comes with a sad tale: Boldt had the castle built over the course of 4 years to give to his wife on her birthday in 1904—Valentine's Day—but she died a month before and the castle, 80% complete, was never occupied. After falling into disrepair it's been slowly restored, but by design will never be more than 80% complete. The few restored areas are gorgeous: There's an oval stained-glass window in the foyer ceiling, a formal dining room, and an impressive billiards room. But most of the house is still gutted, so you won't spend as much time as you might think during your self-guided tour. Still, bring a picnic lunch and spend some time on the 5-acre island's grounds. Then take a shuttle from Heart Island to the Yacht House and check out Boldt's amazing collection of antique wooden boats.

Heart Island. ℭ 800/847-5263. Admission is $4.75 adults, $3 children 6–12. Open Mother's Day to Columbus Day 10am–6:30pm; July–Aug 10am–7:30pm. Yacht House admission is $3 adults, $2 children; daily mid-May to Sept 10:30am–6:30pm. Uncle Sam Boat Tours, on the water in Alexandria Bay (ℭ 315/482-2611), runs a shuttle for the 10-min trip to the castle, with frequent departures from mid-May to mid-Oct for $6.75.

Remington Museum ⭐ You'd expect to find an impressive collection of Remington's Western-themed paintings and bronzes in the town he called home for many years, and fans of that genre won't be disappointed. Cowboys, Indians, and the horses they rode in on are depicted in lifelike grandeur, cast in action poses for eternity. But what makes this museum interesting is its treasure trove of work that only diehard fans know about: Remington's later-in-life Impressionist landscape paintings of his beloved New York State north country. You'll also get a look at some of the tools, furniture, and artifacts from his studio.

303 Washington St., Ogdensburg. ℭ 315/393-2425. Admission $6, senior/students $5, free for children 5 and under. May–Oct Mon–Sat 10am–5pm, Sun 1–5pm; Nov–Apr Wed–Sat 11am–5pm, Sun 1–5pm.

Thousand Islands Museum This tiny museum is only worth a half hour of time, but to anyone with an interest in the area's history, it does have some interesting displays and artifacts. You'll find remnants of the grand old Frontenac Hotel, lots of duck decoys (a tribute to the importance on hunting in the area), along with some old boats used for waterfowl hunting and fishing, as well as old lures and hooks.

312 James St., Clayton. ℭ 315/686-5794. Admission $2, seniors/students $1, free for children under 6. Mid-May to mid-Oct daily 10am–5pm.

1000 Islands Skydeck ⭐ *Kids* Every place with a view must have an observation tower, right? Even the relatively undeveloped 1000 Islands have a candy-cane-looking deck hovering high in the sky. Take the elevator up 400 feet and on a good day you'll get a 25-mile view out over the St. Lawrence River. Three decks (one of them is enclosed) let you take in the scattered islands sitting in the river. You do have to cross the Canadian border to get here, so bring your passport.

Hill Island, Lansdowne, Ontario. ℭ 613/659-2335. www.1000islandsskydeck.com. Admission C$7.95 ($5.70) adults, kids 6–12 C$4.45 ($3.20), free for children 5 and under. Daily May to late June and Labor Day to Oct 9am–6pm; late June to Labor Day 8:30am–8:30pm.

SPORTS & OUTDOOR PURSUITS

BOAT TOURS Lots of tour ships run the island circuit all summer, offering close-up views of the islands and occasionally interesting narration peppered with the standard bad jokes. Take an hour tour and you'll pass Boldt Castle (with an unlimited stop to jump off and check out the grounds), Millionnaire's Row (with amazing mansions, called "cottages"), and interesting points like **Tom Thumb Island**—the region's smallest at 3 square feet. You'll cross over into Canadian waters, pass under the international bridges, and see that some islands are just big enough for a shack, while others are up to a whopping 45 square miles in area. Go with **Uncle Sam Boat Tours,** 45 James St., Alexandria Bay (ℭ 315/482-2611), and those 12 and under will get to drive the boat for a few seconds and get a captain's license. The two-nation, 2-hour tour is $14, a 1-hour tour is $10. Uncle Sam also offers lunch and dinner cruises ($22–$30).

DIVING   Mix complicated currents and deep depths and you'll usually find shipwrecks. That's certainly true here, making it an ideal place for interesting diving. But currents that make it hard for boat captains also make it hard for divers—the waters here are Class V (out of 5)—so you should go with a guide. Jump in and explore wrecks dating to the 1700s, in water where the visibility is quite good—about 75 feet. **1000 Islands Diving Adventures,** 335 Riverside Dr., Clayton (© **877/544-4241**), offers supervised dives as well as complete packages.

FISHING   To say that the St. Lawrence is a haven for fishermen would be an understatement. The creatures that ply these waters are the main reason many people venture up this way during the season (which generally runs Apr–Nov)—it's truly a world-class area for fishing. Why? Because of areas like Henderson Trench, a glacier-cut area west of Henderson Harbor between Stony Island and Stony Point, that averages 120 feet in depth. In late summer, the waters attract mature king salmon; as they wait for their ancient call to head up the Black River to spawn and die, they pig out and grow to some 30 pounds or more. What other beasts will you encounter? In eastern Lake Ontario, you'll hook salmon, lake trout, steelhead, and walleye. On the St. Lawrence, there's walleye, pike, perch, muskellunge (get your muscles ready—these grow up to 35 lb.), and bass. In the inland waters, expect trout, walleye, muskellunge, and pike. Some of the less expensive fishing charters are out of Clayton: **Ferguson Fishing Charters** (© **315/686-3100**), **St. Lawrence Charters** (© **315/686-1216**), and **1000 Islands Fishing Charters** (© **877/544-4241** or 315/686-3030).

GOLF   The flat, lush riverside terrain makes for some nice golf courses. Play in the middle of the river out on Wellesley Island at the **Thousand Islands Country Club,** Route 100 (© **315/482-9454;** www.ticountryclub.com), which boasts two 18-hole courses; greens fees are $21 to $31 weekdays, $26 to $36 weekends. Or try the par-71 **C-Way Golf Club,** Route 12, Clayton (© **315/686-4562;** www.cwayresort.com); greens fee are $17.

KAYAKING   Get an up-close and personal tour of the islands as you skim along the surface in a kayak. With all the water traffic out here, especially the enormous tankers, it's good to go with a guide. Besides, it's easy to get lost among all the islands! Kayak past **Grass Point Marsh** and keep an eye out for wildlife as you work your way toward historic **Rock Island,** with some of the area's most beautiful cottages. Paddle through the **French Creek Wildlife Preserve** and look for birds. Or take on something seriously adventuresome and spend the day circumnavigating the region's third-largest land plot, **Grindstone Island.** Go with **T.I. Adventures,** 38714 Rte. 12E, Clayton (© **315/686-2000**), or **Whitewater Challengers** (© **315/639-6100**).

RAFTING   The 1000 Islands are home to some of the nation's most renowned white water, namely the **Black River Canyon.** From May to October, the Black gushes with pounding white water, and scores of paddlers fly down it on rafts. It's Class III and IV, which means there's some serious rollicking going on (and that you must be at least 14 years old to go). As you cruise through Rocket Ride and Knife's Edge, you'll see fabulous waterfalls cascade from the canyon walls and jump in the water at Swimmer's Rapids. Go with **Whitewater Challengers** (© **800/ 443-RAFT**); it's around $60 for a day trip. Trips depart from Black River Bay

Campground in Dexter. Or go with **ARO Adventures** out of Old Forge (℗ **800/ 525-RAFT**).

ESPECIALLY FOR KIDS

Check out the **Family Fun Park at Colonial Village** (Rte. 11B, east of Potsdam; ℗ **315/265-PARK**), with go-karts, laser tag, and a ball crawl. In the winter there's a virtual roller coaster, tubing hill, and ice skating. You can get your speed-on at **Alex Bay Go-Karts** on Route 12, a quarter mile north of the 1000 Islands Bridge (℗ **315/482-2021**). Or, get lost in the 7-foot-high hedges of **Mazeland,** also on Route 12, ¾ mile north of the bridge (℗ **315/482-2186**).

WHERE TO STAY

The old Frontenac Hotel was a 300-room grand dame patronized by Vanderbilts and President U.S. Grant at the turn of the 20th century. Unfortunately, the Frontenac and the other grand hotels were all claimed by fire, so you won't find any old classics like the Adirondacks's Sagamore. The historic properties were replaced by motels and two-story resorts, which have the benefit of being on the water, but generally promise little else. Fortunately, there are a couple of gems (reviewed below). Few spots are open year-round, and virtually all hotels require a 2-night minimum stay on summer weekends.

For chain options, you'll have to stay in Watertown, a 30-minute drive from the 1000 Islands, where you'll find a **Microtel**, 8000 Virginia Smith Dr. (℗ **800/ 447-9660** or 315/629-5000). Farther north in Ogdensburg, there's a **Quality Inn,** 6765 State Hwy. 37 (℗ **800/392-4550** or 315/393-4550), and a **Ramada,** 119 W. River St. (℗ **315/393-2222**).

EXPENSIVE

Hart House *(Finds* ★★★   Overlooking the 1000 Islands Golf Course on huge Wellesley Island, this wood-shingled inn is a luxurious getaway off the beaten track. The inn is actually what remains of a mansion where Waldorf=Astoria owner George Boldt lived while his Heart Island castle was being built. Today it boasts bright public spaces that are formal (though of course not nearly as stuffy as in the Boldt era). In the small nonsmoking rooms, you'll find nice touches like Tiffany-style lamps, propane fireplaces, and old-time radios. Opt for a room the "luxury area," which are nicer and larger, with added amenities like sleigh or canopy beds, whirlpools, skylights, and sitting areas. The Hart Room has a deck overlooking the golf course, while the Kashmir Garden Suite is one of the most romantic rooms I've seen. Dramatic without being cheesy, it has an elaborate canopy bed and huge bathroom with gorgeous hand-painted walls, whirlpool, and a propane fireplace that can be seen from both bedroom and bathroom.

P.O. Box 70, Wellesley Island, NY 13640. ℗ **888/481-LOVE.** Fax 315/482-LOVE. www.harthouseinn.com. 8 units. May–Oct $125–$295 double; Nov–Apr $115–$265 double. Rates include full breakfast. Packages available. 2-night minimum summer weekends. AE, DISC, MC, V. From I-81, take exit 51 on Wellesley Island to the stop sign and turn right. Turn left at the next stop sign. Turn right on Club Rd. **Amenities:** Free use of bikes. *In room:* A/C, some rooms with TV/VCR, hair dryer, no phone.

Riveredge ★★★   Sitting on the water in the heart of Alexandria Bay, this is the area's most luxurious accommodation, boasting two pools, a great restaurant (reviewed below), and other amenities. The very comfortable (though cookie-cutter standard) rooms, with decent-size bathrooms, are in the middle of a face-lift, as the Florida pinks and blues of the previous owners give way to creams and earthen tones of its current Kentucky owners. All are fitted with elegant blonde wood furniture and comfortable beds and balconies with water views (request one with a view of Boldt Castle). Even the Jacuzzi rooms feel elegant and not at all tacky. Standard rooms have a desk and sitting chairs; the concierge-level floors have a cool circular staircase and loft but no desk.

17 Holland St., Alexandria Bay, NY 13607. © **800/ENJOY-US** or 315/482-9917. Fax: 315/482-5010. www. riveredge.com. 129 units. Late June to late Aug weekdays $179–$253 double, weekends $238–$338 double; Sept–Oct weekdays $126–$217 double, weekend $168–$288 double; late Oct to mid-Apr weekdays $99–$149 double, weekends $132–$198 double; mid-Apr to late June weekdays $126–$217 double, weekends $168–$288 double. Packages available. 2-night weekend minimums. AE, DC, DISC, MC, V. Free valet parking. At Rte. 12 and Church St. turn left, turn right onto Walton St. and left onto Holland St. Pets allowed with a $20 fee. **Amenities:** 2 restaurants; lounge; small indoor and heated outdoor pools; tiny fitness area; 2 Jacuzzis; concierge; secretarial services; limited room service; massage (can do in-room); babysitting; concierge-level floor. *In room:* A/C, TV w/pay movies, dataport, coffeemaker, hair dryer, iron, safe.

MODERATE

Bonnie Castle ⭐ *Kids*   Don't let the name fool you: This hotel is much more Holiday Inn than castle. The grounds sit right on the water and right next to the upscale Riveredge, yet many of this hotel's basic rooms are unfortunately across the parking lot in a two-story motel-like structure. Rooms are spacious, with more comfortable furniture than you'd expect at first glance, and some even have nice touches like a wet bar or Jacuzzi. But the river-view rooms are where you want to be: right across from Boldt Castle.

Holland St., P.O. Box 219, Alexandria Bay, NY 13607. © **800/955-4511** or 315/482-4511. Fax 315/482-9600. www.bonniecastle.com. 128 units. Summer: $114–$185 double; $210–$250 suite. Off season: $49–$129 double; $88–$149 suite. Packages available. 2-night minimum in summer. AE, DISC, MC, V. **Amenities:** Restaurant; lounge; outdoor heated and indoor pool; 2 tennis courts; sauna; limited room service. *In room:* TV/VCR, fridges in some, coffeemaker, hair dryer.

Edgewood ⭐⭐ *Kids*   Recently purchased out of bankruptcy, this 40-acre waterfront property is being completely renovated, with exciting results. Set back from the road, the grounds are nice and quiet. All rooms have balconies or porches, and many look directly over the water—some people even fish from their balconies! Some rooms boast mahogany decks and cedar posts, giving an upscale, woodsy touch to the roomy but otherwise basic sleeping areas. Done in earthy greens and browns, the guest rooms are simply furnished with industrial carpeting, scratchy sofas, and wildlife stencils on the walls. But the rooms have a fine deck, so you'll hardly want to sit indoors. The Edgewood also offers a great lounge and snack bar with a huge deck overlooking the water.

Edgewood Park Rd., Alexandria Bay, NY 13607. © **888/EDGEWOOD** or 315/482-9923. www.1000islands. com/edgewood/edgewood.htm. 101 units. May–Oct and July–Aug Sun–Thurs $119–$229 double, Fri–Sat $129–$259 double; May–June Sun–Thurs $89–$189 double, Fri–Sat $99–$219 double; Sept–Oct Sun–Thurs $89–$189 double, Fri–Sat $99–$219 double. Packages available. July–Aug 2-night weekend minimum. AE, DC, DISC, MC, V. **Amenities:** 3 restaurants; 2 lounges, large outdoor pool, small exercise room, game room, limited room service. *In room:* A/C, TV, hair dryer, iron.

McKinley House ⭐⭐⭐   This old Victorian in the tiny town of Clayton was completely restored just 3 years ago, and the results are stunning, both inside and out. Turrets, round windows, and high ceilings open up the spacious rooms even more, giving them a bright and airy feel. Stained glass, hardwood floors, crystal chandeliers, and unique antiques add elegance to this three-unit property. It's formal (perhaps a bit too much so for this laid-back area) and flowery, but doesn't cross the line into froufrou.

505 Hugunin St., Clayton, NY 13624. © **866/393-8059** or 315/686-3405. Fax 315/686-5564. www.mckinley house.com. 3 units, 2 with private bathroom. $125–$145 double. Rates include full breakfast. 2-night summer weekend minimum. No credit cards. Open Memorial Day to Columbus Day. *In room:* No phone.

Pine Tree Point Resort ★ Step into the lobby of this sprawling resort and you'll feel like you're stepping back in time. That's not necessarily a good thing: This property is run by a second generation 1000 Islands family, which has kept many of the heavy antique velvet furnishings and old family photos instead of opening the place up to the light. Fortunately, the dining room and patio don't feel so dark, and some rooms have balconies for enjoying the view. Each room is slightly different, but all have a motel feel to them (some with worn vinyl furnishings, some with old TVs). The resort's location just outside of town and among the pine trees is key; if you don't have a water view, at least you look out onto the pine forest. Try to score a room with great outdoor space: 201 has a huge balcony with an amazing castle view and 311 had an enormous split-level deck. In general, go for a room in the "Chateau" or "Cliff" buildings; those rooms are newer and usually better outfitted. Cottages have knotty pine walls and kitchenettes but surprisingly not that much more space, so they don't end up being a great investment.

P.O. Box 99, Anthony St., Alexandria Bay, NY 13607. © **888/PINE-BAY** or 315/482-9911. Fax 315/482-6420. www.pinetreepointresort.com. 99 units. Mid-June to Labor Day $99–$209 double, $139 and way up cottage; mid-May to mid-June and Labor Day to Columbus Day $79–$189 double, $119 and way up cottage. Packages available. 2-night summer weekend minimum. AE, DC, DISC, MC, V. Open Mother's Day to Columbus Day. Pets allowed in some rooms. **Amenities:** Restaurant; lounge; outdoor heated pool; small exercise room; Jacuzzi; sauna; video arcade; limited room service. *In room:* A/C, TV, dataport, some with kitchenette, coffeemaker, most with hair dryer.

INEXPENSIVE

Capt. Thomson's Resort ★ Occupying the prime water-view grounds of the historic Frontenac Hotel, this two-story motel is decidedly less glamorous but offers an equally grand view. Rooms are nothing more than standard motel-type accommodations—industrial carpeting, IKEA-ish furniture, cramped bathrooms—but with historic photos on the walls. The payoff is in the views; those rooms not facing the parking lot offer picture-perfect scenes of the river and islands.

47 James St., P.O. Box 160, Alexandria Bay, NY 13507. © **315/482-9961.** Fax 315/482-5013. www.capt thomsons.com. 68 units. July–Aug Sun–Thurs $86–$179 double, Fri–Sat $96–$179 double; May–June and Sept to mid-Oct Sun–Thurs $59–$119 double, Fri–Sat $76–$129 double. Packages available. 2-night minimums during summer weekends. AE, DC, DISC, MC, V. Open May to mid-Oct. **Amenities:** Restaurant; outdoor heated pool; limited room service. *In room:* A/C, TV, 2 units with kitchenettes.

Tibbet's Point Hostel Ever stayed on the grounds of a lighthouse? Here's your chance. Set out by itself on a lonely stretch of the river, this hostel has rooms that are right beneath a lighthouse that dates from 1827. As with any hostel, it's not glamorous—single-sex rooms with bunk beds, shared bathrooms, a kitchen, and a TV room, and a couple of private rooms. It's very clean but don't expect new (or even newish furniture). Still, the location can't be beat: Walk out by the water and take in the amazing view—but take your bug repellent, too!

33439 County Rd. 6, Cape Vincent, NY 13618. © **315/654-3450.** www.hiayh.org. 26 units. $14 for AYH members, $17 for nonmembers. Maximum stay of 3 days. Open mid-May to Oct. No credit cards. From Rte. 12E in Cape Vincent, turn left on Broadway for 2½ miles. *In room:* No phone.

CAMPGROUNDS

Fortunately, some very choice properties in this region are state parklands, making for fantastic campsites with great views. One of the best options is **Long Point State Park,** 7495 State Park Rd., Three Mile Bay (© **315/649-5258**), on a long narrow peninsula facing one of Lake Ontario's bays. With 85 campsites, only 18 of them are electric, assuring a relatively peaceful experience. **Cedar**

Moments   A Fishin' Tradition

In this hugely popular fishing destination, it only makes sense that there be traditions surrounding the consumption of fish. One that began in the early 1900s is that of the shore dinner: River guides would set out in their skiffs, fish all morning, and set up on one of the islands to prepare and eat the feast. Thankfully, this tradition continues today.

Here's how it works: After a full morning of fishing, you'll stop on a deserted or nearly deserted island and relax around picnic tables as the guide sets up, starting with a fire. Traditional shore dinners begin with the guide putting sliced fat-back in the skillet—100% fat from the back of a pig. Why all fat? The grease that's rendered from the fat-back is used to fry the fish and dessert. As the fat fries, slices of bread are loaded up with sliced onion and pieces of fat and folded into a sandwich. There's your appetizer. You may also enjoy a salad (with 1000 Island dressing, of course). Meanwhile, the guide is frying up the just-caught fish, as well as cooking potatoes and corn on the cob.

As you chow on the fish, dessert preparations begin. Eggs, sugar, and cream go into a dish, along with bread that has been drying in the sun. When the mixture is thrown into the hot fat-back grease, the batter puffs up, making the French toast–like concoction resemble a puff pastry. Top it with butter, maple syrup, cream, and brandy. *Mmmm.*

Note: Most of the fishing companies mentioned in the fishing section earlier in this section offer a traditional shore dinner for an extra charge.

Point State Park, 36661 Cedar Point State Park Dr., Clayton (✆ **315/654-2522**), also offers some tent sites right on the water. Rent a cabin on the water at **Burnham Point State Park,** 34075 Rte. 12E, Clayton (✆ **315/654-2324**). The view is unbeatable, even if the cabins have bunk beds and no facilities. Also off by itself is **Association Island RV Resort and Marina,** Showshoe Road, Henderson Harbor (✆ **866/-223-2244**), which juts out into Lake Ontario. The entire island is devoted to camping, but with 300 RV sites, cottages, and a marina, you'll hardly be alone.

WHERE TO DINE
With few exceptions, restaurants here follow the hotel trend—decent and reliable without being anything fancy. And only a few are located right on the water. But these places do have personality: They're local hangouts where menus make inside jokes about residents and where most meals come with a loaf of bread for carving and a presentation of relishes that you may or may not want to spoon onto your plate. But try to at least nab one dinner on the river as the sun sets—it makes for a magical moment.

EXPENSIVE
Clipper Inn ★★ AMERICAN   Ask most locals where they go for a "night out" and they'll direct you to this building on Route 12. The nicest place not on the water, the Clipper definitely caters to a hometown crowd, with references to locals and inside jokes typed on the specials page. The dining room, while not

large, is cordoned off into more intimate sections: get a table in back, where fans and a huge canoe hang from the ceiling. It's the type of place that calls its own appetizers unnecessary, and they are, since food comes with salad, a loaf of warm bread, and the de rigueur relishes. The menu is standard American but has some dashes of brilliance: Lamb comes moist and tender, slow-cooked in a brown sauce accented with Jack Daniels, currants, and mirepoix. Shrimp and scallops in a marinara sauce with cream and a hint of brandy are served over noodles with asparagus and broccoli. Homemade desserts are good; the white chocolate raspberry bread pudding with white chocolate sauce is not to be missed. One drawback: The service, while friendly, is frustratingly slow.

126 State St., Clayton. ✆ 315/686-3842. Reservations suggested. Main courses $14–$21. AE, DC, DISC, MC, V. Early Apr to late Oct daily 5–10pm.

Jacques Cartier ★★★ FRENCH AMERICAN   One-of-a-kind culinary combinations and amazing views make for the best dining experience not only in the region but one of the best in the state. On the fourth floor of the Riveredge Hotel, this summer-only dining room is elegantly done up in flowery blues and small chandeliers. But three walls boast no decor: They're floor-to-ceiling windows, looking out onto the water and castle, which is lit at night. Go at sunset as a pianist gently tickles keys. The action in the open kitchen gets lost with the better view outdoors, but it does allow the delicious aromas to waft over the room. The food is dramatically presented by very attentive waiters in black tie. You might start with something like smoked salmon stuffed with flaky, moist lump crabmeat and drizzled with balsamic vinaigrette. Main courses have included herb-crusted rack of lamb, served over a strong and delicious tomato risotto with house-smoked caponata and baby spinach and finished with a minted rosemary demi-glace of almond apples and the thinnest of eggplant chips, and Chilean sea bass encrusted with pistachio nuts and orange zest, sautéed in butter, and finished with pineapple and carrot-juice reduction, Polynesian salsa, jasmine rice, and julienne vegetables. The very good wine list has lots of New York State wines. The only downside: inconsistent desserts that, though creative, don't live up to the rest of the menu.

At the Riveredge Hotel, 17 Holland St., Alexandria Bay. ✆ 800/ENJOY-US or 315/482-9917. Reservations recommended. Main courses $28–$35. AE, DC, DISC, MC, V. Mid-May to mid-Oct daily 6–9:30pm.

Thousand Islands Inn ★★ AMERICAN   Have dinner at the place where Thousand Island salad dressing was invented. Disregard the unattractive dark interior and the sculpted carpeting; this restaurant has some of the area's best food, and they're still inventing new dishes. You'll of course start off with a salad topped with a certain dressing. Then try the sautéed pork chops: two loin chops sautéed in butter and spices, topped with Swiss cheese and mushrooms and served flaming in brandy. Another original dish is the beef steak continental— two beef fillets, one served with a Bordelaise sauce and the other with an herbed blue cheese sauce. Venison, quail, fish, chicken, seafood (try the seafood crepes), and pastas are also on the menu. Homemade desserts finish the meal nicely.

335 Riverside Dr., Clayton. ✆ 800/544-4241 or 315/686-3030. Main courses $11–$18. AE, DC, DISC, MC, V. Mid-May to mid-Sept. Sun–Thurs 5:30–9pm, Fri–Sat 5:30–10pm; July 1 to Labor Day from 7am.

MODERATE

Captain Thomson's *Kids* ★ AMERICAN   To reach this fun floating restaurant, you have to step across the creaking docks. Inside it's dark and candlelit, but the wide open space makes it less romantic and more family-friendly. Go with the chicken tenders or order a Cajun prime rib, the crab legs, or sea scallops. There's no need for appetizers, since dinners come with bread, vegetable, baked or mashed potatoes, rice, or fries, and a tossed salad. In fact, after all that you may not have room for the entree! But for the huge appetite, or to share, nice appetizer choices include baked Brie topped with strawberry sauce and crab-stuffed mushroom caps topped with a cheese sauce.

47 James St., Alexandria Bay. ✆ 315/482-9961. Main courses $10–$19, lunch $4.50–$8. AE, DC, DISC, MC, V. Daily mid-May to mid-Oct 7am–10pm.

Cavallario's Steak House ⭐ AMERICAN   While steaks are the specialty in this large restaurant with a faux castle facade, the menu actually features only a few red meat options; the rest focuses on fish, chicken, and veal. You can even get an entire "shore dinner" brought to your table. While the standard menu offers no surprises, the well-prepared food gets high marks. You'll find sautéed honey-mustard chicken breast topped with macadamia nuts, along with fish dishes like broiled buttercrumb scrod, served with béarnaise sauce. Don't want the soup or salad? Cut expenses by ordering from the a la carte menu.

26 Church St., Alexandria Bay. ✆ 315/482-9867. Main courses $14–$20; a la carte entrees $9–$12. AE, DC, DISC, MC, V. May–Oct daily 5–10pm.

Foxy's ⭐⭐ *Finds* *Kids* AMERICAN   Another local favorite that's tucked between Clayton and Alexandria, Foxy's is the best midrange restaurant on the water and those lucky enough to find it come back year after year. Unfortunately there's very little outdoor seating, but come for the sunset outside the many windows. The food is better than the plastic tablecloths and paper napkins would suggest. Lobster bisque comes creamy, spicy, and chock-full of lobster chunks. Entrees include the predictable mix of lasagna, steak, scallops, and haddock. Dishes come simply presented but tasty. Ask about the specials, which tend to be more inventive, like a chicken breast stuffed with cheese, apples, and cranberries. Desserts are generously sized and good, like fried ice cream or turtle cheesecake.

Fishers Landing. ✆ 315/686-1191. Mother's Day to Mid Sept 11am-10pm daily. Main courses $10–$17. AE, DC, DISC, MC, V. From Rte. 12, turn west on Rte. 195, at the blinking light between Clayton and Alexandria Bay.

Sackets Harbor Brewing Company ⭐ BREWPUB   Located in a refurbished railway station of the now extinct New York Central Railroad and right on the shore of Lake Ontario, this brewpub serves up great views and good food that's complemented by fantastic home-brewed beers. Dine outside on the patio or in the dining room that's decked out in deep reds with lots of wood, brass, and ceiling fans. Sample the signature 1812 amber ale and tuck into homey pub food like honey orange pork chops, or barbecued ribs braised in the 1812 ale, brushed with a chipotle barbecue glaze, and served with garlic mashed potatoes. Lighter dishes include sesame-seared salmon, served over soba noodles and spinach in mushroom broth.

212 W. Main St., Sackett's Harbor. ✆ 315/646-2739. Main courses $11–$21. AE, DISC, MC, V. Mon–Fri noon–9pm; Sat–Sun noon–10pm; from mid-Sept to June closed Mon–Tues.

INEXPENSIVE

Aubrey's Inn ⭐⭐ *Kids* AMERICAN   This homey place with the lumpy booth seat cushions is a local fave that's hopping any time it's open. Why? Very simple: mammoth portions of good food at an unbelievable price and friendly service to boot. The only water views are of the murals on the walls, but you don't come for the ambience. You're here for the $5 heaping plate of spaghetti or the enormous pork chops or pancakes the size of manhole covers.

550 Broadway, Cape Vincent. © 315/654-3754. Main courses $5–$12. AE, DISC, MC, V. Winter daily 7am–8pm, summer daily until 9pm.

JReck's DELI   The 1000 Islands' area answer to Subway subs. Get 'em piled high with ham, corned beef, or Italian sausage and your favorite toppings, or order up a burger with sides of onion rings or macaroni salad. It's also a supercheap place to grab a breakfast egg sandwich.

29 Market St., Alexandria Bay. © 315/482-3403. Sandwiches $2–$6. Summer daily 7am–11pm, winter daily 7am–8pm.

THOUSAND ISLANDS AFTER DARK

There's not much to do here after dark, though some of the bars in Alexandria Bay hop till the wee hours. Check out **C.P. Romans,** James St. (© **315/482-7662**), the **Dockside Pub,** Market St. (© **315/482-9849**), and **Rum Runners,** 219 Holland St. (© **315/482-4511**). Or head across the river to Canada, where the **Thousand Islands Playhouse,** 690 Charles St. S., Gananonque, Ontario (© **613/382-7020**), presents dramas, musicals, and live music from May to October. Or try your luck at the **1000 Islands Charity Casino,** 380 Hwy. 2, Gananonque, Ontario (© **866/266-8422**).

13

Western New York

by Rich Beattie

For most travelers, the main draw to this swatch of New York State is tucked up in its northwest corner: world-famous Niagara Falls. The cascading cataracts draw millions of people every year, and it's a pretty cool sight, whether you're up above the 775-foot Skylon Tower or down below in the *Maid of the Mist.*

But the pummeling water isn't the only thing this part of the state has to offer. Buffalo, the area's commercial center, is its only major city. You may know it simply as the home of the chicken wing, but Buffalo is a contender for surprise city of the year. In the early 20th century, Buffalo was one of the richest cities in America, and it still harbors a wealth of architectural treasures that warrant a couple days' stay. Frank Lloyd Wright was just one architect who left his mark on the area; fans will definitely want to check out the Prairie-Style Darwin D. Martin House and Graycliff in nearby Derby. The city's also trying to forge a renaissance during economically hard times by recovering its downtown's glory days. Results are mixed, but there's a lot going on, from renovated hotels to excellent restaurants.

As for the rest of the area, maybe it's the hefty snowfall, the long winters, or something in the water, but western New York is home to some unique characters, quirky museums, and strange foods that are fun to check out.

The legacies don't end there, though. Religious pioneers and other groups have been a major factor shaping the land as well, providing more to explore. Drawn by a rural landscape and gorgeous lake, Methodists arrived in southern New York's Chautauqua in the 1860s and created what is now one of the nation's most preeminent arts retreats, Chautauqua Institution. Elbert Hubbard started a movement of craftsmen in East Aurora, just outside Buffalo, bequeathing a treasure trove of gorgeous furniture and a tradition of craftsmanship. Mediums flocked to teeny Lilydale, and now that area is the epicenter of getting in touch with the deceased. And the Amish have set up camp in a small area of the state, making for an interesting drive.

1 Buffalo

70 miles west of Rochester; 398 northwest of New York City

It's the eighth largest city in America, with more millionaires per capita than any other American city. It's an industrial hub that hosted a world's fair. The country's top architects are flocking here to design and construct landmark buildings, including the world's largest office building.

At least, this is what I'd be writing about Buffalo if it were 100 years ago. It's no secret that Buffalo has seen better days, but the legacy of its past—one that's being renovated with some modern quirks thrown in for good measure—makes Buffalo a worthwhile stop for a couple days' stay.

I grew up in nearby Rochester, and all I knew about Buffalo was that it created the chicken wing and it got more snow than anywhere else in the universe. My loss. When industrialists realized that the Great Lakes/Erie Canal/Hudson River route was the way to get things from America's heartland to Europe, it inspired a boom. And those businessmen put their money back into the city: They brought Frederick Law Olmsted, fresh off his creation of Central Park in New York City, to design Buffalo's park system. They summoned architects Frank Lloyd Wright, H. H. Sullivan, and E. B. Green to fulfill their every architectural whim for business and personal space, and many of their treasures still stand downtown.

The economy is still hurting, but Buffalo is forging ahead with renovations anyway, and the result is a couple of cool hotels and some fantastic restaurants. Though you can cover all the sites here in a couple days, it's also easy to base yourself here for exploring western New York, since the city's easy to get in and out of.

Oh, and just for the record: Chicken wings aren't the only quirky food this city created; and though the city does indeed get some 90 inches of snow each year, it also averages 85 days with temperatures over 75.

ESSENTIALS

GETTING THERE   The **Buffalo Niagara International Airport** (© 800/ FLY-BNIA or 716/630-6000; www.nfta.com/airport), 10 miles east of downtown, is served by a number of airlines including **JetBlue** (© 800/538-2580), which has lots of cheap one-way flights other parts of New York, **AirTran Airways** (© 800/ AIRTRAN), **American** (© 800/433-7300), **Continental** (© 800/525-0280), **Delta** (© 800/221-1212), **Northwest** (© 800/225-2525), **Southwest** (© 800/ 435-9792), **United** (© 800/241-6522), and **US Airways** (© 800/428-4322).

The **ITA Shuttle** (© 800/551-9369 or 716/633-8294) can take you from the airport to the downtown hotels. It's $15 per person one-way and shuttles leave every hour on the hour from 6:30am to 10pm. If you'd prefer to rent a car—and you'll need one if you want to get beyond the downtown Buffalo attractions—**Avis** (© 800/331-1212), **Budget** (© 800/527-0700), **Hertz** (© 800/654-3131), and **Enterprise** (© 800/325-8007) all have rental counters at the airport.

By car, Buffalo is reachable via the New York State Thruway (I-90).

Amtrak (© **800/USA-RAIL**) rolls into Buffalo's train station at 75 Exchange St. (at Washington St.).

Greyhound (© **800/231-2222** or 716/855-7531) and **New York Trailways** (© 800/295-5555 or 716/852-1750) make their way to the station at 181 Ellicott St. (at N. Division).

VISITOR INFORMATION   The **Buffalo Convention and Visitors Bureau,** 617 Main St. (© **800/BUFFALO;** www.buffalocvb.com), is located in the Market Arcade downtown. It's open Monday to Friday, from 8am to 5pm. Drop by and pick up brochures.

GETTING AROUND   While Buffalo has a rail and bus system, driving is still recommended. The **Metro Rail** runs along Main Street from HSBC Arena to the South Campus of the University of Buffalo, with several stops in between. Along Main Street, aboveground, it's free; once it goes underground at the Theater stop, it's $1.25 per ride (exact change not necessary). If you want a taxi, it's best to call, since they're hard to find on the street. Try **Broadway Taxi** (© **716/896-4600**).

EXPLORING THE AREA

WALK DOWNTOWN   Don't just drive by Buffalo's architectural gems. Take a couple hours and hoof it downtown to check out the sights—they are truly beautiful. Start at the E. B. Green and William S. Wicks–designed **Market Arcade** at 617 Main St., just north of Chippewa Street. Built in 1922, the arcade now houses shops, cafes, and the Visitors Center. Continue south on Main; just south of Chippewa is Green's Neoclassical, beaux arts **Buffalo Savings Bank** (1901), now the M&T Center. Continue down Main Street past **Lafayette**

(Fun Fact **Where the Buffalo Roam?**

The bushy beasts never even lived in the area. Most think the city's name comes from French explorers, who called the Niagara River "Beau Fleuve" or beautiful river. Another possibility? A mistranslation of the Indian word for "beaver," since the words are similar.

Downtown Buffalo

Buffalo
NEW YORK ★ Albany

ACCOMMODATIONS ■
Adam's Mark **9**
Doubletree by Hilton **22**
Hampton Inn **7**
Hyatt Regency **18**
The Mansion on
  Delaware **4**
Radisson Suite Hotel
Buffalo **20**

DINING ◆
Anchor Bar **23**
Bacchus **5**
Charlie the Butcher's Kitchen **14**
Cozumel Grill **2**
E.B. Green's **18**
Mothers Restaurant **3**
Pearl St. Grill & Brewery **12**
Spot Coffee **6**
Ya Ya Bayou Brewhouse **7**

ATTRACTIONS ●
Buffalo Transportation/Pierce-Arrow Museum **13**
City Hall **8**
Dun Building **11**
Ellicott Square **14**
Guaranty Building **10**
M&T Center (formerly Buffalo Savings Bank) **19**
Market Arcade **21**
Lafayette Square **17**
Liberty Bank **16**
St. Paul's Episcopal Cathedral **15**
Theodore Roosevelt National Historic Site **1**

Square and imagine the 19th-century great orators Daniel Webster and Henry Clay speaking there. Now, on summer Thursdays, there's live music here from 5 to 8:30pm. On your right is the 352-foot **Liberty Bank,** adorned with two reduced-scale replicas of the Statue of Liberty. At Church Street, on your right, is the gorgeous **St. Paul's Episcopal Cathedral.** And on your left, the **Ellicott Square** building; with 500,000 square feet, it was the world's largest office building for 16 years after it opened in 1896. Step inside to see the majestic interior courtyard with its glass roof and Italian marble mosaic floor. It's also a good place to stop and try a Buffalo's take on the roast beef sandwich, called Beef on Weck, from Charlie the Butcher Express, right in the lobby. Cut over Swan Street to Pearl Street; on your left is E. B. Green's **Dun Building,** named for Robert Dun, who founded the nation's largest credit-reporting agency, Dun & Bradstreet. Walk north on Pearl Street, and just before Church Street on your left is Louis Sullivan's stunning **Guaranty Building** from 1895, with its terra-cotta tiles. Make a left onto Eagle Street and then an immediate right on Niagara Street, down to the **Buffalo City Hall,** an Art Deco gem with a brightly colored crown. Go up to the 28th floor observation deck (free) for a great panoramic view of the city (℃ **716/ 851-5891;** Mon–Fri 8am–3pm). Continue up Court Street, make a left on to Pearl, and finish with a coffee at **Spot,** 227 Delaware Ave. (℃ **716/856-2739**), at the corner of Chippewa, where people flock at all times of day and night.

OUTDOOR PURSUITS

BOATING   Unfortunately, Buffalo doesn't have much in the way of a developed waterfront, but you can find out what Lake Erie is all about on a trip aboard the *Miss Buffalo* or *Niagara Clipper* sightseeing cruises. Narrated tours and dining cruises, which offer views of Buffalo's unique architecture, depart from the Erie Basin Marina downtown from May through October (cruise Tues–Sun). Call ℃ **800/244-8684** or 716/856-6696 (www.missbuffalo.com).

PLAYING IN THE PARKS   In Buffalo's heyday, the city hired New York Central Park designer Frederick Law Olmsted to create a parks system unrivaled at the time. That's exactly what he did. Olmsted's Buffalo system of parks and parkways was the first of its kind in the nation; it represents one of his largest bodies of work. His system now comprises 75% of the city's parkland and it's worth walking through at least a couple of them. If you only have time for one, **Delaware Park** is a 350-acre gem with wide-open spaces and quiet walkways. On some summer evenings, you can enjoy Shakespearean plays performed al fresco. The other parks are Martin Luther King, Jr., Front, South, Cazenovia, and Riverside.

SPECTATOR SPORTS

Though the city's hockey team, the Buffalo Sabres, is in danger of being sold, right now the city boasts about professional hockey and football. The **Buffalo Bills** play

---

⁄ *Fun Fact*   Sears Model Homes

Between 1908 and 1940, Sears, Roebuck and Co. sold as many as 100,000 build-it-yourself kit homes: order one up and a full 30,000 pieces, including 750 pounds of nails and 27 gallons of paint and varnish, would arrive on your plot of land. A 75-page instruction book showed you how to assemble it. One of them still stands at the corner of Jewett and Parkside, across from Delaware Park.

just outside the city in Orchard Park, 1 Bills Dr., Orchard Park (© **716/649-0015;** www.buffalobills.com). The **Sabres** play downtown at the HSBC Center, One Seymour Knox Plaza (© **716/888-4000;** www.sabres.com).

MUSEUMS

Albright-Knox Art Gallery ★★★   The gorgeous Albright-Knox is one of Buffalo's can't-miss attractions, a treasure trove of 5,000 works that should attract more attention than it does. This Greek Revival building with 18 dramatic marble columns on its facade nabs some exhibits that don't even make it to New York City. The original wing dates from 1905, but the Albright has focused on collecting more modern works for its newer wing, which opened in 1962. Gaugin, Picasso, Pollock, de Kooning, and Warhol are all represented in the permanent collection, while some artists of the moment and cutting-edge photographers have works here as well. And unlike some museums, the collection is well organized and not overwhelming. Still, plan on a half-day to take it all in—and have lunch in their excellent cafe.

1285 Elmwood Ave. © **716/882-8700.** Admission $6 adults, free for children under 12, free to all Sat 11am–1pm. Tues–Sat 11am–5pm; Sun noon–5pm.

Buffalo Transportation/Pierce-Arrow Museum ★★   In the early 20th century, the Pierce-Arrow Company was manufacturing some of America's highest high-end cars. It supplied wheels to the White House, the royal families of Japan and Saudi Arabia, and some of the wealthy local industrialists. Now this museum pulls together some of these behemoth autos in its huge open space, along with the bikes and motorcycles the company also made until the Depression helped send it spiraling downward. Perhaps most interesting, the museum broke ground in the spring of 2003 to build the only gas station designed by Frank Lloyd Wright. Built to Wright's specs, it's a filling station he designed but never realized in his lifetime.

263 Michigan Ave. (at Seneca St.). © **716/853-0084.** www.pierce-arrow.com. Admission $7. Usually open Wed–Sat noon–5pm; always call first. Closed holidays, and open only limited hours in winter.

Darwin D. Martin House ★★★   A must for any lover of Frank Lloyd Wright architecture. One of Wright's greatest works, this Prairie Style home was designed and constructed between 1903 and 1906. Wright imagined the 10,000-square-foot residence for Martin, who was one of Buffalo's wealthy industrialists and one of Wright's biggest boosters; its low-slung profile with an emphasis on the horizontal was and remains an amazing piece of architecture. A tour of the inside reveals the architect's genius for expanding spaces and hiding bookcases. A huge restoration is underway to restore all the buildings and build a new visitor center, so expect construction. Until the renovations are complete, you'll have to schedule your 90-minute tour in advance.

118 Summit Ave. © **716/856-3858.** www.darwinmartinhouse.org. Admission $10. Tours by reservation only. Oct–May weekends only; June–Sept weekends and some weekdays. From downtown, take Rte. 33 east to NY 198 west to Parkside Ave. exit, bear right off Rte. 198 onto Parkside Ave. go 2 lights to Jewett Pkwy., and turn right. Martin House is 2 blocks up at corner of Jewett and Summit.

Pedaling History Bicycling Museum ★★ *Kids*   You don't have to be a two-wheeling fanatic for the world's largest bicycle museum to grab your attention. Amid the crammed collection of historic frames and spokes, you'll find army bikes mounted with machine guns, and unique tandem bikes with side-by-side seating. You'll see folding paratrooper bikes from WWII, the only surviving floating marine bike from the 1880s, and a bicycle built for five. Families can easily

spend an hour here perusing the collection and picking the brains of the bike fanatics who run the place.

3943 N. Buffalo Rd. (Rte. 277), Orchard Park. ℂ 716/662-3853. www.pedalinghistory.com. Admission $6 adults, $5.40 seniors, $3.75 children ages 7–15. Apr–Jan 14 Mon–Sat 11am–5pm and Sun 1:30–5pm; Jan 15–Mar Fri–Mon 11am–5pm. Closed major holidays. From I-90, take exit 56, go east on Mile Strip Rd., turn right on Rte. 277, go ⅘ mile.

Theodore Roosevelt National Historic Site ☆ This mansion, the home of Roosevelt's friend Ansley Wilcox, became famous on September 14, 1901, when T. R. was sworn in as the 26th president of the United States in the home's library. Hours earlier, President William McKinley had died by an assassin's bullet, taken at the Pan-American Exposition, and Roosevelt had been summoned to Buffalo. Now the library has been re-created to reflect what it looked like on the inaugural day, and the rest of the home is an interesting glimpse into how Buffalo's wealthiest families lived. There's also an exhibit on the exposition, a fair that made Buffalo internationally renowned.

641 Delaware Ave. (between North and Allen). ℂ 716/884-0095. Admission $3. Mon–Fri 9am–5pm; Sat–Sun noon–5pm.

WHERE TO STAY

The downtown hotel scene in Buffalo is dominated by a couple of large chain hotels that serve both the convention and the visitor population. But they're by no means your only options.

Situated in a great locale, right on millionaire's row and close to downtown you'll find **Best Western on the Avenue,** 510 Delaware Ave. (ℂ **888/868-3033** or 716/886-8333), and **Holiday Inn Buffalo Downtown,** 620 Delaware Ave. (ℂ **800/HOLIDAY** or 716/886-2121). A little farther out, you'll find more options, such as **Buffalo/Amherst Courtyard by Marriott,** 4100 Sheridan Dr. (ℂ **800/321-2211** or 716/626-2300); **Holiday Inn Express & Suites,** 601 Dingens St. (ℂ **800/HOLIDAY** or 716/896-2900); and the **Travelodge/University District,** 3612 Main St. (ℂ **800/578-7878** or 716/837-3344).

EXPENSIVE

Hyatt Regency ★★★ With a prime downtown location right on Main Street, the dramatic 395-room Hyatt soars into the sky and above its competition, as the most elegant of the downtown chains. A former office building, it's now a French Renaissance–style structure—with its spectacular glass-topped lobby and sizeable rooms. Since it's connected to the convention center, it attracts a business-focused clientele, but its location makes it a great option for the leisure traveler, too. Rooms, though uniformly decorated, aren't cookie-cutter at all, since designers had to transform them from variously shaped offices. Comfy and spacious, the bedrooms have a brand-new feel to them; grab one above the 8th floor facing Lake Erie and you'll get the added bonus of a fantastic view. Their excellent steakhouse, E. B. Green's, is reviewed below.

Two Fountain Plaza, Buffalo, NY 14202. ℂ 716/856-1234. Fax 716/852-6157. www.buffalo.hyatt.com. 395 units. $160–$175 double; $199–$450 suite. Packages available, AE, DC, DISC, MC, V. Self-parking $7. **Amenities:** 2 restaurants; small exercise room; access to nearby health club; small business center; salon; limited room service; laundry service; same-day dry cleaning; executive-level rooms. *In room:* A/C, TV w/pay movies, fax (some units), dataport, coffeemaker, hair dryer, iron.

The Mansion on Delaware ★★★ *(Finds)* Buffalo's most luxurious hotel blends right in with the elegant homes on Millionaire's Row; without its tiny—and I mean tiny—sign, you'd never expect to be allowed in the door. It's also one of Buffalo's recent success stories; the 1860s building was brought back from the brink of complete collapse to become the city's swankiest place to stay. The service is excellent, and the sleekly designed (and completely nonsmoking) rooms with their very modern furniture, workstations, and amenities have attracted everyone from Hillary Clinton to Keifer Sutherland. Big bathrooms are fitted with multihead showers and whirlpool tubs; personalized stationery and business cards make for memorable touches. The "grand" rooms are larger and worth the extra money, but suites are a disappointment, a little too small for two separate rooms. My favorites: 202, a "grand" room with high ceilings and huge floor-to-ceiling bay windows; and 212, cozy and quietly situated in the back.

414 Delaware Ave., Buffalo, NY 14202. ℂ 716/886-3300. Fax 716/883-3923. www.mansionondelaware. com. 28 units. $145–$250 double. AE, DC, DISC, MC, V. Rates include continental breakfast. Free valet parking. **Amenities:** Exercise room; concierge; courtesy car within 3 miles; 24-hr. room service; laundry; same-day dry cleaning. *In room:* A/C TV/DVD, dataport, coffeemaker, hair dryer.

MODERATE

Adam's Mark ★★ You may think you've died and gone to Las Vegas when you enter the sprawling, 486-room Adam's Mark. This enormous member of the chain clearly caters to the convention crowd, with huge ballrooms and meeting spaces filled with everyone from bridge players to motivational speakers. What's the benefit to you? Since conventioneers rarely leave the hotel, the hotel offers lots of amenities, like a nice pool and exercise area. From the outside, the place looks like an East German bunker, but inside, rooms are comfortable and spacious (if bland and cookie-cutter). And though the Hyatt and Radisson occupy the best locales, this one is also central and downtown.

120 Church St., Buffalo, NY 14202. ℂ 716/845-5100. Fax 716/845-0310. www.adamsmark.com. 486 units. $69–$199 double; $160–$299 suite. AE, DC, DISC, MC, V. Valet parking $12 per day. **Amenities:** Restaurant; 2 lounges; indoor pool; exercise room; sauna; tour desk; courtesy car; small business center; 24-hr. room service; laundry; same-day dry cleaning; executive-level rooms. *In room:* A/C, TV w/pay movies, some with fax, dataport, coffeemaker, hair dryer, iron, safe in some rooms.

Doubletree by Hilton ★ Located across the street from a hospital, the hotel caters to hospital visitors and a corporate crowd, which tend to be longer-term residents. That works out perfectly for leisure travelers, since you'll get added amenities. The decor is simple and plain (think corporate monotone), but rooms are generally quite spacious. All of them have fridges and microwaves, while some have full kitchenettes. You'll also find comfy public areas like a library where you can sit and read or play board games.

125 High St., Buffalo, NY 14203. ℂ 716/845-0112. Fax 716/845-0125. $119–$149 double. AE, DC, DISC, MC, V. **Amenities:** Restaurant; small exercise room; game room; concierge; car-rental desk; courtesy car; small business center; limited room service; coin-op washers and dryers; laundry; same-day dry cleaning. *In room:* A/C, TV w/pay movies, some with fax, dataport, some with kitchenettes, fridge, coffeemaker, hair dryer, iron, safe.

Radisson Suite Hotel Buffalo ★★ The Radisson gives you plenty of living space in a superb downtown location, right on Main Street. While this property doesn't have the Hyatt's chic or its amenities, the Radisson is a worthy, affordable alternative—with an unbeatable location. The all-suite hotel offers lots of square footage, and French doors that divide the living room from the bedroom. While you're not paying for exquisite furniture or huge bathrooms, you'll still find plenty of breathing space.

601 Main St., Buffalo, NY 14203. ℂ 800/333-3333 or 716/854-5500. Fax 716/854-4836. www.radisson.com/buffalony_main. 146 suites. $169 suite. AE, DC, DISC, MC, V. Free self-parking. **Amenities:**

Restaurant; exercise room; limited room service; laundry service; same-day dry cleaning. *In room:* A/C, TV, dataport, fridge, coffeemaker, hair dryer, iron, microwave.

INEXPENSIVE

Hampton Inn ★★ *Value* The ancient Greek-style statue overlooking the pool is your first indication that this isn't your standard Hampton Inn. In fact, it's one of the nicest members of this chain I've seen. Set right in the heart of downtown's theater and nightlife area, the newly renovated building offers comfy rooms done in Hampton Inn green; they're predictably plain, but all are outfitted with free high-speed Internet access. Upgraded rooms are the shining stars of this hotel—they're enormous and come loaded with amenities such as Jacuzzis, fireplaces, and big, flat-screen TVs. And of course everyone can enjoy the Hampton Inn breakfast, which here is more like a full-blown buffet spread.

220 Delaware Ave., Buffalo, NY 14202. © **800/HAMPTON** or 716/855-2223. Fax 716/856-5221. 137 units. $99–$125 double; $129–$189 suite. Rates include breakfast. AE, DC, DISC, MC, V. **Amenities:** Indoor pool; small exercise room; Jacuzzi; small business center; coin-op washers/dryers; laundry service; same-day dry cleaning. *In room:* A/C, TV w/pay movies, dataport, some with kitchenette, coffeemaker, hair dryer, iron.

Holiday Inn, Buffalo International Airport It's the nicest of the airport hotels, and its location east of the city makes it ideal for those early-morning flights or for spending the night if you're heading east. In true airport-hotel style, it's pretty bland on the outside, but the rooms, though dressed in chain-quality furnishings, are spacious and quiet.

4600 Genesee St., Cheektowaga, NY. © **716/634-6969.** Fax 716/634-0920. www.holidayinnbuffaloairport. com. 207 units. $89–$139 double; $129–$189 suite. Packages available. AE, DC, DISC, MC, V. **Amenities:** Restaurant; outdoor heated pool; exercise room; Jacuzzi; sauna; courtesy car; limited room service; coin-op washers and dryers; laundry service; same-day dry cleaning; business-class rooms. *In room:* A/C, TV w/pay movies, dataport, coffeemaker, hair dryer, iron.

WHERE TO DINE

The home of the Buffalo wing, Buffalo is renowned for creating or passionately embracing somewhat suspect food items. Who would have thought to dump chicken wings into a deep fryer? Why, the same folks who still gravitate toward the Friday fish fry, who maintain a passion for the hot dog that borders on obsession, and who are positively mad for a homegrown concoction called Beef on Weck. Fortunately, amid the unhealthy oddities, you'll also find that some of the renovations downtown have brought about some excellent, upscale restaurants.

VERY EXPENSIVE

E.B. Green's ★★★ STEAKHOUSE Nothing comes small in the huge, spectacular Hyatt Regency, least of all in its top-notch steakhouse. Serving the best cuts of beef in Buffalo, E.B. Green's has a classy interior with a lush, sunken dining room. The hook here is that you get to pick your own piece of beef from a cart rolled up table side (you don't need to be a butcher, they'll help you choose). Sides are a la carte, as at any self-respecting steakhouse, and while the spinach is creamy and the mac-and-cheese perfectly crusted over, they're not necessary— each entree comes with salad and a choice of potato. Desserts, such the lemon-meringue and the chocolate cake, serve two.

In the Hyatt Regency, Two Fountain Plaza. © **716/855-4870.** Reservations recommended. Main courses $19–$37. AE, DC, DISC, MC, V. Daily 5–11pm.

Oliver's ★★★ CONTINENTAL A short drive from downtown, this upscale restaurant serves a less hip clientele than some of its downtown competitors, but even hipsters will want to put up with the cheesy piano bar out front. Decorated in candlelight and muted olive tones, the real show happens on your plate. You can start with a rich soup or heavy porcini gnocchi, but what you absolutely must order is the spinach loaf, a delicious garlic bread loaf filled with fresh crushed spinach. Dramatically displayed entrees then arrive; some, like the Hawaiian butterfish with peekytoe crab Rangoon, Shanghai bok choy, and lemongrass-curry sauce, are only for the more adventuresome. But its impossible to find fault with the simpler dishes; for example, the chestnut honey-glazed pork tenderloin, with brioche and applewood smoked bacon stuffing, spaghetti squash, and spiced pecans is tender and complex. Desserts also shine; the caramel apple bread pudding comes wonderfully unsoggy. One drawback: The service can be spotty.

2095 Delaware Ave. (north of Delaware Park). 🕐 **716/877-9662.** Reservations recommended. Main courses $19–$35. AE, MC, V. Mon–Thurs 5–10pm; Fri–Sat 5–11pm; Sun 4:30–9:30pm.

EXPENSIVE

Bacchus ★★★ INTERNATIONAL TAPAS   A hip new restaurant in downtown's busiest area, Bacchus lives up to the promise of its name—it's indeed a wine mecca, offering more than 200 bottles, all available by the glass. And they prove delicious accompaniments to the excellent food. Big windows look out onto the crowded sidewalks of Chippewa Street, but it's even more packed inside—on weekend evenings the noise from the crowded bar spills over into the chic candlelit dining room. Don't think regular tapas here; the plates are larger than traditional tapas (two per person will do), and trade the typical Spanish flair for a decidedly Asian one, like the seared ahi tuna, honey coconut wasabi, and sticky rice. But dishes span the rainbow of flavors, like a Maine lobster ravioli and baby spinach in brandy cream. Crowds form early, but a wait at the classy bar is hardly a bore.

54 West Chippewa St. 🕐 **716/854-WINE.** Reservations recommended. Tapas $8–$16. AE, DISC, MC, V. Tues–Thurs 5–11pm; Fri–Sat 5pm–midnight.

Mothers Restaurant ★★★ *Finds* AMERICAN   Step inside from the alleyway and you'll find a quiet, brick-wall-lined, candle-lit hideaway that every local will recommended as historic Allentown's finest. The handwritten menu boasts a suffusion of flavors and a wealth of ingredients. The grilled lamb rib chops, for example, come with an orzo, toasted almond, and caramelized onion salad and apple-pear compote. The equally complex appetizers shine, too, with offerings like potato gnocchi topped with fresh tomato sauce with mushrooms, peas, hot peppers and fresh mozzarella. Full dinners served until 3am every night make it ideal for late-night gourmet diners. Bonus: There's an outdoor patio.

33 Virginia Place (between Virginia and Allen sts.). 🕐 **716/882-2989.** Reservations accepted. Main courses $15–$25. AE, MC, V. Daily 5pm–3am.

MODERATE

Cozumel Grill MEXICAN-AMERICAN   While you won't find anything amazing on the menu, Cozumel does an above-average job with its basic burritos/taco/fajita menu. You'll often find red and blue corn tortillas, and their salsa is excellent. You can get basic steaks and burgers, but why? Their best entrees have a healthy dose of south-of-the-border flair, like the Drunken Chicken, which comes sautéed with Sauza Hornitos tequila, red and green peppers, onions, mushrooms, and sausage.

153 Elmwood Ave., between Allen and North. 🕐 **716/884-3866.** Reservations accepted. Main courses $8–$17. AE, DC, DISC, MC, V. Sun–Thurs 11am–11pm; Fri–Sat 11am–midnight.

Pearl Street Grill & Brewery ★ AMERICAN BREWPUB   One of downtown's most happening scenes, Pearl Street attracts college kids and families alike.

Set in an old warehouse with leaded windows, exposed brick, and wood beams, and low-level lights, Pearl Street is two floors of nonstop beer-pouring, food-running, and pool playing. Though the warehouse-cum-microbrewery is a stereotype by now, not all places can do it well, but Pearl Street pulls it off. The menu offer basic burgers and salads, but upgrades with tasty pasta and pizza, excellent kielbasa, and more upscale options like sesame-crusted ahi tuna. Definitely sample their beer; the Lake Effect Pale Ale and Burnie's Brown are both excellent.

76 Pearl St. at Seneca. ℂ **716/856-BEER.** Reservations accepted. Main courses $9–$18. AE, DC, DISC, MC, V. Sun–Thurs 11am–10pm; Fri–Sat noon–midnight.

Saigon Café ★★ *Finds* VIETNAMESE/THAI FUSION   Outside of the Chinese take-out shops, Asian food isn't easy to find here. Fortunately, one of the few sit-down Asian restaurants is also quite good. With a small dining room and a seasonal patio, the cafe dips from cuisines other than Vietnamese, so besides the expected dishes like the noodle soup *pho,* you'll find other standards like pad thai. But the restaurant succeeds most in its more exotic dishes: Dancing Seafood, for example, is shrimp, squid, scallops, and mussels doing a tango among lime leaves, lemongrass, peppers, onions, and a sweet, spicy sauce. Or try the caramel catfish, simmered with a spicy caramel sauce and served in clay pot topped with scallions and cilantro.

1098 Elmwood Ave. (between Forest and Bidwell). ℂ **716/883-1252.** Reservations recommended. Main courses $7–$17. AE, MC, V. Mon–Thurs 11am–10pm; Fri 11am–11pm; Sat noon–11pm; Sun noon–9pm.

Ya Ya Bayou Brewhouse ★★ NEW ORLEANS CAJUN   This hip downtown hangout serves up fresh beer and good Cajun-tinged food. Score a table in the candlelit area behind the crowded bar and next to the brewing kettles; start with the breaded oysters or hush puppies and pecan-crusted chicken fingers. Move on to a full southern menu of po' boys, catfish, chicken, or an excellent grilled pork T-bone, served with oyster cornbread stuffing, roasted sweet potato, and pan gravy. Whatever your taste, don't skip the $2 side of mac-and-cheese. If you like dark beer, don't miss Ya Ya's very flavorful "Great Satchmo" stout.

617 Main St. at Chippewa. ℂ **716/854-YAYA (9292).** Reservations recommended. Main courses $12–$22. AE, DC, DISC, MC, V. Sun–Thurs 4:30–11pm; Fri–Sat 4:30pm–midnight.

INEXPENSIVE

Anchor Bar *Overrated* CHICKEN WINGS   Okay, it's kinda cool to eat chicken wings in the restaurant where they were accidentally discovered in 1964, but the wings are nothing exceptional—after all, there's not much you can do with chicken wings but deep fry 'em and serve 'em with hot sauce, blue cheese, and celery—and there are certainly nicer places to eat them than in this divey bar. Come only if you want to pay tribute to an American culinary tradition.

1047 Main St. at North St. ℂ **716/853-1791.** Reservations not accepted. Wings are 20 for $11, 50 for $24. AE, DC, DISC, MC, V. Mon–Thurs 11am–11pm; Fri 11am–1am; Sat–Sun noon–1am.

Charlie the Butcher's Kitchen ✿ DELI   Beef on Weck is a one of those "only in Buffalo" creations, and Charlie has made the sandwich into a science—and an experience. What the heck is weck? It's short for kummelweck, a German kaiser roll sprinkled with caraway seeds and pretzel salt and baked again for several minutes until crusty. Add sliced, rare roast beef and you'll have the basic sandwich, but Charlie insists on dipping the top of the roll in au jus and adding horseradish. He's set up in the food court of the gorgeous Ellicott building downtown; grab a sandwich and enjoy the Italian mosaic floors and the skylight.

295 Main St. (in the Ellicott Square bldg.). © **716/855-8646**. Beef on Weck $4.25; other sandwiches $3–$6. AE, MC, V. Mon–Fri 11am–4:30pm.

Louie's Texas Red Hots HOT DOGS   No, the hot dog wasn't invented here, but Buffalonians have embraced it with an unequaled passion. So forget the Texas reference—this is a Buffalo institution. The dogs do taste better here (all that practice cooking 'em); at Louie's they come nicely seared and bursting with flavor. Best of all you can getcha hot dogs 24 hours a day.

2350 Delaware Ave. © **716/877-6618**. Hot dogs $1.50. No credit cards. 24 hr.

BUFFALO AFTER DARK
PERFORMING ARTS
Shea's Performing Arts Center, 646 Main St. (© **716/847-0850**), is a gorgeous former movie palace dating from 1926 and built in the style of a European opera house. It now hosts touring shows, concerts, opera, and dance performances. The **Buffalo Philharmonic Orchestra** performs at the acoustically perfect Kleinhans Music Hall, 71 Symphony Circle (© **800/699-3168** or 716/885-5000), every week from mid-September to the end of June. For theater, head to **Studio Arena,** 710 Main St. (© **800/77-STAGE** or 716/856-5650), one of the finest regional theaters in the country. Each season (Sept–Apr) features six productions.

NIGHTCLUBS & LIVE MUSIC
The bar scene is centered around two streets: the most happening is Chippewa Street, downtown, where you'll find loud bars pouring local brew Genesee and others; try the down-home **Big Shotz,** 45 W. Chippewa St. (© **716/852-7230**), and the more upscale **La Luna,** 52 W. Chippewa St. (© **716/855-1292**). Allen Street is a bit quieter, but you can also find some good bars like **Gabriel's Gate,** 45 Allen St. (© **716/886-0602**), and **Colter Bay,** at Delaware and Allen (© **716/ 882-1330**). This is also where you'll find Buffalo's gay scene, in bars like **Cathode Ray,** 26 Allen St. (© **716/884-3615**). For live music, join the slightly older set at the 450-seat music hall, the **Tralf,** 622 Main St. (© **716/851-8725**), which hosts jazz, blues, R&B, and/or rock groups several times a week; they're mostly local acts, but sometimes you'll get a national name, like Roomful of Blues. Sit at long tables to take in the show and there's a small dance space up front by the stage. The **Lafayette Tap Room,** 391 Washington St. (© **716/854-2466**), is committed to the blues and offers a full schedule of local and national acts in their small space.

2 Day Trips from Buffalo

Since it's only 70 miles or so from Buffalo to the Pennsylvania border, consider making Buffalo your base to explore the area if you don't want to stay in small towns. Niagara Falls, of course, should be one of your destinations and is discussed later, in section 5. Another thing you'll likely want to do is to take a drive either south along Lake Erie or northeast along Lake Ontario—the views out over both of these Great Lakes are spectacular. Inland, however, is a different story. Outside the city, the landscape quickly changes into rural farmland and it's not all that exciting a drive—you probably won't want to do much random exploring through the back roads. However, there's plenty worth seeing. You'll find quirky museums celebrating everything from the kazoo to Lucille Ball, one of the nation's premier educational vacation spots, and one of the state's best parks.

ESSENTIALS

GETTING AROUND A car is absolutely essential in this rural part of the state. See Buffalo section for car-rental options.

VISITOR INFORMATION The **Cattaraugus County Tourism,** 303 Court St., Little Valley (© **800/242-4569**), is open Monday to Friday from 8am to 5pm.

MUSEUMS & ATTRACTIONS

Graycliff ★★★ Any worshipper of Frank Lloyd Wright will want to make the pilgrimage to Graycliff. Set on a 70-foot cliff overlooking Lake Erie, this 1927 home that Wright built for his most generous patron, industrialist Darwin D. Martin, is set on more than 8 acres, and the two-story, 6,500-square-foot house was Martin's summer home through the mid-1940s. Full of sunlight and air, abundant in windows, long and narrow in plan, the home captures the summer light and the cool lake breezes. And the house blends into the natural landscape. It's a transitional point from Wright's earlier Prairie Style—found in Buffalo's Martin House (p. 391)—to his late concrete designs like Fallingwater in Pennsylvania. It's also a fascinating walk, even for those not familiar with Wright's work. Check out the beautiful vistas from the cantilevered balconies of the house, or just wander the gardens and wooded landscape.

6472 Old Lake Shore Rd., Derby. © 716/947-9217. $10. 1-hr. tours mid-Apr to mid-Nov Tues–Sun. Reservations required. I-90 to exit 57, Rte. 75 north to Rte. 20W, go 7 miles, turn right on S. Creek Rd. to end, turn left on Old Lake Shore Rd.

Herschell Carousel Factory Museum ★ Lovers of old carousels, bygone ages, or just exquisite woodworking shouldn't miss this museum. The world's only museum housed in an original carousel factory building, this one opened in 1915 to carve wood into fanciful carousel horses. You'll see some 20 hand-carved carousel animals and music-roll production equipment from the Wurlitzer Company. There are also two historic carousels to ride, one of which dates from 1915.

180 Thompson St., North Tonawanda. © 716/693-1885. $4. Apr–June and Sept–Dec Wed–Sun 1–5pm; July–Aug daily 11–5pm. I-290 to exit 2. Rte. 425 north for 2 miles, left on Christiana, right on Payne, left on Thompson.

Kazoo Museum ★ The enormous kazoo on the roof of this house may make you feel like you're in Oz, but this museum is one of those upstate quirks that makes this area an interesting exploration. Unless you're a kazoo fanatic—or lover of the offbeat—you probably shouldn't drive out of your way for this museum, but lovers of quirk will be in heaven. You'll find kazoos of all shapes and sizes: wooden kazoos, liquor bottle–shaped kazoos that celebrated the end of prohibition, silver and gold kazoos, and many more. Due to a recent ownership change, they stopped making kazoos on the original equipment; with any luck they'll start it up again.

8703 S. Main St., Eden. © 716/992-3960. Free admission. Tues–Sat 10am–5pm; Sun noon–5pm. Take I-90 west to exit 57A, turn left to Rt. 62, turn right.

Lucy-Desi Museum Yes, tiny Jamestown gave birth to the famous actress and comedienne Lucille Ball, and now this tiny museum celebrates her with video tributes and memorabilia. Learn how Lucy and Desi met and how they collaborated on what the museum calls "the most famous comedy series of all time." Hmm. Still, if you're a fan of *I Love Lucy* you'll love the collection of Lucy's clothes and the volumes of merchandise produced in connection with the show. If you're not a fan, skip it.

212 Pine St., Jamestown. ☎ 716/484-0800. May–Oct Mon–Sat 10am–5:30pm, Sun 1–5pm; Nov–Apr Sat 10am–5:30pm, Sun 1–5pm, weekdays by appointment. $5 for adults, seniors/children $3.50. Take I-90 to exit 59, toward Dunkirk/Fredonia, turn left onto Rte. 60/Bennett Rd., turn right onto Rte. 60N, which turns into N. Main St., turn left onto E. 2nd St.

Toy Town Museum ★★ *Kids*   The tiny town of East Aurora is where toy gurus Fisher and Price started their company. Now this small museum preserves some of America's earliest dolls and playthings, as well as some of the latest toy crazes. There's a great play space for the kids, with lots of interactive toys. But adults also love this place: Since the museum exhibits toys by decade from the early 1900s, it's easy to find trinkets from your formative years, which leads to lots of reminiscing about the toys you had and the ones you always wanted.

636 Girard Ave., East Aurora. ☎ 716/687-5151. Free admission. Mon–Sat 10am–4pm. From I-90 take exit 54, take Rte. 400 to Maple St. exit, make a right to Girard Ave., and turn left at the blinking signal.

SHOPPING

Elbert Hubbard started his furniture-building movement, and founded the Roycroft Arts and Crafts Community, more than 100 years ago in the tiny town of East Aurora; now, craftspeople carry on the fine workmanship of the Roycrofters and have made it a big business here. Browse their galleries and shops; with any luck you'll see them at work. Go to **Schoolhouse Gallery & Cabinet Shop,** 1054 Olean Rd. (☎ 716/655-4080), for some of the most beautiful works. Other

"No séances, please."

That's the sign you'll find in Lily Dale's Maplewood Hotel. If you're a follower of clairvoyance, you probably know what Lily Dale is already. For those of you who aren't in touch with the dead, around 30 registered mediums reside in this tiny Victorian enclave.

How did it happen that this small corner of the state became the centerpiece of the spiritualist movement? Was it the isolation of the frontier or just something in the water? Whatever the explanation, the three Fox sisters of sleepy Hydesville in Wayne County created an international stir in 1848 with their claims to have heard "rappings" from beyond the grave and public exhibitions of their ability to communicate with the dead. From these small beginnings the modern role of a medium evolved.

These days you can visit anytime; the town isn't much to look at, so most of the year you shouldn't bother coming unless you're getting a reading. Summer is the exception, though: From June to early September, travelers descend on the place for daily events that include meditation and healing services, clairvoyant demonstrations, and workshops. The summer of 2004 will be a big one, as it's the town's 125th summer season.

Workshops and speakers run $20 to $400, but you can watch the basic activities simply by paying the gate fee of $7. A hotel and private homes can put you up for the night, and there's camping as well. Lily Dale is 1 hour south of Buffalo. For more information, call ☎ 716/95-8721 or visit www.lilydale.org.

Fun Fact **Watching It Wiggle**

Jell-O was discovered long before Bill Cosby was born, and the world-famous dessert can trace its roots to this area—in particular, the town of LeRoy. In 1897, a local carpenter stumbled upon a fruit-flavored gelatinous dessert that his wife called Jell-O. Without the capital or experience to market it, though, he sold his patent in 1899 for the sum of $450. The dessert took off thanks to an innovative and slick marketing campaign. By 1909, the company had posted sales earnings of more than a million dollars. For the entire history—likely more than you ever wanted to know—visit the Jell-O Museum, 23 East Main St. in LeRoy (55 miles from Buffalo; © 585/768-7433). The museum is open May through October, Monday to Saturday, 10am to 4pm, Sunday 1 to 4pm.

---

craftspeople sell their work at **West End Gallery,** 48 Douglas Lane (© 716/652-5860).

For a step back in time of a different kind, visit **Vidler's 5¢ & 10¢ Store,** 676-694 Main St., East Aurora (© 877/VIDLERS). Since 1930, this quaint store has been selling candies, confections, dry goods, and knickknacks. There's even a section of the store with the original wood floors and brass cash register.

The **Amish** maintain a small enclave on the eastern border of Chautauqua County and the western border of Cattaraugus County, bisected by Route 62 in the Conewango Valley area. Drive along Route 62 and you'll run across numerous shops selling cheese, crafts, and baked goods. Shops aren't open on Sunday and they request that you not take photographs.

OUTDOOR PURSUITS

ERIE CANAL EXPERIENCES   Take a ride on the manmade water route that transformed upstate New York. Get on a boat with **Lockport Locks and Erie Canal Cruises,** 210 Market St., Lockport (© 800/378-0352 or 716/433-6155), for the 2-hour experience of being raised through the 49-foot elevation of the Niagara Escarpment in the only double set of locks on the canal (open mid-May to mid-Oct, $13). Pass under bridges, see water cascade over locks, and travel through the solid walls of the "rock cut." No, it's no speedboat ride, but for anyone who hasn't experienced going through a lock, it's pretty cool. Or go through the **Lockport Cave and Underground Boat Ride,** 2 Pine St. (© 716/438-0174). You'll walk through a 1,600-foot tunnel, blasted out of solid rock in the 1800s, then ride a boat to see the start of geologic cave formations and miner artifacts (open mid-May to Oct; $8).

PARKS   You can explore cliffs, crevices, cavernous dens, and caves of quartz in two parks with tons of the hardened rock. **Rock City,** Rte. 16 South, Olean (© 716/372-7790), open early May to end of October, is the world's largest exposure to quartz conglomerate, with gigantic rocks that climb stories high. Admission is $4.50. Native Americans used the rocks as a fortress for protection; now the narrow alleys of rock harbor wildflowers and mountain laurel. And **Panama Rocks,** Route 10, Panama (© 716/782-2845), open early May to mid-October (admission $6), is the world's most extensive outcrop of glacially cut ocean quartz conglomerate—a technical distinction, as both parks are pretty much the same. Take an hour for either. Or get out among the trees in **Alleghany State Park** (© 716/354-9121); its 65,000 acres, most of it primitive woodland, make it the largest state park in the system, with sand beaches as well as hiking and nature trails. See below for camping details.

SKIING   It's not exactly Colorado, or Vermont, or even, well, the Adirondacks. But here's where to go when you absolutely must get your schuss-on. At **Kissing Bridge,** in Glenwood (© **716/592-4963;** www.kissing-bridge.com), you'll find 36 snow-covered slopes, encompassing 700 acres of terrain and served by nine lifts. And **Holiday Valley,** in Ellicottville (© **716/699-2345;** www.holidayvalley.com), offers 13 lifts, 52 slopes spread over 1,100 acres, and a 750-foot vertical drop—so you'll get good variety no matter what kind of skiing or riding you like.

WINERIES   It's not just in the Finger Lakes region that you'll find nice upstate New York State wines. The southern shore of Lake Erie, with just a thin strip of soil suitable for grape production, has its own grape and wine heritage; the wineries makes for a fun stop-off. Check out **Johnson Estate Winery,** 8419 West Main Rd., Westfield (© **800/374-6569**); **Woodbury Vineyards,** 3230 S. Roberts Rd., Fredonia (© **888/697-9463**), and **Merritt Estate Winery,** 2264 King Rd., Forestville (© **888/965-4800**).

WHERE TO STAY
EXPENSIVE

The Roycroft Inn ★★★ *(Finds)*   Get a touch of history and a dash of artistry in your hotel stay. The small country inn in its current form was opened in 1995, but the property dates from 1895, when the Roycroft Arts and Crafts Community was founded by Elbert Hubbard. Hubbard's self-contained community supported hundreds of craftspeople, and he opened his door to those journeying to this craftsman's mecca. Common areas are intimately rustic, with lots of Roycroft originals that you're actually allowed to sit on. All rooms are nonsmoking and all are suites; though not huge, they're hardly cramped. There's a touch of history in all the guest rooms, which are outfitted with at least one original Roycroft piece, plus some reproductions: they're heavy, solid wooden pieces that lend a distinguished air to your stay. But there's nothing stuffy about the place—it's comfy and thoroughly modern, as are the sizeable bathrooms. The restaurant is fantastic and listed separately.

40 S. Grove St., East Aurora, NY 14052. © 716/652-5552. Fax 716/655-5345. www.roycroftinn.com. $120–$230 double. Rates include continental breakfast. Packages available. AE, DC, DISC, MC, V. I-90 to Rte. 400 to Maple St. exit, turn right, turn left on Main and make your first right onto South Grove St. **Amenities:** Restaurant; access to nearby health club; limited room service. *In room:* A/C, TV/VCR, dataport, hair dryer, iron.

MODERATE

Old Library ★   Located right next door to the Old Library Restaurant, a former Carnegie home, this pink house looks decidedly un-Carnegie, as it's more frilly than stately. It is an historic home, dating from 1895, though it's only been hosting guests since 1988. Beautifully decorated inside with a rich woodwork of oak, blistered maple, mahogany, and parquet floors, you'll also find stained-glass windows and tons of antiques. None of the units, however, can boast the charm of the public spaces; they are unfortunately carpeted and done in pastel colors, and the standard rooms are quite cramped. Upgrade to one of the huge suites if you can.

120 S. Union St., Olean, NY 14760. © 716/373-9804. www.oldlibraryrestaurant.com. 9 units. $75–$95 double; $125–$165 suite. Rates include breakfast. Packages available. AE, DC, DISC, MC, V. I-86 to exit 26, which leads you right onto S. Union St. **Amenities:** Restaurant; lounge; nonsmoking hotel. *In room:* A/C, TV, dataport, hair dryer.

CAMPING

Allegany State Park   With 65,000 acres, most of it primitive woodland, it's easy to find your own patch of earth. Bring a tent, drive an RV, or rent a cabin. You'll find 86 sites for tents and 144 cabins, all within an easy walk of the park's lake. Cabins are primitive, with no running water or linens, but you will find a couple cots, a fridge, and a stove.

2373 ASP, Rte. 1, Salamanca, NY 14779. ℂ **716/354-9121**. Campsites are $13 for nonelectric hookups, $19 for electric. Cabins are $36–$74 a day; from late June to late Aug you must rent for a full week ($145–$295). DISC, MC, V. Rte. 17 (Southern Tier Expressway) to exit 18 and follow the signs.

Lake Erie State Park 🌟🌟   Set on high bluffs overlooking Lake Erie, this campground is all about the view; the park features a shoreline of over three-quarters of a mile bordering the shallowest of the Great Lakes. Full of great hiking (and in the winter cross-country skiing) trails, the park is also a prime place to bird-watch: it's a natural stopping place for birds before they fly across the lake. Cabins are primitive, with bunk beds and no indoor plumbing, and you must bring your own bedding. If you can get one, grab one of the "prime" sites—these line the lake, so that your first view in the morning will be the sun rising over the water.

5905 Lake Rd., Brockton, NY 14716. ℂ **716/792-9214**. 97 campsites, $13 for nonelectric hookups, $19–$23 for electric. 10 cabins, $55–$75, from late June to late Aug you must rent for a full week ($220–$232). AE, DISC, MC, V. New York State Thruway West (I-90) to exit 59 to Rte. 60 north. Left on Rte. 5. Park is located 5 miles west of Dunkirk.

WHERE TO DINE
EXPENSIVE

Patina 🌟🌟🌟 *Finds* AMERICAN & PACIFIC RIM   What other kind of food would you look for in a converted 19th-century home but comfort food? At this rural bistro you'll get plenty of that, dining among the rich red tones of its small dining room downstairs and its sparse upstairs room. The cuisine's not all what it seems, though: The heart-warming options come with a twist. Patina doesn't just serve meatloaf, but chipotle meatloaf, with garlic mashed potatoes. You'll also find similarly adventuresome dishes like red-chile and pecan-crusted yellowfin tuna with poblano risotto.

687 Main St. (at Temple St.), East Aurora. ℂ **716/652-9008**. Main courses $15–$27. AE, DISC, MC, V. Mon–Fri 11:30am–2pm; Sun–Thurs 5–9pm; Fri–Sat 5–10pm. Rte. 400 to East Aurora exit, turn right on Main St.

Roycroft Inn 🌟🌟 AMERICAN   Like the Roycrofters who flocked to the area to make the distinctive furniture that fills the inn, the dishes are simple but well crafted. Get a table in the Larkin Room, which overlooks the serene courtyard garden. Shrimp and corn fritters come with a hot curry oil, and grilled Atlantic salmon comes with a fennel and dill cream sauce. Shrimp and scallops are sautéed with leeks, spinach, pancetta, and garlic, finished with a porcini mushroom cream sauce, and then tossed with penne pasta. And whatever you do, don't miss the Chocolate Terrine; it's chocolate mousse encased in yellow cake and chocolate butter cream, covered with a chocolate ganache. Out of this world.

40 S. Grove St., East Aurora. ℂ **716/652-5552**. Reservations requested. Main courses $13–$25; lunch $6–$13. AE, DC, DISC, MC, V. Lunch Mon–Fri 11:30am– 2pm; Sun–Thurs 5–9pm; Fri–Sat 5–10pm; Sun 10am–2pm. Take I-90 to Rte. 400 to Maple St. exit, turn right, turn left on Main and make your first right onto S. Grove St.

MODERATE

The Old Library 🌟 AMERICAN   A Carnegie library from 1910 to 1974 in tiny Olean, this gorgeous brick building now houses an excellent restaurant. Fortunately, it's held onto its book-loving roots without getting old and musty.

The interior is decorated with ornate woodwork and friezes and laden with antiques. The menu, presented as, what else?, a chapter in a book offers more than 550 wines and a wealth of food choices, everything from pastas to mahimahi to antelope. Can't decide? Consider their specialty: a seafood stew with fresh lobster, shrimp, scallops, clams, fish, potatoes, and carrots in a light cream base and served in a pumpernickel bread bowl.

116 S. Union St., Olean. ✆ 877/241-4348 or 716/372-2226. Main courses $11–$20; lunch $7–$10. AE, DC, DISC, MC, V. Sun–Thurs 11am–10pm; Fri–Sat 11am–11pm.

Portabello's NORTHERN ITALIAN   Set in tiny Olean, Portabello's is heavy on the Italian while trying to cover all its bases. In other words, you can get a good homemade gnocchi, but you can also come for chicken wings or a western New York staple, the Wednesday or Friday fish fry. The small, plainly decorated restaurant serves up some unique dishes, too, like a dandelion appetizer sautéed in garlic and olive oil, as well as a calamari steak. Most of its dishes, though, are traditional Italian staples like chicken parmigiana and shrimp marinara.

5246 Transit Rd., Depew. ✆ 716/683-0100. Main courses $7–$15. AE, DISC, MC, V. Mon–Thurs 11am–9:30pm; Fri 11am–10:30pm; Sat 3–10:30pm; Sun noon–9pm. I-90 to exit 56 and take Transit Rd. south 3 miles.

Root Five ★★ AMERICAN   There's nothing like waterfront noshing as the sun sets over Lake Erie. Set on a magical plot of land that's perfect for sunsets, this lakeside joint jumps, especially in summer, when live blues bands rock the place. The patio area was recently expanded, meaning more room to enjoy the water. With plenty of nachos and potato skins, the menu may seem like typical bar food, and much of it is, but there are upscale choices as well, such as a roast half duck with blueberry demiglaze, and seafood, their specialty, including shrimp- and crab-stuffed sole with lemon buerre blanc.

4914 Lakeshore Rd., Hamburg. ✆ 716/627-5551. Reservations accepted. Main courses $11–$18; lunch $6–$8. AE, MC, V, DISC. Daily noon–3pm and 4–10pm. Take Rte. 5 south from downtown Buffalo.

INEXPENSIVE

Ted's Jumbo Red Hots *Kids* HOT DOGS   For more than 75 years, Ted and his local chain have been perfecting the hot dog—and now his delectable dogs come regular size and foot-long, and are served plain, with cheese, and/or chili. Buffalo knows hot dogs, and they flock here to get 'em hot off the charcoal grill, often with an old-fashioned milkshake. Not into hot dogs? You can also order a burger or chicken sandwich. And with eight locations around the Buffalo area, you'll never be too far from one.

All locations open daily for lunch and dinner. 2351 Niagara Falls Blvd., Amherst (✆ 716/691-7883); One Galleria Dr., Cheektowaga (✆ 716/683-7713); 4878 Transit Rd., Depew (✆ 716/668-7533); 6230 Shimer Rd., Lockport (✆ 716/439-4386); 333 Meadow Dr., North Tonawanda (✆ 716/693-1960); 3193 Orchard Park Rd., Orchard Park (✆ 716/675-4662); 2312 Sheridan Dr., Tonawanda (✆ 716/834-6287); 7018 Transit Rd., Williamsville (✆ 716/633-1700).

3 Letchworth State Park

60 miles from Buffalo; 35 miles south of Rochester

Of all the places that call themselves the "Grand Canyon of the East," Letchworth comes closest in living up to that claim. Stretched along a thin strip of the Genesee River, this park is one of the state's best, and a destination unto itself as one of the most scenically magnificent areas in the eastern U.S.

Lush woodlands sprawl over the park's 14,350 acres, bisected by the roaring Genesee River, which cuts a gorge through it, creating all sorts of waterfalls along the way. You can get up close and personal with the falls just by driving through the park; for an even closer view, go hiking along some of the 66 miles of trails.

Stick to the southern end; as the park moves north the land flattens out and isn't that interesting or dramatic. But down south, cliffs climb as high as 600 feet; there's also wonderfully dense forest. Keep an eye out for the park's beavers, deer, eagles, hawks, river otters, and tons of birds.

ESSENTIALS

GETTING HERE   From Buffalo, take the New York State Thruway (I-90) West to Route 400 South and take the East Aurora exit. Turn left onto Route 20A East. Follow 20A to Warsaw. Make a right onto Route 19 South to Route 19A, to Denton Corners Road. Turn left on Denton Corners Road and into the park. From Rochester, take I-390 to Exit 7.

VISITOR INFORMATION   The park office at Letchworth State Park, Castile (℡ 585/493-3600), is open from 6am to 11pm year-round.

OUTDOOR PURSUITS

BALLOONING   One of the more unique ways to see this gorgeous split in the earth is from overhead in a hot-air balloon with **Balloons Over Letchworth** (℡ 585/493-3340). Float over the canyon in a seven-story hot-air balloon and look down on the many waterfalls and 600-foot cliffs. End the flight with a champagne celebration. Price is $189 per person, $199 in October when the leaves are gorgeous. Plan on 3 hours; you'll be in the air 45 minutes to an hour. Leaves from the Middle/Upper Falls picnic area.

HIKING   The park's most scenic hike is the Gorge Trail, which follows the cut of the river as it meanders through the park, creating deep cuts in the earth. It's a 7-mile trail one-way and moderately difficult, so don't do the whole thing unless you're feeling adventuresome. For an easy .75-mile hike, and one you can do with the kids, the Pond Trail takes you out to a small pond stocked with fish (no fishing—unless you have a license).

RAFTING   See the park from the bottom up, screaming as you course through the rollicking white water. Take a 5½-mile trip along the Genesee River through Class II white water with **Adventure Calls Outfitters** (℡ **888/270-2410** or 585/343-4710; www.adventure-calls.com). The trip is perfect for novices and families. You can even get out of the rafts and go body surfing at the "New Wave Rapids" or get soaking wet at the "Leap of Faith." Open April to early November, Saturday, Sunday, and holidays, $28; from June 25 to end of August, also open Tuesday to Friday, $25.

WHERE TO STAY

EXPENSIVE

Glen Iris Inn ★★★ *(Finds)*   This historic former home of William Pryor Letchworth is the only inn inside the park. Rustically formal, it's been a hotel since 1914; today it's a yellow-and-green wooden home that's been restored to its roots. Rooms are on the small side, but tastefully decorated in antiques, floral prints, and lacy table coverings. Public spaces are done with dark woods in formal Victorian style but are very cozy and comfortable. Step out onto the porch and take in the view of the Middle Falls and the rush of water, surrounded by the dense woodlands of the park. Though "lodge rooms" are more spacious, they're also more modern and bland: stay at the inn. There, the Cherry Suite is spacious and exquisite with gorgeous floors, but the real prize is the huge balcony with a view of the Middle Falls. Two huge separate homes, Caroline's Cottage and the Stone House, offer lots of space and your own swath of land in the park. A word of warning: rooms book up quickly, and up to a year in advance. The restaurant is reviewed below.

7 Letchworth State Park, Castile, NY 14427. ⓒ **585/493-2622**. www.glenirisinn.com. 24 units. $80–$170 double; $185–$285 cottage. AE, DISC, MC, V. Open Good Friday through the first week in Nov. **Amenities:** Restaurant; lounge; limited room service. *In room:* A/C, TV (VCR in lodge rooms and cottages), fridge and coffeemaker in lodge rooms and cottages, hair dryer, iron.

INEXPENSIVE

Broman's Genesee Falls Inn   This red-brick building is a decent and cheap option for staying right outside Letchworth Park. The cramped rooms are decked out in period furnishings and simple decor—hardly the lap of luxury, but they're not uncomfortable, either. Get more space by upgrading to the master suite, which gives you breathing room and, oddly, leather furniture. For even more space, the big Blue Stone House sits on its own 2½ acres and comes loaded with amenities. All units are nonsmoking. The restaurant is reviewed below.

Main and Hamilton sts., Portageville, NY. ⓒ **585/493-2484**. Fax 585/468-5654. www.10kvacationrentals. com/geneseefallsinn. 16 units. Dec–Apr $45–$55 double; Apr–Dec $55–$65 double; $125–$150 suite and home year-round. Add $10 to rates in Oct. MC, V. Pets allowed. Take Rte. 400 South to 20A East to 19A South to 436 East, just past Portageville entrance to the park. **Amenities:** Restaurant. *In room:* A/C, some with TV, some with fridges, cabins and home have full kitchens, some with coffeemakers, no phone.

CAMPING

Letchworth offers camping and cabins set deep in the woods. Unfortunately, the 270 tent and trailer sites are located at the northern end of the park, far from the falls, and are only open mid-May to late October. Some of the 82 cabins are available year-round, while others are only open April to December. The cabins range from simple, rustic one-roomers to three-room spreads with kitchens and electric heat ($29–$85 a night, 2-night minimum; slightly lower rates Sept to early June). Call ⓒ **800/456-2267** or 585/237-3303 to reserve.

WHERE TO DINE
EXPENSIVE

Glen Iris Inn ★★ *Finds* AMERICAN   Serving a small menu of classic American dishes, the Glen Iris is the area's best dining experience. Set in a formal Victorian dining room, you'll tuck into dishes like excellent sautéed pork cutlets crusted in crushed almonds, flamed in amaretto, and served with caramelized onions. Fish dishes are also delicious: sample Genesee jumbo shrimp stuffed with feta cheese, wrapped in bacon, and served over sautéed spinach in a light cream sauce. Rich desserts, such as bananas Foster and bourbon pecan pie, take the meal out on a high note.

7 Letchworth State Park, Castile. ⓒ **716/493-2622**. Reservations recommended. Lunch entrees $7.50–$10; dinner entrees $18–$23. AE, DISC, MC, V. Daily 8–10am and noon–4pm; Sun–Thurs 5–8pm; Fri–Sat 5–9pm.

MODERATE

Broman's Genesee Falls Inn ★ AMERICAN   Though the dining room's decor is as simple as the room decor, Broman's offers better-than-expected dishes at a good price. They cover the steak and pasta basics, but also do nice appetizers like seafood bisque, and tasty entrees such as broiled scallops or a chicken breast stuffed with crabmeat and shrimp.

Main and Hamilton sts., Portageville. ⓒ **585/493-2484**. Lunch $5–$8; dinner entrees $13–$21. MC, V. Daily 11am–10pm.

4 Chautauqua Institution ⭐⭐

77 miles south of Buffalo; 142 miles southwest of Rochester; 406 miles northwest of New York City.

Chautauqua Lake is more than just a gorgeous 18-mile-long body of water surrounded by woods. Every summer, thousands of people flock to this tiny section of southwestern New York State for a learning vacation at one of the nation's most renowned arts institutes: Chautauqua Institution. A learning vacation's certainly more palatable when it's set among Victorian mansions on a stunning lake amid 750 acres of beautiful wooded grounds. And this is no mere school: during its nine-week summer season, some 7,500 people are in residence here daily, taking courses in art, music, dance, theater, and foreign languages. Others flock here for lectures by leading intellectuals, and for operas and concerts. You can choose from more than 2,000 events every summer, and some 150,000 people come here to do just that. Though many guests are on the far side of 70, there are extensive programs, from sailing to dancing, for kids of all ages. Even recreational day camp is offered at the Children's School (for kids ages 3–5) and the Boys' & Girls' Club (for kids 6–15).

All this began in 1874 when two Methodists founded the institution as an educational experiment in vacation learning. It grew quickly to include academic subjects, music, art, and physical education. The Institute now boasts its own symphony, operatic, and ballet companies, and has popular entertainers perform in its 5,000-seat amphitheater.

Recreation and relaxation are an important part of the mix: Sand beaches, swimming, fishing, sailing, and watersports, and 36 holes of golf, are all on premises, as well as a gorgeous Victorian hotel with a first-class restaurant.

ESSENTIALS

THE SEASON   The 9-week summer season runs from mid-June to mid-August. Each week has a theme, which might be about governance, the Middle East, or science and ethics. Not much happens in the off season; only the library and archives are open year-round.

GETTING THERE   You'll need to drive here. Chautauqua is 70 miles from Buffalo. From the New York State Thruway (I-90), take exit 60, then Route 394 west. From the Southern Tier Expressway (I-86/Rte. 17) if eastbound, take Exit 7, then Route 33 north, and Route 394 east. If westbound, take Exit 8, then Route 394 west.

VISITOR INFORMATION   The **Chautauqua County Tourism Bureau** is located at the gates of Chautauqua Institution, Route 394 (© **800/242-4569**). For information on the Institution, call © **800/386-ARTS** or visit www.chautauqua-inst.org.

ADMISSION TO THE INSTITUTION   To get through the gates of the Institution costs $37 per day, plus another $3 if you're spending the night. (That's in addition to any hotel charges.) Your gate fee gets you into all the lectures and entertainment (with the exception of opera and theater) that you can squeeze in. You can also take a dip in the lake. Additional sporting options, of which there are many, all cost extra.

OUTDOOR PURSUITS

The grounds of the Institution have a wealth of activities, all of which cost extra beyond the gate fee. Activities include a state-of-the-art fitness center ($7 a day), a swimming pool ($2 per swim session), weeklong sailing instruction (call for rates), bike rental ($45 per week), tennis ($12–$16 per hour), and nearby golf (greens fees: $32 weekday, $40 weekend), or you could always go swimming in the lake for free.

WHERE TO STAY

Thousands of Chautauqua guests choose to stay right on the Institution's grounds in privately owned accommodations that range from quaint rooming houses and inns to luxury homes and condominiums. Some recommended properties include **The Ashland** (10 Vincent; © **888/598-5969** or 716/357-2257 [in season] or 716/837-3711 [off season]; ashlandguesthouse@yahoo.com), **The Vera** (25 S. Terrace; same contact info as the Ashland), **The Cambridge** (9 Roberts Ave.; © **716/357-3292** [May 15–Oct 15] or 727/866-7965 [Oct 22–May 1]; scluehrs@cs.com, **The Gleason** (12 N. Lake Drive; © **716/357-2595;** patricia@netsync.net), and the **Tally Ho Apartments** (16 Maris; © **716/357-3325** [May–Sept] or 954/920-2088 [Sept–May]). Rooms may be available by the day, week, and/or season and amenities run the gamut from a single bed with shared bathroom to gorgeous, fully loaded lakefront condos that go for a few thousand a week. For a complete list of accommodations, try the Institution's online "Webrevations" system, which can help match your needs with appropriate lodgings.

A few chains in the area provide basic accommodation, including: **Days Inn,** 10455 Bennett Rd., Fredonia (© **716/673-1351**); **Holiday Inn Express,** 2675 Shadyside Rd., Findley Lake (© **800/HOLIDAY**); and **Best Western,** 3912 Vineyard Drive, Dunkirk (© **716/366-7100**).

Athenaeum Hotel ★★★   A step back in time, this Victorian grand dame sits on a tree-shaded hill overlooking Chautauqua Lake on the grounds of the Institution. It's only open regularly during the Chautauqua Institute's season, (mid-June to mid-Aug), and may be open at scattered times after that until October. It's unfortunate that such a gorgeous place has such a short season: Around since 1881 (and the first hotel in the world to have electric lights), the hotel retains its grandiose lobby with soaring ceilings and old woodwork. It feels very presidential, and indeed, no less than 9 U.S. presidents have stayed here, from Grant to Clinton. Rooms have been renovated and though quite comfortable, the basic structure hasn't been changed since it was built—so don't count on tons of space, and be prepared for cramped bathrooms. But you'll want to spend your time outdoors anyway, enjoying the grounds and the lake, or just lounging on the deck under the soaring arches and pillars of the outdoor space.

P.O. Box 66, Chautauqua, NY 14722. © **800/821-1881** or 716/357-4444. Fax 716/357-4175. 156 units. $277–$401 double. Rates include 3 meals daily. AE, DISC, MC, V. Parking $5 per day, valet $5 in, $5 out. **Amenities:** Restaurant; limited room service; laundry service, dry cleaning. *In room:* A/C, TV, hair dryer, iron.

CAMPGROUNDS

Right on Chautauqua Lake, you'll find 250 campsites with 2,000 feet of lakefront at the sprawling **Camp Chautauqua,** Route 394 (© **800/578-4849** or 716/789-3435). Count on lots of RV traffic. Still, you'll be able to find a spot for yourself to pop a tent. You'll also get tons of amenities like a teen center, coin-op laundry, heated pools, and tennis.

WHERE TO DINE

In addition to meals at the glorious Athenaeum (see below), casual dining for breakfast, lunch, or dinner is available on the Institution's grounds at the **Refectory** and **Sadie J's.** In Mayville, 4 miles away, there's **The Watermark,** 188 South Erie St. (© **716/753-2900**) and **Webb's Captain's Table,** 115 West Lake

Rd., Route 394 (© **716/753-2161**) overlooking Chautauqua Lake, for American dining and **Olive's at the Country Grill,** 43 South Erie St. (© **716/573-2331**).

Athenaeum Hotel ⭐⭐ AMERICAN   Though most people who dine here are guests of the hotel, you can still enjoy a meal in this gorgeous grand hotel with a reservation and proper attire. Recently renovated, it now shimmers with a fresh coat of formal elegance. Look out onto the lake as you dine on the five-course American menu. Like the hotel, meals are very traditional, classic American dishes. You'll have a couple different appetizers, soups, and salads to choose from: you may start off with a smoked salmon or tortellini bolognese, move through soup and salad and onto a choice of four or five entrees, like a roast half duck or crab cakes a la Newport.

P.O. Box 66, Chautauqua. © **800/821-1881** or 716/357-4444. Jacket and tie required for men at dinner. Reservations required. Breakfast $15; lunch $20; dinner $33. AE, DISC, MC, V. Daily during summer season 8am–9:30am; noon–1:30pm; 5–7:30pm.

5 Niagara Falls ⭐⭐

21 miles northwest of Buffalo; 165 miles northwest of Ithaca

Okay, let's ignore the wedding and honeymoon thing for a minute and just focus on the water. It flows down the Niagara River, picking up speed as it courses along its ancient migratory pathway, reaching speeds of up to 30 mph before tumbling, hundreds of thousands of gallons at a time, over the craggy rocks of Niagara Falls. You can get the view with your toes just inches from both sets of falls, the American Falls and the Horseshoe Falls; you can also check them out from way up high, from your hotel room, or from down below, with the mist spraying up in your face.

That's the cool part of the falls. And since we share the attraction with Canada, you can take in the view from the New York side or the Ontario side. On the American side you can see the pre-falls rapids and get varied views of the water. Across the border is a gorgeous panorama of both the American Falls and Horseshoe Falls. The Canadian side is much better set up for travelers, with a wealth of hotels, restaurants, and activities that you won't find on the economically depressed American side.

Now let's get to the kitsch. Ever since two American aristocrats honeymooned here in 1801, followed by Jerome Bonaparte (Napoleon's younger brother) and his bride 3 years later, the area surrounding the falls has been a draw for elopers and honeymooners, complete with heart-shaped whirlpool tubs and mirrored ceilings, along with wax museums and souvenir shops.

That Niagara Falls still exists, and people love it: Hotel owners say the heart-shaped-tub rooms are their most popular. But it's changing. When the Canadian side opened a casino a few years ago, chain hotels came chasing the money, building high-rise properties on the most scenic land. That building frenzy is still happening: Today, the Canadian side is awash in cranes and construction—more hotels are going up, along with a second casino, scheduled to open in 2004.

In a desperate attempt to keep up, the American side just opened its own casino, but the sad truth is that Niagara Falls, New York, is full of boarded-up buildings and run-down hotels. While both sides offer falls attractions and cool water views, the Canadian side is where the fun is. Best of all, the exchange rate makes for some great deals. Bring your passport.

ESSENTIALS

GETTING THERE   Niagara Falls International Airport is for charter and cargo planes only, so plan to fly into **Buffalo Niagara International Airport** (4200 Genesee St.; ℰ **800/FLY-BNIA;** www.nfta.com). See Buffalo section for all airline listings. **ITA Shuttle** runs from Buffalo Niagara International airport to both the American and Canadian side of the falls (ℰ **800/551-9369** or 716/633-8294) five times a day. Cost is $25 per person one-way to the American side, $30 to Canadian side.

When driving from I-90, take Route 290 to Route 190 to the Robert Moses Parkway—this will put you in downtown Niagara Falls, New York, and you'll see signs for the Rainbow Bridge to Canada. The **Greyhound station** (ℰ **800/ 231-2222**) is at 343 4th St.; **Amtrak** (ℰ **800/USA-RAIL**) comes right into the Niagara Falls station at 27th Street and Lockport Road.

VISITOR INFORMATION   On the American side, the **Niagara Tourism and Convention Corporation** is at 345 Third St., Ste. 605, Niagara Falls, NY (ℰ **800/338-7890** or 716/282-8992; www.niagara-usa.com). Office hours are Monday to Friday from 8:30am to 5pm. On the Canadian side, contact **Niagara Falls Ontario Convention and Visitors Bureau,** 5515 Stanley Ave., Niagara Falls, Ontario (ℰ **800/563-2557;** www.discoverniagara.com). They're open daily, June to August 10am to 7pm, and September to May from 9am to 5pm.

Note: At press time, US$1=C$1.39.

WHEN TO GO   While hotels and restaurants stay open here year-round, several of the top falls attractions, like *Maid of the Mist* and Cave of the Winds, only operate when the ice has melted, which could be in April or as late as May. The season usually goes through October.

GETTING AROUND   A car is not essential for getting around on either side of the falls; in fact, if you're just planning on seeing the in-town attractions on either side, you'd be better off without one—traffic and parking in the summer are nightmarish, and parking at the attractions is expensive year-round. Though most attractions are fairly close to each other, you don't even have to walk: free shuttles on both sides of the falls will take you to the major hotels and the major attractions.

CROSSING THE BORDER   You can get to Canada either by driving or walking. I recommend hoofing it. The walk across the river is only a couple city blocks long and you'll get great views along the way. More importantly, you'll avoid the lineup of cars—the wait can be an hour or more in summer. Either way, be sure you have proper documentation of citizenship: a passport is best, but at least have your driver's license *and* birth certificate. Customs folks on both sides will ask why you're going, how long you'll be, and, upon your return, if you're bringing anything back with you. If you're in a car, be prepared to pop the trunk.

SEEING THE FALLS

Start off in the **Niagara Falls State Park** (ℰ **716/278-1796;** www.niagarafalls statepark.com), the oldest state park in the United States. Designed by Frederick Law Olmsted, it's also the best thing about the American side of the Falls. In

---

Fun Fact **Niagara Falls for Marilyn**

Marilyn Monroe strutted her stuff at the falls in the 1953 flick *Niagara*. The following year, visitations to the falls skyrocketed.

winter it's quiet and serene; the summer brings a crush of people. You can either walk or ride the trolley ($5 adults, $3 kids in summer, operates year-round) along its 3-mile route. Parking is $10. Walk out on to the **Observation Tower,** which stretches into the river ($1; open Apr or May–Oct).

In the park, visit **Cave of the Winds** (© **716/278-1790;** $8 adults, $7 kids), where you'll take an elevator down 175 feet and emerge onto boardwalks to walk around the base of the American Falls. They'll give you a raincoat and sandals.

Accessible from the New York Observation Tower and from the Canadian side is the famous *Maid of the Mist* boat ride (© **716/284-8897;** www.maidof themist.com; Apr or May–Oct, $11 adults, $6.25 kids). Hands down, this is the coolest way to see the falls. From up top, the water can look like a painting in slo-mo. But board this famous boat and chug upriver toward the deafening roar of both the American and Horseshoe Falls. You'll sail right up the base of both, with the mist spraying up in your face. Don't worry, they'll provide the slicker to keep you dry. The downside: The trip is only 30 minutes, and the boat will be packed.

Over on the Canadian side, the view is pure panorama and absolutely stunning. A walkway stretches along the Niagara River, offering picture-perfect view with every step. When you get out to Table Rock, take the **Journey Behind the Falls** (© **905/354-1551**). An elevator takes you down to tunnels, where you'll get to view the blur of water right behind Horseshoe Falls through little portholes cut in the rock. There's also a midfalls platform that gets you a dramatic midfalls view of Horseshoe, just off to its side. Admission is C$7.50 ($5.40).

BIRD'S-EYE VIEWS

Creating Niagara Falls's distinctive skyline is **Skylon Tower,** 52 Robinson St., Niagara Falls, Ontario (© **905/356-2651;** www.skylontower.com), the 775-foot tower that pierces the clouds. It's been shooting people up above the falls since 1965, and it's a pretty cool view. Take one of the yellow elevators up the outside of the tower (C$9.50/US$7.60 adults; C$8.50/US$6.80 seniors; C$5.50/US$4.40 children 12 and under). Helicopter tours are more expensive, but clearly provide for the most dramatic views. Go with **Niagara Helicopters,** 3731 Victoria Blvd., Niagara Falls, Ontario (© **905/357-5672;** www.niagarahelicopters.com), or **Rainbow Air,** 454 Main St., Niagara Falls, New York (© **716/284-2800**). It's about $60 per person for a quick 10-minute ride. If you prefer to stay in touch with the earth but still get an aerial view, you can go up 400 feet in a balloon that's still tethered to the ground with the **Great American Balloon Company,** Rainbow Boulevard South, Niagara Falls, New York (© **716/278-0824**).

Value **Niagara Falls Attractions Passes**

If you plan on doing several of the Falls attractions, consider buying a pass. On the American side, the Park Service's **Master Pass** (© **716/278-1796**), will gain admission to *Maid of the Mist,* Cave of the Winds, the trolley, the Aquarium, and a couple other attractions, along with tons of discounts ($28 adults, $19 for ages 6–12, free under 6). Pick up your pass at the visitor center inside the park. On the Canadian side, the **Niagara Falls and Great Gorge Pass** gets you into the Journey Behind the Falls, *Maid of the Mist,* Whitewater Walk, and the Butterfly Conservatory (plus transportation and discount coupons) for C$35 ($25) adults, C$20 ($14) children 6 to 12, 5 and under are free.

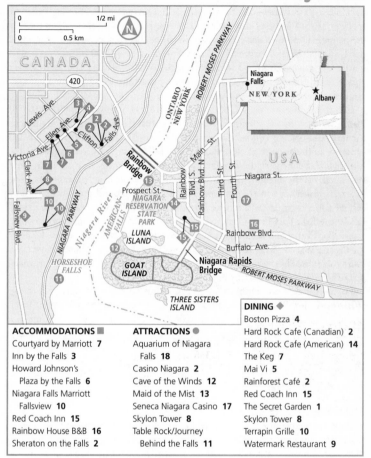

| 0 | 1/2 mi |
| 0 | 0.5 km |

ACCOMMODATIONS ■

Courtyard by Marriott **7**

Inn by the Falls **3**

Howard Johnson's
 Plaza by the Falls **6**

Niagara Falls Marriott
 Fallsview **10**

Red Coach Inn **15**

Rainbow House B&B **16**

Sheraton on the Falls **2**

ATTRACTIONS ●

Aquarium of Niagara
 Falls **18**

Casino Niagara **2**

Cave of the Winds **12**

Maid of the Mist **13**

Seneca Niagara Casino **17**

Skylon Tower **8**

Table Rock/Journey
 Behind the Falls **11**

DINING ◆

Boston Pizza **4**

Hard Rock Cafe (Canadian) **2**

Hard Rock Cafe (American) **14**

The Keg **7**

Mai Vi **5**

Rainforest Café **2**

Red Coach Inn **15**

The Secret Garden **1**

Skylon Tower **8**

Terrapin Grille **10**

Watermark Restaurant **9**

Take a 15-minute "ride over the falls" from May to October. It's $20 for adults, $10 for kids.

OTHER ATTRACTIONS

The **Whirlpool Aero Car,** 3 miles north of the falls, at 3850 Niagara Pkwy. (© **905/354-5711**), is a cable car that takes you high above the churning white water of the **Niagara Whirlpool,** created by an abrupt change in the river's direction. Admission is C$6.50 (US$4.70). The **Whitewater Walk,** 2 miles north of the falls, at 4330 Niagara Pkwy. (© **905/374-1221**), is just a walk down by the white-water rapids on a boardwalk. If you're going to skip an attraction, this would be it, especially in winter, when some of the boardwalk is closed. Admission is C$6 (US$4.30). The **Botanical Gardens,** 9 miles north of the falls (2565 Niagara Pkwy; © **905/358-0025**), boast 100 acres of formal and informal gardens, plus a **Butterfly Conservatory,** which has more than 2,000 free-flying tropical butterflies in a rainforest-like setting. Admission is C$10 (US$7.20).

On the American side, the small, year-round **Aquarium of Niagara Falls,** 701 Whirlpool St., Niagara Falls (© **800/500-4609** or 716/285-3575), lets you get up close and personal with penguins, sea lions, and sharks, among other rare species of fish. The best time to come is just before 2:30pm; that's when they feed the penguins (quite a sight). Then stay for the sea lion demonstration at 3pm. On the Canadian side, **Marineland,** 7657 Portage Rd. (© **905/356-9565;** www. marinelandcanada.com), is a lot more like SeaWorld—a huge, summertime-only park with killer and beluga whales jumping out of the water, a petting zoo, and amusement park rides.

On the American side, **Old Fort Niagara,** in Youngstown (© **716/745-7611;** www.oldfortniagara.org), is a 17th-century fort on one of the most scenic (and strategic, of course) pieces of land in upstate New York—right on Lake Ontario at the mouth of the Niagara River. The carefully arranged buildings form what's believed to the longest continuously operating fort in North America. Used by the French, British, and now Americans, it has cannons, living quarters decked out in the time period, and underground gunpowder holding rooms. On a clear day you can see Toronto. Over in Canada, **Old Fort Erie,** 50 Lakeshore Rd., Fort Erie, Ontario (© **905/871-0540;** www.oldforterie.com), is a series of flint-stone buildings 17 miles south of the falls that only saw action during the War of 1812. Interiors are reconstructed similar to Fort Niagara, with gunpowder storage, officer's quarters, and soldier's living areas giving insight into the living conditions at the time.

For a boat ride you won't soon forget, climb aboard a 48-person craft with **Whirlpool Jet Boat Tours,** 61 Melville St., Niagara-on-the-Lake, Ontario (© **905/468-4800;** www.whirlpooljet.com). Crashing along at speeds up to 65 mph, you splash along the Niagara River through the Niagara Gorge and into the Whirlpool on this 1-hour, 18-mile ride. With all the white-water splash, you'll get wet—soaking wet, actually. (Bring a complete change of clothes.) You won't see the falls on this trip, but you do get to see what happens after the water goes over the brink and through the river canyon.

SHOPPING

Yes, there are tons of souvenir shops here selling everything from commemorative spoons to snow globes. But there are a couple of things you can only get on the Canadian side, such as a Cuban cigar (which, of course, you're not supposed to bring back over the border). Lots of places sell them (you'll see the signs): One

---

(Kids   Kid Stuff in Canada's Clifton Hill

Set up to keep kids entertained all day and night, the Clifton Hill area on the Canadian side (www.cliftonhill.com) abounds with haunted houses, Disney-esque rides, and nonstop video-game action. Walk down the strip and duck into whatever grabs your attention. Put on a pair of 3-D glasses at **Ripley's Moving Theater,** 4983 Clifton Hill (© **905/356-2261**), ride the virtual roller coaster (your seat moves in sync with the roller-coaster movie). You can skip the Ripley's Believe It Or Not Museum; the **Guinness World of Records,** 4943 Clifton Hill (© **905/356-2299**), is more interesting—you'll learn useless trivia like the largest collection of naval fluff (.54 oz.). And the **Adventure Dome,** 4943 Clifton Hill (© **905/357-4330**), is a four-story screen with virtual rides on everything from a bobsled to a tank.

of the better places is **Gordon's Cigars and Pipes,** 5860 Ferry St., Niagara Falls, Ontario (℗ **905/358-7425**). His best cigars are in the back room. And for something emblazoned with the red coats of the Canadian Mounties, head to the **Mounted Police Trading Post,** 5685 Falls Ave. (℗ **800/372-0472** or 905/374-2288). If outlet malls are your thing, you have a couple of options: **Niagara Falls USA Prime Outlets,** 1900 Military Rd. (℗ **800/414-0475**), has J. Crew, Eddie Bauer, and Nine West, among others, while on the other side, head to **Canada One Factory Outlets,** 7500 Lundy's Lane, Niagara Falls, Ontario (℗ **866/284-5781** or 905/356-8989), with Club Monaco, Nike, and the Rocky Mountain Chocolate Factory—*mmmm.*

WHERE TO STAY

Accommodations range from huge chains to quaint B&Bs to disgusting motels. In general, hotels are much nicer on the Canadian side. Rates from June to August are decidedly higher than the rest of the year and fluctuate wildly depending on the particular week, if any events are in town, and of course availability. So if you call to book and the rates are astronomical, try the following week.

Both sides abound in chain hotels. On the American side, good choices include **Comfort Inn,** 1 Prospect Pointe (℗ **800/28-HOTEL** or 716/284-6835), which is superclose to the water; **Holiday Inn at the Falls,** 231 Third St., (℗ **800/955-2211** or 716/282-2211); and the **Hampton Inn,** 501 Rainbow Blvd. (℗ **800/426-7866** or 716/285-6666).

On the Canadian side: The **Quality Inn,** 4946 Clifton Hill (℗ **800/263-7137** or 905/358-3601), puts you in the middle of all the Disney-like action, as does the **Super 8,** 5706 Ferry St. (℗ **888/442-6095** or 905/356-0052). You'll also find a **Four Points Sheraton,** 6045 Stanley Ave. (℗ **800/263-2566** or 905/374-4142), and a **Best Western,** 5289 Fallsview Ave. (℗ **800/263-2580** or 905/356-0551).

EXPENSIVE

Niagara Falls Marriott Fallsview ★★★   For the most up-close and personal view of the falls, combined with luxury accommodations, this is the place to stay. Closer to the falls than anyone (just 300 ft.) and built in a curving design that allows virtually every room an unobstructed view of the falls, the hotel also boasts loads of amenities and excellent service. Even standard rooms are big with large bathrooms; upgraded rooms let you take a whirlpool bath with the falls just a glance away. With comfy beds, a spa, great restaurant (reviewed below), pool, and the best hotel falls view in town, you may never want to leave your hotel. The only annoyance: There's no parking lot, so you valet park your car whether you like it or not.

6740 Fallsview Blvd., Niagara Falls, Ontario, Canada L2G 3W6. ℗ **888/501-8916** or 905/357-7300. Fax: 905/357-0490. www.niagarafallsmarriott.com. 427 units. June–Aug C$159–C$399 (US$114–US$287) double, C$199 ($143) and way up suite; Jan–May and Sept–Dec C$99–$399 (US$71–US$287) double, C$189 (US$136) and way up suite. Packages available, AE, DC, DISC, MC, V. Valet parking C$13 (US$9.35). **Amenities:** Restaurant; lounge; large indoor pool; small exercise room; spa; 2 Jacuzzis; sauna; children's programs; game room; concierge; tour desk; courtesy car; small business center; limited room service; massage; babysitting; laundry service; same-day dry cleaning; executive-level rooms. *In room:* A/C, TV w/pay movies, dataport, minibar, coffeemaker, hair dryer, iron, safe.

Red Coach Inn ★★★ *(Finds*   Just across the street from the rapids, this 1920s-era Tudor-style hotel with a distinctive gabled roof is the most luxurious property on the American side—by a lot—and the most comfortably intimate hotel on either side. Skip the tiny standard rooms and go with a suite; these are more like apartments, with full kitchens, dining tables, comfy chairs and sofas, and tons of amenities. The guest rooms at the nonsmoking hotel are carpeted and decked out in antiques, but you won't find them stuffy or musty at all; staying here feels just like relaxing at home. In fact, there's not even a formal front desk—you just check in at the restaurant. All suites have a view of the rapids, a separate bedroom, and spacious bathrooms.

2 Buffalo Ave., Niagara Falls, NY 14303. © **800/282-1459** or 716/282-1459. www.redcoach.com. 15 units. July–Aug $139–$179 double, $189–$339 suite; Jan–Mar $89–$119 double, $129–$249 suite. Rates change monthly in spring and fall and are in between low and high. Packages available. DISC, MC, V. **Amenities:** Restaurant; lounge. *In room:* A/C, TV/VCR, dataport, kitchens (some units), fridge, coffeemaker, hair dryer, CD player, microwave.

Sheraton On The Falls ★★★ The most upscale hotel in the area is also right in the heart of the touristy Clifton Hill neighborhood. This enormous glass-walled high-rise sits directly across from the American Falls and is attached to so many family-oriented distractions—Hard Rock Cafe, Planet Hollywood, and a new amusement complex, to name a few—you may forget to leave the complex. In fact, you may be running to the spa or your room to escape the crush of people. Rooms are spacious and some even possess a feature the other upscale high-rises don't—balconies overlooking the falls. Another bonus: the spa's location lets you get a massage while overlooking the falls.

5875 Falls Ave. Niagara Falls, Ontario, Canada L2G 3K7 © **905/374-4445.** Fax 905/371-0157. 670 units. Nov–Apr C$129–C$399 (US$93–US$287); May–June and Sept–Oct C$169–C$399 (US$122–US$287); July–Aug C$179–C$499 (US$129–US$359). Packages available. AE, DC, DISC, MC, V. Valet parking C$12 (US$ 8.65) (higher in summer). **Amenities:** 4 restaurants; lounge; 2 pools (indoor, heated outdoor); health club; spa; sauna; children's programs in summer; concierge; tour desk; small business center; shopping arcade; 24-hr. room service; in-room massage; laundry service; dry cleaning; amusement park. *In room:* A/C, TV w/pay movies, coffeemaker, hair dryer, iron.

MODERATE

Courtyard by Marriott ★★ Right across the street from the HoJo's, the Courtyard offers rooms that are a little larger in a hotel that's decidedly newer and less kitschy. You'll find an upscale restaurant and large pool area, and all in the same great location—close to everything without being inside the mayhem of Clifton Hill. Rooms are spacious and simply furnished. It's great option for families; but with fireplace and Jacuzzi rooms available, it's also an affordable option for couples.

5950 Victoria Ave., Niagara Falls, Ontario, Canada L2G 3L7. © **800/321-2211** or 905/358-3083. Fax 905/358-8720. www.nfcourtyard.com. 258 units. June–Aug C$99–C$399 (US$72–US$287) double, C$159–C$399 (US$114–US$287) suite; Sept–May C$69–C$399 (US$50–US$287) double, C$99–C$399 (US$72–US$287) suite. Packages available. AE, DC, DISC, MC, V. Self-parking June–Aug C$8 ((US$5.75), other times free. **Amenities:** Indoor/outdoor pool; small exercise room; Jacuzzi; sauna; children's programs; game room; tour desk; limited room service; laundry service; coin-op laundry; same-day dry cleaning. *In room:* A/C, TV w/pay movies, dataport, coffeemaker, hair dryer, iron, safe.

Howard Johnson's Plaza by the Falls ★ *Kids* Some places consciously preserve the kitsch of the falls, but many of them are run-down motels where you wouldn't even have your mother-in-law stay. If you're looking for classic falls touches like a heart-shaped Jacuzzi tub in your room and a mirror over your bed, look no farther than Howard Johnson's Plaza by the Falls. Yes, the rooms are basic and only quasi-comfortable, but they're spacious and some even have balconies. The hotel outside may look drab, but it's filled with nice amenities and it's a short walk from Clifton Hill.

5905 Victoria Ave., Niagara Falls, Ontario, Canada L2G 3L8. © **800/446-4656** or 905/357-4040. Fax 905/357-6202. www.hojobythefalls.com. 200 units. June–Aug C$69–C$399 (US$50–US$287) double, C$159–C$399

(US$114–US$287) suite; Sept–May C$69–C$199 (US$50–US$143) double, C$99–C$399 (US$72–US$287) suite. Packages available. AE, DC, DISC, MC, V. Self-parking C$8 (US$5.75) June–Aug, other times free. **Amenities:** Food court; indoor/outdoor pool; sauna; Jacuzzi; children's programs; game room; tour desk; limited room service; laundry service; coin-op washers and dryers. *In room:* A/C, TV, coffeemaker, hair dryer, safe.

INEXPENSIVE

Inn by the Falls 🔥 *Value*   This inn offers stripped-down accommodations for travelers who don't plan on spending much time in the rooms. And though rooms are sparsely and simply furnished, they're clean and spacious. They're also in a great location; just slightly set apart from the casino and Clifton Hill, you'll be in the heart of the mayhem without being overwhelmed by it. And even though rooms are wildly cheap, you'll still find a pool and a nice courtyard area. Get a room in the back near the courtyard; those in the front can get noisy. And, for those who want to indulge in kitsch, you can get a room with a heart-shaped Jacuzzi tub.

5525 Victoria Ave., Niagara Falls, Ontario, Canada L2G 3L3. ℭ 800/263-2571 or 905/374-6040. Fax 905 /374-7715. www.innbythefalls.net. 80 units. Memorial Day to Labor Day C$79–C$189 (US$57–US$136) double, C$99–C$249 (US$72–US$179) suite; Labor Day to Memorial Day C$45–C$599 (US$32–US$72) double, C$69–C$149 (US$50–US$107) suite. Packages available. AE, DISC, DC, MC, V. **Amenities:** Outdoor pool; Jacuzzi. *In room:* TV, coffeemaker, hair dryer.

Rainbow House B&B   Staying at this small inn is like visiting your favorite grandmother's house. Owner Laura Lee's home is charmingly cluttered and extremely cheery and welcoming. The nonsmoking rooms are decked out in wicker and wood furnishings and filled with knickknacks; though they aren't huge, they all have private bathrooms. Stick with one of the standard rooms— the suite isn't worth the extra dough. Bonus: The place has a wedding chapel if you get the itch to tie the knot.

423 Rainbow Blvd. South, Niagara Falls, NY 14303. ℭ 800/724-3536 or 716/282-1135; www.rainbow chapel.com. 4 units. Rates include breakfast. MC, V. Mar–Nov $85–$150 double; Nov–Mar weekday $55–$90 double, weekend $85–$150 double. Take Robert Moses Pkwy. to Fourth St., turn right onto Rainbow Blvd. *In room:* A/C, no phone.

CAMPGROUNDS

Set right on the shore of Lake Erie, **Four Mile Creek State Park,** Lake Road, Youngstown (ℭ 716/745-3802), is a huge expanse of park with 266 campsites and great views—on a clear day you can see Toronto. Be sure to pay the $4 extra for a prime site, which puts you right on the water. There's lots of exploring to do around here: The marsh at the mouth of Four Mile Creek is home to many varieties of wildlife, like great blue herons, along with hiking trails along densely wooded bluffs.

WHERE TO DINE
EXPENSIVE

Red Coach Inn ★★★ AMERICAN   Hands down, the Red Coach is the best place to eat on the American side of the falls, and it's some of the area's best food as well. The main section of the dining room is dark, wooded, and elegant, but skip that in favor of a seat on the glassed-in patio so you can get a view of the rapids. Appetizers are worth the splurge: Start with the excellent coconut and toasted almond fried shrimp. Then move on to their specialty, red meat—from steak to veal, everything is flavorful and perfectly prepared. Not feeling extravagant? A burger's only $8.

2 Buffalo Ave., Niagara Falls, NY. ℭ 800/282-1459 or 716/282-1459. Reservations recommended. Main courses $8–$26. DISC, MC, V. Mon–Thurs 11:30am–10pm; Fri–Sat 11:30am–11pm.

Skylon Tower *(Overrated* AMERICAN   Why is it that revolving restaurants always serve up amazing views and less-than-amazing food? Sadly, the Skylon doesn't buck the trend. In 1 hour, you'll get a view of the falls for about half the time—and since they're illuminated at night, it does make for an ever-changing spectacle. The other 30 minutes are a wash, with views only of the flat Canadian landscape. And despite the high-class pretension (black-tie servers, French-named entrees, high prices), the food is frustratingly average. Skip the salads: iceberg lettuce comes mixed in with them. Entrees are a little better; a broiled salmon came nicely done, and meats are well prepared, if not the most flavorful cuts. Desserts, too, are fine, but come prepared to be underwhelmed. Or, skip the meal entirely, and come for a drink.

5200 Robinson St., Niagara Falls, Ontario. ℂ **905/356-2651**. Reservations recommended. Main courses C$25–C$44 (US$18–US$32). AE, DC, DISC, MC, V. Daily May–Aug 11:30am–2:30pm and 4:30–9:30pm; Sept–Apr 11:30am–2:30pm and 4:30–9pm.

Terrapin Grille ★★★ AMERICAN   Combining one of the best restaurants in town with the best unobstructed falls view, the Marriott Hotel's restaurant is an ideal—if pricey—fine dining experience. Yes, every table has a view of the falls, but with just one wall of floor-to-ceiling windows, obviously some tables are better than others—try to get one as close as possible to the windows. The restaurant, done in classic deep reds with low lighting, makes for a romantic experience. And the cuisine is some of the city's best, fusing traditional Italian, French, and Oriental cuisines. There are pastas on the menu, but you'll want to come for steak and/or seafood, their specialties. Consider delicious entrees such as rack of lamb crusted with Dijon mustard and fresh rosemary and served with cracked peppercorn sauce, or grilled tiger prawns, 10 jumbo prawns marinated with lemon and garlic and grilled to perfection. There's also an extensive wine list featuring area wines.

At the Marriott Fallsview, 6740 Fallsview Blvd. Niagara Falls, Ontario. ℂ **905/357-7300**, ext. 4220. Reservations suggested. Main courses C$28–C$70 (US$20–US$50). AE, DC, DISC, MC, V. Daily 7am–midnight.

Watermark Restaurant ★★★ CONTINENTAL   Lifting you up 34 stories above the falls, this modern restaurant gets you 555 feet above the gorge, about as high as you can get this close to Horseshoe Falls and still have a great meal (see Skylon Tower review, above). Floor-to-ceiling windows afford an unforgettable view. Yes, the real show happens below, with the colored lights shining on the falls, but the food's good enough to distract you. Relying on local ingredients, the chefs create memorable meals such as roasted rack of Ontario lamb, with Dijon and rosemary crust, Merlot sauce, and garlic whipped potatoes, and roasted cedar plank Atlantic salmon with Ontario maple chili glaze. Save room for the bread pudding, made with currants, nutmeg, and cinnamon and served warm with Scotch whiskey sauce.

At the Hilton Hotel, 6361 Fallsview Blvd., Niagara Falls, Ontario. ℂ **905/354-7887**. Reservations recommended. Main courses C$40–C$70 (US$29–US$50); lunch C$9–$C11 (US$6.50–US$8). AE, DC, DISC, MC, V. Daily 7am–10:30am and 11:30am–10:30pm.

MODERATE

Hard Rock Cafe *(Kids* AMERICAN   This ubiquitous and überpopular chain has hedged its bets by putting its music memorabilia–filled restaurant on both sides of the falls. In both, they serve their standard menu—an assortment of fried goods, along with chicken, pork, and rib dishes and sandwiches that are heavy on the barbecue sauce. You may find a shorter wait at the American outlet. Across the river, the Hard Rock is right next to the jam-packed casino; it's always open until 2am, making for late-night barbecue binges.

5701 Falls Ave., Niagara Falls, Ontario. ☎ **905/356-7625**. Daily 11am–2am. Also at 333 Prospect St. Niagara Falls, New York. ☎ 716/282-0007. Summer Sun–Thurs 11am–midnight, Fri–Sat 11am–1am. They close an hour earlier in winter. Reservations not accepted. Main courses at either are $10–$30. AE, DC, DISC, MC, V.

The Keg ⭐ STEAKHOUSE   This Canadian steakhouse chain feels more expensive than it is, with it's classic wood decor, relaxed setting, and stone fireplace. You might be fooled into believing it's not a chain; their food, too, is a cut above chain-restaurant cuisine. Excellent steaks are their specialty, but don't overlook the chicken and ribs. Everything comes keg-sized (in America we say "supersized") so there's no need to order appetizers. Do grab a side dish: the steamed asparagus, garlic cheese toast, and others come big enough to share.

5950 Victoria Ave., Niagara Falls, Ontario. ☎ **905/353-4022**. Main courses C$15–C$30 (US$11–US$22). AE, DC, DISC, MC, V. Daily 1pm–1am.

Rainforest Café ⭐ *Kids* AMERICAN   Family fun in a place straight out of Disney. Predictably set in the kid-centered Clifton Hill neighborhood, this outlet of the Rainforest Café chain boasts faux rain and trees with comical touches like bar stools painted to resemble animal tail-ends (complete with tails). There are endless distractions: with an 80-foot erupting volcano and a shark exhibit, it's every kid's dream come true. The food is fine and comes humorously named, like the Planet Earth Pasta and the Rumble in the Jungle turkey wrap, and it spans the range from chicken fried steak to coconut shrimp, burgers, and pizza.

5785 Falls Ave., Niagara Falls, Ontario. ☎ **905/374-4444**. Reservations recommended. Main courses C$13–$23 (US$9.35–US$17). AE, DC, DISC, MC, V. June to Labor Day daily 11am–2am; Labor Day to May Sun–Thurs 11am–10pm, Fri–Sat 11am–midnight.

INEXPENSIVE

Boston Pizza ⭐ *Kids* PIZZA   Games, games, and more games. Oh yeah, and food. Boston Pizza combines every video game on earth with a restaurant under the same roof. Right in the heart of the Clifton Hill action, the place runs on its own pace, which is usually fast forward. Kids pour into the video game area nonstop, returning to their tables for a bite of burger. Adults crowd around the noisy bar to watch sports on the many TVs. Food-wise, most folks come for the pizza, with more than 20 specialties.

4950 Clifton Hill, Niagara Falls, Ontario. ☎ **905/358-2750**. Main courses C$9–C$15 (US$6.45–US$11). AE, DC, DISC, MC, V. Daily 11am–2am.

Mai Vi ⭐ VIETNAMESE   Serving the best Asian food in the area, this small Vietnamese restaurant in the heavily trafficked tourist area doesn't feel touristy at all. With a storefront facade and a simple design, the emphasis here is on fresh ingredients in traditional Vietnamese dishes. The *pho* (noodle soup) comes stocked with goodies, and the spring rolls are full of garlic-marinated shrimp, pork, and vermicelli, and peanut sauce. The crispy duck is fantastic.

5713 Victoria Ave., Niagara Falls, Ontario. ☎ **905/358-0697**. Main courses C$8–C$13 (US$5.65–US$9.35). AE, MC, V. Sun–Thurs 11am–10pm; Fri–Sat 11am–11pm.

The Secret Garden ITALIAN AMERICAN   Hardly a secret, since this restaurant, oft frequented by large tour groups, is front and center on River Road, overlooking the falls. There is a beautiful garden outside; unfortunately you can't see it from inside the restaurant. In fact, one wall of windows just gives you a view of the gift shop. The other windows do give you a good view of the

---

Moments **A Little Peace, Please**

It's not easy to escape the crush of people jostling for prime viewing space next to the falls. But there are a couple of places where you can escape the major crowds.

On the American side, head to **Three Sisters Islands,** tiny islands that jut out from Goat Island. You'll be close enough to the swirling rapids to dip your toes in, and looking out over the rapids it's easy to forget all the people behind you.

On the Canadian side, head to **Navy Island,** located opposite Ussher's Creek in Chippawa, at the northern tip of Grand Island, closest to the Canadian shore. Home to French, Brits, and Canadian rebels and farmers, Navy Island was considered for both the 1960 World's Fair and the home of the United Nations. Neither came to fruition. Now it's home to many species of wildlife, including deer. It's a popular spot for fishermen, nature lovers, bird-watchers, and campers. The terrain is lush with vegetation even wild raspberries and grapes. There are also a variety of trees, pawpaw, oak, hickory, and blue beech. Be aware however when venturing out as the island is also loaded with poison ivy.

---

falls, but only come here during the summer months, when you can sit outside and take in the view of the falls from the patio. The view almost makes up for the predictable and very average menu of salads, sandwiches, and pastas.

5827 River Rd., Niagara Falls, Ontario. © 905/358-4588. Reservations suggested. Lunch C$7–C$15 (US$5–US$11); dinner main courses C$10–C$20 (US$7.20–US$14). AE, DC, DISC, MC, V. May–Oct daily 8am–11pm; Nov–Apr daily 8am–8pm.

NIAGARA FALLS AFTER DARK

CASINOS In 2002, **Seneca Niagara Casino,** 310 Fourth St., Niagara Falls (© 877/8-SENECA or 716/299-1100), opened on the American side, operated by the Seneca Indians in the old airplane hangar–like convention center. Over the river, **Casino Niagara,** 5705 Falls Ave., Niagara Falls, Ontario (© 888/946-3255), has been open for several years, and a second, superhuge casino is scheduled to open in the spring of 2004. Both the Americans and Canadians have ubiquitous slots, as well as blackjack, craps, roulette, music, bars, restaurants, and nonstop action.

NIGHTCLUBS The drinking age in Canada is 19, so Canadian and American youth make good use of it, to such a degree that the only place you'll find any nightlife is on the Canadian side. Most clubs there cater to the younger (read: much younger) set. **Pumps Nightclub & Patio,** 5815 Victoria Ave. (© 905/371-8646), offers a great outdoor space for those hot summer nights. **Rumours Night Club,** 4960 Clifton Hill (© 905/358-6152), is smack in the middle of the tourist district and regularly sees lines out the door. **Club Rialto,** 5875 Victoria Ave. (© 905/356-5646), is the one place in town that caters to an over-30 crowd, with music that's a little less hip-hop and a little more Billy Joel.

Index

Frommer's®

WITH KIDS

Traveling with kids ages 2 to 14 has never been this easy!

Frommer's Chicago with Kids
Frommer's Las Vegas with Kids
Frommer's New York City with Kids
Frommer's Ottawa with Kids

Frommer's San Francisco with Kids
Frommer's Toronto with Kids
Frommer's Vancouver with Kids
Frommer's Washington, D.C. with Kids

"Every page of this comprehensive book is full of tips."
—*Parenting*

Available at bookstores everywhere.

FROMMER'S® COMPLETE TRAVEL GUIDES

Alaska
Alaska Cruises & Ports of Call
Amsterdam
Argentina & Chile
Arizona
Atlanta
Australia
Austria
Bahamas
Barcelona, Madrid & Seville
Beijing
Belgium, Holland & Luxembourg
Bermuda
Boston
Brazil
British Columbia & the Canadian
   Rockies
Brussels & Bruges
Budapest & the Best of Hungary
California
Canada
Cancún, Cozumel & the Yucatán
Cape Cod, Nantucket & Martha's
   Vineyard
Caribbean
Caribbean Cruises & Ports of Call
Caribbean Ports of Call
Carolinas & Georgia
Chicago
China
Colorado
Costa Rica
Cuba
Denmark
Denver, Boulder & Colorado Springs
England
Europe
European Cruises & Ports of Call

Florida
France
Germany
Great Britain
Greece
Greek Islands
Hawaii
Hong Kong
Honolulu, Waikiki & Oahu
Ireland
Israel
Italy
Jamaica
Japan
Las Vegas
London
Los Angeles
Maryland & Delaware
Maui
Mexico
Montana & Wyoming
Montréal & Québec City
Munich & the Bavarian Alps
Nashville & Memphis
New England
New Mexico
New Orleans
New York City
New Zealand
Northern Italy
Norway
Nova Scotia, New Brunswick &
   Prince Edward Island
Oregon
Paris
Peru
Philadelphia & the Amish Country
Portugal

Prague & the Best of the Czech
   Republic
Provence & the Riviera
Puerto Rico
Rome
San Antonio & Austin
San Diego
San Francisco
Santa Fe, Taos & Albuquerque
Scandinavia
Scotland
Seattle & Portland
Shanghai
Sicily
Singapore & Malaysia
South Africa
South America
South Florida
South Pacific
Southeast Asia
Spain
Sweden
Switzerland
Texas
Thailand
Tokyo
Toronto
Tuscany & Umbria
USA
Utah
Vancouver & Victoria
Vermont, New Hampshire & Maine
Vienna & the Danube Valley
Virgin Islands
Virginia
Walt Disney World® & Orlando
Washington, D.C.
Washington State

FROMMER'S® DOLLAR-A-DAY GUIDES

Australia from $50 a Day
California from $70 a Day
England from $75 a Day
Europe from $70 a Day
Florida from $70 a Day
Hawaii from $80 a Day

Ireland from $60 a Day
Italy from $70 a Day
London from $85 a Day
New York from $90 a Day
Paris from $80 a Day

San Francisco from $70 a Day
Washington, D.C. from $80 a Day
Portable London from $85 a Day
Portable New York City from $90
   a Day

FROMMER'S® PORTABLE GUIDES

Acapulco, Ixtapa & Zihuatanejo
Amsterdam
Aruba
Australia's Great Barrier Reef
Bahamas
Berlin
Big Island of Hawaii
Boston
California Wine Country
Cancún
Cayman Islands
Charleston
Chicago
Disneyland®
Dublin
Florence

Frankfurt
Hong Kong
Houston
Las Vegas
Las Vegas for Non-Gamblers
London
Los Angeles
Los Cabos & Baja
Maine Coast
Maui
Miami
Nantucket & Martha's Vineyard
New Orleans
New York City
Paris
Phoenix & Scottsdale

Portland
Puerto Rico
Puerto Vallarta, Manzanillo &
   Guadalajara
Rio de Janeiro
San Diego
San Francisco
Savannah
Seattle
Sydney
Tampa & St. Petersburg
Vancouver
Venice
Virgin Islands
Washington, D.C.

FROMMER'S® NATIONAL PARK GUIDES

Banff & Jasper
Family Vacations in the National
   Parks

Grand Canyon
National Parks of the American West
Rocky Mountain

Yellowstone & Grand Teton
Yosemite & Sequoia/Kings Canyon
Zion & Bryce Canyon

FROMMER'S® MEMORABLE WALKS

Chicago	New York	San Francisco
London	Paris	

FROMMER'S® WITH KIDS GUIDES

Chicago	Ottawa	Vancouver
Las Vegas	San Francisco	Washington, D.C.
New York City	Toronto	

SUZY GERSHMAN'S BORN TO SHOP GUIDES

Born to Shop: France	Born to Shop: Italy	Born to Shop: New York
Born to Shop: Hong Kong, Shanghai & Beijing	Born to Shop: London	Born to Shop: Paris

FROMMER'S® IRREVERENT GUIDES

Amsterdam	Los Angeles	San Francisco
Boston	Manhattan	Seattle & Portland
Chicago	New Orleans	Vancouver
Las Vegas	Paris	Walt Disney World®
London	Rome	Washington, D.C.

FROMMER'S® BEST-LOVED DRIVING TOURS

Britain	Germany	Northern Italy
California	Ireland	Scotland
Florida	Italy	Spain
France	New England	Tuscany & Umbria

HANGING OUT™ GUIDES

Hanging Out in England	Hanging Out in France	Hanging Out in Italy
Hanging Out in Europe	Hanging Out in Ireland	Hanging Out in Spain

THE UNOFFICIAL GUIDES®

Bed & Breakfasts and Country Inns in:	Southwest & South Central Plains	Mexio's Best Beach Resorts
California	U.S.A.	Mid-Atlantic with Kids
Great Lakes States	Beyond Disney	Mini Las Vegas
Mid-Atlantic	Branson, Missouri	Mini-Mickey
New England	California with Kids	New England & New York with Kids
Northwest	Central Italy	New Orleans
Rockies	Chicago	New York City
Southeast	Cruises	Paris
Southwest	Disneyland®	San Francisco
Best RV & Tent Campgrounds in:	Florida with Kids	Skiing & Snowboarding in the West
California & the West	Golf Vacations in the Eastern U.S.	Southeast with Kids
Florida & the Southeast	Great Smoky & Blue Ridge Region	Walt Disney World®
Great Lakes States	Inside Disney	Walt Disney World® for Grown-ups
Mid-Atlantic	Hawaii	
Northeast	Las Vegas	Walt Disney World® with Kids
Northwest & Central Plains	London	Washington, D.C.
	Maui	World's Best Diving Vacations

SPECIAL-INTEREST TITLES

Frommer's Adventure Guide to Australia & New Zealand
Frommer's Adventure Guide to Central America
Frommer's Adventure Guide to India & Pakistan
Frommer's Adventure Guide to South America
Frommer's Adventure Guide to Southeast Asia
Frommer's Adventure Guide to Southern Africa
Frommer's Britain's Best Bed & Breakfasts and Country Inns
Frommer's Caribbean Hideaways
Frommer's Exploring America by RV
Frommer's Fly Safe, Fly Smart

Frommer's France's Best Bed & Breakfasts and Country Inns
Frommer's Gay & Lesbian Europe
Frommer's Italy's Best Bed & Breakfasts and Country Inns
Frommer's Road Atlas Britain
Frommer's Road Atlas Europe
Frommer's Road Atlas France
The New York Times' Guide to Unforgettable Weekends
Places Rated Almanac
Retirement Places Rated
Rome Past & Present

AOL Keyword: Travel

Booked aisle seat.

Reserved room with a view.

With a queen – no, make that a king-size bed.

With Travelocity, you can book your flights and hotels together, so you can get even better deals than if you booked them separately. You'll save time and money without compromising the quality of your trip. Choose your airline seat, search for alternate airports, pick your hotel room type, even choose the neighborhood you'd like to stay in

Travelocity

Visit www.travelocity.com
or call 1-888-TRAVELOCITY

Fly.
Sleep.
Save.

Now you can book your flights and
hotels together, so you can get even better deals
than if you booked them separately.

Visit www.travelocity.com
or call 1-888-TRAVELOCITY

Travelocity,® Travelocity.com® and the Travelocity skyline logo are trademarks and/or service
marks of Travelocity.com LP. © 2003 Travelocity.com LP. All rights reserved.